**HMH** |  into **Reading**™

Writing Workshop
Teacher's Guide

GRADE 5

Program Author
Joyce Armstrong Carroll

Welcome to
HMH Into Reading™
Writing Workshop

The *HMH Into Reading*™ Writing Workshop from Houghton Mifflin Harcourt represents a new generation of writing instruction. Developed through years of classroom experience and research, this method puts the writing workshop theory into practice. Teachers will find explicit modeling and instruction in process, technique, and the integration of grammar. Students have the chance to hone their craft through daily writing practice and regular conferences with teachers and peers. The Writing Workshop encourages students to grow into their own voices and share their ideas with the world.

PROGRAM OVERVIEW

HMH Into Reading™ Writing Workshop

PROGRAM AUTHOR

My Very Dear Teachers,

How I would have reveled in *HMH Into Reading*™ 60 years ago when I walked into that third-grade classroom in Emma Arleth Elementary for my first year in teaching! Then we had Dick and Jane readers, but nothing for or about writing. Oh, we had isolated grammar exercises that put the yawn in teaching and made kids actually hate writing anything. But now we have a handle on writing as a process, and we know how to integrate grammar within that process. So hug this book and use it. Nowhere will you find so consistent a writing scaffold, so integrated a curriculum, such a research-based and pedagogically proven approach to teaching ELAR. You are lucky indeed!

With my deepest respect for you all,

—Joyce Armstrong Carroll, a.k.a. Dr. JAC

Joyce Armstrong Carroll, Ed.D., H.L.D.

In her 60-year career, Joyce Armstrong Carroll has taught every grade level from primary through graduate school. In the past 40 years, working in tandem with her husband Edward Wilson, she has trained thousands of teachers, who, in turn, have taught hundreds of thousands of students. A nationally-known consultant, she has served as president of TCTE and on NCTE's Commission on Composition and its Standing Committee Against Censorship. Recipient of the Edmund J. Farrell Lifetime Achievement Award in Education and the Honorary Doctorate of Humane Letters for her work in Education, Dr. Carroll has written numerous articles and over twenty books—most on teaching writing. She and her husband have authored a national writing and grammar series as well as *AbydosPRO: An Integrated Writing and Grammar Curriculum*. She co-directs Abydos Literacy Learning.

Teaching Writing Workshop

The *Into Reading* Writing Workshop focuses on the writing process and the use of mentor texts, emphasizing student ownership of their own writing.

WRITING PROCESS

- Teacher's Guide provides explicit modeling and instruction for each stage of the writing process.

- Routines build strong habits.

- Recursive development of ideas and language encourages the development of voice.

STUDENT OWNERSHIP

- Students write daily, exercising their choice of topics.

- Students set and own their writing goals.

- Students confer regularly with teachers and peers.

MENTOR TEXTS

- Twelve focal texts—authentic trade literature—serve as mentor texts, modeling the development of themes, topics, and writing techniques.

- The focal texts double as a student choice trade library.

- Aspirational writing models provide strong examples of responses to module prompts.

WRITING WORKSHOP • MODULES

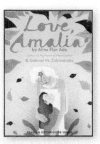

Lesson at a Glance

The Writing Workshop Teacher's Guide holds the blueprint for each day's lesson.

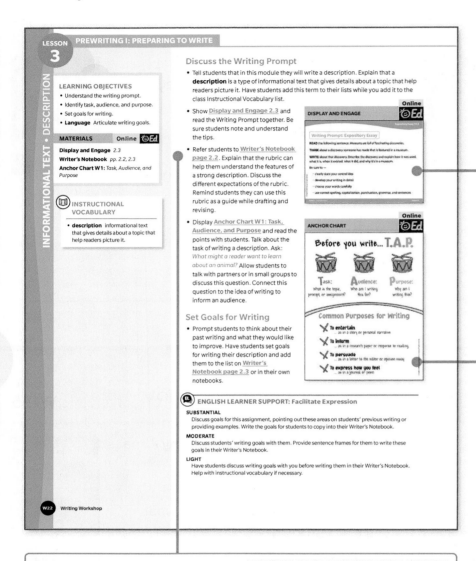

Display & Engage Projectable content for whole-class instruction

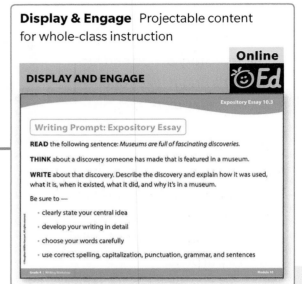

Anchor Charts Projectable and printable illustrations of key writing topics

Writer's Notebook
Direct support for student writing—no abstract practice or busy work

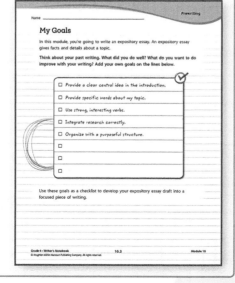

Scaffolded Writing Instruction for English Learners

As English learners participate in the Writing Workshop, scaffolded instruction helps the teacher meet them at their own language proficiency levels and leverage what they already know.

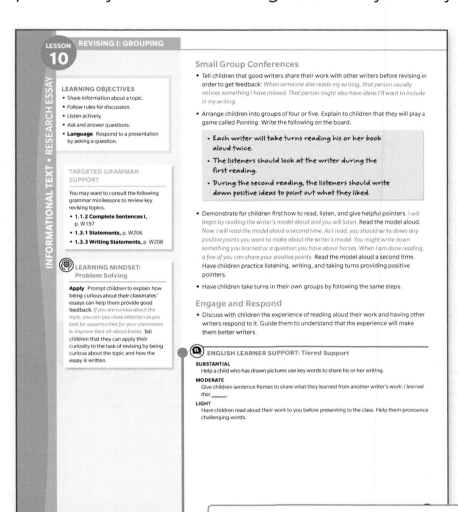

Support English learners using a variety of research-based strategies to

- focus on academic language and vocabulary
- link background knowledge and culture to learning
- increase comprehensible input
- support language output with sentence frames
- promote classroom interaction

 ENGLISH LEARNER SUPPORT: Tiered Support

SUBSTANTIAL
Help a child who has drawn pictures use key words to share his or her writing.

MODERATE
Give children sentence frames to share what they learned from another writer's work: *I learned that _____.*

LIGHT
Have children read aloud their work to you before presenting to the class. Help them pronounce challenging words.

Grammar in the Context of Writing

Grammar is most effectively taught in the context of writing instruction. The revising and editing stages of the writing process present the best opportunities for students to master the grammar skills needed to write strong, clear sentences.

Into Reading Writing Workshop provides a multifaceted approach to grammar:

INTEGRATED Writing Workshop lessons teach grammar in the context of revising and editing. Grammar minilessons supplement the revising and editing lessons as students' needs dictate.

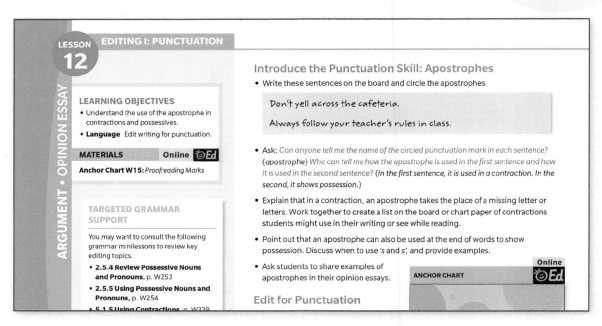

DIFFERENTIATED Grammar minilessons provide customized support for students who need help with other grammar and language skills.

SYSTEMATIC Teachers who want a comprehensive, systematic grammar curriculum can teach the minilessons according to the scope and sequence.

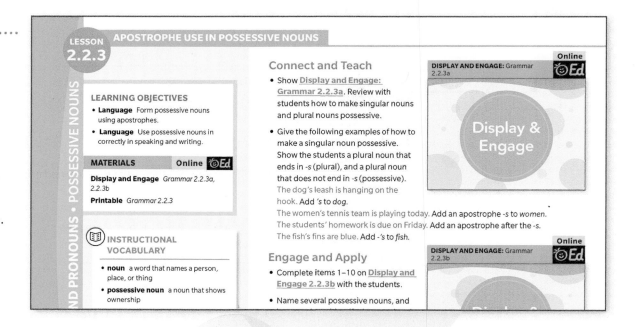

GRAMMAR MINILESSONS • TOPICS AND SKILLS

Writing Conferences and Assessment

Integrated into daily instruction, various types of assessment enable teachers to target individual needs, helping writers grow into their own voices.

RUBRICS

Multi-trait rubrics provided at point of use offer focused guidance to score and guide student writing. One rubric for every mode is provided.

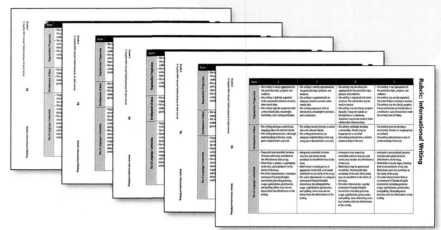

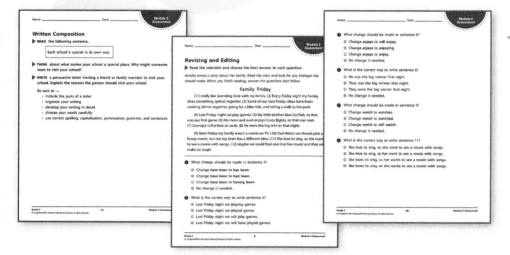

WEEKLY AND MODULE ASSESSMENTS

- Weekly Assessments include editing tasks that assess application of key grammar skills.

- Module Assessments include editing tasks and writing prompts that assess each Module's key grammar and writing skills.

WRITING CONFERENCES

As students work on their writing, teachers circulate the room and offer targeted assistance on the day's lesson, another writing topic, or an area of grammar that needs work. These regular, informal conferences provide students with actionable feedback to help them on their path to becoming great writers.

Writing
Workshop

WRITING WORKSHOP • MODULES

WRITING WORKSHOP • MODULES

WRITING WORKSHOP • MODULES

The Writing Conference

There can be no substitute for the writing conference. For teachers, it is an unbeatable opportunity to stay in touch with student work in progress. For students, it's a precious chance to have a conversation with their teacher about their writing and feel noticed as a writer.

Knowing that they have an actual audience gives students a reason to write; knowing how that audience is responding to their work gives them a reason to improve.

What happens during a writing conference?

A good writing conference is a conversation between teacher and student. This conversation has several parts:

1. **Listen** The first step is always to ask the student about his or her writing and pay close attention to the answer.

2. **Affirm** Based on what you hear, offer praise for some element of the student's writing to reinforce his or her strengths. This is essential.

3. **Teach** Focus on a general principle rather than providing a specific correction. Draw upon the focal text, writing model, or other familiar texts to provide clear examples of the principle.

4. **Apply** Finally, suggest that the student try it out for him- or herself.

How often should I confer with my students?

During independent writing time, circulate the room and confer with a few students every day, as time allows. A focused four- or five-minute conference gives you enough time to listen, deliver personalized instruction, and show students that you are paying attention.

What can I possibly cover in four or five minutes?

You don't have to do it all—focus on one or two writing elements based on the day's lesson and what the student shows you in his or her work. Provide a teaching strategy and a way to try it out. Don't edit for grammar or mechanics; use this valuable time to explore ideas, text structure, and language techniques.

Can I hold conferences with small groups?

Students with similar needs can benefit from informal small-group conferences. Feel free to call an impromptu small-group discussion during independent writing time, based on what you have seen during your individual conferences.

What about peer conferences?

During revising and editing lessons, this Teacher's Guide provides explicit direction for peer conferences. Students do best when prompted to focus on a limited set of writing traits or features in a given conference.

When is the best time to correct students' grammar?

Teaching grammar in the context of revising and editing shows students how writing good sentences will improve the clarity and impact of their writing. Rather than correcting errors, look for opportunities to emphasize principles taught in the day's grammar lesson. You can also bring in a minilesson for individual students or small groups based on demonstrated need.

What do I do with students who are sensitive to feedback?

Research shows that all students learn best from affirmative, targeted instruction about their writing. Writing is an emotionally charged activity; students who feel safe and confident will write more freely and with greater meaning.

Expository Essay

FOCUS STATEMENT Even great ideas for inventions require a lot of hard work.

FOCAL TEXT

Girls Think of Everything: Stories of Ingenious Inventions by Women

Author: Catherine Thimmesh

Illustrator: Melissa Sweet

Summary: This nonfiction book offers accounts of women inventors. There are addresses at the back for finding more information, a list of sources, and an index.

WRITING PROMPT

READ this sentence: *Today, in living rooms and labs, people are inventing.*

THINK about an inventor you have learned about.

WRITE an expository essay about how the inventor had to work hard to make the idea for an invention a reality.

LESSONS

1. **Introducing the Focal Text**

2. **The Read**

3. **Vocabulary**

4. **The Writing Process**

5. **Prewriting I: Preparing to Write**

6. **Drafting I: Beginning the Draft**

7. **Drafting II: Using Organization Strategies**

8. **Drafting III: Completing the Draft**

9. **Revising I: Group Conferencing**

10. **Revising II: Varying Sentence Types**

11. **Revising III: Organizing**

12. **Editing I: Grammar, Usage, and Punctuation**

13. **Editing II: Peer Proofreading**

14. **Publishing**

15. **Sharing**

LEARNING MINDSET: Trying Again

Display Anchor Chart 32: My Learning Mindset throughout the year. Refer to it to introduce Trying Again.

INFORMATIONAL TEXT • EXPOSITORY ESSAY

LEARNING OBJECTIVES

- Understand an expository essay or informational text.
- Discuss the features of an expository essay.
- Understand and discuss that expository essays can be organized in many ways.
- **Language** Understand and use instructional vocabulary.

MATERIALS   Online Ed

Display and Engage *1.1*

Classroom materials *books about inventors and their inventions*

Focal Text *Girls Think of Everything*

 INSTRUCTIONAL VOCABULARY

- **expository essay** a piece of writing that explains.
- **thesis** the main idea of an expository essay
- **organization** the way a text is arranged to help readers understand the information
- **elaboration** the process of developing and strengthening an idea with evidence and details

Priming the Students

Explore the Topic

- Tell students that Benjamin Franklin was a famous American who helped create the United States government system. He was an ambassador to France and England and was friends with George Washington.

- Say: *What do you know about Ben Franklin and his kite?* (*Answers will vary but should include the discovery of electricity.*) Explain: *Ben Franklin was curious. He liked to solve problems, so he invented helpful and practical things.*

- Ask: *What were some of Ben Franklin's inventions?* (*Answers may vary but may include bifocals, Franklin stove, lightning rod, swim fins, odometer, or long arm to reach for books on his tall library shelf.*) Write answers on chart paper.

- Use photos or real representations of the inventions and explain that many of these inventions are still in use today.

- Suggest to students that not all inventors are adults. Earmuffs, wrist-warmers, and the trampoline were all invented by boys and girls younger than 16.

- Read aloud to students a sample or two from books about inventors and their inventions, such as the Wright Brothers and their airplane or George Washington Ferris, Jr., and his Ferris Wheel invented for the 1893 Chicago World's Fair.

- After reading descriptions of how these inventors overcame setbacks and problems, ask: *What were some challenges that the inventors faced?* Discuss with students that the path from idea to invention is often a long and challenging journey.

Online ◉Ed

DISPLAY AND ENGAGE

Expository Essay 1.1

Focus Statement

Even great ideas for inventions require a lot of hard work.

Discuss the Focus Statement

- Show **Display and Engage 1.1**. Read the statement aloud to students. Ask: *What does this mean: "Even great ideas require hard work?"* Have partners TURN AND TALK for three minutes. Have student volunteers explain what they think the Focus Statement means and how it relates to the inventors and inventions they have discussed.

 ENGLISH LEARNER SUPPORT: Build Vocabulary

ALL LEVELS Supply a word list to support students' discussions of the Focus Statement, ranging from simple, lower-level words and phrases (e.g., *problem, try again*) to higher-level words (e.g., *overcome challenges, persist*).

Priming the Text

Prepare to Read

Girls Think of Everything

- Show the cover of *Girls Think of Everything*. Ask: *How does this illustration remind you of an inventor?* (*Answers will vary.*) Have students talk for three minutes with partners about the things they see in the illustration. Then have volunteers tell what they noticed and why it reminded them of inventors.

- Take a moment to define "Stories" in the subtitle of the book. Explain that these stories are about real people and real inventions. They are expository writing, not fiction.

- Tell students that in this module, they will be writing an **expository essay** about an inventor who worked hard to turn an idea into a real invention. Say: *Expository writing explains a topic or informs the reader about a subject.*

Explore the Writing Form

- Draw an open umbrella on the board or chart paper. Say: *Expository writing is an umbrella term for writing that explains.*

- Suggest to students that the parts of the umbrella represent the features of expository writing. Point to the umbrella's handle. Say: *Writing that explains has a main idea, or a **thesis**, that expresses the writer's purpose.*

- Point out the spokes that support the umbrella's circle. Explain: *An author supports a thesis by using facts and details. Usually expository writing follows a logical order.*

- On the board or chart paper, write the first sentence of a potential expository paragraph on inventors, such as "Ben Franklin had an idea for an invention."
  THINK ALOUD *If I wanted to write an expository paragraph on Ben Franklin's long arm invention, I would give information that explains the topic to readers. I could explain why he wanted to invent the device by telling about the high shelves in his library. I could list the steps in his invention process in chronological order. I could also give examples of ways that Ben Franklin used his invention.*

- Ask: *What else could I include to explain the invention of the long arm?* (*Possible answers: You could define long arm, tell how the invention is still used today, or compare it to similar inventions used in industry today.*) Write students' answers on the chart paper and discuss.

- Say: *Using one or more ways to explain Franklin's idea for an invention makes the point of the expository paragraph clear.*

- Tell students that in the next lesson you will read to them from a book about women inventors.

 LEARNING MINDSET: Trying Again

Introduce: Throughout this module, students will learn that people can create amazing things using innovation, perseverance, and problem solving. Inventors, for example, sometimes create several versions of their inventions before they work. Explain that inventors learned from their mistakes, and they kept trying. *Overcoming challenges by trying again is a good strategy for learning and life. We can all learn from our mistakes.*

Introduce Instructional Vocabulary

- Create a class Instructional Vocabulary list on chart paper, and add *the term expository essay* to it (*a piece of writing that explains*). You will be adding to this list throughout the year.

- Next, tell students that the method of developing an expository paragraph or essay is called **organization**. Add the term to your list.

- Point again to the umbrella you drew on the board. Say: *The handle of the umbrella is like the thesis sentence. It opens the umbrella. The spokes, or organization, keep the umbrella open to do its task. The organization is the way the thesis connects to the spokes, through description, examples, definitions, and reasons—details that support the thesis.* Point to the fabric of the umbrella. Say: *The fabric covering the spokes is the* **elaboration**. *Elaboration is the process of developing and strengthening an idea with evidence and details. In an expository essay, you want to provide information that interests and informs your reader. You need to give details to flesh out the facts.*

- Direct students to create an Instructional Vocabulary Glossary at the back of their notebooks and add these terms and definitions to it.

Engage and Respond

- Tell students that in this module they will be writing an expository essay about an inventor who worked hard to turn an idea into a real invention.

- Have students TURN AND TALK with a partner. Have them discuss how a writer might show that an inventor worked hard during the process of inventing.

 ENGLISH LEARNER SUPPORT: Build Vocabulary

SUBSTANTIAL
Have students repeat the Instructional Vocabulary terms after you and practice saying their definitions.

MODERATE
Have students create their own flashcards with an Instructional Vocabulary term on one side and the definition on the other. Have them use the flashcards to quiz a partner.

LIGHT
Have students work with partners or in small groups to use the Instructional Vocabulary to discuss an expository text they have read.

LEARNING OBJECTIVES

- Understand the elements of expository writing.
- Discuss the craft of expository writing.
- Ask and answer questions about a selection from *Girls Think of Everything*.
- **Language** Read to understand and discuss texts and vocabulary.

MATERIALS Online

Focal Text *Girls Think of Everything*

 INSTRUCTIONAL VOCABULARY

- **chronological order** the order in which events happen

Read the Focal Text

- Today you will read aloud a section from *Girls Think of Everything*. Before you begin, page through the text and point out that a different inventor is featured every few pages.

- Have students scan the images. Ask: *What kinds of things do the images seem to be showing?* (*the inventors and inventions*)

- Explain to students that you will be reading aloud the section that tells about Bette Nesmith Graham, the inventor of a product called Liquid Paper®.

- Ask: *What do you think Liquid Paper® is used for?* (*Answers will vary.*) Explain that Liquid Paper® is white fluid that typists use to cover up writing or typing errors on paper. Then point out: *When Bette Nesmith Graham invented Liquid Paper®, everyone used typewriters and made carbon copies. Correcting mistakes was a messy business. Her invention revolutionized how secretaries and business people worked. Liquid paper® is still used today, even though we do not use typewriters much at all.*

- Read aloud pages 19–22.

  » Ask: *What were some of the challenges Bette faced and how did she overcome them?* (*She had several challenges. She was creating a product and needed help to meet the demand. She changed the formula and its name. She also got advice and publicity.*)

  » Ask: *What made Bette a good inventor?* (*Answers will vary.*) Explain: *She wanted to solve a problem. She created a practical solution. She did not give up.*

  » Say: *We are going to look at this selection again. This time, we'll notice the author's craft.* Have students look at the first paragraph and discuss the main idea, or thesis, of the selection.

  » Say: *This selection presents events in the order in which they happened. Do you know what that is called?* (**chronological order**)

  » Point out the italicized portions in the text and ask: *Why are these sentences in italics?* (*They are quotations from Bette Nesmith Graham.*)

- Add the term *chronological order* to the class Instructional Vocabulary list, and have students add it to their glossaries.

Engage and Respond

- Have students write in their notebooks or on paper questions they have about the reading passage. Provide models of question, such as the following: *How did Bette change the formula of her paint? Why did she first think she needed a chemist?* Have partners compare questions and discuss possible answers to their inquiries.

EL **ENGLISH LEARNER SUPPORT: Support Comprehension**

ALL LEVELS Have pairs of students alternate reading paragraphs from the selection and discussing them. Provide sentence frames, such as the following: *This paragraph is about _____. The next paragraph is about _____.*

LEARNING OBJECTIVES

- Acquire new vocabulary words.
- Generate a list of vocabulary words for writing essays.
- Explain the meaning of content area words.
- Categorize words and label parts of speech.
- **Language** Write sentences using content-based vocabulary.

MATERIALS   Online

Focal Text *Girls Think of Everything*
Writer's Notebook *p. 1.1*
Display and Engage *1.2*

TARGETED GRAMMAR SUPPORT

You may want to consult the following grammar minilessons to review key editing topics.

- **2.1.1 Recognizing Common and Proper Nouns,** p. W218
- **3.3.1 Regular Verbs,** p. W258
- **4.2.1 Adverbs That Tell How, Where, When, How Often,** p. W283

Review the Focal Text

- Review with students the selection on Bette Nesmith Graham in *Girls Think of Everything* and other passages, if time allows.

- Scan through the selection and take note of any special vocabulary that has to do with the invention, process of creation, or marketing of the product, such as *tempera paint, chemist, formula,* or *organized sales campaign.* Discuss with students the meaning of these words.

- Page through other selections and have students identify additional words and phrases that they find interesting, such as the words below. Have students enter them into the Word Bank on **Writer's Notebook page 1.1** or have them create a Word Bank in their own notebooks. Explain that the Word Bank is a resource for them to build a vocabulary list.

investment	inspiration	creative solution
determination	ingenuity	innovation
manufacture	develop	research
professional	success	triumphantly

- Show **Display and Engage 1.2**. Review the directions with students about notating words in their Word Banks. Provide dictionaries or other resources as needed.

- Conduct a grammar minilesson for those who need additional help identifying nouns, verbs, and adverbs.

Online

DISPLAY AND ENGAGE

Expository Essay 1.2

Vocabulary

Use the Word Bank page in your Writer's Notebook to build your vocabulary.

- Select words about inventors or inventing from your reading.
- Write each word in your Word Bank.
- Identify the part of speech: noun (N); verb (V); adjective (Adj); adverb (Adv).

Engage and Respond

- Have students write a sentence that uses two Word Bank words with different parts of speech. Then tell them to share the sentence with a partner.

 ENGLISH LEARNER SUPPORT: Build Vocabulary

SUBSTANTIAL
Give students five content-specific words to write in their Word Banks. Have partners write sentences using the words and read them aloud to each other.

MODERATE
Guide partners to select five content-specific words from their reading and write a sentence with each word. Then tell them to compare their sentences for accuracy of word usage.

LIGHT
Have students collect ten words for their Word Banks and use each word in a sentence. Then tell partners to identify the parts of speech for each word.

INFORMATIONAL TEXT • EXPOSITORY ESSAY

LEARNING OBJECTIVES

- Understand the steps in the writing process.
- **Language** Discuss terms and goals for writing an expository essay.

MATERIALS — Online Ed

Anchor Chart W8: *Elements of Informational Text*

● *Professional Learning*

TEACHING TERMS

Anchor charts are engaging, visual representations of skills, strategies, concepts, or processes that can be prepared by the teacher or co-created during a lesson by the teacher and class. Anchor charts are displayed in the classroom to make thinking visible, to keep learning relevant, and to help build a collaborative culture of literacy.

See the **GPS guide** to learn more.

Review the Writing Process

- Review the writing process with students as you write the following steps on the board or on chart paper for display in the classroom.

> 1. Prewriting: choose a topic and organize your ideas
> 2. Drafting: write your ideas down
> 3. Revising: make improvements to the ideas, organization, and style of your writing
> 4. Editing: correct errors in grammar, spelling, and punctuation
> 5. Publishing/Sharing: share your completed work with others

ANCHOR CHART — Online Ed

Informational Text

Introduction	Body	Conclusion
• hooks the readers • includes the central idea	• supports the central idea with facts and details • gives reasons and examples • uses an organizational strategy	• restates the central idea • leaves readers with a thought

Purpose
Informational texts often

- ✦ describe things, people, or events
- ✗ show sequence
- ✗ compare things
- ✗ show cause and effect
- ✗ show a problem and its solution

- Point out that writers may need to return to earlier steps throughout the process as they work to develop their ideas.

- Encourage students' questions and answer all those that may arise.

- Remind students that in this module they will be writing an expository essay. Explain that an expository essay is a kind of informational text. Show **Anchor Chart W8: Elements of Informational Text** and read the points with students. Point out that informational text is nonfiction—it tells about real people, places, things, processes, and ideas.

- Give students an example of a type of informational text, such as a newspaper article, and ask them to suggest other types as you write them on the board. (*Sample answers: textbook, biography, encyclopedia entry, informational web site, how-to manual, etc.*)

- Explain that an expository essay is a short form of informational writing that gives information on a single, focused topic. Write the following points on the board:

> An expository essay has a thesis sentence.
>
> It is organized by paragraphs that support the thesis with details.

- Have students TURN AND TALK to a partner about how *Girls Think of Everything* meets the criteria for an informational text. As a class, discuss possible answers. (*It informs, it hooks the reader with humor, includes vivid details, etc.*)

 ENGLISH LEARNER SUPPORT: Support Discussion

ALL LEVELS Explain to students that most of the terms used to discuss an expository essay have Spanish equivalents: *información* (information); *ensayo* (essay); *tesis* (thesis); *organización* (organization); *gol* (goal).

INFORMATIONAL TEXT • EXPOSITORY ESSAY

LEARNING OBJECTIVES

• Discuss writing prompt.

• Use a planning chart to explore topics.

• Discuss and write goals for completing an expository essay.

• **Language** Discuss writing prompt and topic choices using content-based vocabulary.

• **Language** Complete prewriting activities.

MATERIALS   Online 😊Ed

Display and Engage *1.3*

Writer's Notebook *pp. 1.2, 1.3, 1.4*

Classroom materials *books about inventors or inventions*

LEARNING MINDSET: Trying Again

Apply Point out to students that, like inventors, they can learn from their mistakes. Encourage students to take risks in their writing. *It's okay to make mistakes when you write because you can always try again. All good writing is rewriting!*

● *Professional Learning*

RESEARCH FOUNDATIONS

Why does mindset matter? Students with a learning mindset are curious, challenge-seeking students who recognize that taking on challenges and learning from mistakes creates opportunities to develop their intelligence, practice skills, and increase their potential to be successful.

See the **GPS guide** to learn more.

Prepare to Write

• Show **Display and Engage 1.3** and read the Writing Prompt together. Use the prompt to discuss with students the requirements for writing their expository essays. Say: *The essay must have a central idea (thesis), a pattern of organization, supporting details (elaboration), a strong conclusion, and proper spelling, capitalization, punctuation, and grammar.*

> **Online**
> 😊Ed
>
> **DISPLAY AND ENGAGE**
>
> Expository Essay 1.3
>
> **Writing Prompt: Expository Essay**
>
> **READ** the following sentence: *Today, in living rooms and labs, people are inventing. They are combining their curiosity and creativity with persistence and optimism.*
>
> **THINK** about an inventor you have learned about.
>
> **WRITE** an expository essay about how that inventor had to work extremely hard to make the idea for an invention a reality.
>
> Be sure to —
> • clearly state your central idea in a thesis sentence
> • organize your writing
> • use proper spelling, capitalization, punctuation, and grammar
>
> Grade 5 • Writing Workshop   Module 1

• Distribute **Writer's Notebook page 1.2**. Discuss the rubric. Remind students they can use this rubric as a resource as they draft and revise their papers.

• Explain: *Good writers think about how they can improve with each new piece they write.* Have students TURN AND TALK for three minutes about setting goals for themselves and their expository essays. Then have them add their goals to the list on **Writer's Notebook page 1.3** or in their own notebooks.

Choosing a Topic

• Tell students it is time to think about the topic for their essay. Model thinking about a topic:

THINK ALOUD *An invention that interests me is the electric light, created by Thomas Edison. He had to try thousands of different materials to make the filament. He also invented the wiring and switches that turn a light bulb on and off. It took him years to develop the light. The story of this invention would make a good expository essay topic.*

• Say: *To choose an inventor for your topic, you may need to research inventors and inventions.* Direct small groups of students to spend a few minutes searching the Internet for famous inventors or recent inventions that interest them. Encourage students to find an equal number of women and men inventors.

• Bring the class back together to share their findings. List the inventors or inventions on the board or chart paper.

• Have students turn to the planning chart on **Writer's Notebook page 1.4**. Explain to students that planning their essays is an important prewriting step.

• Have students complete the column for Prompt. In the Topics column, have them write the names of two or three inventors and inventions that interest them the most. Explain that they may have to do a bit more research to decide which one to write about. Students will complete the chart in the next lesson.

Engage and Respond

• Have students discuss in small groups the topics they are considering.

 ENGLISH LEARNER SUPPORT: Facilitate Choices

ALL LEVELS Provide sentence frames to facilitate discussion. For example: *I want to write about _____ because _____.*

INFORMATIONAL TEXT • EXPOSITORY ESSAY

LEARNING OBJECTIVES

- Develop working thesis statements for an expository essay.
- Research ideas to draft an expository essay.
- **Language** Explain and summarize ideas in writing.

MATERIALS   Online Ed

Display and Engage *1.4a–1.4d*
Writer's Notebook *pp. 1.4, 1.5, 1.6*

 LEARNING MINDSET:
Trying Again

Apply Explain to students that even though a thesis statement is only one sentence, it is unlikely that they will get it right the first time. *A "working" thesis statement is a writer's best try at summarizing his or her main idea. In later drafts, when the essay takes shape, writers can try again to craft an even better thesis statement. When writing a thesis statement, trying again helps you become a better writer.*

Conduct Research and Write a Thesis Statement

- Have students review their topic ideas and choose one that feels most interesting to them. Explain that writers do their best work when they write about something that interests them.

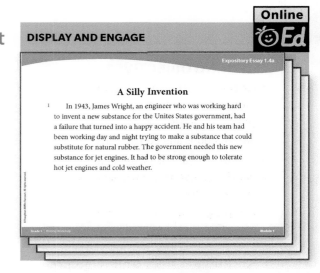

- Show **Display and Engage 1.4a–1.4d** and distribute **Writer's Notebook pages 1.5–1.6**. Have volunteers read the model essay aloud.

- Write "Thesis Statement" on the board and ask: *What do you know about a thesis statement?* Write responses on the board. (*Thesis Statement: a sentence that summarizes the main idea in an expository essay*)

- Ask: *What is the thesis statement in the model?* Write the response on the board and have students underline it in their Writer's Notebooks. (*Thesis Statement in Model: "In 1943, James Wright, an engineer who was working hard to invent a new substance for the US government, had a failure that turned into a happy accident."*)

- Ask: *If a thesis statement summarizes the main idea of the essay, what do you think we need to do before we can write our thesis statements?* (*research the topic; know what points we want to make*)

- Show how to begin research by using the model topic as an example. Discuss using keywords to search and how to take notes on main ideas. Remind students to write down quotations exactly and to always note their sources.

- Bring the discussion back to the thesis statement. Model using research notes to draft a thesis statement.
  THINK ALOUD *My research notes say "James Wright was the inventor of silly putty. He was not trying to invent a toy. He was trying to invent a new kind of rubber." I see that Wright invented silly putty by accident, which is interesting. I think my main idea will be that silly putty was invented by accident. Now I am ready to write a working thesis sentence.*

- Write the following "working thesis statement" on the board:

> James Wright was working hard to make a new kind of rubber when he made a toy by mistake.

Begin to Draft

- Allow time for students to conduct research and draft a working thesis statement (or two). Remind students to use the planning chart on **Writer's Notebook page 1.4** to record their notes and ideas.

- Make sure students understand that they need to create and follow a research plan in order to write their expository essay and this tool will help them do that.

INFORMATIONAL TEXT • EXPOSITORY ESSAY

LEARNING OBJECTIVES

- Organize an expository essay with purposeful structure.
- Write an expository essay with clear introductions and conclusions.
- Include relevant facts, definitions, details, quotations, and examples in an expository essay.
- **Language** Write an expository essay that explains and describes.

MATERIALS   Online Ed

Display and Engage *1.5a–c*
Writer's Notebook *pp. 1.5, 1.6, 1.7*

Introduce the Skill

- Show **Display and Engage 1.5a–c** and have students look at **Writer's Notebook pages 1.5 and 1.6**. Go over the organizational structure with students and help them make connections between the chart and the model.

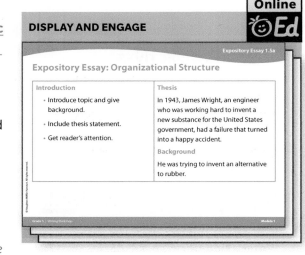

- Ask: *Does the introduction in the model get the reader's attention?* (*Answers will vary but may include that a failure becoming a happy accident is intriguing.*) Ask: *What are some ways that a writer can get a reader's attention?* (*write something surprising; tell an interesting story; humor*)

- Have students identify facts, concrete details, and examples used in the body of the model. Point out that these details come from researching.

- Point out that quotations and definitions are also good supports to use in the body of an expository essay.

  THINK ALOUD *If I were writing this model essay and I found in my research a quote from an astronaut about how useful silly putty was during a mission, I could include that quote in the body of my essay.*

- Point out that the conclusion to the essay summarizes things already discussed in the essay and does not contain new information.

Continue to Draft

- Give students time to continue drafting. Have them focus today on fleshing out the structure of their essays. Distribute **Writer's Notebook page 1.7** or tell students they may use their own notebooks to make notes on how their essays are organized.

- Reassure students they do not need to worry about making their writing perfect at this time—they should just get some ideas down.

- Encourage them to spend the bulk of their time drafting the body of their essays.

- Circulate the room, providing assistance to students as needed.

EL **ENGLISH LEARNER SUPPORT: Facilitate Writing**

ALL LEVELS Group students who have questions about any of the words or terms listed on **Writer's Notebook page 1.7**. Define problematic words and terms and provide examples, as needed, to clarify the activity. Let students know you are available to provide individual help as they write.

LESSON 8

DRAFTING III: COMPLETING THE DRAFT

LEARNING OBJECTIVES

- Organize drafts with a purposeful and logical structure.
- **Language** Write an expository essay using a variety of sentence types.

MATERIALS   Online ⊙ Ed

Anchor Chart W8: *Elements of Informational Text*

Display and Engage *1.4d*

TEACHER TIP

You might have students work with partners to review their drafts for organization. Circulate the room and provide help in situations where partners seem stuck.

Focus on Organization

- Display **Anchor Chart W8: Elements of Informational Text** and review the elements with students. Give students time to look at their own essays and confirm that they have included each element. Students who find a missing element should note what they have missed.

- Write the following questions on the board. Have students review their drafts for organization using the questions.

> Do you have a thesis statement?
>
> Does your introductory paragraph give background?
>
> Does the body include facts, details, examples, quotations, or definitions?
>
> Do your paragraphs build on each other?
>
> Does the order you used make sense?
>
> Does your conclusion relate to the thesis?

ANCHOR CHART   Online ⊙ Ed

Informational Text

Introduction	Body	Conclusion
• hooks the readers • includes the central idea	• supports the central idea with facts and details • gives reasons and examples • uses an organizational strategy	• restates the central idea • leaves readers with a thought

Purpose
Informational texts often
- describe things, people, or events
- show sequence
- compare things
- show cause and effect
- show a problem and its solution

- If students answer "no" to any of the questions, have them make notes for what to add as they revise.

Focus on Conclusions

- Next, explain that the best conclusions restate the author's main idea and then leave the reader with something to think about. Remind students that the conclusion is not the place to add new information.

- Show **Display and Engage 1.4d** and have a volunteer read the model conclusion. Ask: *What makes this an effective conclusion?* Discuss how the conclusion returns to the writer's main ideas and leaves readers with a fresh way to think about a silly invention.

Continue to Draft

- Have students return to their drafts to tighten up the organization and create a strong conclusion.

- Circulate the room, providing support as needed.

EL **ENGLISH LEARNER SUPPORT: Support Writing**

ALL LEVELS Provide support to help students compose simple, compound, and complex sentences, as appropriate for their writing level, that are effective in getting the idea across.

REVISING I: GROUP CONFERENCING

LEARNING OBJECTIVES
- Revise an expository essay.
- **Language** Use small group conferences to give peer feedback on expository essays.

MATERIALS Online

Display and Engage *1.6*

LEARNING MINDSET:
Trying Again

Normalize At this point in the writing process, some students may be frustrated about working with the same essay again. Let students know that it is normal to feel frustrated while revising a piece of writing. A good writer keeps revisiting his or her work, trying again and again to make it the best it can be. If you approach revision with patience, you will continue to discover things that can be improved.

Small Group Conferences

- Tell students that they will have group conferences to examine the following elements in their expository essays:
  » a strong thesis statement;
  » an introduction that gets the reader's attention;
  » interesting details, examples, facts, definitions, or quotations;
  » a conclusion that ties back to thesis sentence.

- Ask students to listen for interesting facts and details as you read aloud the following paragraph from the model. Have them jot down any words, phrases, or sentences that interest them:

  After a full year of hard work, Wright and his team came up with a putty that was a failure. It was gooey and not at all what they needed. Wright threw it on the floor. To his surprise, it bounced. Soon, Wright discovered that the putty had other interesting properties. It could stretch. When pressed onto a newspaper or comic book, it could pick up images.

- Ask: *What did you jot down?* (*gooey, it bounced, it could pick up images*)

- Divide students into groups of four or five. Each group member will need a pen, paper, their essays, and a highlighter.

- Tell students that their group will use a strategy called "Highlighting."

- Project **Display and Engage 1.6** and go over the rules of highlighting.

- Assign each group member a number, so they have an order in which writers will read. Then begin the activity.

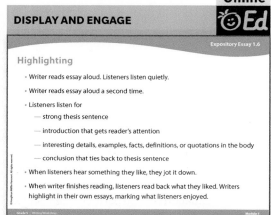

DISPLAY AND ENGAGE Online

Expository Essay 1.6

Highlighting
- Writer reads essay aloud. Listeners listen quietly.
- Writer reads essay aloud a second time.
- Listeners listen for
  — strong thesis sentence
  — introduction that gets reader's attention
  — interesting details, examples, facts, definitions, or quotations in the body
  — conclusion that ties back to thesis sentence
- When listeners hear something they like, they jot it down.
- When writer finishes reading, listeners read back what they liked. Writers highlight in their own essays, marking what listeners enjoyed.

Continue to Revise

- After the highlighting activity, have students revisit their essays. Tell them to look for sections that contain few or no highlights. Students should consider revising these sections to make them more appealing.

 ENGLISH LEARNER SUPPORT: Facilitate Conferences

ALL LEVELS Lead a group of students with limited proficiency through the highlighting exercise. Go through the steps but customize the exercise to the needs of the group. Modifications may include the following: allowing writers to clarify pronunciation of words in their writing before they read; asking writers to pause after each sentence or paragraph during the second reading to allow time for note-takers to write; or allowing listeners to clarify meanings of words they do not know during the second reading.

INFORMATIONAL TEXT • EXPOSITORY ESSAY

LEARNING OBJECTIVES

- Revise essays.
- **Language** Use complex and compounds sentences.

MATERIALS   Online

Display and Engage *1.4a–1.4d*

TEACHER TIP

If students are having trouble writing compound and/or complex sentences, have them start with simple sentences. Then, provide one-on-one assistance to help students learn how to combine these sentences.

TARGETED GRAMMAR SUPPORT

You may want to consult the following grammar minilessons to review key revising topics.

- **1.2.4 Review Kinds of Sentences,** p. W206
- **1.3.3 Compound Sentences,** p. W210
- **1.4.1 Complex Sentences With Conjunctions,** p. W213

Introduce the Revision Skill

- Review with students the characteristics of the following kinds of sentences: simple, compound, and complex.

- Tell students that varying sentence lengths and sentences types will make their expository essays more engaging to the reader.

- Show **Display and Engage 1.4a–1.4d**. Read the first sentence aloud. Ask: *What kind of sentence is this?* (*complex*) Help students analyze the independent and dependent clauses in this sentence by writing the sentence on the board and coding the dependent clauses in a different color. With students' help, break down the sentence into a series of simple sentences.

> The year was 1943.
>
> James Wright was an engineer.
>
> He was working hard.
>
> He was trying to invent a new substance.
>
> It was for the United States government.
>
> He failed.
>
> His failure was a happy accident.

- Read the simple sentences aloud. Ask: *How would you describe the rhythm of these sentences?* (*short, choppy, monotonous*) Ask: *Why is the complex sentence a better choice?* (*more interesting to read*)

- Point out that when a writer varies the kinds of sentences he or she uses, the sentence lengths will vary, too.

- Ask: *Who can combine two of the simple sentences on the board to make a compound sentence?* (*Answers will vary. Example: He was trying to invent a new substance for the United States government and he failed.*) Explain to students that there are many ways to write the same information and writers will make different choices.

- Read and analyze with students a few more sentences from the model.

Revise to Vary Sentences

- Have students re-enter their writing to vary the kinds of sentences in their expository essays.

- Circulate the room and assist students. If students need help with a particular sentence type, do a direct teach, using the grammar minilessons as needed.

LEARNING OBJECTIVES

- **Language** Revise an expository essay for organization.

MATERIALS	Online

Display and Engage 1.5a–c
Writer's Notebook p. 1.7

TEACHER TIP

Tell students that when a writer has worked with a piece of writing for a long time, it can be difficult to step back and evaluate it. We become too close to the writing and are unable to see it clearly. If this rings true for some students, give them the option of trading papers with a partner to get help evaluating their organization.

Introduce the Revision Skill

- Show <u>**Display and Engage 1.5a–c**</u>. Review the three parts of an expository essay with students (introduction, body, conclusion) and discuss the elements of each part. Answer any questions students may have.

- Have students turn to <u>**Writer's Notebook page 1.7**</u> and review the notes they took when planning their essays. Ask: *Are there notes in your organization charts that you did not include in your essay?* If student see variations between their notes and their essays, have volunteers share discrepancies with the class. Help them evaluate whether their original notes or plans should be incorporated into their essay or discarded.

- To facilitate decision making, ask volunteers questions such as the following: *What information have you not included in your essay? In which section might this information belong? Would the information strengthen that section? How?*

- Using volunteer examples, explain to students that not all of their original notes must be included in their essays.
  THINK ALOUD *Sometimes at the planning stages, we think information will be relevant. But, as the draft takes shape, we see that the information is not needed because it will not add anything valuable to the essay.*

- Write the following questions on the board and discuss them with students.

> Do you have a thesis statement?
>
> Does the introduction get the reader's attention?
>
> Did you develop the topic with facts, definitions, details, quotations, and/or examples?
>
> Does the information make sense?
>
> Does each sentence follow the next in a logical way?
>
> Does the conclusion relate back to the thesis sentence?

Continue to Revise

- Have students evaluate and revise their essays for organization using their notes and the questions on the board.

- Circulate the room, providing assistance as needed.

INFORMATIONAL TEXT • EXPOSITORY ESSAY

LEARNING OBJECTIVES

- **Language** Edit expository essays for proper capitalization, correct spelling, and subject/verb agreement.

MATERIALS   Online *Ed*

Display and Engage *1.7a–1.7b*

TEACHER TIP

If individual students are having trouble using resources to answer their questions about proper capitalization, correct spelling, or subject-verb agreement, you may want to pair them with a partner. Partners can assist each other to answer questions.

TARGETED GRAMMAR SUPPORT

You may want to consult the following grammar minilessons to review key editing topics.

- **1.3.2 Subject-Verb Agreement,** p. W209
- **2.1.2 Capitalizing Proper Nouns,** p. W219
- **8.1.4 Review Spelling,** p. W346

Introduce the Editing Skill

- Tell students that they will proofread and edit their expository essays to check for proper capitalization, spelling, and subject-verb agreement. As needed, revisit grammar minilessons for additional review.

- Explain that students will use a strategy called *ratiocination* to proofread their own papers. Show **Display and Engage 1.7a–1.7b**.

DISPLAY AND ENGAGE   Online *Ed*

Expository Essay 1.7a

Ratiocination

Be an editing detective. Code your expository essay. Then, check it and make corrections.

Codes	What?	Check
Capitalization Underline in green	words that are capitalized / words that may need to be capitalized	Did you use capital letters correctly? Do you need to capitalize anything that is not yet capitalized?

Grade 3 | Writing Workshop   Module 1

- Point out to students that the left column shows a way to "code" their essays. The middle column tells them what kinds of words they will code. The last column tells them what questions to ask themselves about the words.

  THINK ALOUD *To code my essay for capitalization, I will look at the first row, first column of the chart. It tells me to underline in green. The second column tells me to underline words that I capitalized and words I did not capitalize but think may need to be capitalized.*

- Ask: *What types of words may need capitalization?* (*words in a title; proper nouns; direct quotations after dialogue tags, etc.*)

- Demonstrate the strategy by writing the following example from the model on the board and going through all the steps on the chart.

> In 1943, <u>James</u> <u>Wright,</u> an <u>engineer</u> who was working hard to invent a new substance for the <u>Unites States government,</u> had a failure that turned into a happy accident.

- Ask: *Did I properly capitalize James Wright?* (*yes*) Should "engineer" be capitalized? (*no*) What about the three words "United States government"? (*They are correct.*)

- Tell students that once they have finished proofing for capitalization, they can go on to code and investigate spelling. After spelling, they may go on to subject-verb agreement.

- Tell students they may use print and online resources to help them answer their questions about capitalization, spelling, and subject-verb agreement.

Proofread Writing

- Have students work independently to edit their essays using the ratiocination strategy.

- Circulate the room and provide assistance as needed. Group students who need support on similar grammar topics and use the grammar minilessons or students' own writing to provide targeted review and support.

INFORMATIONAL TEXT · EXPOSITORY ESSAY

LEARNING OBJECTIVES

- **Language** Edit writing for proper use of past tense of irregular verbs.
- **Language** Edit writing for proper use of collective nouns.
- **Language** Edit writing for proper use of adjectives.
- **Language** Edit writing for proper use of pronouns.

MATERIALS   Online

Display and Engage *1.8*

Writer's Notebook *p. 1.8*

TARGETED GRAMMAR SUPPORT

You may want to consult the following grammar minilessons to review key editing topics.

- **2.2.3 Collective Nouns,** p. W225
- **3.3.1 Regular Verbs,** p. W258
- **3.3.2 Irregular Verbs,** p. W259
- **3.3.3 Past Tense Forms of Irregular Verbs,** p. W260
- **3.4.1 Verbs Be and Have,** p. W263

Clocking Activity

- Tell students they will proofread each other's expository essays.

- Show **Display and Engage 1.8**. Review the items on the proofreading checklist. As needed, review the grammar minilessons.

- Review with students the steps for clocking to prepare them for the activity. Then go through the steps below.

  » Students sit in concentric circles.

  » Distribute **Writer's Notebook page 1.8** and have students write their names at the top of their editing page. The page will travel with their essay.

  » As students receive a peer's essay, they become the editor of that paper. Editors write their initials to the left of the item they are checking. No marks are made on student essays.

  » Refer to **Display and Engage 1.8** and call out what item is to be checked by the editor.

  » The editor notes corrections to be made.

  » After a couple of items, have students move so that each paper is read by several editors.

  » When the editing process is completed, students take their editing page and make corrections, if any. If they are confused by an edit, they may ask the editor or their teacher.

Edit Writing

- Have students do a final pass through their expository essays, integrating the notes from the clocking activity into their writing.

- Circulate the room, providing assistance as needed.

(EL) ENGLISH LEARNER SUPPORT: Facilitate Feedback

ALL LEVELS As you circulate the room, check in with students who may not understand their classmates' edits due to language limitations. Provide support as needed.

DISPLAY AND ENGAGE   Online Ed

Expository Essay 1.8

Peer Proofreading

What to Check

1. Is there a name on the paper?
2. Check for correct use of the verbs *be* and *have*.
3. Check for correct use of all other verbs.
4. Check for correct use of verb tense.
5. Check whether irregular verbs that are in past tense are written correctly.
6. Do all sentences have correct subject-verb agreement?
7. Do all sentences have proper punctuation?
8. Are there any spelling errors?

INFORMATIONAL TEXT • EXPOSITORY ESSAY

LEARNING OBJECTIVES

- Discuss publishing opportunities for a wider audience.
- Decide upon a publishing option.
- Reassess goals for writing expository essays.
- **Language** Participate in and discuss the publishing experience.

MATERIALS   Online

Focal Text *Girls Think of Everything*
Writer's Notebook *p. 1.9*

 LEARNING MINDSET:
Trying Again

Review Remind students about the importance of trying again. *When you review your goals, you will see evidence of your successes. However, you may also discover places where you did not meet your goals. These become opportunities for you to try to do better in your next writing assignment.* Remind students that mistakes and failures for inventors and their inventions were just challenges to overcome. They kept tinkering with their inventions until they succeeded.

TEACHER TIP

Consider allowing your students to collect their expository essays into a class book or binder for display in your school's library. If your school has a newspaper, encourage students to submit all or part of their essay for publication in a special "Spotlight on Authors" feature.

Prepare the Final Copy

- Show the front cover of *Girls Think of Everything*. Ask: *How does this illustration sum up the contents of the book?* (*Answers will vary.*) Direct students to consider creating an illustration that will reflect the main idea of their expository essays.

- Flip through the pages of *Girls Think of Everything,* pointing out the titles and subtitles of each entry. Explain: *The titles are the names of the inventors, and the subtitles are the things they invented. Each entry has an illustration of the inventor.*

- Have students create titles for their essays.

- Tell students that "the printing press made everyone a reader. The computer made everyone a publisher." Provide a few examples of how students might use the computer to publish their expository essays.

  - Use software programs to create book-like pages or oral presentations of their essays.
  - Post the essay on a class page for the school's website.
  - Participate in a class blog that publishes information about inventors or inventions.
  - Make a video of the writer reading the expository essay and post on an approved website.
  - Record a re-enactment of the inventor and the invention to show in class, using classmates, dialogue, costumes, and equipment.

Publish Writing

- Have partners TURN AND TALK for five minutes to discuss their preferences for publishing options. Have volunteers explain their preferences to the class. Record preferences on the board or chart paper. Discuss the options and decide the type of publishing option to use either as a class or individually.

Engage and Respond

- After students have published their expository essays, have them turn to their Writer's Notebook page 1.9.

- Discuss the page and ask students to write their thoughts about meeting their goals.

 ENGLISH LEARNER SUPPORT: Support Discussion

ALL LEVELS Have students of different levels work in small groups to prepare their final copies. Monitor the groups, giving tips and advice when needed.

LEARNING OBJECTIVES

- Present expository essays to an audience.
- Ask and answer questions about writing.
- **Language** Exhibit comprehension of expository essays read aloud.
- **Language** Participate in a collaborative discussion of the writing experience.

MATERIALS   Online

Display and Engage *1.9*

 Professional Learning

BEST PRACTICES

Parents, caretakers, and friends are critical to the learning process. Communication with those at home is essential to building a successful classroom environment. Caretakers should be aware of the topics and skills students are learning about at school. Students should also be encouraged to share and discuss their writing.

See the **GPS guide** to learn more.

Share Writing

- Have students share their expository essays by reading them aloud. Discuss options for reading aloud, such as a Round Table Reading, in which every person in a small group reads aloud an essay to the others in the group. As another option, mention having a special Author's Chair in which each student sits to read his or her essay.

- Invite the class to decide how they would like to share their expository essays with others. Suggest that students may broaden their audiences by reading to friends, parents, or other classes.

- Encourage students to ask each author follow-up questions. Remind students of the rules for classroom collaboration. Ask students to listen politely, be respectful of the author, and be courteous when asking the author for more details.

Engage and Respond

- Conclude with an informal debriefing. Show **Display and Engage 1.9**. Have partners ask and answer the questions. Tell students to take notes in their Writer's Notebook or on their own paper.

- Ask students to save the information to help them with their next writing assignments.

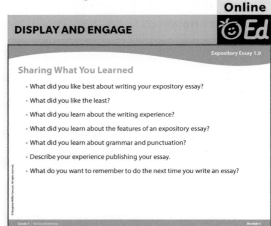

Online

DISPLAY AND ENGAGE

Expository Essay 1.9

Sharing What You Learned

- What did you like best about writing your expository essay?
- What did you like the least?
- What did you learn about the writing experience?
- What did you learn about the features of an expository essay?
- What did you learn about grammar and punctuation?
- Describe your experience publishing your essay.
- What do you want to remember to do the next time you write an essay?

EL **ENGLISH LEARNER SUPPORT: Support Presentations**

ALL LEVELS Before students take part in the Round Table Reading or sit in the Author's Chair, allow them to practice reading their expository essays aloud to themselves or to a partner.

Story

FOCUS STATEMENT There are many different ways to tell a story.

FOCAL TEXT

The Mesmer Menace

Author: Kersten Hamilton

Illustrator: James Hamilton

Summary: Twelve-year-old inventor Wally Kennewicket and his dog ,Noodles, live at the Amazing Automated Inn. They work together to foil the evil plans of hypnotists, the Mesmers, in this sci-fi steampunk adventure.

WRITING PROMPT

READ this sentence: *There are many different ways to tell a story.*

THINK of all the different kinds of fiction that you have read.

WRITE a story about a character that is on a journey to discover something. Choose a subgenre for your story.

LESSONS

1. **Introducing the Focal Text**

2. **The Read**

3. **Vocabulary**

4. **Prewriting: Preparing to Write**

5. **Drafting I: Beginning the Draft**

6. **Drafting II: Narrative Structure**

7. **Drafting III: Completing the Draft**

8. **Revising I: Organization and Elaboration**

9. **Revising II: Including Dialogue**

10. **Revising III: Conferencing**

11. **Revising IV: Developing Interesting Characters**

12. **Editing I: Grammar, Usage, and Mechanics**

13. **Editing II: Peer Proofreading**

14. **Publishing**

15. **Sharing**

LEARNING MINDSET: Wonder

Display Anchor Chart 32: My Learning Mindset throughout the year. Refer to it to introduce Wonder and to reinforce the skills you introduced in previous modules.

NARRATIVE • STORY

INSTRUCTIONAL VOCABULARY

- **narrative** a story
- **genre** a kind of literature with certain characteristics
- **subgenre** a category of a genre
- **steampunk** a blend of science fiction and fantasy typically set during the Industrial Revolution with futuristic elements.

LEARNING MINDSET:
Wonder

Introduce Tell students that humans are naturally curious. *in* The Mesmer Menace, *a character reads about flying then uses what he learned to create an invention that helps solve a problem.* Tell students that curiosity can lead them to read and learn new things.

● *Professional Learning*

RESEARCH FOUNDATIONS

A student's mindset is how he or she feels about learning. A learning mindset is a set of beliefs—including growth mindset, belonging, and purpose and relevance—that help students accept challenges, embrace mistakes, and value hard work.

See the **GPS guide** to learn more.

Priming the Students

Explore Narratives

- Tell students that another word for *story* is **narrative**. Ask: *What are the characteristics of a narrative?* Have students Turn and Talk for three minutes. Have student volunteers name several characteristics, such as plot, character, setting, theme, as you write their responses on the board or chart paper.

- Continue the discussion by writing the word **genre** on the board or chart paper. Model looking up the word in a student dictionary. Read aloud the definition.

The Mesmer Menace

  THINK ALOUD *I know that there are four main literary genres: poetry, drama, fiction, and nonfiction. They are different kinds, or types, of literature, and each has defining characteristics.*

- List the four main genres on the board or chart paper. Then introduce the concept of **subgenre**. Say: *A subgenre is a category of a genre.* Ask: *What are your favorite kinds of stories to read?* Add students' answers to your list. Point out that the kinds of stories, such as mysteries or adventure stories, are subgenres of fiction.

- Show students the cover of the focal text, *The Mesmer Menace.* Say: The Mesmer Menace *is an example of the subgenre* **steampunk**. *If you have not heard of this subgenre, think about each part of the compound word:* steam *and* punk. *What might the words mean together as a subgenre of science fiction?*

- Ask: *What do you notice about the cover of* The Mesmer Menace *that might also be a clue to the meaning of steampunk?*

- Explain that steampunk is a blend of science fiction and fantasy. The setting for steampunk stories is usually during the Industrial Revolution of the 1800s. The characters, however, invent or use devices from the future, such as flying machines, robots, or devices powered by steam.

Engage and Respond

- Show **Display and Engage 2.1** and read the Focus Statement aloud. Then refer to the list of genres and subgenres on the chart paper and ask: *What are your favorite kinds of stories to read and write?* Have students write responses in their notebooks.

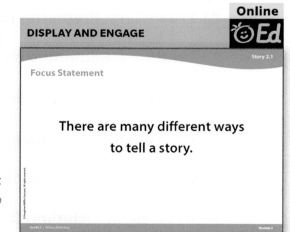

Online

DISPLAY AND ENGAGE

Story 2.1

Focus Statement

There are many different ways to tell a story.

LEARNING OBJECTIVES

- Use background knowledge to prepare to read.
- Brainstorm words and phrases on a topic.
- Discuss audience and purpose.
- Analyze a narrative text for author's craft.
- **Language** Discuss the elements of narrative using academic language.

MATERIALS
Online

Anchor Chart W4: *Elements of Narrative*

Focal Text *The Mesmer Menace*

Writer's Notebook *p. 2.1*

INSTRUCTIONAL VOCABULARY

- **narrator** the person or animal that tells the story
- **setting** where and when a story takes place
- **foreshadowing** hints at future happenings in the plot
- **character** the people or animals that the story is about
- **conflict** the problem in a story
- **plot** the series of events in a story

Priming the Text

Prepare to Read

- Introduce <u>Anchor Chart W4: Narrative Elements</u>. Discuss each term listed.

- Remind students of genre discussion. Then show the cover of *The Mesmer Menace*. Explain that this book is an example of the steampunk subgenre. Ask: *What clues about the story do the title and the illustration suggest?* Discuss the author's audience and purpose. Ask: *Why do you think the author wrote the book? Who is the audience?*

- Explain to students that a **narrator** tells the story. Say: *The narrator in this story is a type of dog called a dachshund.* Ask: *What do you know about dachshunds?*

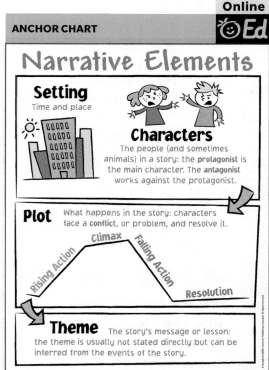

The Read

Read the Focal Text

- Read the first three chapters of *The Mesmer Menace,* or more if time allows. As you read, stop at these points for discussion.

  » Show the first illustration of the building on the edge of the cliff. Ask: *What do you notice about this building? Why do you think it may be important?* (*Answers will vary.*)

  » Read the introduction. Ask: *What do you think automatons are? What do you think has happened?* (*Answers will vary.*)

  » Read the first three paragraphs and point out the date and **setting** of the story.

  » Ask: *Why do you think the first chapter begins with the word* Danger? (*Answers will vary.*) Introduce the term **foreshadowing**. Explain that foreshadowing increases suspense.

  » Have students think about the main **characters**. Ask: *What have you learned about Wally? What other characters seem to be important?* (*Answers will vary.*)

  » Remind students that stories have **conflict** and a **plot**. Ask: *Why is the arrival of the hobo important to the plot?* (*Answers will vary.*) Tell students to listen for descriptions of other people in disguise.

  » Continue reading *The Mesmer Menace*. Have students write interesting words, sentences, or ideas on <u>Writer's Notebook page 2.1</u>.

Engage and Respond

- Have students write two or three sentences to answer the following question: *What narrative element is most interesting to you? Why?* Have partners share their ideas.

LEARNING OBJECTIVES

- Read and understand newly encountered vocabulary.
- Explain the meaning of vocabulary words.
- Label parts of speech.
- **Language** Discuss and define new vocabulary.
- **Language** Write about vocabulary using academic language.

MATERIALS   Online

Focal Text *The Mesmer Menace*
Writer's Notebook *p. 2.1*
Display and Engage *2.2*
Classroom materials *chart paper, markers*

Review the Focal Text

- Review with students the first three chapters of *The Mesmer Menace*. Explain that the narrative is rich with vocabulary used in a humorous fashion. Remind them that the narrator is a dog that uses an advanced vocabulary and defines certain words for the reader.

- Ask students what comes to mind when they hear the word *bank*. List these words on the board or chart paper. If students have not mentioned the word *deposit*, write it on the list of words. Link *deposit* to the word *bank*.

- Say: *A word bank is a place where you can deposit words you want to remember.*

- Have students return to **Writer's Notebook page 2.1**. Page through *The Mesmer Menace* and have students identify interesting and unusual words. Write the words the students select on chart paper for a class resource.

- Point out the part of speech (noun, verb, adverb) of some of the words below. Remind students that dictionaries identify a word's part of speech.

automaton	meticulously	tricks
menace	tidied	skullduggery
profundity	velocipede	Pasha
cunningly	Mesmers	espionage

- Pause to ask students why certain words are interesting to them. Have students add those words to their Word Banks.

- Show **Display and Engage 2.2**. Read the directions. Have students refer to their Word Bank and, with partners, make drawings, create games, and otherwise get familiar with the words. If they don't know the meanings of the words, they can look them up using print and digital resources.

Engage and Respond

- Direct students to have a conversation with their partner. Each student should use at least three words from his or her Word Bank during the conversation.

EL **ENGLISH LEARNER SUPPORT: Vocabulary Support**

SUBSTANTIAL
Ask yes/no questions about the Word Bank terms, such as *Would a teacher be happy with a student who uses tricks and skullduggery? Yes or no?*

MODERATE
Ask questions about the Word Bank terms, and have students choose from two possible answers. For example: *If a girl very carefully cleaned every part of her bicycle, did she act cunningly or meticulously?*

LIGHT
Have students use three terms from their Word Banks to write a short paragraph about a villain.

LEARNING OBJECTIVES

- Understand elements of narrative writing.
- Use multiple prewriting strategies to plan.
- **Language** Discuss fiction by using the words *setting, character,* and *conflict.*
- **Language** Write sentences in response to a prompt.

MATERIALS   Online

Focal Text *The Mesmer Menace*
Display and Engage *2.3, 2.4*
Writer's Notebook, *pp. 2.2, 2.3, 2.4*

● *Professional Learning*

BEST PRACTICES

Students learn more when they are directly involved and clearly understand their own goals and objectives. Remind students that it's important to return to the goals they set as they work.

TEACHER TIP

Consider grouping students according to their genre preferences. Allow them to share ideas about the genre and discuss responses to the story starters.

Review the Elements of Narrative

- Review the sections of *The Mesmer Menace* that you have already read. Then read another chapter or two of the book if you have time.

- Discuss the narrative elements in the story. Ask: *What is the setting? Who are the major characters? What events have happened? What conflicts have you noticed? What do you predict might happen based on the foreshadowing?* (*Answers will vary.*)

Introduce the Prompt and Brainstorm

- Explain to students that they will create their own imaginative story. They will choose a subgenre for this story, such as science fiction or fantasy.

- Show **Display and Engage 2.3**. Read the prompt together. Make note of the tips.

- Show **Display and Engage 2.4** and have students read along using **Writer's Notebook page 2.2**. As you read the Writing Model to students, point out the underlined phrase. Discuss other possibilities for finishing the sentence. To model using the story starter (the underlined words) for a different genre, ask: *What might you add if you wanted to write a science fiction story? A fantasy? An adventure or fairy tale?*

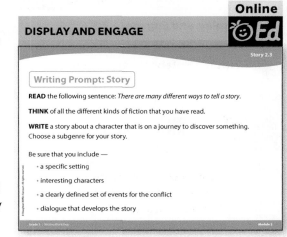

DISPLAY AND ENGAGE   Online Ed   Story 2.3

Writing Prompt: Story

READ the following sentence: *There are many different ways to tell a story.*

THINK of all the different kinds of fiction that you have read.

WRITE a story about a character that is on a journey to discover something. Choose a subgenre for your story.

Be sure that you include —
- a specific setting
- interesting characters
- a clearly defined set of events for the conflict
- dialogue that develops the story

Set Goals and Review the Rubric

- Point out that good fiction writers try to write stories readers will find interesting. Have students write goals for their stories on **Writer's Notebook page 2.3**.

- Have students refer to **Writer's Notebook page 2.4** as you discuss with them what you will be looking for in their stories.

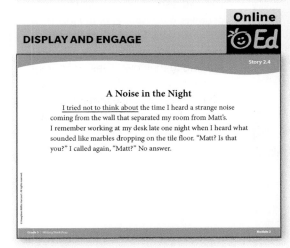

DISPLAY AND ENGAGE   Online Ed   Story 2.4

A Noise in the Night

I tried not to think about the time I heard a strange noise coming from the wall that separated my room from Matt's. I remember working at my desk late one night when I heard what sounded like marbles dropping on the tile floor. "Matt? Is that you?" I called again. "Matt?" No answer.

Engage and Respond

- Write on the board or chart paper the following story starters: "Lying on the ground like a dead chicken, I looked up to see . . ." or "Suddenly, we found ourselves lost in the wilderness and without any . . . ."

- Ask: *What kind of story could you write with the first starter? What kind for the second?* (*Answers will vary.*) Explain that finishing these sentences will help students generate ideas for their own stories. Have them freewrite in their notebooks.

LEARNING OBJECTIVES

- Understand how to turn prewriting into the beginning of a draft.
- **Language** Compose goals for narrative writing.
- **Language** Write narrative sentences to complete a story idea.

MATERIALS   Online

Display and Engage *2.3, 2.5*

Anchor Chart W4: *Elements of Narrative*

Writer's Notebook *pp. 2.5, 2.6*

 LEARNING MINDSET:
Wonder

Apply Remind students that curiosity, or a sense of wonder, leads them to learn about new and interesting things. *You can learn about your interests by reading different kinds of books, a newspaper or magazine, or online articles.* Tell students that they can apply information they gain while reading to their own lives. Encourage students to use the kinds of stories (the genres) they like to read as models for the stories they will write.

Prepare to Draft

- Show **Display and Engage 2.3**. Review the prompt, clarifying the requirements: a character on a journey, a series of events, an interesting setting, and dialogue.

- Suggest to students that the genre they choose will define the setting. Say: *A science fiction story may take place on another planet. A fantasy may take place in a dream world in which animals and objects can talk. A steampunk narrative is set in the past but has futuristic inventions.*

- Show **Anchor Chart W4: Elements of Narrative**. Review the narrative elements to help students begin to structure their stories.

- Explain that today they will choose a genre for their story. Say: *We worked with story starters to generate ideas for a story.* Write on the board or chart paper the story starters from the prewriting exercise.

> Lying on the ground like a dead chicken, I looked up to see...
>
> Suddenly, we found ourselves lost in the wilderness without any...

THINK ALOUD *I like the starter with the phrase "lying on the ground like a dead chicken" because it sounds funny, and I think I can build a story from it.*

Begin to Draft

- Direct students to use **Writer's Notebook page 2.5** as they continue to explore ideas for their stories.

- Have students review their freewrites from the previous lesson and begin drafting. Remind students to first create an environment and then let the story unfold as the characters interact.

- To model how a story unfolds, show students **Display and Engage 2.5**. Read aloud the second section and have students read along using **Writer's Notebook page 2.6**. Give students time to write. Circulate the room to provide help as needed.

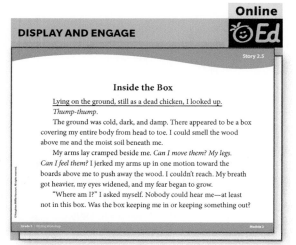

DISPLAY AND ENGAGE   Online

Story 2.5

Inside the Box

Lying on the ground, still as a dead chicken, I looked up. *Thump-thump.*

The ground was cold, dark, and damp. There appeared to be a box covering my entire body from head to toe. I could smell the wood above me and the moist soil beneath me.

My arms lay cramped beside me. *Can I move them? My legs. Can I feel them?* I jerked my arms up in one motion toward the boards above me to push away the wood. I couldn't reach. My breath got heavier, my eyes widened, and my fear began to grow.

"Where am I?" I asked myself. Nobody could hear me—at least not in this box. Was the box keeping me in or keeping something out?

 ENGLISH LEARNER SUPPORT:
Elicit Participation

SUBSTANTIAL

Give students sentences frames to complete, such as *My goals for writing my story are _____ and _____. The genre for my story is _____.*

MODERATE

Ask students to answer these questions in writing: *What are two of your goals for writing your story? What genre have you chosen for your story?*

LIGHT

Have pairs discuss their goals and the genres they have chosen for their story before drafting.

LEARNING OBJECTIVES

- Understand genre characteristics.
- Understand narrative structure.
- Develop drafts into focused, structured, and coherent pieces of writing.
- **Language** Explain stories using academic language, including *genre, setting, plot,* and *character.*

MATERIALS   Online

Anchor Chart W4: *Elements of Narrative*

Anchor Chart W6: *Narrative Structure*

 INSTRUCTIONAL VOCABULARY

- **exposition** the beginning of the story
- **rising action** a series of conflicts leading up to the climax
- **climax** the turning point in the story
- **falling action** the action following the climax
- **resolution** the conclusion that ties all the parts together

TEACHER TIP

Be sure to add the vocabulary terms in this lesson to the class Instructional Vocabulary list. Direct students to add the terms to their glossaries as well.

Introduce Narrative Structure

- Remind students of the narrative elements as shown on <u>Anchor Chart W4: Elements of Narrative</u>.

- Explain to students that using the nursery rhyme "Little Miss Muffet" will help them remember the narrative elements of character, setting, and plot. They will also learn about narrative structure.

- Have students recite the nursery rhyme. Then have students fold an 8 1/2 x 11" sheet of paper into quadrants. In each quadrant have students draw one part of the nursery rhyme: Miss Muffet on her tuffet, the appearance of the spider, the shock in Miss Muffet's reaction, and Miss Muffet running away.

  THINK ALOUD *I can see in quadrant 1 that Miss Muffet is the main character of the narrative. She is sitting on a grassy tuffet, which is the setting. In quadrant 2, the spider slowly makes its appearance in the story. It causes trouble, or conflict in the story. In quadrant 3, the spider sits down beside Miss Muffet, and she becomes frightened, which is an event in the plot*. *In quadrant 4, Miss Muffet runs away.*

- Show <u>Anchor Chart W6: Narrative Structure</u>. Say: *To remember narrative structure, think of a pyramid.* Extend the discussion of narrative structure by showing where the four quadrants of the Miss Muffet story align on the pyramid. Say: *Quadrant 1 shows the* **exposition**. *Quadrant 2 shows the conflict and* **rising action**. *Quadrant 3 shows the* **climax**. *Quadrant 4 shows the* **falling action** *and* **resolution**.

- Review and explain the meanings of instructional vocabulary as you point to the various sections of the pyramid.

- Explain to students that the basic narrative structure for all stories, no matter the length, is the same as on the pyramid.

ANCHOR CHART   **Online**

Narrative Structure

The narrative structure is also called the plot. It usually has five stages:

Climax the turning point in the story

Rising action: what happens in the story that leads to the climax

Falling action: the events that happen after the climax

Exposition any important background information about the setting and characters

Resolution the conclusion of the story

Continue to Draft

- As students work on their drafts, circulate and assist as needed.

ENGLISH LEARNER SUPPORT: Support Drafting

SUBSTANTIAL
Provide copies of the narrative structure pyramid. Have students point to the steps on the pyramid as you identify *exposition, rising action, climax, falling action,* and *resolution.*

MODERATE
Ask students to rephrase the steps on the narrative pyramid and explain what the steps mean, either in their home language or in English.

LIGHT
Have students apply the narrative structure pyramid to another story, such as a commonly known myth or fable.

LEARNING OBJECTIVES
• Draft narratives.
• Add conclusions to drafts.
• **Language** Write a draft of a story with a clearly defined genre.

MATERIALS   Online ⓔ**Ed**

Display and Engage 2.3, 2.6a, 2.6b
Writer's Notebook p. 2.7
Anchor Chart W6: *Narrative Structure*

Imagine Characters

• Have students look at the names of the characters in *The Mesmer Menace.* Ask: *What makes the following characters' names memorable: Wally Kennewickett, Calypso, Noodles, Melvin, Priscilla or Prissy, Theodore Roosevelt?* (Answers may vary.)

• Explain to students that naming characters gives them life. Suggest that they think about the names and personality traits of people they know to help them create characters for their stories.

THINK ALOUD *I had an odd and funny neighbor once. I might use some of her traits for one of my characters. I also like to ask my characters questions: For example:* How would someone describe your looks or your actions? What are you good at? What are you afraid of? What do and don't you want people to know about you? *Answering these questions helps me understand my characters.*

Write a Conclusion

• Review the Writing Prompt on **Display and Engage 2.3**. Read aloud the third model story section on **Display and Engage 2.6a–2.6b** and have students follow along, using **Writer's Notebook page 2.7**. Explain that the story is at a critical point—the climax. The character needs to escape from the trap, and the story needs to end. Ask: *What conclusions can you suggest?* Have students discuss their ideas as you write on the board.

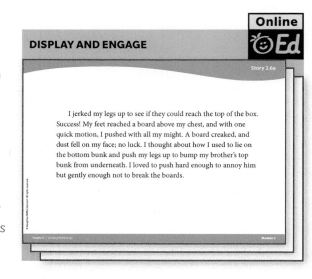

DISPLAY AND ENGAGE

Online ⓔ**Ed**

Story 2.6a

I jerked my legs up to see if they could reach the top of the box. Success! My feet reached a board above my chest, and with one quick motion, I pushed with all my might. A board creaked, and dust fell on my face; no luck. I thought about how I used to lie on the bottom bunk and push my legs up to bump my brother's top bunk from underneath. I loved to push hard enough to annoy him but gently enough not to break the boards.

• Use **Anchor Chart W6: Narrative Structure** to remind students that their stories should end with falling action and a resolution. Say: *Remember to conclude your story within the genre you have chosen. For example, in* The Mesmer Menace, *Noodles uses Wally's flying invention to save the train from disaster. The flying machine is a good conclusion because the genre is steampunk.*

• Allow students time to continue drafting their stories. Circulate the room to offer assistance as needed.

(EL) ENGLISH LEARNER SUPPORT: Support Discussion

SUBSTANTIAL
Have partners read each other's stories aloud. Have them identify the setting, characters, and conflict of each other's story using sentence frames, such as *The setting of your story is _____. The characters in your story are _____. The conflict in your story is _____.*

MODERATE
Have partners read each other's stories. Have them respond orally by using sentence frames, such as *I like _____ about your story. I need more information about _____ in your story.*

LIGHT
Have partners take turns reading their drafts aloud. Have them discuss the climax and ending of each story and make notes about how to improve those plot points.

LEARNING OBJECTIVES

- Review narrative structure.
- Revise drafts for organization.
- Revise drafts to add any needed information.
- **Language** Write correctly formed sentences.

MATERIALS Online

Anchor Chart W6: *Narrative Structure*
Classroom materials *chart paper, markers*

TARGETED GRAMMAR SUPPORT

You may want to consult the following grammar minilessons to review key revising topics.

- **1.1.1 Complete Sentences,** p. W198
- **1.1.3 Writing Sentences,** p. W200
- **1.2.1 Declarative and Interrogative Sentences,** p. W203

Introduce the Revision Skill

- Explain that when revising, it's important for students to go back and check that their narrative stories are structured and organized correctly. Review narrative structural elements from Lesson 6 (*beginning, middle,* and *end*) using "Little Miss Muffet" as your guide.

- Have students revisit their illustrations of the quadrants depicting the structure of the rhyme. Display a Miss Muffet quadrant that you've drawn on chart paper and filled in, except leave the bottom right quadrant blank.

- Point out that without the information in the missing quadrant, we don't know what happens to the main character, Miss Muffet.

  THINK ALOUD *If narrative stories have missing elements, then the stories aren't complete. If elements, such as the ending, are missing, the story is hard to follow and understand. It's important that the story's structure be complete.*

- Now fill in the fourth quadrant on the chart paper. Review the quadrants and how the information aligns to the five sections of the pyramid: 1) exposition: the beginning of the story; 2) rising action: a series of conflicts leading up to the climax; 3) climax: the turning point in the story; 4) falling action: the action following the climax; and 5) resolution: the conclusion tying all the parts together.

- Explain that revisions should clarify ideas and use narrative techniques such as dialogue and description to properly develop events in the story.

- Review that both short narratives such as "Little Miss Muffet" and longer ones, similar to the students' stories, have the same narrative structure.

  THINK ALOUD *All the narrative elements we just discussed must be included for the story to be complete. As you read back over your stories and make revisions, check to see that all narrative elements have been included and that your stories make sense. When checking that events are sequenced clearly, be sure you're using transitional phrases to guide the reader from one event to the next.*

Revise for Organization and Elaboration

- Use <u>Anchor Chart W6: Narrative Structure</u> as a guideline for students to check for complete and coherent narratives.

- Guide students as they revise their drafts for elements such as word choice and sentence structure as well as checking that dialogue and descriptions support and enhance their story.

- Emphasize the use of sensory details to create more vivid events and experiences, as applicable.

- Devote extended class time to implementing revisions.

ANCHOR CHART Online

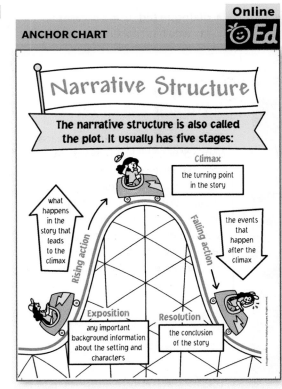

Narrative Structure

The narrative structure is also called the plot. It usually has five stages:

Climax
the turning point in the story

what happens in the story that leads to the climax

Rising action

Falling action

the events that happen after the climax

Exposition
any important background information about the setting and characters

Resolution
the conclusion of the story

NARRATIVE • STORY

LEARNING OBJECTIVES

- Strengthen the use of dialogue.
- **Language** Explain the meaning of a dialogue tag.
- **Language** Write correctly formed dialogue sentences.

MATERIALS Online ⓔEd

Display and Engage 2.7

TARGETED GRAMMAR SUPPORT

You may want to consult the following grammar minilessons to review key revising topics.

- **2.5.2 Possessive Pronouns,** p. W239
- **5.3.4 Review Contractions,** p. W311
- **6.1.3 Interjections and Dialogue,** p. W315

 INSTRUCTIONAL VOCABULARY

- **dialogue** the words characters in a story say out loud to each other
- **dialogue tag** using phrases to say who has spoken

 LEARNING MINDSET: Wonder

Normalize Remind students that a sense of wonder can make them stronger writers. *It is normal to allow your sense of wonder to help you learn about new and interesting things. You can apply those new ideas to your writing.* Encourage students to see if a sense of wonder comes through as they review each other's stories.

Exploring Dialogue

- Lead a discussion about how strong **dialogue** can add to a story and how weak dialogue can detract from it. Read the following lines of dialogue:

  "Hi, how are you?"

  "I'm fine. How about you?"

  "I'm fine but in a hurry!"

  "Okay, see you later."

- Discuss why this type of dialogue would not add complexity to any story.
  THINK ALOUD *The main purpose of dialogue should be to bring characters to life and add interest to the story. Dialogue should do more than just duplicate speech.*

- Explain that a few lines of dialogue can reveal more about a character than several lines of details and descriptions. Explore a strong example of dialogue, using a quote from *The Mesmer Menace*. Show **Display and Engage 2.7**. Discuss what this dialogue reveals about the story. Students might suggest that the dialogue provides information, reveals the characters' thoughts and feelings, and shows how the characters respond to what happened.

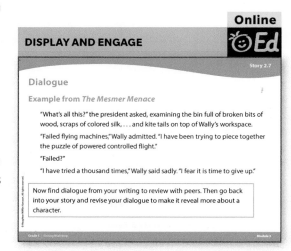

- Define a **dialogue tag** as using phrases after a spoken statement, such as "she said" and "he said." Then explain that a dialogue tag is not always necessary: if it's clear to the reader who is speaking, then the dialogue tag can be omitted.

- Have students use their own writing as a springboard for discussion about dialogue in their stories.

  » Divide the class into small groups.

  » Ask students to find dialogue from their writing to review with peers.

  » Have students take turns discussing where dialogue tags can be omitted or added for clarity and conciseness.

Revising Dialogue

- To help students revise dialogue they have written, instruct them to cover their dialogue with their finger, one line at a time. Then have them read the dialogue without the covered line. If the story makes sense without the covered line, direct students to change or eliminate the dialogue as necessary.

- Provide ample time for students to work on revisions, which may include adding, deleting, combining, or rearranging dialogue.

 ENGLISH LEARNER SUPPORT: Tiered Support

ALL LEVELS Have partners read dialogue aloud to one another and suggest improvements. If pairs are struggling, ask leading questions, such as: *This character is angry. What can he say to show his anger?*

LESSON
10

REVISING III: CONFERENCING

LEARNING OBJECTIVES

- Give and receive peer feedback.
- Revise drafts to reflect peer suggestions.
- **Language** Review key grammar topics.
- **Language** Write correctly formed sentences.
- **Language** Use different sentence lengths.

MATERIALS   Online

Display and Engage 2.8

TARGETED GRAMMAR SUPPORT

You may want to consult the following grammar minilessons to review key revising topics.

- **1.2.1 Declarative and Interrogative Sentences,** p. W203
- **1.4.4 Review Complex Sentences,** p. W216
- **4.1.1 Adjectives,** p. W278

Small Group Conferences

- Divide the class into small groups of four or five students. Show **Display and Engage 2.8** and use it to explain the highlighting strategy. Explain that this strategy provides verbal and written feedback. The writer learns what the listeners find effective in his or her writing. In their groups, students should use the highlighting strategy to give and get feedback.

- Debrief with the whole class. Discuss students' responses to the following questions.

DISPLAY AND ENGAGE   Online Ed

Story 2.8

Conferencing: Highlighting Strategy

Students will work together in groups of four or five. Each student should have a highlighter.

1. Each person in the group takes turns as a listener and as a writer. Listeners listen as the writer shares aloud.
2. Listeners give verbal and written feedback. Focus on the positive!
3. During the first reading, listeners listen. During the second reading, listeners write notes about what they liked about the writer's writing.
4. After the readings, listeners share their notes aloud. Writers highlight on their own writing what the listeners shared.

Grade 5 | Writing Workshop   Module 2

> - How will you use the feedback from your writing group to revise your draft during the next lesson?
> - Which section of your story needs the most revision? How can you tell?
> - What are you starting to notice about yourself as a writer?

Continue to Revise

- Have students re-enter their writing and continue to revise, using the feedback they received in small group conferences.

- Circulate the room and assist students with revising. If students need help with a specific grammar topic, do a direct teach.

- As you circulate, group students who need support on similar grammar topics. Use the grammar minilessons or the students' own writing to provide targeted review and support. Remind students that they must make revisions if readers don't understand what they're saying in their stories.

(EL) ENGLISH LANGUAGE SUPPORT: Support Participation

SUBSTANTIAL
Review examples students identified during the highlighting exercise. Talk with students about how they will use the feedback to make changes to their writing.

MODERATE
Direct partners to take turns reading a section aloud then paraphrasing aloud. Pairs should pause to incorporate feedback and make changes to their writing.

LIGHT
Assign partners the roles of writer and listener. Revisit highlighted parts together and take turns describing and explaining why sections were highlighted. Discuss how to strengthen other parts of their writing similarly, emphasizing clarity.

LEARNING OBJECTIVES

- Use strategies to develop characters.
- **Language** Elaborate on character traits.

MATERIALS   Online Ed

Display and Engage *2.9*

Writer's Notebook *p. 2.8*

TARGETED GRAMMAR SUPPORT

You may want to consult the following grammar minilessons to review key revising topics.

- **2.2.4 Review Singular and Plural Nouns,** p. W226
- **4.3.1 Comparative/Superlative Adjectives,** p. W288
- **4.4.2 Prepositional Phrases,** p. W294

 INSTRUCTIONAL VOCABULARY

- **characterization** the creation of a fictional character
- **trait** a quality belonging to a character

Introduce Characterization

- Explain that students will be studying a short passage from a story to see how the author brings characters to life.
- Show **Display and Engage 2.9**. Have a volunteer read aloud the excerpt to the class. Ask students to consider how the author of this passage developed King Barf.

> **Online Ed**
>
> **DISPLAY AND ENGAGE**   Story 2.9
>
> **Characterization Model**
>
> Read this passage and think about how the author brings King Barf to life.
>
> If I had just looked at his royal costume, I suppose I could have been impressed, though gold wasn't so impressive to me anymore. King Barf wore a gold crown on his head, gold chains around his neck, gold armor on his chest, gold rings on all of his fingers. There were servants on all sides of the king with giant paddles, and they swatted at the pixies trying to converge on the king and all his glorious gold.
>
> But King Bartholomew Archibald Reginald Fife . . .
> King Barf was chubby.
> He had a turned-up nose and floppy ears.
> He looked like a pink pig with a crown on his head.
> "My people of The Mountain," he said, double chins wobbling. He sounded like a pig with a stuffy nose. "Your work is so valuable to The Kingdom."

- Ask students: *Where does the name King Barf originate? (the first letter of each of the king's names: Bartholomew Archibald Reginald Fife)*

  THINK ALOUD *How does the author portray King Barf? As good? Or evil? Or maybe a combination of the two? How does the author reveal this character?*

- Have students open to **Writer's Notebook page 2.8**. Review each of the eight sections on the chart as follows.

1. Name	5. Dialogue
2. Description	6. Impact
3. Inner Qualities	7. Comparisons
4. Actions	8. Reactions

- Facilitate completing the chart.
  - » 1) Fill in King Barf's Name.
  - » 2) Describe what he looks like.
  - » 3) Describe his personality **traits**, mannerisms, and beliefs.
  - » 4) Write verbs that fit him.
  - » 5) Select significant dialogue.
  - » 6) Analyze how you think he'd influence other characters.
  - » 7) Compare him to animals or other beings to open your perspective and shift your writing angle.
  - » 8) Write your reaction to him. Start with this question: "Would I want to be friends with him?"

- Lead a discussion and have students brainstorm ideas about King Barf, stopping after each section to add ideas to the chart.

Revise for Character Development

- Have students think about the characters in their story and how they might revise to bring them more fully to life. Direct them to use **Writer's Notebook page 2.8** as a mechanism for brainstorming characteristics for their characters.

- Students should then re-enter their writing to more fully develop their characters.

LEARNING OBJECTIVES

- Proofread writing for grammar, usage, and mechanics.
- **Language** Proofread writing for spelling.
- **Language** Edit writing for capitalization and punctuation.

MATERIALS   Online

Anchor Chart W16: *Proofreading Marks*

TARGETED GRAMMAR SUPPORT

You may want to consult the following grammar minilessons to review key editing topics.

- **1.2.4 Review Kinds of Sentences,** p. W206
- **5.2.3 Transitions in Writing,** p. W305
- **7.4.4 Review Punctuation,** p. W341

Review Proofreading Marks

- Share **Anchor Chart W16: Proofreading Marks** with students. Point out that students will be using these proofreading marks as they proofread their writing. Remind students that proofreading is a type of editing that is done to make sure their writing is clear and understandable to all who read it.

- Walk students through examples of how proofreading marks are applied in writing.

Proofread Writing

- Remind students that if their stories are not written clearly, then their audience may not understand what is happening. It may be that they haven't properly used types of sentences, punctuation, or transitions. Have students independently edit their writing, using ratiocination from Module 1 for sentence types, punctuation, and transitions.

- Circulate the room and provide assistance as needed.

- As you circulate, group students who need support on similar grammar topics. Use the grammar minilessons or the students' own writing to provide targeted review and support.

ANCHOR CHART   **Online** Ed

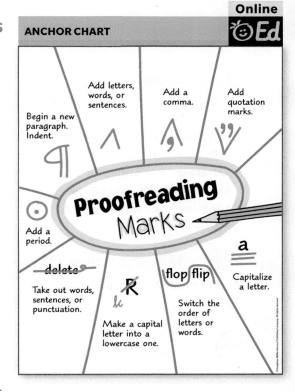

EL ENGLISH LEARNER SUPPORT: Tiered Support

SUBSTANTIAL
Read students' writing. Write sentences with grammatical errors on a separate piece of paper, showing only one at a time. Discuss errors and guide students to correct the mistakes in their own writing.

MODERATE
Read students' writing. Encourage them to identify errors and suggest revisions, using simple phrases to seek clarification where needed.

LIGHT
Read students' writing. Guide them as they identify errors. Have students suggest revisions. Ask questions such as the following: *Why do you think this is a mistake? How can you improve or fix this sentence?*

NARRATIVE • STORY

LEARNING OBJECTIVES

- Proofread writing for grammar, usage, and mechanics.
- **Language** Proofread writing for spelling.
- **Language** Edit writing for capitalization and punctuation.
- **Language** Edit writing with peer support.

MATERIALS	Online Ed

Anchor Chart W15: *Editing Checklist*

LEARNING MINDSET:
Wonder

Review Tell students that it's surprising and remarkable that each one of us learns in a different way. *Just as no two people see the world the same way, no two people learn exactly the same way. That's why it's important to be flexible learners and thinkers. But what makes us similar is that we never stop learning. We can all learn from one another.* As students give and receive edits, encourage them to be mindful and respectful of each other's opinions and insights.

TARGETED GRAMMAR SUPPORT

You may want to consult the following grammar minilessons to review key editing topics.

- **1.3.3 Compound Sentences,** p. W210
- **3.2.3 Consistent Use of Tenses,** p. W255
- **7.2.3 Using Commas in Sentences,** p. W330

Clocking Activity

- Before students begin proofreading each other's papers, display **Anchor Chart W15: Editing Checklist** and review the items. Add the items to the board or chart paper that are specific to this module, such as dialogue.

- Review the rules for clocking.

  » Students form concentric circles or sit opposite each other in rows, hence the term "clocking"; sitting in rows is "digital clocking." As students receive a peer's paper, they become that paper's editor.

  » Call out what item is to be checked by the editor, such as the following: dialogue uses quotation marks correctly, each sentence begins with a capital letter, and sentence ends with proper punctuation.

  » Have students move positions after a couple of items so each student's paper is read by several editors.

  » No marks are made on the actual paper. All papers should have a proofreading page with the writer's name at the top.

  » Each editor writes his or her name next to the number in turn and writes the concept to be checked.

  » When the editing process is completed, have students take their editing page and make any corrections. If there is a problem, they may address it with their editor or teacher.

Edit Writing

- Have students do a final pass through their narrative stories, integrating the notes from the clocking activity into their own writing.

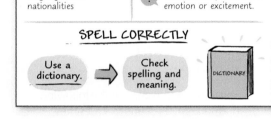

LEARNING OBJECTIVES

- Create a title.
- Publish writing.
- Use technology to assist with writing.
- **Language** Ask and answer questions using academic language.

MATERIALS   Online

Display and Engage *2.10*

TEACHER TIP

Throughout the publishing process, you may wish to assign student pairs to a computer to support each other as they publish and produce their work, including logging on, utilizing software, and navigating the Internet.

Prepare the Final Copy

- Tell students they will write a final copy of their stories. They will also work on the titles of their pieces and publishing their written work.

- Have students evaluate the titles of their stories before writing the final copy and publishing.

  THINK ALOUD *The first title a writer puts on a rough draft isn't necessarily the final title. The title may be the first thing you write before starting your story, but it should really be one of the last elements you work on before the story is complete. Your title should draw readers in and hint at what is to come in the story. If you're not happy with your title, now is the time to change it.*

Publish Writing

- Discuss students' publishing options with **Display and Engage 2.10**. Invite students to share their ideas. Consider multiple ways to publish students' stories, such as using blank hardcover books, creating a class anthology, or investigating online apps that support book creation.

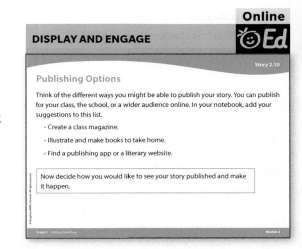

- Have student pairs work together to plan their final copies. Circulate the room and give them tips.

- For the remainder of the time, have students work on their final draft and how they plan to publish their stories.

- Use computers if they are available to type final drafts. Login in and set up students on an account as needed. Reinforce keyboarding skills. Encourage students to set a goal of typing at least two pages in a single session.

EL   ENGLISH LEARNER SUPPORT: Tiered Support

SUBSTANTIAL
Assist students with formulating appropriate titles for their published works. Start by asking them to think of a word or phrase that describes their story. Use responses as a jumping off point to brainstorm titles.

MODERATE
Discuss students' ideas for titles. Have students share ideas with a partner, negotiating to figure out a word or phrase that represents or describes each other's stories.

LIGHT
Have student pairs brainstorm title ideas for each other's work, taking turns leading a conversation and sharing ideas.

LEARNING OBJECTIVES

- Share writing.
- Engage in collaborative discussion.
- **Language** Ask and answer questions using academic language.

MATERIALS   Online

Anchor Chart W17: *Tips on How to Present*

Display and Engage *2.11*

Writer's Notebook *pp. 2.3, 2.9*

● *Professional Learning*

BEST PRACTICES

At regular intervals, request family conferences to share students' independent writing progress and assignments. Positive reinforcement of progress outside the classroom supports the development of a student's identity as a writer.

See the **GPS guide** to learn more.

TEACHER TIP

Before students present their published work, review language and conventions for oral speaking, encouraging the use of formal English when appropriate to express ideas.

Share Writing

- Revisit <u>Anchor Chart W17: Tips on How to Present</u>. Review the tips for presenting.

- Have students share their narrative stories by reading them aloud. Encourage students to ask the presenter questions about their story.

- Encourage the use of multimedia components and visual displays where appropriate to enhance the development of ideas or themes.

Engage and Respond

- Using <u>Display and Engage 2.11</u>, make a running list of additional options for sharing student work. Options can include written, oral, or multimodal presentations.

- Have students turn to <u>Writer's Notebook page 2.3</u>, the list of goals they set at the beginning of this Writing Workshop. Tell them to revisit the goals. Have them Turn and Talk with a partner about how they feel they met their goals and take notes about what goals they might set for the next writing assignment.

1. What did you like best about writing your narrative story?

2. What did you like least?

3. What did you learn about writing? How did you learn it?

4. What do you want to remember to do the next time you write a story?

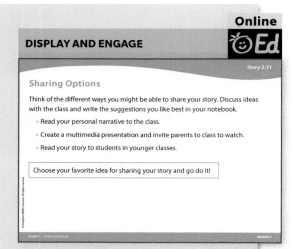

- Then have students fill out <u>Writer's Notebook page 2.9</u>.

EL **ENGLISH LEARNER SUPPORT: Tiered Support**

SUBSTANTIAL

Together, review students' writing goals from <u>Writer's Notebook page 2.3</u>. Talk about ways they met their goals or did not. Write down students' thoughts and have them copy their thoughts on <u>Writer's Notebook page 2.9</u>.

MODERATE

Discuss students' original writing goals. Provide sentence frames as needed to facilitate revisiting their goals. For example: *I did _____ well, but I need to work on _____.*

LIGHT

Have student pairs discuss their writing goals before filling out <u>Writer's Notebook page 2.9</u>.

Persuasive Essay

FOCUS STATEMENT Using persuasion is much more powerful than fighting.

FOCAL TEXT

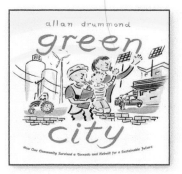

Green City: How One Community Survived a Tornado and Rebuilt for a Sustainable Future

Author and Illustrator: Allan Drummond

Summary: A community survives a tornado and rebuilds their city using sustainable design.

WRITING PROMPT

READ this sentence: *Using persuasion is much more powerful than fighting.*

THINK about the times you struggled to get your way. Did you yell or did you reasonably explain your idea?

WRITE a persuasive essay stating what you would do if a natural disaster destroyed your town. Stay or go?

·········· LESSONS ··········

1. **Priming the Students**

2. **Priming the Text**

3. **The Read**

4. **Vocabulary**

5. **Prewriting: Preparing to Write**

6. **Drafting I: Beginning the Draft**

7. **Drafting II: About Persuasive Writing**

8. **Drafting III: Completing the Draft**

9. **Revising I: Elaboration and Organization**

10. **Revising II: Group Conferencing**

11. **Revising III: Incorporating Feedback**

12. **Editing I: Grammar, Usage, and Mechanics**

13. **Editing II: Peer Proofreading**

14. **Publishing**

15. **Sharing**

**LEARNING MINDSET:
Seeking Challenges**

Display <u>Anchor Chart 32: My Learning Mindset</u> throughout the year. Refer to it to introduce Seeking Challenges and to reinforce the skills you introduced in previous modules.

LEARNING OBJECTIVES

- Prepare for reading by discussing natural disasters.
- Make connections between the text and personal experiences with natural disasters.
- **Language** Express spoken or written ideas about natural disasters.

MATERIALS   Online Ed

Anchor Chart W9: *Elements of an Argument*

Display and Engage *3.1*

 LEARNING MINDSET:
Seeking Challenges

Introduce For some students it will be a challenge to talk or write about these frightening events. With mindful support, these students may accept and even triumph over the challenge. Remind students that when we seek out challenges, our brains grow.

TEACHER TIP

If students have lived through a traumatic experience related to a natural disaster, take extra care with them and their writing. Explain that although their writing may stir up difficult feelings, writing can be a way of healing difficult emotions.

Explore the Topic

- Tell students that they will be reading about a city that was destroyed by a tornado. Explain that a tornado is a type of natural disaster. Ask: *What happens during a tornado?* Have volunteers use available resources to answer the question.

- Ask: *What are other types of natural disasters?* Make a list on the board and discuss each type briefly. Have volunteers use available resources to find definitions and facts. Record definitions on the board.

> tornado: violent, destructive rotating wind
>
> hurricane: a rainstorm with violent winds
>
> earthquake: vibrations in the earth's crust
>
> wildfire: a large fire the spreads rapidly
>
> tsunami: an unusually large wave caused by an undersea quake or volcanic eruption

- Ask whether any students have lived through a natural disaster. Encourage willing students to share experiences.

- Ask: *What do you think happens before, during, and after a natural disaster?*

- Tell students they will be writing a persuasive essay about whether they would choose to rebuild or move away after a severe natural disaster.

- Display **Anchor Chart W9: Elements of an Argument** and point out what it takes to write a good persuasive essay.

Discuss the Focus Statement

- Show **Display and Engage 3.1**. Have students write a few sentences about the focus statement. Have volunteers share their writing with the class.

 ENGLISH LEARNER SUPPORT:
Facilitate Participation

ALL LEVELS Students who are more comfortable speaking than writing might meet in a small group to discuss the focus statement rather than write their responses.

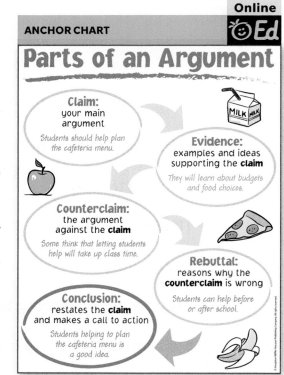

ANCHOR CHART   Online Ed

Parts of an Argument

Claim: your main argument
Students should help plan the cafeteria menu.

Evidence: examples and ideas supporting the **claim**
They will learn about budgets and food choices.

Counterclaim: the argument against the **claim**
Some think that letting students help will take up class time.

Rebuttal: reasons why the **counterclaim** is wrong
Students can help before or after school.

Conclusion: restates the **claim** and makes a call to action
Students helping to plan the cafeteria menu is a good idea.

DISPLAY AND ENGAGE   Online Ed

Persuasive Essay 3.1

Focus Statement

How can learning about natural disasters make us safer from them?

ARGUMENT • PERSUASIVE ESSAY

LEARNING OBJECTIVES

- Generate and clarify questions on a topic.
- **Language** Use prereading support to make predictions about a text.
- **Language** Explain predictions in writing.

MATERIALS   Online

Focal Text *Green City*
Writer's Notebook pp. 3.1, 3.2
Display and Engage 3.2

TEACHER TIP

Explain that a "book walk" prepares the reader for what he or she is about to read. It includes a look at the front and back covers, the table of contents, and some of the pages, including pictures. For personal reading, book walks can help readers decide whether a book interests them.

Prepare to Read

- Show the cover of *Green City*. Point out that the subtitle tells what this book is about.

- Ask: *What does the word "sustainable" mean?* (*able to last in the long term*) *What does "green" mean in this title?* (*environmentally friendly*)

- Turn to the copyright page and discuss the illustrations, asking for student observations.

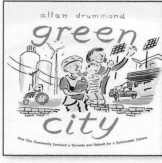

Green City

  THINK ALOUD *I see a car, a door, and a stoplight flying in the air. There is a water tower that is about to fall over. Words are scattered: "Get down into the basement!"; "There goes the stoplight!"; "Total darkness! All the power is out!"; and "Watch out—the water tower". A summary on this page says the book tells the story of Greensburg, Kansas. I am not sure if this is an informational book or a fictional story. Let's look at the back cover to find out.*

- Turn to the back cover and have a volunteer read "Source Notes." Ask: *Is the book fiction or informational?* (*It is a fictional story based on real events.*)

- Go through the book page by page and have students comment on illustrations, talk bubbles, and other features.

- Pause on page 8 and have students read the talk bubbles. Ask: *What information does the author give in these talk bubbles?* (*different ideas residents have about what to do*)

- On page 15, point out the feature "Going Green." Ask: *Do you think this feature is fictional or informational?* (*informational*) *How do you know?*

- Point out the Author's Note and ask: *Why might an author include a note in a book like this?* (*to share his or her personal story; to show why the story means a lot*)

Engage and Respond

- Have students use **Writer's Notebook page 3.1** or their own notebooks to make predictions about the characters, setting, story, and fictional versus nonfictional aspects of the book. Ask them to generate three questions about the book.

- Show **Display and Engage 3.2**. Explain that sometimes we generate questions that are unclear or not useful. Model clarifying questions to make them clearer and more specific.

- Have students use **Writer's Notebook page 3.2** to clarify questions. They should work in pairs and take turns asking questions and having partners paraphrase the questions. If a partner has trouble paraphrasing a question, the writer should consider clarifying it.

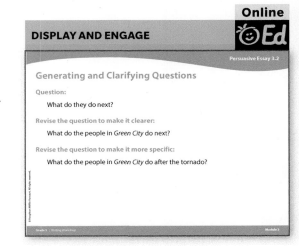

Online
Ed

DISPLAY AND ENGAGE

Persuasive Essay 3.2

Generating and Clarifying Questions

Question:
  What do they do next?

Revise the question to make it clearer:
  What do the people in *Green City* do next?

Revise the question to make it more specific:
  What do the people in *Green City* do after the tornado?

ARGUMENT • PERSUASIVE ESSAY

LEARNING OBJECTIVES

- Analyze an informational text for organization and structure.
- Identify the central idea and author's message in an informational text.
- Identify author's purpose in an informational text.
- **Language** Use strategic techniques to understand vocabulary in reading.

MATERIALS   Online

Focal Text *Green City*
Display and Engage *3.3*
Writer's Notebook *p. 3.3*

Read the Focal Text

- Remind students that *Green City* is based on actual events. Tell students that as you read, they should jot down questions they have about the information in the book.

- Read aloud *Green City*. As you read, stop at these points.

  » Read page 2. Point out that the book is written in first person. Ask: *Who is the narrator in the story?* (*a person who lives in Greensburg*) Read the talk bubbles. Ask: *What information do these talk bubbles provide?* (*They give an idea of what it was like for members of the community right after the tornado hit.*)

  » Read pages 8–9. Read the talk bubbles. Ask: *What do the talk bubbles tell you here?* (*Residents disagreed about what to do.*)

  » Read pages 15–25. Ask: *What is the author's point of view about "green" building? How can you tell?* (*He has a positive view of green building. He presents sustainable development as exciting and futuristic.*)

- Read the author's note. Ask: *Does this page answer some of the questions you had about the book? Which ones? What questions do you still have?*

- Ask: *What is the author's purpose in this book? How do you know?* (*telling the story of a green city and how it came to be; telling about life of a community after disaster strikes*)

- Show the questions on **Display and Engage 3.3**. Explain that writers craft persuasive essays to discuss an issue, take a position, provide arguments supporting the position, and convince the reader of the position. Tell students that the four questions will help them craft their own persuasive essays.

DISPLAY AND ENGAGE

Online Ed

Persuasive Essay 3.3

Questions about Persuasive Essays

- What is the issue?
- What is the author's position?
- What are the arguments that support this position?
- How does the text change how the reader feels?

Engage and Respond

- Distribute **Writer's Notebook page 3.3**. Have students work individually to answer the questions. Then, have small groups discuss their responses.

- Group students who need support on similar grammar topics. Use the grammar minilessons or the students' own writing to provide targeted review and support.

(EL) ENGLISH LEARNER SUPPORT: Scaffold Vocabulary Acquisition

SUBSTANTIAL
Use simplified language to explain that "building green" means building in a way that is environmentally friendly.

MODERATE
As you read, use simplified language to explain the meanings of words such as *reclaimed, wind-resistant, geodesic, sustainable,* and *affordable.*

LIGHT
As you read, have students jot down words they are unfamiliar with and use resources to determine the definitions.

LEARNING OBJECTIVES

- Identify and define vocabulary used to describe natural disasters.
- Brainstorm to come up with words that are useful in describing natural disasters.
- Use various strategies to determine meaning.
- **Language** Work cooperatively to come up with descriptive words in writing.

MATERIALS   Online

Focal Text *Green City*
Writer's Notebook p. 3.4

TEACHER TIP

Be sensitive to students who may have lived through a natural disaster, being sure to include words on the list about cleaning up and building things new from scratch. Emphasize working together and rebuilding community.

 LEARNING MINDSET:
Seeking Challenges

Apply Tell students that in order to become confident learners, it's important to seek out challenges. Maybe learning new vocabulary is difficult for some students. Urge them to take on the challenge of learning and using five new words during this module. Encourage the class to help and support each other.

Review the Focal Text

- Point out that *Green City* uses many descriptive words that are related to natural disasters.
- Have students use <u>Writer's Notebook page 3.4</u> or their own notebooks as Word Banks. Page through the chapters with students and have them identify words and phrases that are related to natural disasters. List their selections on the board.
- Then, encourage students to add their own words that may be related to the destruction that happens when natural disaster strikes. Add those words to the list. Encourage students to be creative with their word choices. (Any word that describes a "big mess" can be used.)

> <u>Words from Green City</u>
>
> destroyed, gone, shredded, gigantic mess, rubble, emergency, disaster area, cleanup
>
> <u>Other disaster-related words</u>
>
> danger, wreckage, ruins, catastrophe, calamity, restart, rebuild

- As students come up with other words and phrases that relate to a natural disaster or disaster recovery, ask volunteers to help figure out the definitions, using context and/or digital or print resources.

Engage and Respond

- Ask students to work individually to come up with more words and phrases that they may want to use in their essays. Have them brainstorm words and phrases about cleaning up, relocating, and rebuilding. Suggest that they look again at *Green City*, use a thesaurus or other resources, and draw on words they already know. Have students add the words and their definitions to their Word Banks.
- Have students select three of their favorite words and write sentences using them.
- Ask volunteers to share their sentences with the class.

 ENGLISH LEARNER SUPPORT: Build Vocabulary

SUBSTANTIAL
Work with students in a small group to help them come up with additional words for their Word Banks.

MODERATE
Have students work with partners and take turns brainstorming additional words for their Word Banks.

LIGHT
Encourage students to use a thesaurus and other digital resources and challenge themselves to come up with at least three words they did not know before.

ARGUMENT • PERSUASIVE ESSAY

LEARNING OBJECTIVES

- Plan a persuasive essay by choosing a topic and a position.
- Set goals for writing a persuasive essay.
- **Language** Work in a group to plan a position for a persuasive essay.

MATERIALS   Online

Display and Engage *3.4a–b*

Writer's Notebook *pp. 3.5, 3.6, 3.7*

TEACHER TIP

Explain that the t-chart from this lesson will serve as a guide when they write their persuasive essays. Without the t-chart, a writer may have problems organizing ideas and getting to the point and may also risk forgetting to include some ideas.

INSTRUCTIONAL VOCABULARY

- **graphic organizer** a chart or other visual representation of information

Review the Writing Prompt

- Show <u>Display and Engage 3.4a–b</u>. Read through and discuss the writing prompt as a class. Note the tips.

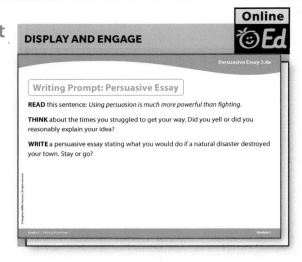

DISPLAY AND ENGAGE

Persuasive Essay 3.4a

Writing Prompt: Persuasive Essay

READ this sentence: *Using persuasion is much more powerful than fighting.*

THINK about the times you struggled to get your way. Did you yell or did you reasonably explain your idea?

WRITE a persuasive essay stating what you would do if a natural disaster destroyed your town. Stay or go?

- Lead a class discussion on the pros and cons of rebuilding and the pros and cons of moving away, based on the events in *Green City*. Record the discussion on the board using a t-chart **graphic organizer**, like the one below.

Rebuilding Pros	Rebuilding Cons
build green	expensive
keep community together	relocate temporarily
fresh start	neighbors disagree

- Have students choose a natural disaster to work on.

- Divide students into small groups, according to the natural disasters they choose (for example, an earthquake group, a tsunami group, etc.).

- Have groups discuss what they would want to do if the natural disaster they chose destroyed their town: rebuild or move away.

- Distribute <u>Writer's Notebook page 3.5</u> and have students work individually to fill in the pros and cons of rebuilding and starting over in the case of the natural disaster they chose. Have students work in pairs or small groups to discuss the pros and cons and then clearly state their position at the bottom of the graphic organizer.

Begin Prewriting and Set Goals

- Distribute <u>Writer's Notebook page 3.6</u>. Discuss the expectations listed in the rubric.

- Have students decide on goals for their persuasive essays. Have them add their goals to the list on <u>Writer's Notebook page 3.7</u> or in their own notebooks Tell students they can use items from the rubric to add to their writing goals.

ENGLISH LEARNER SUPPORT: Scaffold Planning and Writing

SUBSTANTIAL

Lead a small group to help students fill out the pros and cons chart.

MODERATE

Invite students to work in a small group to help each other with the pros and cons chart.

LIGHT

Give students the option of working with a partner on the pros and cons chart.

LEARNING OBJECTIVES

- Identify and gather relevant information.
- Develop a list of sources (bibliography).
- Demonstrate understanding of information.
- **Language** Generate research questions for inclusion in a persuasive text.

MATERIALS   Online

Display and Engage *3.3, 3.5a–d*
Writer's Notebook *pp. 3.5, 3.8, 3.9, 3.10, 3.11*

TEACHER TIP

Arrange to have students work on computers in your classroom or in a computer lab, so they can do their research online. Remind students not to give out any personal information online.

Prepare to Draft

- Show **Display and Engage 3.5a–d** and have students follow along using **Writer's Notebook pages 3.8–3.9**. Read through the model essay with students.

- Ask: *What does the first paragraph do?* (*begins with a hook; sets out the argument*) *What is the writer's argument?* (*Her family has compelling reasons to stay, despite the volcano.*)

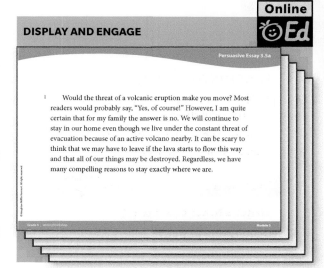

DISPLAY AND ENGAGE

Persuasive Essay 3.5a

1   Would the threat of a volcanic eruption make you move? Most readers would probably say, "Yes, of course!" However, I am quite certain that for my family the answer is no. We will continue to stay in our home even though we live under the constant threat of evacuation because of an active volcano nearby. It can be scary to think that we may have to leave if the lava starts to flow this way and that all of our things may be destroyed. Regardless, we have many compelling reasons to stay exactly where we are.

- Ask: *What reasons does the author give?* (*history in the home, roots in community, natural beauty of town*) Point out that the writer has crafted the essay so that each reason has its own paragraph containing details and examples. Have students identify the supporting details and examples for each reason.

- Ask: *What does the last paragraph do?* (*summarizes reasons, relates back to the intro*)

- Show **Display and Engage 3.3**. Remind students of the four questions central to a persuasive essay and ask them to answer the questions with regard to the model. Tell students to keep these questions in mind as they research and draft.

- Have students use available print or digital resources to gather facts about the natural disaster they have chosen. Ask: *What questions will you research?* Record student questions on the board.

> What kind of damage can this natural disaster do?
>
> Is there a risk of it happening again?
>
> Would there be a warning?
>
> How much time and money would it take to rebuild?

- Distribute **Writer's Notebook page 3.10**, and have students fill it in as they gather information from print or digital sources. Tell them to note the sources of information and keep a list of sources on **Writer's Notebook page 3.11**.

- Give students time to begin their research on the natural disaster they chose.

- As needed, help students identify the information that is most relevant.

Begin to Draft

- Have students use the position stated on **Writer's Notebook page 3.5** to write a clear thesis statement focusing on the main idea and expressing their position.

- Have them also refer to **Writer's Notebook page 3.10** for facts to support their thesis statement as they draft their essays.

 ENGLISH LEARNER SUPPORT: Support Research

ALL LEVELS Where needed, pair students with fluent speakers who are researching the same or similar topics.

ARGUMENT • PERSUASIVE ESSAY

LEARNING OBJECTIVES

- Develop drafts by organizing with purposeful structure.
- **Language** Use persuasive words and transitions in writing.

MATERIALS Online

Writer's Notebook *pp. 3.8, 3.9, 3.12*

Display and Engage *3.5a–d, 3.6*

 **INSTRUCTIONAL VOCABULARY**

- **transitional word or phrase** a word or phrase that shows the relationship between ideas

TEACHER TIP

Tell students that they should carefully select effective, persuasive words and phrases and be careful not to overuse them. Persuasive words and phrases are effective only when they support good reasons that also have supporting facts and details. Persuasive words cannot stand on their own.

Persuasive Words and Transitions

- Remind students that in a persuasive essay their job is to make an argument that convinces readers of a position. Say: *Some words and phrases help persuade readers.*

- Distribute **Writer's Notebook page 3.12** and consider the persuasive words at the top with students. Ask why each word is persuasive.

- Have students suggest additional persuasive words, and record the ones they like on **Writer's Notebook page 3.12** or in their own notebooks.

- Tell students that a **transitional word or phrase** can also be persuasive. Ask: *What are transitional words and phrases?* (*words and phrases that connect ideas*) Ask students for examples of transitional words and phrases. Write them on the board.

> also, in addition to, obviously, furthermore, although, on the other hand, while, since, in other words, importantly

- Point out that many of the transitional words and phrases are neutral and are not persuasive. Underline any persuasive words and phrases that students suggest.

- Show **Display and Engage 3.5a–d** and have students turn to **Writer's Notebook pages 3.8–3.9**. Give students a few minutes to read through the model and circle transitional words and phrases.

- Ask: *Which transitional words did you circle in the model?* (*However, Regardless, Most importantly, Additionally, Then, Moreover, also, at that point, But*)

- Show **Display and Engage 3.6** and discuss when each word or phrase might be used. Have volunteers suggest possible sentences for some of the words or phrases.

- Tell students to record persuasive transitional words or phrases on **Writer's Notebook page 3.12** or in their own notebooks.

Online

DISPLAY AND ENGAGE

Persuasive Essay 3.6

Transition Words for Persuasive Essays

Equally important . . .	Nevertheless . . .	On the contrary . . .
I'm sure you can see that . . .	Obviously . . .	Most importantly . . .
On the other hand . . .	Regardless . . .	What needs to be done/what we need to do . . .
If . . . , then . . .	Although . . .	

Continue to Draft

- Have students continue to draft. Encourage students to use persuasive and transitional words. Students may consult **Writer's Notebook page 3.12**, **Display and Engage 3.6**, and online or print resources.

 ENGLISH LEARNER SUPPORT: Scaffold Writing

SUBSTANTIAL

Help students find one or two places in their essays where they can incorporate a persuasive or transitional word.

MODERATE

Ask partners to add at least two persuasive or transitional words into their essays.

LIGHT

Ask students to add at least three transitional words or phrases to their essays.

ARGUMENT • PERSUASIVE ESSAY

LEARNING OBJECTIVES

- Draft a persuasive essay with a strong conclusion and a purposeful structure.
- **Language** Use and identify the elements of a persuasive essay.

MATERIALS　　Online

Display and Engage 3.3
Writer's Notebook pp. 3.8 , 3.9

TEACHER TIP

If students need more time to finish their drafts, you may want to extend the writing period.

 LEARNING MINDSET:
Seeking Challenges

Apply If students are satisfied with the organization of their essays, encourage them to challenge themselves to strengthen their arguments. Students can decide whether their essays will benefit most from incorporating additional reasons or examples in support of existing arguments or from adding more arguments to their essays. Remind students that when they seek challenges in their writing, they grow as writers.

Introduce the Skill

- Show **Display and Engage 3.3** and remind students of the guiding questions for persuasive writing. Say: *Your essays will address these questions.*
- Have students turn to **Writer's Notebook pages 3.8–3.9**. Ask students to find, circle, and label the issue the model essay is about.
- Next, ask students to underline and label the author's position.
- Then, ask students to number each argument the author makes.
- Finally, ask students to make a squiggly line under the essay's conclusion.
- Ask: *What is the issue in the model?* (*whether the family should move because of the volcano threat*) *Where in the essay does it appear?* (*paragraph 1*) *What is the author's position?* (*The family should not move.*) *Where in the essay does it appear?* (*paragraph 1*) Ask similar questions for each argument and have students identify the reasons and examples supporting each argument.
- Record an outline of the model on the board.

> Structure of a persuasive essay:
>
> Paragraph 1: issue and author's position
>
> Paragraph 2: argument 1
>
> Paragraph 3: argument 2
>
> Paragraph 4: argument 3
>
> Paragraph 5: conclusion

- Summarize the structure of the model with students.
  THINK ALOUD *When I look at the model, I see that the first paragraph introduces the issue and gives the author's position on the issue. The author then gives three arguments, each in a separate paragraph. Each argument has reasons and examples contained in the same paragraph. The conclusion is in the last paragraph.*
- Give students a few minutes to check the organization of their own persuasive essays. Instruct students to note anything in their essays that seems out of order.
- Ask: *Why is an essay's conclusion important?* (*final opportunity to convince the reader*)
- Have a volunteer read aloud the model's last paragraph. Ask: *What does the model's conclusion do?* (*It adds to the argument in favor of staying by painting a picture of how hard it would be to start new somewhere else.*) *How does it link to the introduction?* (*by mentioning the possibility of evacuation, by reviewing the many reasons for staying*)

Continue to Draft

- Have students return to their persuasive essays to work on purposeful organization and a strong conclusion.

 ENGLISH LEARNER SUPPORT: Support Drafting

ALL LEVELS As you circulate the room, help students organize their essays or draft conclusions.

LEARNING OBJECTIVES

- Revise drafts using reorganization and elaboration to improve clarity and coherence.
- **Language** Revise drafts to clearly explain.

MATERIALS Online

Display and Engage 3.7, 3.8a–b

LEARNING MINDSET:
Seeking Challenges

Apply It can be difficult for students to challenge themselves when revising their writing. Take opportunities to share some of the writing challenges that you have taken on. *I didn't know how to _____, but I wanted to learn how. So I _____.*

INSTRUCTIONAL VOCABULARY

- **plagiarism** using information or ideas from another source without crediting the source

TEACHER TIP

Modeling is a powerful teaching strategy. Model for students how you make changes to your own writing to normalize revising. *Almost every good writer, no matter how experienced, revises his or her writing. It is part of the writing process.*

Revise for Craft: Organization and Elaboration

- Explain to students that sometimes in early drafts ideas are not organized clearly or are written in ways that are not clear or complete enough for the reader to grasp.

  THINK ALOUD *I have gotten my thoughts down on paper. I read them and I see that they are out of order or incomplete. That's okay. Revision is the time to step back and evaluate how clear my ideas are. When I revise, I can make my ideas clearer.*

- Explain to students that, in addition to reorganizing, they may need to elaborate in order to convey complete ideas. To elaborate is to add information or explanations.

- Show **Display and Engage 3.7** and have a volunteer read the paragraph aloud. Ask students to work on improving the paragraph in their notebooks to make it more coherent and comprehensible. Tell students you will then discuss it as a class.

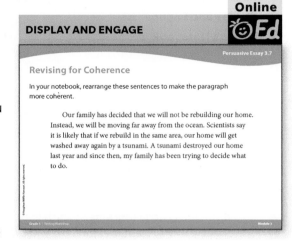

- After students have worked on the paragraph, ask: *Which sentence should come first? What should be next? What information is missing?* Students should note that the issue—Should we rebuild or move away?—is not stated clearly. Record student answers on the board, as in the following example. Underline information that is added.

(1) A tsunami destroyed our home last year and since then, my family has been trying to decide what to do. (2) <u>Should we rebuild in the same place, or should we move somewhere else and start fresh?</u> (3) <u>Yesterday,</u> our family decided we will not be rebuilding our home. (4) Instead we will be moving far away from the ocean. (5) <u>The reason for this is that</u> scientists say it is likely that if we rebuild in the same area, our home will get washed away again by <u>another</u> tsunami.

Credit Your Sources

- Show **Display and Engage 3.8a–b**. Remind students that failing to credit sources is called **plagiarism**. Have students go back into their drafts and revise to avoid plagiarism.

- If time allows, have students continue revising their writing for organization and clarity. Remind them to elaborate (add information or explanations).

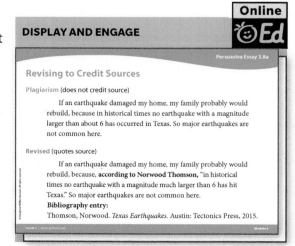

ARGUMENT · PERSUASIVE ESSAY

LEARNING OBJECTIVES

- Revise persuasive essays based on peer feedback.
- **Language** Participate in group conferences to provide and receive feedback on persuasive essays.

MATERIALS   Online

Display and Engage *3.9a–3.9c*

Anchor Chart W9: *Elements of an Argument*

TEACHER TIP

Expect some noise during this exercise. As long as you can tell that students are on task, tolerate the volume (up to a point).

Small Group Conferencing

- Tell students that they are going to listen to each other read their persuasive essays and provide feedback. Writers will use the feedback as they revise their work.

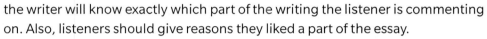

- Show **Display and Engage 3.9a–3.9c** and walk through the steps of the Say Back exercise.

- Tell students to take notes in their notebooks.

- Explain that listeners should take notes on writers' exact words, so the writer will know exactly which part of the writing the listener is commenting on. Also, listeners should give reasons they liked a part of the essay.

  THINK ALOUD *I am listening to a persuasive essay and I like this sentence: "Scientists say it is likely that if we rebuild in the same area, our home will get washed away again by a tsunami." It would take me too long to write the whole sentence, but I could jot the words "Scientists say . . ." Then, when it is my turn to give feedback, I could say, "I like the sentence that starts with the words 'Scientists say.' I like it because it is convincing evidence." Then, I would say what I want to know more about. "I would like to know more about how likely a tsunami is to strike again."*

- Answer questions about the Say Back exercise and divide the class into groups. Give each group member a number. Writer 1 will go first, then Writer 2, and so on.

- Have students conduct the exercise.

- After, give writers time to study the feedback and circle the comments in their notebooks that they want to address in their revision.

  » Students may consider areas in their essays where they did not have any positive comments and evaluate what they might want to change or add.

  » Students should also consider the areas where listeners want to know more and evaluate whether to add additional information.

  » Remind writers that they do not have to act on every comment they receive, but they should carefully consider each one.

Revise Based on Conference

- Have students return to their persuasive essays and revise based on feedback.

- After students have revised, have them use **Anchor Chart W9: Elements of an Argument** to help confirm that their essay clearly is crafted to employ the characteristics of an argumentative text.

EL **ENGLISH LEARNER SUPPORT: Support Conferencing**

ALL LEVELS Integrate students into groups with native speakers. Allow students to decide on their level of participation, based on their comfort level with reading aloud and speaking to the group. For example, beginning students might simply listen to the conferences without participating. Encourage students to ask questions when they do not understand what is said.

LEARNING OBJECTIVES
- Revise drafts to improve word choice.
- **Language** Revise persuasive essays to improve word choice.

MATERIALS   Online ⊙Ed

Anchor Chart W14: *Revising Checklist*
Display and Engage *3.10a–b*

TEACHER TIP

Consider inviting students who are busy making revisions and students who are having trouble making revisions to meet as a group with you and share their experiences. Encourage students to learn from each other.

Introduce the Revision Skill

- Tell students that they will continue to revise their essays, based on feedback from conferences. They will also replace general words and phrases in their essays.

- Write the following sentence on the board: *Building a new home will allow my family to do some cool things that are good for the world.* Ask: *What do you think of this sentence?* Students should recognize vague words. Help students replace them.

> Building a new home will allow my family to ~~do some cool things~~ use green building materials ~~that are good for the world~~ won't harm the environment.

- Ask: *Why is it better to use precise words and phrases in your persuasive essays?* (*They convey ideas better and are more convincing.*)

- Have students search their essays for words, phrases, or statements they can make more specific. Ask volunteers to share general words, phrases, or statements. Have the class suggest specific language.

Revise for Clarity and Coherence

- Review **Anchor Chart W14: Revising Checklist** with students. Say that in addition to replacing general language, they can add, delete, or rearrange words.

- Project **Display and Engage 3.10a–b.** Discuss the way the writer revised the sentences to make them clearer.

- Have students return to their essays to continue incorporating peer feedback, replace general language, and delete any extra words or ideas.

EL ENGLISH LEARNER SUPPORT:
Supporting Revision

SUBSTANTIAL
Select two or three general words or phrases used by students and help them brainstorm more specific words and phrases.

MODERATE
Ask students to select from their essays at least three general words or phrases. Help students brainstorm or use print or digital resources to come up with more specific words and phrases.

LIGHT
Ask students to select at least four general words or phrases in their essays. Have students use print or digital resources to come up with more specific words and phrases.

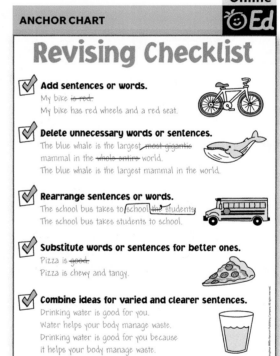

Online ⊙Ed

ANCHOR CHART

Revising Checklist

☑ **Add sentences or words.**
My bike ~~is red.~~
My bike has red wheels and a red seat.

☑ **Delete unnecessary words or sentences.**
The blue whale is the largest ~~most gigantic~~ mammal in the ~~whole entire~~ world.
The blue whale is the largest mammal in the world.

☑ **Rearrange sentences or words.**
The school bus takes to school the students.
The school bus takes students to school.

☑ **Substitute words or sentences for better ones.**
Pizza is ~~good.~~
Pizza is chewy and tangy.

☑ **Combine ideas for varied and clearer sentences.**
Drinking water is good for you.
Water helps your body manage waste.
Drinking water is good for you because it helps your body manage waste.

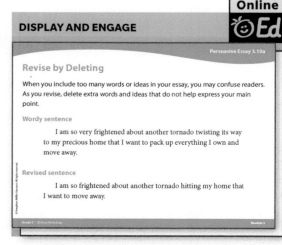

Online ⊙Ed

DISPLAY AND ENGAGE

Persuasive Essay 3.10a

Revise by Deleting

When you include too many words or ideas in your essay, you may confuse readers. As you revise, delete extra words and ideas that do not help express your main point.

Wordy sentence

I am so very frightened about another tornado twisting its way to my precious home that I want to pack up everything I own and move away.

Revised sentence

I am so frightened about another tornado hitting my home that I want to move away.

ARGUMENT • PERSUASIVE ESSAY

LEARNING OBJECTIVES

- **Language** Edit persuasive essay drafts for proper usage of irregular verbs, collective nouns, persuasive language, and transitions.

MATERIALS

Online **Ed**

Display and Engage *3.11a–c*

TEACHER TIP

Explain to students that *proofread* means "to read something and mark errors." Tell students that proofreading is a type of editing. After errors are marked, they are corrected.

TARGETED GRAMMAR SUPPORT

You may want to consult the following grammar minilessons to review key editing topics.

- **2.2.3 Collective Nouns,** p. W225
- **3.3.1–3.3.5 Regular and Irregular Verbs,** pp. W258–W262
- **3.4.1–3.4.5 The Verbs *Be* and *Have*,** pp. W263–W267
- **5.2.1–5.2.5 Transitions,** pp. W303–W307

Introduce the Editing Skill

- Tell students they will be proofreading their papers for correct use of irregular verbs, collective nouns, and persuasive words and transitions.

- If needed, go over relevant grammar minilessons with the class.

- Ask: *Why is it important to use the correct form of an irregular verb?* (*so writing will be clear; so readers can understand the argument; so readers will see you as authoritative*)

- Ask: *Why is it important to know how to use collective nouns?* (*Arguments will be taken more seriously by readers if grammar and usage are correct.*)

- Show **Display and Engage 3.11a–c**. Review the ratiocination procedure.

  » Students code their own papers by going through the entire essay three times to apply each code (underline irregular verbs; box collective nouns; circle persuasive language and transitions).

  » Students use the questions in column 3 to check their work. They mark any errors.

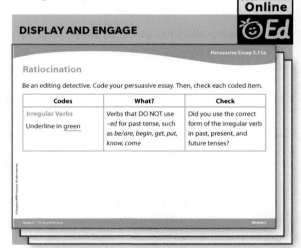

- Demonstrate the ratiocination process. Write the following on the board.

> Our community are aware that we live dangerously close to a volcano. Most of us knowed this before we made the decision to move here.

- Go through the ratiocination steps by asking: *Do you see any irregular verbs?* (*are, knowed, made*) *Do you see any collective nouns?* (*community*) *Do you see any persuasive language or transitions?* (*no*) Mark the words according to the chart. Say: *Explain whether you should add any persuasive language here.* (Sample answer: *No—this is background information and not an argument.*)

- Ask students to identify and correct the errors (*Are* should be *is* to agree with the collective noun; the irregular verb *knowed* should be *knew*.)

- Ask: *What transition could we add?* (*In fact could be added before the last sentence.*)

Edit Writing

- Students use the ratiocination exercise to edit their essays.

- Circulate the room and assist students who have questions or seem stuck.

EL **ENGLISH LEARNER SUPPORT: Support Language Skills**

ALL LEVELS Gather students who are having problems with ratiocination and work with them in a small group. Each student reads his or her essay aloud, and the group helps him or her locate words and phrases to code.

ARGUMENT • PERSUASIVE ESSAY

LEARNING OBJECTIVES

- **Language** Edit writing for complete sentences and proper capitalization, punctuation, and spelling.

MATERIALS   Online

Anchor Chart W9: *Elements of an Argument*

Display and Engage *3.12*

Writer's Notebook *p. 3.13*

TEACHER TIP

At this point, students should be able to proofread each other's texts for capitalization, complete sentences, and punctuation marks. If they can't, use the grammar minilessons to review with those who need additional help.

TARGETED GRAMMAR SUPPORT

You may want to consult the following grammar minilessons to review key editing topics.

- **1.1.1–1.1.5 Complete Sentences,** pp. W198–W202
- **7.4.3 Using Punctuation,** p. W340
- **8.1.5 Connect to Writing: Using Correct Spelling,** p. W347

Clocking Activity

- Display <u>Anchor Chart W9: Elements of an Argument</u> and ask students to have a last look at the genre features of their persuasive essay.

- Review the rules for clocking.

- Show <u>Display and Engage 3.12</u> and call out what item is to be checked by the editor: For example, ask: *Is there a name on the paper? Are there any sentence fragments?*

  THINK ALOUD *If I find an error in the paper I am editing, I write it down on the lines following the item I am checking. I include details to help the writer find the error. For example, I might write "Sentence 2 in paragraph 2 is a fragment."*

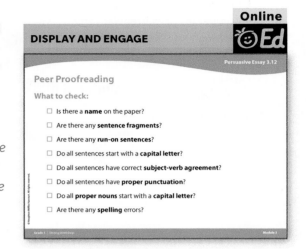

- Have students use <u>Writer's Notebook page 3.13</u> or their notebooks for the clocking activity.

- Continue with and complete the clocking exercise.

Edit Writing

- Have students do a final pass through their persuasive essays, integrating the notes from the clocking activity into their writing.

(EL) ENGLISH LEARNER SUPPORT: Support Editing

ALL LEVELS As you circulate the room, help students recognize and correct incomplete sentences and sentence fragments in their writing.

LEARNING OBJECTIVES

- Publish persuasive essays.
- Use technology to assist with writing.
- **Language**: Title persuasive essays.

MATERIALS	Online

Display and Engage *3.5a–d, 3.13*

TEACHER TIP

Arrange to have as many computers available as possible, so students can work at the same time on their final essays. Consider having them use apps that can help them publish their persuasive essays.

Prepare the Final Copy

- Tell students that now that their essay is complete, they will need to come up with a title. Ask: *What makes a good title?* (*short, catchy, gives an idea of content*)

- Show **Display and Engage 3.5a–d** and tell students that the class will create a title for the model together.

- Have volunteers read the model aloud to remind the class of its contents. Then, ask: *What is the model mostly about?* Record students' ideas on the board as below:

> A difficult choice; the writer's love of her home; a volcano that may erupt; staying at home for as long as possible

- Say: *Based on these ideas, suggest a short, catchy title that would grab a reader's attention.* Record suggestions on the board and, with the class, discuss the pros and cons of each.

- Once the class is satisfied with one or two options for a title of the model, tell them that they will select a title for their own essays.

- Have students work in pairs. Instruct pairs to take turns reading each other's work and brainstorming titles. Provide assistance if students are stuck.

- Once students have settled on a title, use **Display and Engage 3.13** to brainstorm publishing options with the class. Record their ideas on the board:

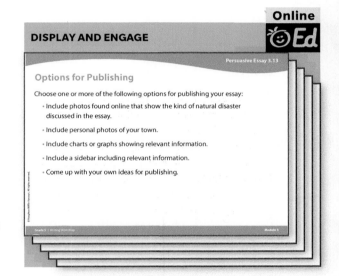

DISPLAY AND ENGAGE — Online

Persuasive Essay 3.13

Options for Publishing

Choose one or more of the following options for publishing your essay:

- Include photos found online that show the kind of natural disaster discussed in the essay.
- Include personal photos of your town.
- Include charts or graphs showing relevant information.
- Include a sidebar including relevant information.
- Come up with your own ideas for publishing.

> - include a chart showing how often the kind of disaster discussed has affected the area
> - include a sidebar that tells someone's personal story about surviving or rebuilding the kind of disaster discussed
> - include hand-drawn illustrations of the disaster

Publish Writing

- Have students plan their final drafts. Allow them the option of discussing their plans with a partner.

- Have students use computers to type and print their final drafts.

 ENGLISH LEARNER SUPPORT: Support Publishing

ALL LEVELS Pair students with native speakers to brainstorm for titles.

LEARNING OBJECTIVES

- Participate in a collaborative discussion about the writing process.
- Review and evaluate writing goals.
- **Language** Share persuasive essays by orally presenting them to the class.

MATERIALS   Online

Anchor Chart W17: *Tips on How to Present*

Display and Engage *3.14*

Writer's Notebook *pp. 3.7, 3.14*

TEACHER TIP

Students who are shy or soft-spoken may have trouble projecting their voices. Have one-on-one meetings and explain that soft-spoken students should raise their voices so much that they almost feel they are yelling. Arrange to sit at the back of the room and offer silent signals to help them find the right volume.

LEARNING MINDSET:
Seeking Challenges

Review Discuss with students what the biggest challenges were for them in this module. Remind them that there will always be things we don't know, so it's important to challenge ourselves to learn as much as possible. When you come across something that you don't know, think of it as a challenge, something you are going to learn how to do.

Share Writing

- Review <u>Anchor Chart W17: Tips on How to Present</u>.
- Have students use <u>Display and Engage 3.14</u> to choose a mode of delivery, such as reading their essays aloud and sharing any visuals they included.
- Write the following debriefing questions on the board and have student volunteers answer each question.

> What did you like best about writing your essay?
>
> What was the greatest challenge in writing this essay?
>
> What did you learn about writing?
>
> What did you learn about grammar?
>
> What do you want to remember from this experience?

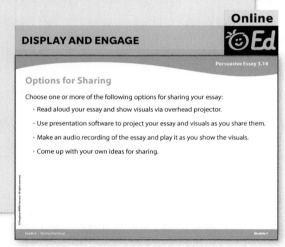

ANCHOR CHART   Online

Tips on How to Present

Express the Main Idea Make sure the point of the presentation is clear.	
Look at the Audience Eye contact brings people into your presentation.	
Speak Clearly and Loudly Make sure people can hear and understand you.	
Use Natural Body Language Smile and use your hands when you talk.	
Avoid Informal Language and Slang Speak more formally than you would to friends.	slang

DISPLAY AND ENGAGE   Online

Persuasive Essay 3.14

Options for Sharing

Choose one or more of the following options for sharing your essay:
- Read aloud your essay and show visuals via overhead projector.
- Use presentation software to project your essay and visuals as you share them.
- Make an audio recording of the essay and play it as you show the visuals.
- Come up with your own ideas for sharing.

Engage and Respond

- Have students turn to <u>Writer's Notebook page 3.7</u> or the list of goals they wrote at the beginning of this module.
- Then, tells students to TURN AND TALK with a partner about whether and how they met their goals.
- Have students use <u>Writer's Notebook page 3.14</u> to set new goals for future writing assignments.

 ENGLISH LEARNER SUPPORT: Support Fluency

SUBSTANTIAL
Lead a small group of students to help them practice reading aloud with fluency and proper pronunciation.

MODERATE
Pair students with native speakers to help them practice reading aloud with fluency and proper pronunciation.

LIGHT
Pair students to help each other practice reading aloud with fluency and proper pronunciation.

Letter

FOCUS STATEMENT The people who moved west in the 1850s had much to learn.

FOCAL TEXT

Along the Santa Fe Trail: Marion Russell's Own Story

Author: Ginger Wadsworth

Illustrator: James Watling

Summary: An adaptation of Marion Russell's account of traveling the Santa Fe trail in the 1800s

WRITING PROMPT

READ this sentence: *The people who moved west in the 1850s had much to learn.*

THINK about what a person moving west might need to know.

WRITE a letter to a historical society requesting information about what it was like to travel west back then.

· · · · · · · · · LESSONS · · · · · · · · ·

1. **Introducing the Focal Text**

2. **The Read**

3. **Vocabulary**

4. **Prewriting I: Task, Audience, Purpose**

5. **Prewriting II: Parts of a Letter**

6. **Drafting I: The Body of a Letter**

7. **Drafting II: Integrating Genre Elements**

8. **Drafting III: Completing the Draft**

9. **Revising I: Elaboration and Organization**

10. **Revising II: Peer Conferencing**

11. **Revising III: Incorporating Feedback**

12. **Editing I: Grammar, Usage, and Mechanics**

13. **Editing II: Peer Proofreading**

14. **Publishing**

15. **Sharing**

LEARNING MINDSET:
Grit

Display Anchor Chart 32: My Learning Mindset throughout the year. Refer to it to introduce Grit and to reinforce the skills you introduced in previous modules.

INFORMATIONAL TEXT • LETTER

LEARNING OBJECTIVES
- Connect to the focal text by generating questions about the topic.
- **Language** Engage in prereading discussions to prepare to read the focal text.

MATERIALS Online

Focal Text *Along the Santa Fe Trail*
Writer's Notebook *p. 4.1*
Display and Engage *4.1*

 LEARNING MINDSET:
Grit

Introduce Tell students that people who moved out west about 150 years ago had grit. They dealt with a lot of hardships, but they kept on going. It takes grit to keep on writing when it's difficult for us, but the more we do it the better we get at it.

TEACHER TIP

Show students the map at the beginning of *Along the Santa Fe Trail* and trace the trail with them. Have volunteers discuss any personal knowledge they have about the states included in the trail.

Priming the Students

Explore the Topic

- Tell students that in this module the class will read a book that takes place in the 1850s. It is a true story of a young girl and her family as they move to California. The book is mainly about their trip on a wagon train.

- Ask: *What do you already know about California in the 1850s?* (*travel was difficult; West was not yet developed; many people moved there; gold rush*) *Who can share background knowledge about the dreams that motivated people to leave the east coast for California?* (*people dreamed of striking it rich/finding gold*)

- Show students the illustrations in *Along the Santa Fe Trail* to orient them to the time in history, the mode of transportation, and the trip the characters take.

- Ask: *Now that you have seen the pictures in the book, what do you think it would be like to make that move?* Record students' answers on the board.

> It would take many days.
>
> They would have to take a lot of food/supplies.
>
> They would encounter others making the same trip.
>
> They might encounter hardship/danger.

THINK ALOUD *The illustrations in the book help me imagine the journey and the hardships the travelers faced, but I wonder how people got information about the trip they were about to take. I realize that I find travel information online. In the 1850s, information was harder to get. The travelers must have had many questions before they began their journey.*

- Tell students they will be writing to a museum or historical society to ask for information about traveling west in the 1850s.

- Distribute **Writer's Notebook page 4.1** or tell students to use their own notebooks to brainstorm questions about traveling west in the 1850s. They can ask the questions in one of two ways:
  » as if they are travelers in the 1850s
  » as present-day students looking for historical information

- If some students are struggling to come up with questions, assign them to work with partners.

Discuss the Focus Statement

- Show **Display and Engage 4.1**. Read the Focus Statement with students. Have students TURN AND TALK to a partner and share their thoughts about the Focus Statement.

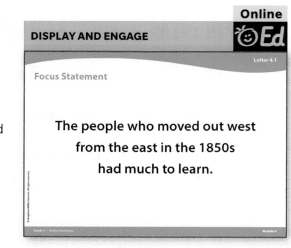

DISPLAY AND ENGAGE Online

Focus Statement

The people who moved out west from the east in the 1850s had much to learn.

LEARNING OBJECTIVES

- Discuss the author's purpose and audience for a text.
- **Language** Work as a group to generate questions about the focal text.

MATERIALS	Online

Focal Text *Along the Santa Fe Trail*

Writer's Notebook *p. 4.1*

Priming the Text

- Show the cover of *Along the Santa Fe Trail*. Read the introduction. Ask: *What was Marion Russel's purpose for dictating/writing her original story?* (*Answers will vary but should include that the author wanted to tell about her trip; record history.*) *What was Ginger Wadsworth's purpose in retelling it?* (*to bring it to today's readers*) Ask: *Who is the audience for this book?* (*students; people curious about history of traveling west*)

Along the Santa Fe Trail

- Tell students to think of questions they may have as you read. Explain that these questions will help them write their letters.

Read The Focal Text

- Begin reading *Along the Santa Fe Trail*. After each page, ask students what questions they have. Remind students that they will be asking questions about information that is NOT included in the book. They will not be getting answers to their questions at the moment.

- Model asking questions about the text by posing your own questions at the following points:

- Read page 6. Say: *On this page, these are my questions:* What kind of meals did Mother prepare? What supplies and ingredients did they take with them for meals?

- Read page 9. Say: *On this page, these are my questions:* What is cholera? What were they burning and why?

- Read page 15. Say: *On this page, these are my questions:* How many miles were they able to travel a day? How fast do the horses go?

- Read page 21. Say: *On this page, these are my questions:* What is leap frog? What is dare base?

- Read page 36. Say: *On this page, this is my question:* How common was theft along the trail?

Engage and Respond

- Have students meet in small groups to discuss the questions that came up during the read.

- Have students record the questions that are most interesting and intriguing to them. They may add those questions to **Writer's Notebook page 4.1** or write them in their own notebooks.

 ENGLISH LEARNER SUPPORT: Support Discussion

ALL LEVELS Have students work in groups with native speakers for the Engage and Respond activity.

TEACHER TIP

Plan enough time to read and discuss the whole book in one session. Alternatively, if time is limited, read until page 24.

LEARNING OBJECTIVES

- **Language** Work cooperatively to identify and define vocabulary that sparks curiosity.
- **Language** Use various strategies to determine word meaning.

MATERIALS Online

Focal Text *Along the Santa Fe Trail*

Display and Engage *4.2*

Writer's Notebook *p. 4.2*

TEACHER TIP

If a student struggles to find interesting vocabulary words, you might want to pair them with a student who is having no trouble coming up with words or ideas that they are curious about.

Review the Focal Text

- Point out that *Along the Santa Fe Trail* includes many words and phrases that can help students identify what they are curious about.

- Remind students that they will be writing letters requesting information about traveling west in the 1850s. Explain that these words and phrases will help them brainstorm questions.

- Show **Display and Engage 4.2** and distribute **Writer's Notebook page 4.2** or have students write in their own notebooks.

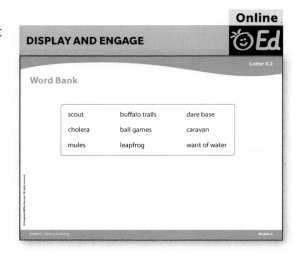

Online

DISPLAY AND ENGAGE

Letter 4.2

Word Bank

scout	buffalo trails	dare base
cholera	ball games	caravan
mules	leapfrog	want of water

- Direct student attention to the first word in the Word Bank: *scout*. Ask students to find the word in *Along the Santa Fe Trail* and have a volunteer read the sentence.

- Ask: *Based on the context of the sentence, what do you think the word* scout *means?* (*Answers will vary.*) Ask a volunteer to look up the word *scout* in a print or online dictionary and help students determine which definition applies: a person sent ahead to determine conditions.

- Ask: *Why would this word be helpful in a letter requesting information about traveling west in the 1850s?* (*Answers will vary.*)

- Repeat the above procedure with each word in the Word Bank. Have students add words and phrases that they may use in their letters to their Word Banks.

- Page through *Along the Santa Fe Trail* with students and have volunteers suggest additional words to add to their Word Banks. Tell students to look for words that they find interesting or unusual, even if they already know the definitions.

  THINK ALOUD *As I look for words in the book, I come across the word* buffalo. *I know that a buffalo is a type of animal. I even know what a buffalo looks like. But, I also have many questions about the buffalo. I want to know if the travelers ate buffalo. I also want to know if it was dangerous to encounter a buffalo on the trail. I am wondering if a single buffalo ever travels alone or do they only travel in herds. Because I am curious about it, I am going to add* buffalo *to my Word Bank even though I already know its definition.*

Engage and Respond

- Have students choose 3-5 of their favorite words in their Word Banks and write a sentence for each that tells what they want to know about that word.

 ENGLISH LEARNER SUPPORT: Support Vocabulary

ALL LEVELS Pair students with native English speakers to lend support when filling in their Word Banks.

INFORMATIONAL TEXT • LETTER

LEARNING OBJECTIVES

- Understand purpose, audience, and task for writing a letter requesting information.
- **Language** Set realistic goals for writing.

MATERIALS
Online Ed

Anchor Chart W1: *Task, Audience, and Purpose*

Display and Engage *4.3a–b*

Writer's Notebook *pp. 4.3, 4.4*

TEACHER TIP

Give students the option to research real museums and/or historical societies that actually have this information. Students may have to make a phone call to obtain the name and address of a person to whom they can address their letters. Alternatively, allow students to write to the director of a fictional society using the salutation "To Whom It May Concern."

LEARNING MINDSET:
Grit

Apply Some students will find the rubric daunting. Remind them that they may think they can't do some of the things on the rubric, but maybe they can't do them *yet*. If they keep trying, eventually they will succeed. *Remember, your classmates and your teacher are here to support you. We are a community.*

Discuss the Writing Prompt

- Tell students that in this module they will write a letter that requests information from a museum or historical society.

- Show **Anchor Chart W1: Task, Audience, and Purpose** and read the points with students. Ask: *How is a letter that requests information similar to an informational text? How is it different?* (*Answers will vary but should include that the writer must apply information he or she knows and create questions to obtain new information.*)

- Show **Display and Engage 4.3a–b** and read the Writing Prompt together.

- Ask volunteers to name the letter's purpose, audience, and task and record student responses as below:

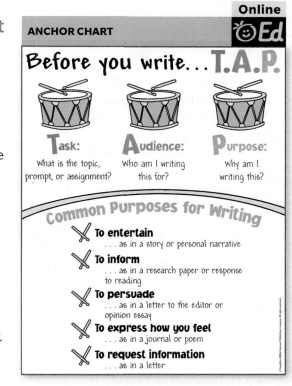

ANCHOR CHART Online Ed

Letter Requesting Information:

Purpose: to get facts and details in preparation for a trip, or to get historical facts about traveling west in the 1850s

Audience: employee of a museum or historical society, or a person who has access to the needed facts/records

Task: ask detailed questions, be specific about what information is needed

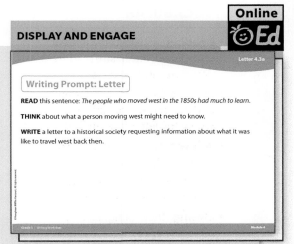

DISPLAY AND ENGAGE Online Ed

Letter 4.3a

Writing Prompt: Letter

READ this sentence: *The people who moved west in the 1850s had much to learn.*

THINK about what a person moving west might need to know.

WRITE a letter to a historical society requesting information about what it was like to travel west back then.

- Distribute **Writer's Notebook page 4.3** and explain that the rubric shows what students should know and be able to do by the end of the module. Remind students that they can use this as a resource while drafting.

Set Goals for Writing

- Point out that good writers think about what they want to improve with each new piece of writing. Have students think about the goals they want to set for their letters and add these goals to the list on **Writer's Notebook page 4.4** or in their own notebooks.

INFORMATIONAL TEXT • LETTER

LEARNING OBJECTIVES

- Understand and organize the parts of a formal letter.
- **Language** Understand the differences between formal and informal letters.
- **Language** Complete planning of formal letter.

MATERIALS   Online **❍Ed**

Anchor Chart W13: *Parts of a Formal Letter*

Display and Engage *4.4a–d*

Writer's Notebook *pp. 4.5, 4.6, 4.7*

INSTRUCTIONAL VOCABULARY

- **heading** usually three lines of text: date of letter, street address, city, state, and zip code
- **inside address** the name and address of the organization to whom the letter is addressed
- **salutation** the greeting, usually *Dear _____,*
- **body** the information of the letter, and any requests for responses
- **closing** the ending, usually *Sincerely,* or *Yours truly,*
- **signature** name of the letter writer, hand written in ink

Parts of a Formal Letter

- Display <u>Anchor Chart W13: Parts of a Formal Letter</u>. Explain that a formal or business letter has six parts: the **heading**, the **inside address**, the **salutation**, the **body** of the letter, the **closing**, and the **signature**.

- Explain that a formal letter uses a student's school address and is typed or written neatly with all six parts aligned on the left-hand side of the page. The letter should be polite, use formal English, and get to the point.

  THINK ALOUD *I want to know more about how many wagon trains went west in a year along the Sante Fe Trail, and what the conditions were like for children. In my online research, I learned that the Santa Fe Trail is called The Great Prairie Highway. It is now under the supervision of the National Parks Service. I plan to ask for a list of books that have first-hand accounts of the trail.*

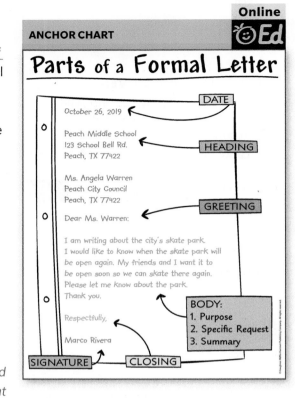

- Show <u>Display and Engage 4.4a–d</u>. Point out the six parts of a formal letter.

- Refer students to <u>Writer's Notebook pages 4.5–4.6</u>. Say: *The greeting of this letter is To Whom It May Concern because the name of the Director of the National Trails Intermountain Region is not listed on the website.* Explain that if the director is identified, the letter could address that person by name. Say: *Using Dear Sir or Dear Madam is also acceptable.*

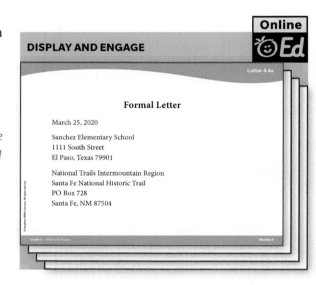

- Ask: *As you read the letter, what do you notice about the tone and the word choices?* (*Possible Answers: The tone is formal, and the letter is polite*).

- Tell students that a friendly letter has only five parts: heading, greeting, body, closing, and signature. Say: *A friendly letter uses informal language and indents each paragraph of the body. Use a friendly letter format to write thank-you letters.*

- Remind students that if they did not do research on a specific organization, they may write a formal letter to a fictional library, museum, or other organization.

Engage and Respond

- Have students turn to <u>Writer's Notebook page 4.7</u> and complete their letter organizer. If time allows, have partners discuss the real or fictional formal letters and exchange ideas.

INFORMATIONAL TEXT • LETTER

LEARNING OBJECTIVES

- Plan and organize a letter requesting information about a topic.
- Write first draft of a formal letter.
- **Language** Ask and answer questions about topics for a formal letter.
- **Language** Write a list of questions for a formal letter.

MATERIALS   Online Ed

Writer's Notebook pp. 4.1, 4.2

 INSTRUCTIONAL VOCABULARY

- **request for information** polite question that asks for specific answers
- **topic** the subject of a text

 LEARNING MINDSET: Grit

Practice Tell students that sometimes they might get stuck on a topic for their writing. They might not think that they know what to say in their formal letters. Remind them that learning from others can help get them unstuck. Encourage them to keep trying; with practice, they will figure things out.

Prepare to Draft

- Tell students that this lesson will help them develop the body paragraphs of their formal letters. Say: *Generally, the three parts of the body of a formal letter are: (1) an introduction; (2) a* **request for information***, including additional questions that you would like answered; and (3) a final paragraph to summarize and express your appreciation. The body of a formal letter may be three or four paragraphs.*

- Have students return to **Writer's Notebook page 4.2** to review the words that they have written there. Ask: *What words do you want to know more about?* Write suggestions from students on the board or on chart paper.

- Explain that the words will help them settle on a **topic** for their formal letter. Say: *For example, if you wrote the words* buffalo wallow, drenching water, *and* thunderstorms, *you may want to ask for more information about the weather. If you wrote* no-man's land, leapfrog, *and* dare base, *you may want to know more about games children played along the Santa Fe Trail. The weather or games would be your topic for your formal letter.*

- Divide the class into small groups of students. Have each group discuss their word lists and exchange information about topics. Then ask students to choose one topic and record it in their notebooks.

- Say: *Begin to think about questions you want to ask. If your topic is weather, you might want to ask "What was the best time to travel west along the Santa Fe Trail and why?" or "What kind of weather might the travelers expect if they started too late on their journey?"*

- Have students review **Writer's Notebook page 4.1**. Remind them that their questions can become more specific based on their topics.

- Have groups generate and write down questions, based on their topics. Then have students exchange questions with a partner from the group and read and discuss each other's questions. Say: *If you do not understand something in your partner's set of questions, ask "What do you mean by this?"* Have partners respond and make changes to their questions to ensure clarity.

Begin to Draft

- Have students begin to draft their formal letters using their topic notes and list of questions.

- Circulate the room and assist with topics and questions, as needed.

 ENGLISH LEARNER SUPPORT: Asking and Answering Questions

SUBSTANTIAL
Pair students and have them ask and answer questions, such as *What is your topic? What do you want to know more about?* Provide the following sentence frames: *My topic is _____. I want to know _____ about my topic.*

MODERATE
Have partners write a statement of what they want to know more about. Provide the following sentence frame: *I want to know more about _____.* Then have the partners turn their statements into questions.

LIGHT
Have students collaborate on their list of topics and questions. Encourage students to use academic language as they ask questions: *What words belong with your topic? What questions do you have about my requests for information?*

LEARNING OBJECTIVES

- Develop drafts by adding details.
- Revise drafts for clarity by deleting ideas to improve word choice.
- **Language** Discuss drafts by using academic language.
- **Language** Write to include details in different kinds of sentences.

MATERIALS Online ⊙ Ed

Display and Engage *4.4a–d, 4.5*
Writer's Notebook *pp. 4.5, 4.6, 4.8*

TEACHER TIP

Make yourself available to students who are struggling with details. Model out loud for them how you might approach writing a formal letter requesting information about a particular topic.

Introduce the Skill

- Show **Display and Engage 4.4 a–d**. Suggest that students look at **Writer's Notebook pages 4.5–4.6** and follow along as you discuss how the writer added clarifying details to the paragraphs.

- Say: *Notice in the first paragraph that the writer asks for information about the conditions of the journey for children. In paragraph 2, the writer requests maps, any films, or a list of books by people who were travelers as children along the Santa Fe Trail.*

- Explain to students that the writer asks first for general information. Then, the writer adds details about the kinds of information that might be helpful. Say: *Finally, the writer provides a list of specific questions about the life of the children along the Trail: Did the children attend school? What were the chores that children might do? These questions focus on details about the conditions of the journey for children.*

- Show **Display and Engage 4.5**. Say: *Sometimes writers use too many words to communicate ideas. The result is overwriting.* Read aloud the first set of sentences. Ask volunteers to name phrases that can be deleted, such as "At this point in time" and "I happen to be." Say: *Getting rid of the extra ideas helps sharpen the writing.*

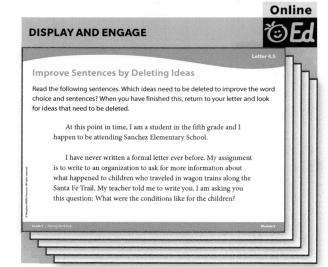

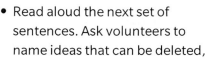

Online ⊙ Ed

DISPLAY AND ENGAGE

Letter 4.5

Improve Sentences by Deleting Ideas

Read the following sentences. Which ideas need to be deleted to improve the word choice and sentences? When you have finished this, return to your letter and look for ideas that need to be deleted.

At this point in time, I am a student in the fifth grade and I happen to be attending Sanchez Elementary School.

I have never written a formal letter ever before. My assignment is to write to an organization to ask for more information about what happened to children who traveled in wagon trains along the Santa Fe Trail. My teacher told me to write you. I am asking you this question: What were the conditions like for the children?

Grade 5 Writing Workshop   Module 4

- Read aloud the next set of sentences. Ask volunteers to name ideas that can be deleted, such as "I have never written a formal letter before"; "My assignment is to . . ."; "My teacher told me to write to you;" and "I am asking you this question." Say: *Deleting the extra ideas improves the word choice and sentences.*

- Direct students to the **Writer's Notebook page 4.8**. Have partners work together to delete ideas (phrases and sentences) to improve clarity and word choice before they return to their drafts.

Continue to Draft

- Have students read their drafts and look for places to add clarifying details and to improve word choice by deleting ideas.

 ENGLISH LEARNER SUPPORT: Practicing the Skill

SUBSTANTIAL

Confirm understanding of *draft, details, word choice, ideas,* and *delete.* Have students read aloud a sentence from their writing and point out the details. Help students craft a clear sentence.

MODERATE

Have partners read aloud the opening paragraphs of their formal letters. Have students underline the details and discuss how to improve word choice. Provide sentence frames such as the following: *The important detail is _____. To improve word choice, delete _____.*

LIGHT

Have a native speaker and a non-native speaker work together to revise the sentences in the Writing Model and to discuss their own formal letters.

LEARNING OBJECTIVES

- Draft a strong conclusion to a formal letter.
- Complete draft of formal letter.
- **Language** Write a request for information in a formal letter.
- **Language** Use content-based vocabulary within the formal letter.
- **Language** Confirm understanding of academic language.

MATERIALS   Online Ed

Display and Engage *4.4a–d*

Writer's Notebook *pp. 4.5, 4.6*

 INSTRUCTIONAL VOCABULARY

- **conclusion** The end of a piece of writing, usually the last paragraph

TEACHER TIP

If students need more time to revise their drafts and add a conclusion, consider giving them extra class time to do so.

Write Conclusions

- Explain to students that in this lesson they will work to complete their drafts and learn more about how to write a **conclusion** for a formal letter.

- Show <u>Display and Engage 4.4 a–d</u>. Click through the Writer's Model, stopping briefly to note highlights of each section. Remind students that they can follow along in the <u>Writer's Notebook pages 4.5–4.6</u>.

  THINK ALOUD *I am going to look at a model of a formal letter and think about how to organize and conclude a letter. First, I notice that the writer included a heading, the inside address, and the salutation. I notice that the salutation is addressed* To Whom It May Concern *because the writer did not know the name of a specific person in charge.*

- Read aloud the first paragraph of the Writer's Model.

  THINK ALOUD *The writer explains that more information about conditions for children along the Santa Fe Trail would help to complete a class project. Notice that the writer's tone is polite and friendly.*

- Read aloud the second paragraph of the Writer's Model.

  THINK ALOUD *This writer wants to know if other authors have written firsthand accounts of their travels. These books would be useful in researching, as would the maps and films about the camping stops along the trail.*

- Read aloud the next paragraph of the Writer's Model.

  THINK ALOUD *The writer wants to know about children's schooling and chores.*

- Point to the last paragraph and identify each part of the conclusion as you spend time to explain its structure.

  THINK ALOUD *I want to take a special look at the conclusion. Because a concluding paragraph is the last impression a writer will leave upon a reader, I know that the it needs to be strong and polite. The writer wants the request for information to be answered. The writer briefly summarizes the request and the need for a response. The writer also expresses appreciation. Do you think the conclusion will cause the person to respond?* (yes, or answers may vary)

Finish the Drafts

- Give students time in class to finish their drafts. As they write, offer assistance as needed. Use the most efficient manner to get from student to student, including moving between groups in a rolling chair.

 ENGLISH LEARNER SUPPORT: Support Vocabulary

SUBSTANTIAL

Review academic language, such as *request for information* and *conclusion*. Have students point to the conclusion. Provide a sentence frame, such as the following: *My conclusion says _____.*

MODERATE

Have partners read each other's formal letters and highlight the content-based vocabulary. Then have partners discuss the conclusions and make suggestions. Provide sentence frames, such as the following: *Your conclusion is _____. It needs _____.*

LIGHT

Have students read and discuss their formal letters. Encourage them to use academic vocabulary, such as *conclusion*, in their discussions. Have students ask for more information about any content-based vocabulary that is unclear in the formal letter.

INFORMATIONAL TEXT • LETTER

LEARNING OBJECTIVES

- Revise drafts to combine and rearrange ideas for coherence.
- Revise drafts to elaborate ideas.
- **Language** Analyze formal letters for organization and elaboration.
- **Language** Write sentences with elaboration.

MATERIALS Online

Anchor Chart W14: *Revising Checklist*
Display and Engage *4.6a–b*
Writer's Notebook *p. 4.7*

INSTRUCTIONAL VOCABULARY

- **coherence** quality of being clear and consistent in writing
- **elaboration** process of providing support or development for an idea

LEARNING MINDSET: Grit

Normalize Remind students that learning to write takes effort. It is normal to feel discouraged at times. If they are disappointed by their progress so far with the formal letter, explain that hard work will lead to success. Receiving suggestions from friends or teachers about how to use detailed language will help them improve their writing.

Introduce the Revision Skill

- Show **Anchor Chart W14: Revising Checklist**. Review the revision steps.

- Explain to students that they will combine or rearrange ideas to make their drafts more **coherent**. Say: *The word* coherent *means "to be clear or consistent." Your writing is coherent if your ideas are arranged logically and your sentences are connected.*

- Show **Display and Engage 4.6a**. Ask students to TURN AND TALK about how they might rearrange the sentences at the top of the page to make them more coherent. Discuss the various options with students and when you and they have agreed upon the best way to do it, write the improved sentences on the board. You may need to explain why some ideas work better than others.

- Explain to students that another kind of revision strategy is **elaboration**. Say: *The word* elaboration *means "to support or develop an idea."*

- Ask students to read the request for information on **Display and Engage 4.6b**. Help students see that this request is not very polite and does not include enough information. Discuss their ideas as a class and agree upon the best way to make changes. Then, write the new sentences on the board. Make sure students understand why the new sentences are more skillful than the original request.

- Explain to students that revising means to make decisions about their own writing. Say: *Can your sentences be combined, rearranged, or elaborated upon?*

- Explain to students as they revise their drafts, they should also check their prewriting strategies and the format for writing. They may look back at **Writer's Notebook page 4.7** for guidance.

Engage and Respond

- Provide plenty of class time for students, in groups or individually, to revise drafts of their letters for organization and elaboration.

- If time permits, allow student to discuss their revisions. Encourage them to explain their successes in combining sentences, rearranging ideas, or elaborating.

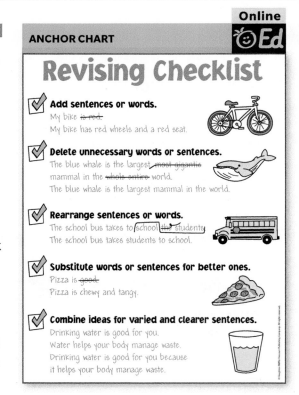

ANCHOR CHART Online Ed

Revising Checklist

☑ **Add sentences or words.**
My bike ~~is red.~~
My bike has red wheels and a red seat.

☑ **Delete unnecessary words or sentences.**
The blue whale is the largest, ~~most gigantic~~ mammal in the ~~whole entire~~ world.
The blue whale is the largest mammal in the world.

☑ **Rearrange sentences or words.**
The school bus takes to school ~~the~~ students
The school bus takes students to school.

☑ **Substitute words or sentences for better ones.**
Pizza is ~~good.~~
Pizza is chewy and tangy.

☑ **Combine ideas for varied and clearer sentences.**
Drinking water is good for you.
Water helps your body manage waste.
Drinking water is good for you because it helps your body manage waste.

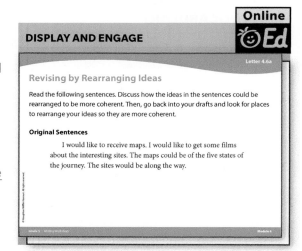

DISPLAY AND ENGAGE Online Ed

Letter 4.6a

Revising by Rearranging Ideas

Read the following sentences. Discuss how the ideas in the sentences could be rearranged to be more coherent. Then, go back into your drafts and look for places to rearrange your ideas so they are more coherent.

Original Sentences

I would like to receive maps. I would like to get some films about the interesting sites. The maps could be of the five states of the journey. The sites would be along the way.

LEARNING OBJECTIVES

- Participate in peer review of formal letters by offering suggestions for improvement.
- Incorporate feedback into formal letters.
- Revise to add transitions to formal letters.
- **Language** Confirm understanding of suggestions about formal letters.
- **Language** Express ideas about formal letters.

MATERIALS   Online 🍎Ed

Anchor Chart W1: *Task, Audience, and Purpose*

Anchor Chart W14: *Revising Checklist*

INSTRUCTIONAL VOCABULARY

- **transitions** words or phrases that make the relationship between sentences or paragraphs clear
- **revise** to rewrite for improvement in ideas, sentence structure, and word choice

TARGETED GRAMMAR SUPPORT

You may want to consult the following grammar minilessons to review key revising topics.

- **5.2.3 Transitions in Writing,** p. W305

Use Small Group Conferences

- Show <u>**Anchor Chart W1: Task, Audience, and Purpose**</u> and remind students that their task is to compose a formal letter. The audience is a director of the Westward Expansion Historical Society or a museum, and the purpose is to ask for information. Explain to students that today, their audience will be their classmates who will read the formal letters and provide feedback.

- Show <u>**Anchor Chart W14: Revising Checklist**</u>. Say: *Today you will listen to each other's formal letters and provide feedback.* Point to each item on the chart as you say: *Remember to listen for ways to add information, combine ideas, and rearrange or delete ideas.*

- Divide class into groups of four. Say: *In turn, writers will read aloud their formal letters, pause, and then read the letters again. Listeners will listen to each letter and jot down what they liked and what part of the letter they wanted to know more about. Listeners will then read aloud their feedback to the writer.*

- As students participate in the peer conferencing, visit each group to answer questions or offer assistance.

Continue to Revise

- After the groups have completed the peer conferencing activity, provide instruction about using transitions between paragraphs in their letters.

- Say: ***Transitions*** *are words or phrases that lead readers from one sentence or paragraph to another, such as* moreover, similarly, also, however, nevertheless, as a result, first, *and* next. Write the transition words on the board or chart paper. Explain to students that transitions help make writing flow logically from one point to another.

- Have students continue to **revise** drafts based on feedback from the peer conferencing. Have students look at inserting transitions between paragraphs.

- Some students may be resistant to changing their formal letters or incorporating feedback from peers. Work with each reluctant student one on one, encouraging them to make at least one or two changes.

- As you circulate, group students who need support on similar grammar topics. Use the grammar minilessons or the students' own writing to provide targeted review and support.

 ENGLISH LEARNER SUPPORT: Conferencing

SUBSTANTIAL

Have pairs of students read aloud paragraphs from their letters. Model saying a feedback sentence. Repeat the routine as you help students revise.

MODERATE

Have pairs of students read aloud paragraphs from their letters. Provide sentence frames for the listener to use in providing feedback, such as the following: *I like your idea about _____. I want to know more about _____.*

LIGHT

Have partners read aloud letters to one another and provide feedback. Encourage listeners to use complete sentences in their feedback. Encourage readers to use the feedback to revise their letters.

INFORMATIONAL TEXT • LETTER

Incorporate Feedback

- Explain to students that in this lesson they will incorporate feedback and revise to improve sentence structures.

- As a reminder about revising for sentence structure, show <u>Anchor Chart W14: Revising Checklist</u>. Point out the features of revision.

  THINK ALOUD *When I write a formal letter, I want to present my ideas in the best way possible. Since I don't know the person to whom I will write, my sentences should be clear and concise. I know the person is busy and I don't want to waste time with unnecessary details, so I should ask for information directly. For example, in the Writer's Model, the writer asks, "Would you please send me any materials you have about the conditions along the trail?" This is a simple, direct request.*

- Write the sentence on the board or on chart paper. Say: *If I remove the first three words from the sentence ("Would you please"), the sentence becomes a command, instead of a request. I may sound rude to the reader. If I add a clause to the end of the sentence, such as "if you have time and don't mind responding to me, a fifth grader," I complicate my request with unnecessary information.*

- Show <u>Display and Engage 4.7</u>. Read aloud the *Before* and *After* sentences. Explain that the longer versions of the sentences contain ideas that could be deleted. Words such as "amazing" and "thrilling" are unnecessary. Phrases such as "as I said before" are also extra ideas that can be deleted.

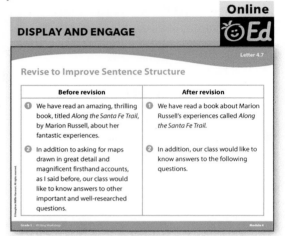

- Have students refer to the <u>Writer's Notebook page 4.8</u> and practice deleting ideas from the sentences.

Revise for Sentence Structure

- Have students continue to revise to incorporate feedback from other students. Circulate the room to check on groups or students needing assistance or conferencing help.

(EL) ENGLISH LEARNER SUPPORT: Revise for Sentence Structure

SUBSTANTIAL
Read aloud a sentence from a student's formal letter. Ask pairs of students: *Can this sentence be revised? (yes) How?* Provide the following sentence frame: *I can revise to improve _____. (sentence structure)* Have pairs of students work together to revise.

MODERATE
Have partners read aloud sentences and ask: *Should this sentence be revised?* Provide the following sentence frame: *This sentence can be revised by _____.*

LIGHT
Have students continue to collaborate on their formal letters. Have them discuss the sentences and provide possible revisions to each other. Encourage them to use full sentences in their discussions.

INFORMATIONAL TEXT • LETTER

LEARNING OBJECTIVES

- Edit writing for proper use of complete sentences, subject-verb agreement, capitalization, and punctuation.
- **Language** Include complete sentences in writing.

MATERIALS   Online

Anchor Chart W16: *Proofreading Marks*

Display and Engage *4.8a–b*

TARGETED GRAMMAR SUPPORT

You may want to consult the following grammar minilessons to review key editing topics.

- **1.1.1 Complete Sentences,** p. W198
- **1.2.4 Review Kinds of Sentences,** p. W206
- **1.3.2 Subject-Verb Agreement,** p. W209
- **7.4.3 Using Punctuation,** p. W340

TEACHER TIP

Use the grammar minilessons with those students who are still having issues with proper sentence structure, capitalization, or punctuation.

Introduce the Editing Skill

- Display <u>Anchor Chart W16: Proofreading Marks</u> and go over the marks with students.

- Tell students they will be proofreading their own papers for

  » correctly written and correctly punctuated complete sentences

  » proper subject-verb agreement

  » proper capitalization

- Remind students that they will send these letters to people they don't know. Proper grammar and mechanics show the writer is serious and has paid attention to details.

  THINK ALOUD *When I get a letter from a stranger, the only thing I know about them is the way he or she writes. If I look at the letter and see that the person included incomplete or run-on sentences, I will think the person rushed the letter.*

ANCHOR CHART   Online

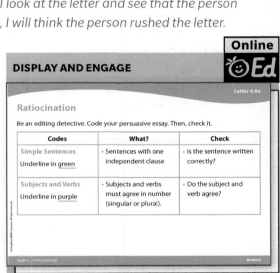

- Show **Display and Engage 4.8a–b**. Review the ratiocination procedure.

  » Students code their own papers by going through the essay three times to apply each code.

  » Students check each coded word based on the questions in column 3. They mark any errors.

- Demonstrate the ratiocination process on the board by writing this phrase:

DISPLAY AND ENGAGE   Online

Letter 4.8a

Ratiocination

Be an editing detective. Code your persuasive essay. Then, check it.

Codes	What?	Check
Simple Sentences Underline in green	• Sentences with one independent clause	• Is the sentence written correctly?
Subjects and Verbs Underline in purple	• Subjects and verbs must agree in number (singular or plural).	• Do the subject and verb agree?

To whom it may concern

Ask: *What can you tell me about this salutation?* (*all words should be capitalized; needs a colon at end*) Correct the salutation on the board.

Draw a red box around each letter that is red below. Draw a blue circle around the colon.

To Whom It May Concern:

Edit Writing

- Have students edit their letters using the ratiocination procedure.
- Circulate the room and assist students who have questions or seem stuck.

LEARNING OBJECTIVES

• **Language** Edit classmates' writing for complete sentences and proper capitalization, punctuation, and spelling.

MATERIALS   Online

Anchor Chart W15: *Editing Checklist*
Writer's Notebook *p. 4.9*
Display and Engage *4.9*

TARGETED GRAMMAR SUPPORT

You may want to consult the following grammar minilessons to review key editing topics.

• **1.1.4 Review Complete Sentences,** p. W201
• **1.3.3 Compound Sentences,** p. W210
• **2.1.1 Recognizing Common and Proper Nouns,** p. W218
• **7.1.1 Punctuation in Compound and Complex Sentences,** p. W323

TEACHER TIP

Students may feel they did something wrong if their peers find errors that they missed on their own papers. Reassure them that it is normal to miss errors on one's own writing. Writers may get too close to their own work and become unable to pick out errors. A second set of eyes is always useful to edit work. This is true even for experienced writers.

Clocking Activity

• Display **Anchor Chart W15: Editing Checklist** and discuss the points with students.

• Tell students they will use clocking to double-check each other's sentence structure, proper use of capital letters, and punctuation.

• Distribute **Writer's Notebook page 4.9** and have students write their names at the top of their editing page.

• Show **Display and Engage 4.9** and use the checklist to lead the clocking activity.

• When the clocking activity is complete, have students review their editing pages.

• Give students an opportunity to ask questions of the editors whose comments they do not understand. Tell students to take notes on their editing pages to help them clarify the comments.

Edit Writing

• Have students complete a final pass through their letters, integrating the notes from the clocking activity into their writing.

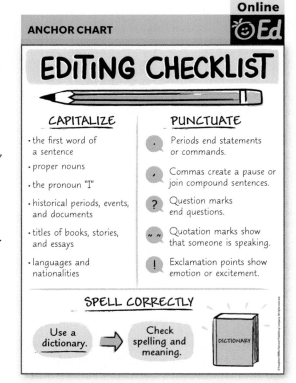

ANCHOR CHART   Online

EDITING CHECKLIST

CAPITALIZE
• the first word of a sentence
• proper nouns
• the pronoun "I"
• historical periods, events, and documents
• titles of books, stories, and essays
• languages and nationalities

PUNCTUATE
. Periods end statements or commands.
, Commas create a pause or join compound sentences.
? Question marks end questions.
" " Quotation marks show that someone is speaking.
! Exclamation points show emotion or excitement.

SPELL CORRECTLY
Use a dictionary. → Check spelling and meaning. DICTIONARY

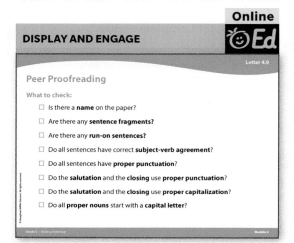

DISPLAY AND ENGAGE   Online

Letter 4.9

Peer Proofreading

What to check:
☐ Is there a **name** on the paper?
☐ Are there any **sentence fragments**?
☐ Are there any **run-on sentences**?
☐ Do all sentences have correct **subject-verb agreement**?
☐ Do all sentences have **proper punctuation**?
☐ Do the **salutation** and the **closing** use proper punctuation?
☐ Do the **salutation** and the **closing** use proper capitalization?
☐ Do all **proper nouns** start with a **capital letter**?

(EL) **ENGLISH LEARNER SUPPORT: Support Editing**

ALL LEVELS As you circulate the room, help students understand their peers' edits and make any needed corrections.

LEARNING OBJECTIVES

- Finalize and send letters requesting information to appropriate museums or historical societies.
- **Language** Work in a group to come up with an appropriate audience for formal letters.

MATERIALS	Online

Display and Engage *4.10*

TEACHER TIP

Some students may want to send letters to email addresses. Have those students prepare formal letters and send them as attachments to an email. Gather a group of students who need help with the body of the email. It should give their names, grade, and school. It should also say that the attached letter requesting information is part of a school assignment.

Prepare the Final Copy

- Show <u>Display and Engage 4.10</u>. Discuss the publishing options with students.

- Have students TURN AND TALK with a partner to come up with additional ideas for publishing their work. If students do not want to send out their letters, have them come up with appropriate alternatives. Have students record ideas in their notebooks.

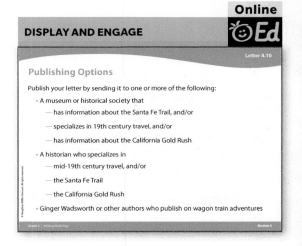

- Tell students that even if they chose not to send their letters to a real person in an earlier lesson, they will have an opportunity to change their minds and send their letters to one or more people.

    THINK ALOUD *I decided to write my letter for practice and not actually send it. But now, as I reread my letter, I am really very curious to get the answers to my questions. I worked hard on this letter and I want to send it out. To do this, I go online and research museums and historical societies that specialize in the 1850s and westward travel during that time. If I find two or three choices, I might send my letter to all of them.*

- Encourage students to publish their letters in this way, explaining that they will feel satisfied when they get a response.

- Ask: *Who wants to research places to send their letters?* Place students in small groups based on the type of information they are requesting and have them collaborate to find appropriate places and/or people to send their letters.

- Have students use their own notebooks to write down the information they find.

- Explain that it is best to come up with specific names of people to whom they can address the letter. If students cannot find specific contacts on the Internet, they may consider calling places that look promising and asking for names, addresses, and/or email addresses.

- Remind students that if they cannot find a particular name, they may use the salutation *To Whom It May Concern.*

Publish Writing

- Have students work on computers to prepare their final copy.

- Allow students to confer with you or a partner if they have questions.

 ENGLISH LEARNER SUPPORT: Support Research

ALL LEVELS Place students in groups with native English speakers for the online research portion of the lesson.

INFORMATIONAL TEXT • LETTER

LEARNING OBJECTIVES

- Share letters by reading aloud to the class.
- **Language** Answer questions to reflect on the process of writing a formal letter.

MATERIALS   Online

Anchor Chart W17: *Tips on How to Present*

Display and Engage *4.11*

Writer's Notebook *pp. 4.4, 4.10*

 LEARNING MINDSET:
    Grit

Review Congratulate students on their grit in finishing their letters. Tell students that you know it is not easy, but they all deserve a lot of credit for having worked so hard on their writing and finishing their correspondence.

TEACHER TIP

Tell students who sent out their letters to let you know when they get responses. Make time in future class periods to allow students to share their responses.

Share Writing

- Review **Anchor Chart W17: Tips on How to Present**. Answer any questions.

- Show **Display and Engage 4.11**. Review with students the ideas for sharing their letters.

- In a class discussion, have students brainstorm additional ideas for sharing their work. Tell students to record ideas they like in their Writer's Notebook or in their own notebooks.

- Give students a chance to prepare their presentations, either by recording their presentations or practicing for an oral presentation.

- When it is time for the presentations, write the following questions on the board. After each presentation, have the presenter answer these questions:

> • Did you send out your letter? To whom? Why did you choose the recipient?
>
> • What did you learn about writing a formal letter? How did you learn it?
>
> • What was your favorite part of writing this letter?
>
> • What was the most challenging part?

Tips on How to Present

Express the Main Idea
Make sure the point of the presentation is clear.

Look at the Audience
Eye contact brings people into your presentation.

Speak Clearly and Loudly
Make sure people can hear and understand you.

Use Natural Body Language
Smile and use your hands when you talk.

Avoid Informal Language and Slang
Speak more formally than you would to friends.

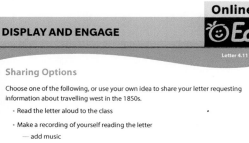

Letter 4.11

Sharing Options

Choose one of the following, or use your own idea to share your letter requesting information about travelling west in the 1850s.
- Read the letter aloud to the class
- Make a recording of yourself reading the letter
  — add music
  — add sound effects
- Make a video
  — use a voice over to read the letter
  — include images that show travel in the 1850s related to your questions

Engage and Respond

- Conclude with an informal debriefing on how students felt about the entire process, including listening to the presentations.

- Have students turn to **Writer's Notebook page 4.4** or the list of goals in their notebooks. Have them TURN AND TALK with a partner about whether they feel they have met each goal.

- Ask students to use **Writer's Notebook page 4.10** to take notes about their goals for the next writing assignment.

EL **ENGLISH LEARNER SUPPORT: Elicit Participation**

ALL LEVELS In preparation for their presentations, pair students with a native English speaker to help with pronunciation and/or expression for reading aloud.

Editorial

FOCUS STATEMENT People see things in different ways.

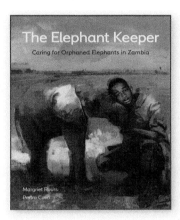

FOCAL TEXT

The Elephant Keeper: Caring for Orphaned Elephants in Zambia

Author: Margriet Ruurs

Illustrator: Pedro Covo

Summary: The true story of a keeper named Aaron and the elephant he helped to rehabilitate

WRITING PROMPT

READ this sentence: *People see things in different ways.*

THINK about what it means that people have different points of view about caring for Earth.

WRITE an editorial for your local newspaper about an environmental issue you feel strongly about.

·········· LESSONS ··········

1 **Introducing the Focal Text**

2 **The Read**

3 **Vocabulary**

4 **Prewriting: Preparing to Write**

5 **Drafting I: Beginning the Draft**

6 **Drafting II: Elements of Persuasive Writing**

7 **Drafting III: Teacher Conferencing**

8 **Drafting IV: Finishing the Draft**

9 **Revising I: Elaboration**

10 **Revising II: Grouping/Conferencing**

11 **Revising III: Incorporating Feedback**

12 **Editing I: Grammar, Usage, and Mechanics**

13 **Editing II: Peer Proofreading**

14 **Publishing**

15 **Sharing**

LEARNING MINDSET: Setting Goals

Display <u>Anchor Chart 32: My Learning Mindset</u> throughout the year. Refer to it to introduce Setting Goals and to reinforce the skills you introduced in previous modules.

LEARNING OBJECTIVES

- Establish a purpose for reading.
- Generate questions about a text.
- Evaluate details in a text.
- **Language** Discuss reasons for reading an editorial.

MATERIALS   Online

Display and Engage *5.1, 5.2*
Classroom materials *news article and editorial from a local newspaper or student news website*
Anchor Chart W9: *Elements of an Argument*
Focal Text *The Elephant Keeper*

 INSTRUCTIONAL VOCABULARY

- **fact** information that can be proved
- **editorial** an article that uses facts to support an opinion
- **opinion** an idea or belief that cannot be proved
- **thesis** the main idea of an argument; also called a **claim**
- **argument** a form of writing that attempts to convince readers

 LEARNING MINDSET:
Setting Goals

Introduce Tell students that it is important to set goals in their schoolwork and their personal life. When we set a goal, we can break down the steps it will take to achieve the goal. Then the goal won't seem as overwhelming. *Every big job can be broken down into smaller steps. When you are accomplishing the smaller steps, you know you are on your way to achieving your goal.*

Priming the Students

Explore the Focus Statement

- Tell students that they will be reading a book about rescuing elephants in the country of Zambia on the continent of Africa. Then they will write an editorial about an environmental topic they feel strongly about.

- Invite students to share any knowledge they have about elephants and their habitat in Africa or the need to protect the animals. Ask: *Do you think people have different ideas about elephants and rescuing them?*

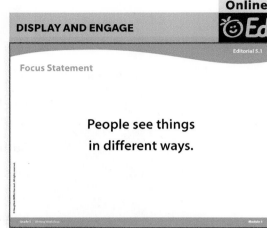

- Display the Focus Statement on **Display and Engage 5.1** and read it aloud: "People see things in different ways."

- Engage students in a discussion about why people see things in different ways. Begin with a discussion of the weather; adapt the following comment to the weather in your area. For example, say: *I have never lived in a place where there was snow in the winter, so when I visit friends up north, I can watch it snow for hours. I think it's beautiful. But my friends hardly pay attention to it. To them, it's very ordinary.*

- Elicit from students the ways that "people see things in different ways."

- Point out that people may have different opinions about issues in your community, too. Explain a specific instance. For example, say: *When I was growing up, the people who owned factories in my town wanted to build a wide highway so that they would have an easier way to send their products to other towns. If they could sell more products, they could hire more people. The factory owners said that having more jobs would be good for the community. The farmers who owned the land that was needed for the highway didn't want to sell their land. They were using it to grow crops for food. The farmers thought the highway was bad for the community. Why do these groups see the same idea in different ways?*

- Elicit the idea that people on both sides of the issue had valid reasons for their thoughts.

- Reread the Focus Statement with students. Have them write a few sentences that share their thoughts about the Focus Statement.

 ENGLISH LEARNER SUPPORT: Support Discussion

ALL LEVELS Explain that the word *see* in the focus sentence does not mean seeing things with your eyes in the literal sense. To *see things differently* means "to consider and form an idea about something from a different point of view."

Discuss Newspapers

- Find an editorial and a news article from an online news site aimed at students or from a local newspaper.

- Make and distribute copies of the news article. Point out that news articles present **facts**, or information that can be proved. With students, determine what the facts are in the article.

- Write *facts* on the Class Instructional Vocabulary List. As you continue the lesson, have students add this and other terms in this lesson to their personal Instructional Vocabulary glossaries.

- Make and distribute copies of the **editorial**. Explain that it is an article that uses facts to support an **opinion**. Define *opinion* as an idea or belief that cannot be proved.

- Do a popcorn read of the editorial; choose students at random to read a section of the editorial aloud.

- Have students summarize the main idea of the editorial; point out that this is the same as a **thesis** or a **claim**.

- Project **Display and Engage 5.2** and discuss the following questions about the editorial:

  » *What is the issue?*

  » *What is the author's position, or claim?*

  » *How does the author support this position?*

  » *How does this editorial change how I feel?*

- Point out that editorials are a form of writing called an **argument**. In this context, an argument is not a fight; it is a form of writing that attempts to convince readers.

- Reinforce the difference between a news article and an editorial: news articles are meant to inform, but editorials are meant to change the way people think.

- With students, underline the facts and opinions in the editorial. Ask: *Why would an editorial contain both facts and opinions?* (*because the writer uses facts to back up the opinion*)

- Display **Anchor Chart W9: Elements of an Argument** and review it with students.

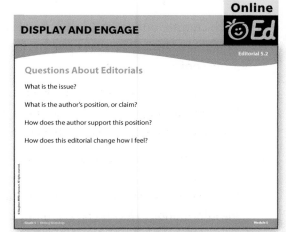

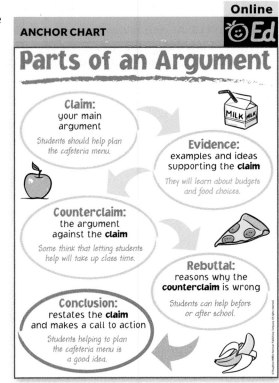

Priming the Text

Prepare to Read

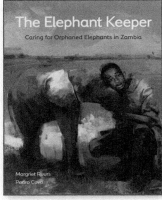

The Elephant Keeper

- Show the cover of *The Elephant Keeper*. Point out the subtitle: *Caring for Orphaned Elephants in Zambia.* Talk about why books have subtitles: to tell more about what the book is about and to make readers more interested in the book.

- Point out that this book is a persuasive text that gives detailed information about a topic. Page through the book with students, pointing out chapters, headings, illustrations (both photographs and artist-drawn pictures), and words in italics.

- Ask: *Why might the author have included these text features?* (*to help readers better understand the text; to help readers know what each section is about; to show how important the work of the elephant orphanage is*)

- As you page through the book with students, ask them to describe what they see. Ask students if they can tell what the author's point of view is.

- Each chapter ends with two pages of short factual articles about elephants. Challenge students to see how this information might support the writer's argument.

- As you reach the end of the book, call attention to the glossary—the alphabetical list of words and their meanings. Point out that the italicized words that students noticed throughout the text are explained on this page.

- Read aloud the acknowledgments on the last page of the book. Ask: *What important information do the acknowledgments show about how the author wrote the book?* (*The author visited an elephant nursery in Zambia; she worked hard to make sure the information in it was correct; many people helped her with the book.*)

EL **ENGLISH LEARNER SUPPORT: Facilitate Language Connections**

ALL LEVELS As you preview the book, call attention to English-Spanish cognates that will help students understand the story. These cognates include elephant (*elefante*), hippopotamus (*hipopótamo*), complicated (*complicado*), and preservation (*preservación*).

Read the Focal Text

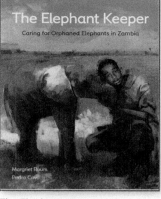

The Elephant Keeper

• Before reading, ask students to keep a list of words that catch their attention. These can be words that they like or don't understand.

• Read the first ten pages of the text, up to the end of the first chapter. Ask:

   » *How do the people in the village feel about elephants?* (They dislike them because the elephants steal their crops and kill humans.)

   » *What does Aaron's mother say about what he did?* (She says he "did the right thing. You don't just let an animal die.")

• Remark that this is a complex issue with good arguments on both sides.

• Point out the informational text about elephants. Ask:

   » *Why do you think the author included this nonfiction text in a fictional story?* (to inform readers about elephants so that they would be interested in helping them)

   » *How do you feel when you read words like "can be in deep trouble," "killed," and "leaving orphaned babies behind"?* Point out that using such emotional language is a persuasive technique.

   » *How do you feel as you look at the photos of the baby elephants with their mothers and the baby elephant drinking milk from a bottle?* Again, point out that using photos to elicit an emotional response is a persuasive technique.

• Continue reading, stopping occasionally to ask comprehension and analysis questions. Point out and discuss persuasive techniques as they occur (for example, comparing the social bonds of elephants with those of humans).

• After reading, ask:

   » *For what audience did the author write this book?* (general readers; people who like animals)

   » *Why did the author write this book?* Elicit from students that the purpose was beyond telling a story; it is meant to make people want to help elephants.

Engage and Respond

• Have students write two or three sentences that answer the following question: *How did the author of* The Elephant Keeper *try to convince readers that her position was correct?* Have student share their ideas with a partner.

(EL) ENGLISH LEARNER SUPPORT: Elicit Participation

SUBSTANTIAL
Allow students to point or use simple words or phrases to answer the question.

MODERATE
Supply the following sentence frame: *The author tried to convince readers by _____.*

LIGHT
Allow time for students to recite their sentences before sharing them with a partner.

LEARNING OBJECTIVES

- Use print and digital resources to determine meanings of words.
- Use context to determine word meanings.
- **Language** Articulate definitions of new words based on research in resources or context.

MATERIALS   Online

Focal Text *The Elephant Keeper*
Writer's Notebook p. 5.1

INSTRUCTIONAL VOCABULARY

- **sound reasoning** a logical chain of thought that leads to a rational conclusion
- **position** an opinion
- **viewpoint** the perspective that influences an author's position on an issue

Review the Focal Text

- Page through *The Elephant Keeper*, selecting words and phrases that are especially descriptive or may be new to students. Write the terms on the board or on paper and discuss them with students. Read the sentence containing each term to allow students to determine the meaning from the context. Possibilities include:

thatch	converged	impressed
debris	poachers	mingled
prod	complicated	traumatized

- Distribute **Writer's Notebook page 5.1**. Instruct students to add to the Word Bank any words or phrases from the focal text that they find interesting.

- If students cannot determine the meaning of a term from context, provide print or digital resources for them. Suggest that they add the meanings to their **Writer's Notebook page 5.1**.

Discuss Vocabulary for Editorials

- Point out to students that their editorials will be about an environmental issue. As a group, brainstorm words that may be useful for this assignment. Possibilities include:

environment	caution	avoid
future	catastrophe	solution

- Suggest that students add words that will be helpful to their Word Banks.

- Also point out that as students discuss their editorials, some terms will be helpful to know. Remind students that they already know what a thesis statement and an argument are. Introduce **sound reasoning, position,** and **viewpoint** and share their definitions.

- Add these terms to the Class Instructional Vocabulary List and have students add the terms to their glossaries.

Engage and Respond

- Have students select one word or term from today's lesson and write a few sentences explaining how it might be a useful word for writing or evaluating editorials.

(EL) ENGLISH LEARNER SUPPORT: Elicit Participation

SUBSTANTIAL
Allow students to explain their chosen word orally to you or a partner.

MODERATE
Provide sentence frames, such as the following: *I think _____ would be useful because _____.*

LIGHT
Have student pairs discuss their chosen term aloud before writing their thoughts.

LESSON 4

ARGUMENT • EDITORIAL

LEARNING OBJECTIVES

- Set writing goals.
- Determine a topic for an argumentative text.
- Develop a research plan.
- **Language** Discuss topics for an editorial.
- **Language** Articulate goals for writing an editorial.

MATERIALS   Online

Display and Engage 5.3
Writer's Notebook pp. 5.2, 5.3, 5.4

TEACHER TIP

Some students may need more time to discuss what it means for people to see things in different ways. If so, put them in a small group and use simple examples to start a conversation about opinions, such as the following: *Who likes chocolate? Who likes strawberry? Why do people disagree about the best flavor?*

LEARNING MINDSET: Setting Goals

Apply Point out that students already have some skills in setting goals. *Writing down your assignments each day is a form of goal setting. The list tells you what you must do before tomorrow. Checking off assignments as you finish them shows that you are making progress. A good way to set writing goals is to use the rubric as a model of skills you want to achieve.*

Discuss the Writing Prompt

- Tell students that in this lesson they will begin to write an editorial about an environmental topic.

- Show **Display and Engage 5.3** and read the Writing Prompt aloud. Encourage students to listen and formulate questions about the prompt.

  THINK ALOUD *This makes me think about the book we read. Aaron cared for an elephant, but his neighbors thought that elephants were dangerous and took food from humans. So, people can feel differently about environmental issues. There can be good arguments on both sides of an environmental issue.*

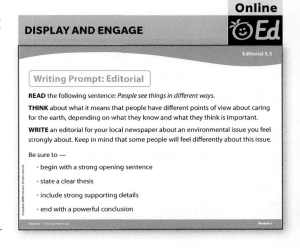

Set Goals for Writing

- Refer students to **Writer's Notebook page 5.2**. Discuss different expectations of the rubric. Remind students that they can use this rubric as a resource for setting goals as well as while drafting, revising, and editing their editorials.

- Point out that good writers want to improve with each piece of writing that they do. Ask: *What do you think you want to do better as you write your editorial?*

- Have students add their new goals to the list on **Writer's Notebook page 5.3**.

Select a Topic and Develop a Plan

- Write the following topics on the board.

reusable bags versus plastic bags	protecting wildlife
water conservation	recycling programs
street lights and light pollution	tree-planting programs
energy conservation	composting programs

- As a class, brainstorm additional environmental topics and add these to the list.

- Invite discussion and questions about the possible topics. Then have students choose one as the topic of their editorial.

- Refer students to **Writer's Notebook page 5.4**. Have them enter their topic and then ask: *How do you feel about your topic? Write your position down. You will develop your position into a thesis statement in the next lesson.*

- Encourage students to think of facts they already know that support their position and to include them on the worksheet. Explain that they will also develop this plan in the next lesson.

LEARNING OBJECTIVES

- Analyze an argumentative text.
- Plan and begin a first draft.
- Develop and follow a research plan.
- Generate and clarify questions for inquiry.
- Identify and gather relevant information.
- **Language** Articulate research questions.

MATERIALS Online ⊙Ed

Display and Engage 5.2, 5.4a–e, 5.5
Writer's Notebook pp. 5.4, 5.5, 5.6, 5.7

TEACHER TIP

If necessary, set up a plan with the technology group to have enough computers available for your students.

Analyze the Model

- Project **Display and Engage 5.4a–e** and have students follow along on **Writer's Notebook pages 5.5–5.6** as you read the model aloud.

- After you have finished reading the editorial, project **Display and Engage 5.2** again and discuss the questions as they pertain to the model.

  » *What is the issue? (the use of plastic water bottles)*

  » *What is the author's position? (Sports teams should use recyclable water bottles.)* Point out that this position is the last sentence in the first paragraph. Say: *This sentence is the author's thesis statement. It's engaging because it makes you think, and it's a statement that can be supported.*

  » *How does the author support this position? (Arguments include ease of use, taste, and impact on the environment.)* Point out that, taken together, the arguments are sound reasoning—a logical chain of thought that leads to a sound conclusion.

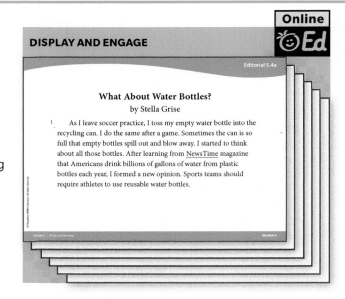

Online ⊙Ed

DISPLAY AND ENGAGE

Editorial 5.4a

What About Water Bottles?
by Stella Grise

1   As I leave soccer practice, I toss my empty water bottle into the recycling can. I do the same after a game. Sometimes the can is so full that empty bottles spill out and blow away. I started to think about all those bottles. After learning from NewsTime magazine that Americans drink billions of gallons of water from plastic bottles each year, I formed a new opinion. Sports teams should require athletes to use reusable water bottles.

Expand Research Plan

- Show and discuss **Display and Engage 5.5**. Tell students the writer of the model developed these inquiry questions as part of her research plan. Generating and clarifying these questions helped her gather information to support her position.

- Allow time for students to think about and complete **Writer's Notebook page 5.7** about their editorials.

Online ⊙Ed

DISPLAY AND ENGAGE

Editorial 5.5

Generating and Clarifying Questions

❶ What is a broad question about my topic?
   Why do people use disposable water bottles?

❷ How can I clarify the question, or make it more focused?
   What makes disposable water bottles more convenient for athletes?

❸ What questions should my research focus on?
   How much time does it take to fill a reusable water bottle?
   Does bottled water taste better than tap water?
   How might manufacturing bottled water harm the environment?
   How many/what percentage of disposable plastic water bottles are recycled?

Begin to Draft

- Have students return to **Writer's Notebook page 5.4**. Guide them to develop a working thesis statement based on their position and notes thus far. Say: *Start your draft by looking at your plan. Write one sentence that states your position. Be sure it will engage readers and can be supported. This sentence will be your working thesis statement. It's like a topic sentence that focuses on your main idea. You can refine it as you discover more about your topic, which is why we call it a working statement.*

- Have students use their inquiry questions to research facts to support their working thesis and record the facts in the graphic organizer. They may need to add more boxes to their plan.

LEARNING OBJECTIVES

- Compose an argumentative text.
- Evaluate sources.
- **Language** Compose a draft of an argumentative text.
- **Language** Rephrase information.

MATERIALS   Online

Display and Engage *5.4a–e, 5.6*
Writer's Notebook *pp. 5.5, 5.6, 5.8*
Anchor Chart W9: *Elements of an Argument*

 INSTRUCTIONAL VOCABULARY

- **secondary source** a book, article, or report by someone who did research on the subject
- **primary source** a document, interview, or information from someone who has personally witnessed an event

TEACHER TIP

Students do not need to do an enormous amount of research for this editorial. Tell them they need three or four strong facts to support their opinion.

Revisit the Model

- Project **Display and Engage 5.4a–e** and have students follow along on **Writer's Notebook pages 5.5–5.6**. Point out how the model demonstrates the elements listed in **Anchor Chart W9: Elements of an Argument**. Help students see the structure of the model and how the writer integrated research into it to persuade her audience. Have students mark up the model noting these elements:

  » **First paragraph:** *Topic* is introduced. *Thesis* is stated. Explain that the thesis is strong because it's clearly stated and can have more than one opinion about it.

  » **Second paragraph:** Lists reasons to use disposable bottles. Point out that these are *opposing arguments.*

  » **Third and fourth paragraphs:** Opposing arguments are disputed by *evidence*—facts that support a position—gained *from personal research.*

  » **Fifth and sixth paragraphs:** Offer *evidence* for position *from research sources.*

Using Sources

- On **Display and Engage 5.4e**, review the author's sources. Point out that each is a **secondary source:** a book, article, or report by someone who did research on the subject. The writer used **primary sources** when she tested how long it takes to fill a water bottle and whether people could taste the difference. A *primary source* is a document, interview, or information from someone who has personally witnessed an event. Add these terms to the Class Instructional Vocabulary List, and have students add them to their glossaries.

- Say: *Credibility means "believability." If a source has credibility, you can generally believe it. But not all sources are credible.* Discuss what makes a source credible:

  » the person or organization that produced it

  » how the information was gathered

  » how old the information is

- Say: *Besides selecting credible sources, you need to understand the source information. One way to be sure you understand information is to restate it accurately in your notes.*

- Use **Display and Engage 5.6** to show how the author of the model restated information from her sources.

- Have students use **Writer's Notebook page 5.8** to classify and list their sources, evaluate credibility, and demonstrate understanding by restating information.

- Encourage students to pattern their work after the model as they do research and draft their editorials.

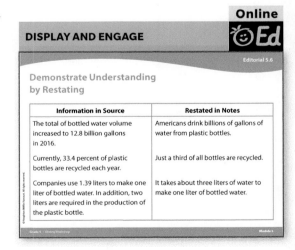

DISPLAY AND ENGAGE   Online

Editorial 5.6

Demonstrate Understanding by Restating

Information in Source	Restated in Notes
The total of bottled water volume increased to 12.8 billion gallons in 2016.	Americans drink billions of gallons of water from plastic bottles.
Currently, 33.4 percent of plastic bottles are recycled each year.	Just a third of all bottles are recycled.
Companies use 1.39 liters to make one liter of bottled water. In addition, two liters are required in the production of the plastic bottle.	It takes about three liters of water to make one liter of bottled water.

 ENGLISH LEARNER SUPPORT: Support Writing

ALL LEVELS Monitor and, if necessary, work with students to restate rather than copy verbatim the information they gather.

LEARNING OBJECTIVES

- Write a strong opening paragraph for an editorial.
- Revise drafts of an editorial.
- **Language** Discuss writing in small groups.

MATERIALS   Online

Display and Engage *5.7*

Writer's Notebook *pp. 5.5, 5.6*

TEACHER TIP

Encourage students to conference with you about their introduction. If they already have a strong opening, let them know that you are available to discuss whatever pieces of their editorial they are struggling with.

Write a Strong Introduction

- Tell students that writing a strong introduction to their editorial is important because they are trying to persuade people to agree with their viewpoint. They want readers to be "hooked" by the introduction so that they continue to read.

- Show students **Display and Engage 5.7** and discuss what the writers have included in their thesis statements.

> **Sample 1:** Ask: *What are the pros and cons of stating your opinion at the very beginning of your editorial?* (It could turn away the people who disagree with you; it could bring along those who agree with you.)

> **Sample 2:** Ask: *Here, the writer tells you that she has held her viewpoint since she was little. Is this a strong opening sentence? Why or why not?* (Some people may not care; others may think that makes her beliefs even stronger.)

> **Sample 3:** Ask: *In this sample, the writer gives an opinion and a fact to back it up. Is this a strong thesis statement? Why or why not?* (Facts make opinions stronger; it could persuade some people to agree with you.)

DISPLAY AND ENGAGE

Online

Editorial 5.7

Write a Strong Introduction

Read and discuss these thesis sentences. Confer with your teacher about yours. Then revise your introduction until it as powerful as it can be.

Sample 1
It is simply cruel and inhumane to kill elephants for their ivory tusks.

Sample 2
Ever since I was a little girl, I have told my parents to turn off the water when they brushed their teeth.

Sample 3
Plastic bags should be outlawed because many of them end up in our rivers and oceans and pose a danger to the animals that live there.

Grade 5 | Writing Workshop   Module 5

Circulate and Confer

- As students draft, suggest they refer to their marked-up models on **Writer's Notebook pages 5.5–5.6** to help structure their work. Encourage them to use their working thesis statement to develop a strong opening paragraph.

- Determine who wants to conference. Have students identify what they want to discuss during the conference. Group students with similar issues together.

- Invite students to read their problem sections so that you and peers may respond.

- If the question or concern has been answered to the satisfaction of the student who raised it or to the satisfaction of other participating students, they may choose to stay or to return to their drafting.

- Students not conferring may continue their drafting. If a student who is not participating in a conference group needs immediate help, some agreed-upon signal may be used, such as raising a hand.

EL **ENGLISH LEARNER SUPPORT: Scaffold Writing**

SUBSTANTIAL
Work with students to identify problem areas and supply helpful sentence frames as necessary.

MODERATE
If students identify a problem area, ask specific questions, such as *What do you think is the problem? What do you want to say here?* Discuss specific solutions.

LIGHT
Help students articulate what they think the problem is, and ask guiding questions to lead them to a solution.

LEARNING OBJECTIVES

- Understand plagiarism and the need to paraphrase and cite.
- Draft a strong conclusion to an editorial.
- **Language** Rephrase to avoid plagiarism.
- **Language** Discuss how to develop a conclusion for an editorial.

MATERIALS   Online

Display and Engage *5.4a, 5.4d, 5.8a–b, 5.9a–b*

Writer's Notebook *p. 5.9*

INSTRUCTIONAL VOCABULARY

- **plagiarism** copying someone else's work without giving credit
- **paraphrase** to state information in your own words

TEACHER TIP

Return to your local newspaper editorials for more examples of effective conclusions.

Distinguish Between Plagiarism and Paraphrasing

- Point out that whenever a writer does research, **plagiarism**—copying another person's work without giving credit— is possible. Discuss <u>Display and Engage 5.8a–b</u>. Emphasize that plagiarism can be avoided by either directly quoting or by **paraphrasing**, but in both instances the source must be credited. Read through the statements and have students write them in their notebooks; then do a quick spot check to see if they understand the concepts. Ask:

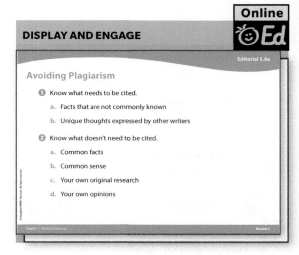

  » *Would I need to credit a statement that California touches the Pacific Ocean?* (*No, because that is a common fact.*)

  » *Should I credit a source that tells how much plastic is in the Pacific Ocean?* (*Yes, because that is not commonly known.*)

  » *In the editorial, did the writer need to give the source for her survey of players?* (*No, because it was her own research.*)

- Say: *Paraphrasing, or accurately restating material from a source, and then naming the source is not only a good way to avoid plagiarism, but it's also a good way to help you demonstrate that you understand the information you are using*

- Have students complete <u>Writer's Notebook page 5.9</u>. Then discuss the examples and students' paraphrasing. Be sure the paraphrasing shows an accurate understanding of the original information.

- Add *plagiarism* and *paraphrase* to the Class Instructional Vocabulary List, and have students add the terms to their glossaries.

Write Conclusions

- Recall with students that their editorials are meant to persuade readers. Explain that a conclusion is a writer's last chance to persuade.

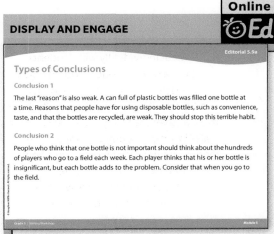

- Say: *Here are three possible conclusions for the editorial about plastic water bottles.* Uncover each conclusion on <u>Display and Engage 5.9a–b</u> as you read it aloud. Ask: *Which conclusion is most likely to inspire action? Why?* (*Possible response: Conclusion 3; It shows that team rules can make a difference and gives a reasonable suggestion. It makes readers feel more involved.*)

- Show <u>Display and Engage 5.4a and 5.4d</u>. Read aloud the introduction and the conclusion. Ask: *How does the ending echo the beginning?* (*It restates the introduction in slightly different words.*) Say: *Strong conclusions usually refer to the introduction.*

- Monitor as students write their conclusions and finalize their drafts.

LEARNING OBJECTIVES

- Revise sentence structure by deleting, combining, and rearranging ideas.
- **Language** Revise to improve sentence structure.

MATERIALS   Online

Anchor Chart W14: *Revising Checklist*
Display and Engage *5.10a–b*
Writer's Notebook *p. 5.10*

TARGETED GRAMMAR SUPPORT

You may want to consult the following grammar minilesson to review key revising topics.

- **5.1.2 Combine Sentences and Ideas,** p. W299

TEACHER TIP

Meet individually with students who are having trouble adding details and persuasive language to their editorials. As you read their drafts, help them answer the four questions: *What is the issue? What is the author's position? What are the arguments that support this position? How does this text change how I feel?* If you and the student can't answer the questions, then revision is necessary.

Introduce Revising Sentence Structure and Word Choice

- Return to the editorial from a local paper or website that you used during Lesson 1. Have students underline the facts in red and the opinions in blue. Say: *Using facts to support opinion is a characteristic of writing an editorial.*

- Have students underline the facts in their editorials in red and the opinions in blue. Ask: *Does your editorial have enough facts to support your opinions? Have you included enough details to make your thoughts clear?* Suggest that students add information, or elaborate, as they revise for sentence structure and word choice.

- Display **Anchor Chart W14: Revising Checklist**. Point out the types of revision students might do.

- On **Display and Engage 5.10a–b**, explain that the first sentence in each pair was in the draft of the model. The second sentence is how it was revised. Make these points:

  » **A:** The second sentence is more coherent because it gives the cause first and then the result. Say: *When writing is coherent, the ideas are logically connected; they "hold together."*

  » **B:** The second sentence combines ideas and reduces wordiness.

  » **C:** Unnecessary ideas in the first group were deleted in the revision.

  » **D:** The second sentence is better because it makes clear what the last reason is.

- Say: *A good writer experiments with sentence structure and word choice to express ideas in the best way. That's the craft involved in writing an argument like an editorial.*

- Write on the board: "Getting a bottle ready took less than a minute." Ask: *How could we add details to make this sentence more informative? (Possible response: The whole operation, from taking the bottle out of the cupboard and filling it to putting on the lid, took less than a minute.)*

Revise

- Keep **Anchor Chart W14: Revising Checklist** on display. Have students revisit their work to experiment with revising sentence structure and word choice for elaboration and coherence. Have them use the checklist on **Writer's Notebook page 5.10**.

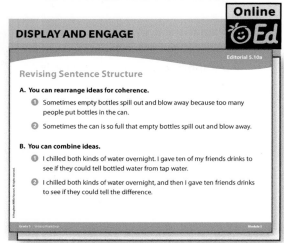

ARGUMENT · EDITORIAL

LEARNING OBJECTIVES

- Share suggestions for peers' writing.
- Revise writing.
- **Language** Discuss peers' editorials and verbalize revisions.

MATERIALS   Online

Display and Engage *5.11*

TEACHER TIP

Some students may be shy about reading their work out loud to a large group. Talk with the class about being respectful and helpful in this situation. Their goal is to help their peers improve their writing.

 LEARNING MINDSET:
Setting Goals

Apply As you introduce the conferencing points, mention that these questions are a form of setting goals. *You are thinking about what you want to achieve in your own editorial, and by using a list of points to focus on, you are targeting goals that are important to you.*

Group Conferences

- Tell students that it is time to read their classmates' writing and provide suggestions for revision.

- Project **Display and Engage 5.11** and review the conferencing points with students. Clarify any instructions as necessary.

- Conferences should proceed as follows:

  » Divide the class into groups of four or five.

  » A designated writer should read his or her editorial aloud all the way through, pause, and then read it again.

  » Listeners listen carefully. During the second reading, they take notes to help them remember what they want to comment on.

  » After the second reading, the group discusses the editorial and makes comments and suggestions using the questions from **Display and Engage 5.11**.

  » Continue until all group members have shared their editorials.

- Remind writers that information from the conference will help them revise their editorials.

- Debrief with the class. Ask students:

  - What are you noticing about yourself as a writer?
  - How is writing an editorial different from writing an informational essay?
  - Which type of writing do you think is most interesting to write? Why?

 ENGLISH LEARNER SUPPORT: Facilitate Reading

ALL LEVELS Provide time and private space for students to practice reading their editorials aloud before sharing. Ask native speakers to help with pronunciation and other issues that might concern students. Help them make notes about the feedback they receive.

Online
Ed

DISPLAY AND ENGAGE

Editorial 5.11

Conferencing

As you listen to a group member's editorial, think about these questions.

1. Did the introduction hook me? Would I keep reading?
2. What is the issue?
3. What is the author's position? Where is it clearly stated?
4. What are the arguments that support this position? What other arguments could the writer use?
5. Does the author support each opinion with facts?
6. Does the author mention sources where they are needed?
7. How does this editorial change how I feel?

ARGUMENT • EDITORIAL

LEARNING OBJECTIVES

- Incorporate feedback to finalize drafts.
- Improve sentence structure and word choice.
- List sources.
- **Language** Apply spoken suggestions to revise drafts.
- **Language** Revise drafts for sentence structure and word choice.

MATERIALS   Online Ed

Display and Engage *5.4e, 5.12a–b*

Review Revising

- Tell students that in this lesson they will finalize their drafts.

- Using **Display and Engage 5.12a–b**, say: *Let's look at two versions of some sentences to see how the writer made improvements when finalizing a draft.* Make these points:

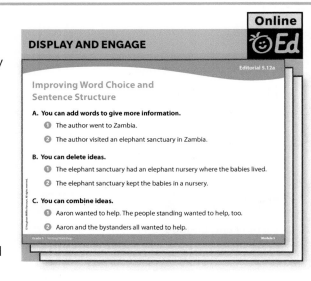

- » **A:** The second sentence adds an idea to show what the author did in Zambia.

- » **B:** The first sentence was wordier than it needed to be.

- » **C:** The writer combined the sentences and chose "bystanders" to replace "people standing by" to make the idea shorter without changing the meaning.

- » **D:** The second sentence changes the order of ideas and adds words to logically connect the events. It's also more specific by using "Bezi" and "bottle."

- » **E:** The second uses shorter words and gets to the point quickly.

- Release students to revise their editorials using input from the conferencing as well as insights from the instruction on word choice and sentence structure.

List Sources

- Tell students that once they finalize their drafts and know what information they are definitely using, they should list their sources. Review **Display and Engage 5.4e** and discuss how the magazine article, website, and book are listed.

- On the board write the following general formats for listing sources, and have students copy them in their notebooks. Point out that website and sometimes magazine articles do not always have the author's name. If no author is named, the source is alphabetized by the title.

TEACHER TIP

Consider having an online or printed thesaurus handy for students to find alternative word choices.

> Alphabetize by author's last name.
> BOOK:
> Author (Last name, First name). <u>Book Title</u>. Publisher Location: Publisher, Copyright year.
>
> MAGAZINE:
> Author (Last name, First name). "Article Title." <u>Magazine Name</u>, Date Published. Pages.
>
> WEBSITE:
> Author (Last name, First name). "Article/Website Title." url, Date you read it.

- Remind students that when handwriting, they should underline book titles and magazine names. When they type on a computer, they can italicize these sources.

- Have students list the sources for their editorials on a separate sheet of paper.

LEARNING OBJECTIVES

- Edit for pronoun usage.
- Edit for subordinating conjunctions.
- **Language** Edit sentences for correct pronoun use.
- **Language** Edit complex sentences for use of subordinating conjunctions.

MATERIALS   Online

Display and Engage *5.13*

 **INSTRUCTIONAL VOCABULARY**

- **pronoun** a word used in place of a noun
- **complex sentence** a sentence with one main clause and one subordinate clause
- **subordinate clause** a clause that is not a sentence on its own
- **subordinating conjunction** a word that acts as a transition and begins a subordinate clause

TARGETED GRAMMAR SUPPORT

You may want to consult the following grammar minilessons to review key editing topics.

- **1.4.1 Complex Sentences with Conjunctions,** p. W213
- **2.4.5 Connect to Writing: Using Subject and Object Pronouns,** p. W237
- **5.1.3 Subordinating Conjunctions,** p. W300

Work with Pronouns

- Review with students that a **pronoun** is a word that stands for a noun. Elicit examples of pronouns, such as *I, her, them, you, your, it,* and *itself.*

- Point out that pronouns help readers keep track of the people and things they name. Pronouns can also be very useful for reducing wordiness. Say: *But problems arise when it's not clear what a pronoun is referring to.* Write on the board: *Jim and his dad will take a walk when he gets home.* Ask: *Who is not home yet—Jim or his dad? How can you revise the sentence to clarify this?* (*Jim and his dad will take a walk when his dad gets home; When Jim gets home, he will take a walk with his dad.*)

- Review the pronoun examples on **Display and Engage 5.13**. Ask students why the second sentence is clearer than the first.

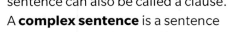

DISPLAY AND ENGAGE   Online

Editorial 5.13

Editing Drafts

After reading these examples, return to your drafts to check for correct pronoun usage and subordinating conjunctions.

Tom and Angelo talked. Then he made his choice.
After Tom and Angelo talked, Angelo made his choice.

Sofia and her friend Maria went for a walk. She decided to stop for some water.
Sofia decided to stop for some water while she walked with her friend Maria.

The doorbell and the phone rang at the same time. Maybel ran to answer it.
When the doorbell and phone rang at the same time, Maybel ran to answer the door.

Work with Complex Sentences

- Review with students that a sentence is a complete thought with a subject and a predicate. A simple sentence can also be called a clause. A **complex sentence** is a sentence with one main clause and a **subordinate clause**, which is not a complete thought. A subordinate clause is introduced by a **subordinating conjunction**.

- Write the following subordinating conjunctions on the board: *although, because, even if, so that, until, when.* See if students can list others.

- Write the following sentences on the board and read them aloud: *Kelly wants to read this book. It's written by her favorite author.*

  THINK ALOUD *I'm going to combine these ideas into a complex sentence.*

  » *I could write: "Kelly wants to read this book because it's written by her favorite author." Because is the subordinating conjunction.*

  » *I can also reverse the order of the clauses: "Because this book is written by Kelly's favorite author, she wants to read it."*

- Tell students that subordinating conjunctions help show readers how ideas are related. Complex sentences also make writing more interesting and varied.

- Review the examples of the use of subordinating conjunctions (*After, while, When*) on **Display and Engage 5.13**. Ask students why the second sentence is clearer than the first.

Edit Writing

- Add the grammatical terms used in the lesson to the Classroom Instructional Vocabulary List, and have students add them to their personal glossaries.

- Have students edit their writing for pronoun and subordinating conjunction use.

ARGUMENT • EDITORIAL

TEACHER TIP

In editing for pronouns and subordinate conjunctions to form complex sentences, peers are repeating what students looked for on their own in the previous lesson. These areas pose difficulty for some students, and more advanced students can help those who are struggling.

TARGETED GRAMMAR SUPPORT

You may want to consult the following grammar minilessons to review key editing topics.

- **1.4.2 Dependent and Independent Clauses,** p. W214
- **1.4.5 Connect to Writing: Using Complex Sentences,** p. W217
- **7.4.3 Using Punctuation,** p. W340
- **8.1.5 Connect to Writing: Using Correct Spelling,** p. W347

Clocking Activity

- Tell students that in this lesson they will use the clocking activity to edit each other's editorials.

- Project **Display and Engage 5.14** and discuss the items to be checked by editors. Keep the checklist visible during the clocking activity.

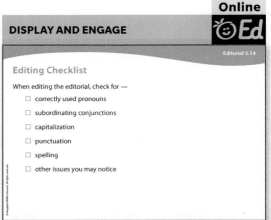

- Review the rules for clocking:

  » Each writer prepares a cover page for his or her editorial. This page should have the writer's name at the top and be divided into several sections. Each section is labeled 1–6; each number corresponds to an editing task.

  » Students form concentric circles. Students in the inner circle trade papers with their classmate in the outer circle. As students receive a peer's editorial, they become the editor of that editorial.

  » No marks are made on the actual editorial. Each editor writes his or her name in a section on the editing page and makes comments on each editing task.

  » Call out which item is to be checked by the editor: (1) correctly used pronouns; (2) subordinating conjunctions; (3) capitalization; (4) punctuation; (5) spelling; (6) other issues.

  » After students have completed the full set of editing tasks for the first time, have writers collect their editorials and move to another editor. Do the entire process until each section of the editing page is used.

Edit Writing

- When the editing process is completed, the editing page and editorial are returned to the writer. Tell students to use the editing page to guide further changes they make to their drafts.

LEARNING OBJECTIVES

- Choose an option for publishing a written work.
- **Language** Discuss options for publishing an editorial.

TEACHER TIP

Invite your technology team and other tech-savvy students and teachers to come to class and discuss safe ways to use the Internet to publish students' writing.

Prepare the Final Copy

- Allow time for last-minute changes as students work to finalize their editorials.
- Have students write titles for their editorials and prepare a final copy on a computer.

Discuss Publishing

- Hold a class brainstorming session about publishing the editorials. List all students' ideas on the board or on chart paper.
- Ask students to think of options that would be particularly good for an editorial. Record student ideas as they are generated. Then discuss each one.
- Have students confer in small groups about how they might publish their editorials.

Publish

- Assist students with publishing their editorials as needed.

EL ENGLISH LEARNER SUPPORT: Elicit Participation

SUBSTANTIAL
Show students the various options to publish and help them select the most appropriate one for them.

MODERATE
Discuss the publishing options with students. Then have them orally complete the following sentence frame: *I will publish my editorial by _____ because _____.*

LIGHT
Have partners discuss their chosen option for publishing and explain their choice.

LEARNING OBJECTIVES

- Share writing.
- Hold a collaborative discussion.
- Use appropriate delivery to present results.
- **Language** Discuss editorials and the editorial writing process.

MATERIALS Online

Writer's Notebook *pp. 5.3, 5.11*

TEACHER TIP

Point out that writing an editorial is a sophisticated task. Congratulate students on their achievement!

 **LEARNING MINDSET: Setting Goals**

Review Tell students they are now going to measure their progress toward their goals. Remind students: *When you set goals, you need to place some markers along the way so you know how much progress you are making toward your goals.* As they set new goals for their next writing assignment, remind students to consider the steps they will need to take to track their progress toward their goals.

Share Writing

- Have students brainstorm and discuss options for sharing their editorials.
- Record student ideas on the board as they are generated.
- Have students choose how to share their editorials.
- If students read their editorials aloud to the class, encourage students to ask the presenters questions about their editorials. Remind students of the rules for listening and asking questions and promoting positive feedback. Encourage speakers to answer with details they learned as they were writing.

Revisit Goals

- Have students revisit **Writer's Notebook page 5.3** for their goals list from the beginning of the module. Ask students to TURN AND TALK with a partner about how they feel they met their goals.
- Have students record their progress toward their goals on **Writer's Notebook page 5.11**.

Engage and Respond

- Conclude with an informal debriefing about how students felt about writing editorials. Ask the following questions:
  - » *How did your attitude toward editorials change as you worked on this assignment?*
  - » *What did you like best about writing your editorial?*
  - » *What did you like least?*
  - » *Describe your thoughts about publishing your editorial.*
  - » *Do you think the editorials would convince an audience? Why or why not?*

EL **ENGLISH LEARNER SUPPORT: Practice Reading**

ALL LEVELS Allow time for students to practice reading their editorials aloud before they present their writing to the group. They could rehearse their reading with you, another adult, a student partner, or by themselves.

Personal Narrative

FOCUS STATEMENT Only you can tell your story.

FOCAL TEXT

Miss Alaineus: A Vocabulary Disaster

Author and Illustrator: Debra Frasier

Summary: A girl in fifth grade misunderstands a vocabulary assignment.

WRITING PROMPT

READ this sentence: *Only you can tell your story.*

THINK about a memory from your life. Maybe it's a funny family story or something important you think about often.

WRITE a personal narrative that tells the story of what happened.

LESSONS

1. **Introducing the Focal Text**

2. **The Read**

3. **Vocabulary**

4. **Prewriting: Preparing to Write**

5. **Drafting I: Beginning the Draft**

6. **Drafting II: Understanding Plot Structure**

7. **Drafting III: Completing the Draft**

8. **Revising I: Elaboration**

9. **Revising II: Conferencing**

10. **Revising III: Incorporating Feedback**

11. **Revising IV: Varying Sentences**

12. **Editing I: Grammar, Usage, and Mechanics**

13. **Editing II: Peer Proofreading**

14. **Publishing**

15. **Sharing**

LEARNING MINDSET: Belonging

Display <u>Anchor Chart 32: My Learning Mindset</u> throughout the year. Refer to it to introduce Belonging and to reinforce the skills you introduced in previous modules.

NARRATIVE • PERSONAL NARRATIVE

LEARNING OBJECTIVES

- Describe a personal connection to a source.
- Connect to background knowledge.
- **Language** Use accessible language to learn new words.
- **Language** Share information orally in cooperative settings.

MATERIALS   Online

Writer's Notebook *p. 6.1*
Display and Engage *6.1*

 INSTRUCTIONAL VOCABULARY

- **personal narrative** a story about a person's own experiences
- **narrative** a story

 LEARNING MINDSET: Belonging

Remind students that together they are a community of learners. *I learn from you every single day, just as you learn from each other and from me. We are all in this together, and we depend on each other for help.* Tell students that they are about to share stories of misunderstandings. Rather than laugh at each other, encourage students to use these stories to get to know one another better.

Priming the Students

Making Connections

- Tell students that in this module they will be writing a **personal narrative**. Remind students that a **narrative** is a story, so a personal narrative is a story about a personal experience—something that happened to them—and it is told in their own words. Add these terms to the Class Instructional Vocabulary List, and have students add them to their glossaries, creating their own definitions.

- Point out to students that hearing about someone else's experience sometimes triggers a similar memory that happened in their own lives. Ask: *Did you ever realize you were singing the lyrics of a song incorrectly?* Encourage students who answer yes to describe the mistake they made.

- Share your own funny memory about misunderstanding song lyrics.
  THINK ALOUD *Have you ever heard of the Beatles? When I first heard their music, I loved it, but because they were British, I sometimes misunderstood what they sang. For example, for a long time, I thought they were singing "Lucy's in a fight with Linus!" Then someone told me that the lyrics were "Lucy in the sky with diamonds."*

- If students can't recall a misunderstood song lyric, have them think about a time they misunderstood a direction from a parent or teacher, something in a show, or a friend's comment. Encourage students to share their experiences.

- List examples of misunderstood words on the board with the title "Misunderstood Words and Phrases." Add other examples, including your own.

- Have students add the examples to the Word Bank on **Writer's Notebook page 6.1** or their own notebooks as a resource for writing.

- Point out that funny memories like these can sometimes give writers good ideas for their personal narratives. Encourage students to freewrite or journal about a funny memory.

Discuss the Focus Statement

- Show **Display and Engage 6.1**. Read the Focus Statement aloud. Have students share their thoughts about it in small groups. Ask students what they think it means to say, "Only you can tell your story."

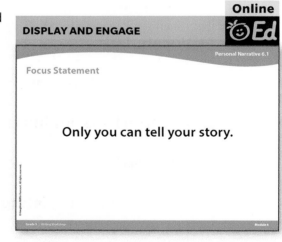

Online

DISPLAY AND ENGAGE   Personal Narrative 6.1

Focus Statement

Only you can tell your story.

 ENGLISH LEARNER SUPPORT: Build Background

SUBSTANTIAL
Explain that when people misunderstand, they have a wrong understanding. Encourage students to think of song lyrics or other words they have misunderstood in their home language.

MODERATE
Ask students to describe English words or phrases they have misunderstood: *I thought _____ was _____.* Have them write examples in their notebooks.

LIGHT
Help students expand on their misunderstanding of an English word or phrase: *I thought _____ was _____ when I heard _____. Because I misunderstood, _____.*

NARRATIVE • PERSONAL NARRATIVE

LEARNING OBJECTIVES

- Use background knowledge to prepare to read.
- Discuss author's purpose.
- Analyze a narrative text for author's craft.
- **Language** Discuss author's usage and treatment of words.

MATERIALS Online ⓔEd

Writer's Notebook *p. 6.1*

Focal Text *Miss Alaineus: A Vocabulary Disaster*

⚙ LEARNING MINDSET:
Belonging

Introduce Tell students that even though they are all different, they are all an important part of the class. *Your contributions to the class are good for everyone because they help us think of things in a different way and broaden our ideas for what is possible.* Encourage students to feel comfortable when asking for help and giving help to others.

Priming the Text

Prepare to Read

- Invite students to think about how they best learn new words. Ask: *What are your favorite ways to learn new words? Do you enjoy learning new words? Why or why not?*

- Create a list of ways to learn new words. Begin by writing the following suggestions on the board, and then invite students to add their own ideas. Encourage students to copy the list in their notebooks.

  - Print a new word in large letters with different colors.
  - Draw a colorful cartoon showing the word's meaning.

The Read

Read the Focal Text

- Show students the cover of the text. Read the title aloud, pausing between the words *Miss* and *Alaineus*. Encourage students to discover the play on words. Then read the text, stopping as indicated below:

Miss Alaineus

  » Begin reading page A. Notice the font change to italics for definitions. When reading those definitions, change your tone of voice from conversational to "official," so that it sounds as if you're reading from a dictionary. After reading pages B and C, stop and ask: *Why did I read some of the text in a different voice?* Help students understand that these are definitions of words.

  » Write the vocabulary words on page C on the board or chart paper. Have students write the words they like most on **Writer's Notebook page 6.1**.

  » Read pages D and E. Then read the definitions for the words *hypothesis* and *category*. Ask: *Why is the narrator making up the definitions?* (*Sample answer: Because it's too hard to look them up in bed.*)

  » Continue reading the text as time allows, stressing boldfaced words to give students auditory cues. Allow them to discover the play on words as they listen.

- Point out the sentences at the bottom of some pages. *Ask: Why did the author include those sentences?* (*Sample answer: to give examples of words that start with that letter*) *What are the sentences about?* (*Sample answer: how the narrator feels*)

- Discuss the purpose of the pages at the end of the book and how they add interest.

Engage and Respond

- Have students answer these questions in their notebooks: *How did the author of Miss Alaineus keep readers interested? How might I use some of those ideas in my own writing?* Ask students to share their ideas with a partner.

LEARNING OBJECTIVES

- Read and understand new vocabulary.
- Use context to determine meaning.
- Use word parts to clarify meaning.
- **Language** Use strategies to learn new words.
- **Language** Identify and use word parts.

MATERIALS   Online

Focal Text *Miss Alaineus: A Vocabulary Disaster*

Writer's Notebook *p. 6.1*

 **INSTRUCTIONAL VOCABULARY**

- **pun** a play on words
- **homonym** a word that looks and sounds the same as another word but has a different meaning

Review the Focal Text

- Review with students the story *Miss Alaineus: A Vocabulary Disaster*. Point out that the text is rich with vocabulary definitions and **puns**. A *pun* is a play on words. Say: *In* Miss Alaineus, *the author uses a technique called a "play on words," or a pun. A pun uses words that sound and look alike in a humorous way. When I write a personal narrative, I sometimes add puns to make the reader laugh. For example, I might say, "Insects bug me."*

- Explain that this is a play on the word *bug*, which means "an insect" and also "to bother or annoy." The word *bug* is a **homonym**: it's a word that looks and sounds like another word but has a different meaning. Homonyms are perfect words to use to make a pun. Add the words *pun* and *homonym* to the Class Instructional Vocabulary List, and have students add the terms and their own definitions to the lists in their glossaries.

- Have students suggest other puns they think are funny. Explain that the title *Miss Alaineus* is a type of pun because Sage thought it was a person, but it was really a word that describes a collection of things: *miscellaneous*.

- Have students return to their Word Bank on **Writer's Notebook page 6.1**.

- Ask students to name some words from their Word Banks. Write them down on chart paper or the board. Ask students which words, if any, could be puns. Make sure they understand why.

- Provide these two words from *Miss Alaineus* to help students understand how a word can be a pun: *star:* a heavenly body or a famous person; *cliff:* a person's name or the high, steep face of a rock.

- Put students in pairs to identify any homonyms in their Word Banks. If they can't find one, challenge them to list two or three homonyms that don't appear in the text. Then have them work together to write a pun with one of the homonyms. For example, "The stars are out tonight at the opening of the new blockbuster movie."

- Write students' puns on chart paper or the board.

EL ENGLISH LEARNER SUPPORT: Build Vocabulary

ALL LEVELS Students may have particular difficulty understanding English puns. Elicit examples of puns in their home language as examples.

NARRATIVE · PERSONAL NARRATIVE

LEARNING OBJECTIVES

- Use multiple prewriting strategies to plan.
- Understand elements of narrative writing.
- **Language** List ideas for writing.

MATERIALS   Online

Writer's Notebook *pp. 6.2, 6.3, 6.4*

Display and Engage *6.2*

Anchor Chart W5: *Elements of a Personal Narrative*

TEACHER TIP

Students might also ask family members or friends for ideas to add to their three-column charts.

Generate Ideas

- Ask: *What will Sage in* Miss Alaineus *most likely never forget? Why? (She'll never forget mistaking* miscellaneous *for a name because she was so embarrassed.)*

- Explain to students that to begin prewriting for their personal narratives they should think about experiences they will never forget.

- To help them generate ideas, draw a three-column chart on the board. Label the first column *Names,* the second *Descriptions,* and the third *Anecdotes.* Above the third column, write the sentence frame *I'll never forget when. . . .*

- Model adding information to the chart. Quickly write names of family, friends, pets, places, and things in column one.

- Model brainstorming adjectives associated with the names in column one, and add them to column two as they come to you.

- In the third column, model using "I'll never forget when. . . " to add memorable moments associated with the items in column one.

- Tell students to brainstorm ideas on **Writer's Notebook page 6.2**. Allow time for the activity, and remind students they can add to their chart at any time.

Discuss the Writing Prompt

- Show **Display and Engage 6.2** and read the Writing Prompt together. Have students copy it into their notebooks. Invite them to review their list of brainstormed anecdotes to see which ones they could write about.

- Point out that students will be writing a personal narrative. Show **Anchor Chart W5: Elements of a Personal Narrative** and walk through it with students. Encourage students to copy the features into their notebooks.

Set Goals for Writing

- Remind students that good writers set goals before writing.

  THINK ALOUD *I want to use sensory words to show rather than tell, so my readers feel like they are experiencing the event themselves.*

- Have students think about goals they would like to set for their personal narrative, and write them on **Writer's Notebook page 6.3**.

- Review the rubric for a personal narrative on **Writer's Notebook page 6.4** with students.

Online **Ed**

DISPLAY AND ENGAGE   Personal Narrative 6.2

Writing Prompt: Personal Narrative

READ the following sentence: *Only you can tell your story.*

THINK about a memory from your life. Maybe it's a funny family story or something important that you think about often. It may have been a time when you learned a lesson or overcame a challenge.

WRITE a personal narrative that tells the story of what happened. Include vivid details and make sure your narrative has a beginning, middle, and end.

Be sure to —
- include a beginning, middle, and end
- use vivid details

Online **Ed**

ANCHOR CHART

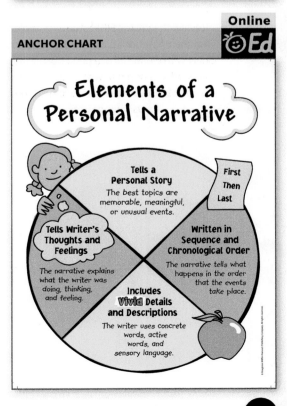

Elements of a Personal Narrative

Tells a Personal Story
The best topics are memorable, meaningful, or unusual events.

First Then Last

Tells Writer's Thoughts and Feelings
The narrative explains what the writer was doing, thinking, and feeling.

Written in Sequence and Chronological Order
The narrative tells what happens in the order that the events take place.

Includes Vivid Details and Descriptions
The writer uses concrete words, active words, and sensory language.

LEARNING OBJECTIVES

- Turn prewriting into the beginning of a draft.
- Use organizational patterns.
- **Language** Use academic language to discuss writing tasks.

MATERIALS   Online

Writer's Notebook pp. 6.2, 6.5, 6.6
Display and Engage 6.3a–c

 INSTRUCTIONAL VOCABULARY

- **first-person point of view** the narrator is part of the story and uses words such as *I*, *me*, and *we*

TEACHER TIP

Review the prompt that students copied into their notebooks, as well as the Anchor Chart with elements of a personal narrative. As students begin to write, suggest they keep these resources handy to help them focus their narrative.

Prepare to Draft

- Say: *Today, you'll begin turning your prewriting notes into a draft of your personal narrative.* Have students return to **Writer's Notebook page 6.2**. Give them several minutes to add ideas they may have remembered since the last lesson.

- In small groups, have students share two or three ideas they are considering for their personal narrative and elicit feedback. Then ask students to select a topic.

- As students begin writing, remind them to

  » write from the **first-person point of view**, using pronouns such as *I*, *me*, *my*, and *mine*. Add the term *first-person point of view* to the Class Instructional Vocabulary List, and have students add it to their glossaries;

  » begin with a strong opening sentence that will catch the interest of the reader;

  » include vivid details;

  » make sure their story has a beginning, middle, and end.

- Tell students you will share a personal narrative about an exciting experience. Show **Display and Engage 6.3a** and have students follow along on **Writer's Notebook pages 6.5 and 6.6** as you read the model. Discuss how the writer has included the features above. Say: *Part of a narrative is setting the scene. The story opens with a vivid description that helps the reader experience what the writer was seeing, hearing, and feeling. The writer tells why she was so excited in the last sentence.*

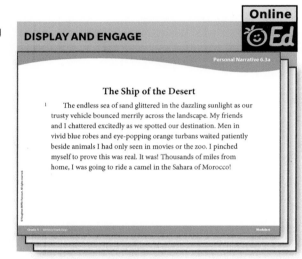

DISPLAY AND ENGAGE   Online

Personal Narrative 6.3a

The Ship of the Desert

1   The endless sea of sand glittered in the dazzling sunlight as our trusty vehicle bounced merrily across the landscape. My friends and I chattered excitedly as we spotted our destination. Men in vivid blue robes and eye-popping orange turbans waited patiently beside animals I had only seen in movies or the zoo. I pinched myself to prove this was real. It was! Thousands of miles from home, I was going to ride a camel in the Sahara of Morocco!

- Point out that the last sentence could also have been the first sentence. Explain that students can choose when to reveal information as long as there is a clear sequence to the story.

- As you present and read **Display and Engage 6.3b–6.3c**, invite students to identify other features of a personal narrative. Point out that the last paragraph brings the story to a close.

Begin to Draft

- Have students begin to draft their personal narratives, using their prewriting notes.

 ENGLISH LEARNER SUPPORT: Scaffold Writing

SUBSTANTIAL
Students may draw their narrative. Tell them to include a sequence of pictures with a beginning, middle, and end and then add a brief caption to each frame.

MODERATE
Provide a graphic organizer such as a story map for students to use in writing their narrative. You might also want to include an opening sentence frame in each part of the map.

LIGHT
Provide paragraph frames for students to use in writing their narrative.

NARRATIVE • PERSONAL NARRATIVE

LEARNING OBJECTIVES

- Understand plot structure.
- Develop a draft into a focused, structured, and coherent piece of writing.
- **Language** Write about events using a plot structure.

MATERIALS   Online

Focal Text *Miss Alaineus: A Vocabulary Disaster*

Anchor Chart W6: *Narrative Structure*

Anchor Chart W5: *Elements of a Personal Narrative*

Writer's Notebook *pp. 6.5, 6.6*

 INSTRUCTIONAL VOCABULARY

- **plot** the conflict, events, and resolution that make up a story
- **exposition** the part of the story that introduces the characters and the setting
- **rising action** series of events that lead to the climax
- **climax** the moment of greatest intensity; the turning point in a story
- **resolution** the conclusion of the action

Understanding Plot Structure

- Remind students that a personal narrative includes a **plot**: the conflict, events, and resolution that make up a story.

- Use the focal text to review the narrative structure of a plot. As students fold an 8-1/2" x 11" sheet of paper into quadrants, draw quadrants on the board. Invite students to think about *Miss Alaineus*. Ask: *How did the story begin?* (*Sample answer: Sage caught a cold from Forest and had to stay home from school.*) In the top left quadrant, draw a picture of Sage in bed. Add a box of tissues. Ask: *What part of the story does this quadrant represent?* (*the beginning*) Print the word *Beginning* at the top of the quadrant. Have students replicate what you draw on their own paper as you move through the quadrants.

- Move to the second quadrant. Ask: *What happened next in the story?* (*Sample answer: Sage got the vocabulary list from Starr and made up definitions for the words.*) In the second quadrant, draw a picture that represents that part of the story.

- In the third quadrant, draw a picture of Sage giving her definition of *Miss Alaineus* with other students laughing. Draw an arrow between the second and third quadrants. Ask: *What part of the plot do these two quadrants represent?* (*the middle*)

- In the fourth quadrant, draw Sage in her "Miss Alaineus" cape holding up a trophy. Ask: *What part of the plot does this quadrant represent?* (*the ending*)

- Show Anchor Chart W6: Narrative Structure. Review the narrative structure components. Then have students figure out which quadrant in the drawing represents each part of the plot diagram. Ask: *Where does quadrant one belong on the plot diagram?* (**exposition**) *Which quadrant represents **rising action**?* (*the second quadrant*) Discuss the **climax** with students. Some students may think it was when Sage was embarrassed by defining *Miss Alaineus* incorrectly (*the third quadrant*). Others may argue that it was when Sage and her mother came up with the idea of dressing her like Miss Alaineus. Ask: *Why does quadrant four represent the **resolution**?* (*Sample answer: It shows it is possible to turn an embarrassing situation into a win.*)

- If you have not already done so, add the terms related to narrative structure to the Class Instructional Vocabulary List, and have students add them to their glossaries.

Continue to Draft

- Have students continue to draft their personal narratives, using their notes and other prewriting documents. You may want to post Anchor Chart W5 Elements of a Personal Narrative as well. Encourage students to reread the model on Writer's Notebook pages 6.5 and 6.6 if they need a reminder. Move around the room, offering assistance as needed.

ANCHOR CHART   Online

Narrative Structure

The narrative structure is also called the plot. It usually has five stages:

Climax — the turning point in the story

Rising action — what happens in the story that leads to the climax

Falling action — the events that happen after the climax

Exposition — any important background information about the setting and characters

Resolution — the conclusion of the story

NARRATIVE • PERSONAL NARRATIVE

LEARNING OBJECTIVES

• Draft a narrative.

• Write a conclusion.

• **Language** Write a satisfying conclusion.

MATERIALS   Online

Display and Engage 6.4

Writer's Notebook *pp. 6.4, 6.6*

Focal Text *Miss Alaineus: A Vocabulary Disaster*

 LEARNING MINDSET:
Belonging

Review Remind students that a personal narrative helps members of the classroom community understand more about one another. *By telling us more about your experiences, you help us get to know you better. That brings the community closer.* Have students think about what their personal narrative reveals about their attitude toward life.

Develop a Conclusion

• Ask students if they have ever watched gymnastics. Ask: *Do you know what it means to "stick the landing" in gymnastics? (to land on both feet without falling or taking extra steps) Why does the crowd cheer when a gymnast sticks the landing? (It shows that the gymnast was in perfect control and has brought the routine to a satisfying end.)*

• Explain that the conclusion to a personal narrative should be like sticking the landing in gymnastics. Say: *A good conclusion completes your message and leaves your reader satisfied.*

• Point out that there are several ways to conclude a narrative. Use **Display and Engage 6.4**, and discuss the ideas:

  » End with an image. Summarize the experience in a vivid and descriptive way.

  » End with dialogue. If you used dialogue in your narrative, use dialogue to have a character comment in a memorable way on the experience.

  » End with action. Example: I walked away from . . ., but I would never escape the memory.

  » End with emotion. Reflect on your emotions about the experience to help the reader connect with your story. How did the experience make you feel? What did you learn?

• Have students review the end of the model on **Writer's Notebook page 6.6**. Ask: *How did the narrative end? (with an emotion and a reflection)*

• Read the page for Y and Z in *Miss Alaineus*. Ask: *How did the author end the narrative? (with an image of Sage in next year's vocabulary show)*

• Invite students to finish their draft with a powerful conclusion.

Complete the Draft

• Discuss the rubric on **Writer's Notebook page 6.4**. Remind students that they can use the rubric as a resource while they are drafting.

• Have students complete the draft of their personal narrative.

• If it is feasible in your classroom setting, sit in a chair on wheels and simply roll from student to student, offering support and answering questions. If a student needs immediate help, use an agreed upon signal, such as raising a hand. If a student is deeply engaged in writing, consider skipping that student until another time.

 ENGLISH LEARNER SUPPORT: Elicit Participation

ALL LEVELS Have students work together as they complete their conclusions. Encourage them to discuss their ideas and get feedback as they write.

NARRATIVE • PERSONAL NARRATIVE

LEARNING OBJECTIVES

- Understand how to elaborate a draft.
- Revise drafts.
- **Language** Elaborate writing with figurative details.

MATERIALS   Online

Focal Text *Miss Alaineous*

Display and Engage *6.5*

Anchor Chart W12: *Elements of Figurative Language*

INSTRUCTIONAL VOCABULARY

- **simile** a comparison of two unlike things that uses the word *like* or *as*
- **metaphor** a comparison of two unlike things that does not contain the word *like* or *as*
- **personification** the giving of human qualities to an animal, object, or idea
- **imagery** words and phrases that appeal to the five senses
- **hyperbole** exaggeration

TEACHER TIP

You may wish to create lists of sensory words to trigger students' ideas. Place each of these categories on a separate piece of chart paper: Sight Words, Sound Words, Touch Words, Taste Words, Smell Words. Add a few examples to each list and challenge students to add more. Locate examples by searching the Internet for "sensory words." Post the lists for students to use as a resource.

Focus on Elaboration

- Write the following sentence on the board and read it aloud.

> Even though I was sick in bed, I had to finish writing definitions for the vocabulary words.

- Ask: *What do you think of this writing?* Elicit that it is telling not showing.

- Read aloud the first paragraph on page E of the focal text. Then ask: *How did the author elaborate on the sentence on the board? What effect does it have on you, the reader?* Help students see how the text shows rather than tells.

- Use **Display and Engage 6.5** to discuss elaboration. Explain that when you elaborate, you add details such as explanations, examples, and descriptions with sensory words.

- Show **Anchor Chart W12: Elements of Figurative Language**. Explain that elaboration can also be figurative language, or words that don't mean exactly what they say.

- Discuss how each type of figurative language adds details and is an example of showing and not telling.

- Add **simile**, **metaphor**, **personification**, **imagery**, and **hyperbole** to your Class Instructional Vocabulary List and direct students to add them to their glossaries.

Use Elaboration to Revise the Draft

- Challenge students to reread their drafts, highlight parts of their writing that tell rather than show, and then elaborate with details and figurative language.

- Ask volunteers to share their revisions. Students should read their original sentences and then the revised versions. Ask listeners to point out what they can imagine seeing, hearing, smelling, tasting, or feeling.

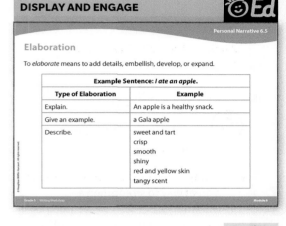

DISPLAY AND ENGAGE Online

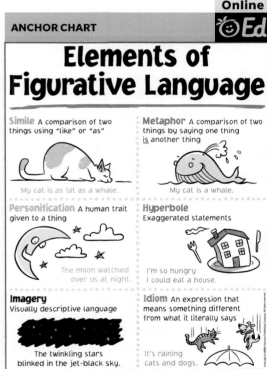

ANCHOR CHART Online

NARRATIVE • PERSONAL NARRATIVE

LEARNING OBJECTIVES

- Give and receive peer feedback.
- Revise drafts.
- **Language** Articulate and understand verbal feedback.

MATERIALS   Online

Anchor Chart W5: *Elements of a Personal Narrative*

 LEARNING MINDSET:
Belonging

Apply Explain that a writer's group is a great way to strengthen a community. *Everyone in the group is trying to help other members succeed. Pointing out what is memorable is positive feedback that can reinforce a writer's effort to do better.* Have students think about what they noticed about themselves as writers from the feedback. Ask: *How did this grouping strategy help you as a writer?*

TEACHER TIP

Listen carefully to what students say during the debriefing session. Make notes of the discussion as this will give you qualitative data concerning next steps for minilessons and/or data for future grouping strategies.

Pointing

- Remind students that working with a writing group gives them practice in collaborating with others, developing "people skills" while listening and responding, discovering how their writing affects others, and experiencing a writing group as a helpful and nonthreatening place. Begin the lesson by reviewing the writing group strategy of pointing.

> 1. Students form groups of four or five.
> 2. Writers read their whole personal narrative while listeners listen.
> 3. Writers read the narrative a second time while listeners jot down words, phrases, images, or anything that sticks in their minds.
> 4. After the second reading, listeners point out what they liked as writers jot down notes.
> 5. No negative comments are allowed. It is students' responsibility to focus on and share only what they liked and found memorable.

- Have students form groups of four or five and begin their pointing exercise. Move around the room, listening carefully to what students in different groups say. You may want to display **Anchor Chart W5: Elements of a Personal Narrative** again to help guide discussion. If a student gives negative comments, gently remind the group to focus only on what each person likes and remembers from the story.

- After all writers have read their narratives, ask students to come back together as a whole class to debrief about what they learned from their writing groups. Make this a pleasant experience. Encourage students to think about how they can use the feedback to make their narratives more appealing and memorable.

Continue to Revise

- Have students re-enter their writing and continue to revise using the feedback they received in their writing group conferences.

🔵 ENGLISH LEARNER SUPPORT: Elicit Participation

SUBSTANTIAL

Provide simple sentence frames for students to use to provide feedback: *I remembered _____. I liked _____ because _____. The sentence _____ was good because _____.*
You may wish to have English learners work together in their writers' groups.

MODERATE

Help students frame their comments by providing the following questions: *What do you remember? What did you like? What did you see, hear, or feel when you were listening to the story?*

LIGHT

Encourage students to think about and share why some parts of the narratives were easier to remember than others.

NARRATIVE • PERSONAL NARRATIVE

LEARNING OBJECTIVES
- Revise drafts using feedback.
- **Language** Understand verbal feedback.

Prepare to Revise

- Tell students that they will use feedback from their writing groups to continue the revision process.

- Begin with the whole class. Ask: *What kinds of things did most peers point out in your writing group?* As students respond, help them recognize that specific details that engage the senses are more easily remembered than simple telling.

- Use this brief model to review elaboration. Read the sentences aloud.

> **Before:** I could smell the boxes I placed in the living room.
>
> **After:** I could smell the musty cardboard boxes consuming every inch of available floor space as they patiently waited to be packed, sealed, and shipped.

- Ask: *How does the first sentence make you feel? Why?* (*Sample answer: It's kind of boring because I only see boxes in the living room and that's not interesting.*) *How is the second sentence different?* (*Sample answer: The details show. I can smell the boxes and see them piled all around.*)

- Point out that *boxes patiently waiting to be packed* is an example of *personification*—giving human qualities to inanimate objects.

- If some students haven't finished their writing group activity from the previous lesson, give them time to finish so that every writer has feedback.

Use Feedback to Revise a Draft

- Have students return to revising their drafts, using the feedback they received from their peers. Remind them to locate parts of their narrative where they tell, rather than show, and to focus on adding explanations, examples, description, and figurative language. As they work, confer with students who need extra help.

 ENGLISH LEARNER SUPPORT: Scaffold Writing

SUBSTANTIAL
Students may benefit from drawing a storyboard about their experience before revising their narrative. Encourage them to include color and speech bubbles to add details. If they have difficulty converting the pictures into words and constructing grammatically correct sentences from scratch, provide them with sentence frames. Reference the sensory word charts to help them add details.

MODERATE
Provide students with simple examples in pictures and words of each of the types of figurative language: simile, metaphor, personification, imagery, and hyperbole.

LIGHT
If students are having trouble understanding the meaning of the term *figurative language,* remind them that figurative language includes similes, metaphors, personification, imagery, and hyperbole. Have students review the definitions for these terms that they recorded in their notebooks during Lesson 8. For more support, provide simple examples for each term.

NARRATIVE • PERSONAL NARRATIVE

LEARNING OBJECTIVES

- Vary sentence lengths in drafts.
- Revise drafts.
- **Language** Write a variety of sentence types.

INSTRUCTIONAL VOCABULARY

- **simple sentence** a sentence that has only one independent clause
- **compound sentence** a sentence that contains two independent clauses joined by a comma and coordinating conjunction

TARGETED GRAMMAR SUPPORT

You may want to consult the following grammar minilesson to review a key revising topic.

- **1.3.3 Compound Sentences,** p. W210

TEACHER TIP

If students have difficulty identifying compound sentences, tell them to use different colored pens to underline the subjects and verbs in the sentence. Encourage students to break longer sentences into parts to see if each part has a subject and verb. Ask: *Can each part stand alone as a sentence? Is there a comma and a conjunction joining the parts?*

Review Sentence Types

- Begin by reviewing simple and compound sentences.

- Remind students that a **simple sentence** has one independent clause and no subordinate clauses. It may have phrases or even a compound subject or predicate but only one independent clause. Say: *An example of a simple sentence is "Sage made up definitions for her vocabulary words."*

- A **compound sentence** has two independent clauses (or sentences) joined together by a comma and a coordinating conjunction. Say: *An example of a compound sentence is "Sage made up definitions, but she misunderstood one of the words."*

- Add these terms and definitions to the Class Instructional Vocabulary List that you started, and direct students to include the terms in their glossaries.

- Write on the board this excerpt from a personal narrative.

> I can still remember receiving the dreaded news. I was sitting at home. My cell phone hummed. I started to feel sick. I shifted in my chair, and my stomach churned. I knew good and well what was going to happen. We would have to move. I didn't want to leave my home and my hometown. I had no choice.

- Read the passage aloud. Discuss how the sentences vary. Point out that a simple sentence can be short or long. Ask students to say which sentences are simple (S), compound (C), or other (O). You may need to show how to identify sentences that are neither simple nor compound (the sixth sentence). As students volunteer their answers, label each sentence with S, C, or O. When you have finished writing, make a list at the side of the passage, so the pattern of sentence variety becomes evident.

- Model combining the second and third sentences into a compound sentence. Ask: *What other simple sentences could you combine into a compound sentence?* (*Sample answer: I didn't want to leave my home and my hometown, but I had no choice.*)

Revise by Varying Sentences

- Have students use the coding method to revise their drafts, focusing on coding, identifying, and revising types of sentences. Students can also reference their elaboration notes from Lesson 9 to add depth to their sentences. As they work, move around the room so that you are available when students need help.

- End the lesson by asking volunteers to share original and revised sentences. Discuss how coding for sentence variety turns a random revision process into a systematic approach.

- Encourage students to make a clean copy of their revised draft, leaving space between each line for proofreading.

NARRATIVE • PERSONAL NARRATIVE

LEARNING OBJECTIVES

- Edit for complete sentences.
- Edit for subject-verb agreement.
- Edit for spelling.
- **Language** Increase understanding of English conventions.

MATERIALS   Online

Anchor Chart W16: *Proofreading Marks*
Writer's Notebook *pp. 6.4, 6.5, 6.6*

TARGETED GRAMMAR SUPPORT

You may want to have students consult the following grammar minilessons to review key editing topics.

- **1.3.1 Complete Subjects and Predicates,** p. W208
- **1.3.2 Subject-Verb Agreement,** p. W209
- **8.1.1 Spelling: Homophones,** p. W343
- **8.1.2 Spelling: Words with Endings,** p. W344
- **8.1.3 Spelling: Words with Suffixes,** p. W345

Prepare to Proofread

- Display **Anchor Chart W16: Proofreading Marks**. Explain that students will edit their personal narratives for complete sentences, subject-verb agreement, and misspelled words. Briefly review the specific marks used to edit those features.

- As needed, revisit relevant grammar topics to remind students what to look for. Say: *Remember that proofreading is a type of editing. When you proofread, you check to make sure there are no mistakes in your narrative.*

  THINK ALOUD *As I proofread this personal narrative, I like to look at one rule at a time. I first check that every sentence is complete. Then I check subject-verb agreement. Then I check for misspelled words.*

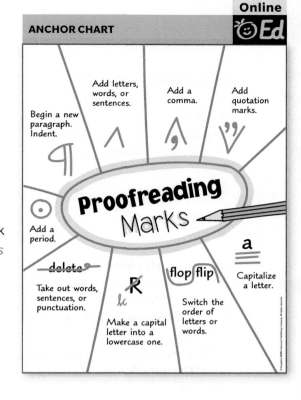

ANCHOR CHART — Online Ed

- Have students retrieve the narrative model on **Writer's Notebook pages 6.5 and 6.6**. Although there are no errors in the text, model editing by first checking for complete subjects and predicates. Remind students that writers sometimes use sentence fragments, such as "Whew!" or "Right?" to add interest. They are called interjections.

- Next, check each sentence for subject-verb agreement.

- Finally, check for frequently misspelled words, such as *its/it's* and *there/their/they're*.

Proofread Drafts for Grammar, Usage, and Mechanics

- Have students use proofreading marks to edit their narratives.

- Encourage students to review the rubric on **Writer's Notebook page 6.4** to make sure they have written the best possible personal narrative.

- Walk around the room, monitoring student progress and offering suggestions where needed. As you circulate, group students who need support on similar grammar topics. Use the grammar minilessons or the students' own writing to provide targeted review and support.

LEARNING OBJECTIVES

- Edit writing for grammar and mechanics.
- **Language** Apply English language conventions with peer support.

TARGETED GRAMMAR SUPPORT

You may want to have students use the following grammar minilessons to review key editing topics.

- **1.3.2 Subject-Verb Agreement,** p. W209
- **7.1.1 Punctuation in Compound and Complex Sentences,** p. W323

Review the Clocking Activity

- Explain that proofreading is done silently, unlike writing groups in which students read their papers to one another.
- Give students the following directions.

> - Write your name on a sheet of blank paper and label it "Proofreading Page." Then write the following numbers and items that will be checked.
>   1. there, their, they're
>   2. its and it's
>   3. punctuation in compound sentences
>   4. subject/verb agreement
> - Place the proofreading page on top of your narrative draft.

Clocking Activity

- Have students sit either in concentric circles or in rows facing each other.
- Tell them to exchange papers with the classmate they are facing and proofread for the first item on the list above. If students find any errors they should note them on the proofreading page, not on the draft itself.
- After a suitable amount of time, tell students in one row (or one circle) to take back their papers, move one seat over, exchange papers with the next student, and proofread for the second item on the list.
- Keep students moving until all have had the opportunity to proofread for each item on the list at least once.

Integrate Proofreading Edits

- Have students read their proofreading sheets and decide which, if any, corrections need to be made based on what the editors pointed out. For example, they may look up words in the dictionary or discuss a correction with the editor.
- If the writer decides an editor has found a valid error, the writer has the opportunity to correct it. Tell students that if they disagree with an editor's correction, they are free to ask the opinion of the teacher.
- After students have had sufficient time to look over their proofreading sheets and edit their drafts, have them sign off on the proofreading sheet and store it with their draft.
- If there is time, debrief the clocking activity with students.

LEARNING OBJECTIVES

- Create a title.
- Publish writing.
- Use technology to assist with writing.
- **Language** Demonstrate increased comprehension of English.

MATERIALS   Online 😊 **Ed**

Focal Text *Miss Alaineus: A Vocabulary Disaster*

Display and Engage *6.6*

TEACHER TIP

Remind students that it's not legal to download images they find on the Internet without permission. Some schools subscribe to a website that provides them with a license to download images or clip art throughout the year. Assist students who prefer to download images rather than draw illustrations for their narratives.

Prepare the Final Copy

- Explain that students will prepare and publish their narratives. If students have not yet chosen a title for their personal narrative, spend a few minutes discussing the purpose of the title. Say: *A title on a draft is just a placeholder. When I think about a title for my personal narrative, I want it to intrigue and interest the reader without giving away the story. In the focal text, the title (Miss Alaineus) sounds strange, and the subtitle (A Vocabulary Disaster) makes the reader wonder what kind of disaster could happen with vocabulary words! The title of the model, "Ship of the Desert," is intriguing because a ship and the desert don't go together.*

- Give students time to finalize their titles.

- Tell students that they can choose to handwrite their narratives or use a computer to type them. Remind students to use their best handwriting if they handwrite their personal narratives, start each line directly under the previous line, and indent the first line of each paragraph. If they use unlined paper, encourage students to place the paper over a sheet of lined paper to keep their lines straight.

- If computers are available, encourage students to type their final copy. Use the model narrative to demonstrate setting margins and selecting a font and font size.

- Ask: *What are some ways an author might publish a personal narrative?* (*Sample answers: in a collection of stories; as a stand-alone story; in an online personal blog*)

- Show and discuss the options on **Display and Engage 6.6**. Ask students if they can add to the list of publishing ideas for their personal narratives. The list should include traditional outlets such as magazines as well as online possibilities.

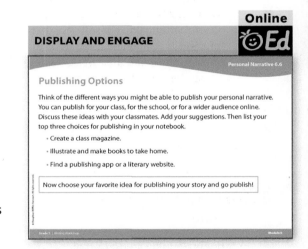

- Have students list their top three choices for publishing. Working with a partner, have each student choose their top publishing choice.

Embellish the Personal Narrative

- Point out that students elaborated on their personal narratives by adding details. Similarly, they can elaborate on, or embellish, their stories by adding illustrations. Focus on the illustrations and design of *Miss Alaineus* as you show students the cover of the book and page through it, discussing how each illustration adds to the narrative. Encourage students to think about where and how (e.g., drawing, cutting out pictures) they might add illustrations to their own narratives.

- If students use a computer to type their final copy, use the model narrative to demonstrate how to insert and format graphics throughout the text.

- Some students may wish to create their own books. Students might place the pages in a report cover with fasteners. Encourage students to use their imaginations when designing a cover for their personal narrative.

NARRATIVE • PERSONAL NARRATIVE

LEARNING OBJECTIVES

- Share writing.
- Engage in collaborative discussion.
- **Language** Ask and answer questions using academic language.

MATERIALS   Online

Display and Engage 6.7

Writer's Notebook pp. 6.3, 6.7

TEACHER TIP

You may wish to work with your school or district IT director to identify safe, useful writing apps or software that students might enjoy using to write, publish, and share their work. Remind students not to share personal information online.

 LEARNING MINDSET: Belonging

Review Remind students that the better community members understand one another, the stronger the community becomes. *Sharing personal experiences, as you did in your personal narratives, helps your teacher and classmates understand more about what you enjoy and what your life is like.* Encourage students to think about what more they would like to know about the people in their classroom and school communities.

Share Writing

- Explain that there are many ways students might choose to share their writing with others. Broaden students' ideas about publishing by discussing ways in which they can share in the digital world. Explain that there are many writing apps that allow writers to write, publish, and share their work online.

- Show **Display and Engage 6.7**. Read each idea and discuss how it might make sharing more fun and add interest for the reader. Ask students if they can add their own ideas.

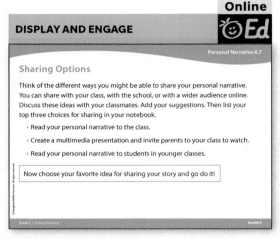

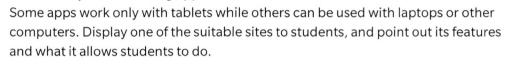
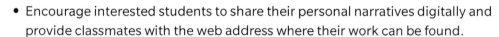

- Ask students to choose their favorite way of sharing their writing and describe how they will make it happen.

- Locate appropriate apps and online software by searching the Internet for "elementary school writing apps." Some apps work only with tablets while others can be used with laptops or other computers. Display one of the suitable sites to students, and point out its features and what it allows students to do.

- Encourage interested students to share their personal narratives digitally and provide classmates with the web address where their work can be found.

- Some students may wish to read their narratives aloud in small groups. When each student has finished reading, encourage listeners to ask the presenter questions.

Reflect on Writing

- Tell students to return to the goals they set at the beginning of this Writing Workshop on **Writer's Notebook page 6.3** or in their notebooks. Then have them keep a written record of the ways in which they met and didn't meet their goals with **Writer's Notebook page 6.7**.

- After students reflect on their goals, have them Turn and Talk with a partner about the goals they did or didn't meet. Encourage students to note what they would like to improve in their next writing assignment.

- As a class, engage in an informal discussion of this writing assignment. Encourage students to think about and express their feelings about the following topics.

> - What did you like best about writing your personal narrative?
> - What did you like least?
> - What did you learn about writing? How did you learn it?
> - What ideas or emotions did you want to convey to your reader? Do you think you were successful? Why or why not?
> - What do you want to remember to do the next time you write a narrative?

Research Report

FOCUS STATEMENT Research and curiosity are flip sides of the same coin. Research is questioning and investigating with a purpose.

FOCAL TEXT

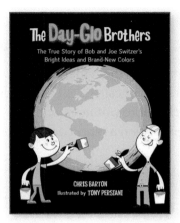

The Day Glo Brothers: The True Story of Bob and Joe Switzer's Bright Ideas and Brand-New Colors

Author: Chris Barton

Illustrator: Tony Persiani

Summary: The story of how two brothers invented day-glo colors

WRITING PROMPT

READ this sentence: *Research and curiosity are flip sides of the same coin.*

THINK about what you already know about how to investigate a topic.

WRITE a research report about a discovery that was made in the past that affects your life today.

LESSONS

1. **Introducing the Focal Text**

2. **The Read**

3. **Vocabulary**

4. **Prewriting I: Preparing to Write**

5. **Prewriting II: Gathering Sources**

6. **Drafting I: Following the Research**

7. **Drafting II: Incorporating the Research**

8. **Drafting III: Finishing the Draft**

9. **Revising I: Paraphrasing vs. Plagiarizing**

10. **Revising II: Peer Conferencing**

11. **Editing I: Grammar, Usage, Mechanics**

12. **Editing II: Peer Proofreading**

13. **Editing III: Developing a Bibliography**

14. **Publishing**

15. **Sharing**

LEARNING MINDSET:
Questioning

Display Anchor Chart 32: My Learning Mindset throughout the year. Refer to it to introduce Questioning and to reinforce the skills you introduced in previous modules.

LEARNING OBJECTIVES

- Recall background knowledge about researching topics.
- Learn a new approach to researching a topic.
- Tell students about the focal text.
- **Language** Discuss features of a research report with academic language.

MATERIALS Online Ed

Focal Text *The Day-Glo Brothers*

Anchor Chart W10: *Elements of Research*

Display and Engage *7.1*

INSTRUCTIONAL VOCABULARY

- **data** facts and figures that give information about a topic
- **hypothesis** a proposed explanation about a topic
- **research** 1. *v.* to study and find information; 2. *n.* information about a topic

TEACHER TIP

Make sure students understand that a hypothesis is an idea you develop based on some information, but additional research is needed to make certain it's true.

Priming the Students

Discuss the Focus Statement

- Show **Display and Engage 7.1**. Read the Focus Statement. Have students share their experiences on previous research projects. Ask: *Why did you research that topic? Where did you find your **data** about the topic? What was fun about doing the research?*

DISPLAY AND ENGAGE

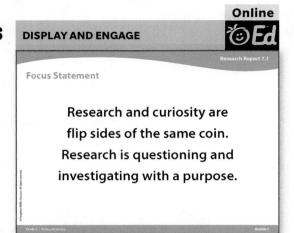

Research Report 7.1

Focus Statement

> Research and curiosity are flip sides of the same coin. Research is questioning and investigating with a purpose.

- Call attention to the focal text *The Day-Glo Brothers*. Tell them that they will be reading this book about the discovery of a special paint called Day-Glo. Explain that the authors of this book did a lot of research before writing about the inventors. Then tell students that they will begin writing a report on an invention that they like.

Discuss a New Approach

- Display **Anchor Chart W10: Elements of Research** and list characteristics of inquiry and research students may use as they develop their research report.

- Explain that they will learn a new way to write a research report. In this new way, they will form a **hypothesis** and then follow the research as the report is developed.

- Encourage students to add **research** and other research and inquiry terms along with their definitions to their Instructional Vocabulary glossaries. Add the terms to the class Instructional Vocabulary list as well.

ANCHOR CHART Online Ed

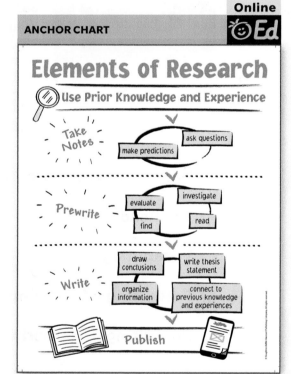

Elements of Research

Use Prior Knowledge and Experience

Take Notes — make predictions — ask questions

Prewrite — evaluate — investigate — find — read

Write — draw conclusions — write thesis statement — organize information — connect to previous knowledge and experiences

Publish

EL **ENGLISH LEARNER SUPPORT: Build Vocabulary**

SUBSTANTIAL

Write the following two sentences on the board: *I will research dogs to find out why they wag their tails. This research explains why cats purr.* Explain that *research* can have two meanings. Circle *research* in each sentence and have students identify it as a noun or verb.

MODERATE

Discuss the two meanings of *research*. Have students complete the following sentence frames: *This research says _____. Duncan and Emily research _____.*

LIGHT

Ask students to use *research* as a verb and then as a noun. Write their responses on the board. Then have them discuss the meaning of *research* in each sentence.

LEARNING OBJECTIVES

- Discuss the motivation of the Switzer brothers in inventing Day-Glo paints.
- Analyze how the Switzer brothers' discoveries were made.
- Make a list of the subjects or inventions that interest students that they may want to research.
- **Language** Discuss a research report using academic language.

MATERIALS

Online Ed

Focal Text *The Day-Glo Brothers*

TEACHER TIP

Encourage students' questions about *The Day-Glo Brothers* as well as the inventions they discuss at the end of the lesson.

 LEARNING MINDSET: Questioning

Introduce Students will be asking many questions about their topic in order to do their research. Tell them that questioning means looking for the how and why of what's going on, not only in their classroom but also in the world around them. Emphasize that curious students want to know how things work.

Priming the Text

Prepare to Read

- Show the cover of *The Day-Glo Brothers* and explain that the book is a research report.

Read

- Read the book aloud. Stop periodically to discuss exactly what the brothers had to do to finally get the paint they wanted. After reading, ask:

  » *What is this book mainly about?*

  » *Why did the brothers invent Day-Glo paints?*

  » *How did Bob's accident have an effect on their first invention?*

  » *How did they invent the paints?*

  » *Why do you think the author uses dates in this report?*

  » *What character traits of Bob and Joe made their inventions possible?*

- Conclude by discussing the research report aspects in *The Day-Glo Brothers.* Ask:

  » *How does the author help the reader understand how the inventions were made?*

  » *How does the author use research to tell the story?*

  » *How is this report organized?*

After Reading

- Explain that Bob and Joe were interested in colors that glowed, and this interest propelled them to make more and more discoveries. Use a Think Aloud similar to the following one to start students' thinking.

  THINK ALOUD *When I read about the Day-Glo brothers and their inventions, I began to think about things that really interest me—things I want to find more about. For example, I love biking. I wonder how the first bicycle was invented. Or what about popcorn? I love popcorn. How were these things invented? I'm also interested in cell phones, computers, and skateboards. Who invented all that stuff?*

- Have students make a list of inventions that they might wish to find out more about for a research report. Record their responses on the board.

 ENGLISH LEARNER SUPPORT: Build Background

SUBSTANTIAL
Before class begins, have a sampling of familiar inventions for students to explore, such as markers, books, erasers, and paper clips. Have them ask questions about what they would like to know about each invention.

MODERATE
Hold up a common invention from the classroom such as an ink pen. Ask pairs of students to come up with two questions about the invention. If necessary, provide sentence frames, such as the following: *Why was the _____ invented? Who invented the _____?*

LIGHT
Ask students to name inventions of common objects in the classroom, such as a pencil sharpener, chalk, a television, and a computer. Allow students to contribute any information they know about these commonly used inventions.

The Day-Glo Brothers

The Day-Glo Brothers

LEARNING OBJECTIVES

- Read and understand new vocabulary words.
- Use Word Bank to list words students might want to use in their research.
- **Language** Discuss features of a research report using academic language.

MATERIALS   Online

Focal Text *The Day-Glo Brothers*
Display and Engage 7.2
Writer's Notebook *p. 7.1*

 INSTRUCTIONAL VOCABULARY

- **hypothesis** a proposed explanation about a topic
- **data** facts and figures that give information about a topic

---

TEACHER TIP

Point out that the use of idioms in *The Day-Glo Brothers* (*scrounged around, souped up, more his speed, jazzed up*) make the research report more informal and create a sense of fun, making the text more interesting to the reader.

Review the Focal Text

- Review pages 3–13 of *The Day-Glo Brothers* with students.

- Have students use the Word Bank on **Writer's Notebook page 7.1** or their own notebooks. Page through *The Day-Glo Brothers* and have students identify and record words and phrases that they don't understand or that they find interesting.

DISPLAY AND ENGAGE   Online Ed

Research Report 7.2

Word Bank

illuminating	imagination	cavorted
souped-up	library	gullible
experiment	discovery	scrounged around

Grade 5 | Writing Workshop   Module 7

- Write students' word choices on the board and then show **Display and Engage 7.2** to see how many words match.

illuminating	imagination	cavorted
souped-up	library	gullible
experiment	discovery	scrounged around

- Discuss the images suggested by some of the words and phrases. Ask: *What images do these words suggest? Can you use these words in your research report?* Make sure students understand that they will need both specific, technical words in their report as well as vivid, descriptive words.

- Add research terms, such as **hypothesis** and **data** to the class Instructional Vocabulary list as you encounter examples of these terms in *The Day-Glo Brothers*. Students should add these research terms to their glossaries. Ask:

   » *What is a hypothesis that you could use for this book?*

   » *What kind of data does the author use to tell the story?*

Continue Brainstorming

- Have students use the Word Bank on **Writer's Notebook page 7.1** or their own notebooks to record words that relate to the topics they find interesting.

- Have students continue brainstorming inventions from the previous lesson.

EL **ENGLISH LEARNER SUPPORT: Build Vocabulary**

SUBSTANTIAL
Have students draw pictures of idioms from the book that explain their meaning—for example, a souped-up car or scrounging around for something to eat in the refrigerator.

MODERATE
Explain that using idioms when speaking will help students sound like a native speaker. Have them complete the following sentence frames: *I want to get a souped-up _____. I hate it when I have to scrounge around for _____.*

LIGHT
Provide the following sentence frames for students: *A souped-up _____ can _____. _____ scrounged around for _____.*

LEARNING OBJECTIVES

- Use prior knowledge.
- Discuss a writing prompt.
- Ask and clarify questions about a topic.
- Set goals for writing.
- **Language** Discuss writing tasks using academic language.

MATERIALS   Online

Anchor Chart W3: *Asking Questions*
Display and Engage *7.3*
Writer's Notebook pp. 7.2, 7.3

TEACHER TIP

Students may or may not have done a research project before. Make sure they understand that they are going to be asking questions and gathering information about a topic of interest to them and then writing about it.

LEARNING MINDSET:
Questioning

Apply Tell students that curiosity leads to questioning and questioning leads to learning. Encourage students to ask a lot of questions and explore new ideas, materials, and skills.

Preview the Research Report Writing Process

- Tell students that in this module they will write a research report.

- Display **Anchor Chart W3: Asking Questions** to preview how to generate and clarify questions on a topic. Explain that students will develop a hypothesis about an invention and use questions to guide their research.

- Display an opened shoebox, holding onto its lid. Explain that this will be a place where they can keep their ideas and research documents for their research report.

- Tell students to bring in a shoebox to class tomorrow to hold all their information.

- Project **Display and Engage 7.3** and read the Writing Prompt aloud. Have students brainstorm possibilities for a topic as they think about the Writing Prompt. Point out and discuss the genre characteristics.

Exploring the Topic

- Lead students in a Think Aloud to show them how to write what they know about a topic and the questions they have.

THINK ALOUD *One invention that has changed my life is the invention of the cell phone. The first thing I'll do is write what I do know. I'll write this under the heading* What I Know. *Then, I'll ask questions about what I want to find out under the heading* What I Want to Know. *I'll use questions that begin with* what, why, how, who, *and* when. *These questions will help guide my research.*

- Distribute **Writer's Notebook page 7.2**. Have students choose a topic they want to explore. Then, have them write what they know about the invention in the first column. Next, ask students to generate questions for inquiry on their topic and have them write those questions in the second column.

- Then allow students to discuss their charts in small groups.

Set Goals for Writing

- Point out to students that their writing must include the important elements of a research report. Have students consider the goals that are provided. Then tell them to think about and add their personal goals for this assignment to the list on **Writer's Notebook page 7.3** or in their notebooks.

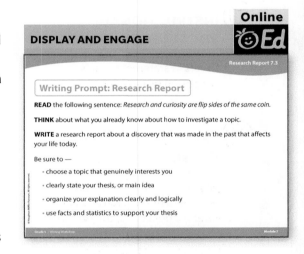

LEARNING OBJECTIVES

- Discuss a research report model.
- Take notes for a research report.
- Review a rubric for writing.
- **Language** Discuss writing tasks using academic language.

MATERIALS   Online

Display and Engage *7.4a–7.4b*

Writer's Notebook *pp. 7.2, 7.4, 7.5, 7.6, and 7.7*

Anchor Chart W2: *Research Sources*

Classroom materials *shoebox (1 per student), index cards (at least 5 per student)*

INSTRUCTIONAL VOCABULARY

- **thesis** a statement that is supported by research

LEARNING MINDSET: Questioning

Apply Explain that, as students delve into their research and find answers to questions, they will likely come up with new questions. Encourage them to add new questions to **Writer's Notebook page 7.2**.

Preview a Model

- Tell students that they are going to be reading a model of a research report on the invention of the cell phone. Project **Display and Engage 7.4a–7.4b.** Before reading, tell students to listen for a **thesis** statement and data that supports it. Then read aloud the first two paragraphs. Have students follow along on **Writer's Notebook pages 7.5 and 7.6**.

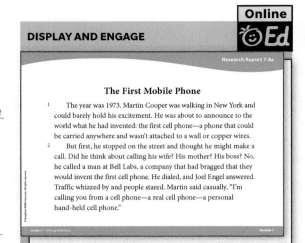

DISPLAY AND ENGAGE   Online

Research Report 7.4a

The First Mobile Phone

1   The year was 1973. Martin Cooper was walking in New York and could barely hold his excitement. He was about to announce to the world what he had invented: the first cell phone—a phone that could be carried anywhere and wasn't attached to a wall or copper wires.

2   But first, he stopped on the street and thought he might make a call. Did he think about calling his wife? His mother? His boss? No, he called a man at Bell Labs, a company that had bragged that they would invent the first cell phone. He dialed, and Joel Engel answered. Traffic whizzed by and people stared. Martin said casually, "I'm calling you from a cell phone—a real cell phone—a personal hand-held cell phone."

- After reading, lead students in a Think Aloud.

  THINK ALOUD *The thesis is "The first cell phone was invented by Martin Cooper." Once the researcher found out that Martin Cooper invented the first cell phone, the writer searched for information about it. Then, the writer used the research to include facts about the cell phone. For example, the writer included what happened the day Cooper announced the new invention and who received the first phone call. The writer also gave 1973 as the year the cell phone was invented. These useful facts, or data, came from the research.*

Research the Topic

- Have students form a thesis, which will state what their research is about.

- Have students take out their shoeboxes. Explain they will keep their notes in the box. Have them use the questions from **Writer's Notebook page 7.2** to develop their research plan. Explain that recording their notes and research on index cards will help them keep the research organized.

- Give students time to research their topics. Display **Anchor Chart W2: Research Sources** to give them ideas of where to look. Have students keep a record of all their sources on **Writer's Notebook page 7.7**.

ANCHOR CHART   Online

Research
is using sources to find information.

CHICAGO DAILY
OCTOBER 4, 1871
Chicago Is Burning

A **primary source** gives direct information about a topic.

Great Fires in History

A **secondary source** uses information from primary sources.

Good Sources ✓
- nonfiction books
- print or online magazines or newspapers
- respected websites

Avoid Plagiarism ✗
- Always list the sources you used for your ideas and information.
- Put the information you find in your own words.

Introduce the Rubric

- Distribute **Writer's Notebook page 7.4**. Share the rubric with students and remind them that this tells them what they need to understand and include when writing their research report.

 ENGLISH LEARNER SUPPORT: Facilitate Discussion

ALL LEVELS Build on students' writing successes. Discuss how writing a report will increase their vocabulary. Aid them in writing goals that center on researching a topic.

INFORMATIONAL TEXT • RESEARCH REPORT

LEARNING OBJECTIVES

- Organize data and connect it to experiences related to the topic.
- Organize writing and continue to research.
- Identify credible primary and secondary sources.
- **Language** Discuss writing tasks using academic language.

MATERIALS   Online

Display and Engage *7.5a–7.5b*

Anchor Chart W10: *Elements of Research*

Writer's Notebook *p. 7.2*

Classroom materials *shoeboxes (one per student)*

 INSTRUCTIONAL VOCABULARY

- **primary source** an original document, interview, speech, or information from someone who has witnessed an event
- **secondary source** book, article, or report based on research someone else did
- **credible source** a trustworthy source of information

 LEARNING MINDSET: Questioning

Apply Explain that students may question the credibility of the research they find. Have them ask themselves these questions: *Do I trust this source? Is this source believable, or credible? Or is it biased, or slanted to one particular point of view?* Also point out that primary sources are usually trustworthy (unless the primary source is not telling the truth).

Distinguish Between Primary and Secondary Sources

- Display **Anchor Chart W10: Elements of Research** to remind students of how to follow the research model.

- Discuss the meanings of **primary** and **secondary sources**. Encourage students to add *primary source* and *secondary source* and their definitions to their glossaries. Also add these terms to the class Instructional Vocabulary list.

- Explain that both primary and secondary sources can be used in order to gather information for their research topic. Project **Display and Engage 7.5a–7.5b**. Lead students in a Think Aloud to help them distinguish between the two.

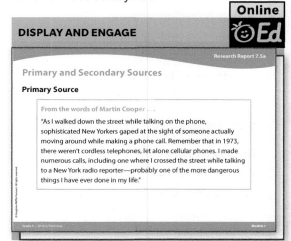

THINK ALOUD *When I write a research report, I look for information, but I also consider the source. Let's read the words of Martin Cooper. Martin Cooper is a primary source because he was there when he used his phone for the first time. He observed what people were doing as he made the calls. So, I can trust this source because Martin Cooper was there, and he is reporting what he saw and did. Now, let's read an excerpt from a secondary source. These are words that were printed in an article. This is a good writer, but we have no knowledge that the reporter saw all this happening. The reporter probably looked at a lot of sources to write this observation. Now, both of these sources are probably reliable, but the primary source is more reliable because it comes directly from the person who was there.*

Continue the Research Process

- Have students organize the information in their shoeboxes into **credible sources**, both primary and secondary sources.

- Have students meet in small groups and explain what research and sources they have so far. Invite students to give suggestions on what other information they might collect using other sources, including interviews with experts who can help clarify the topic. They may also want to add to their **Writer's Notebook page 7.2** to record new questions that come up as they work.

- Have students continue to gather information and place it in their shoeboxes. Have them note particularly which research comes from a primary source.

- If necessary, aid students in setting up interviews with experts.

 ENGLISH LEARNER SUPPORT: Facilitate Discussion

ALL LEVELS To help students process the meanings of primary and secondary sources, explain that the Spanish cognate for *primary* is *primero*, and the cognate for *secondary* is *secundario*.

INFORMATIONAL TEXT • RESEARCH REPORT

LEARNING OBJECTIVES

- Continue to ask questions and look for answers.
- Keep track of used sources.
- Identify credible sources.
- Conference with peers.
- Work on a first draft.
- **Language** Discuss writing tasks using academic language.

MATERIALS   Online 🍊 **Ed**

Display and Engage 7.6
Writer's Notebook pp. 7.7, 7.8
Classroom materials shoeboxes

 INSTRUCTIONAL VOCABULARY

- **credible source** a trustworthy source of information

TEACHER TIP

To help students who are struggling and to make sure their papers contain strong information and a logical flow, you may wish to periodically meet with them in small discussion groups, so they can learn from each other and you.

Identifying Credible Sources

- Discuss with students of the meaning of *credible*.

- Explain that using **credible sources** for their research will give their research report validity and accuracy. Add the term to the class Instructional Vocabulary list and tell students to add it to their glossaries.

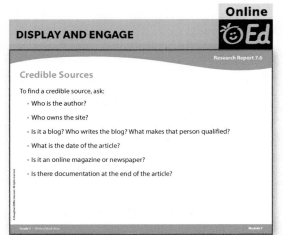

- Project and read aloud **Display and Engage 7.6**. Lead students in a Think Aloud to help them identify credible sources.

THINK ALOUD

1. *When I research from a book or magazine, I read the article. Then, I look to see if the author is an expert. That will tell me if the source is credible.*

2. *But when I go online, I have to remember that anyone can post anything on the Internet. A person could say that hippos speak French and publish it as fact. So, I have to be extra careful with this kind of source. The first thing I do is read about the author. Is he or she an expert? If not, that source may not be reliable.*

3. *Then, I think about who owns the website. Are they trying to sell me something? If so, that might not be a reliable source.*

4. *Then, I ask if it is a blog. People can write anything on blogs, which are often filled with opinions. I can't always trust these sites—unless the author is an expert.*

5. *Then, I look at the date. If the information is old, it may no longer be true.*

6. *If the information is from an online newspaper or magazine, I can usually trust that source.*

7. *Last, I look at the bottom of the article. Are there sources that tell me where the author got his or her information? If so, the information is probably trustworthy.*

Verify Sources

- Have students meet in groups. Ask volunteers to offer up articles they have read and identified the source as credible or not, explaining their reasons.

- Have students use **Writer's Notebook 7.8** to list and verify the articles they have used as credible or not credible.

- Meet one on one with students who seem to be unsure of the identification of credible sources for their research report.

Writing the Drafts

- Have students continue asking and answering questions from their research.

- Remind them to keep track of the websites they visit by writing them down on **Writer's Notebook page 7.7** or printing the articles and placing them in their shoeboxes.

- Have them use their research to begin writing their draft.

LEARNING OBJECTIVES

- Identify and gather research.
- Review credibility of primary and secondary sources.
- Interpret research to create a focused, organized, and coherent piece of writing.
- **Language** Discuss writing tasks using academic language.

MATERIALS   Online Ed

Display and Engage *7.4a–7.4b*
Anchor Chart W2: *Research Sources*
Writer's Notebook *pp. 7.5, 7.6, 7.8, 7.9*
Classroom materials *shoeboxes*

TEACHER TIP

To assess student's understanding of the important concept of determining the credibility of both primary and secondary sources, you may wish to lead a discussion in order to review and clarify these concepts and to address any confusion.

Identify and Gather Information

- Project and revisit **Display and Engage 7.4a–7.4b**. Read aloud the research report on the invention of the cell phone, focusing on the first two paragraphs. Have students follow along on **Writer's Notebook page 7.5**. Then use a Think Aloud to explain how to identify information that will support the thesis.

  THINK ALOUD

  My thesis is to tell about Martin Cooper who invented the cell phone. I want to continue to identify research about this thesis. So, I will identify articles that support this thesis. I will look at an article titled "Martin Cooper and the History of the Cell Phone." I'll see if I can find some good information there. I also found an article titled "The Motorola DynaTAC 8000X Phone." Then, I'll look at a website that gives quotes by Martin Cooper.

  1. *The next thing I'll do is gather these three research articles and read them to see if I can possibly use information from them in my report. If they are online, I'll print them.*

Assess Credibility of Primary and Secondary Sources

- Display **Anchor Chart W2: Research Sources.** Explain that when we research, we have to continually determine if the source is reliable, or credible. Use a Think Aloud to model how to assess credibility.

  THINK ALOUD

  1. *First, let's look at an article or book that is a secondary source. To assess if it's credible or not, I look to see who wrote the information. The article that is written by a scientist for a science magazine is usually credible. However, another source is written by middle school students. Not knowing how knowledgeable they are, I'll put that source aside. I'll keep looking for a more reliable source.*

  2. *When I look at a primary source, I'll evaluate how knowledgeable that author is. The quote I found was made by Martin Cooper. He is an expert who is the center of my research, so I'll consider his words credible.*

- Have students continue to use **Writer's Notebook page 7.8** to evaluate the credibility of their sources.

Demonstrate Understanding

- Project **Display and Engage 7.4a–7.4b**. Ask students to follow along on **Writer's Notebook page 7.6**. This time focus on the last two paragraphs that continue the research report on the invention of the cell phone. Read the text aloud and ask students determine if the author has gathered and used the information in a clear and logical way.
- Read together **Writer's Notebook page 7.9**. As students continue to write their drafts, have them use the checklist to guide their writing.

Teacher Conferences

- Have students meet one on one with you to discuss their drafts. Be sure to advise students about the credibility of the researched information in their draft.
- After students have checked their sources, have them finish their drafts as you continue meeting with individual students as necessary.

LEARNING OBJECTIVES

- Review drafts to make sure they are complete.
- Reread drafts to make sure all the words are original.
- Use quotation marks when using another writer's words.
- **Language** Discuss writing tasks using academic language.

MATERIALS   Online

Display and Engage *7.7a–7.7b*

Writer's Notebook *p. 7.10*

Classroom materials *shoeboxes*

INSTRUCTIONAL VOCABULARY

- **paraphrasing** stating someone else's ideas using your own words
- **plagiarism** copying someone else's work without giving credit

Distinguishing Between Paraphrasing and Plagiarism

- Discuss the meanings of **paraphrasing** and **plagiarizing**. Encourage students to add the words and their definitions to their glossaries. Also add these terms to the class Instructional Vocabulary list.

- Explain that it is important to use your own words when writing a research report. Point out that, if you do not, you are using someone else's words and representing them as your own.

- Project **Display and Engage 7.7a–7.7b**. Read aloud the Original Source box. Then read the plagiarized version. Use a Think Aloud to explain the difference between plagiarism and paraphrasing.

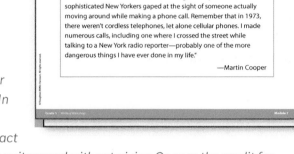

Online Ed

DISPLAY AND ENGAGE

Research Report 7.7a

Avoid Plagiarizing

Original Source

"As I walked down the street while talking on the phone, sophisticated New Yorkers gaped at the sight of someone actually moving around while making a phone call. Remember that in 1973, there weren't cordless telephones, let alone cellular phones. I made numerous calls, including one where I crossed the street while talking to a New York radio reporter—probably one of the more dangerous things I have ever done in my life."

—Martin Cooper

THINK ALOUD

1. *The quote from Martin Cooper shows Cooper's exact words. In the Plagiarizing box, the underlined words show the exact words from the quote that the writer used without giving Cooper the credit for saying them. In doing this, the writer is plagiarizing the material.*

2. Read aloud the Quoting without Plagiarizing sentence. *This sentence gives Martin Cooper credit for his thoughts and words. The use of quotation marks makes using his exact words okay because they show the words are not the writer's words but Cooper's.*

3. Reads aloud the Paraphrasing sentence. *This sentence is written by telling about Martin's thoughts not using the author's own words. Paraphrasing is an acceptable practice in writing a research report.*

Review Drafts

- Read aloud the list on **Writer's Notebook page 7.10** and discuss each item.

- Conclude by discussing how to avoid plagiarism. Ask:

  » *How can using more than one source help you avoid plagiarism?*

  » *How can writing a draft without looking at your sources help you avoid plagiarism?*

  » *How can quotations help you avoid plagiarism?*

- Have students use their checklist as they return to their drafts. Have them compare their drafts to their sources to make sure they did not plagiarize text.

- After students have checked their work, allow them to continue writing. Make sure the source materials are put back into the shoebox to help ensure that students will use their own words when writing.

 ENGLISH LEARNER SUPPORT: Facilitate Revising

ALL LEVELS Work with students one on one and review paragraphs from their drafts. Have them compare their work to the original source. Supervise students as they locate and circle any words in their drafts that are exact words from the original source.

INFORMATIONAL TEXT • RESEARCH REPORT

LEARNING OBJECTIVES
- Give and receive peer feedback.
- Revise drafts based on feedback.
- Revise drafts to improve word choice.
- **Language** Discuss writing tasks using academic language.

MATERIALS	Online

Display and Engage *7.8*

Writer's Notebook *p. 7.11*

LEARNING MINDSET:
Questioning

Apply Just as students ask questions about their topic, it's important to ask questions about their writing. If they get stuck, they can question where they are and how they got there by asking themselves, "Can I try this in a different way?"

Give and Receive Feedback

- Explain that when you revise, you improve your writing. Say: *Getting feedback from your peers is a great way to find out what you've done well and what you can do to make your writing better. Today, we will focus on whether or not your research report has enough or too much information, if the research follows a logical flow, and if there are any parts that are confusing or difficult to understand.*

- Project **Display and Engage 7.8**. Read aloud the questions.

- Divide students in groups of four or five.

- Have writers take turns reading their reports aloud as the rest of the group listens.

- After a second read, have the writer ask the group the questions from **Writer's Notebook page 7.11**. As their peers respond to the questions, have writers record their responses.

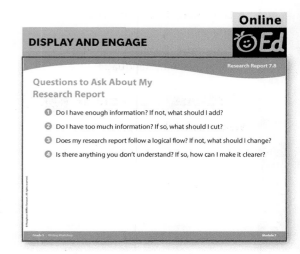

Revise Drafts

- Have students incorporate the feedback from their peers as they revise their reports. Point out that if they do not agree with the feedback, they do not have to use it.

- As students revise, also have them improve word choice by deleting vague or unclear ideas or words and substituting with clearer, more vivid and specific words.

- Be sure to give students enough time to revise their drafts.

 ENGLISH LEARNER SUPPORT: Facilitate Discussion

SUBSTANTIAL
Work with students one on one and have them ask each of the conferencing questions. Assist students to make sure they fill in the chart to answer the questions. Then have them join the group and ask the questions on their own.

MODERATE
Have students work in pairs to review their work, asking and answering the peer conferencing questions. Monitor students to be sure they have a clear understanding of the feedback they are receiving.

LIGHT
To facilitate peer conferencing, you may want to have students work in smaller groups of two or three students in order to ask and answer each of the conferencing questions.

INFORMATIONAL TEXT • RESEARCH REPORT

LEARNING OBJECTIVES

- Edit writing for proper use of adverbs.
- Edit writing for proper use of pronouns.
- Edit writing for proper use of prepositions.
- **Language** Discuss writing tasks using academic language.

MATERIALS   Online

Writer's Notebook *p. 7.12*

TARGETED GRAMMAR SUPPORT

You may want to consult the following grammar minilessons to review key editing topics.

- **2.4.1 Subject Pronouns,** p. W233
- **2.5.2 Possessive Pronouns,** p. W239
- **4.2.3 Using Adverbs,** p. W285
- **4.4.1 Prepositions,** p. W293
- **4.4.2 Prepositional Phrases,** p. W294

Prepare to Edit

- Write the following sentences on the board or chart paper: *First, Jeff quickly punched the volleyball with his hands. Then, he fell awkwardly on the sand.*

- Discuss the meanings of adverbs, pronouns, and prepositions and have volunteers name an example of each from the first sentence.

- Frame the first sentence and say: *An adverb tells when or how something is done. The adverb First tells when the action happened. The word* quickly *tells how Jeff punched the ball. Using adverbs in your writing makes it easier for the reader to know when and how something happened.* Remind students that many but not all adverbs end with the suffix *-ly*.

- Point to the word *with*. Say: *With is a preposition, and* with his hands *is a prepositional phrase. This prepositional phrase further clarifies how Jeff punched the ball.*

- Point to the word *his*. Explain that this is a possessive pronoun that refers back to Jeff.

- Have students look at the second sentence and identify the other preposition (*on*), prepositional phrase (*on the sand*), two adverbs (*Then, awkwardly*), and pronoun (*he*). Ask:

  » *Which word tells us how something happened?* (*awkwardly*)

  » *Which word tells us when something happened?* (*Then*)

  » *Which word stands for* Jeff? (*he*)

- Conclude by explaining that the proper use of pronouns helps readers know who is doing what, adverbs tell when and how things are done, and prepositions and prepositional phrases help to make clear where something takes place or how something is done. Reinforce that all of these grammar elements work together to make a research report more clearly understood.

Self-Editing

- Remind students to use ratiocination to proofread their drafts for adverbs, pronouns, and prepositions. They can first look for adverbs and in addition find places to insert them. Next, they can check their pronouns to make sure each agrees with its subject. Last, they can check their prepositions and prepositional phrases to make sure they are accurate and make sense.

- Have students use **Writer's Notebook page 7.12** to guide them as they edit their work.

- Conclude the lesson by providing time to have students write a fresh copy of their report.

 ENGLISH LEARNER SUPPORT: Facilitate Editing

SUBSTANTIAL
Circle each pronoun on a student's draft. Then, have them name the word to which the pronoun refers.

MODERATE
Before editing, have students work in groups to brainstorm adverbs to complement action verbs.

LIGHT
Have students work in pairs to review their checklist against their drafts.

INFORMATIONAL TEXT • RESEARCH REPORT

LEARNING OBJECTIVES

- Review peers' papers for grammar, usage, and mechanics.
- **Language** Discuss writing tasks using academic language.

MATERIALS   Online

Display and Engage *7.9*

Writer's Notebook *p. 7.13*

Anchor Chart W16: *Proofreading Marks*

TEACHER TIP

Since these are research reports, students who review a report might not know the correct spelling of some specialized words. Before they mark them for spelling, have them check the words in a digital or print dictionary.

Clocking Activity

- Review the rules for clocking.

- Have students sit in concentric circles. Distribute <u>Writer's Notebook page 7.13</u> and have students write their names at the top of their editing page. The page will travel with their research reports.

- Show <u>Display and Engage 7.9</u> and call out what item is to be checked by the editor.

   THINK ALOUD *When I find an error in the report, I'll put my name by the number and explain where I found the error. For example, for number 1, I'll check to make sure all proper nouns and the first word of each sentence begins with a capital letter. If they are capitalized, I won't mark the student page. I will just make notes where corrections need to be made.*

- As students receive a peer's research report, they become the editor of that paper. Editors write their names to the left of the item they are checking.

- After a couple of editing items, have students move so that each paper is read by several editors.

Edit Writing

- Display <u>Anchor Chart W16: Proofreading Marks</u> and remind students how to use proofreading marks on their reports now that they have feedback from their classmates.

- If they are confused by an edit, allow them to ask you or the editor.

(EL) **ENGLISH LEARNER SUPPORT: Support Editing**

ALL LEVELS Circulate as the clocking activity proceeds. When you see an error that is common to two or more students, create a sentence that is similar with the same mistake. Explain how to correct the error and guide them to correct the same mistake in their own writing.

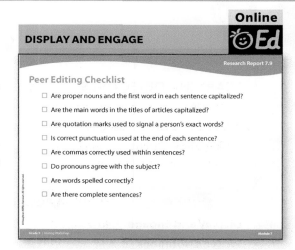

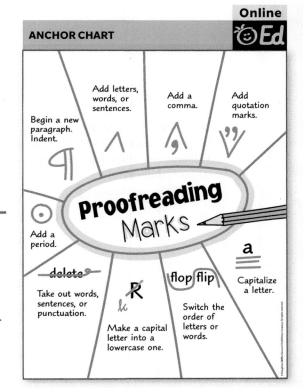

LEARNING OBJECTIVES

- Include sources for research reports.
- Properly record a bibliography.
- **Language** Discuss writing tasks using academic language.

MATERIALS	**Online**

Display and Engage 7.4a–7.4b, 7.10

Writer's Notebook p. 7.14

TEACHER TIP

Sometimes URLs are too long and complex to copy or retype. There are websites you can find that will teach you and your students how to shorten web addresses.

Reference Your Work

- Explain that it is very important to give credit to the sources that helped you write your report. Say: *There are two ways of giving credit to your sources. One is within the text of your report. The other is a bibliography.*

- Project **Display and Engage 7.4a–7.4b** and point to the reference at the end of the third paragraph. Say: *This gives credit to my source. I put it in parentheses and included the last name of the author. Then, I put a comma and the date the text was written.*

Develop a Bibliography

- Show **Display and Engage 7.10**. Use a Think Aloud to help students understand the four kinds of bibliography items: online article, encyclopedia, magazine, and book.

Online

DISPLAY AND ENGAGE

Research Report 7.10

Bibliography

Keith, Robert. "The Cell Phone Time Line." http://cellphone.example.com, April 25, 2018.

Marsalis, Delfeayo. No Cell Phone Day. New Orleans, LA: Kidstown Press, 2013.

Manning, Sharon. "How Cell Phones Changed Lives." Time, April 2015. pp. 21-22.

Encyclopedia Britannica: 16th Ed., "Mobile Telephones."

THINK ALOUD

1. *In this bibliography, I have four kinds of sources. Let's look at the first one. It is from an online article, and I include the author's name (last name first, comma, first name last, and a period). Then, I put the name of the article in quotation marks and add a period. Then, I note the web address where the article can be found ending with a comma, and followed by the date of the article, ending with a period.*

2. *The second source is from a book. In this item, I list the author's name first followed by a period. Notice again how I list the last name first, comma, and then the first name. Then, I write the title of the book followed by a period. Note that I underline the title of the book. Next, I list the city, comma, and state abbreviation where the book was published, followed by a colon and the name of the publisher. After that, I add a comma and the year it was published, followed by a period.*

3. *The third source is from a magazine. First, I list the author's last name, comma, first name, and a period. Then, I give the title of the article in quotation marks, ending with a period. Lastly, I give the name of the magazine, underlined, a comma, and the month and year of the publication along with the page numbers I read, ending with a period.*

4. *The last source is from an encyclopedia. In this item, I list the name of the encyclopedia, colon, the edition, a comma, and the title of the article in quotation marks, followed by a period.*

Add References

- Have students check their shoeboxes for their sources. Instruct them sort their sources by type: online articles, books, magazines, and encyclopedias.

- Ask students to scan their reports and find paragraphs where they need to add a reference within the text. Allow time for them to make these additions.

- Have students use **Writer's Notebook page 7.14** to guide them as they generate a bibliography for their research report.

LEARNING OBJECTIVES

- Write a title for a research paper.
- Publish the final copy using computer software or write neatly by hand.
- Decide on publishing options.
- **Language** Discuss the publishing process using academic language.

MATERIALS

Online

Display and Engage *7.11*

Classroom materials *computer, printer, video camera*

TEACHER TIP

If students choose to present their writing in a video, they could print their text in a larger size font for easier reading.

Write a Title

- Explain that a title is a good way to both sum up the main idea of a research report as well as capture the attention of listeners or readers. Have students experiment with a variety of titles before deciding on their final, most appropriate title.

- You may wish to first have small groups work together to summarize their work and then suggest a title. Encourage peers to suggest alternate options before students decide which title to use.

Prepare the Final Copy

- Have students type their research paper on a computer and print out their final copy.

- Encourage them to experiment with different types and sizes of fonts.

- If computers are unavailable, allow students to neatly write their final copy by hand.

Publish

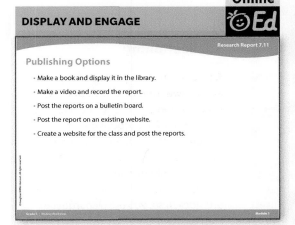

- Tell students that they have several options for publishing their reports. Project **Display and Engage 7.11** and discuss the value of each option. Remind students that, if they go on the Internet, they should not give out any personal information.

DISPLAY AND ENGAGE

Online

Research Report 7.11

Publishing Options

- Make a book and display it in the library.
- Make a video and record the report.
- Post the reports on a bulletin board.
- Post the report on an existing website.
- Create a website for the class and post the reports.

- Have students talk with a partner to explore publication options before selecting one. Circulate and help advise students as they share their preferences. If there are two or more students who wish to work together on any of the options, allow them to publish as a group.

- Give students sufficient time to publish their reports according to their preferences. Encourage them to add illustrations, photographs, or videos to enhance their presentations.

LEARNING OBJECTIVES

- Share writing.
- Participate in a collaborative discussion about writing experiences.
- **Language** Use academic language to engage in a discussion about writing.

MATERIALS   Online

Anchor Chart W17: *Tips on How to Present*

Writer's Notebook *pp. 7.3, 7.4, 7.15*

 LEARNING MINDSET:
Questioning

Review Encourage students to ask and answer questions about what they learned as writers. *You might be open to new ideas about how to research a report differently in the future. If so, you are a curious learner. You also might be comfortable asking questions and asking for help when you are stuck. If so, you are a courageous learner.*

Share Writing

- Share <u>Anchor Chart W17: Tips on How to Present</u>. Review and discuss the tips for presentations.

- Have students share their reports in their preferred method. Encourage students to be attentive and applaud each presentation.

- After each presentation, have students share their before and after drafts with the class. Give them a chance to discuss how they revised their work to get their final product.

Revisit Goals

- Have students review the goals on <u>Writer's Notebook page 7.3</u>. Ask: *How well did you meet your goals? What will be your goals for your next piece of writing?* Distribute <u>Writer's Notebook page 7.15</u>. Have them TURN AND TALK with a partner about how they feel they met their goals. Encourage students to take notes about what goals they would like to set for their next writing assignment.

- If time permits, have students take a look at the rubric on <u>Writer's Notebook page 7.4</u> to evaluate how they met all of the standards for writing a research report.

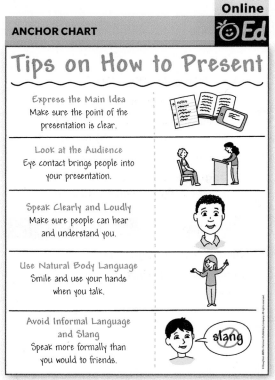

ANCHOR CHART   **Online**

Tips on How to Present

Express the Main Idea
Make sure the point of the presentation is clear.

Look at the Audience
Eye contact brings people into your presentation.

Speak Clearly and Loudly
Make sure people can hear and understand you.

Use Natural Body Language
Smile and use your hands when you talk.

Avoid Informal Language and Slang
Speak more formally than you would to friends.
slang

Lyric Poem

FOCUS STATEMENT   Home is where the heart is.

FOCAL TEXT

SHARON CREECH
WINNER OF THE NEWBERY MEDAL FOR WALK TWO MOONS

LOVE THAT DOG

a novel

Love That Dog

Author: Sharon Creech

Summary: A boy learns to write and appreciate poetry.

WRITING PROMPT

READ this sentence: *Home is where the heart is.*

THINK about a place you love, where you feel most comfortable.

WRITE several pieces of poems to practice using poetic techniques. Then use those skills to write a lyric poem describing a place you love to be.

LESSONS

1. **Introducing the Focal Text**

2. **The Read**

3. **Vocabulary**

4. **Prewriting: Preparing to Write**

5. **Drafting I: Beginning the Draft**

6. **Drafting II: Figurative Language**

7. **Drafting III: Features of Poetry**

8. **Drafting IV: Poetic Techniques**

9. **Revising I: Using Descriptive Verbs**

10. **Revising II: Conferencing**

11. **Revising III: Incorporating Feedback**

12. **Editing I: Grammar, Usage, and Mechanics**

13. **Editing II: Peer Proofreading**

14. **Publishing**

15. **Sharing**

**LEARNING MINDSET:
Growth Mindset**

Display <u>Anchor Chart 32: My Learning Mindset</u> throughout the year. Refer to it to introduce Growth Mindset and to reinforce the skills you introduced in previous modules.

LEARNING OBJECTIVES

- Use background knowledge to discuss poetry.
- Discuss genre features of poetry.
- Read poetry for enjoyment and understanding.
- **Language** Discuss features of poetry with academic language.

MATERIALS Online

Classroom materials *poetry books*
Anchor Chart W11: *Elements of Poetry*
Display and Engage *8.1*

📖 **INSTRUCTIONAL VOCABULARY**

- **poetry** text that uses varied line length, rhythm, rhyme, or other devices to express feelings or a story

TEACHER TIP

Many students will approach poetry with apprehension. The first two lessons in this module are meant to show students that poetry is enjoyable. Encourage them to be comfortable as they listen to you read and to engage with the feelings conveyed in each poem.

Priming the Students

Explore the Topic

- Before students enter the classroom, flood the classroom with **poetry** books. Be sure to display books that include elements such as internal rhyme, alliteration, onomatopoeia, similes, metaphors, and graphic elements. Present a variety of poems, including narratives, sonnets, haikus, silly poems, long and short poems, concrete poems, and current and classic poems.

- Tell students that in this module, they will learn about poetry and become poets themselves. Ask them what questions they have about poetry.

- Allow students to explore the books and ask them to share their favorite poems.

- Prompt discussion of poetry with the following questions.

  » *Why is this poem one of your favorites today?*

  » *Which details in this poem appeal to you?*

  » *How can you tell that this is a poem?*

  » *How is poetry like/unlike other genres?*

  » *What are the challenges of reading poetry?*

- Brainstorm poetry terms, discuss the terms, and add them to the Class Instructional Vocabulary List as a resource for understanding poetry. Students should also add these terms to their glossaries.

- Encourage students to bring in their favorite poems to share with the class.

Discuss the Focus Statement

- Show **Display and Engage 8.1**. Read with students the Focus Statement. Ask: *What do "home" and "heart" mean in this statement? What sort of feeling do you think this statement is meant to express?* Have students share their thoughts about the Focus Statement.

- Show **Anchor Chart W11: Elements of Poetry**, and tell students that they will become familiar with these elements by the end of the module.

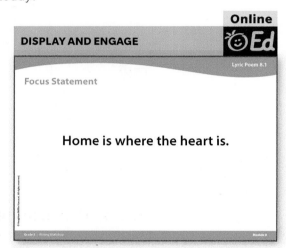

DISPLAY AND ENGAGE Online Lyric Poem 8.1

Focus Statement

Home is where the heart is.

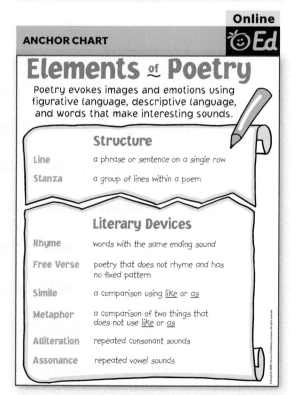

ANCHOR CHART Online

Elements of Poetry

Poetry evokes images and emotions using figurative language, descriptive language, and words that make interesting sounds.

Structure

| Line | a phrase or sentence on a single row |
| Stanza | a group of lines within a poem |

Literary Devices

Rhyme	words with the same ending sound
Free Verse	poetry that does not rhyme and has no fixed pattern
Simile	a comparison using *like* or *as*
Metaphor	a comparison of two things that does not use *like* or *as*
Alliteration	repeated consonant sounds
Assonance	repeated vowel sounds

LEARNING OBJECTIVES

- Discuss elements and characteristics of poetry.
- Read poetry for enjoyment and understanding.
- Discuss the meaning of punctuation marks used in poetry.
- **Language** Discuss features of poetry with academic language.

MATERIALS   Online **⬤Ed**

Focal Text *Love That Dog*
Writer's Notebook *p. 8.1*

 INSTRUCTIONAL VOCABULARY

- **stanza** a group of lines in a poem, usually set off by spaces

 LEARNING MINDSET: Growth Mindset

Introduce Explain to students that experiences help us grow. *Part of growing up is learning from the experiences you have. As we read* Love That Dog, *you'll see how a boy learns about poetry through experiences with it. He is uncomfortable with it at first, but he works on understanding it and eventually writes poems himself. His hard work leads to his enjoyment of poetry.* Tell students that when poetry seems difficult or unfamiliar, they might think about Jack and how he worked to understand and enjoy poetry.

Priming the Text

Prepare to Read

- Allow students who brought poems to class to read them aloud. Be prepared to share one of your favorite poems if students did not bring any.

- Show the cover of *Love That Dog* and briefly explain that the book is about a boy who is learning about poetry. Explain that the story mentions several poems that you will read first. Suggest that students close their eyes as they listen.

Love That Dog

- Point out the two poems at the back of *Love That Dog*: "Stopping by Woods on a Snowy Evening" by Robert Frost and the first stanza of "The Tiger" by William Blake. Briefly explain the building blocks of poems: lines and **stanzas**. Add *stanza* to the class Instructional Vocabulary list, and have students add it to their glossaries.

- Read each poem aloud. After each poem, ask the following questions.

  » *What idea do you think the writer wanted to share?*

  » *How do the lines and stanzas divide the ideas?*

  » *What feeling do you get from the poem?*

- Point out to students that they may have to read a poem several times to understand it. Invite them to listen to the poems again. Ask:

  » *What did you notice the second time I read the poem?*

  » *How is reading a poem on the page different from listening to it?*

- Point out that poets use punctuation to give signals about how to read a poem. Commas, dashes, and semicolons indicate short pauses. Periods and colons indicate longer pauses.

The Read

- Tell students that you will begin reading the main part of the book. Read pages 1–11 of the book. Ask:

  » *What does Jack think about poetry as the story begins?*

  » *Do you think he will change his mind?*

  THINK ALOUD *When I hear Jack's poems, I hear the same word patterns that were in the poems I read earlier. Jack might be writing poems like the ones he heard.*

- Have students record words, phrases, and ideas from the poems in the Word Bank on **Writer's Notebook page 8.1** or in their own notebooks as a resource for writing.

LEARNING OBJECTIVES

- Understand poetry terms.
- Recognize elements of poetry.
- **Language** Discuss features of poetry using academic language.

MATERIALS   Online

Classroom materials *poetry books*

Focal Text *Love That Dog*

Writer's Notebook *p. 8.1*

Anchor Chart W11: *Elements of Poetry*

 INSTRUCTIONAL VOCABULARY

- **narrative poem** a poem that tells a story
- **lyric poem** a poem that describes a person or thing
- **rhyme** words that end in the same sounds, such as *boat* and *coat*
- **line length** the width of a line of poetry
- **mood** the feeling a poem shares, such as happy, sad, or puzzled

TEACHER TIP

Students will best understand the language of poetry if it is taught as they encounter examples of it. As you reread poems, pause to point out stanzas, poetic devices, or other elements.

Review the Focal Text

- Review with students pages 1–11 of *Love That Dog*.

- Have students return to the Word Bank on **Writer's Notebook page 8.1** or in their own notebooks. Page through *Love That Dog* and have students identify words and phrases that they find interesting, such as those listed below.

Brain's empty	tottery	a squashed pea
splattered	clash	taptaptaptaptap
miles to go	screech	blooming words
shining bright	straggly	sprouting books

- Discuss the images suggested by some of the words and phrases. Point out that poetry relies on vivid language. Encourage students to add vivid words and phrases to their notebook as they read poetry.

- Point out that working with poetry will be easier if students are familiar with poetry terms. Explain that *Love That Dog* is a **narrative poem**, a poem that tells a story. Add poetry terms to the class Instructional Vocabulary list as you discuss them. Students should add poetry terms to their developing glossaries.

- Explain that a **lyric poem** is another kind of poetry. Most of the short poems at the back of the book are lyric poems because they describe a person or a thing. Revisit the wheelbarrow poem, the woods poem, and the tiger poem to illustrate the terms **rhyme**, **line length**, and stanza.

- Point out that poetry conveys a **mood**, or a feeling. Tell students that clues in the poem will help them figure out the mood of the poem. Ask students to think about the mood of "dog" by Valerie Worth as you read it aloud.

  THINK ALOUD *When I read "dog," I see words like "lies down," "lolls his limp tongue," and "rests." What feeling, or mood, do these words create?*

- Challenge students to determine the mood of the woods poem and the tiger poem.

- End the lesson by asking students to think about how the words make them feel as you read pages 12–30 of *Love That Dog*. Reread the text and discuss the mood of the poem. Point out **Anchor Chart W11: Elements of Poetry**, and discuss which elements students can see in *Love That Dog*.

ⓔ ENGLISH LEARNER SUPPORT: Build Vocabulary

SUBSTANTIAL
Ask students to choose words that they think are vivid. Allow students to explain their selected words and phrases to a partner.

MODERATE
Provide sentence frames for students, such as *I think _____ is a vivid word because _____.*

LIGHT
Have students discuss their chosen words before writing their thoughts about them.

LEARNING OBJECTIVES

- Use multiple prewriting strategies to plan writing.
- Explore focal statement, writing prompt, and rubric.
- Set goals for writing.
- Brainstorm topics for a lyric poem.
- **Language** Discuss writing tasks using academic language.

MATERIALS   Online

Display and Engage *8.2, 8.3*

Writer's Notebook *pp. 8.2, 8.3*

LEARNING MINDSET:
Growth Mindset

Apply Tell students that one way we learn new skills is by testing them out. *When you hear a sound or a line in a poem you like, pay attention. Can you write a poem with the same rhyme scheme or use a certain word you heard in a line of your own poetry?* Explain that we learn by playing with and applying new ideas. Writing poems can be playful and fun.

Preview the Poetry Writing Process

- Tell students that in this module they will write a lyric poem. Project **Display and Engage 8.2** and read the Writing Prompt aloud. Suggest that students begin thinking about the focus statement as their topic.

- Remind students about the elements of poetry they discussed in lesson 3. Then show them **Display and Engage 8.3**. Discuss similarities and differences between poetry in general and a lyric poem. Let students know that they will be learning more about poetic techniques and figurative language in future lessons.

- Distribute **Writer's Notebook page 8.2**. Discuss the rubric. Remind students that this rubric can be a resource while they draft and revise.

- Brainstorm poetry topics per the prompt. Write them on the board or chart paper and have students write them in their notebooks. Encourage students to continue to explore topics as they learn about poetry.

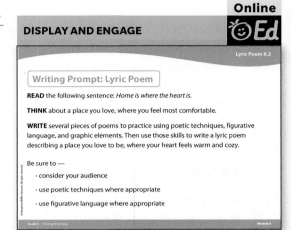

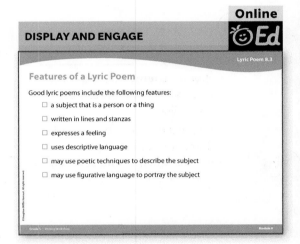

Set Goals for Writing

- Point out that writing poetry can be enjoyable. Have students add personal goals for the assignment to the list on **Writer's Notebook page 8.3** or to their notebooks.

 ENGLISH LEARNER SUPPORT: Scaffold Writing

SUBSTANTIAL
Build on students' writing successes. Talk about how writing a poem will increase their descriptive vocabularies. Write goals that center on using descriptive language, and have students copy those goals into their notebooks.

MODERATE
Discuss students' writing goals. Provide sentence frames that challenge students to be more descriptive writers. For example, *The _____ cat _____ ate her _____ dinner.*

LIGHT
Have students draft their personal writing goals before they discuss the goals with a partner and record them.

LEARNING OBJECTIVES

- Discuss genre features in poetry.
- Draft poetry incorporating rhyme.
- Discuss features of poetry with academic language.
- **Language** Discuss writing tasks with academic language.

MATERIALS   Online

Focal Text *Love that Dog*

Display and Engage *8.2, 8.4*

 INSTRUCTIONAL VOCABULARY

- **rhyme scheme** the pattern of rhyming words at the ends of poetry lines
- **internal rhyme** when a word at the center of a line of poetry rhymes with the word at the end of the same line

TEACHER TIP

Consider having students suggest lines for a class poem to ease reluctant writers into writing and sharing poetry.

Learn About Rhyme

- Recall that students will be experimenting with poetic devices as they write poetry.

- Project and read aloud the first two stanzas of "Stopping by the Woods on a Snowy Evening." Evaluate and label the **rhyme scheme** for the first stanza: *a, a, b, a*. Ask: *Which line from the first stanza rhymes with lines in the second stanza?* With the class, label the rhyme scheme for the second stanza: *b, b, c, b*.

- Project **Display and Engage 8.4**. Read aloud "My Attic." Ask: *What do you notice about the rhymes in this poem?* As students point out the rhyme within each line of the poem, tell them that the term for this device is **internal rhyme**. Define *internal rhyme* as rhyming a word in the center of a line of poetry with a word at the end of the same line. Add the new terms to the class Instructional Vocabulary list, and have students add them to their glossaries.

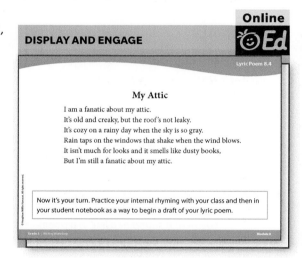

- Using **Display and Engage 8.4**, ask the class to add their own examples of internal rhymes. Begin by making up one of your own.

  THINK ALOUD *Internal rhymes can add a musical element to a poem. This poet is using internal rhymes to make what might be a boring subject more interesting.*

- Ask: *How does the rhyming of words like* creaky *and* leaky *make the poem about an attic more interesting? Here's an internal rhyme I like: The moon is a flashlight, it lights up my nights.*

Begin to Draft

- Project **Display and Engage 8.2** and review the Writing Prompt by reading it aloud. Remind students that in the next lessons they will draft lines of poetry. Later they will select lines to create a poem.

- Allow time for students to freewrite lines of poetry incorporating rhyme scheme and internal rhymes in their notebooks.

- Walk among students to offer assistance.

 ENGLISH LANGUAGE SUPPORT: Build Vocabulary

SUBSTANTIAL

Provide lists of rhyming words on the topic, such as *home/roam/dome, warm/storm/form*, and so on to show that words can rhyme despite spelling differences.

MODERATE

Show students how to use a print or online rhyming dictionary.

LIGHT

Have students work in pairs to list rhyming words related to the topic.

LEARNING OBJECTIVES

- Discuss genre features of poetry.
- Draft poetry incorporating poetic techniques.
- **Language** Discuss features of poetry with academic language.

MATERIALS   Online

Focal Text *Love That Dog*
Anchor Chart W11: *Elements of Poetry*
Display and Engage *8.2*

 INSTRUCTIONAL VOCABULARY

- **poetic techniques** ways that poets use words to convey their ideas
- **onomatopoeia** using a word that sounds like the noise that it represents, such as *buzz*
- **alliteration** the repetition of a sound at the beginning of more than one word, such as the *s* sound in *slid on the soft slope.*

TEACHER TIP

Encourage students to experiment with poetic devices that they may have seen in other poems, even if they have not studied them in class. They may want to try personification, for example.

Learn About Poetic Techniques

- Remind students that they will be drafting lines of poetry for a poem.

- Recall the lesson about rhyme scheme and internal rhyme. Tell students that today's lesson will be about other **poetic techniques**, or ways that writers play with words to convey ideas and feelings.

- Read aloud "Street Music" from page 100–101 of *Love That Dog.* Write the following words on the board:

grinding	clash	roar
slamming	screeching	blasts

- Repeat the words aloud, emphasizing their sounds. Ask: *What do you notice about the sounds of these words?* Elicit from students that the words sound like the ideas they represent. Explain that **onomatopoeia** is the term used for such words.

  THINK ALOUD *I'm thinking about how it would change the meaning of this poem if the poet had said "coming up from the subway" instead of "grinding up from the subways." I think the poem would be a lot less interesting without onomatopoeia.*

- Read aloud the first stanza of "Stopping by Woods on a Snowy Evening" from *Love That Dog.* Then write these pairs of words on the board:

these, think	see, stopping
His, house	watch, woods

- Read the words aloud, emphasizing their initial sounds. Ask: *What do you notice about the sounds of these words?* Elicit that the paired words begin with the same sound. Tell students that **alliteration** is the term for that technique.

- Add the terms to the class Instructional Vocabulary list and have students add the words and their own definitions to their glossaries.

Continue Drafting

- Project **Display and Engage 8.2** again to remind students of the writing prompt.

- Keep **Anchor Chart W11: Elements of Poetry** visible to help students as they draft lines of poetry per the prompt. Challenge them to use onomatopoeia and alliteration in their lines.

- As students write, circulate among them offering assistance.

 ENGLISH LEARNER SUPPORT: Discuss Vocabulary

ALL LEVELS Point out that because English sometimes uses different letters to represent the same sound, alliterative words will not always begin with the same letters. For example, *photograph* and *fun* begin with the same sound, even though that sound is spelled differently.

POETRY • LYRIC POEM

LEARNING OBJECTIVES

- Discuss elements and characteristics of poetry.
- Read poetry for enjoyment and understanding.
- **Language** Discuss features of poetry using academic language.

MATERIALS   Online

Focal Text *Love That Dog*

Anchor Chart W12: *Elements of Figurative Language*

Display and Engage 8.2

Writer's Notebook p. 8.4

INSTRUCTIONAL VOCABULARY

- **figurative language** phrases that use words to mean something other than their dictionary definitions, such as similes and metaphors

- **simile** a description that makes a direct comparison of two unlike things using the word *like* or *as*; for example, "Jill was like a tornado as she tossed the game pieces out of the box."

- **metaphor** a description that makes an indirect comparison between two unlike things; for example, "the cloak of nightfall" compares night to a piece of clothing

Learn About Figurative Language

- Challenge students to name poetry terms. Write them on the board as students define them: *rhyme scheme, internal rhyme, line length, alliteration, onomatopoeia.*

- Tell students that today they will learn about **figurative language**, another device used by poets.

- Read aloud the poem "Love That Boy" from page 105 of *Love That Dog*. Read the poem again, omitting "like a rabbit loves to run." Ask: *How does the meaning of the poem change when those lines are gone? Why do you think the poet included the words? What does the line compare?*

- Point out that poets and other writers often compare unlike things to make a point. Ask: *How does comparing the father's love to a rabbit's love of running help you understand the father's feelings?* Tell students that comparisons using *like* or *as* are called **similes**.

- Read aloud "The Tiger" from page 95 of *Love That Dog*. Then reread the first line. Ask: *Does the poet mean that the tiger is really burning? What does the poet mean with this comparison? How would the poem be different if the poet said, "The tiger is very bright"?*

- Explain that this phrase is a **metaphor**, and the poet is indirectly comparing a tiger to a fire or another bright object.

- Review the new terms using **Anchor Chart W12: Elements of Figurative Language**. Ask students to provide examples.

- Add the new terms to the class Instructional Vocabulary list and have students add the terms, creating their own definitions, to their glossaries.

Continue to Draft

- Project **Display and Engage 8.2** to remind students of the writing prompt.

- Distribute **Writer's Notebook page 8.4**. Have students use the page to write similes and metaphors on their topic.

- As students write, circulate among them offering assistance.

EL ENGLISH LANGUAGE SUPPORT: Support Discusssion

ALL LEVELS Provide sentence frames for students to construct similes and metaphors. For example: *The sun is like _____. The river was a ribbon of _____.*

POETRY • LYRIC POEM

LEARNING OBJECTIVES
- Use features of poetry in writing.
- Use multiple prewriting strategies to plan writing.
- **Language** Discuss features of poetry using academic language.

MATERIALS   Online

Display and Engage 8.2, 8.5
Writer's Notebook p. 8.5

 **LEARNING MINDSET:**
Growth Mindset

Apply Explain to students that sometimes learning feels difficult. *You have been learning a lot of terms about poetry, so you might be feeling like you are standing under a waterfall of vocabulary. Take a deep breath and remember that you can consult your vocabulary list or ask me or a classmate if you forget a term. Eventually, you will remember the terms and be able to use them in your writing. Just keep trying, and understanding poetry and poetic terms will get easier.* Point out that brains are like muscles, they will get stronger when they work hard.

TARGETED GRAMMAR SUPPORT

You may want to consult the following grammar minilessons to review key descriptive writing topics.

- **4.1.1 Adjectives,** p. W278
- **4.2.1 Adverbs that Tell How, Where, When, How Often,** p. W283

Selecting Lines for Development

- Project **Display and Engage 8.2** and review the writing prompt. Remind students that they have been drafting lines of poetry for their lyric poems. Preview the lesson by saying that today they will build a poem from those lines.

- Project **Display and Engage 8.5**.

  THINK ALOUD *Over the past few lessons, I have been thinking about the prompt and writing lines for a poem about "Home is where the heart is." Now I am going to see which lines will work best in a poem. I'm just beginning, so anything can change.*

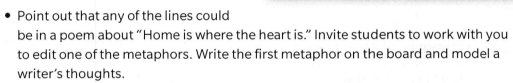

DISPLAY AND ENGAGE
Online
Lyric Poem 8.5

Lines of Poetry

Internal Rhyme
No matter where I roam, I always think of home.

Onomatopoeia and Alliteration
I hear the plopping sound of soup simmering on the stove.

Similes
A room as bright and warm as a summer day.
Our kitchen table is like the control tower at an airport.

Metaphors
Home is the station I leave each day to travel out into the world.
Our kitchen table is the heart of our home.

- Elicit from students the poetic terms that describe the lines: internal rhyme, alliteration, onomatopoeia, simile, and metaphor.

- Point out that any of the lines could be in a poem about "Home is where the heart is." Invite students to work with you to edit one of the metaphors. Write the first metaphor on the board and model a writer's thoughts.

  THINK ALOUD *I really like the idea of writing about traveling to and from home, so I want to work with "Home is the station I leave each day to travel out in the world." I think I want to make it sound more exciting, so maybe I will change it to "Home is the airport I leave each day to fly out into the world." I can add lines about returning home to refuel or rest or get directions. I'll look at the other lines to see if there are ideas that fit with this metaphor. And I need to remember to show that home is a special place connected to the heart and love.*

- Invite students to share lines that they have written.

Circulate the Room

- Distribute **Writer's Notebook page 8.5**. Have students use the page to select lines and expand on them.

- As students work, circulate to assist as necessary.

- Consider grouping students who are uncertain about which lines to revise with those who are confident about how to proceed to allow for peer insights and encouragement.

EL **ENGLISH LEARNER SUPPORT: Poetic Conventions**

ALL LEVELS Review characteristics of poetry with students. Point out that poets have greater freedom than other writers because lines of poetry do not need to follow punctuation rules and grammatical conventions.

LEARNING OBJECTIVES

- Revise drafts for descriptive verbs.
- Understand and use dictionaries and thesauruses.
- **Language** Discuss features of poetry using academic language.

MATERIALS   Online

Display and Engage 8.6

Writer's Notebook p. 8.6

Classroom materials *dictionary, thesaurus*

 INSTRUCTIONAL VOCABULARY

- **thesaurus** an online or hard copy reference work that contains synonyms and antonyms

TARGETED GRAMMAR SUPPORT

You may want to consult the following grammar minilessons to review key revising topics.

- **3.1.1 Linking and Action Verbs,** p. W248
- **4.1.2 Adjectives and Linking Verbs,** p. W279
- **4.2.2 Conjunctive Adverbs,** p. W284

Introduce the Revision Skill

- Point out that poems rely on vivid language to convey a mood or idea.

- Project **Display and Engage 8.6**.

- Distribute **Writer's Notebook page 8.6**. Read the poem aloud. Model revising the poem and invite students to revise the poem in their Writer's Notebook, using their own words.

- Say: *I'm going to pretend I wrote this poem. I like it, but it needs some changes to show the mood I want to share. I think it needs words that are more descriptive.*

DISPLAY AND ENGAGE

Online

Lyric Poem 8.6

The Blue Bird

The blue bird sits
upon

the dry round brown
nest

on the dark black
branch

near the green
leaves.

Grade 5 · Writing Workshop   Module 8

- Begin by saying: *First, let's look at the verbs in the poem. Can you think of verbs that would be more descriptive than the word sits? There are a lot of choices, but I want the best one.* (*Possibilities include crouches, sings, clutches, hides*)

- Next say: *In the last stanza, near isn't a verb, but it's not very descriptive. Maybe I can put a verb in its place. How about "sheltered by"? Other ideas? I might have to change other words in a line to make the new choice fit.* (*Possibilities include "hidden by" and "encircled by"*)

- Finally, say: *Maybe I should look at the third stanza, too. The adjective dark means the same thing as black, so maybe I can replace it. What else might describe a branch? Thick? Twisted? What will fit the mood I want to share?* (*Possibilities include solid, wet, weak, gnarled*)

- Say that writers often use a **thesaurus** to find synonyms and a dictionary to check definitions, as needed. Demonstrate how to use a print or an online thesaurus, whichever is available to your students. Some dictionaries also contain synonyms, so make those available, too.

Revise for Descriptive Verbs

- Have students revise their own poems for descriptive verbs and other parts of speech. Remind them that every word in a poem is important.

 ENGLISH LANGUAGE SUPPORT: Build Vocabulary

SUBSTANTIAL

Work with students individually to target verbs and other words for revision.

MODERATE

Encourage students to work with a thesaurus, but point out that shades of meaning may make some words less appropriate choices. They may want to consult a dictionary or a more expert speaker to verify that a word conveys the right mood.

LIGHT

Have partners list synonyms for words, then rank the words according to mood. For example, *residence* feels formal, *house* is neutral, and *home* feels warm. Have pairs explain which choice best fits the poem.

LEARNING OBJECTIVES

- Revise drafts.
- Give and receive peer feedback.
- Discuss revision suggestions using academic language.
- **Language** Discuss features of poetry using academic language.

MATERIALS   Online

Display and Engage 8.7
Writer's Notebook p. 8.7

 LEARNING MINDSET:
Growth Mindset

Review Tell students that revising is a skill that will help them grow as a writer. Remind them that they are developing writing skills that require practice. *I think that yet is a very useful word. When I think, "Oh, that's too hard. I can't do it," I add the word yet. That makes me want to try harder because I know if I keep trying, I will reach my goal. If I keep working on finding the right words for a poem, I will find them.*

TARGETED GRAMMAR SUPPORT

You may want to consult the following grammar minilessons to review key revising topics.

- **3.1.2 Main and Helping Verbs,** p. W249
- **4.1.3 Articles,** p. W280
- **4.2.3 Using Adverbs,** p. W285

Small Group Conference

- Show <u>Display and Engage 8.7</u> and have students follow along with <u>Writer's Notebook page 8.7</u>. Read the conferencing checklist with students and tell them that they will use this checklist in their small group conferences.

- Tell students that it is time to share their poems and receive feedback.

  » Divide students into groups of four.

  » Each poet reads his or her poem, pauses, and reads again.

  » Listeners pay attention closely. Upon second reading, listeners jot down ideas in words or pictures that match the writing.

  » After the reading, listeners share their words or sketches and talk about their responses.

- After each poem has been shared aloud, have students use the conferencing checklist to guide the discussion.

- Encourage writers to take notes and record the feedback they receive about their poems in their notebooks.

- As conferences are proceeding, walk among the groups to assist as needed.

DISPLAY AND ENGAGE Online **Ed**

Lyric Poem 8.7

Conferencing

1. How does the poem reflect the idea that "home is where the heart is"?
2. Do the lines and stanzas break in logical places?
3. Could the poet add any internal rhymes?
4. Did the poet use onomatopoeia or alliteration? If so, where? Could any be added?
5. Did the poet include similes or metaphors? If so, where? Could any be added?
6. Are there any words that could be replaced with more descriptive words? Which ones?

Continue to Revise

- Have students re-enter their writing and continue to revise using the feedback they gained in the small group conferences.

- As you circulate, group students who need support on similar grammar topics. Use the Grammar minilessons or the students' own writing to provide targeted review and support.

EL **ENGLISH LANGUAGE SUPPORT: Scaffold Revision**

SUBSTANTIAL
Point out that adjectives, adverbs, and verbs tend to be the most descriptive words. Help students find these words in their poems.

MODERATE
Review parts of speech for students to target words for revision.

LIGHT
Have students find adjectives, adverbs, and verbs on their own in their poems and work in pairs to determine whether the words should be replaced.

POETRY • LYRIC POEM

LEARNING OBJECTIVES
- Revise drafts.
- Discuss revision using academic language.
- **Language** Discuss features of poetry using academic language.

MATERIALS Online

Writer's Notebook p. 8.7

Anchor Chart W14: *Revising Checklist*

Display and Engage 8.8

TEACHER TIP

Some students may be unsatisfied with their work so far. Because lyric poems are short poems, tell students that they still have time to begin fresh.

TARGETED GRAMMAR SUPPORT

You may want to consult the following grammar minilessons to review key revising topics.

- **3.1.3 Verbs Tenses,** p. W250
- **4.1.4 Review Adjectives and Articles,** p. W281
- **4.2.4 Review Adverbs,** p. W286

Revision Ideas

- This lesson will require flexibility because students will be in varying stages of the writing process. Some may elect to begin again while others may be working in groups, incorporating feedback, or conferring with the teacher.

- Before students work on their poems, explain that the suggestions from their writing groups can be used to revise their poems. Remind students to use the notes they took on **Writer's Notebook page 8.7** to guide their revisions.

- Display **Anchor Chart W14: Revising Checklist** to show ways of revising.

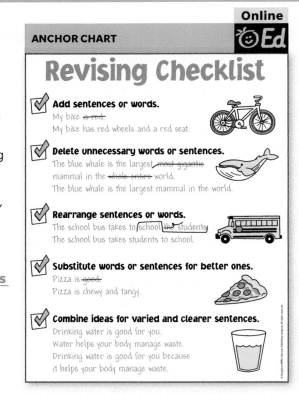

- Show **Display and Engage 8.8** to help students carefully choose words to improve their drafts. Remind them that sometimes they need to delete ideas to improve their word choice.

- You may need to model revising for sound devices. Write this line on the board:

> Whenever I leave, I come back to rest.

THINK ALOUD *I like this line, but maybe I can make it sound better.*

» *How about trying to add alliteration? Is there a word beginning with the w sound I can add? I'll take out* leave *and put in* wander.

» *I like the idea of "rest," so maybe I should look for a word beginning with the r sound that fits the meaning of the line. Perhaps* return.

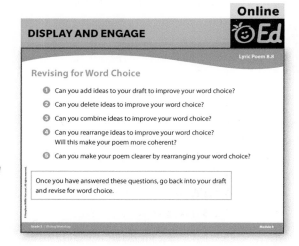

- Write the new line on the board:

> Whenever I wander, I return to rest.

- Permit students to work alone, consult with their group members, or confer with the teacher.

EDITING I: GRAMMAR, USAGE, AND MECHANICS

LEARNING OBJECTIVES

- Edit a poem.
- **Language** Edit writing for spelling, capitalization, punctuation, and stanzas.

MATERIALS

Online ⊙Ed

Display and Engage 8.8

TEACHER TIP

Editing poetry can be difficult when poets use non-standard language to make a point. Explain that poets do not have to conform to standard punctuation and capitalization when the changes detract from their intended meaning.

INSTRUCTIONAL VOCABULARY

- **mechanics** writing skills including spelling, punctuation, capitalization, and paragraphing

TARGETED GRAMMAR SUPPORT

You may want to consult the following grammar minilessons to review key editing topics.

- **7.4.4 Review Punctuation,** p. W341
- **8.1.5 Connect to Writing: Using Correct Spelling,** p. W347

Self Editing with Ratiocination

- Students will begin by proofreading and revising their own poems.

- Point out that proofreading poetry is different from proofreading other writing. Because poems have a different structure and poets can break some writing rules, not all the rules of punctuation and capitalization will apply here. Proofreading today will focus on **mechanics**, or spelling, punctuation, capitalization, and stanzas, as well as specific language. Encourage students to review their poems for unusual use of grammar, punctuation, and spelling to be certain that it is the way they want it.

- Project **Display and Engage 8.8** and discuss the suggestions for editing poetry. Remind students that sometimes poets may break editing rules for poetic effect. In this case, suggest edits that support students' poetic choices, for example, no capital letters or some words in all capital letters. Sometimes the words may make a visual design.

DISPLAY AND ENGAGE

Lyric Poem 8.8

Revising for Word Choice

1. Can you add ideas to your draft to improve your word choice?
2. Can you delete ideas to improve your word choice?
3. Can you combine ideas to improve your word choice?
4. Can you rearrange ideas to improve your word choice? Will this make your poem more coherent?
5. Can you make your poem clearer by rearranging your word choice?

Once you have answered these questions, go back into your draft and revise for word choice.

- Use this ratiocination activity with poetry, keeping in mind students are also looking for items from the Editing Checklist.

> - Circle all "to be" verbs.
> - Underline each line in a different color. (Should any line be longer or shorter?)
> - Make a rectangle around each stanza. (Should any stanza be longer or shorter?)
> - Mark words that might not be specific enough with a check.
> - X out the word "very."
> - Draw two vertical lines next to anything that still needs your attention.
> - Put the word "it" in a triangle.

Edit Writing

- When the process is completed, have students look at the markups to get a sense of where they've possibly been too vague: heavy use of the word *it*, too many uses of *very*, lots of check marks and vertical lines.

- Have writers go back into their poems to make corrections and revise for specific language and details. You may wish to confer individually to focus on specificity in your students' writing development.

EDITING II: PEER PROOFREADING

LEARNING OBJECTIVES

- Edit writing.
- **Language** Proofread writing for mechanics.

MATERIALS   Online

Display and Engage 8.9

TARGETED GRAMMAR SUPPORT

You may want to consult the following grammar minilessons to review key editing topics.

- **7.4.4 Review Punctuation,** p. W341
- **8.1.5 Connect to Writing: Using Correct Spelling,** p. W347

Review Clocking Activity

- Show **Display and Engage 8.9**, and review the items on the Editing Checklist. Point out that, as proofreaders, students will focus on punctuation, spelling, and capitalization. Remind students that poets can disregard some writing rules to emphasize their message.

- Tell students that if any ideas in their peers' poems are not clear to them, they need to point it out to the poet. As needed, review additional grammar topics.

- Review the rules for clocking.

> **Online** ⓔEd
>
> **DISPLAY AND ENGAGE**
>
> Lyric Poem 8.9
>
> **Editing Checklist**
>
> As you edit a poem, use this checklist.
>
> ☐ Check for capitalization of names and the first letter of a sentence. Some poets may begin each line with a capital letter, too.
>
> ☐ Check for punctuation that makes sense with the way the line reads.
>
> ☐ Look for misspelled words.
>
> ☐ Should any lines or stanzas be longer or shorter?
>
> ☐ Check for correct use of past tense and irregular verbs.
>
> ☐ Do you have any other comments for the poet?
>
> Make all corrections to your poem.
>
> Grade 5 | Writing Workshop   Module #

- Each poet prepares a cover page for his or her poem. This page should have the poet's name at the top and be divided into several sections. Each section is labeled from 1-6 with each number corresponding to an editing task.

- Students form concentric circles or sit opposite each other in rows, hence the term clocking; in rows, it is called digital clocking. When students receive a peer's poem, they become that poem's editor.

- No marks are made on the actual poem. Each editor writes his or her name on the editing page and makes comments on each editing task.

- Call out which item is to be checked by the editor: 1) capitalization; 2) punctuation; 3) spelling; 4) line length; 5) stanza length; and 6) other comments.

- After you call out one or two editing tasks, have students collect their poems and move to another editor. Do the entire process several times.

Incorporate Suggestions

- When all group members have proofread the poems, tell poets to take their comment sheet and make changes as needed. Remind poets that they are in charge of deciding which edits to apply to their poems.

 ENGLISH LEARNER SUPPORT: Scaffold Writing

ALL LEVELS Show students how to use software or online resources to check their spelling. Warn students that spell-checking programs will not necessarily find all errors. Software will not find correctly spelled words that are misused, such as *two/to/too* or *who's/whose.*

LESSON 14

PUBLISHING

LEARNING OBJECTIVES

- Create a title.
- Create a legible final version of a poem.
- Publish a poem.
- Use technology to assist with writing.
- **Language** Discuss the publishing process using academic terms.

MATERIALS   Online

Display and Engage *8.10*

TEACHER TIP

Recall whether any students were particularly nervous about working with poetry. In a private moment, commend those students for their progress.

 LEARNING MINDSET:
Growth Mindset

Normalize Point out to students that, similar to Jack in *Love That Dog,* they have been discovering poetry and trying their hands at writing poetry. Explain that it is normal to struggle when we acquire new skills. *Congratulations on finishing your poems! I know you are better writers and readers because you worked on understanding and writing poetry.* Ask students how they can apply this attitude in the future.

Write a Title

- Discuss the purpose of a title: to preview a poem, to show the main idea, to provoke an emotion, or to name the subject. Because students have been working on their poems for some time, they may already have titles in mind. Allow time for students to formulate or change their title.

Prepare the Final Copy

- Have students write a clean copy of the poem by hand or use computers to enter and print their final copy. Permit last-minute changes in fonts or type size if students wish to add graphic elements.

Consider Publication Options

- Tell students that the content of their poem may help them decide how to present it. Provide a few examples for presenting a poem about "Home is where the heart is."

> a. Make a drawing to illustrate the poem.
>
> b. Make a collage of images that illustrate the ideas in the poem. Images could come from magazines or online resources.
>
> c. Make a video of themselves reading the poem with background images from their own home or neighborhood.
>
> d. Find or write a song to play as background music as they read the poem aloud.

- Use **Display and Engage 8.10** to stimulate a class discussion about the different ways of publishing a poem. Ask students to Turn and Talk with a partner about how they would like to publish. Finally have them choose their favorite option and publish their poem.

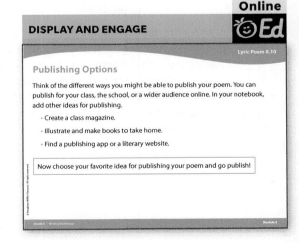

LEARNING OBJECTIVES

- Share writing.
- Participate in a collaborative discussion.
- **Language** Use academic language to engage in a discussion about writing.

MATERIALS   Online

Anchor Chart W17: *Tips on How to Present*

Display and Engage *8.11*

Writer's Notebook pp. 8.3, 8.8

TEACHER TIP

Make this session into a celebration. Consider adding a few decorations associated with the assignment's theme to the classroom. Be considerate of those students who do not wish to perform or read aloud their poems. Allow them to take a pass or play a recording of their poem.

Share Writing

- Share <u>Anchor Chart W17: Tips on How to Present</u>. Review the tips for presenting writing.

- Show <u>Display and Engage 8.11</u> and ask students to add their ideas for ways of sharing their poetry. Let them choose the way they would most like to share.

- Begin by having students share their poems by reading them aloud. You may wish to organize a class "poetry slam" and encourage students to perform their poems. The class as a whole can choose the poet who gave the most engaging performance.

- After each poetry reading, encourage students to ask the poet questions about his or her work. Encourage each poet to share insights that he or she gleaned about the poetry writing process.

ANCHOR CHART   Online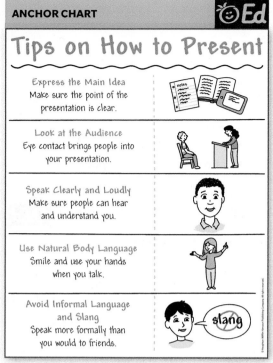

» What did you like best and least about writing your lyric poem? Why?

» What did you learn about writing? How did you learn it?

» What did you learn about the structure of poetry (that is, lines and stanzas)?

» What did you learn about poetic elements, such as rhyme and alliteration?

» What did you learn about presenting poetry to an audience? Did you enjoy presenting your work?

» What do you want to remember to do the next time you write a lyric poem?

Engage and Respond

- Conclude with an informal debriefing about how students felt about writing and presenting poetry.

- Have students review <u>Writer's Notebook page 8.3</u> to review the goals they set at the beginning of this module. Have them Turn and Talk with a partner about how they met their goals and take notes about what goals they might set for the next writing assignment. Students can use <u>Writer's Notebook page 8.8</u> to reflect on and plan their new goals.

Imaginative Story

FOCUS STATEMENT Characters are at the heart of stories.

FOCAL TEXT

The Egypt Game

Author: Zilpha Keatley Snyder

Illustrator: Alton Raible

Summary: Two girls get involved in an elaborate "Egypt game," an imaginative game that soon leads to strange, mysterious happenings.

WRITING PROMPT

READ this sentence: *Characters are at the heart of stories.*

THINK about the books you've enjoyed and how the characters have driven the action.

WRITE an imaginative story in which you develop a character whose personality and actions are responsible for driving the plot.

LESSONS

1. **Introducing the Focal Text**

2. **The Read**

3. **Vocabulary**

4. **Prewriting: Preparing to Write**

5. **Drafting I: Beginning the Draft**

6. **Drafting II: Elements of a Narrative**

7. **Drafting III: Understanding Characters**

8. **Drafting IV: Completing the Draft**

9. **Revising I: Using Dialogue**

10. **Revising II: Grouping/Conferencing**

11. **Revising III: Incorporating Feedback**

12. **Editing I: Grammar, Usage, Mechanics**

13. **Editing II: Peer Proofreading**

14. **Publishing**

15. **Sharing**

LEARNING MINDSET:
Problem Solving

Display Anchor Chart 32: My Learning Mindset throughout the year. Refer to it to introduce Problem Solving and to reinforce the skills you introduced in previous modules.

LEARNING OBJECTIVES

- Discuss features of imaginative fiction.
- Recount stories, using details.
- **Language** Express opinions and describe details of fictional stories.

MATERIALS Online Ed

Anchor Chart W6 *Narrative Structure*
Display and Engage *9.1*

 INSTRUCTIONAL VOCABULARY

- **character** a person or animal in a story
- **plot** the events, problem, solution, and action in a story

LEARNING MINDSET: Problem Solving

Introduce Throughout the module, students will be challenged to solve problems in their writing. Tell them that there are many strategies that they can use to solve problems. Give feedback when students are struggling with problems. *Sometimes it is difficult to solve a problem. If one strategy doesn't work, it might be time to think of a new strategy.*

Priming the Students

Explore the Topic

- Tell students that in this module they will read and write an imaginative story. Explain that not all imaginative fiction is a fantasy or fairy tale. Imaginative fiction also includes made-up stories about events that could happen in real life.

- Tell students that many authors use their own real-life events to inspire stories. Say: *That doesn't mean they tell the whole truth. If they did, the story wouldn't be fiction.*

- Ask: *How do you think authors use real events when they write fiction? (Real events can be a jumping-off point to inspire an imaginative story or can be woven into a story.)*
  THINK ALOUD *I might write a story about the teacher of a fifth-grade class because I know something about that. I think about an ordinary day in the classroom. Then I ask "what if" questions. For example, "What if a bird flew into the room and landed on my shoulder?" I can then explore what happens next.*

- Display **Anchor Chart W6: Narrative Structure** and go over it with students.

- Tell students that the book they will read, *The Egypt Game,* was written in 1967. Ask: *How was life different in 1967?* Students should recognize that there were no cellphones, computers, or Internet.

- Explain that the children in the story play an imaginative game that may be similar to games their parents or grandparents played as children.

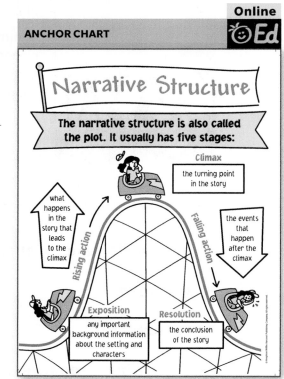

Discuss the Focus Statement

- Show **Display and Engage 9.1**. Read the Focus Statement with students.

- Have students add **character** and **plot** to their Instructional Vocabulary glossaries.

- Have students write answers to these questions: Are characters at the heart of a story? Are they more or less important than plot? Explain.

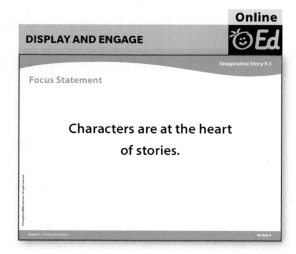

 ENGLISH LEARNER SUPPORT: Facilitate Discussion

ALL LEVELS Give students the option to meet in mixed groups to discuss the Focus Statement rather than write responses.

NARRATIVE • IMAGINATIVE STORY

LEARNING OBJECTIVES
- Discuss author's purpose and audience.
- Infer and identify character traits and character motivations based on reading.
- **Language** Listen to gain information about characters in a story.
- **Language** Discuss characters in a story.

MATERIALS   Online 🍊Ed

Focal Text *The Egypt Game*
Writer's Notebook p. 9.1

TEACHER TIP

If time allows, discuss what students learn about the minor characters Marshall and Mrs. Ross, as well as how students learn about them. Ask whether they also know something about Dorothea, even though she does not appear in the story directly. Discuss the reliability of what is said about her.

Priming the Text

Prepare to Read

The Egypt Game

- Show students the cover of *The Egypt Game* and preview some of the pictures inside. Explain that the book is an imaginative story written for young people.

- Ask: *Why did the author write this story? (to entertain)*

- Tell students that you will be reading aloud the third chapter in the book.

- Before you read, give students the following context. Say: *We will read about Melanie and her little brother, Marshall, who live in an apartment building in California. Marshall always carries a stuffed animal. They will meet April, who has moved there to live with her grandmother.*

- Read the chapter "Enter Melanie and Marshall" without stopping to discuss.

- Ask: *What kinds of things can you learn about the characters in the story? (how they look, what they want, what they like/dislike, how they act and feel, etc.)*

- Tell students you will read the chapter a second time. Explain that when they hear something interesting about Melanie or April, they can pause the reading by saying the character's name.

- When a student says a character's name, say: *In one word or phrase, describe what you learned about Melanie/April. Which sentence from the story gives you this information?* Ask whether the class agrees, disagrees, or has anything to add.

- Record student observations on the board as well as the quotes that students use to support each characteristic. See the example below.

> Melanie
> - friendly: "Melanie always looked forward to meeting new tenants..."
> - wants a new friend: "To have a handy friend again...would be great."
> - surprised: "...she was almost speechless."
>
> April
> - playing dress up: "Her hair was stacked up...."
> - proud of her mother: "...my mother is Dorothea Dawn."

- Have students use **Writer's Notebook page 9.1** or their own notebooks to record what they learn about Melanie and April.

Engage and Respond

- Have students discuss the following questions with a partner: *What do you still want to know about April? What do you still want to know about Melanie?*

LEARNING OBJECTIVES

- Identify and define vocabulary used to describe characters.
- List adjectives and adverbs that are useful in character descriptions.
- Use various strategies to determine meaning.
- **Language** Work cooperatively to come up with descriptive words for characters in writing.

MATERIALS   Online Ed

Focal Text *The Egypt Game*

Anchor Chart W12: *Elements of Figurative Language*

Writer's Notebook *pp. 9.2, 9.3*

 INSTRUCTIONAL VOCABULARY

- **figurative language** words or phrases that mean something different from their dictionary definitions
- **literal language** words that are used according to their dictionary definitions

TEACHER TIP

Encourage students to use markers or crayons to write their descriptive words in color. Students who enjoy drawing may even want to draw a picture of their characters.

Review the Focal Text

- Point out that the chapter "Enter Melanie and Marshall" from *The Egypt Game* contains many vivid character descriptions.

- Have students turn to their Word Banks on **Writer's Notebook page 9.2** or in their own notebooks. Page through the chapter with students and have them identify words and phrases that they like, such as the words and phrases below.

hair teetering forward	to thaw her out	wadded it all up
high winging eyebrows	yellowish-white fur thing	warily
Girl Scout cookie caper	showboating	haughty face
	more exciting escapades	frozen spells
		like a lasso

- Have students identify words or phrases that they do not understand.

- As students offer words and phrases, ask volunteers to use context and/or digital or print resources to determine meanings.

- Have students add to their Word Banks words and phrases that they can use to write about characters.

- Point out that some of the phrases used in the text are **figurative language**. Go over the definitions of *figurative language* and **literal language**. Have students add these words to their Instructional Vocabulary glossaries, and add them to your Class Instructional Vocabulary List.

- Ask volunteers to change some of the figurative language into literal language: *hair teetering forward—her hair was tilted above her face; frozen spells—times when she became unfriendly.* Ask: *Why do you think the author uses figurative language instead of literal language in these instances?* (*to make the descriptions more interesting*)

Engage and Respond

- Tell students that they will be writing their own imaginative story. Have students imagine a character they want to write about. Then, have them turn to **Writer's Notebook page 9.3** to brainstorm words that tell about the character.

- Encourage students to be creative with their descriptive words and phrases. Have them focus on adjectives, adverbs, and phrases, including figurative language.

EL **ENGLISH LEARNER SUPPORT: Scaffold Writing**

SUBSTANTIAL

Work with students in a small group to help them come up with descriptive words for their characters.

MODERATE

Have students work with partners and take turns brainstorming descriptive words for each of their characters.

LIGHT

Encourage students to use one or more similes, or unusual comparisons using *like* or *as*, in their descriptions.

LEARNING OBJECTIVES

- Use freewriting to create imaginative stories.
- Set goals for writing.
- **Language** Write using sound-letter relationships.

MATERIALS   Online

Display and Engage *9.2a–b*
Writer's Notebook *pp. 9.4, 9.5, 9.6*

TEACHER TIP

Make sure students understand that although the sentence frames used in the freewriting are from the focal text, they are free to write anything that pops into their minds. Their freewriting should not necessarily relate to the focal text.

LEARNING MINDSET: Problem Solving

Explain that writers may sometimes have trouble coming up with an idea for a story. One way of problem solving is to use freewriting, which allows your imagination to lead the way. *Not every freewrite will lead you to a great idea. If one freewrite doesn't work out, try starting another. The only way to problem solve is to keep trying.*

Review the Writing Process

- Distribute **Writer's Notebook page 9.4**. Discuss the expectations in the rubric. Tell students to refer to the rubric as they draft, edit, and revise.

- Show **Display and Engage 9.2a–b** and read the writing prompt together. Note the list under "Be sure to."

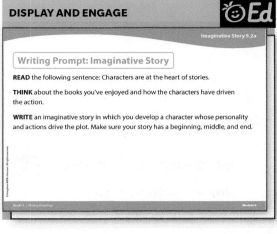
- Explain to students that freewriting is a way to spark their imagination. The idea is to write the first thing that comes into your mind. Ask: *Why do you think it helps to write without thinking too much?* (*Sometimes we second-guess ourselves and rule out great ideas.*)

  THINK ALOUD *I start to write about a family with a dog named Ralph and want to write "Ralph couldn't wait until the family left. That was his time to sit at the table and read the newspaper." I stop myself. "A dog that can read is ridiculous," I say to myself, so I don't write down this idea. When I freewrite, though, I don't worry about whether it's a good idea. Later, I can decide if I want to use the idea.*

- Write the following freewriting rules on the board. Go over the rules with students and answer any questions.

  > - Keep your hand moving. DO NOT stop to think.
  > - Make mistakes. DO NOT worry about spelling, punctuation, or grammar.
  > - Write anything. DO NOT worry about what others will think.
  > - Keep going. DO NOT erase, cross out, or stop writing.

- Distribute **Writer's Notebook page 9.5** or have students use their own notebooks. Tell students that they will freewrite using sentence frames. These are beginnings of sentences from "Enter Melanie and Marshall."

Set Goals for Writing

- Point out that some writers think about what they want to improve with each new piece they write. Have students set goals for their imaginative stories by adding to the list on **Writer's Notebook page 9.6** or in their own notebooks.

ENGLISH LEARNER SUPPORT: Support Writing

SUBSTANTIAL
Students with limited speaking and writing ability in English may better access their imagination by drawing pictures of characters and story events.

MODERATE
Students with limited writing ability might opt for a spoken free-association game in which one partner completes the sentence frame and then both partners take turns adding sentences.

LIGHT
Students may be self-conscious about mistakes. Let them know they need not share freewrites.

NARRATIVE • IMAGINATIVE STORY

TEACHER TIP
Reassure students that there will be time in later lessons to add to their drafts as well as to correct spelling, grammar, and punctuation.

Prepare to Draft

- Show <u>Display and Engage 9.3a–c</u> and distribute <u>Writer's Notebook pages 9.7 and 9.8</u>. Read the first paragraph of the model aloud. Point out to students that the first paragraph is written using one of the sentence frames from "Enter Melanie and Marshall."

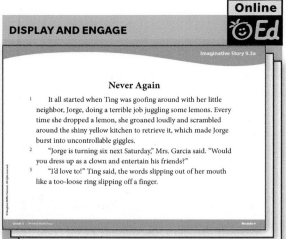

- Give students a few minutes to look over their freewrites on <u>Writer's Notebook page 9.5</u>. Ask volunteers to select and read one or more of their freewrites aloud to the class.

- Ask: *What was it like to freewrite? Did anyone write something that surprised you? Why?*

- Tell students they will select one of their freewrites to use as a starting point for their draft. Inform students they do not need to know where the story will go. They should just choose the freewrite that is most interesting to them.

  THINK ALOUD *Here is a freewrite that I want to work on. It says:* All through the month of August, it rained. So much rain made Celeste cranky because she had to stay indoors much of the time. But that all changed when Celeste discovered a small white button lying on the floor in the kitchen. *I wrote this but I have no idea why the button made staying indoors better. What I do know is that it seems interesting. So I am going to explore this idea.*

- Pair students to discuss which freewrite to choose. If students have already selected freewrites, have them tell their partners what they chose and why. If students are not sure which freewrite to select, they can ask for their partner's help.

Begin to Draft

- Tell students they will freewrite once again. Have volunteers remind the class of the freewriting rules. Ask students whether they have any questions about freewriting.

- Have students begin to draft their imaginative stories using the freewrite of their choice. Encourage students to continue using freewriting to develop their stories.

LEARNING OBJECTIVES

- Understand and use plot structure in story writing.
- Write stories that include a setting.
- Analyze and incorporate into writing the effect of setting on mood.
- Use sensory details in writing.
- **Language** Expand vocabulary by replacing general descriptive words with specific descriptive words.

MATERIALS   Online ⊙Ed

Anchor Chart W6: *Narrative Structure*

 INSTRUCTIONAL VOCABULARY

- **setting** the time and place in which a story takes place
- **conflict** something in a story that creates a challenge for characters; a problem
- **resolution** how the problem in the story is solved; how the story ends

The Elements of Plot

- Display **Anchor Chart W6: Narrative Structure**. Write the following chart on the board and go over plot structure with students.

Plot Structure		
Beginning	Middle	End
introduce character and setting	problem (conflict) rising action	solution (resolution)

- As you discuss plot, have students add words to their Instructional Vocabulary list: **setting, conflict, resolution**. You may want to add the words to the Class Instructional Vocabulary List.

Create a Setting

- Tell students that authors often use setting to help create mood. Read aloud the second full paragraph from page 17 of *The Egypt Game* ("It was dusky . . . being watched").

- Ask: *What do you learn about the setting in this paragraph?* (It is inside a store, maybe an antique store. The store is dark, though it is daytime. There are not many people around.) *What mood does the setting create?* (The dark, the old items, and the lack of clerks help create a scary or dreary mood.)

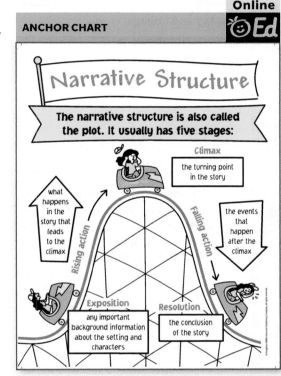

- Tell students you will read the paragraph again. Say: *Listen for sensory details.*

- Ask: *What words does the author use to convey sensory details?* (*dusky; vases and jars, some partly cracked or broken; crudely made jewelry; tiny statues*) Point out that specific sensory details like these help create a clear picture for the reader. Say: *Use specific sensory details to develop setting and mood in your stories.*

Continue to Draft

- Circulate the room, offering assistance as needed.

 ENGLISH LEARNER SUPPORT: Scaffold Writing

SUBSTANTIAL
Help students who are having trouble coming up with descriptive words and sensory details.

MODERATE
Point out general descriptive words in student stories, such as *hot*, *cold*, and *pretty,* and model using online or print resources to replace them with specific words.

LIGHT
Encourage students to use print and online resources to locate and replace general descriptive words in their stories with specific words that create an image.

LEARNING OBJECTIVES

- Analyze texts to determine what makes a literary character unique and interesting.
- **Language** Write a literary text that includes interesting, unique characters.

MATERIALS Online

Display and Engage 9.3a–c
Writer's Notebook pp. 9.7, 9.8, 9.9
Anchor Chart W3: *Asking Questions*

TEACHER TIP

If students base their character on a person they know, tell them that it might help to use the person's name during the draft phase of writing. They can change the name in the revision stage. *Using a real person's name may help you get deeper into the heart and soul of your character.*

 **LEARNING MINDSET: Problem Solving**

Characters Students may be struggling to make their characters unique. Suggest that they take time and be patient as they ask and answer questions about their characters' likes, dislikes, and unique history. *Even if you don't include this information in your story, knowing it will help you create a rich, unique character.* Tell students that with patience, they can create characters who will interest readers.

Introduce the Skill

- Show <u>**Display and Engage 9.3a–c**</u> and ask students to turn to <u>**Writer's Notebook pages 9.7 and 9.8**</u>.

- Before you read the model aloud, say: *As I read, mark each place in the story where you learn something about Ting.*

- After you read, have volunteers tell what they learned about Ting. Write responses on the board, as shown.

> Ting: likes to goof around; hates to dress in costume; has trouble saying no; likes to make people happy

- Ask: *What makes Ting a believable character?* (*She is goofy; she has faults; she makes mistakes; she wants to do her best.*) *What details tell you these things?* (*She is a bad juggler; she says yes without thinking about it first; she struggles to learn to say no.*)

- Advise students that good writers get to know their characters and what is unique and interesting about them. Ask: *Without naming the person you are thinking of, name an interesting characteristic of someone you know.* Encourage students to use specific characteristics as they create their characters.

- Ask volunteers: *What is your character's name, and why did you choose that name?* Encourage students to be intentional with naming characters. Students can think about names of friends, family members, or favorite characters.

  THINK ALOUD *I can make up a name that tells something about a character. For example, if I were writing about a man who kept dropping things, I could name him Slip Butterfingers. I could give his son, who is constantly busy, the nickname Ant.*

- Give students the option of conferencing in small groups to work on deepening their characters. Have each group use <u>**Writer's Notebook 9.9**</u> or their own notebooks to come up with five questions that will help them flesh out the characters in believable and unique ways.

- Review <u>**Anchor Chart W3: Asking Questions**</u> with students to help them learn how to clarify the questions they ask, so they will get needed answers.

ANCHOR CHART Online

Asking Questions

We ask questions to help us focus our thinking about a topic so that we can write about it.

Generate questions on a topic.	Think about your questions.	Clarify your questions for research.
Ask "big" questions about a topic.	Think about the topic and what you need to find out.	Ask questions that you can look up in a book or on the Internet.

What will happen to elephants in the future?

I need to know more about elephants living today.

Where do elephants live?

What are the biggest dangers for elephants?

Continue the Draft

- Have students continue, focusing on making characters unique.

- Circulate the room, offering assistance to students as needed.

NARRATIVE · IMAGINATIVE STORY

LEARNING OBJECTIVES

- Develop drafts that include all the elements of literary plot structure.
- Develop drafts with strong, unique characters and an interesting setting.
- **Language** Incorporate a variety of sentence types in writing.

MATERIALS   Online

Anchor Chart W4: *Elements of Narrative*

 LEARNING MINDSET: Problem Solving

Normalize Tell students that when a writer returns to a draft after time away, it is normal to notice problems. Encourage students to spend time rethinking and rewriting words, phrases, paragraphs, or descriptions that they notice are not effective. *When you see problem areas in your own writing and work to make them better, you grow as a writer.*

Review the Skill

- Display <u>Anchor Chart W4: Elements of Narrative</u> and review the elements of a narrative story. Ask whether students have questions or are encountering problems with any of the elements. Address any questions or problems.

- Tell students that as they complete their drafts, they should check to make sure they have included all the elements of a narrative story. Suggest that now is the time to strengthen any elements that seem weak.

- Encourage students to use a variety of sentence types. Short, simple sentences create emphasis, as long as they are not overused. Compound and complex sentences add variety and show relationships between ideas.

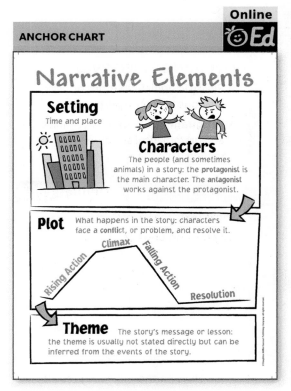

ANCHOR CHART   Online **Ed**

Circulate the Room

- Let students know you are available for one-on-one assistance and have them return to their stories.

- Circulate the room, providing help as needed.

EL **ENGLISH LEARNER SUPPORT: Discuss Language Structures**

SUBSTANTIAL
Help students write complete simple sentences, pointing out and helping them correct fragments.

MODERATE
Students who are able to write complete simple sentences can be challenged to include two or three compound sentences in their stories.

LIGHT
Challenge students to vary sentence structure to include a variety of simple, compound, and complex sentences in their stories.

NARRATIVE • IMAGINATIVE STORY

LEARNING OBJECTIVES

- Revise imaginative stories by using dialogue to serve a purpose.
- **Language** Use proper mechanics and grammatical structure when writing dialogue.

MATERIALS Online *Ed*

Focal Text *The Egypt Game*
Display and Engage *9.4a–b*

TEACHER TIP

Have partners exchange stories and read dialogue aloud to each other. Writers should listen to the dialogue they wrote to decide if it sounds like something a person might really say. After listening, writers may want to edit their dialogue so it sounds more conversational.

TARGETED GRAMMAR SUPPORT

You may want to consult the following grammar minilessons to review key revising topics.

- **6.1.3 Interjections and Dialogue,** p. W315
- **7.1.3 Commas with Direct Address and Tag Questions,** p. W325

Introduce the Revision Skill

- Ask: *What does it mean to "show rather than tell" in writing?* (*to use action and dialogue rather than description and narration, so readers can "see" or "feel" what is happening*) *Does this sentence show or tell? It was freezing cold outside.* (*tell*) *How could I show it is cold?* (*Sample answer: Jake shivered and zipped up his jacket.*)

- How could I use dialogue to show it is cold? (*Sample answer: "Brrr . . . Let's go indoors," Jake said.*)

- Show **Display and Engage 9.4a–b** and read with students. Discuss each purpose and example with students.

- Read the dialogue aloud from pages 30 and 31 of *The Egypt Game,* beginning with "Do you really still play with paper dolls . . ." and ending with "the girls could go to the house pretending to sell Girl Scout cookies to see if it really was the crooks."

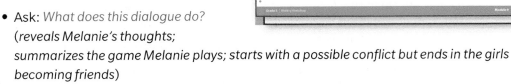

DISPLAY AND ENGAGE Online *Ed*

Imaginative Story 9.4a

Using Dialogue

Dialogue must have a purpose. Look at the chart for some examples of purpose for dialogue in narrative writing.

Purpose	Example
Describe a place	"Wow, it's dark in here," Lisa said.
Describe a character	"Julia never gets anywhere on time," Scott remarked.
Create a sense of time	Mom looked at her watch and said, "It's almost midnight."
Reveal a character's thoughts	"I have always wanted to go for a walk in the forest," said John.

- Ask: *What does this dialogue do?* (*reveals Melanie's thoughts; summarizes the game Melanie plays; starts with a possible conflict but ends in the girls becoming friends*)

- Show **Display and Engage 9.4a–b** again and ask: *What special punctuation for dialogue do you see on the examples?* (*quotation marks; commas setting off dialogue tags; commas, periods, question marks inside quotation marks*)

- Remind students that they can use dialogue tags to help them show how characters speak. Ask for dialogue tag suggestions and write them on the board:

> she whispered; he shouted suddenly; he cried; she said quietly; they yelled angrily

Revise for Dialogue

- Have students revisit their own writing to discover where they can use dialogue with purpose. If they find dialogue with no purpose, they should delete it or replace it to add to the clarity and coherence of the story.

- Remind students that as they add and revise dialogue, they are also improving sentence structure and word choice for coherence by adding or deleting ideas.

EL **ENGLISH LEARNER SUPPORT: Support Writing**

SUBSTANTIAL
As you circulate, help students find at least one place in their stories where they can insert purposeful dialogue. Provide support with grammatical structure as needed.

MODERATE
As you circulate, make sure students have at least two lines of dialogue in their stories. Provide grammar support as needed. Work with students to refine dialogue so it serves a purpose.

LIGHT
Make sure students include at least three lines of dialogue. Help students vary dialogue tags and craft dialogue so it sounds natural and serves a purpose.

NARRATIVE • IMAGINATIVE STORY

LEARNING OBJECTIVES

- Revise drafts by receiving and incorporating peer feedback.
- **Language** Listen, take notes, and respond to peer stories.

MATERIALS   Online

Display and Engage 9.3b, 9.5

Anchor Chart W14: *Revising Checklist*

Small Group Conferences

- Remind students that using specific details in writing helps readers picture what is happening. Read from the model (**Display and Engage 9.3b**): "Kids were everywhere . . . orange wig." Ask: *What specific details help you picture what's happening?* (*squeaky red clown nose; red and white polka-dotted jumpsuit; crazy orange wig*)

- Tell students that their groups will use a strategy called highlighting. Show **Display and Engage 9.5** and go over the rules of highlighting.

- Ask a volunteer to help you model the highlighting strategy. Sit across from the volunteer and serve as listener while the volunteer takes the role of writer. After you have modeled the strategy, discuss with students what they observed.

- Divide students into small groups. Assign each group member a number. That is the order in which they will read their story.

Online

DISPLAY AND ENGAGE

Imaginative Story 9.5

Highlighting

- Writer reads story aloud. Listeners listen quietly.
- Writer pauses. Listeners make sure they are prepared with pen and paper.
- Writer reads story aloud a second time. When listeners hear a specific detail they like, they jot it down.
- When writer finishes reading, listeners read back what they liked. Writers highlight in their own stories what listeners enjoyed.

Listeners can jot down words, phrases, sentences, images, and dialogue that they like.

When you go back into your stories to revise, notice if there are places where you have too many details. If so, delete them. You may also wish to combine ideas.

Continue to Revise

- After the highlighting activity, students should revisit their stories. Tell them to notice sections that have few or no highlights. Use **Anchor Chart W14: Revising Checklist** to show students how to use specific details to make these sections more appealing. If they feel they have too many details, they can delete some. Sometimes they can improve word choice by combining ideas.

Online

ANCHOR CHART

Revising Checklist

☑ **Add sentences or words.**
My bike ~~is red.~~
My bike has red wheels and a red seat.

☑ **Delete unnecessary words or sentences.**
The blue whale is the largest ~~most gigantic~~ mammal in the ~~whole entire~~ world.
The blue whale is the largest mammal in the world.

☑ **Rearrange sentences or words.**
The school bus takes to ~~school the students~~
The school bus takes students to school.

☑ **Substitute words or sentences for better ones.**
Pizza is ~~good~~
Pizza is chewy and tangy.

☑ **Combine ideas for varied and clearer sentences.**
Drinking water is good for you.
Water helps your body manage waste.
Drinking water is good for you because it helps your body manage waste.

 ENGLISH LEARNER SUPPORT: Elicit Participation

ALL LEVELS Modify the highlighting strategy to allow for language limitations. You might have writers look up pronunciation of words before they read; ask writers to pause after each paragraph during their second reading to allow time to write notes; or let listeners ask for meanings of words during the second reading.

NARRATIVE • IMAGINATIVE STORY

LEARNING OBJECTIVES
- Revise drafts to include specific details and images.
- **Language** Use sensory details in writing.

TEACHER TIP

Let students know that in early drafts it is perfectly fine to have general descriptions. Sometimes not worrying about the details is a good way to get a story on the page. Revision is usually the time to add specific details.

LEARNING MINDSET: Problem Solving

Normalize Reassure students that it is hard work to find the exact words, phrases, and sentences that create an image for the reader. They may know in their minds what they are trying to convey, but getting it down on paper may take several tries. *Do your best to create an image using specific words and then move to another section of your story. After a while, revisit what you have written. Each time you revisit your words, you may find that you can improve them. That doesn't mean you did a bad job the last time! It means you are slowly solving a difficult problem and you are growing as a writer.*

Introduce the Revision Skill

- Have volunteers share with the class words or excerpts that they highlighted during the highlighting activity in Lesson 10.

- Point out examples of specific details that "paint a picture" or create an image for the reader. Write those student examples on the board. Then, come up with and write a more general version of each example, as shown below. Ask students why the student examples are better.

> Lisa was struggling under the weight of a huge red suitcase. / Lisa carried a heavy suitcase.
>
> His eyes were the color of the sky. / His eyes were blue.
>
> Greg's hand trembled, and his voice shook. / Greg felt nervous.

- Remind students that when they create images in writing they should think about using all five senses.

THINK ALOUD *My character is swimming in the ocean. I think about how many senses I can use. I can write that my character **sees** the color of the water, **hears** the sound of the waves, **tastes** the salty water, **feels** a chill on her skin, and **smells** the ocean air. The ocean is a good vehicle for all five senses! Not everything will be.*

Revise for Specificity

- Have students return to their writing. Students should focus on looking for general statements or words they used. Have them revise to add specific details that create images for the reader.

- Conference with individual students and help them identify general statements that can be made more specific.

 ENGLISH LEARNER SUPPORT: Scaffold Writing

SUBSTANTIAL
Assist students in finding one place in their stories where they can create an image that appeals to at least one of the senses.

MODERATE
Challenge students to find two places in their stories where they can create an image and use two or three senses in their descriptions.

LIGHT
Challenge students to find four places in their stories where they can create an image and use four or five senses in their story.

NARRATIVE • IMAGINATIVE STORY

LEARNING OBJECTIVES

- Edit stories for grammar, usage, and mechanics.
- **Language** Use proper punctuation for dialogue in writing.

MATERIALS
Online Ed

Anchor Chart W15: *Editing Checklist*

TARGETED GRAMMAR SUPPORT

You may want to consult the following grammar minilessons to review key editing topics.

- **6.1.1–6.1.5,** Direct Quotations and Interjections, pp. W313–W317

Review the Editing Checklist

- Revisit <u>Anchor Chart W15: Editing Checklist</u>. Review the items on the checklist.

- If needed, review how to use proofreading marks.

- As needed, revisit grammar topics on which students need additional review or practice.

Proofread Writing

- Use ratiocination as students return to their writing to edit for grammar, spelling, and punctuation.

- Have students pay particular attention to quotation marks and punctuation in dialogue.

- Circulate the room. Group students who need support on similar grammar topics. Use grammar minilessons or students' own writing to provide targeted review and support.

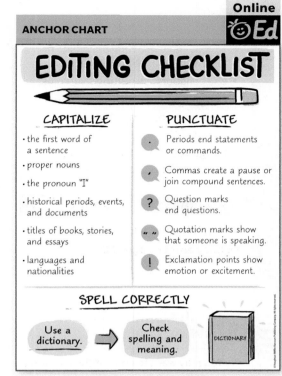

ANCHOR CHART — Online Ed

EDITING CHECKLIST

CAPITALIZE
- the first word of a sentence
- proper nouns
- the pronoun "I"
- historical periods, events, and documents
- titles of books, stories, and essays
- languages and nationalities

PUNCTUATE
- . Periods end statements or commands.
- , Commas create a pause or join compound sentences.
- ? Question marks end questions.
- " " Quotation marks show that someone is speaking.
- ! Exclamation points show emotion or excitement.

SPELL CORRECTLY
Use a dictionary. → Check spelling and meaning. DICTIONARY

EL **ENGLISH LEARNER SUPPORT: Support Editing**

ALL LEVELS Review students' writing as you circulate the room. Look for repeated grammatical, mechanical, or usage errors. Focus on one example of the error, modeling how to correct it. Then, ask students to find and correct other similar errors in the story. Provide guidance as needed.

LEARNING OBJECTIVES

- Use collaborative editing strategies.
- **Language** Edit stories for complete sentences and subject-verb agreement.
- **Language** Edit stories for proper punctuation.

MATERIALS   Online

Writer's Notebook *p. 9.10*

Display and Engage *9.6*

TARGETED GRAMMAR SUPPORT

You may want to consult the following grammar minilessons to review key editing topics.

- **1.1.1 Complete Sentences,** p. W198
- **1.1.2 Sentence Fragments and Run-ons,** p. W199

Clocking Activity

- Review the rules for clocking.

- Students sit in concentric circles. Distribute **Writer's Notebook page 9.10** and have students write their names at the top of their editing pages. Each page will travel with its imaginative story.

- As students receive a peer's imaginative story, they become the editor of that paper. Editors write their names to the left of the items they are checking.

- Show **Display and Engage 9.6** and call out what item the editor is to check. Ask: *Is there a name on the paper?*

  THINK ALOUD *If I find an error in the paper I am editing, I write it down on the lines following the item I am checking. I include details to help the writer find the error. For example, I might write "Sentence 2 in paragraph 2 is a run-on."*

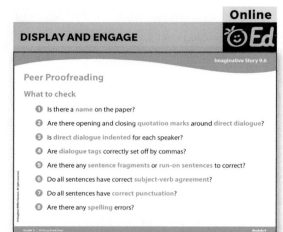

- After reviewing a couple of items, have students pass the story with its editing page so that each paper is read by several editors.

- Remind students that each editor should place his or her name next to the number of the item being checked on **Writer's Notebook page 9.10**. Then the editor notes corrections to make. Remind students that no marks are made on the author's story.

- When the editing process is complete, tell students to take their editing page and make corrections, if any. If they are confused by or disagree with an edit, they may ask the editor or the teacher.

Edit Writing

- Have students do a final pass through their imaginative stories, integrating the notes from the clocking activity into their writing.

 ENGLISH LEARNER SUPPORT: Support Grammar Instruction

ALL LEVELS As you circulate the room, help students recognize and correct incomplete sentences and subject-verb agreement issues in their writing.

LEARNING OBJECTIVES

- Publish imaginative stories.
- Use technology to publish imaginative stories.
- **Language** Create titles that describe the story and entice readers.

LEARNING MINDSET: Problem Solving

Tell students that creating a good title can be like solving a puzzle. *It is easier to problem-solve when you take your time and have patience. Write the text of your story before making your title page. As you copy your story in its final form, look for clues that will lead you to a great title. Patience can lead to creative solutions to your problems.*

Prepare the Final Copy

- Have students take another look at the titles they chose for their stories. Ask: *How did you come up with the title of your story? Has your story changed since you titled it?* Discuss.

- Explain that their original titles may no longer be the best ones for their stories since stories evolve and change with each revision.

- Tell students that the title of a story is an entryway for readers. If it sounds appealing, a reader is more likely to want to read the story. Ask: *What are titles that have enticed you to read a book or watch a movie?* Discuss the reasons that certain titles have intrigued students.

- Have students pair with a partner to discuss their titles. Instruct them to read each other's stories and titles and provide feedback.

- Tell students they will make a simple book to publish their stories.

- Write the following options on the board and go over each one with students. Ask students whether they have other creative ideas for their books, and add students' ideas to the options.

> - Handwrite the text.
> - Use a computer to type the text.
> - Use colors and/or fonts creatively.
> - Draw illustrations.
> - Find photos or illustrations online.
> - Include a short summary or excerpt on the back cover to entice readers.
> - Write a dedication to someone who has inspired or helped you.
> - Include an "About the Author" page with your photo and some information about you or how you got the idea for the story.

Publish Writing

- Have students TURN AND TALK to their partners to share their publishing ideas and plans.

- Have students work on the final copy for the remainder of their time. Circulate the room, providing assistance as needed.

 ENGLISH LEARNER SUPPORT: Scaffold Writing

ALL LEVELS As you circulate the room, support students as needed to help them create intriguing titles for their stories.

LESSON 15

LEARNING OBJECTIVES
- Present imaginative stories.
- Respond to presentations of imaginative stories.
- **Language** Practice presentations.

MATERIALS   Online

Anchor Chart W17: *Tips on How to Present*

Writer's Notebook *pp. 9.6, 9.11*

TEACHER TIP
You may want to allow students to ask questions about the writer's creative process after each reading. Explain to students that they should ask about aspects of the story that they admire so they can learn about how other writers get ideas.

Share Writing

- Revisit **Anchor Chart W17: Tips on How to Present**. Review tips for presenting.

- Give students time to practice for their presentations by reading their stories quietly aloud several times. Tell students to work on expressive reading and fluidity.

- Have students read their stories aloud to the class, sharing any illustrations as they go.

- After each presenter has read, encourage students to raise their hands and say what they enjoyed about the story or the presentation.

Engage and Respond

- Conclude with an informal debriefing. Ask students to respond to the following questions:

> What was your favorite part of writing this story?
>
> What was most difficult for you?
>
> What did you learn?

- Have students turn to **Writer's Notebook page 9.6** or the list of goals they set at the beginning of this module. Ask students to TURN AND TALK with a partner about whether or not they have met their goals. Then have students complete **Writer's Notebook page 9.11**.

 ENGLISH LEARNER SUPPORT: Support Speaking

SUBSTANTIAL
Help students with pronunciation and fluid reading before their presentations.

MODERATE
Pair students with fluent English speakers for help with pronunciation and fluid reading before their presentations.

LIGHT
Have students check their stories for words that they have trouble pronouncing and use resources, such as a fluent speaker or an online resource, to learn correct pronunciation.

Letter to the Editor

FOCUS STATEMENT Some things are worth fighting for.

FOCAL TEXT

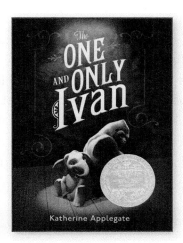

The One and Only Ivan

Author: Katherine Applegate

Illustrator: Patricia Castelao

Summary: Ivan is a gorilla who lives in a shopping mall. When a baby elephant named Ruby shows up, she helps him gain a new perspective.

WRITING PROMPT

READ this sentence: *Some things are worth fighting for*.

THINK about organizations that care for animals.

WRITE a letter to the editor of your local newspaper. In your letter, explain why people should support the organization with their money or time.

·········· LESSONS ··········

1. **Priming the Students**

2. **Priming the Text**

3. **The Read**

4. **Vocabulary**

5. **Prewriting: Preparing to Write**

6. **Drafting I: Beginning the Draft**

7. **Drafting II: Elements of the Genre**

8. **Drafting III: Completing the Draft**

9. **Revising I: Writing Effective Paragraphs**

10. **Revising II: Peer Conferencing**

11. **Revising III: Incorporating Feedback**

12. **Revising IV: Transitions**

13. **Editing I: Peer Proofreading**

14. **Publishing**

15. **Sharing**

LEARNING MINDSET: Noticing

Display <u>Anchor Chart 32: My Learning Mindset</u> throughout the year. Refer to it to introduce Noticing and to reinforce the skills you introduced in previous modules.

LEARNING OBJECTIVES

- Discuss the purpose of letters to the editor.
- Generate a list of organizations or programs that help animals.
- **Language** Discuss features of text with academic language.

MATERIALS   Online

Classroom materials *list of animal welfare programs and organizations*

Display and Engage *10.1*

 INSTRUCTIONAL VOCABULARY

- **letter to the editor** a letter written to a newspaper or magazine that shares an opinion or attempts to inspire action

 LEARNING MINDSET: Noticing

Introduce Throughout this module, students may be exposed to new ideas or have new insights into the ways that animals are cared for. Encourage students to be alert to information about community organizations that help animals. *Pay attention to posted notices or news reports about animal organizations. You may find one that interests you!*

Discuss the Focus Statement

Prepare to Read

- Invite students to share their experiences with animals. Possible areas to explore include:

  » pets, including their own or those that belong to others

  » animals in their neighborhood or the wilderness

  » zoo animals

- If students have not mentioned the issue of how animals are treated, ask: *Can you think of examples of organizations that encourage the proper treatment of animals?* Begin recording students' ideas about animals and these organizations, which could include shelters, animal rights groups, organizations that educate pet owners, and so on. You may want to compile a list of organizations that promote humane treatment of animals beforehand.

- Encourage students to notice and remember how organizations help animals because they will be writing about this topic soon.

- Show **Display and Engage 10.1**. Read the Focus Statement aloud. Ask: *What might "fighting" mean in this statement?* Elicit from students that "fighting" can mean speaking up strongly for a cause or working with a group to change a bad situation. It does not necessarily mean being violent.

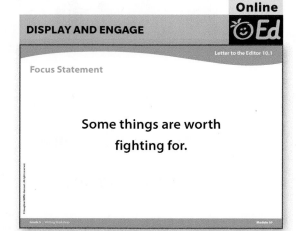

- Ask: *Can a person "fight" with written words?* Point out that many writers have called attention to problems and made people want to work for changes because of what they wrote. Some people write **letters to the editor**. Have students add the definition of *letter to the editor* to the Instructional Vocabulary glossary in their notebooks: a letter written to a newspaper or magazine that shares an opinion or attempts to inspire action. You may want to add the term to the Class Instructional Vocabulary List.

 ENGLISH LEARNER SUPPORT: Facilitate Discussion

ALL LEVELS If students have difficulty naming animals, find pictures of animals that are common to your area or zoo animals . Then show the pictures and name the animals. Ask students for the names in their home languages. Encourage them to discuss which animals they have seen.

LEARNING OBJECTIVES

- Read a letter to the editor as a class.
- Discuss the meaning of the letter.
- **Language** Discuss a letter to the editor using academic language.

MATERIALS   Online

Classroom materials *letter to the editor from an outside source*

Anchor Chart W9: *Elements of an Argument*

 INSTRUCTIONAL VOCABULARY

- **argument** a reason or set of reasons that supports an idea
- **fact** information that can be proved to be true
- **opinion** an idea or a belief that cannot be proved

TEACHER TIP

Reading the letter to the editor may spark student interest in newspapers. Consider including newspapers in the reading materials available in your room, or investigate whether your local paper has a program that supplies newspapers for classroom use.

Priming the Text

Read a Letter to the Editor

- Scan your local newspaper, news websites, or magazines for a letter to the editor on an issue that will interest students. Make individual copies of the letter for students.

- Recall with students that this module is about how animals are treated. Remind them that a letter to the editor is an opinion. Tell them that the letter writer presents an **argument**, that is, he or she gives and explains reasons to support a point of view.

- Display and discuss <u>Anchor Chart W9: Elements of an Argument</u>.

- Do a "popcorn" read of the letter to the editor: call on students in random order to read aloud a selection from the text.

- Discuss the following questions as they relate to the letter:

  » *What is the issue?*

  » *What is the writer's position on the issue?*

  » *What are the reasons that support this position?*

  » *Is the argument convincing? Why or why not?*

  » *Does the writer mention opposing views? How?*

  » *Does this letter change how you feel or inspire you to act? Explain.*

- Write **fact** and **opinion** on the Class Instructional Vocabulary List. Discuss with students the differences between a fact (information that can be proved to be true) and an opinion (an idea or belief that cannot be proved).

- Have partners mark the facts and opinions in the letter in different colors. Walk among the pairs to assist as necessary.

- Ask pairs to share their assessments of the letter to the editor. Discuss any statements on which there is disagreement.

- Have students add the new vocabulary words to their personal Instructional Vocabulary glossaries.

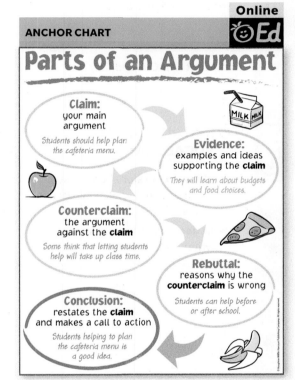

ANCHOR CHART   Online

Parts of an Argument

Claim: your main argument

Students should help plan the cafeteria menu.

Evidence: examples and ideas supporting the **claim**

They will learn about budgets and food choices.

Counterclaim: the argument against the **claim**

Some think that letting students help will take up class time.

Rebuttal: reasons why the **counterclaim** is wrong

Students can help before or after school.

Conclusion: restates the **claim** and makes a call to action

Students helping to plan the cafeteria menu is a good idea.

LEARNING OBJECTIVES

- Discuss an author's audience and purpose.
- Read fiction with purpose and understanding.
- Analyze a fiction text for author's craft.
- **Language** Discuss features of text with instructional language.

MATERIALS Online **Ed**

Focal Text *The One and Only Ivan*

 INSTRUCTIONAL VOCABULARY

- **glossary** an alphabetical list of words and their meanings used in a book
- **fiction** writing that is from a writer's imagination

TEACHER TIP

Students may want to find out more about Ivan. An Internet search will yield information, but be aware that the real Ivan died in 2012. Students who have recently lost a pet or a loved one may be affected by this news.

The Read

Read the Focal Text

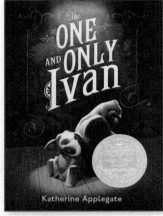

The One and Only Ivan

- Show the cover of *The One and Only Ivan*.

- Display the **glossary** pages. Point out that a glossary is an unusual feature in a book of **fiction**, or a story that is made up by the author. Share a few of the definitions and invite students to speculate on the book's subject.

- Read from the beginning of the book to the top of page 16, pausing after "Tag was my twin sister's name."

- Begin a discussion of the text with these questions:

  » *Who is the speaker in the book?*

  » *Why might the author have chosen this character to be the speaker?*

  » *Which audience might the author be trying to reach?*

  » *How does the author want readers to feel about Ivan?*

  » *What does the author show about Ivan's life?*

  » *What do you think might happen in the rest of the book?*

  » *What problem might the author be exploring in this book?*

- Turn to the Author's Note on page 303. Read the first and third paragraphs of the note to provide background about Ivan. With students' permission, read the second, fourth, and fifth paragraphs, but first warn them that the paragraphs will reveal what happens in the book. The last paragraph on page 304 does not reveal plot, so read it aloud to provide additional background information.

- Continue reading as time permits. Share illustrations with the students. Add *glossary* (an alphabetical list of words and their meanings used in a book) and *fiction* (writing that is from a writer's imagination) to the Class Instructional Vocabulary List, and have students add the words and definitions to their Instructional Vocabulary glossaries.

Engage and Respond

- Have students TURN AND TALK to a partner about why readers would be interested in Ivan's story.

EL ENGLISH LEARNER SUPPORT: Utilize Language Transfer

ALL LEVELS Spanish-speaking students may recognize that several of the animal names in the text are cognates: *gorilla/gorila, elephant/elefante,* and *chimpanzee/chimpancé.*

ARGUMENT • LETTER TO THE EDITOR

LEARNING OBJECTIVES

- Use context to understand domain-specific vocabulary.
- Use word choice to determine the author's message.
- **Language** Read to understand domain-specific vocabulary.

MATERIALS   Online ⊙Ed

Focal Text *The One and Only Ivan*
Display and Engage *10.2*
Writer's Notebook *p. 10.1*

TEACHER TIP

Make an effort to use vivid verbs as you interact with students. Note and praise their use of such words in conversations.

Review the Focal Text

- Review with students the pages from *The One and Only Ivan* that you read during the previous lesson.

- Use **Display and Engage 10.2** as you model how to tease out clues that reveal the author's message. Say:

  I'm getting a feeling for the author's attitude toward Ivan's situation. Now I want to look at specific word choices made by the author to see how the author shows that attitude.

- Read the sentence "My domain is made of thick glass and rusty metal and rough cement" aloud. Point to "domain" in the first column.

  THINK ALOUD *"Domain" makes me think of a kingdom or place where Ivan rules, so I think it's the place where he lives and is in charge. But when I continue reading, I see phrases like (point to each as you say them) "thick glass," "rusty metal," and "rough cement." I get a totally different feeling. They make me feel confined, unsafe, and unpleasant. Together, those phrases make his home sound like a prison.*

- Ask: *Isn't it interesting how the author uses negative, unpleasant words to make us understand her message?* Invite discussion.

- As students scan the pages of the book, have them identify words and phrases that show the author's message about Ivan's situation and write them on **Writer's Notebook page 10.1**. These may include the following:

  » "Patient is a useful way to be when you're an ape."

  » "At present, I do not have any gorilla friends."

- As students record the words and phrases, they should also record the message that is conveyed.

- Write the following verbs from the selection on the board:

| waste | forages | scurry | flatten |

- Point out that these verbs vividly describe actions. Have students discuss the action each verb describes and why the author chose them. Have students add vivid verbs and verbs they find interesting to their Word Bank.

LEARNING OBJECTIVES

- Review the writing prompt.
- Plan a first draft.
- Generate and select topics for writing.
- Set goals for writing.
- Gather relevant information for a letter to the editor.
- **Language** Articulate goals for writing.

MATERIALS   Online

Classroom materials *list of animal welfare programs and organizations*

Display and Engage *10.3*

Writer's Notebook *pp. 10.2, 10.3*

TEACHER TIP

If students cannot find a topic that interests them on the chart or during the class discussion, you may want to allow them to use their research time to find an organization or program that interests them.

 LEARNING MINDSET:
Noticing

Apply Have students notice details about animal programs. *When you notice details, you get a clearer idea of how a program works. Watch for details as you do your research.* Follow up with questions about details as you discuss students' topics.

Work with the Prompt

- Display the list of animal organizations you began. Invite students to add animal programs or organizations and details that they have noticed since you began the chart.

- Show **Display and Engage 10.3** and read the writing prompt aloud. Invite questions about the assignment.

- Have students use a sheet of paper to make a quick sketch based on one of the topics on the list. This exercise can release visual images that will enrich each student's treatment of a topic.

- Invite students to explain their drawings to partners.

Set Goals

- Refer to the rubric on **Writer's Notebook page 10.2**. Inform students that they will be working on acquiring these skills as they write their letters to the editor.

- Discuss the goals list on **Writer's Notebook page 10.3**. As you share the goals with students, point out that they are related to the items on the rubric.

Conduct Research

- Have students write their topic and what they think will be their main points.

- Explain that if students are conducting research on a local organization, they will need to find local sources of information. List sources with them, which may include:

  » websites

  » the local newspaper

  » interviews with staff members or volunteers

- Tell students to use their notebook to record information from their research that supports their main points. Point out that as they find information, they may change their main points.

- Even though students will be primarily offering support for a program, challenge them to think of some arguments against their idea. Encourage them to find four or five strong ideas for when they begin drafting.

- As students do their research, walk among them offering assistance.

 ENGLISH LEARNER SUPPORT: Facilitate Expression of Ideas

SUBSTANTIAL
Review students' previous writing. Discuss goals for this assignment. Write the goals out, and have them copy the goals into their Writer's Notebooks.

MODERATE
Discuss student's writing goals. Provide sentence frames for them to write new goals.

LIGHT
Have student pairs discuss writing goals before recording them.

LEARNING OBJECTIVES

- Evaluate a model letter to the editor.
- Synthesize and organize information for a letter.
- Begin a first draft.
- **Language** Read and discuss persuasive writing.

MATERIALS   Online

Display and Engage *10.4a–c*

Writer's Notebook *p. 10.4*

Classroom materials *yellow, pink, and blue index cards*

 INSTRUCTIONAL VOCABULARY

- **salutation** the part of the letter that greets the person receiving it
- **closing** the part of the letter after the message

TEACHER TIP

If several students are researching one organization in your area, consider inviting a staff member into your class or having an electronic conference with a staff member to aid the research process.

Work with the Model

- Remind students that they will be writing a letter to the editor about an animal program or organization. Say: *Let's look at what one student wrote in a letter to the editor.*

- Show the model on **Display and Engage 10.4a–c**. Read the letter aloud as students follow along on **Writer's Notebook page 10.4**. Point out the **salutation**, body paragraphs, **closing**, and name on the letter. At an appropriate moment, add *salutation* and *closing* to the Class Instructional Vocabulary List and have students add them to their own Instructional Vocabulary glossaries.

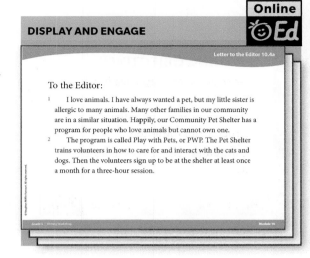

- Discuss the letter, beginning with these questions:

  » *What is the purpose of the letter?* (*to call for volunteers at an animal organization*)

  » *How does the writer support the main idea that people should volunteer?* (*with information from various sources*)

  » *Is the letter convincing? Why or why not?* (*Responses will vary.*)

- Show how the author transferred his ideas to writing. Say: *I want to look at how the author put his paragraphs together. What ideas does he write about in each?*

  » *The first paragraph talks about why the program exists and how it works.*

  » *The second paragraph shows how animals benefit from the program. Where do you think he got information for this paragraph?* (*from Virginia Petrini*)

  » *The third paragraph shows how people benefit from the program. What would have been his source for this paragraph?* (*his personal experiences*)

  » *The last paragraph tells people how to get involved. Did he use facts, opinions, or both?* (*both*)

  » *I see that the writer mentions only the good things about the program. Does that make sense?* (*Yes, because he wants others to volunteer.*)

Begin to Draft

- Have students get out their notes from the previous lesson. Allow them two or three minutes to add ideas.

- Ask students to circle two or three strong arguments that support their main point.

- Distribute three colors of index cards. Tell students to transfer reasons supporting their purpose and main idea to pink cards and reasons against their purpose (if any) on blue cards. They should put information for the introduction and conclusion on yellow cards.

- Have students begin a draft of their letter by getting a statement of their opinion down. Explain that they will expand this statement into an introductory paragraph later.

LEARNING OBJECTIVES

- Learn about two organizational patterns.
- Determine an organizational structure for the letter.
- **Language** Discuss key features of text.

MATERIALS   Online

Classroom materials *index cards from previous lesson, large sheet of paper*

Writer's Notebook *p. 10.4*

Anchor Chart W9: *Elements of an Argument*

Discuss Organizational Structures

- Have students take out their colored index cards from the previous lesson. Provide time to write new cards if they have done additional research. Say: *Today we will talk about organizing your letter and begin writing it.*

- Have students select two or three pink cards that best support their position and number the cards, labeling #1 as the best support, #2 as the next best, and so on.

- Have students pick the blue cards with the strongest arguments against their main point, and then number the best point as #1, the next best as #2, and so on. Note that some students might not have cards for arguments against their position.

- Write *Straw Man* on the left half of a large sheet of paper. Explain that a straw man is easily defeated, so this pattern knocks over any objections before presenting its strongest argument. To illustrate, tape cards to the paper in this order:

  1. The yellow introduction card

  2. The strongest point against your position (a blue card): the writer will need to supply evidence to defeat this position.

  3. The strongest point supporting your position (a pink card)

  4. The yellow conclusion card

- Write *Two Reasons* on the right half of the same paper. Say *This is another organizational structure. This one is simple: your argument is supported by two strong reasons.* To illustrate this structure, tape cards to the paper in this order:

  1. The yellow introduction card

  2. The first point supporting your position (a pink card)

  3. The second point supporting your position (a pink card)

  4. The yellow conclusion card

- Point out that the two-reasons structure does not include arguments against the position.

- Have students look at the model on **Writer's Notebook page 10.4**. Ask: *Which organizational structure did this writer use? (two reasons)*

  THINK ALOUD *Now I want to think about my research and pick the structure that will work best with it.*

  » *I have one point that works against my position and three that support it.*

  » *I think I want to use Straw Man, so that I can state the opposition and then use an argument to tear it down.*

  » *In the next paragraph, I'll present another argument supporting my position. I have at least two arguments left, so I'll pick the strongest one and set the other aside.*

  » *Then I'll finish off with a strong conclusion.*

- Remind students that **Anchor Chart W9: Elements of an Argument** will help them craft their writing as they continue their drafts.

- Allow time for students to determine which organizational structure they want to use and then to continue drafting their letters.

ARGUMENT • LETTER TO THE EDITOR

LEARNING OBJECTIVES
- Write an introduction and conclusion.
- Confer with teacher and peers about drafts.
- **Language** Discuss and evaluate writing using instructional language.

MATERIALS	Online

Writer's Notebook p. 10.4

Display and Engage 10.5

 LEARNING MINDSET:
Noticing

Apply Encourage students to identify how conferencing helped them develop and express their ideas. *What did you learn about your draft that you might also be able to use the next time you write something?*

Introductions and Conclusions

- Say: *When you have completed the argument for your letter, you need to write your introduction and conclusion.*

- Point out that an introduction needs to get the reader's attention. Students can start with the statement of opinion they wrote when they began drafting and expand it. Suggest that writers use an attention-getting fact or common problem in the introduction.

- Explain that the best conclusions restate the author's main point and then leave the reader with something to think about.

- Invite students to look again at <u>Writer's Notebook page 10.4</u> to see how the writer constructed his introduction and conclusion.

- Show <u>Display and Engage 10.5</u> to help guide students in drafting an introduction and conclusion for their letter. Allow time for pairs to discuss the model introduction and conclusion.

DISPLAY AND ENGAGE

Online

Letter to the Editor 10.5

Introductions and Conclusions

Review the introduction and conclusion that the model writer used in his letter to the editor. Discuss with a partner:

- What did you like best about the introduction?
- What did you like best about the conclusion?
- What could you improve upon?

Now go back into your letter and draft an introduction and a conclusion. You will have time to revise and edit them later.

Small Group Conferences

- As students continue drafting, implement small group conferences as needed.

- Begin by asking students how many want to conference. Then ask students to identify what they want to discuss during the conference. For students who have similar problems or questions, suggest they conference together.

- Tell students who conference to take turns reading their problematic sections and listen actively to the others' responses. Encourage them to ask relevant questions about the author's purpose and meaning, so that they can respond helpfully.

- Set up an agreed-upon signal that students who are not conferencing may use if they need help, such as raising their hand or putting their writing to the left of their desks.

EL ENGLISH LEARNER SUPPORT: Support Language Structures

SUBSTANTIAL
Provide simple sentence frames for students to state their main arguments and supporting evidence.

MODERATE
Provide outlines with paragraph starters for students to fill in with their main argument and supporting evidence.

LIGHT
Have partners explain their main argument and supporting evidence to each other and discuss ways they might express their ideas. Monitor and offer feedback.

ARGUMENT • LETTER TO THE EDITOR

LEARNING OBJECTIVES

- Explore ways to include details to make paragraphs more effective.
- Revise paragraphs.
- **Language** Discuss writing details using instructional language.

MATERIALS	Online

Display and Engage *10.4a–c, 10.6*

INSTRUCTIONAL VOCABULARY

- **statistic** a fact that is exact or estimated and is usually stated in numbers
- **quotation** the exact words said by a person
- **description** words and phrases that paint pictures through images
- **anecdote** a brief story

LEARNING MINDSET: Noticing

Apply Point out to students that noticing what is missing can be as important as noticing what is already in their letters. *Ask yourself these questions: What more would a reader want to know about my subject? What detail would make my letter come to life and be more convincing?* Encourage students to be detectives, so they can determine which important pieces are missing from their writing.

Revising to Strengthen Support

- Tell students that today they will be revising their drafts to make them more convincing. Say: *There are different ways to convince people.*

- Project **Display and Engage 10.6**. As you discuss each type of detail, write it on the Class Instructional Vocabulary List and have students add it to the Instructional Vocabulary glossaries in their notebooks.

DISPLAY AND ENGAGE

Letter to the Editor 10.6

Adding Details to Writing

Anecdote: a brief story

Description: words and phrases that paint pictures through images

Fact: a statement that can be proved

Quotation: the exact words a person said

Statistic: a fact that is exact or estimated and is usually stated in numbers

- As you discuss ways to revise, project **Display and Engage 10.4a–c**, showing the model. Point out that students already know about facts, or statements that can be proved.

   THINK ALOUD *Suppose I had written this letter, and I want to add some details to help convince readers.*

   » *At the end of the first paragraph, I could add a **statistic**. I go back to the group's website and read, "52 volunteers average 318 hours/month." I would add, "The 52 volunteers do more than the minimum. They play with pets about 318 hours each month."*

   » *Most of the second paragraph summarizes what Virginia Petrini said. I could add a **quotation** from her at the end. Suppose from my notes I could quote her saying, "'That will help them when they get placed in a home,' explained Ms. Petrini."*

   » *Maybe the third paragraph needs some **description**. After the third sentence, I might add, "The dogs greet us by wagging their tails and jumping for treats we bring." I like the vivid verbs* wagging *and* jumping *because they are so descriptive.*

- Point out that students may need to do more research. Say that this is common because writers may find that they need more details. Also point out that not all letters will need all types of elaboration; writers should tailor their choices to their subject.

- As students revise to strengthen their support, be available for consultation.

EL ENGLISH LEARNER SUPPORT: Support Language Structures

SUBSTANTIAL
Provide a short, simple sentence frame for students to use with a quotation: "_____," _____ *said*. Offer vivid verbs they might use in a detail, gesturing their meanings.

MODERATE
Provide a simple sentence frame for students to use with a quotation: _____ *told me,* "_____." Discuss verbs they might use in their details.

LIGHT
Provide a complex sentence frame for students to use with a quotation: *According to* _____, "_____." Have partners discuss descriptive details and vivid verbs they plan to use.

REVISING II: PEER CONFERENCING

LEARNING OBJECTIVES

• Discuss drafts with peers.

• **Language** Discuss writing using instructional language.

MATERIALS	Online

Writer's Notebook *p. 10.5*

Display and Engage *10.7*

TEACHER TIP

If students have not had much experience conferencing, demonstrate with a volunteer. Have other students note what the student as writer/reader and what you as listener do during the reading. List these tasks, gestures, and vocal expressions in a two-column chart for reference during conferencing.

Small Group Conferences

• Tell students that it's time to read their classmates' writing and provide feedback.

• Read over **Writer's Notebook page 10.5** with students before they begin their conferences.

• Be sure students understand the Say Back process. Explain that each student in a small group will read his or her letter aloud, pause, and then read it again. Upon the second reading, listeners make notes and then share them.

• Groups may also want to use the questions on **Display and Engage 10.7** to add specific comments to the discussion. Project the questions as students confer.

Online

DISPLAY AND ENGAGE

Letter to the Editor 10.7

Conferencing

As you read or listen to a group member's paper, think about these questions.

❶ What is interesting about the first paragraph? How does it preview the letter's topic?

❷ What is the writer's main point? Where is it clearly stated?

❸ How does each paragraph contribute to the main idea?

❹ Does the writer need to add any facts, statistics, quotations, descriptions, or other types of information to support the main idea? If so, where?

❺ How does the conclusion restate the writer's main point and encourage readers to act?

❻ Was the letter effective enough to convince you? Why or why not?

• Walk among the groups to offer support as needed.

• Debrief with the class. Elicit students' responses to the following questions.

> • What have you learned about using writing to convince people?
>
> • How is writing a letter to the editor different from writing a personal letter?
>
> • What are you starting to notice about yourself as a writer?

• End this lesson with a discussion about how writers will use the information they received from their group to revise their writing during the next session.

EL ENGLISH LEARNER SUPPORT: Support Speaking

ALL LEVELS Provide an opportunity for students to practice reading their letters to you or to another student before they read aloud to the small group.

ARGUMENT • LETTER TO THE EDITOR

LEARNING OBJECTIVES

- Incorporate feedback from peer reviews.
- Revise drafts.
- **Language** Discuss writing using instructional language.

MATERIALS	Online ⊚*Ed*

Display and Engage *10.4a–c*

Revising to Strengthen Sentences

- In this lesson, students will use feedback from their small group conferences to continue the revision process.

- Before students begin to work independently, conduct a minilesson on strengthening sentences by adding details. Project **Display and Engage 10.4a–c** for students. Model expanding a sentence by adding information.

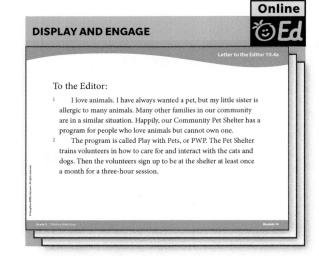

DISPLAY AND ENGAGE

Letter to the Editor 10.4a

To the Editor:

1   I love animals. I have always wanted a pet, but my little sister is allergic to many animals. Many other families in our community are in a similar situation. Happily, our Community Pet Shelter has a program for people who love animals but cannot own one.

2   The program is called Play with Pets, or PWP. The Pet Shelter trains volunteers in how to care for and interact with the cats and dogs. Then the volunteers sign up to be at the shelter at least once a month for a three-hour session.

THINK ALOUD *As I look at this letter, I see a place that would be even more interesting if more information were added. The sentence in the second paragraph, "The program is called Play with Pets, or PWP," could tell more about the program.*

» *If I were the writer, I would expand the sentence to include more information. Maybe it should read, "The program is called Play with Pets, or PWP, because volunteers get to go to the shelter and play with the animals there."*

» *Now I think that readers will have a better idea of what the program is. And the phrases "get to go" and "play" help catch readers' interest by explaining that the program offers a fun opportunity.*

- Have students use their small group feedback to revise their letters to the editor.

TEACHER TIP

Tell students that this stage of revising is a good time to strengthen their concluding paragraphs with a sentence that leaves their readers with a final, interesting thought.

EL ENGLISH LEARNER SUPPORT: Expanding Language

SUBSTANTIAL

Work with each student to target two or three sentences that need additional information. Work together on expanding them. Invite students to try to expand other sentences on their own.

MODERATE

Work together with each student on expanding one sentence with details, and have the student use that sentence as a model to expand others.

LIGHT

If students cannot determine where they need additional details, have them read their sentences and see if they can add information that answers *who, what, when, where, why,* or *how* questions.

ARGUMENT • LETTER TO THE EDITOR

LEARNING OBJECTIVES

- Incorporate transitions into writing.
- **Language** Express relationships with transitions.
- **Language** Edit for grammar, usage, and mechanics.

MATERIALS	Online

Display and Engage *10.8*

 INSTRUCTIONAL VOCABULARY

- **external coherence** a logical flow of ideas between paragraphs in a text
- **internal coherence** a logical flow of ideas between sentences within a paragraph
- **transitions** words that connect the ideas in text

TARGETED GRAMMAR SUPPORT

You may want to consult the following grammar minilessons to review key editing topics.

- **1.3.3 Compound Sentences,** p. W210
- **1.4.1 Complex Sentences with Conjunctions,** p. W213
- **5.2.5 Connect to Writing: Using Transitions,** p. W307

Transitions

- Point out that readers get confused when the ideas in a piece of writing are disconnected. Write **external coherence** on the Class Instructional Vocabulary List and explain that writing that has external coherence "holds together"—that means the paragraphs all relate to the central idea and there is a clear flow of ideas between the paragraphs.

- Ask: *What would be the term for writing that has a clear flow of ideas within a paragraph?* See if students can deduce the term **internal coherence**; add it to the Class Instructional Vocabulary List.

- Add **transitions** to the Class Instructional Vocabulary List and explain that transitions are words that join ideas. Say: *Transition is from a Latin word that means "to go across." Transitions "go across," or join, two ideas in a text. They help readers see the coherence of the writing.* Have students add the new vocabulary terms to their glossaries.

- Project **Display and Engage 10.8**. Explain that this is a draft of the model letter. Read the paragraph aloud. Model editing as if you were the author.

  THINK ALOUD *I'm not sure that the connection between "I have always wanted a pet" and "My little sister is allergic to many animals" is clear.*

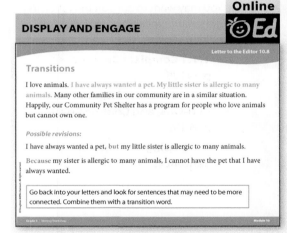

  » *Maybe I could write* (point to and read the following):

  I have always wanted a pet, but my little sister is allergic to many animals.

  » *Or I could write* (point to and read the following):

  Because my sister is allergic to many animals, I cannot have the pet I have always wanted.

- Say: *In these sentences,* but *and* because *are transitions connecting ideas. There's more than one way to connect ideas, so a writer experiments to find the best way.*

- As you circulate, group students who need support on similar grammar topics. Use the grammar minilessons or the students' own writing to provide targeted review and support.

EL **ENGLISH LEARNER SUPPORT: Express Relationships**

SUBSTANTIAL
Work with students to determine where transitions are needed in their letters. Underline problem areas and ask how the ideas are related. Have students find a suitable transition from a list you have supplied. Model inserting the transition.

MODERATE
Have students work in pairs to discern where transitions may be necessary in their work, select transitions from a list that you have supplied, and insert them into the sentence.

LIGHT
Supply a list of transitions for students to consider as they revise and edit their work.

LEARNING OBJECTIVES

- Proofread peers' letters.
- **Language** Edit writing with peer support.

MATERIALS   Online

Display and Engage *10.9*

TARGETED GRAMMAR SUPPORT

You may want to consult the following grammar minilessons to review key editing topics.

- **1.1.1 Complete Sentences,** p. W198
- **1.1.2 Sentence Fragments, Run-Ons, and Comma Splices,** p. W199
- **7.2.3 Using Commas in Sentences,** p. W330

Clocking Activity

- Tell students they will help each other proofread their writing by using the activity called Clocking.

- Project **Display and Engage 10.9** and quickly review the items to be checked by editors. Keep the checklist visible during the clocking exercise.

- Review the rules for clocking:

  » Each writer prepares a cover page for his or her letter. This page should have the writer's name at the top and be divided into several sections. Each section is labeled 1–6 with each number corresponding to an editing task.

  » Students form concentric circles. Students in the inner circle trade letters with their classmate in the outer circle. As students receive a peer's letter, they become that letter's editor.

  » No marks are made on the actual letter. Each editor writes his or her name in a section on the editing page and makes comments on each editing task.

  » Call out which item is to be checked by the editor: (1) capitalization; (2) punctuation within sentences; (3) complete sentences; (4) punctuation at the end of sentences; (5) parts of a letter; (6) other comments.

  » After you call out the full set of editing tasks, have students collect their letters and move to another editor. Continue the process until each section of the editing page is used.

DISPLAY AND ENGAGE

Online Ed

Letter to the Editor 10.9

Editing Checklist

As you review your classmate's letter, use this checklist.

- ☐ Check the letter for proper capitalization.
- ☐ Check the letter for proper punctuation within sentences.
- ☐ Check to be certain all sentences are complete. There should be no run-ons or fragments.
- ☐ Check punctuation at the end of each sentence.
- ☐ Check for parts of a letter: salutation and closing.
- ☐ Mention any other comments you may have.

Once you receive your editing checklists from your classmates, go back into your letters and make the changes. Your goal is to have a letter with no mistakes.

Grade 5 | Writing Workshop   Module 10

Edit Writing

- When the editing process is completed, the editing page and letter are returned to the writer. The writer then uses the editing page to make further changes.

- As you circulate, group students who need support on similar grammar topics. Use the grammar minilessons or the students' own writing to provide targeted review and support.

EL ENGLISH LEARNER SUPPORT: Focus on English Grammar

SUBSTANTIAL

Share sample sentences that contain a grammar topic that students need to practice. Have students copy a few of the sentences to provide practice with the grammar topic.

MODERATE

Provide sentences with blanks where grammar choices need to be made. Have students work together to complete the sentences. Ensure students have used grammar correctly and discuss changes if needed.

LIGHT

Have students review their writing for grammar topics that have been especially tricky for them.

LEARNING OBJECTIVES

- Write a title that reflects the main idea of the letter.
- Use technology to assist with writing.
- Publish writing.
- **Language** Express a main idea in a title.

MATERIALS   Online

Display and Engage *p. 10.4a–c*

TEACHER TIP

Explain to students that the layout of a letter in a newspaper will affect the headline, so items submitted to a paper do not need titles. The newspaper itself will often add titles to letters. However, it is useful for students to title their letters to demonstrate their understanding of the main idea.

 **LEARNING MINDSET:**
Noticing

Review Remind students about the importance of noticing. *When you notice things, you learn more about the world. You make connections between things that you know and your new observation.* Ask students how noticing new things helped them write and edit their letters to the editor.

Prepare the Final Copy

- Allow time for last-minute changes as student pairs work together to finalize their letters.
- Discuss what makes a good title. Show the model letter on **Display and Engage 10.4a–c**. Work with students to write a title for it. Then have students write titles for their letters and prepare a final copy.
- Circulate among the students and offer assistance as needed.

Online
Ed

DISPLAY AND ENGAGE

Letter to the Editor 10.4a

To the Editor:

1   I love animals. I have always wanted a pet, but my little sister is allergic to many animals. Many other families in our community are in a similar situation. Happily, our Community Pet Shelter has a program for people who love animals but cannot own one.

2   The program is called Play with Pets, or PWP. The Pet Shelter trains volunteers in how to care for and interact with the cats and dogs. Then the volunteers sign up to be at the shelter at least once a month for a three-hour session.

Publish Writing

- Point out to students that they have options for publishing their letters.
- Tell students that the content of their letters to the editor will give them hints about places where they can be published. Although the obvious choice would be any newspapers in your community, other choices may occur to them.

> a. Send the letter to the organization that is the subject of the letter so that it can be included in its newsletter.
>
> b. Post the letter on the website of the organization.
>
> c. Post the letter on a social media website with their parents' permission.
>
> d. Post parts of the letter on a bulletin board at the organization or on another community bulletin board.

- Have students confer about how they will publish their letters.
- Finally, help students publish their letters.

ARGUMENT • LETTER TO THE EDITOR

LEARNING OBJECTIVES
- Share letters to the editor.
- Hold a collaborative discussion.
- **Language** Discuss using instructional language.

MATERIALS   Online

Anchor Chart W17: *Tips on How to Present*

Writer's Notebook *pp. 10.3, 10.6*

TEACHER TIP

Be sure to congratulate students on their work. Point out that they have learned a lot about an animal organization and they can use this knowledge to be better community members.

Share Writing

- Review the tips on **Anchor Chart W17: Tips on How to Present**.

- Invite students to share their letters to the editor by reading them aloud.

- Encourage students to ask the presenters questions about their letters. Remind students of the rules for asking questions. Encourage speakers to answer with details they learned from their research.

Engage and Respond

- Conclude with an informal debriefing about how students felt about writing their letters. Ask the following questions:

  » *What did you like best about writing your letter?*

  » *What did you like least?*

  » *What did you learn about writing? How did you learn it?*

  » *What did you learn about grammar? How did you learn it?*

  » *What did you learn about punctuation? How did you learn it?*

  » *Describe your thoughts about publishing your letter.*

  » *What do you want to remember to do the next time you write a letter to the editor?*

- Have students turn to **Writer's Notebook page 10.3** containing the list of goals they set at the beginning of this module. Ask them to review their original goals and then TURN AND TALK with a partner about whether they feel they met their goals.

- Have students work on **Writer's Notebook page 10.6** to reflect on this assignment and look ahead to the next writing assignment.

Online
Ed

ANCHOR CHART

Tips on How to Present

Express the Main Idea Make sure the point of the presentation is clear.	
Look at the Audience Eye contact brings people into your presentation.	
Speak Clearly and Loudly Make sure people can hear and understand you.	
Use Natural Body Language Smile and use your hands when you talk.	
Avoid Informal Language and Slang Speak more formally than you would to friends.	slang

---

EL **ENGLISH LEARNER SUPPORT: Support Presentations**

ALL LEVELS Before they share with the class, allow students to practice reading their letters aloud to themselves or to a partner.

Realistic Story

FOCUS STATEMENT Write what you know.

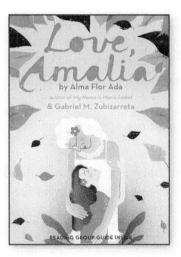

FOCAL TEXT

Love, Amalia

Author: Alma Flor Ada and Gabriel M. Zubizarreta

Summary: Amalia's best friend moves away and then her grandmother dies. She learns lessons about loss and the ways we carry those we love with us.

LESSONS

1. **Introducing the Focal Text**

2. **The Read**

3. **Vocabulary**

4. **Prewriting: Preparing to Write**

5. **Drafting I: Beginning the Draft**

6. **Drafting II: Understanding Plot Structure**

7. **Drafting III: Completing the Draft**

8. **Revising I: Elaboration**

9. **Revising II: Conferencing**

10. **Revising III: Incorporating Feedback**

11. **Revising IV: Varying Sentence Length**

12. **Editing I: Grammar, Usage, and Mechanics**

13. **Editing II: Peer Proofreading**

14. **Publishing**

15. **Sharing**

**LEARNING MINDSET:
Self-Reflection**

Display **Anchor Chart 32: My Learning Mindset** throughout the year. Refer to it to introduce Self-Reflection and to reinforce the skills you introduced in previous modules.

LEARNING OBJECTIVES

- Make connections to prior knowledge.
- **Language** Express memories.

MATERIALS   Online

Classroom materials *objects that evoke a memory, such as photos, souvenirs, ticket stubs, trophies*

Display and Engage *11.1*

Writer's Notebook *p. 11.1*

 INSTRUCTIONAL VOCABULARY

- **narrative** a story

LEARNING MINDSET: Self-Reflection

Tell students that in this module there will be many opportunities for self-reflection about their experiences and their writing. *Remember that looking back and self-reflecting allow us to learn from mistakes as well as learn new things.*

TEACHER TIP

As you discuss students' objects and memories, be aware that some students may get emotional.

Priming the Students

Explore the Topic

- Tell students that they will be exploring their memories in order to tell stories.

- Bring a few objects that evoke special memories for you. Explain that they are objects that you treasure. Describe the memories each evokes. For example:

    THINK ALOUD *This ticket stub makes me happy. It's from a concert my son took me to last year. Not only does he know how much I like this band's music, but he likes it too. I'm happy thinking of the evening we spent listening to music we both enjoy.*

- Ask students if they have treasured objects that remind them of events or people. Encourage students to add these objects and memories to **Writer's Notebook page 11.1** or their own notebooks to use as a resource for writing. Note how writing things down extends memory.

- Talk about how things such as objects, smells, pictures, and songs often trigger not only memories but also emotions.

- Remind students that a **narrative** is a story and that narratives can be fictional or nonfictional. Say: *We are going to write fictional stories. That means they are made up. But fictional stories can be based on real-life events or memories. That's a strategy many writers use called "writing what you know."*

- Explain to students that they will pull from their memories to write fictional stories. Note that actual events from their past will make their stories seem more realistic.

Discuss the Focus Statement

- Show **Display and Engage 11.1**. Read the Focus Statement with students. Point out that the prompt says, "what you know" not "what you know about." Ask: *What does "what you know" mean?*

- As a follow-up, offer students the opportunity to bring in a treasured object to the next class session and share the memories associated with this object.

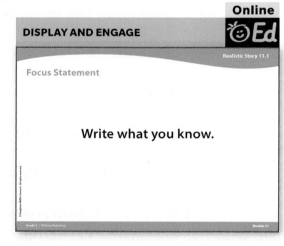

DISPLAY AND ENGAGE   Online   Realistic Story 11.1

Focus Statement

Write what you know.

 ENGLISH LEARNER SUPPORT: Facilitate Discussion and Writing

SUBSTANTIAL

Talk with students about the objects that bring back memories to them. Tell students to choose one, and ask them questions such as *How does it make you feel? Who does it remind you of?*

MODERATE

Provide sentence frames to help students articulate their memories: When I see _____, it reminds me about _____. When I look at _____, I feel _____ because _____.

LIGHT

Have partners discuss the objects that bring back memories to them.

LEARNING OBJECTIVES

- Use background knowledge to prepare to read.
- Read a fictional story with purpose and understanding.
- Infer basic themes and use text evidence as support.
- **Language** Discuss a short story using academic language.

MATERIALS Online

Writer's Notebook p. 11.2
Focal Text *Love, Amalia*

 INSTRUCTIONAL VOCABULARY

- **theme** a message about life that the writer shares with the reader

 LEARNING MINDSET: Self-Reflection

Introduce Tell students that we write what we know because then we are sure about what we are saying. *We have to look inside ourselves to be sure of what we know. We have to question honestly how we feel or why we do what we do. Part of good writing is self-reflection.* Help students realize that truthful writing comes from finding the words to express feelings and reactions.

Priming the Text

Preparing to Read

- Remind students that in the previous lesson they were encouraged to explore memories that are associated with objects that had special meaning.

- Ask: *Why do you think we remember certain things and not others? Do you think our memories capture exactly what happened?* Help students realize that we attach meaning to what we remember, even if we don't remember the details exactly. Note that we often remember things the way we want to.

- Allow students to share their happy memories associated with past events or the objects they may have brought from home.

- Encourage students to link their memories with the web graphic organizer on **Writer's Notebook page 11.2** as a resource for later writing. Students should identify how memories are often connected.

The Read

Read the Focal Text

- Preview *Love, Amalia* before reading it aloud to students. Be aware that it includes many Spanish words and phrases, but the author provides context to aid comprehension. Challenge students to use context to figure out the meanings of the Spanish words.

- Read aloud the first three chapters of *Love, Amalia* or as much as time allows. As you read, have students look for memories that the characters discuss and how they present them. Stop to point out these moments and also to ask comprehension questions.

- Introduce the element of **theme**. Ask: *What message or messages do you think the writer is trying to express? What evidence in the story makes you think that? Why might you need to read more to really understand the book's themes?*

- Add *theme* to the Class Instructional Vocabulary List, and encourage students to include it in the glossaries in their notebooks.

Love, Amalia

 ENGLISH LEARNER SUPPORT: Elicit Participation

ALL LEVELS Allow Spanish speakers to help you translate the Spanish words and phrases as you read *Love, Amalia*.

LEARNING OBJECTIVES
- Read and understand newly encountered vocabulary.
- Label parts of speech.
- **Language** Explain meanings of vocabulary words.

MATERIALS   Online

Focal Text   *Love, Amalia*
Writer's Notebook   p. 11.3
Display and Engage   11.2

TEACHER TIP

Carefully pronounce each word that students suggest for their Word Banks as you browse *Love, Amalia* and use it in a sentence.

Review the Focal Text

- Review with students the first chapters of *Love, Amalia*. Help students appreciate the author's use of descriptive vocabulary.

- Have students begin a Word Bank on **Writer's Notebook page 11.3**. Browse *Love, Amalia* and encourage volunteers to suggest words, such as those below, that they find vivid or descriptive or whose meaning they would like to learn.

subtle	slathered	crimson
lush	fascinating	tasteful
extraordinary	elegy	prelude
enthusiasm		

- Show **Display and Engage 11.2**. Read the directions with students. Then have students form pairs to notate each entry in their Word Banks.

Online

DISPLAY AND ENGAGE

Realistic Story 11.2

Vocabulary

Identify each entry in your Word Bank as one of the following.
- Write **CN** next to each common noun.
- Write **A** next to each adjective.
- Write **V** next to each verb.

- Create a class copy of the Word Bank on chart paper to keep displayed while you work through the writing process for students' narratives.

- Have students use a dictionary or online resource to define each word on their list.

- Ask students to select a word and convert it from its current part of speech to another part of speech, such as an adjective into an adverb or a verb into a noun. Students should then use this new word in a sentence. Model with this example: *The crowd became enthusiastic because of the speaker's enthusiasm.*

- Ask students to think about the adjectives in the list. Have them create images using nouns that would be described by these adjectives.

Engage and Respond

- Have students choose three words from the entries in their Word Bank and use them to write a short description of a person or place.

EL **ENGLISH LEARNER SUPPORT: Build Vocabulary**

SUBSTANTIAL

Show students pictures and use the vocabulary words in sentences to help them understand. For example, show a verdant, green forest and say: *This is a lush forest because it has so many trees and plants.*

MODERATE

Have students work with partners to find pictures of the following: a subtle tan, a lush forest, an extraordinary play in sports, and so on.

LIGHT

Have students share ideas for their descriptions with a partner. After writing, they can read aloud their descriptions to one another.

NARRATIVE • REALISTIC STORY

LEARNING OBJECTIVES

- Choose a topic.
- Set writing goals.
- Use prewriting strategies to plan.
- **Language** Articulate prewriting plan.

MATERIALS   Online Ed

Display and Engage *11.3*

Writer's Notebook *pp. 11.4, 11.5, 11.6*

 INSTRUCTIONAL VOCABULARY

- **topic** the person or thing a text is about
- **brainstorming** thinking of many ideas quickly before thinking about them more carefully later
- **audience** people who read a text
- **author's purpose** the reason a writer writes something

 LEARNING MINDSET: Self-Reflection

As students set goals for their writing, encourage them to self-reflect about the writing they've done in previous modules. Perhaps they've made mistakes or feel they are not a good writer. *As you set your goals for this module, think about the things you've learned about writing in previous modules. You have probably become a much better writer over the course of this year. Moving forward, try to think of your mistakes as something to celebrate because they give you opportunities to self-reflect and think about how to improve.*

Discuss the Writing Prompt

- Remind students that in this module, they will write a realistic narrative.

- Show <u>**Display and Engage 11.3**</u> and read the Writing Prompt together. Discuss each point and make sure students understand what they are being asked to do.

Prewriting

- Note that there are several things students need to think about before they can start drafting. The first step is to pick a **topic**.

- Explain that sometimes writers use **brainstorming** to arrive at a suitable topic for their work. Say: *When you brainstorm, you allow your mind to go from one idea to another. Don't force your thinking; just let it flow.* Model brainstorming for a topic.
  THINK ALOUD *One place that pops into my mind is my local bike shop. That makes me think of an employee there who was chomping on an apple while showing me a bike. That makes me think about the candy apples they used to sell at school fairs—and a funny event that once happened. I'll write a story about a character who goes to a school fair and has a funny experience involving a candy apple.*

- Have students use <u>**Writer's Notebook page 11.4**</u> to brainstorm ideas. Encourage them to come up with at least three ideas under each column. Have students discuss their ideas with a partner and then circle the topic they choose.

- Point out that writers think about their **audience**: what the readers know and what they might be interested in. Note that authors also write with a **purpose**, typically to entertain, to inform, or to persuade their audience. Ask: *Which of those is usually the purpose of storywriters? (to entertain)* Encourage students to think about their audience and purpose using <u>**Writer's Notebook page 11.5**</u>.

- If you have not already done so, add the terms *topic, brainstorming, audience,* and *author's purpose* to the Class Instructional Vocabulary List, and have students add the terms to the glossaries in their notebooks.

Set Goals for Writing

- Have students set goals for their stories by adding to the list on <u>**Writer's Notebook page 11.6**</u> or in their own notebooks.

EL **ENGLISH LEARNER SUPPORT: Scaffold Writing**

SUBSTANTIAL
Talk about different goals students can work toward with their story. Write down these goals for students, and then have them copy those goals into their Writer's Notebook.

MODERATE
Discuss students' writing goals. Provide sentence frames to write their goals, as needed. For example: *In this story, I am going to _____ and watch out for _____.*

LIGHT
Have partners discuss their writing goals before entering them in their Writer's Notebook.

DRAFTING I: BEGINNING THE DRAFT

LEARNING OBJECTIVES
- Understand how to turn prewriting into the beginning of a draft.
- **Language** Understand and practice using academic vocabulary such as *setting, characters, plot,* and *conflict.*

MATERIALS   Online

Display and Engage *11.3, 11.4a–11.4f*
Focal Text *Love, Amalia*
Writer's Notebook *pp. 11.7–11.9, 11.10*

 INSTRUCTIONAL VOCABULARY

- **setting** the place and time in which story events occur
- **characters** the people or animals that a story is about
- **plot** the events of a story
- **conflict** the problem or struggle in a story

TEACHER TIP

Explain to students that reflecting upon their own memories will help make their writing more realistic. Encourage them to think about specific details, events, and emotions that they can use in their stories.

Prepare to Draft

- Review the prompt with students on <u>**Display and Engage 11.3**</u> and the requirements for the narrative. Say: *When you write about what you know, you don't have to write about an exotic person in an exotic land. Write about what is familiar to you.*

- Review the meanings and importance of **setting**, **characters**, **plot**, and **conflict**. Explain that the main characters, setting, and conflict are typically introduced near the beginning of a story.

- Reread or remind students of the first chapter of *Love, Amalia.* Ask: *What is the setting?* (*grandmother's kitchen*) *Who are the characters?* (*Amalia and her grandmother*) *What is the conflict?* (*Amalia's best friend is moving away.*)

- Show <u>**Display and Engage 11.4a–11.4f**</u> and have students turn to <u>**Writer's Notebook pages 11.7–11.9**</u>. Read through the model story with students. Encourage them to circle the main characters, underline descriptions of the setting, and put a star next to the paragraph that shows when the conflict begins. Then say: *Something like this happened to me when I was in grade school. I based my story on my memories—especially on the feelings I had about what happened. It helps to have something to start with when you are writing. But I also changed a lot and added characters and details to make this fiction story come alive.*

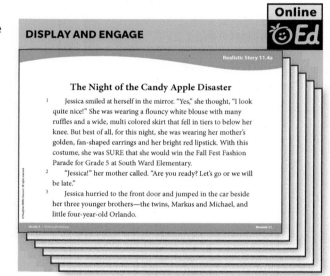

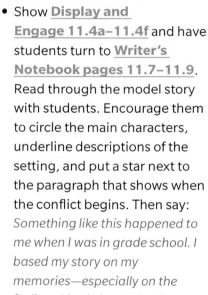

Begin to Draft

- Discuss the different expectations of the rubric on <u>**Writer's Notebook page 11.10**</u>. Remind students they can use this rubric as a resource while drafting and revising.

- Have students begin to draft their stories, using their prewriting notes to help focus their writing.

 ENGLISH LEARNER SUPPORT: Build Vocabulary

ALL LEVELS For Spanish-speaking students, point out that the word *conflict* has a cognate: *conflicto*; and for French-speaking students, the cognate is *conflit*. For Spanish-speaking students, the word *character* has the cognate *carácter*.

LEARNING OBJECTIVES

- Understand plot structure.
- Develop drafts into a focused, structured, and coherent piece of writing.
- **Language** Understand and use academic language for narrative structure.

MATERIALS   Online

Anchor Chart W6: *Narrative Structure*

Writer's Notebook *pp. 11.7–11.9, 11.11*

Display and Engage *11.5*

 INSTRUCTIONAL VOCABULARY

- **exposition** the beginning of a story; introduces the characters and setting
- **protagonist** main character
- **climax** moment of the most tension in a story's conflict
- **falling action** the events that follow the climax
- **resolution** the end of the story, when the conflict is resolved

Focus on Narrative Structure

- Display **Anchor Chart W6: Narrative Structure** and discuss the elements of a story's plot.

- Explain that the **exposition** identifies the setting and introduces the characters. Say: *The main character is called the* **protagonist**. *Who is the protagonist in* Love, Amalia? *(Amalia)*

- Explain that events in the plot develop the conflict until the **climax**, the turning point in the action. Say: *The events increase in tension until the climax.*

- Explain that after the turning point comes the **falling action**, in which the main character begins to resolve the conflict, and the **resolution**, in which the conflict is resolved and all the loose ends are tied up.

- As students refer to **Writer's Notebook pages 11.7-11.9**, show **Display and Engage 11.5** and discuss how it relates to the model.

- If you have not already done so, add *exposition, protagonist, climax, falling action,* and *resolution* to the Class Instructional Vocabulary List, and have students add these terms and definitions to their own glossaries.

- Encourage students to use the graphic organizer on **Writer's Notebook page 11.11** to organize the structure of their stories as they draft.

Continue to Draft

- Allow students to continue working on their stories. Circulate the room, stopping to answer questions or provide advice as needed.

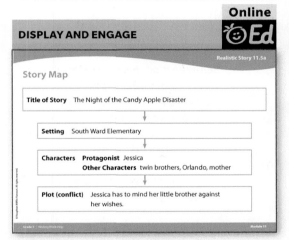

ANCHOR CHART   Online

Narrative Structure

The narrative structure is also called the plot. It usually has five stages:

Climax — the turning point in the story

Rising action — what happens in the story that leads to the climax

Falling action — the events that happen after the climax

Exposition — any important background information about the setting and characters

Resolution — the conclusion of the story

DISPLAY AND ENGAGE   Online

Realistic Story 11.5a

Story Map

| Title of Story | The Night of the Candy Apple Disaster |

| Setting | South Ward Elementary |

| Characters | Protagonist Jessica
Other Characters twin brothers, Orlando, mother |

| Plot (conflict) | Jessica has to mind her little brother against her wishes. |

 ENGLISH LEARNER SUPPORT: Build Vocabulary

SUBSTANTIAL

Have students point to the name of the main character, or protagonist, in the first paragraph of the model. Ask students to complete the following sentence frame: The protagonist's name is _____.

MODERATE

Ask: *Who is the protagonist?* Provide the following sentence frames: _____ is the main character. Another word for main character is _____.

LIGHT

Ask partners to name and explain the protagonist to one another. Have partners review other Instructional Vocabulary, such as *climax* and *resolution*.

NARRATIVE • REALISTIC STORY

LEARNING OBJECTIVES

- Draft stories.
- Add conclusions to drafts.
- **Language** Understand narrative structure (conclusions).

MATERIALS   Online 🍊 Ed

Writer's Notebook p. 11.9

Display and Engage 11.6

 **INSTRUCTIONAL VOCABULARY**

- **conclusion** the end of a story

 LEARNING MINDSET:
Self-Reflection

Self-reflection means looking at your work and determining how you might do it better. *In this lesson, consider any improvements you might make to bring your story to a satisfactory close. When you reread your draft, ask yourself, "What details can I improve?" Then go ahead and put your knowledge to work to improve your writing.*

Write a Satisfying Conclusion

- Ask students: *Think about stories you have read and enjoyed. How did they end? What things do you think help make a good ending?*

- Point out that the **conclusion** is the last thing in a story that readers will read, so it will likely be what they remember most. Explain that it's important to come up with an ending that resolves the conflict and leaves a lasting impression on readers.

- Have students think again about their purpose and audience. Ask: *Why did you write this story? What do you want readers to get from it?* Tell them their conclusion should make sure to fulfill the purpose of their story and leave their audience satisfied.

- Have students return to the end of the writing model on **Writer's Notebook page 11.9**. Ask: *Was this the ending you had expected while you were reading? How did the writer surprise you? How did the writer add humor?*

- Show **Display and Engage 11.6**. Explain that there are many different ways that writers can end a story. Share the examples and ask students to brainstorm more ways. List their ideas on the board or chart paper.

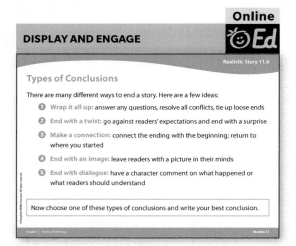

Complete the Draft

- Have students work with partners to come up with ideas for how to end their stories. Encourage them to try at least two different endings to see which works best. Remind them to refer to **Display and Engage 11.6** and the ideas you listed on the board for different options they could try. Suggest they choose one of these ways to write their final conclusion.

- Have students complete the draft of their stories. Encourage them to review the prompt and the rubric to make sure they have included all the necessary parts.

- Circulate to provide support and direction to students.

EL **ENGLISH LEARNER SUPPORT: Support Comprehension**

SUBSTANTIAL

Confirm understanding of the term *conclusion*. Have students point to the conclusion in the model. Supply the following sentence frame: *The end of the story is the _____.*

MODERATE

Explain that *conclusion* comes from the verb *conclude,* which means "to end." Ask: *What is a conclusion?* Provide the following sentence frame: *A conclusion is _____.*

LIGHT

Point out that *conclusion* is the noun form of the verb *conclude,* which means "to end." Pair a native speaker with a nonnative speaker. Have the partners discuss how the conclusion of the model ends the story.

LEARNING OBJECTIVES

- Add details to drafts.
- Revise drafts to add any needed information.
- **Language** Understand and use the word *elaboration*.

MATERIALS   Online

Focal Text *Love, Amalia*

 **INSTRUCTIONAL VOCABULARY**

- **elaboration** details added to show rather than tell
- **dialogue** conversation between two characters

TARGETED GRAMMAR SUPPORT

You may want to consult the following grammar minilessons to review key revising topics.

- **4.1.1 Adjectives,** p. W278
- **4.2.1 Adverbs That Tell How, Where, When, How Often,** p. W283
- **6.1.1 Quotations,** p. W313

Focus on Elaboration

- Explain to students that an important part of revising is making sure that they have added details to their descriptions or plot events. Say: *Remember that the process of adding details is called* **elaboration***. When you elaborate, you show the reader, rather than tell the reader about something.*

- Reread the first paragraph of Chapter 2, page 7, in *Love, Amalia*. Say: *Doesn't this show rather than tell about the experience? Note how many words invite you to hear, see, taste, smell, or feel the moment that Amalia and her grandmother examine letters.*

- Ask: *What details tell you more about the moment Amalia and her grandmother sat down to talk?* Write student responses on the chart paper or board. Point out sensory details. Say: *Sensory details help create a vivid image for the reader. They make readers feel like they are there.*

- Write and read aloud the following text to students:

> The first time Carlos tried to ice skate, it didn't go very well. He fell a lot. He got wet and cranky.

- Ask: *How could you make this scene more interesting?* Have volunteers name ways that a writer could show, not tell, about Carlos and his actions. Then have students rewrite the sentences in their notebooks to add elaboration. Have three volunteers share their new sentences and discuss the different ways they added elaboration.

- Explain that another excellent way to elaborate a narrative is to add **dialogue**. *Dialogue* is conversation between characters.

- Read the second paragraph on page 7 and the first paragraph on page 8 of *Love, Amalia*. Read the characters' words with expression.

- Write the following on the board. Have students compare the impact of this text with the actual text in *Love, Amalia*.

> Amalia asked Abuelita why she was already writing her Christmas cards and what the dry leaves were for. Abuelita replied that she liked to write her cards slowly so that she could think about what to write.

- Point out that dialogue helps readers "hear" the characters.

- Add *dialogue* to the Class Instructional Vocabulary List, and have students add the term to the lists in their glossaries.

Revise to Elaborate

- Tell students that using the letters D.I.D.D. can help them remember ways they can add elaboration: D=description; I=illustration; D=detail; D=dialogue.

- Have students review their drafts and highlight sentences that would benefit from adding descriptions, illustration, or details. Have them identify spots where dialogue will help readers hear the characters. Then have them revise their drafts.

NARRATIVE • REALISTIC STORY

LEARNING OBJECTIVES
- Give and receive peer feedback.
- Revise drafts.
- **Language** Use academic language to discuss peers' stories.

MATERIALS   Online 🍎 **Ed**

Focal Text *Love, Amalia*
Display and Engage *11.7*
Writer's Notebook *p. 11.12*

INSTRUCTIONAL VOCABULARY

- **conferencing** talking to one another about how to improve writing

LEARNING MINDSET: Self-Reflection

Explain that self-reflection is a valuable strategy that helps people learn. *In this lesson, you're going to be looking for ways to improve your peers' drafts, and they will be looking for ways to improve yours.* Suggest that noting weak areas that could use strengthening provides opportunities to reflect upon ways to change and to improve.

Focus on Conferencing

- Read pages 77–78 of *Love, Amalia.* Say: *Amalia's grandmother reads Amalia's first essay. They discuss with one another how Amalia might improve her first draft. In other words, they have a conference. What changes does Amalia's grandmother suggest? (use more details; write from her heart)*

- Explain to students that today they will be **conferencing** just like Amalia and her grandmother did.

- Show **Display and Engage 11.7**. Review the questions and any vocabulary, if necessary.

- Ask a volunteer to join you at the front of the class. Suggest to students that you are in a fishbowl. Say: *The two of us are going to model conferencing. At the end of our conference, we'll discuss what you have observed about the process.*

- Explain that conferencing is a way to improve writing that published authors use. As you model conferencing, reinforce that encouragement is an important part of the process.

- As the volunteer reads his or her story, refer to the questions on **Display and Engage 11.7**, pausing to discuss and provide constructive advice. Also note how the volunteer has followed the prompt.

- When you have concluded the model conferencing, ask the volunteer: *Now that you have reflected upon your writing, what do you think you should do to improve your story? (Possible answer: Look for places that I might show rather than tell the story.)*

- Make sure students understand what they can gain from peer conferencing. Add *conferencing* to the Class Instructional Vocabulary List if you have not already done so, and have students add it to their glossaries.

- Pair students and give them time to conference with each other, taking turns reading their drafts. Have students use **Writer's Notebook page 11.12** to keep track of their notes for their partner.

Revising

- Have students re-enter their writing and continue to revise, using the feedback they gained in conferences.

ENGLISH LEARNER SUPPORT: Scaffold Revision

SUBSTANTIAL
Simplify the language of the conferencing questions on the Display and Engage. Ask: *Can you tell the setting?*

MODERATE
Ask students the questions on the Display and Engage and, if necessary, point to specific areas in their stories that relate to each question.

LIGHT
Be sure students understand the questions on the Display and Engage, especially idioms such as "grab your attention" and "make the story come alive."

LEARNING OBJECTIVES

- Give and receive feedback.
- Revise drafts.
- **Language** Discuss student stories using academic language and the conferencing process.

MATERIALS Online Ed

Display and Engage 11.8

TEACHER TIP

Students can be undisciplined when working in small groups or pairs. Before you start conferencing, make sure your students understand and are focused on the task at hand. If there are students who are off task, ask them to conference with you so you can show them how it's done.

Conference with Peers

- Remind students of the fishbowl activity from the previous lesson. Explain that students will continue to conference with each other.

- Review that in a peer conference listeners ask questions and give feedback that can help the writer improve his or her story. Show **Display and Engage 11.8**. Read aloud the draft. Say: *When I read this early draft of my story during a conference, a listener asked, "How did Jessica react or feel when her mother told her to babysit her little brother?" I remembered how I used to feel when I wanted to go with my friends, but my mother asked me to do something I did not want to do. So I added more details and dialogue to show how Jessica felt.*

Online Ed

DISPLAY AND ENGAGE

Realistic Story 11.8

Incorporating Feedback

Draft

Once they arrived at the school, Jessica's mother said, "Take Orlando with you, while I go with Markus and Michael. Make sure Orlando has fun and don't lose him."

Jessica's heart sank. Disappointed, Jessica started pulling Orlando through the halls.

Revision

Once they arrived at the school, Jessica's mother said, "Take Orlando with you, while I go with Markus and Michael. Make sure Orlando has fun and don't lose him."

Jessica's heart sank. The LAST thing she wanted to do was to take care of her little brother—again. "Oh, Mom, do I HAVE to?" she whined. "He is too much trouble."

- Read aloud the revision. Say: *The revised version is a lot more descriptive and interesting than just saying Jessica was disappointed. The listener's question showed a weakness in the story, which helped me revise to make it stronger.*

- Tell students that in the next conferencing exercise, groups of four or five will listen to writers read their stories in a round robin format.

  » One by one, readers read through their stories once, pause, and then read their stories again.

  » During the second reading, listeners jot down in their notebooks the images or words that they liked in the story.

  » After the second reading, the listeners name the images or words that they have jotted down. The writer highlights the images and words on their draft. The listeners also ask questions and provide other feedback that will help the writer improve his or her story.

Continue to Revise

- After everyone has had time to read and listen to stories, have students continue revising their drafts. Say: *You will make revisions based on listeners' questions and feedback. You may also want to add more details to the sections that listeners pointed out. Your listeners have given you feedback that you can incorporate to make a stronger story.*

EL **ENGLISH LEARNER SUPPORT: Facilitate Discussion**

SUBSTANTIAL
Allow students to point to the parts of the writer's story that they liked or wonder about.

MODERATE
Provide sentence frames for listeners to provide feedback, such as *I liked _____. I don't understand _____. I wonder why _____.*

LIGHT
Encourage students to expand on their comments using sentence frames, such as *I really liked _____ because _____.*

NARRATIVE • REALISTIC STORY

LEARNING OBJECTIVES

- Vary sentence length.
- **Language** Revise sentence structures to vary sentence length.

MATERIALS	Online

Display and Engage *11. 9a–c*

TARGETED GRAMMAR SUPPORT

You may want to consult the following grammar minilessons to review key revising topics.

- **1.3.3 Compound Sentences,** p. W210
- **1.4.1 Complex Sentences With Conjunctions,** p. W213
- **4.4.3 Combining Sentences,** p. W295

Improving Sentences

- In this lesson tell students that they will use the revision strategy called ratiocination to help them vary the lengths of sentences in their writing.

- Show <u>**Display and Engage 11.9a and 11.9b**</u>. Explain that the first paragraph is from an earlier draft of the model. Read the sentences aloud.

- Guide students to realize that the writing sounds choppy and unnatural because all the sentences have a similar short length. Explain that varying the lengths of sentences will make the writing sound more pleasing and keep the reader's interest.

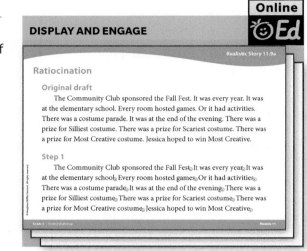

- For step 1, say: *First I circled the periods to help me see how many sentences I had.* Point to the second paragraph. *How many are there? Eleven!*

- For step 2, point to the first three highlighted sentences and note that they all tell about the same subject. Explain that there are several ways to combine them. Work with students to create two variations of longer sentences; for example: *Every year the Community Club sponsored the Fall Fest at the elementary school. The Community Club sponsored the Fall Fest every year at the elementary school.*

- Point to the second group of highlighted sentences. Work with students to combine them; for example: *Every room hosted games or activities, and at the end of the evening, there was a costume parade with prizes for Silliest, Scariest, and Most Creative Costumes.*

- Show <u>**Display and Engage 11.9c**</u>. Read the sample revised paragraph aloud. Point out that there is now one medium-length sentence, one long sentence, and one short sentence. Ask students to comment on how the writing sounds with sentences of varying lengths. Say: *You can use the process of ratiocination to help you figure out which sentences to combine and which ones to leave alone.*

- Have students use the ratiocination process to vary the sentences in their drafts. As you circulate around the room, group students who need support on similar grammar topics. Use the Grammar minilessons or the students' own writing to provide targeted review and support.

EL ENGLISH LEARNER SUPPORT: Scaffold Revision

SUBSTANTIAL

Guide students to find one place in their writing where they might vary the sentence length. Work with students to make the revision and read the revised sentence(s) aloud.

MODERATE

Encourage partners to find two or more places where they could vary the sentence length. Review the ratiocination process with students as necessary.

LIGHT

Ask students to explain where they made changes to their sentences and why their revisions make their realistic stories sound better.

LEARNING OBJECTIVES

- Edit for grammar, usage, and mechanics.
- **Language** Understand and apply English-language conventions.

MATERIALS   Online

Anchor Chart W15: *Editing Checklist*

Anchor Chart W16: *Proofreading Marks*

TEACHER TIP

If students have used a computer to compose their final drafts, show them how to use the spelling and grammar check feature if it is available on the software. Caution them to double check with a grammar book, a dictionary, or a peer after they use this feature because it is not always accurate.

TARGETED GRAMMAR SUPPORT

You may want to consult the following grammar minilessons to review key editing topics.

- **1.3.2 Subject-Verb Agreement,** p. W209
- **6.1.1 Quotations,** p. W313

Prepare to Edit

- Review the items on <u>**Anchor Chart W15: Editing Checklist**</u>. Remind students that proofreading is a type of editing. Now that their drafts are finished, they are going to proofread. Make sure students know that they need to look at everything on the Editing Checklist as well as subject-verb agreement, punctuation, and proper use of quotations.

- Review <u>**Anchor Chart W16: Proofreading Marks**</u>. Ask students to use the proofreading marks to indicate corrections on their drafts.

Edit Drafts

- Have students proofread their drafts using ratiocination as it was modeled in the previous lesson.

- Circulate around the room and provide assistance, as needed.

- As you circulate, group students who need support on similar grammar topics. Use the grammar minilessons or the students' own writing to provide targeted review and support.

(EL) ENGLISH LEARNER SUPPORT: Support Editing

SUBSTANTIAL
Guide students to proofread one area, such as punctuation. Once students are successful, move on to another area.

MODERATE
Group students if they have similar errors, and review that skill. Have students correct the errors in their own papers, and then check them with other group members.

LIGHT
Have students work in pairs to proofread their writing and discuss why the errors are not correct.

ANCHOR CHART   Online **Ed**

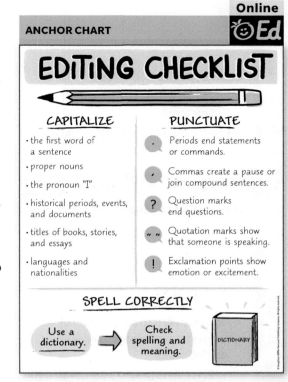

ANCHOR CHART   Online **Ed**

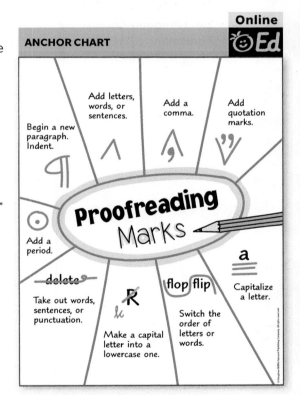

LEARNING OBJECTIVES

- Proofread writing for grammar, usage, and mechanics.
- **Language** Apply English language conventions.

MATERIALS Online

Display and Engage *11.10*

TARGETED GRAMMAR SUPPORT

You may want to consult the following grammar minilessons to review key editing topics.

- **2.1.1 Recognizing Common and Proper Nouns,** p. W218
- **2.4.3 Pronoun-Antecedent Agreement,** p. W235

Clocking Activity

- Review the rules of clocking with students. Since students have used the process several times, use the following sentence frames to help them state the rules.

  » Students form (*concentric circles*) or sit (*opposite each other in rows*).

  » As students receive a peer's paper, they become that paper's (*editor*).

  » The teacher will call out (*the item to the checked by the editor*).

  » The student editors do not make (*marks on the actual paper*).

  » The student editors put their comments on (*an editing page*).

  » Each editor places his or her (*name next to the number*) and writes (*the item to be checked*).

  » When the editing process is completed, (*the students take the editing page and make any corrections*).

  » If there is a problem, (*students discuss it with their teacher or the editor*).

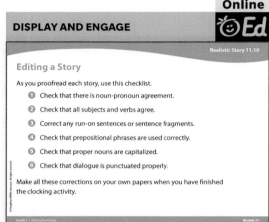

- Show **Display and Engage 11.10** and call out the numbers so students can proofread each other's papers for each of the standard English-language conventions.

Edit Writing

- Have students do a final pass through their realistic stories, integrating the notes from the clocking activity into their own writing.

- Circulate around the room and provide assistance, as needed.

- As you circulate, group students who need support on similar grammar topics. Use the grammar minilessons or the students' own writing to provide targeted review and support.

NARRATIVE • REALISTIC STORY

LEARNING OBJECTIVES

- Create a title.
- Publish writing.
- Use technology to assist with writing.
- **Language** Choose words to create a title.

INSTRUCTIONAL VOCABULARY

- **blog** a diary on a website; weblog
- **attachment** a document that is included with an email

TEACHER TIP

There are several websites where students can publish their work for free. Some allow for the creation of art or the use of previously-created art. There are sites where students can create and share slideshows or make their own comic books. Visit several of these sites before starting the lesson and decide if one or more of them are suitable for your students. Remind students never to give out any personal information.

Prepare the Final Copy

- Have students create a clean final copy of their realistic story using a computer or tablet. Assist students as necessary as they work.

Title the Work

- Remind students that their stories need a title. Explain that the title should not be too long or too short. It should be interesting and catchy so that readers will want to read the story.

- Remind students of the title of the writing model, "The Night of the Candy Apple Disaster." Point out that the title does not tell exactly what happens in the story. Instead, it just refers to something in the story—the candy apple. The word *disaster* in the title signals that something bad will happen. Both the reference and the word create interest and make the reader want to read the story.

- Suggest students make a list of possible titles for their narratives. Encourage students to be imaginative and to use alliteration, rhyme, and figurative language to create interesting titles. Then have them choose the one they like most.

Publish Writing

- Remind students that in *Love, Amalia*, Amalia and her friend Martha talked about keeping in touch by emailing on their computers. At her grandmother's funeral, Amalia's relatives also talked about keeping in touch by using computers.

- Tell students that they will use computers to publish their writing on the Internet.

- Discuss safety issues concerning websites. Point out that students should always work with an adult nearby and should never give out personal information to anyone online.

- Elicit ideas from students for various methods of Internet publication and make a list on the board or chart paper. Bring up the following suggestions if students do not include them: create a class website and publish the stories there; create a class page for an existing school website; post to **blogs** if students have them; email stories as **attachments** to friends and relatives.

- Add the terms *blog* and *attachment* to the Class Instructional Vocabulary List, and have students add them to their glossaries.

- Help students publish their work with their chosen technology.

 ENGLISH LEARNER SUPPORT: Scaffold Writing

SUBSTANTIAL
Ask students to choose a word or phrase from their story that names a key object or event. Use responses as a jumping off point to help them expand into titles.

MODERATE
Have students share ideas with a partner, working together to figure out a word or phrase that represents or describes each other's story.

LIGHT
Tell students to choose a word or phrase from their story that is central to the story. Then tell them to think of words that suggest that something exciting, funny, or strange happens, as appropriate, to include in the title.

LEARNING OBJECTIVES

- Share writing.
- Engage in collaborative discussion.
- **Language** Ask and answer questions using academic language.

MATERIALS	Online

Display and Engage *11.11*

Writer's Notebook *pp. 11.6, 11.13*

INSTRUCTIONAL VOCABULARY

- **graphics** diagrams, graphs, and illustrations
- **audio** a sound recording
- **images** pictures or photographs
- **download** to transfer data from a website to a personal computer
- **upload** to move or transfer data from a computer to a website or another computer

LEARNING MINDSET: Self-Reflection

As students review their goals from the beginning of the module, they will see where they have improved and where they have work to do. Encourage students to celebrate their improvements as well as their mistakes. *Mistakes tell us that we've made progress. Now we know what to work on next and how to improve. And you've got the whole class and me to turn to for help.*

Share Writing

- Have students suggest ways they can use technology to share their realistic stories. For example, they could include multimedia components with their stories, such as **graphics** and **audio**. They might prepare a slideshow and include **images** and other graphics that they **download** from the Internet or **upload** from personal drawings or photographs.

- Use the technology terms and be sure students understand them. You may want to include them on the Class Instructional Vocabulary List and have students note them in their glossaries.

- Ask for volunteers to share their stories.

- Some students may be hesitant to read aloud in front of the class. Allow these students to make an audio recording of their story. Work with them to listen critically to the first reading, find places where they want to improve, and then make a final audio recording. Then they can play the audio recording for the class.

- Encourage listeners to ask the presenter questions about his or her realistic story. Remind students of the rules for listening and asking questions. Encourage the presenter to answer with details from or related to the story.

Engage and Respond

- Review **Display and Engage 11.11**. Have students in small groups take turns using the questions as a springboard for discussions about their writing.

- Have students turn to **Writer's Notebook page 11.6**, the list of goals they set at the beginning of this Writing Workshop. Tell them to revisit the goals. Next, have them Turn and Talk with a partner about how they feel they met their goals and take notes about what goals they might set for the next writing assignment. Then have them fill in their thoughts on **Writer's Notebook page 11.13**.

Online

DISPLAY AND ENGAGE

Realistic Story 11.11

Discussion Ideas

Here are some important questions to consider as you share your published work.

1. What did you like best about writing your realistic story?
2. What did you like least?
3. What did you learn about writing? How did you learn it?
4. What did you learn about grammar? How did you learn it?
5. What did you learn about punctuation? How did you learn it?
6. What ideas or emotions did you want to convey to your reader? Do you think you were successful? Why or why not?
7. What surprised you about your writing?
8. What do you want to remember to do the next time you write a story?

ENGLISH LEARNER SUPPORT: Elicit Participation

ALL LEVELS Before students share their stories with the class, allow them to practice reading their stories aloud to themselves or to a partner. When reading aloud to the class, allow students to read with a partner if they so choose.

Narrative Poem

FOCUS STATEMENT Our words paint the story of our lives.

FOCAL TEXT

Words with Wings

Author: Nikki Grimes

Summary: First-person novel in verse about a young girl named Gabrielle who daydreams as a coping mechanism during her parents' divorce

WRITING PROMPT

READ this sentence: *Our words paint the story of our lives.*

THINK about the story and poetry writing you've done this year. Now you are going to use poetry to tell a story.

WRITE a narrative poem from the first-person perspective. It can be fiction or nonfiction.

· · · · · · · · · · · · · LESSONS · · · · · · · · · · · · ·

1. **Introducing the Focal Text**

2. **The Read**

3. **Vocabulary**

4. **Prewriting: Preparing to Write**

5. **Drafting I: Beginning the Draft**

6. **Drafting II: Integrating Poetry Skills**

7. **Drafting III: Conferencing**

8. **Drafting IV: Completing the Draft**

9. **Revising I: Elaboration**

10. **Revising II: Using Verbs Effectively**

11. **Revising III: Creating Vivid Characters**

12. **Editing I: Grammar, Usage, and Mechanics**

13. **Editing II: Peer Proofreading**

14. **Publishing**

15. **Sharing**

**LEARNING MINDSET:
Resilience**

Display **Anchor Chart 32: My Learning Mindset** throughout the year. Refer to it to introduce Resilience and to reinforce the skills you introduced in previous modules.

POETRY • NARRATIVE POEM

LEARNING OBJECTIVES

- Review what students have already learned about writing poetry.
- Read several narrative poems.
- Discuss how a narrative poem is different from other types of poetry.
- **Language** Discuss features of poetry with academic language.

MATERIALS   Online

Classroom materials *poetry books, images of paintings*

Anchor Chart W11: *Elements of Poetry*

Display and Engage *12.1*

INSTRUCTIONAL VOCABULARY

- **narrative poetry** a form of poetry that tells a story with a beginning, middle, and end
- **figurative language** creative use of words or expressions that mean something different from their dictionary definitions
- **graphic elements** the use of punctuation, shape, line length, and word position to convey a poem's meaning

LEARNING MINDSET: Resilience

Introduce Explain to students that resilience is the ability to keep going even when facing difficulties. *By not giving up when life knocks you down, you show resilience and become stronger.* Tell students that they will read and listen to poems that tell stories of resilience.

Priming the Students

Explore the Topic

- Before students enter the classroom, flood the classroom with examples of **narrative poetry**. Be sure to display narrative poems that include elements such as internal rhyme, free verse, alliteration, **figurative language**, such as onomatopoeia, similes, metaphors, and **graphic elements**. Allow time for students to read the poems on display.

- Tell students that, in this module, they will learn how to write a narrative poem. Explain that narrative poetry tells a story. Say: *Because narrative poetry tells a story, it is often longer than other kinds of poetry. Like other stories, a narrative poem has a beginning, middle, and ending. A narrative poem can rhyme, but it doesn't have to.*

- Display **Anchor Chart W11: Elements of Poetry** and discuss literary techniques poets may use.

- Encourage students to add poetry terms and their definitions to their Instructional Vocabulary glossaries. Also add these terms to your Class Instructional Vocabulary List.

- Explain to students that narrative poets write using the elements of poetry and a narrative story.

Discuss the Focus Statement

- Display a painting that shows action or tells a story. Ask students to use words to describe what they see. Then show **Display and Engage 12.1** and read the Focus Statement with students: *Our words paint the story of our lives.* Explain that, while artists may use paint to tell a story, writers use words. Have students share their thoughts about the Focus Statement.

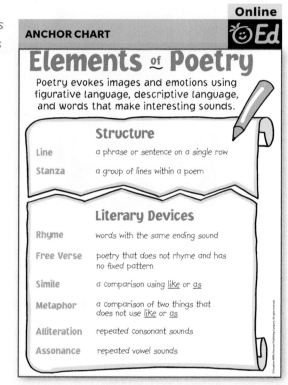

Online

ANCHOR CHART

Elements of Poetry

Poetry evokes images and emotions using figurative language, descriptive language, and words that make interesting sounds.

Structure

| Line | a phrase or sentence on a single row |
| Stanza | a group of lines within a poem |

Literary Devices

Rhyme	words with the same ending sound
Free Verse	poetry that does not rhyme and has no fixed pattern
Simile	a comparison using _like_ or _as_
Metaphor	a comparison of two things that does not use _like_ or _as_
Alliteration	repeated consonant sounds
Assonance	repeated vowel sounds

Online

DISPLAY AND ENGAGE

Narrative Poem 12.1

Focus Statement

Our words paint the story of our lives.

ENGLISH LEARNER SUPPORT: Support Listening

SUBSTANTIAL
Before class begins, select poems that will be accessible for students. Have them draw a picture that shows what happened in the poem.

MODERATE
Have students retell the story that is described in the narrative poem.

LIGHT
Ask students to write a summary of the narrative poem.

LEARNING OBJECTIVES

- Discuss style and characteristics of narrative poetry.
- Read poetry for understanding.
- Discuss meaning of punctuation marks used in poetry.
- **Language** Discuss features of poetry using academic language.

MATERIALS   Online ⒺEd

Focal Text *Words with Wings*

Priming the Text

Prepare to Read

- Show the cover of *Words with Wings* and explain that the book is about a girl who is telling a story. Say: *Gabriella has a problem. In this book of poems, she explains her problem, and, in the end, how she deals with the problem. Each poem is a puzzle piece that when read in order tells how Gabriella works through her problem.*

- Read aloud "Two of a Kind" and have students identify Gabriella's problem: her father no longer lives with her; she and her mother have moved across town.

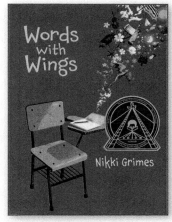

Words with Wings

- Read aloud the poems on pages 3–14. Before reading, review that narrative poetry tells a story, is told in the first person, and can rhyme or not. Also tell them that the poet may use graphic elements, such as laying out the text in a way that helps the reader understand the meaning or feelings within the story.

First Read

- Read each poem aloud. After each poem, ask:

  » *Who is telling the story?*

  » *Who are the characters in this poem?*

  » *Does this poem rhyme?*

Close Read

- Point out to students they may have to read a poem several times to understand it. Turn to pages 3–14 and have them read the poems with you a second time. Ask:

  » *What emotion(s) does Gabriella express?*

  » *How do different characters react to Gabriella?*

  » *How does the layout of the text help her express her feelings?*

- Conclude by discussing the aspects of the narrative poem in *Words with Wings*.

  » *How is narrative poetry different from other poetry?*

  » *Does the poet always use rhyme?*

  » *How does the poet affect the reader by creatively laying out the text?*

After Reading

- Explain that poets want to engage their readers, so they portray their characters in a way that people can understand or relate to.

  THINK ALOUD *When I read about Gabriella and her problems, I felt like I understood what she was feeling. She had difficulty adjusting to a life apart from her father, and she dealt with it by using her imagination and daydreaming. I understand daydreaming because I like to daydream, too. I can see how that would help if you are feeling stressed.*

- Have students record their reactions to Gabriella's poems in their own notebooks.

LEARNING OBJECTIVES

- Recognize graphic elements in poetry.
- Recognize examples of poetic techniques, including figurative language.
- **Language** Discuss features of poetry using academic language.

MATERIALS   Online

Focal Text *Words with Wings*

Anchor Chart W12: *Elements of Figurative Language*

Writer's Notebook *p. 12.1*

 INSTRUCTIONAL VOCABULARY

- **figurative language** creative use of words or expressions that mean something different from their dictionary definitions

TEACHER TIP

Students will best understand figurative language if it is taught as they encounter examples of it. As you select poems to read aloud, choose poems that contain different types of figurative language. As figurative language is encountered, have students discuss the figurative and literal meanings of the words or phrases.

Review the Focal Text

- Review with students pages 3–14 of *Words with Wings*.

- Have students use the Word Bank on **Writer's Notebook page 12.1** or create one in their notebooks. Page through *Words with Wings* and have students identify words and phrases they find interesting or don't understand, such as the following:

braced	dread	color-blind
sway	daydreaming	words have wings
whisper of wind	weird	angry words
		ripping the air

- Discuss the images suggested by some of the words and phrases. Reinforce that these images enable the poet to paint pictures for the reader.

- Display **Anchor Chart W12: Elements of Figurative Language**. Explain that the use of **figurative language** allows a poet to convey feelings and paint vivid pictures. Emphasize that vivid language helps to tell the story as well as create a mood.

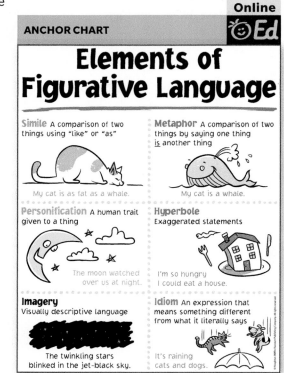

- Read the poem on page 3 and have students identify an example of figurative language.

  THINK ALOUD *When I read "rainbows wrapped round the earth," I imagine the earth being surrounded by rainbows. Rainbows make me happy when I see them, so I think the poet is expressing a world of happiness.*

- Have students locate other examples of figurative language in the poems on pages 4–14, such as *chase away the fear, duck down, words have wings, silent as sunrise, tickle my imagination,* and *buckle up.*

- Point out that a poet can also use graphic elements to help the reader understand the text. Project and read aloud "Sled" on page 28.

  THINK ALOUD *When I read "down down I go," I see the poet going down a hill on a sled because the poet has made the letters of the words look like they are going down a hill. This is an example of using graphic elements to show the action of the poem. It also makes it more fun to read.*

- Ask students to listen as you read pages 15–26 of *Words with Wings*. Elicit from students how the poet uses figurative language to hold the readers' interest and enable them to "see" the story.

- To conclude the lesson, project and read aloud "Canyon" on page 72. Discuss how the poet uses graphic elements to give extra meaning to the poem.

POETRY • NARRATIVE POEM

LEARNING OBJECTIVES

- Demonstrate understanding of poetic terms and techniques.
- Set goals for writing.
- Brainstorm topics for a narrative poem.
- **Language** Discuss writing tasks with academic language.

MATERIALS   Online ⭐Ed

Display and Engage *12.2, 12.3a–12.3b*
Writer's Notebook *pp. 12.2, 12.3*

LEARNING MINDSET: Resilience

Reinforce As students brainstorm poetry topics, have them think about a time when they overcame a problem by being resilient. *When you are resilient, you don't give up. You tackle a problem until you find a solution.* Tell students their poem should feature a challenge or problem they faced with resiliency.

Discuss the Writing Task

- Tell students that in this module they will write a narrative poem. Project **Display and Engage 12.2** and read it aloud. Explain that students will incorporate poetic techniques, graphic elements, and figurative language into their poetry

- Point out that, in many ways, writing narrative poetry is like writing a story.

- Project **Display and Engage 12.3a–12.3b** and read the Writing Prompt aloud. Suggest that students think about the Focus Statement as they consider their topic.

- Distribute **Writer's Notebook page 12.2**. Share the rubric with students and remind them that this tells them what they need to understand and include when writing their narrative poem.

- Brainstorm poetry topics students can explore to tell a story from their life. Ask questions, such as the following:

  » *What problem did you have in the past few years? How did you solve it?*

  » *Has something changed for you recently? How did you deal with this change?*

- Have students use these questions to help them think of and jot down possible topics. Then let students discuss their topics in small groups.

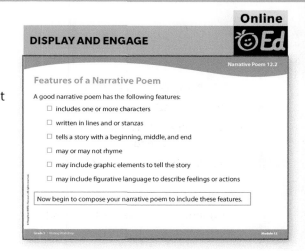

Set Goals for Writing

- Point out that, in writing this kind of poetry, writers must make sure their poem contains all the important elements of a narrative poem. Have students think about and add their personal goals for this assignment to the list on **Writer's Notebook page 12.3** or in their notebooks.

 ENGLISH LEARNER SUPPORT: Planning Support

SUBSTANTIAL
To help students brainstorm, have them draw comic strip boxes showing two or three ideas on paper. Then have them come together and discuss their picture strips and ideas.

MODERATE
To help students brainstorm, provide sentence frames, such as the following: One problem I had was when _____. I solved this problem by _____.

LIGHT
Have students discuss their writing ideas with a partner. Encourage them to listen carefully to any feedback their partners may give them about their topic ideas. Encourage them to consider making changes in their writing based on the value of the feedback.

LEARNING OBJECTIVES

- Commit to a topic.
- Draft poetry with a beginning, a middle, and an end.
- Combine the techniques of poetry with those of a narrative to write a poem.
- **Language** Discuss knowledge and experiences.

MATERIALS   Online

Anchor Chart W4: *Elements of Narrative*
Display and Engage *12.4a-12.4b, 12.3a*
Writer's Notebook *pp. 12.4, 12.5*

📖 **INSTRUCTIONAL VOCABULARY**

- **graphic elements** punctuation, shape, line length, and word position that helps convey a poem's meaning

TEACHER TIP

To encourage using graphic features, consider having students freewrite their poems in a shape that relates to their topic, such as a tree, house, circle, or rectangle.

Learn about Narrative Poetry

- Display **Anchor Chart W4: Elements of Narrative**. Point out that narrative writing has a beginning, a middle, and an end. Note that this kind of writing has a main character who is often the main speaker. Emphasize that this is also true of narrative poetry.

- Explain to students how they can combine elements of the two genres to write a narrative poem.

- Project the model on **Display and Engage 12.4a–12.4b** "Ruffed Grouse in Snow" and have students follow along using **Writer's Notebook page 12.4**. Explain that a ruffed grouse is a large wild bird that lives in the forest. During the snowy months, it doesn't fly south. Instead, it winters in the snow. Read aloud the poem and ask: *What do you notice about the rhymes in this poem?* (*They have an irregular rhyming pattern.*) *What story does this poem tell?* (*A ruffed grouse is disturbed by a passerby and hunters.*)

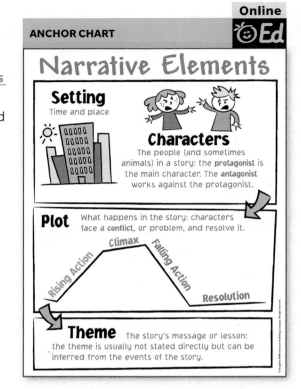

ANCHOR CHART · Online · Ed

Learn about Graphic Elements

- Reread "Ruffed Grouse in Snow."

  THINK ALOUD *This poet arranged the words to stress the grouse's movements. The words are in a downward movement when the bird burrows in the snow.*

- Ask: *How does the spacing of words in lines 5–10 help add to the poem's meaning?* (*symbolizes how deep into the snow the bird is burrowed*) *How do lines 16–20 help show the action of the bird?* (*shows the ascension of the bird into the sky*) Conclude by explaining that these lines are examples of **graphic elements**. Add this term to the Class Instructional Vocabulary List and the student glossaries.

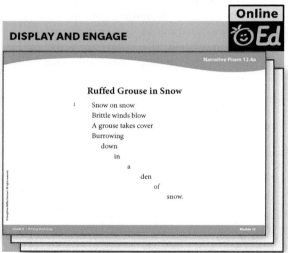

DISPLAY AND ENGAGE · Online · Ed

Begin to Draft

- Project **Display and Engage 12.3a** and review the writing prompt aloud. Remind students that they will be drafting lines for their narrative poem and then selecting from those lines to create a poem.

- Have students use **Writer's Notebook page 12.5** to organize their writing. Have them use the three boxes in the flow chart to show the beginning, middle, and end of their narrative poem.

- Then have students freewrite their narrative poem.

LEARNING OBJECTIVES

- Recognize rhyming words.
- Differentiate rhyming schemes.
- **Language** Discuss rhyming features of poetry using academic language.

MATERIALS   Online

Focal Text *Words with Wings*
Display and Engage *12.3a*
Writer's Notebook *p. 12.5*

INSTRUCTIONAL VOCABULARY

- **rhyme scheme** the pattern of rhymes at the end of the lines in a poem

LEARNING MINDSET: Resilience

Apply Explain to students that sometimes applying what you know can be frustrating. *You have been learning a lot about how to write poetry, and you might be feeling like you will never be able to write skillfully like published poets. Just remember that at one time poets were fifth graders just like you—they all had to start somewhere. However, they kept practicing their writing and didn't give up.* Point out that learning to write poetry is like learning how to kick a ball or sing a song. Being patient about progress, rather than giving up, will keep a person moving forward.

Learn about Poetic Techniques

- Review the writing prompt on **Display and Engage 12.3a** as well as the writing task. Tell students that today's lesson will be about how writers use a **rhyme scheme** in poetry. Add the term *rhyme scheme* to the Class Instructional Vocabulary List, and direct students to add it to their glossaries.

- Read aloud "Correction" from page 43 of *Words with Wings*. Write the last four lines on the board:

> Mr. Spicer sighs
>
> and waves me away.
>
> Good. I've got
>
> nothing else to say.

- Read the poem again, emphasizing the rhyming words in the last four lines. Ask: *Do all lines in the poem rhyme?* (*no*) *What words rhyme?* (*away, say*) *Where do we find these rhyming words?* (*at the end of lines 2 and 4*) Point out to students that this rhyming scheme is ABCB.

- Use a Think Aloud to explain the concept of rhyme scheme.
  THINK ALOUD *When a poet ends lines in a verse with a rhyming word, we assign the letters to each line to describe the rhyming pattern. Any line that ends with a rhyming word is assigned the same letter as the line with a matching rhyming word. For example in the four lines from "Correction," the first line is assigned with the letter A. The second line is B. The third line is assigned the letter C. The end of the fourth line rhymes with the end of the second line, so it is assigned B as well.*

Continue to Draft

- Have students use **Writer's Notebook page 12.5** to guide their writing. As students write, circulate among them to offer assistance when needed.

- If there is time, ask for volunteers to read aloud a stanza from their poem and identify the rhyme scheme.

ENGLISH LEARNER SUPPORT: Build Vocabulary

ALL LEVELS Point out that many rhyming words have similar spellings, as in *snow* and *know*. However, point out that some English words can rhyme but have different spelling patterns. Have them find another word that rhymes with *snow* and *know*, such as *though*. Underline the letters that represent the long-*o* sound. Then have students brainstorm a list of long-*o* words that rhyme, such as *toe/grow/go/although/sew/goat/note*. Write their responses on the board, emphasizing that the rhyming sounds are represented by different spelling patterns.

INSTRUCTIONAL VOCABULARY

- **conferencing** getting together to discuss a topic
- **organizational structure** the way a writer puts together ideas about a topic

Conferencing

- Discuss with students how **conferencing** can be helpful when figuring out how to improve their drafts.

- Ask students to review their drafts and jot down notes about what they want to discuss during a conference.

- Specifically ask students to review their **organizational structure**, making sure their poem has a beginning, a middle, and an end.

- Encourage students to voice their questions and concerns. Allow other students to chime in if they have the same questions.

- Pair students and ask them to share their drafts with one another. Then have students read aloud their troublesome sections. Encourage their peers to respond with constructive suggestions.

- Instruct students to jot down ideas from their discussions in the margins of their draft.

- Write the terms *conferencing* and *organizational structure* on the Class Instructional Vocabulary List and have students add it to their glossaries.

Continue Drafting

- Project **Display and Engage 12.3a** to remind students of the writing prompt.

- Have students use their feedback to continue writing and revising their drafts. As students write, circulate among them to offer any needed assistance.

 ENGLISH LEARNER SUPPORT: Facilitate Discussion

SUBSTANTIAL

Provide sentence frames for students to express their concerns, such as the following: *I wonder if I _____* or *I need help understanding _____*.

MODERATE

Pair students and have them read their drafts one line at a time to each other. Encourage students to discuss each line and bring out any concerns.

LIGHT

Challenge students to work in pairs to discuss their questions and concerns. As necessary, monitor and interact in their discussions.

TEACHER TIP

Before students begin participating in conferencing, remind them that their remarks should be positive and encouraging.

DRAFTING IV: COMPLETING THE DRAFT

LEARNING OBJECTIVES

- Add a conclusion to a draft.
- Finish draft of a narrative poem.
- **Language** Discuss conclusions using academic language.

MATERIALS   Online

Display and Engage *12.3a, 12.4c–12.4d*

Writer's Notebook *pp. 12.6, 12.7*

 **INSTRUCTIONAL VOCABULARY**

- **conclusion** the ending of a story or writing that wraps up everything or tells the big point

TEACHER TIP

Point out that a conclusion can be a sentence, a verse, or even one word that signals that the story has ended.

Adding a Conclusion

- Project **Display and Engage 12.3a** and review the writing prompt. Remind students that they have been drafting lines of poetry for their narrative poems. Preview the lesson by saying that today they will build a poem from those lines.

- Project and read aloud only the first three verses of "My Stuff, His Stuff" on **Display and Engage 12.4c–12.4d**.

THINK ALOUD

1. *In this example poem, the writer wrote a narrative poem with a beginning, a middle, and an end. In the first verse, the problem is revealed.*

2. *In the second verse, details or examples of what is happening in the middle of the story are provided.*

3. *The third verse contains information about what solution is planned to solve the problem. What this poem is missing is a conclusion. A conclusion wraps everything up and tells the main point of the poem.*

- Have students turn to **Writer's Notebook page 12.7** and follow along as you reveal the last stanza of the poem and highlight the last two lines of the poem, reading the stanza aloud.

  THINK ALOUD *This stanza tells the lesson that the brother learns. The last two lines state the point, or **conclusion**, of the poem: two people can respect one another's stuff.*

- Invite students to share the points they would like to use to conclude their poems. Encourage them to incorporate them into a final stanza of poetry.

Choosing a Conclusion

- Distribute **Writer's Notebook page 12.6**. Have students use the page to establish the main point of their poem and try out ways to end the poem.

- Then have students choose one conclusion for their poem.

- Consider grouping students to help one another brainstorm ideas for their conclusions and allow for peer insights and encouragement.

EL ENGLISH LEARNER SUPPORT: Writing Conclusions

SUBSTANTIAL
Have students write their conclusions in prose first. Then work with students to help them turn their conclusions into lines of poetry.

MODERATE
Allow students to work in pairs to develop concluding ideas for their poetry. Tell them to help each other choose the best concluding idea. Allow students to use peer advice and feedback, as well as your help, to create their final lines of poetry.

LIGHT
Challenge students to work in pairs to discuss possibilities for their conclusions. Make suggestions as needed. Then have them work on their own to turn their conclusions into poetry.

LEARNING OBJECTIVES

- Use feedback from peers to clarify a poem's meaning and enhance its style.
- Add elaboration to drafts.
- Add poetic details to drafts.
- **Language** Discuss writing tasks using academic language.

MATERIALS   Online

Anchor Chart W12: *Elements of Figurative Language*

Display and Engage *12.5a–12.5c*

 INSTRUCTIONAL VOCABULARY

- **elaboration** the act of adding more detail

TEACHER TIP

Post samples of similes and metaphors to stimulate thinking so that students can get into the groove of creating their own figurative language.

Introduce Elaboration

- Explain that today students will be revising their poems. They will elaborate on what they have already written by adding figurative language, graphic elements, and poetic language. Write the term **elaboration**, the act of adding more detail, on the Class Instructional Vocabulary List and have students add it to their glossaries.

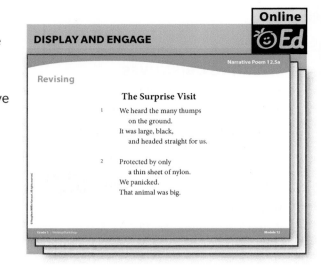

- Show **Display and Engage 12.5a–12.5c**. Read the poem aloud. Use a Think Aloud to model revision.

THINK ALOUD

1. *This narrative poem tells a story about a bear who scared two campers. It's fun to read, but elaboration can make it better.*

2. *In the third line, the poem says "many thumps." To elaborate, the writer could take out "many thumps" and add more words. Plus, repeating the word* thump *would make that idea stand out. So, a good revision would be: "We heard the thump, thump, thump."*

3. *Next, the poem could include more poetic language. In the second stanza, the poet describes the tent as being a thin sheet of nylon. To enhance the danger, a good revision would be "as flimsy as butterfly wings."*

4. *In the second stanza, the poet describes the bear as big. Adding the descriptive word "beastly" will help paint an image of a huge beast.*

5. *There's another way to make the phrase "beastly big" stand out. A good revision would be to make the words bigger and bolder.*

Revise by Elaborating

- Tell students it's time to share their poems with their classmates. Divide students into groups of five. Have each student read his or her poem as the group listens. After the first reading, pass the poem around the group to show any graphic elements that have been used.

- Encourage students to use the group's feedback to revise their poem by elaborating on what they have already written.

- Review **Anchor Chart W12: Elements of Figurative Language** and remind students to use it to help with elaboration.

LEARNING OBJECTIVES
- Revise drafts using vivid verbs.
- Give and receive peer feedback.
- Discuss revision suggestions using academic language.
- **Language** Discuss features of poetry using academic language.

MATERIALS   Online

Display and Engage *12.5a–12.5e*

Classroom materials *dictionary, thesaurus (online or print)*

 LEARNING MINDSET:
Resilience

Review Tell students that ongoing revising requires resilience, or keeping your mind positive and open to realize that changes are necessary during a revision. *Sometimes I think, "Oh, my poem is good enough as it is. I'm tired of making all these changes!" What I need to remember is that revising makes my poem better. For example, yesterday I improved my poem by adding similes and metaphors. Resilience teaches me that sticking with the process will only make me a better writer.*

TARGETED GRAMMAR SUPPORT

You may want to consult the following grammar minilesson to review a key revising topic.
- **3.1.4 Review Verbs,** p. W251

Revising Verbs
- Point out that poems rely on vivid language to help paint a detailed picture for the reader or listener.

- Show **Display and Engage 12.5d** and read aloud the revised sections of the poem "The Surprise Visit." Remind students that this poem was revised to add elaboration. Explain that today you will show how it can be revised again to add vivid verbs.

- You may wish to have students view the original poem to identify each verb and tell whether they think it is vivid or weak. Write their choices in a T-chart on the board under the headings "Weak" and "Vivid." (*Possible responses: **Weak:** hit, ran, fell, found, put; **Vivid:** protected, tearing, unzipped, scrambled, locking, ruled*)

- Use this Think Aloud and the original poem to show how to revise a poem to include vivid verbs.

THINK ALOUD

1. *Consider the word* hit *in the fourth stanza. If I look at my thesaurus, it says that the words* punched, hammered, *and* zapped *are all words that mean almost the same as* hit. *Since Dad is using a flashlight to surprise the bear with the light, a good revision would be to choose a word that is more interesting and doesn't mean "to touch." How about the word* zapped?

2. *In the fifth stanza, the verb* fell *is weak. Can anyone think of a more vivid verb?* (*Possibilities:* stumbled, collapsed, tumbled) *I'll choose the word* stumbled.

3. *Now let's focus on the word* ran *in the last stanza. Think about how mice run around. A word that would make this image more vivid is* scurried.

- After the Think Aloud, show **Display and Engage 12.5e** and read through two of the stanzas that were revised to include vivid verbs. You may wish to allow students to suggest other verb replacements.

Continue to Revise
- Make sure students have access to a thesaurus. Have students continue to identify overused, weak verbs in their writing and replace them with specific, vivid ones.

 ENGLISH LEARNER SUPPORT: Identifying Vivid Words

SUBSTANTIAL
Working in pairs, give students a short list of vague, weak verbs, such as *run, walk, cry,* and *talk.* Using a thesaurus, have students look up the verbs and make a list of synonyms that are more vivid and interesting.

MODERATE
Have students work in pairs to locate weak and vivid verbs in their writing. Monitor students to make sure they are able to determine which verbs are weak and which are vivid.

LIGHT
Have students find and list weak verbs on their own. Then pair students to compile a list of replacement words that are vivid verbs. Allow students to use a thesaurus if necessary.

DISPLAY AND ENGAGE   Online

Revising   Narrative Poem 12.5d

The Surprise Visit (Revision #1)

1   We heard the thump, thump, thump
        on the ground.
     It was large, black,
        and headed straight for us.

2   Protected by only
        a thin sheet of nylon,
     as flimsy as butterfly wings,
        we panicked.
     That animal was **beastly big.**

LEARNING OBJECTIVES
- Create characters with "life."
- Revise character descriptions as needed.
- **Language** Discuss character development using academic language.

TEACHER TIP
Some students may have difficulty describing the characters in the poem. Remind them that they can think about their characters and list their traits, using a word web filled with adjectives.

TARGETED GRAMMAR SUPPORT

You may want to consult the following grammar minilessons to review key revising topics.
- **4.1.1 Adjectives,** p. W278
- **4.2.3 Using Adverbs,** p. W285

Bringing Characters to Life

- Review with students that writers deepen a reader's understanding of characters by developing a character's physical description, actions, and words.
- Write the following line on the board:

> Her hair was red.

- Ask students if this description paints a vivid picture of the girl. Suggest that the poet could add an adjective, such as *fiery* ("fiery red") or rewrite the line to include figurative language, such as "Her hair was a flickering red flame." Write this revision on the on the board.

- Next, focus on how a character's actions can reveal information about the character. Write the following example on the board:

> The little boy cried.

- Have students suggest ways to make the character's actions more vivid. Write a sample revision on the board: "The little boy shrieked with gusto." Ask: *What does this action reveal about the little boy?* (*He is very dramatic when he cries.*)

- Finally, point out that a character's words can also help readers better understand the character. Write the following example on the board:

> The knight offered to help.

- Have students suggest dialogue that would better reveal the knight's character. Write a sample revision on the board: "As usual, I will save the day!" Ask: *What does the dialogue reveal about the knight?* (*He is vain and likes to brag.*)

Revise for Characterization

- Have students work independently to add details to strengthen their character descriptions.

(EL) ENGLISH LEARNER SUPPORT: Description Support

SUBSTANTIAL
Work with students individually. Depending on the poem's topic, ask yes and no questions about the characters, such as: *Is he brave? Is he silly? Is she loyal? Is she shy?* Then have them add these words to the poem.

MODERATE
Have students work in pairs. Have them take turns reading their poems and then describing the characters. Last, have them work together to add these descriptions to their poems.

LIGHT
Have students work in small groups and discuss the meaning of their poems, focusing on character development. Allow students to make changes or add details to their characters based on their conversations with their peers.

LEARNING OBJECTIVES

- Distinguish between action and existence verbs.
- Revise drafts based on action and existence verbs.
- Edit drafts for proper grammar, usage, and mechanics.
- **Language** Edit writing by replacing verbs.

MATERIALS   Online

Display and Engage *12.6a–12.6b*
Anchor Chart W15: *Editing Checklist*

 INSTRUCTIONAL VOCABULARY

- **existence verbs** "to be" verbs that show someone or something exists Examples of existence verbs are *am, is, are, was, were, be, being,* and *been*.

TARGETED GRAMMAR SUPPORT

You may want to consult the following grammar minilessons to review key editing topics.

- **3.1.4 Review Verbs,** p. W251

Identify and Replace Existence Verbs

- Students will begin by proofreading and revising their own poems.
- Point out that, in proofreading their poetry, students are looking for ways to correct their grammar, usage, and mechanics. Explain that proofreading today will focus on replacing **existence verbs** with action verbs.

DISPLAY AND ENGAGE Online Ed

Narrative Poem 12.6a

Editing: Replacing "To Be" Verbs

Original Poem

What Can I Do?
Jackson is a quick sprinter.
He is much faster than I,
Oh yes, it is true.
I am like a slow turtle,
So what can I do?

- Make sure students understand the difference between these two types of verbs. Remind students that existence verbs are "to be" verbs that show someone or something exists. Examples of existence verbs are *am, is, are, was, were, be, being,* and *been*. Have students add the term and examples to their glossaries, while you add them to the Class Instructional Vocabulary List.

- Project **Display and Engage 12.6a–12.6b** and read the first poem "What Can I Do? aloud. Then read the revised version aloud and compare it to the original one at the top. Point out the revisions in lines 1, 2, and 4. Then ask:

  » How is this poem different from the first one? (*It contains more action verbs and fewer existence verbs.*)

  » Which poem do you prefer? Why?

Edit Writing

- Display **Anchor Chart W15: Editing Checklist** and review the items on it.

- Tell students that, using ratiocination, they will review their poems to make sure they use action verbs whenever possible. Tell them they should also use the Editing Checklist to edit their poems for proper usage of grammar, punctuation, and spelling.

- Remind students to review their poems for one correction at a time.

- Circulate the room and provide assistance as needed. You may wish to confer with students individually to guide them on the finer points of grammar and punctuation.

ANCHOR CHART Online Ed

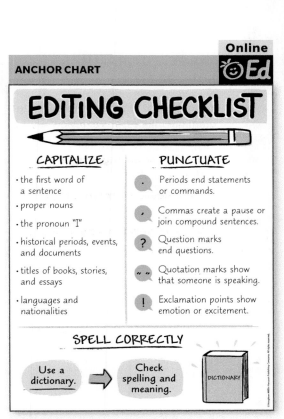

EDITING CHECKLIST

CAPITALIZE
- the first word of a sentence
- proper nouns
- the pronoun "I"
- historical periods, events, and documents
- titles of books, stories, and essays
- languages and nationalities

PUNCTUATE
- Periods end statements or commands.
- Commas create a pause or join compound sentences.
- Question marks end questions.
- Quotation marks show that someone is speaking.
- Exclamation points show emotion or excitement.

SPELL CORRECTLY
Use a dictionary. → Check spelling and meaning. DICTIONARY

LEARNING OBJECTIVES

- **Language** Proofread writing for mechanics.

MATERIALS	Online

Display and Engage *12.7*

Writer's Notebook *p. 12.8*

TEACHER TIP

Editing poetry can be difficult when poets use non-standard language or mechanics to make a point or to create a style. Explain that poets do not have to conform to standard punctuation, spelling, and capitalization when they add to the poem's meaning or style.

TARGETED GRAMMAR SUPPORT

You may want to consult the following grammar minilessons to review key editing topics.

- **2.1.2 Capitalizing Proper Nouns,** p. W219
- **7.4.4 Review Punctuation,** p. W341
- **8.1.4 Review Spelling,** p. W346

Clocking Activity

- Show <u>Display and Engage 12.7</u> and tell students they will be editing their classmates' poems. Point out that they will focus on punctuation, spelling, and capitalization. Remind students that sometimes poets choose to disregard some writing rules, such as punctuation and capitalization, giving special meaning or style to their poems.

- Tell students that, if an idea, phrase, or word is confusing to them, they need to point it out to the poet. Remind students that the purpose of using proper punctuation and spelling, even in poetry, is to help readers understand what the writer is trying to say. As needed, provide additional review of any specific grammar topics.

- Using <u>Writer's Notebook page 12.8</u>, tell each poet to write his or her name.

- Have students form concentric circles or sit opposite each other in rows. Poets exchange their latest edited poems along with <u>Writer's Notebook page 12.8</u>.

- No marks are made on the actual poem. Each editor writes his or her name next to the item to be checked (1, 2, 3, 4, or 5) and makes comments on each editing task.

- Call out which item is to be checked by the editor: (1) capitalization; (2) punctuation; (3) spelling; (4) unclear or vague words; and (5) other comments.

- After editors complete the first editing task, have students collect their poems and move to the next editor. Repeat the process until the entire editing page has been completed.

Incorporate Suggestions

- When all poems have been proofread, poets will take the comment sheets and make changes as needed.

- Remind poets that they are in charge of deciding which changes should be made to their poems.

- Explain that in Lesson 14 they will publish a final copy of their poems on a computer.

Online

DISPLAY AND ENGAGE

Narrative Poem 12.7

Editing

1. Capitalization of proper nouns and the first word in each line
2. Correct use of punctuation within and at the end of lines
3. Correct spelling
4. Unclear or vague words
5. Other comments

Grade 5 | Writing Workshop   Module 12

(EL) ENGLISH LEARNER SUPPORT: Proofreading Support

SUBSTANTIAL
On the first pairing, model for students how to check each item in the poem. Show them how to mark the suggestions on the editing page.

MODERATE
As students pair up for each item, have both students work together to edit the poems.

LIGHT
As students work in pairs to proofread their poems, monitor their ability to give good feedback and amend comments as necessary.

LEARNING OBJECTIVES

- Create a title for a narrative poem.
- Publish final copy on computer software.
- Explore publishing options.
- **Language** Discuss the publishing process using academic vocabulary.

MATERIALS   Online

Display and Engage 12.4c–12.4d
Focal Text *Words with Wings*

TEACHER TIP

As students type their poems on the computer, remind them that spelling software will sometimes correct the spelling of a word that does not need to be corrected. Also, it does not always find correctly spelled words that are misused, such as *pear/pair; their/there; were/we're; sore/ soar.*

LEARNING MINDSET: Resilience

Resilience Point out to students that they have persisted in overcoming difficulties while writing, drafting, editing, and proofreading their work. Explain that now they can enjoy the successful end result of their resilience. *Congratulations on finishing your poems! You have just written a narrative poem, which was in no way an easy task.* Ask students how they might demonstrate resilience in other areas of their lives.

Write a Title

- Explain that a title can grab readers in a way that will entice them to want to read your poem. Tell students that they can state the main idea, provoke an emotion, or name the subject in their title.

- Read aloud "Wishful Thinking" on page 36 of *Words with Wings*. Ask: *Why do you think Gabriella picked this title for the poem?* (*Her mom was wishfully hoping Gabriella would be more like her and less like her dad.*)

- Revisit **Display and Engage 12.4c–12.4d** and read the poem aloud. Then lead students in a Think Aloud.

  THINK ALOUD *The poet who wrote this poem chose a title that summed up the main idea of the poem. Therefore, the poet titled it "My Stuff, His Stuff." Think about the poem. What other title could have the poet used? I can think of other titles like "The Threat," "My Pesky Brother," "The Truce."*

- Because students have been working on their poems for some time, they may already have titles in mind. Allow time for students to formulate or revise their titles.

Prepare the Final Copy

- Have students type the final copy of their narrative poems on the computer. Permit last-minute changes in fonts or type size to enhance their poems through graphic elements.

- Tell students that the content of their poem may help them decide how to present it. Provide a few suggestions for presenting a poem.

  a. Make a drawing to illustrate the poem.

  b. Create a collage of images to illustrate the ideas in the poem. Images could come from magazines or online resources.

  c. Produce a video of themselves reading the poem while students act out the events.

  e. Record their poems, using background music of their choice as they read the poem aloud.

Publish Writing

- Have students TURN AND TALK with a partner to explore publication options before selecting one.

- Have students work on the final copy for the remainder of time.

LEARNING OBJECTIVES

- Share writing.
- Participate in a collaborative discussion about writing.
- **Language** Use academic language to engage in a discussion about writing.

MATERIALS   Online

Anchor Chart W17: *Tips on How to Present*

Writer's Notebook pp. 12.3, 12.9

TEACHER TIP

Make this session festive. Consider playing music between presentations and serving snacks, such as fruit or popcorn, while students enjoy the presentations.

Share Writing

- Share **Anchor Chart W17: Tips on How to Present**. Discuss the tips for presenting writing.

- Have students share their poems by reading them aloud and presenting any drawings or collages as well. Allow students who made videos or recordings to share them. Encourage students to applaud after each presentation.

- After each poetry presentation, encourage students to ask the poets questions about their work. Allow each poet to share insights into the writing process that he or she gleaned from writing narrative poetry.

ANCHOR CHART — Online Ed

Tips on How to Present

Express the Main Idea Make sure the point of the presentation is clear.	
Look at the Audience Eye contact brings people into your presentation.	
Speak Clearly and Loudly Make sure people can hear and understand you.	
Use Natural Body Language Smile and use your hands when you talk.	
Avoid Informal Language and Slang Speak more formally than you would to friends.	slang

Engage and Respond

- Conclude with a discussion about producing a narrative poem. Discussion questions can include:

  » What did you like best about writing your narrative poem?

  » What did you like least?

  » What did you learn about writing? How did you learn it?

  » What did you learn about existence and action verbs? How did you learn it?

  » What did you learn about the importance of punctuation in poetry?

  » How did you publish your narrative? Describe the process.

  » What do you want to remember to do the next time you write a narrative poem?

- Have students turn to **Writer's Notebook page 12.3** to revisit the goals they set at the beginning of this module. Have them TURN AND TALK with a partner about how they feel they met their goals and take notes about what goals they might set for their next writing assignment. Then ask students to use **Writer's Notebook page 12.9** to write down their reflections about their goals.

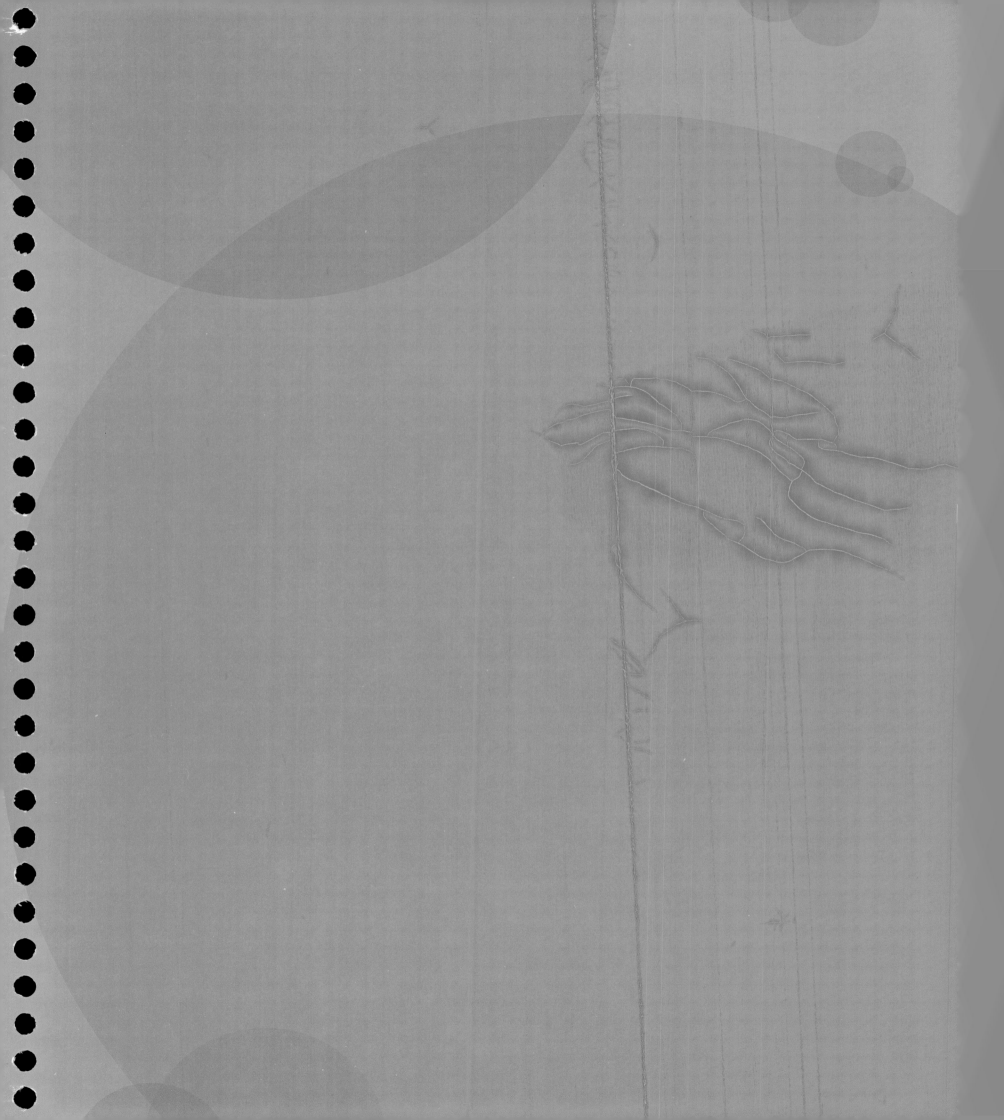

Grammar Minilessons

GRAMMAR MINILESSONS • TOPICS AND SKILLS

Customize your grammar instruction to your classroom needs. These minilessons can be

- **INTEGRATED** Support the grammar instruction in the Writing Workshop revising and editing lessons.
- **DIFFERENTIATED** Deliver based on needs demonstrated in each student's writing.
- **SYSTEMATIC** Teach according to scope and sequence indicated in the weekly planners.

TOPIC 1 — SENTENCES

TOPIC 2 — NOUNS, PRONOUNS, AND OBJECTS

GRAMMAR MINILESSONS • TOPICS AND SKILLS

GRAMMAR MINILESSONS • TOPICS AND SKILLS

LEARNING OBJECTIVES

- **Language** Identify the subject and predicate in a sentence.
- **Language** Use complete sentences correctly in speaking and writing.

MATERIALS   Online

Display and Engage *Grammar 1.1.1a, 1.1.1b*

Printable *Grammar 1.1.1*

 INSTRUCTIONAL VOCABULARY

- **sentence** a group of words expressing a complete thought
- **simple subject** the main word that tells whom or what the sentence is about
- **simple predicate** the main word that tells what the subject is or does

Connect and Teach

- Show **Display and Engage: Grammar 1.1.1a**. Explain that a **sentence** is a group of words that expresses a complete thought. Every sentence needs two parts in order to be complete: a subject and a predicate. The **subject** names the person or thing the sentence is about. The **predicate** tells what the subject is or does.

- Model identifying the simple subject and simple predicate with this sentence: *The students learned about gases on planets.*

  THINK ALOUD *To identify the subject and the predicate, I ask* What word tells whom or what the sentence is about? What word tells what the subject is or does? *The sentence is about the students.* Learned *is the predicate because it tells what the students did.*

Engage and Apply

- Complete items 1–6 on **Display and Engage: Grammar 1.1.1b** with students.

- Have students take turns using each subject and each predicate in new sentences.

- Have students complete **Printable: Grammar 1.1.1** for practice with complete sentences.

- Have students edit a writing draft to change sentence fragments into complete sentences.

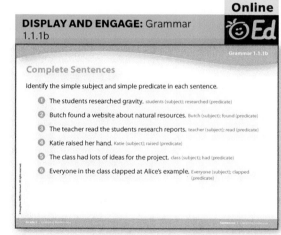

 ENGLISH LEARNER SUPPORT: Facilitate Language Connection

Sentence punctuation may vary from language to language. Students with literacy skills in Cantonese may need practice in starting proper nouns and sentences with a capital letter, since these conventions exist only in alphabetic systems.

Scaffolded Practice

SUBSTANTIAL

Write: *The students study science.* Use sentence frames to help students orally demonstrate how to isolate the subject from the predicate. _____*study science. The students; The students* _____. *study science*

MODERATE

Have students create new sentences using the sentence frames. They should supply new subjects or predicates.

LIGHT

Have students create sentences about the day's activities. Provide them with sentence frames such as *The class* _____. *or* _____ *wrote narrative paragraphs.*

SENTENCES • COMPLETE SENTENCES

LEARNING OBJECTIVES

- **Language** Identify fragments, run-ons, and comma splices.
- **Language** Use complete sentences correctly in speaking and writing.

MATERIALS   Online 🍊 Ed

Display and Engage *Grammar 1.1.2a, 1.1.2b*

Printable *Grammar 1.1.2*

 INSTRUCTIONAL VOCABULARY

- **sentence** a group of words expressing a complete thought
- **fragment** a group of words that does not express a complete thought; not a sentence
- **run-on sentence** two sentences that run into each other
- **comma splice** two complete sentences that are joined by a comma but missing a coordinating conjunction

Connect and Teach

- Show <u>Display and Engage: Grammar 1.1.2a</u>. Remind students that a **sentence** is a group of words that expresses a complete thought. Tell them that a **fragment** is a group of words that does not express a complete thought. A **run-on sentence** is two sentences that run into each other. A **comma splice** is two sentences joined by a comma without a conjunction.

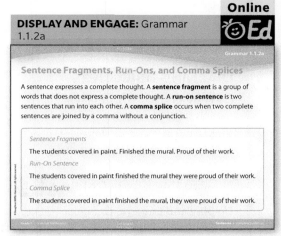

DISPLAY AND ENGAGE: Grammar 1.1.2a — Online 🍊 Ed

Sentence Fragments, Run-Ons, and Comma Splices

A sentence expresses a complete thought. A **sentence fragment** is a group of words that does not express a complete thought. A **run-on sentence** is two sentences that run into each other. A **comma splice** occurs when two complete sentences are joined by a comma without a conjunction.

Sentence Fragments
The students covered in paint. Finished the mural. Proud of their work.
Run-On Sentence
The students covered in paint finished the mural they were proud of their work.
Comma Splice
The students covered in paint finished the mural, they were proud of their work.

- Model identifying fragments with the example: *The art students covered in paint.* Review the examples of run-ons and comma splices as well.

  THINK ALOUD *To identify a fragment, I ask* Does this group of words tell whom or what and also what is or what happens? *This group of words tells who (students), but it does not tell what happens. This group of words is a fragment.*

- Repeat modeling for run-ons and comma splices with these examples:
  Lisa jumped in the lake she was very cold. Corrected: *Lisa jumped in the lake. She was very cold!*
  We went to the store, we bought fruit. Corrected: *We went to the store, and we bought fruit.*

Engage and Apply

- Complete items 1–6 on <u>Display and Engage: Grammar 1.1.2b</u> with students.

- Have students complete <u>Printable: Grammar 1.1.2</u> for practice with sentence fragments.

- Have students edit a writing draft to change sentence fragments, run-ons, or comma splices into complete sentences.

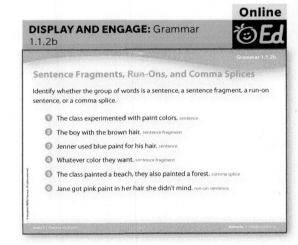

DISPLAY AND ENGAGE: Grammar 1.1.2b — Online 🍊 Ed

Sentence Fragments, Run-Ons, and Comma Splices

Identify whether the group of words is a sentence, a sentence fragment, a run-on sentence, or a comma splice.

1. The class experimented with paint colors. sentence
2. The boy with the brown hair. sentence fragment
3. Jenner used blue paint for his hair. sentence
4. Whatever color they want. sentence fragment
5. The class painted a beach, they also painted a forest. comma splice
6. Jane got pink paint in her hair she didn't mind. run-on sentence

 ENGLISH LEARNER SUPPORT: Scaffolded Practice

ALL LEVELS Explain the terms *simple and complete subject, simple and complete predicate,* and *sentence fragment.* Point out that a sentence fragment (the Spanish *frase*) is a group of words that is not a complete sentence. It does not have both a subject and a predicate, and it does not tell a complete thought. Work with students to distinguish between a complete sentence and a sentence fragment. Point to examples: *The boy in the yard (sentence fragment); The man has a package for the teacher. (complete sentence); Asked the teacher (sentence fragment)* Ask *Is this a complete sentence? Why? Why not?* Model identifying the simple subject and the simple predicate of sentences such as *The students learned about gravity in science class.* Students may respond by pointing or using phrases or sentences.

SENTENCES • COMPLETE SENTENCES

LEARNING OBJECTIVES
- **Language** Identify complete sentences.
- **Language** Use complete sentences correctly in speaking and writing.

MATERIALS	Online

Display and Engage *Grammar 1.1.3a, 1.1.3b*

Printable *Grammar 1.1.3*

 INSTRUCTIONAL VOCABULARY

- **sentence** a group of words expressing a complete thought
- **fragment** a group of words that does not express a complete thought; not a sentence

Connect and Teach

- Show **Display and Engage: Grammar 1.1.3a**. Have students explain the difference between a complete **sentence** and a **fragment**.

- Use the example sentences to model determining which is a fragment and which is a complete sentence: *The soft kittens. The soft kittens slept on a warm blanket.*

  THINK ALOUD *To tell which is a fragment and which is a complete sentence, I ask Does each group of words tell whom or what the sentence is about? Does it tell what is or what happens? The first group of words just tells me who (the soft kittens), so it's a fragment. But the second group of words tells me who (the soft kittens), as well as what they did (slept on a warm blanket). So, the second group of words is a complete sentence.*

- Continue modeling run-on sentences and comma splices using these examples:
  Dad is making roasted vegetables they are my favorite. Corrected: *Dad is making roasted vegetables. They are my favorite.*
  We eat dinner early on Saturdays, then we watch a movie. Corrected: *We eat dinner early on Saturdays, and then we watch a movie.*

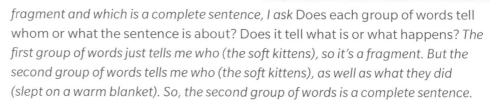

DISPLAY AND ENGAGE: Grammar 1.1.3a — Online Ed

Writing Sentences

A **complete sentence** has a subject and a predicate. The subject tells whom or what the sentence is about. The predicate tells what the subject is or does. The complete sentence expresses a complete thought.

Sentence Fragment
The eager students.

Complete Sentence
The eager students planned a trip to the science museum.

Engage and Apply

- Complete items 1–6 on **Display and Engage: Grammar 1.1.3b** with students.

- Have students work with partners to write sentence frames in which either the subject or the predicate is missing. Have them exchange sentences with another pair to be completed.

- Have students complete **Printable: Grammar 1.1.3** for practice with writing sentences.

- Have students edit a writing draft to be sure every sentence is a complete sentence.

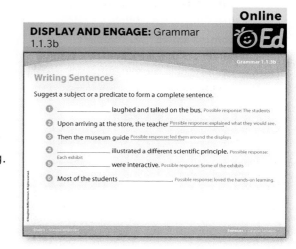

DISPLAY AND ENGAGE: Grammar 1.1.3b — Online Ed

Writing Sentences

Suggest a subject or a predicate to form a complete sentence.

1. _____ laughed and talked on the bus. Possible response: The students
2. Upon arriving at the store, the teacher _____ Possible response: explained what they would see.
3. Then the museum guide _____ Possible response: led them around the displays
4. Each exhibit _____ illustrated a different scientific principle. Possible response:
5. _____ were interactive. Possible response: Some of the exhibits
6. Most of the students _____ Possible response: loved the hands-on learning.

 ENGLISH LEARNER SUPPORT: Scaffolded Practice

ALL LEVELS In Spanish, subject pronouns are usually dropped in everyday speech since the verb can convey their meanings. When speaking and writing, guide students to include subject pronouns. Have them identify or name the subject in their sentences. Then have them identify the predicate.

LEARNING OBJECTIVES

- **Language** Review complete sentences, fragments, run-ons, and comma splices.
- **Language** Use complete sentences correctly in speaking and writing.

MATERIALS   Online

Display and Engage *Grammar 1.1.4a, 1.1.4b, 1.1.4c*

Printable *Grammar 1.1.4*

 INSTRUCTIONAL VOCABULARY

- **sentence** a group of words expressing a complete thought
- **fragment** a group of words that does not express a complete thought; not a sentence
- **run-on sentence** two sentences that run into each other
- **comma splice** two complete sentences that are joined by a comma but missing a coordinating conjunction
- **simple subject** the main word that tells whom or what the sentence is about
- **simple predicate** the main word that tells what the subject is or does

Review Complete Sentences

- Show **Display and Engage: Grammar 1.1.4a** and **Grammar 1.1.4b**. Have students explain the parts of a **sentence** and how to identify **fragments**, **run-ons**, and **comma splices**. Then show **Display and Engage: Grammar 1.1.4c** and work with students to complete the exercises.

DISPLAY AND ENGAGE: Grammar 1.1.4a, 1.1.4b, and 1.1.4c

Online
Ed

Review Complete Sentences

A **sentence** is a group of words that expresses a complete thought. To be complete, a sentence must have both a subject and a predicate. The **simple subject** is the word or words that name the person or thing the sentence is about. The **simple predicate** is the main word or words that tell what the subject is or does.

> simple subject   simple predicate
> The bus drove up to the theater.

> simple subject   simple predicate
> The rock star walked off the bus.

- Write the sentences on the board. Have students determine whether the sentence is complete, a fragment, a run-on, or a comma splice.

  » *Chan raised his hand Mrs. Gonzalez called on him.* run-on

  » *Showed the class how to solve the problem.* fragment

  » *The students silently read their textbooks.* sentence

  » *Maria had a great idea, her classmates cheered.* comma splice

- Remind students that a sentence expresses a complete thought. Every sentence must have a **subject** and a **predicate**. The subject tells whom or what the sentence is about; the predicate tells what the subject is or does. Tell students that sentences missing a subject or a predicate are sentence fragments and cannot be used alone.

- Have students write three sentences and three fragments. Then ask students to exchange their sentences and fragments with a partner. Have partners identify the subjects and predicates in each other's sentences and rewrite the fragments as complete sentences.

- Review run-on sentences and comma splices and ask pairs to write an example of each. Have volunteers share their examples and work as a group to correct them to create complete sentences.

- Have students complete **Printable: Grammar 1.1.4** for more practice with complete sentences.

 ENGLISH LEARNER SUPPORT: Scaffolded Practice

SUBSTANTIAL
Remind students that a complete sentence has both a subject and a predicate. Provide examples of simple subjects that could pair with simple predicates, such as *student-walked*, *box-fell*, *birds-landed*. Model how to make complete sentences with these pairs.

MODERATE
Provide examples of simple subjects that could pair with simple predicates, such as *student-walked*, *box-fell*, *birds-landed*. Have students make complete sentences with these pairs.

LIGHT
Provide examples of simple subjects that could pair with simple predicates, such as *student-walked*, *box-fell*, *birds-landed*. Have students use these pairs and describing words to make complete sentences.

LEARNING OBJECTIVES

- **Language** Use subjects and predicates to convey complete ideas.
- **Language** Use complete sentences correctly in speaking and writing.

MATERIALS   Online

Display and Engage *Grammar 1.1.5*

Printable *Grammar 1.1.5*

 **INSTRUCTIONAL VOCABULARY**

- **sentence** a group of words expressing a complete thought
- **simple subject** the main word that tells whom or what the sentence is about
- **simple predicate** the main word that tells what the subject is or does
- **fragment** a group of words that does not express a complete thought; not a sentence
- **run-on sentence** two sentences that run into each other
- **comma splice** two complete sentences that are joined by a comma but missing a coordinating conjunction

Connect and Teach

- Show **Display and Engage: Grammar 1.1.5**. Remind students to look for **fragments**, **run-ons**, and **comma splices** as they write and revise.

- Tell students that it is important to use complete sentences when writing. If they don't use complete **sentences**, the reader will be confused.

- Point out that an important part of revising is making sure each of your sentences has a **subject** and a **predicate**.

Online
📖 Ed

DISPLAY AND ENGAGE: Grammar 1.1.5

Grammar 1.1.5

Connect to Writing: Using Complete Sentences

Always check your writing to make sure each sentence contains a **subject** and a **predicate**. Change any **fragments** you find into complete sentences. Break **run-ons** and **comma splices** into two sentences.

Incorrect Sentences	Correct Sentences
A package for Ms. Garcia. Handed her the box. Ms. Garcia opened the box she smiled. Her daughter sent a birthday gift, it was a new sweater.	A package for Ms. Garcia arrived this morning. The mail carrier handed her the box. Ms. Garcia opened the box. She smiled. Her daughter sent a birthday gift. It was a new sweater.

Engage and Apply

- Display the correct and incorrect sentence below. Guide students to identify the fragments, run-ons, and comma splices.

> Mrs. Jewls picked up her pen.
> Raised her hand to answer the question. fragment
> The principal visits the class we like it when she is there. run-on
> Mrs. Jewls wrote on the board, we could see the answer.
> comma splice
> The new student. fragment

- Have students complete **Printable: Grammar 1.1.5** for practice with complete sentences.

- Have students return to a piece of their writing. In pairs, have them look for fragments, run-ons, and comma splices. Encourage them to rewrite their sentences to show complete thoughts. Have volunteers share their improvements.

EL **ENGLISH LEARNER SUPPORT: Support Revision**

SUBSTANTIAL

Read students' writing together. Work together to identify the simple subject and simple predicate. Allow students to use their home language to help fill in any missing subject pronouns. Repeat the improved sentence together.

MODERATE

Read students' writing together. Have students identify the subject and predicate of the sentence. Guide them to create complete sentences. Repeat the improved sentence together.

LIGHT

Have partners read their work to each other. Have students identify the subject and predicate of the sentence. Guide them to check that their partners used complete sentences. Have partners work together to choose words to make the sentences more interesting.

SENTENCES • KINDS OF SENTENCES

DECLARATIVE AND INTERROGATIVE SENTENCES

LEARNING OBJECTIVES

- **Language** Identify declarative and interrogative sentences.
- **Language** Use a variety of sentences correctly in speaking and writing.

MATERIALS   Online

Display and Engage *Grammar 1.2.1a, 1.2.1b*

Printable *Grammar 1.2.1*

 INSTRUCTIONAL VOCABULARY

- **declarative sentence** tells something and ends with a period
- **interrogative sentence** asks something and ends with a question mark

Connect and Teach

- Show <u>Display and Engage: Grammar 1.2.1a</u>. Explain that a **declarative sentence** tells something. It ends with a period. An **interrogative sentence** asks something. It ends with a question mark. Changing the order of words can change a declarative sentence into an interrogative sentence.

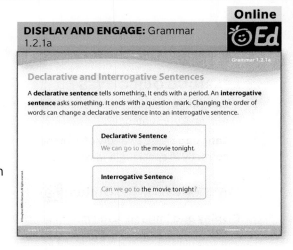

- Model distinguishing between declarative and interrogative sentences with this example sentence: *Can we go to the movie tonight?*

  THINK ALOUD *To identify the kind of sentence, I ask* Does this sentence tell something or ask something? *Since this sentence asks something and ends with a question mark, it must be interrogative. I could change it into a declarative sentence by changing the order of the first two words and the end punctuation to read,* We can go to the movie tonight.

Engage and Apply

- Complete items 1–3 on <u>Display and Engage: Grammar 1.2.1b</u> with students.

- Have students write examples of declarative and interrogative sentences on the board.

- Have students complete <u>Printable: Grammar 1.2.1</u> for practice with declarative and interrogative sentences.

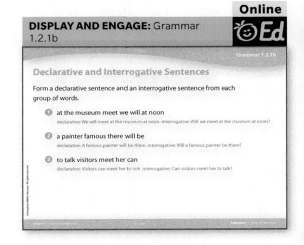

- Have students edit a writing draft to identify declarative and interrogative sentences.

EL **ENGLISH LEARNER SUPPORT: Facilitate Language Connection**

In Spanish, punctuation marks appear at the beginning and end of an exclamatory or interrogative sentence. Remind students that they need to punctuate only the end of a sentence in English.

Scaffolded Practice

ALL LEVELS Explain that a declarative statement tells something. It gives information. *I am wearing a red shirt.* An interrogative statement asks something. *Are you wearing a red shirt?* Divide students into small groups. Give half of the groups a card that says TELL and the other half a card that says ASK. Have the Tell group give a declarative sentence. Have the Ask group change the sentence into an interrogative sentence.

LEARNING OBJECTIVES

- **Language** Identify imperative and exclamatory sentences.
- **Language** Use a variety of sentences correctly in speaking and writing.

MATERIALS   Online

Display and Engage *Grammar 1.2.2a, 1.2.2b*

Printable *Grammar 1.2.2*

INSTRUCTIONAL VOCABULARY

- **imperative sentence** gives an order and ends with a period
- **exclamatory sentence** expresses strong feeling and ends with an exclamation point

Connect and Teach

- Show **Display and Engage: Grammar 1.2.2a**. Explain that an **imperative sentence** gives an order and ends with a period. An **exclamatory sentence** expresses strong feeling and ends with an exclamation point.

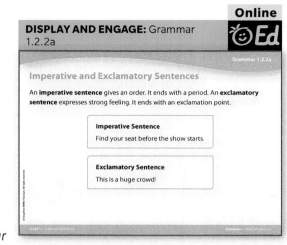

- Model how to identify imperative and exclamatory sentences with these examples: *What a huge crowd! Find your seat before the show starts.*

  THINK ALOUD *To identify the kind of sentence, I ask Does this sentence give an order or express strong feeling? The first sentence expresses a strong feeling. It also ends with an exclamation point, so I know that it's an exclamatory sentence. The second sentence gives an order and ends with a period, so I know it is an imperative sentence.*

Engage and Apply

- Complete items 1–5 on **Display and Engage: Grammar 1.2.2b** with students.

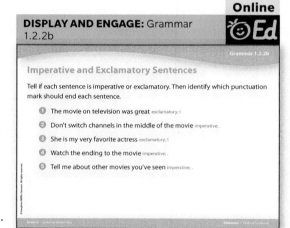

- Have students write examples of imperative and exclamatory sentences on the board.

- Have students complete **Printable: Grammar 1.2.2** for practice with imperative and exclamatory sentences.

- Have students edit a writing draft to identify imperative and exclamatory sentences.

 ENGLISH LEARNER SUPPORT: Scaffolded Practice

ALL LEVELS For Spanish speakers, point out the cognates *imperativa, exclamativa*. Review their meanings. Write examples of imperative and exclamatory sentences. Ask: *Which sentence is an imperative sentence? Which sentence is an exclamatory sentence?* Students may point or say the sentence to answer. Review how each sentence gives an order or expresses a strong feeling.

LESSON 1.2.3

IDENTIFY KINDS OF SENTENCES

LEARNING OBJECTIVES

- **Language** Identify declarative, interrogative, imperative, and exclamatory sentences.
- **Language** Use a variety of sentences correctly in speaking and writing.

MATERIALS   Online

Display and Engage *Grammar 1.2.3a, 1.2.3b*

Printable *Grammar 1.2.3*

 **INSTRUCTIONAL VOCABULARY**

- **declarative sentence** tells something and ends with a period
- **interrogative sentence** asks something and ends with a question mark
- **imperative sentence** gives an order and ends with a period
- **exclamatory sentence** expresses strong feeling and ends with an exclamation point

Connect and Teach

- Show **Display and Engage: Grammar 1.2.3a**. Read through the instruction and review the examples. Then use this sentence to guide students to identify two clues that help them identify which type of sentence it is: *Did you see the movie about Mars?*

  THINK ALOUD *To identify the kind of sentence, I ask Does this sentence tell something, ask something, give an order, or express a feeling? The sentence asks something and ends with a question mark, so I know it is an interrogative sentence.*

Engage and Apply

- Complete items 1–4 on **Display and Engage: Grammar 1.2.3b** with students.

- Have each student write a declarative, an interrogative, an imperative, and an exclamatory sentence without the end punctuation.

- Have students trade sentences, identify their partner's sentence types, and punctuate the sentences correctly.

- Have students complete **Printable: Grammar 1.2.3** for practice with kinds of sentences.

- Have students edit a writing draft to identify kinds of sentences.

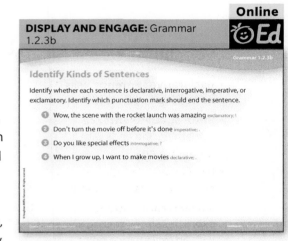

DISPLAY AND ENGAGE: Grammar 1.2.3a — Online Ed

Identify Kinds of Sentences

A **declarative sentence** tells something. It ends with a period. An **interrogative sentence** asks something. It ends with a question mark. An **imperative sentence** gives an order. It ends with a period. An **exclamatory sentence** expresses strong feeling. It ends with an exclamation point.

declarative sentence	imperative sentence
We will have pizza for dinner.	Order pizza for dinner.
interrogative sentence	exclamatory sentence
Will we have pizza for dinner?	Yes, we're having pizza for dinner!

DISPLAY AND ENGAGE: Grammar 1.2.3b — Online Ed

Identify Kinds of Sentences

Identify whether each sentence is declarative, interrogative, imperative, or exclamatory. Identify which punctuation mark should end the sentence.

1. Wow, the scene with the rocket launch was amazing exclamatory; !
2. Don't turn the movie off before it's done imperative; .
3. Do you like special effects interrogative; ?
4. When I grow up, I want to make movies declarative; .

EL **ENGLISH LEARNER SUPPORT: Scaffolded Practice**

SUBSTANTIAL

Use these sentence frames to help students identify each sentence type.

The actress _____ the part. plays; declarative
What was her _____ ? part; interrogative
Learn your lines if you want to act in this _____. play; imperative
I'm going to be a movie _____ ! star; exclamatory

MODERATE

Use the sentences to guide students to identify and label the four types of sentences. Discuss students' responses.

LIGHT

Have students work in pairs to write sentence frames for the four types of sentences. Have them exchange their work with another pair, complete the frames, and then discuss the sentences.

SENTENCES • KINDS OF SENTENCES

LEARNING OBJECTIVES

- **Language** Review declarative, interrogative, imperative, and exclamatory sentences.
- **Language** Use a variety of sentences correctly in speaking and writing.

MATERIALS   Online

Display and Engage *Grammar 1.2.4a, 1.2.4b*

Printable *Grammar 1.2.4*

INSTRUCTIONAL VOCABULARY

- **declarative sentence** tells something and ends with a period
- **interrogative sentence** asks something and ends with a question mark
- **imperative sentence** gives an order and ends with a period
- **exclamatory sentence** expresses strong feeling and ends with an exclamation point

Review Kinds of Sentences

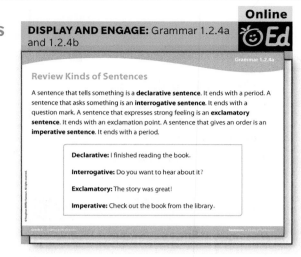

DISPLAY AND ENGAGE: Grammar 1.2.4a and 1.2.4b   Online Ed

- Show **Display and Engage: Grammar 1.2.4a**. Review the four kinds of sentences with students. Remind them that **declarative sentences** tell something, **interrogative sentences** ask something, **imperative sentences** give orders, and **exclamatory sentences** express strong feeling. Remind students that the end punctuation depends on which type of sentence it is. Then have students complete the activity on **Display and Engage: Grammar 1.2.4b**.

- Write the sentences on the board without end marks. Have students determine whether each sentence is declarative, interrogative, imperative, or exclamatory. Then ask students to identify the end punctuation for each sentence.

  » *Wow, what a fantastic movie* exclamatory; !

  » *Did you like the ending* interrogative; ?

  » *Go to the ticket counter* imperative; .

  » *I like science fiction movies* declarative; .

- Have students complete **Printable: Grammar 1.2.4** for more practice with kinds of sentences.

- Have students edit a writing draft to identify kinds of sentences.

EL ENGLISH LEARNER SUPPORT: Scaffolded Practice

ALL LEVELS Remind students that there are four kinds of sentences, and each has its own punctuation. Provide short examples of each, such as: *I am here. Where are you? Go now. We are back.* Make a chart with four wide columns and label the top of each column with each kind of sentence. Have students identify the kind of sentence for each of your examples. Students may point to the column or name the type. Discuss how to distinguish each type by using a think aloud about what each sentence does and what punctuation they see. Remind students that imperative sentences, such as *Stop!* may also have an exclamation point.

LESSON 1.2.5

CONNECT TO WRITING: USING KINDS OF SENTENCES

LEARNING OBJECTIVES

- **Language** Write declarative, interrogative, imperative, and exclamatory sentences.
- **Language** Use a variety of sentences correctly in speaking and writing.

MATERIALS — Online **Ed**

Display and Engage *Grammar 1.2.5*

Printable *Grammar 1.2.5*

INSTRUCTIONAL VOCABULARY

- **declarative sentence** tells something and ends with a period
- **interrogative sentence** asks something and ends with a question mark
- **imperative sentence** gives an order and ends with a period
- **exclamatory sentence** expresses strong feeling and ends with an exclamation point

Connect and Teach

- Show **Display and Engage: Grammar 1.2.5**. Read the example sentences with students.

- Explain that good writers don't use the same sentence type over and over. Instead, they use a variety of sentence types. Read aloud the two examples below.

  Camp Katahdin is a summer camp for girls and boys. The camp is located deep in the woods. There are miles of nature trails and a wide, deep lake. You could come for a visit today. You would like the camp.

  What is Camp Katahdin? It is a summer camp for girls and boys. The camp is located deep in the woods. There are miles of nature trails and a wide, deep lake. Come for a visit today. You'll love it!

- Point out that the second example, which uses all four sentence types, is more interesting for readers and listeners.

Engage and Apply

- Review with students the four kinds of sentences and their end punctuation.

- Have students complete **Printable: Grammar 1.2.5** for practice identifying kinds of sentences.

- Have students return to a piece of their writing. In pairs, have them look for ways to add more variety in sentences to their writing. Encourage them to rewrite their sentences to show more variety. Have volunteers share their improvements.

DISPLAY AND ENGAGE: Grammar 1.2.5

Online **Ed**

Connect to Writing: Using Different Kinds of Sentences

There are four kinds of sentences and each kind does a different job. Using a variety of sentence types can make your writing more lively and interesting.

One Sentence Type	Varied Sentence Types
It would be great if you could listen to my story about camp. Rena seemed like an ordinary camper. I was wrong. No one ever would have guessed that she was a princess.	Listen to what happened at camp. Rena seemed like an ordinary camper. I was totally wrong about that! Who would ever have guessed that she was a princess?

💬 ENGLISH LEARNER SUPPORT: Facilitate Language Connections

In some languages, such as Cantonese, Russian, and Tagalog, word order is the same in some questions and statements. Speakers of some languages may also not be familiar with using a verb like *do/did* to form a question.

Support Revision

ALL LEVELS Read aloud interrogative sentences that students have written. Guide students to consider punctuation and word order. *This is an interrogative sentence. What does an interrogative sentence do? it asks a question What punctuation do we use for an interrogative sentence? a question mark Where do we put the question mark? at the end* When discussing word order, use examples and corrections to show how to form questions.

LEARNING OBJECTIVES

- **Language** Identify complete subjects and predicates.
- **Language** Use compound sentences with subject-verb agreement correctly in speaking and writing.

MATERIALS	Online

Display and Engage *Grammar 1.3.1a, 1.3.1b*

Printable *Grammar 1.3.1*

 **INSTRUCTIONAL VOCABULARY**

- **complete subject** all the words telling whom or what a sentence is about
- **complete predicate** all the words telling what the subject is or does

Connect and Teach

- Show **Display and Engage: Grammar 1.3.1a**. Explain that a **complete subject** contains all of the words that tell whom or what the sentence is about. A **complete predicate** contains all of the words that tell what the subject is or does.

- Model identifying complete subjects and predicates in the example sentence: *The members of the election committee announced the winner.*

  THINK ALOUD *To identify the complete subject and predicate, I ask* What are the words that tell whom or what the sentence is about? What are the words that tell what the subject is or does? The members of the election committee *is the complete subject because these are all of the words that tell whom the sentence is about. The complete predicate is* announced the winner *because all these words together tell what the subject did.*

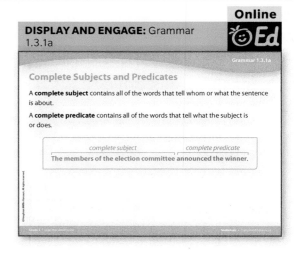

Engage and Apply

- Complete items 1–5 on **Display and Engage: Grammar 1.3.1b** with students.

- Have students write two complete sentences of six to ten words and then exchange papers with a partner. Tell them to underline the complete subjects and predicates in their partner's sentences.

- Have students complete **Printable: Grammar 1.3.1** for practice with complete subjects and predicates.

- Have students edit a writing draft to identify the complete subject and complete predicate in their sentences.

EL **ENGLISH LEARNER SUPPORT: Facilitate Language Connection**

For speakers of Spanish, point out the cognate *conjunción* and explain that it is a word—like *and, but, or*—that joins other words or groups of words. The Spanish word for *and* as a conjunction is *y*; for *but* as a conjunction is *pero*; for *or* as a conjunction is *o*.

Scaffolded Practice

SUBSTANTIAL

Help students understand the conjunctions *and, or,* and *but* by using gestures to indicate *the pencil and the pen, the pencil or the pen,* and *not the pencil but the pen.*

MODERATE

Display these phrases: *the pencil and the pen, the pencil or the pen, not the pencil but the pen.* Act out each scenario, and have students say the correct phrase.

LIGHT

Display these sentences: *I could make a sandwich. I have no bread. I have no peanut butter. I could buy a taco.* Have pairs use *and, or,* and *but* to make as many sensible compound sentences as they can.

LEARNING OBJECTIVES

- **Language** Identify complete subjects and predicates.
- **Language** Use compound sentences with complete subject-verb agreement correctly in speaking and writing.

MATERIALS	Online

Display and Engage *Grammar 1.3.2a, 1.3.2b*

Printable *Grammar 1.3.2*

 **INSTRUCTIONAL VOCABULARY**

- **subject-verb agreement** the use of a singular subject with a singular verb and a plural subject with a plural verb

Connect and Teach

- Show **Display and Engage: Grammar 1.3.2a**. Explain that the subject and verb of a sentence must agree in number.

- Model identifying **subject-verb agreement** in this example sentence: *The student votes tomorrow.*

  THINK ALOUD *To identify whether there is correct subject-verb agreement, I ask* Is the sentence about more than one person, place, thing, or idea? If so, is the verb plural? *In the example sentence, the subject is* The student, *which is singular. Therefore, the verb should be singular. In the example sentence, the singular verb is* votes.

Online

DISPLAY AND ENGAGE: Grammar 1.3.2a

Grammar 1.3.2a

Subject-Verb Agreement

The subject and verb of a sentence should agree. Use a singular verb with a singular subject. Use a plural verb with a plural subject, even if a prepositional phrase stands between the subject and verb.

Singular Subject and Verb	Plural Subject and Verb
The student votes tomorrow.	The students vote tomorrow.
Mary or Ben has my vote.	Mary and Ben have my vote.
One of the candidates is going to win.	Two of the candidates are going to win.

Engage and Apply

- Complete items 1–5 on **Display and Engage: Grammar 1.3.2b** with students.

- Have students write two more sentences, one with a singular subject and the other with a plural subject. Have them exchange papers with a partner to check for subject-verb agreement in each other's sentences.

- Have students complete **Printable: Grammar 1.3.2** for practice with subject-verb agreement.

- Have students edit a writing draft to identify correct subject-verb agreement in their sentences.

Online

DISPLAY AND ENGAGE: Grammar 1.3.2b

Grammar 1.3.2b

Subject-Verb Agreement

Identify the subject. Choose the verb that goes with it.

1. Devon, Marco, and Ellie (want/wants) to run for president.
   Devon, Marco, and Ellie (subject); want (verb)

2. Asha and Ellie (is/are) good friends.
   Asha and Ellie (subject); are (verb)

3. One of the three (was/were) already president last year.
   One (subject); was (verb)

4. They (decide/decides) who has the best ideas.
   They (subject); decide (verb)

5. (Is/Are) anyone surprised that Ellie won the election?
   anyone (subject); Is (verb)

🗨 **ENGLISH LEARNER SUPPORT: Facilitate Language Connection**

In some languages, such as Cantonese, Haitian Creole, and Vietnamese, there is no subject-verb agreement. Speakers of these languages may omit the third-person present-tense ending -s/-es in verbs.

Scaffolded Practice

SUBSTANTIAL

Write sentences, such as *The farmer grows corn.* Read the sentence aloud. Have a volunteer point to the subject of the sentence as you ask if it is about one other person. Then have the student point to the verb. Explain how to form third-person singular verbs.

MODERATE

Write sentence frames, such as *The farmer _____ corn.* and supply verbs, such as *grows.* Model forming third-person singular verbs. Read each sentence aloud with the correct form of the verb.

LIGHT

Guide students to create simple sentences with partners. Have partners review forming third-person singular verbs as needed.

LEARNING OBJECTIVES

- **Language** Identify compound sentences.
- **Language** Use compound sentences with subject-verb agreement correctly in speaking and writing.

MATERIALS   Online

Display and Engage *Grammar 1.3.3a, 1.3.3b*

Printable *Grammar 1.3.3*

 **INSTRUCTIONAL VOCABULARY**

- **compound sentence** two sentences joined by a comma and a conjunction, such as *and, or,* or *but*
- **complete subject** all the words telling whom or what a sentence is about
- **complete predicate** all the words telling what the subject is or does

Connect and Teach

- Show **Display and Engage: Grammar 1.3.3a**. Explain that a **compound sentence** is made up of two smaller sentences. Each smaller sentence has its own **complete subject** and **complete predicate**. The two sentences are joined by a comma and a conjunction, such as *and, or,* or *but*.

DISPLAY AND ENGAGE: Grammar 1.3.3a

Online ꗃEd

Grammar 1.3.3a

Compound Sentences

A **compound sentence** is made up of two smaller sentences. Each smaller sentence has its own subject and predicate. The sentences are joined by a comma and a conjunction such as *and, or,* or *but.*

complete thought	complete thought
Brenda worked hard on the election,	but Max didn't do any work.

- Model identifying correct comma use in the example sentence: *Brenda worked hard on the election, but Max didn't do any work.*

- Explain that this is a compound sentence. Write each of the two smaller sentences on the board and identify their subjects and predicates. Point out the comma and the conjunction that are used to form the compound sentence.

Engage and Apply

- Complete items 1–4 on **Display and Engage: Grammar 1.3.3b** with students.

- Ask students to write two compound sentences. Have them exchange papers with a partner. Partners should circle the conjunctions and use an arrow to indicate where each comma is or should be.

DISPLAY AND ENGAGE: Grammar 1.3.3b

Online ꗃEd

Grammar 1.3.3b

Compound Sentences

Identify each simple sentence in the compound sentences. Tell where the comma should go.

① Dixie could help her friend Janet in the election or she could ride the school bus. Simple sentences: Dixie could help her friend Janet in the election; she could ride the school bus. The comma should be placed after *election.*

② Dominic didn't like to make signs but Logan needed them. Simple sentences: Dominic didn't like to make signs; Logan needed them. The comma should be placed after *signs.*

③ Amaya got together with a few friends and they discussed the candidates they liked. Simple sentences: Amaya got together with a few friends; they discussed the candidates they liked. The comma should be placed after *friends.*

④ Janet didn't win but she had fun running her campaign. Simple sentences: Janet didn't win; she had fun running her campaign. The comma should be placed after *win.*

- Have students complete **Printable: Grammar 1.3.3** for practice with compound sentences.

- Have students edit a writing draft to combine shorter sentences into compound sentences with correct punctuation and an appropriate conjunction.

EL **ENGLISH LEARNER SUPPORT: Scaffolded Practice**

SUBSTANTIAL

Write sentences, such as *My friend buys fruit. He picks red apples. His sisters want apples. They like green apples.* Read each sentence aloud. Model how to join two sentences with a comma and a conjunction. *My friend buys fruit, and he picks red apples. His sisters want apples, but they like green apples.*

MODERATE

Write sentences, such as *My friend buys fruit. He picks red apples. His sisters want apples. They like green apples.* Have students read each sentence aloud with you. Model how to join two sentences with a comma and a conjunction. *My friend buys fruit, and he picks red apples. His sisters want apples, but they like green apples.* Guide students to make other compound sentences.

LIGHT

Write sentences, such as *My friend buys fruit. He picks red apples. His sisters want apples. They like green apples.* Have students read each sentence aloud. Model how to join two sentences with a comma and a conjunction. *My friend buys fruit, and he picks red apples. His sisters want apples, but they like green apples.* Ask students to make compound sentences of their own.

SENTENCES • COMPOUND SENTENCES

LEARNING OBJECTIVES

- **Language** Review complete subjects and predicates, subject-verb agreement, and compound sentences.
- **Language** Use compound sentences with subject-verb agreement correctly in speaking and writing.

MATERIALS   Online

Display and Engage *Grammar 1.3.4a, 1.3.4b, 1.3.4c*

Printable *Grammar 1.3.4*

INSTRUCTIONAL VOCABULARY

- **compound sentence** two sentences joined by a comma and a conjunction, such as *and*, *or*, or *but*
- **complete subject** all the words telling whom or what a sentence is about
- **complete predicate** all the words telling what the subject is or does
- **subject-verb agreement** the use of a singular subject with a singular verb and a plural subject with a plural verb

Connect and Teach

- Show **Display and Engage: Grammar 1.3.4a** and **Grammar 1.3.4b**. Remind students that a **compound sentence** is made up of two smaller sentences joined by a comma and a conjunction. Each smaller sentence has a **complete subject** and a **complete predicate**.

> Grammar 1.3.4a
>
> **Review Compound Sentences**
>
> A **compound sentence** is a sentence made up of two shorter sentences joined by a comma and the **conjunction** *and*, *but*, or *or*. Each part of a compound sentence has its own **complete subject** and **complete predicate**.
>
> complete subject complete predicate complete subject complete predicate
> Tanya gives a speech, and the students listen quietly.

- Remind students that the subject and the verb in a sentence must agree in number.

- Write the sentences on the board without end marks. Have students determine where the comma should be placed to form a compound sentence correctly.

  » *Alejandro wants to go to the museum but his classmates vote for the zoo.* *after* museum

  » *Giraffes are herbivores and lions are carnivores.* *after* herbivores

  » *We can go to the zoo or we can go to the museum.* *after* zoo

- Work with students to complete the exercises on **Display and Engage: Grammar 1.3.4c**.

- Have students complete **Printable: Grammar 1.3.4** for more practice with compound sentences.

- Have students edit a writing draft to combine shorter sentences into compound sentences with correct punctuation and an appropriate conjunction.

ENGLISH LEARNER SUPPORT: Facilitate Language Connection

In Hmong, verbs can be connected without the conjunction *and*. Model for students how to make a compound sentence by using a comma and conjunction to join two sentences. *The election was yesterday, and we went to vote.*

Scaffolded Practice

ALL LEVELS Explain that conjunctions *and, but,* and *or* combine, or join sentences. Model combining sentences, pointing out the comma and the conjunction.
Tina grows carrots in her garden. Tina can't grow corn. Tina grows carrots in her garden, but she can't grow corn.
Explain that conjunction, *but,* connects the two ideas. Display examples of short sentences and work together to combine them.
The cat loves tuna. He does not like cheese. (but)
We visit my aunt in the summer. We visit my grandmother in the winter. (and)
Foxes are red. Some foxes are brown. (or)

LEARNING OBJECTIVES

- **Language** Write compound sentences.
- **Language** Use compound sentences with subject-verb agreement correctly in speaking and writing.

MATERIALS	Online

Display and Engage *Grammar 1.3.5*

Printable *Grammar 1.3.5*

 INSTRUCTIONAL VOCABULARY

- **compound sentence** two sentences joined by a comma and a conjunction, such as *and, or,* or *but*
- **complete subject** all the words telling whom or what a sentence is about
- **complete predicate** all the words telling what the subject is or does
- **subject-verb agreement** the use of a singular subject with a singular verb and a plural subject with a plural verb

Review Compound Sentences

- Show **Display and Engage: Grammar 1.3.5**. Remind students that two short sentences that are closely related in meaning can often be combined to form a **compound sentence**.

- Point out that using compound sentences is a good way to make writing flow more smoothly.

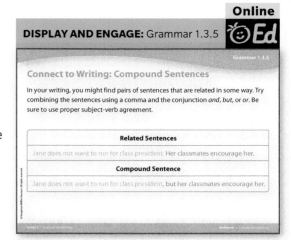

DISPLAY AND ENGAGE: Grammar 1.3.5 **Online** **Ed**

Connect to Writing: Compound Sentences

In your writing, you might find pairs of sentences that are related in some way. Try combining the sentences using a comma and the conjunction *and, but,* or *or.* Be sure to use proper subject-verb agreement.

Related Sentences
Jane does not want to run for class president. Her classmates encourage her.
Compound Sentence
Jane does not want to run for class president, but her classmates encourage her.

Engage and Apply

- Display these examples:

> Susana pitched. Irina played first base.
> Susana pitched, and Irina played first base.

- Explain that in the first example, the two short sentences sound choppy when read together. The second example, in which they are combined into a compound sentence, reads more smoothly. The compound sentence also tells readers that the two ideas are closely connected.

- Have students complete **Printable: Grammar 1.3.5** for practice identifying ways to combine sentences.

- Have students return to a piece of their writing. In pairs, have them look for sentences that can be combined. Encourage them to rewrite their sentences to combine ideas using compound sentences. Remind students to make sure the subject and verb agree in number. Have volunteers share their improvements.

EL **ENGLISH LEARNER SUPPORT: Support Revision**

ALL LEVELS Write: *Miata speaks first. Rudy gives his speech next.* Ask: *How can we combine these two sentences into one?* Then write: *Miata speaks first, and Rudy gives his speech next.*
Have a volunteer circle the comma and the connecting word *and* in the compound sentence. Tell students that they can use the conjunctions *and, but,* and *or* to form compound sentences.
Have a volunteer underline the two simple sentences in the sentence. Point out that there is a subject and a predicate on each side of the connecting word.

Connect to Writing Have partners write paragraphs comparing their interests. Give these sentence frames: *I like_____, and _____ does, too. I like to _____, but _____ would rather _____.*

SENTENCES • COMPLEX SENTENCES

LEARNING OBJECTIVES

- **Language** Identify complex sentences and subordinating conjunctions.
- **Language** Use complex sentences correctly in speaking and writing.

MATERIALS	Online

Display and Engage *Grammar 1.4.1a, 1.4.1b*

Printable *Grammar 1.4.1*

 INSTUCTIONAL VOCABULARY

- **complex sentence** a sentence containing a dependent and an independent clause joined by a subordinating conjunction
- **subordinating conjunction** a conjunction that joins two clauses to form a complex sentence

Connect and Teach

- Show **Display and Engage: Grammar 1.4.1a**. Explain that a **complex sentence** is formed by joining two groups of words, one of which expresses a complete thought. The other group of words adds meaning but does not express a complete thought. It begins with a **subordinating conjunction**, such as *because, although, when,* or *as.*

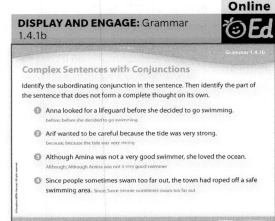

DISPLAY AND ENGAGE: Grammar 1.4.1a

Complex Sentences with Conjunctions

A **complex sentence** is formed by joining two groups of words with a **subordinating conjunction**. One group of words expresses a complete thought. The other group adds meaning but does not form a complete thought on its own. It begins with a subordinating conjunction, such as *because, although, when,* or *as.*

subordinating conjunction
Because a storm had passed through the area, the waves were high.

- Model identifying the elements of a complex sentence in the example sentence: *Because a storm had passed through the area, the waves were high.*

  THINK ALOUD *To identify the elements of a complex sentence, I ask* Which part of the sentence cannot stand on its own? What word does it begin with? Because a storm had passed through the area *cannot stand on its own; it begins with the subordinating conjunction* because.

Engage and Apply

- Complete items 1–4 on **Display and Engage: Grammar 1.4.1b** with students.

- Have students create sentences with subordinating conjunctions. Then have them share their examples with the class and explain the function of each conjunction they have used.

- Have students complete **Printable: Grammar 1.4.1** for practice with complex sentences.

DISPLAY AND ENGAGE: Grammar 1.4.1b

Complex Sentences with Conjunctions

Identify the subordinating conjunction in the sentence. Then identify the part of the sentence that does not form a complete thought on its own.

1. Anna looked for a lifeguard before she decided to go swimming.
   before; before she decided to go swimming

2. Arif wanted to be careful because the tide was very strong.
   because; because the tide was very strong

3. Although Amina was not a very good swimmer, she loved the ocean.
   Although; Although Amina was not a very good swimmer

4. Since people sometimes swam too far out, the town had roped off a safe swimming area. Since; Since people sometimes swam too far out

- Have students edit a writing draft to include complex sentences.

 ENGLISH LEARNER SUPPORT: Facilitate Language Connection

Explain to students that many languages contain subordinating conjunctions with meanings similar to those in English. Have students use bilingual dictionaries to find examples.

Scaffolded Practice

ALL LEVELS Write subordinating conjunctions *because, after, since, if, although, when, as,* and *before.* Remind students that these words begin a dependent clause. Write the following sentences and have students identify the dependent clause in each. *Nathan searched for a blanket because the young boy's clothes were soaked.* because the young boy's clothes were soaked *When sailors saw the lifesaving team, they cheered loudly. When sailors saw the lifesaving team* Students may answer by pointing to the dependent clause or reading it aloud as they are able.

SENTENCES • COMPLEX SENTENCES

LEARNING OBJECTIVES

- **Language** Identify dependent and independent clauses.
- **Language** Use complex sentences correctly in speaking and writing.

MATERIALS	Online 🍊Ed

Display and Engage *Grammar 1.4.2a, 1.4.2b*

Printable *Grammar 1.4.2*

 INSTRUCTIONAL VOCABULARY

- **dependent clause** a group of words that cannot stand on its own as a complete thought
- **independent clause** a group of words that expresses a complete thought and can stand on its own as a sentence

Connect and Teach

- Show **Display and Engage: Grammar 1.4.2a**. Explain that a **dependent clause** cannot stand on its own as a complete thought and is usually introduced by a subordinating conjunction. An **independent clause** can stand on its own as a complete thought. A complex sentence is made up of an independent clause and one or more dependent clauses joined by a subordinating conjunction.

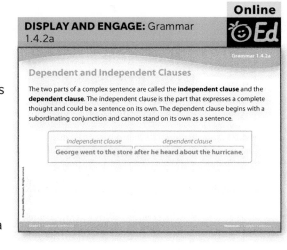

DISPLAY AND ENGAGE: Grammar 1.4.2a — Online 🍊Ed

- Model identifying the dependent and independent clauses in the example sentence: *George went to the store after he heard about the hurricane.*

  THINK ALOUD *To identify the dependent and independent clauses, I ask* Which part of the sentence can stand on its own? Which part just gives extra information? George went to the store *expresses a complete thought and can stand on its own.* After he heard about the hurricane *is extra information.*

Engage and Apply

- Complete items 1–4 on **Display and Engage: Grammar 1.4.2b** with students.

- Have partners write three complex sentences. Then have them identify the independent and dependent clauses in another pair's sentences.

- Have students complete **Printable: Grammar 1.4.2** for practice with complex sentences.

- Have students edit a writing draft to include complex sentences.

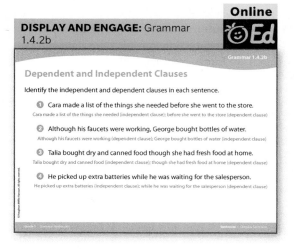

DISPLAY AND ENGAGE: Grammar 1.4.2b — Online 🍊Ed

 ENGLISH LEARNER SUPPORT: Scaffolded Practice

SUBSTANTIAL

Write on the board the words *because* and *when* and remind students these words are subordinating conjunctions. Explain that they are used to combine two related short sentences into a single, longer sentence. Use this model to demonstrate. *The rain stopped. The soccer game started. _____ the rain stopped, the soccer game started.* **When**

MODERATE

Use the same sentence frame to demonstrate how to form complex sentences. Help students identify the dependent and independent clauses. Prompt them with: *Which part of the sentence can stand on its own? Which part cannot?* Then help students form their own complex sentences using subordinating conjunctions.

LIGHT

Provide students with pairs of short, related sentences that can be combined into complex sentences. Have partners combine the sentences and label the conjunction and the dependent clause in each.

LEARNING OBJECTIVES

- **Language** Identify correlative conjunctions.
- **Language** Use complex sentences correctly in speaking and writing.

MATERIALS	Online

Display and Engage *Grammar 1.4.3a, 1.4.3b*

Printable *Grammar 1.4.3*

 INSTRUCTIONAL VOCABULARY

- **correlative conjunctions** a pair of conjunctions that joins parallel words or phrases

Connect and Teach

- Show <u>Display and Engage: Grammar 1.4.3a</u>. Tell students that some conjunctions are always used in pairs. These are called **correlative conjunctions** because they correlate, or bring together, two similar words, phrases, or clauses in a sentence. Correlative conjunctions include *either/or, neither/nor, both/and, whether/or, not only/but also.*

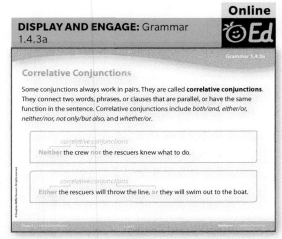

- Model identifying correlative conjunctions in the example sentence: *Neither the crew nor the rescuers knew what to do.*

   THINK ALOUD *To find the correlative conjunctions, I ask this question:* What two words work together to connect parallel parts of the sentence? *The words* Neither *and* nor *link* crew *and* rescuers. *Therefore, they are correlative conjunctions.*

Engage and Apply

- Complete items 1–5 on <u>Display and Engage: Grammar 1.4.3b</u> with students.

- Have students write three sentences using correlative conjunctions. Have them explain the function of the correlative conjunctions in each sentence.

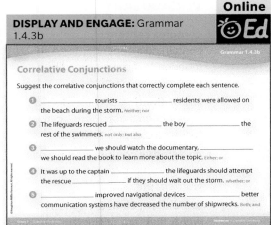

- Have students complete <u>Printable: Grammar 1.4.3</u> for practice with correlative conjunctions.

- Have students edit a writing draft to include sentences using correlative conjunctions.

EL **ENGLISH LEARNER SUPPORT: Facilitate Language Connections**

For Spanish speakers, point out similar correlative conjunctions *o/o* for *either/or*, *ni/ni* for *neither/nor*, *así/como* for *both/and*, *no sólo/sino también* for *not only/but also*.

Scaffolded Practice

SUBSTANTIAL

   Write correlative conjunctions *either/or, neither/nor, both/and, not only/but also* and the following cloze sentences: *Neither my friend _____ I had homework. nor Either we can go to the museum _____ we can go to the library. or _____ did we have fun, but we also learned something new. Not only _____ my friend and I enjoyed the day. Both* Guide students to fill in the correct conjunction. Read aloud the sentences with students.

MODERATE

   Write sentence frames *Neither my friend nor I like _____. Either we eat _____ or we eat _____. Not only did we _____, but we _____. Both _____ and _____ _____.* Guide students to think of how they can complete each sentence. Have students read the sentences aloud.

LIGHT

   Write sentence frames *Neither _____ nor _____. Either _____ or _____. Not only _____, but _____. Both _____ and _____ _____.* Have students work with partners to discuss at least two ways they can complete each sentence. Have students read their sentences aloud.

SENTENCES • COMPLEX SENTENCES

LEARNING OBJECTIVES

- **Language** Review complex sentences and subordinating and correlative conjunctions.
- **Language** Use complex sentences correctly in speaking and writing.

MATERIALS Online

Display and Engage *Grammar 1.4.4a, 1.4.4b, 1.4.4c*

Printable *Grammar 1.4.4*

INSTRUCTIONAL VOCABULARY

- **complex sentence** a sentence containing a dependent and an independent clause joined by a subordinating conjunction
- **subordinating conjunction** a conjunction that joins two clauses to form a complex sentence
- **correlative conjunctions** a pair of conjunctions that joins parallel words or phrases
- **dependent clause** a group of words that cannot stand on its own as a complete thought
- **independent clause** a group of words that expresses a complete thought and can stand on its own as a sentence

Review Complex Sentences

- Show **Display and Engage: Grammar 1.4.4a** and **Grammar 1.4.4b**. Remind students that a **complex sentence** includes an **independent clause** and one or more **dependent clauses**. The clauses often are joined by a **subordinating conjunction**. Other conjunctions called **correlative conjunctions** connect parallel parts of a sentence.

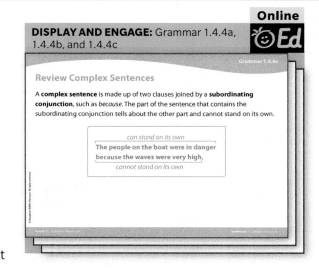

DISPLAY AND ENGAGE: Grammar 1.4.4a, 1.4.4b, and 1.4.4c

Online

Grammar 1.4.4a

Review Complex Sentences

A **complex sentence** is made up of two clauses joined by a **subordinating conjunction**, such as *because*. The part of the sentence that contains the subordinating conjunction tells about the other part and cannot stand on its own.

can stand on its own
The people on the boat were in danger because the waves were very high.
cannot stand on its own

- Write the sentences on the board. Have students identify the conjunctions and tell whether they are subordinating or correlative.

  » *After the game, the coach took the team out for ice cream.* **After; subordinating**

  » *Both Maddie and Tamika hit home runs.* **Both/and; correlative**

  » *The team won the most games this season though it lost the championship game.* **though; subordinating**

- Work with students to complete the exercises on **Display and Engage: Grammar 1.4.4c**. Explain that conjunctions connect words or groups of words in a sentence.

- A complex sentence contains a pair of sentences joined by a subordinating conjunction, such as *because* or *since.* The part of the complex sentence containing the subordinating conjunction tells about the other part. It cannot stand on its own.

- Correlative conjunctions work in pairs. Examples include *both/and, neither/nor,* and *whether/or*. Correlative conjunctions can connect parallel words or phrases, such as two nouns, two verbs, or two adjectives.

- Have students write the following sentence and underline the correlative conjunctions.
  Both King George and the patriots hoped to win the war. **Both, and**

- Have students write sentences using correlative conjunctions.

- Have students complete **Printable: Grammar 1.4.4** for more practice with complex sentences.

- Have students edit a writing draft to include complex sentences.

EL ENGLISH LEARNER SUPPORT: Scaffolded Practice

ALL LEVELS Write subordinating conjunctions *because, after, since, if, although, when , as,* and *before*. Model identifying the elements of a complex sentence in this example: *Because a storm had passed through the area, the waves were high.* Have students identify the elements of a complex sentence in these examples: *The sailors took cover when lightning struck the ship. Both the lightning and the waves were very dangerous.* Students may point to or name elements as you ask such questions as *What is the subordinating conjunction? What is the dependent clause?*

SENTENCES • COMPLEX SENTENCES

LEARNING OBJECTIVES

- **Language** Choose complex sentences to convey ideas.
- **Language** Use complex sentences correctly in speaking and writing.

MATERIALS   Online

Display and Engage *Grammar 1.4.5*

Printable *Grammar 1.4.5*

 INSTRUCTIONAL VOCABULARY

- **complex sentence** a sentence containing a dependent and an independent clause joined by a subordinating conjunction
- **subordinating conjunction** a conjunction that joins two clauses to form a complex sentence
- **correlative conjunctions** a pair of conjunctions that joins parallel words or phrases
- **dependent clause** a group of words that cannot stand on its own as a complete thought
- **independent clause** a group of words that expresses a complete thought and can stand on its own as a sentence

Connect and Teach

- Show <u>Display and Engage: Grammar 1.4.5</u>. Tell students that short sentences do not always show the relationship between ideas clearly.

- Explain that combining short sentences using **subordinating** or **correlative conjunctions** is a way to show the relationships between ideas. Tell students that an important part of revising is to determine which sentences could be linked to more effectively convey meaning.

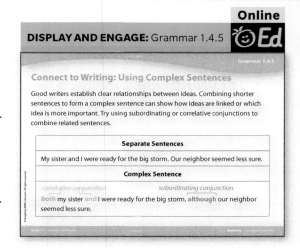

DISPLAY AND ENGAGE: Grammar 1.4.5   Online **Ed**

Connect to Writing: Using Complex Sentences

Good writers establish clear relationships between ideas. Combining shorter sentences to form a complex sentence can show how ideas are linked or which idea is more important. Try using subordinating or correlative conjunctions to combine related sentences.

Separate Sentences
My sister and I were ready for the big storm. Our neighbor seemed less sure.

Complex Sentence

correlative conjunction   *subordinating conjunction*
Both my sister and I were ready for the big storm, although our neighbor seemed less sure.

Engage and Apply

- Display the following sentences. Guide students to use subordinating conjunctions or the correlative conjunctions in parentheses to combine the two ideas.

> The sail ripped. The wind blew so hard. The sail ripped after the wind blew so hard.
> The boat tilted. A man fell overboard. (not only/but also) Not only did the boat tilt, but also a man fell overboard.
> The mate spotted land. The captain ran to the deck. Because the mate spotted land, the captain ran to the deck.

- Have students complete <u>Printable: Grammar 1.4.5</u> for practice using subordinating conjunctions to combine sentences.

- Have students return to a piece of their writing. In pairs, have them look for sentences that can be combined using subordinating or correlative conjunctions. Encourage them to rewrite their sentences to combine ideas. Have volunteers share their improvements.

 ENGLISH LEARNER SUPPORT: Support Revision

ALL LEVELS Explain that a complex sentence is made up of two clauses joined by a subordinating conjunction. Have students read the sentences below and combine them into complex sentences using the conjunction *until*. *Nathan wanted to be a surfman. He realized he was not brave enough to risk his life.* **Nathan wanted to be a surfman until he realized he was not brave enough to risk his life.** Write subordinating conjunctions *since, after, because, when,* and *until*. Have students write several complex sentences using subordinating conjunctions. Provide sentence frames as needed. Read aloud sentences that students have written. Work together to find the conjunction that works best to join the clauses. Allow students to use their home language to clarify the meanings of their sentences. Read aloud the improved sentences together.

NOUNS, PRONOUNS, AND OBJECTS • COMMON AND PROPER NOUNS

LEARNING OBJECTIVES

- **Language** Identify common and proper nouns.
- **Language** Use common and proper nouns correctly in speaking and writing.

MATERIALS   Online 🍊 Ed

Display and Engage *Grammar 2.1.1a, 2.1.1b*

Printable *Grammar 2.1.1*

 INSTRUCTIONAL VOCABULARY

- **common noun** a general person, place, or thing
- **proper noun** a particular person, place, or thing

Connect and Teach

- Show <u>Display and Engage: Grammar 2.1.1a</u>. Explain that a noun is a word that names a person, a place, or a thing. A **common noun** names any person, place, or thing that is general and not specific. A **proper noun** names a particular person, place, or thing.

- Model identifying the nouns in the example sentence: *Coach Greene was concerned about the player.*

    THINK ALOUD *To identify the nouns, I ask:* What word names a person, place, or thing? Is the word general or specific? Coach Greene *is a proper noun because it names a specific person.* Player *is a common noun because it refers to any person who plays.*

DISPLAY AND ENGAGE: Grammar 2.1.1a   Online 🍊 Ed

Grammar 2.1.1a

Recognizing Common and Proper Nouns

A **noun** is a word that names a person, place, or thing. A **common noun** names any person, place, or thing. A **proper noun** names a particular person, place, or thing.

> *proper noun*   *common noun*
> Coach Greene was concerned about the player.

> *proper noun*   *common noun*
> Dr. Tran went to the hospital to meet a new doctor.

Engage and Apply

- Complete items 1–6 on <u>Display and Engage: Grammar 2.1.1b</u> with students.

- Guide students to identify common and proper nouns.

- Have partners list common and proper nouns that they might find in the classroom or at school.

- Have students complete <u>Printable: Grammar 2.1.1</u> for practice recognizing common and proper nouns.

- Have students edit a writing draft to identify proper nouns.

DISPLAY AND ENGAGE: Grammar 2.1.1b   Online 🍊 Ed

Grammar 2.1.1b

Recognizing Common and Proper Nouns

Identify the nouns, and tell whether each is common or proper.

1. Ramona is the best athlete in the class. Ramona (proper); athlete (common); class (common)
2. Jumping rope is Meagan's favorite exercise. rope (common); Meagan's (proper); exercise (common)
3. Playing basketball is also good exercise. basketball (common); exercise (common)
4. Kickball is a popular game during recess. kickball (common); game (common); recess (common)
5. Mrs. Lee's favorite sport is baseball. Mrs. Lee's (proper); sport (common); baseball (common)
6. Many boys and girls play baseball in the spring. boys (common); girls (common); baseball (common); spring (common)

🗨 ENGLISH LEARNER SUPPORT: Facilitate Language Connection

Explain that many languages have common and proper nouns, but capitalization rules differ. Remind students that in English, proper nouns, such as days of the week and months, are capitalized. Point out that in languages such as Russian and Spanish, however, the same proper nouns are not capitalized.

Scaffolded Practice

ALL LEVELS Explain that a common noun names something general, like *city,* but a proper noun names something particular, like *Houston.* Point out that city does not have a capital letter, but *Houston* does. Provide examples that include common nouns and proper nouns that are familiar to students. Discuss how each is a common noun or proper noun. Write each noun and point out how to capitalize the proper nouns. Have volunteers give examples of common nouns and proper nouns as they are able. Students may point to pictures or name nouns.

LEARNING OBJECTIVES

- **Language** Identify and capitalize proper nouns.
- **Language** Use common and proper nouns correctly in speaking and writing.

MATERIALS   Online ⊙Ed

Display and Engage *Grammar 2.1.2a, 2.1.2b*

Printable *Grammar 2.1.2*

 INSTRUCTIONAL VOCABULARY

- **proper noun** a particular person, place, or thing
- **initials** the first letter of each important word
- **acronym** a name made from initials that can be read as a word
- **abbreviation** a shortened form of a word

Connect and Teach

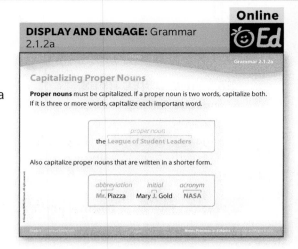

DISPLAY AND ENGAGE: Grammar 2.1.2a — Online ⊙Ed

- Show <u>Display and Engage: Grammar 2.1.2a</u>. Tell students that **proper nouns** must be capitalized. If a proper noun is more than one word, capitalize each important word. Explain that **abbreviations** are capitalized when they represent proper nouns. Names created from **initials** are written with all capital letters.

- Tell students that when the initials of an organization form a word or pronounceable name, such as NASA, those initials are called an **acronym**.

- Model capitalizing proper nouns in the example: *the League of Student Leaders*.
  THINK ALOUD *To capitalize proper nouns, I ask:* How many words make up the proper noun? Which words are important? The League of Student Leaders *is five words; three of them are important and should be capitalized.*

Engage and Apply

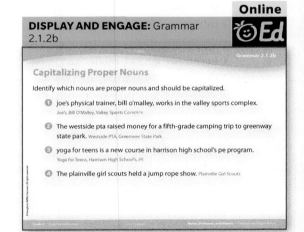

DISPLAY AND ENGAGE: Grammar 2.1.2b — Online ⊙Ed

- Complete items 1–4 on <u>Display and Engage: Grammar 2.1.2b</u> with students.

- Read aloud an article that contains proper nouns and the names of organizations. Have students list and capitalize the proper nouns they hear.

- Have students complete <u>Printable: Grammar 2.1.2</u> for practice capitalizing proper nouns.

- Have students edit a writing draft to be sure all proper nouns have been capitalized.

 ENGLISH LEARNER SUPPORT: Facilitate Language Connection

Some languages, such as Chinese, do not have capital letters. Students may need practice distinguishing between capital and lowercase letters.

Scaffolded Practice

ALL LEVELS Review that a common noun names any person, place, or thing. A proper noun names a specific person, place, or thing. The important words in a proper noun should begin with a capital letter. Model identifying the nouns in the sentence: *Coach Greene was concerned about the player.* Remind students why *Coach Greene* is capitalized. Help students identify each common noun and each proper noun and tell how the proper nouns should be capitalized in the following sentences. *Coach rockett gave the rope to peggy. Rockett, Peggy The girls go to school in long island. Long Island*

NOUNS, PRONOUNS, AND OBJECTS • COMMON AND PROPER NOUNS

LEARNING OBJECTIVES

- **Language** Identify and capitalize organizations.
- **Language** Use common and proper nouns correctly in speaking and writing.

MATERIALS	Online 

Display and Engage *Grammar 2.1.3a, 2.1.3b*

Printable *Grammar 2.1.3*

INSTRUCTIONAL VOCABULARY

- **abbreviation** a shortened form of a word
- **initials** the first letter of each important word
- **acronym** a name made from initials that can be read as a word

Connect and Teach

- Show **Display and Engage: Grammar 2.1.3a**. Explain that the names of organizations are proper nouns. When writing about a specific organization, its name and its abbreviation or acronym should be capitalized.

- Model distinguishing between proper and common nouns in the examples.

  THINK ALOUD *To capitalize proper nouns, I ask:* Do the words name a kind of group or one group in particular?

Engage and Apply

- Complete items 1–4 on **Display and Engage: Grammar 2.1.3b** with students.

- Have partners list organizations. Remind them to capitalize each organization's name.

- Display these proper nouns. Have students rewrite each as an acronym, an abbreviation, or initials.
  Red Glee Group RGG
  National Bowling Society NBS
  Mister Smith Mr. Smith
  Patterson Athletic Training Studio PATS

- Have students complete **Printable: Grammar 2.1.3** for practice capitalizing.

- Have students edit a writing draft for correct capitalization.

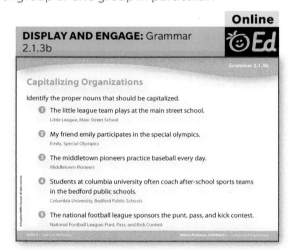

DISPLAY AND ENGAGE: Grammar 2.1.3a — Online

Capitalizing Organizations

The name of a particular organization, or group, is a proper noun. Each important word in the name begins with a capital letter.

proper noun
The Springfield Middle School Parent Teacher Organization is sponsoring a school carnival.

common noun
Parent teacher organizations often help to raise money for schools.

DISPLAY AND ENGAGE: Grammar 2.1.3b — Online

Capitalizing Organizations

Identify the proper nouns that should be capitalized.

1. The little league team plays at the main street school.
   Little League, Main Street School
2. My friend emily participates in the special olympics.
   Emily, Special Olympics
3. The middletown pioneers practice baseball every day.
   Middletown Pioneers
4. Students at columbia university often coach after-school sports teams in the bedford public schools.
   Columbia University, Bedford Public Schools
5. The national football league sponsors the punt, pass, and kick contest.
   National Football League; Punt, Pass, and Kick Contest

ENGLISH LEARNER SUPPORT: Scaffolded Practice

SUBSTANTIAL

Write the following sentences on the board and work with students to identify the nouns: *Ruby kicked the ball. Ruby; ball The class will travel to Washington, DC class; Washington, DC*

MODERATE

Ask students to use words, phrases, or short sentences to identify objects in the room that are common or proper nouns.

LIGHT

Have partners write three sentences on a piece of paper. Ask them to exchange sentences with another pair of students and identify all of the nouns.

LEARNING OBJECTIVES

- **Language** Review common and proper nouns, including initials, acronyms, abbreviations, and names of organizations.

- **Language** Use common and proper nouns correctly in speaking and writing.

MATERIALS   Online ⊙*Ed*

Display and Engage *Grammar 2.1.4a, 2.1.4b, 2.1.4c*

Printable *Grammar 2.1.4*

WORDS ABOUT WRITING

- **common noun** a general person, place, or thing

- **proper noun** a particular person, place, or thing

- **initials** the first letter of each important word

- **acronym** a name made from initials that can be read as a word

- **abbreviation** a shortened form of a word

Review Common and Proper Nouns

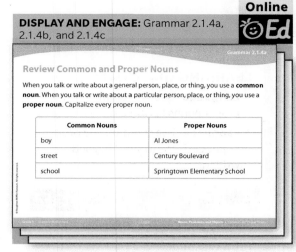

- Show **Display and Engage: Grammar 2.1.4a** and **Grammar 2.1.4b**. Review with students the definition of a noun. Then distinguish a **common noun** from a **proper noun**.

- Remind students that proper nouns are capitalized, while common nouns are not. Explain that the names of specific organizations are proper nouns and that the important words in their names are capitalized.

- Write these sentences on the board. Have students identify the nouns and tell whether they are common or proper.

  » *Myra likes to go to the Museum of Natural History to see the displays of dinosaurs and other prehistoric animals.* Myra (proper), Museum of Natural History (proper), displays (common), dinosaurs (common), animals (common)

  » *The colorful rocks in the case glowed under the lights.* rocks (common), case (common), lights (common)

  » *The director of the museum, Dr. Martinez, talked about meteorites.* director (common), museum (common), Dr. Martinez (proper), meteorites (common)

- Work with students to complete the exercises on **Display and Engage: Grammar 2.1.4c**.

- Have students complete **Printable: Grammar 2.1.4** for more practice with common and proper nouns.

- Have students edit a writing draft to be sure all proper nouns have been capitalized.

EL ENGLISH LEARNER SUPPORT: Scaffolded Practice

ALL LEVELS Draw a T-Map or two-column chart. Label one column *Common Nouns* and the second column *Proper Nouns*. List several pairs of common and proper nouns, such as holiday/Labor Day, month/February, and day/Saturday. Have students identify the common and proper noun in each pair. Record responses in the chart.

LEARNING OBJECTIVES

- **Language** Choose common and proper nouns to convey ideas.
- **Language** Use common and proper nouns correctly in speaking and writing.

MATERIALS   Online

Display and Engage *Grammar 2.1.5*

Printable *Grammar 2.1.5*

 WORDS ABOUT WRITING

- **common noun** a general person, place, or thing
- **proper noun** a particular person, place, or thing
- **initials** the first letter of each important word
- **acronym** a name made from initials that can be read as a word
- **abbreviation** a shortened form of a word

Connect and Teach

- Show **Display and Engage: Grammar 2.1.5**. Tell students that good grammar helps readers focus on the important information in a piece of writing.

- Explain that **proper nouns** are usually important, so correctly capitalizing these words or abbreviations helps readers pay attention to that information.

Online

DISPLAY AND ENGAGE: Grammar 2.1.5

Grammar 2.1.5

Connect to Writing: Using Common and Proper Nouns

When you proofread your work, make sure you have written common and proper nouns correctly. Remember to capitalize proper nouns.

Incorrect Capitalization	Correct Capitalization
Wed., oct. 8 at 7:00 P.M.	Wed., Oct. 8 at 7:00 P.M.
Come to a lecture by dr. Roberta price of the American double dutch Association (Adda).	Come to a lecture by Dr. Roberta Price of the American Double Dutch Association (ADDA).
Dr. price has appeared many times on programs on Pbs, the Public Broadcasting system.	Dr. Price has appeared many times on programs on PBS, the Public Broadcasting System.

Engage and Apply

- Display the following sentences. Guide students to identify the words that should be capitalized:

> dr. smith works in the white house in Washington, DC
> Dr. Smith; White House
> Leon wants to play basketball in the nba. NBA

- Have students complete **Printable: Grammar 2.1.5** for practice capitalizing proper nouns.

- Have students return to a piece of their writing. In pairs, have them look for words that need to be capitalized. Encourage them to rewrite their sentences to capitalize all proper nouns. Have volunteers share their improvements.

EL **ENGLISH LEARNER SUPPORT: Support Revision**

SUBSTANTIAL

Have students choose two sentences with common and proper nouns to copy from a book. Read the sentences aloud with students. Help students identify and circle common nouns, then identify and underline proper nouns. Have students check that the proper nouns are correctly capitalized. Guide students to revise as needed.

MODERATE

Have students choose two sentences with common and proper nouns to copy from a book. Read the sentences aloud with students. Have them circle common nouns and underline proper nouns. Then have students check that the proper nouns are correctly capitalized. Guide students to revise as needed.

LIGHT

Have partners write two sentences with common and proper nouns. Ask students to read their sentences aloud to their partners. Have them circle common nouns and underline proper nouns. Then have students check whether their partner correctly capitalized the proper nouns. Guide students to revise as needed.

NOUNS, PRONOUNS, AND OBJECTS • SINGULAR AND PLURAL NOUNS

LEARNING OBJECTIVES

- **Language** Identify singular and plural nouns.
- **Language** Use singular and plural nouns correctly in speaking and writing.

MATERIALS	Online 🍎Ed

Display and Engage *Grammar 2.2.1a, 2.2.1b*

Printable *Grammar 2.2.1*

INSTRUCTIONAL VOCABULARY

- **singular noun** names one person, place, or thing
- **plural noun** names more than one person, place, or thing

Connect and Teach

- Show <u>**Display and Engage: Grammar 2.2.1a**</u>. Explain that a **singular noun** names one person, place, thing, or idea. A **plural noun** names more than one person, place, thing, or idea. The plural of most nouns is formed by adding *-s* or *-es* to the end of the word. To decide how to form the plural, look at the ending of a singular noun.

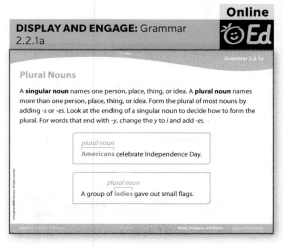

- Model plural nouns in the example sentences: *The students work at the book fair. Some ladies buy a large stack of books.*

  THINK ALOUD *To identify how to form the plural of each noun, I ask, "What is the noun's ending?" Student ends in t. I add an -s to form the plural. Lady ends in y. I change the y to i and add -es. Book ends in k, so I add an -s.*

Engage and Apply

- Complete items 1–6 on <u>**Display and Engage: Grammar 2.2.1b**</u> with students.

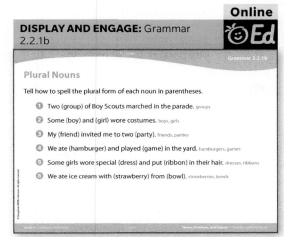

- List the following nouns on the board. Work with students to make them plural. *object objects; sidewalk sidewalks; success successes; bench benches; box boxes; party parties*

- Have students complete <u>**Printable: Grammar 2.2.1**</u> for practice with plural nouns.

- Have students edit a writing draft for the correct usage of plural nouns.

 ENGLISH LEARNER SUPPORT: Facilitate Language Connections

Point out the cognates in the vocabulary list. Then explain that *singular* and *plural* are the same in Spanish as in English. In Spanish, plurals are formed by adding *-s* to words ending in a vowel and *-es* to words ending in a consonant. Students may tend to add *-es* at the end of any word ending in a consonant (*girles*). In Hmong, Vietnamese, and Cantonese, nouns do not have a plural form. Instead, adjectives indicate whether a noun is singular or plural.

Scaffolded Practice

SUBSTANTIAL

Use sentence frames to demonstrate how to change singular nouns to plural by adding *-s* or *-es*. The first sentence should have a singular noun, and the second should have the same noun in plural form.

Ari played one _____ at the park. **game**
Zia played two _____ at the park. **games**

MODERATE

Use sentence frames to demonstrate how to change singular nouns into plural nouns.

Ari's dog had one _____. **puppy**
Zia's dog had three _____. **puppies**

LIGHT

Have pairs of students write similar sentence frames. Partners exchange the frames and check to see if plurals are formed correctly.

NOUNS, PRONOUNS, AND OBJECTS • SINGULAR AND PLURAL NOUNS

LEARNING OBJECTIVES

- **Language** Write the plural forms of nouns correctly.
- **Language** Use singular and plural nouns correctly in speaking and writing.

MATERIALS   Online 🔴 *Ed*

Display and Engage *Grammar 2.2.2a, 2.2.2b*

Printable *Grammar 2.2.2*

 INSTRUCTIONAL VOCABULARY

- **plural noun** names more than one person, place, or thing

Connect and Teach

- Show **Display and Engage: Grammar 2.2.2a**. Explain that to form the plurals of some nouns ending in *f* or *fe*, change the *f* to *v* and add *-s* or *-es*. To form the plurals of nouns ending in *o*, add *-s* or *-es*. Some nouns have the same form whether plural or singular, such as *sheep*.

- Model identifying plural nouns in the example sentence: *Mia's cow had two calves.*

  THINK ALOUD *To identify special plural forms of nouns, I ask, "Does the noun require only adding -s or -es to make it plural, or is the plural formed in another way?" Calves is the plural form of* calf, *so it is not formed by simply adding -s or -es.*

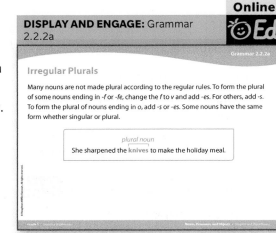

DISPLAY AND ENGAGE: Grammar 2.2.2a   Online 🔴 *Ed*

Grammar 2.2.2a

Irregular Plurals

Many nouns are not made plural according to the regular rules. To form the plural of some nouns ending in -*f* or -*fe*, change the *f* to *v* and add -*es*. For others, add -*s*. To form the plural of nouns ending in *o*, add -*s* or -*es*. Some nouns have the same form whether singular or plural.

plural noun
She sharpened the **knives** to make the holiday meal.

Engage and Apply

- Complete items 1–6 on **Display and Engage: Grammar 2.2.2b** with students.

- Write the following sentences on the board. Have students orally identify special plural nouns.

  My favorite food is mashed potatoes. **potatoes**

  She cut the loaf into two halves. **halves**

DISPLAY AND ENGAGE: Grammar 2.2.2b   Online 🔴 *Ed*

Grammar 2.2.2b

Irregular Plurals

Tell how to spell the plural form of each noun in parentheses.

1. My mother always makes four (loaf) of bread. loaves
2. Some of the (man) help with cooking. men
3. I eat so much I think even my (foot) get bigger. feet
4. Once when we were eating, we saw two (deer) out the window. deer
5. For Thanksgiving, my grandmother always cooks two (turkey). turkeys
6. We work hard to rake up all the (leaf) before people come. leaves

- Have students complete **Printable: Grammar 2.2.2** for practice with irregular plural nouns.

- Have students edit a writing draft for the correct usage of irregular plural nouns.

🟢 **ENGLISH LEARNER SUPPORT: Scaffolded Practice**

SUBSTANTIAL

Play a memory game with students using high-frequency irregular plurals such as *women, children, people, mice, teeth, feet*. Give each student six slips of paper labeled with *woman, child, person, mouse, tooth,* and *foot* and have them identify the plural form of the word. Repeat until students feel confident making the nouns plural.

MODERATE

Use sentence frames to demonstrate how to change singular nouns into plural nouns. Choose nouns that have irregular plurals. For example:

I have a loose _____. **tooth**

I will brush my _____. **teeth**

LIGHT

Have pairs of students write similar sentence frames. Partners exchange the frames and check to see if plurals are formed correctly. Encourage them to use irregular plurals.

LEARNING OBJECTIVES

- **Language** Identify collective nouns.
- **Language** Use collective nouns correctly in speaking and writing.

MATERIALS	Online

Display and Engage *Grammar 2.2.3a, 2.2.3b*

Printable *Grammar 2.2.3*

INSTRUCTIONAL VOCABULARY

- **collective noun** names a group of people, animals, or things that act as a unit

Connect and Teach

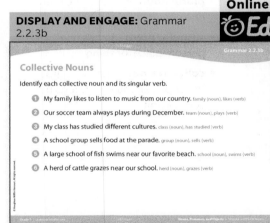

DISPLAY AND ENGAGE: Grammar 2.2.3a — Online Ed

Collective Nouns

A **collective noun** names a group. Even though the group is made up of more than one person, place, thing, or idea, the collective noun is singular. A collective noun is accompanied by a singular verb.

collective noun   singular verb
The class decides to celebrate the holiday together.

- Show **Display and Engage: Grammar 2.2.3a**. Explain that some nouns, called **collective nouns**, name a collection of people, animals, or things that act as a unit. An example of a collective noun is *team*. Collective nouns are treated as singular nouns unless they refer to more than one collection.

- Explain that a collective noun is accompanied by a singular verb.

- Model identifying the collective noun in the example sentence: *The class decides to study for a quiz together.*

  THINK ALOUD *To identify collective nouns, I ask, "Which word names a group of people, places, things, or ideas? Which verb describes what the group does?"* class; decides

Engage and Apply

DISPLAY AND ENGAGE: Grammar 2.2.3b — Online Ed

Collective Nouns

Identify each collective noun and its singular verb.

1. My family likes to listen to music from our country. family (noun), likes (verb)
2. Our soccer team always plays during December. team (noun), plays (verb)
3. My class has studied different cultures. class (noun), has studied (verb)
4. A school group sells food at the parade. group (noun), sells (verb)
5. A large school of fish swims near our favorite beach. school (noun), swims (verb)
6. A herd of cattle grazes near our school. herd (noun), grazes (verb)

- Complete items 1–6 on **Display and Engage: Grammar 2.2.3b** with students.

- Call out a singular noun, a plural noun, and a collective noun. Have students reply by giving an example of a verb to use with it. Ask them to tell whether it is a singular or a plural verb.

- Have students complete **Printable: Grammar 2.2.3** for practice with collective nouns.

- Have students edit a writing draft for the correct usage of collective nouns.

 ENGLISH LEARNER SUPPORT: Scaffolded Practice

SUBSTANTIAL

Work with students to practice using nouns that show a group, such as *class, team,* and *family*. Point out that, even though these nouns stand for more than one person, they are treated like singular nouns. Have students use the words in sentence frames, such as:

The_____ won the game. *team*
The _____ eats dinner together. *family*

MODERATE

Use sentence frames to demonstrate how to use singular verbs with collective nouns. For example:

The team _____ ten points. (score/scores) *scores*
The family _____ in a car. (travel/travels) *travels*

LIGHT

Have pairs of students work together to write sentences using collective nouns. Encourage them to use more challenging nouns in a sentence, such as *army, company,* or *House of Representatives*.

NOUNS, PRONOUNS, AND OBJECTS • SINGULAR AND PLURAL NOUNS

LEARNING OBJECTIVES

- **Language** Review singular and plural nouns.
- **Language** Use singular and plural nouns correctly in speaking and writing.

MATERIALS Online

Display and Engage 2.2.4a, 2.2.4b, 2.2.4c

Printable *Grammar 2.2.4*

 INSTRUCTIONAL VOCABULARY

- **plural noun** names more than one person, place, or thing
- **singular noun** names one person, place, or thing
- **collective noun** names a group of people, animals, or things that act as a unit

Review Singular and Plural Nouns

- Show **Display and Engage: Grammar 2.2.4a** and **Grammar 2.2.4b**. Remind students that adding *-s* or *-es* forms the **plurals** of many nouns. The **singular** and plural forms of some nouns are the same. Others have special plural forms. **Collective nouns** name a group that acts as a single unit. Review examples of each.

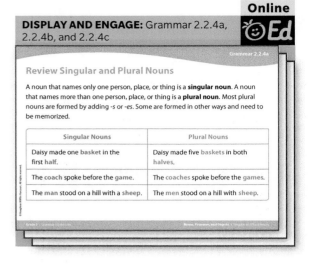

DISPLAY AND ENGAGE: Grammar 2.2.4a, 2.2.4b, and 2.2.4c

Grammar 2.2.4a

Review Singular and Plural Nouns

A noun that names only one person, place, or thing is a **singular noun**. A noun that names more than one person, place, or thing is a **plural noun**. Most plural nouns are formed by adding *-s* or *-es*. Some are formed in other ways and need to be memorized.

Singular Nouns	Plural Nouns
Daisy made one basket in the first half.	Daisy made five baskets in both halves.
The coach spoke before the game.	The coaches spoke before the games.
The man stood on a hill with a sheep.	The men stood on a hill with sheep.

- Work with students to complete the exercises on **Display and Engage: Grammar 2.2.4c**.

- Have students complete **Printable: Grammar 2.2.4** for more practice with singular and plural nouns.

- Have students edit a writing draft for the correct usage of nouns.

 ENGLISH LEARNER SUPPORT: Scaffolded Practice

SUBSTANTIAL

Remind students that most plural nouns are formed by adding *–s* or *–es*. Provide additional examples, such as *boy, box, bench, book*.

MODERATE

Reinforce singular, plural, and collective nouns by presenting the following sentences. Have students identify all the nouns in each sentence and tell whether each is singular (s) or plural (p). Help students identify the collective (c) noun.

- *The team* (c) *rides on a bus* (s) *to the games* (p).
- *The boy* (s) *shows some drawings* (p) *to the class* (c).
- *The mayor* (s) *asks the committee* (c) *some questions* (p).

LIGHT

Have pairs of students work together to identify the singular, plural, and collective nouns from a short passage in a book.

NOUNS, PRONOUNS, AND OBJECTS • SINGULAR AND PLURAL NOUNS

LEARNING OBJECTIVES

- **Language** Write the singular and plural forms of nouns correctly.
- **Language** Use singular and plural nouns correctly in speaking and writing.

MATERIALS   Online

Display and Engage *Grammar 2.2.5*

Printable *Grammar 2.2.5*

 INSTRUCTIONAL VOCABULARY

- **singular noun** names one person, place, or thing
- **plural noun** names more than one person, place, or thing
- **collective noun** names a group of people, animals, or things that act as a unit

Connect and Teach

- Show **Display and Engage: Grammar 2.2.5**. Remind students that it is important to use properly formed plurals in their writing.

Engage and Apply

- Write the following words on the board. Have partners identify whether each is a singular, plural, or collective noun.

  saucers plural
  ounce singular
  bear singular
  auction singular
  churches plural
  class collective
  group collective

- Write these words on the board. Ask the same partners to write the plural forms of the words. Have them use a dictionary if they need help. Then have students use the singular or plural form in sentences. Invite volunteers to share their sentences.

  trench trenches
  mouse mice
  life lives
  candle candles
  tomato tomatoes
  moose moose

- Have students complete **Printable: Grammar 2.2.5** for practice forming singular, plural, and collective nouns.

- Have students return to a piece of their writing. In pairs, have them look for incorrectly spelled plural nouns. Encourage them to rewrite their sentences to form plurals correctly. Have volunteers share their improvements.

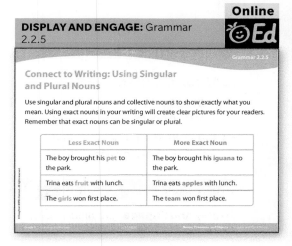

 ENGLISH LEARNER SUPPORT: Support Revision

SUBSTANTIAL

Write: *A girl writes in her diary about her class.*

- Say: *There are three nouns in this sentence. Each noun names one person, place, or thing. They are singular nouns.* Then write: *The girls write in their diaries about their classes.* Ask: *How are these nouns different now? They are plural nouns.*

MODERATE

Write: *The girls write in their diaries about their classes.*

- Say: *I am going to write the rules for changing singular nouns to plural nouns. Tell me which noun in the sentence follows each rule.*
- When a singular noun ends in *s, x, ch,* or *sh,* add *-es. classes*
- When a singular noun ends in a consonant + *y,* change the *y* to *i* and add *-es. diaries*
- For most other singular nouns, just add the letter *-s. girls*

LIGHT

Introduce students to nouns that have special plural forms: *foot/feet, tooth/teeth, child/children.* Have partners write two complete sentences each, one using the singular form and one using the plural form.

NOUNS, PRONOUNS, AND OBJECTS • POSSESSIVE NOUNS

LEARNING OBJECTIVES

• **Language** Identify singular possessive nouns.

• **Language** Use possessive nouns correctly in speaking and writing.

MATERIALS   Online 🍊 **Ed**

Display and Engage *Grammar 2.3.1a, 2.3.1b*

Printable *Grammar 2.3.1*

📖 INSTRUCTIONAL VOCABULARY

• **singular possessive noun** noun in which one person or thing owns something

Connect and Teach

• Show <u>**Display and Engage: Grammar 2.3.1a**</u>. Explain that a **singular possessive noun** shows that one person or thing owns something.

• Model using this sentence: *The coat of the girl was hanging in the closet.*

THINK ALOUD *To make a noun possessive, I ask, "Is there a shorter way to show possession?" I could use the possessive noun girl's to show that she owns the coat. To form the possessive, I add an apostrophe + -s to the end of the noun.*

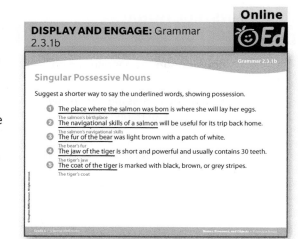

Engage and Apply

• Complete items 1–5 on <u>**Display and Engage: Grammar 2.3.1b**</u> with students.

• Have students ask themselves if there is a shorter way to show possession. Remind them to add an apostrophe + -s to the end of most singular nouns.

• Have students complete <u>**Printable: Grammar 2.3.1**</u> for practice with singular possessive nouns.

• Have students edit a writing draft for the correct usage of singular possessive nouns.

🗨 ENGLISH LEARNER SUPPORT: Scaffolded Practice

SUBSTANTIAL
Have students insert a singular possessive noun for *cat* in the sentence:
The _____ food is here. cat's

MODERATE
Guide students to orally state sentences about objects in the room, using singular possessive nouns.

LIGHT
Have students work with partners to write sentences about objects in the room, using singular possessive nouns.

NOUNS, PRONOUNS, AND OBJECTS • POSSESSIVE NOUNS

LEARNING OBJECTIVES

- **Language** Identify plural possessive nouns.
- **Language** Use possessive nouns correctly in speaking and writing.

MATERIALS	Online

Display and Engage *Grammar 2.3.2a, 2.3.2b*

Printable *Grammar 2.3.2*

 INSTRUCTIONAL VOCABULARY

- **plural possessive noun** noun that shows ownership by more than one person or thing

Connect and Teach

- Show <u>Display and Engage: Grammar 2.3.2a</u>. Explain that a **plural possessive noun** shows ownership by more than one person or thing.

- Model using the sentence: *The laughter of the students can be heard on the playground.*

  THINK ALOUD *I ask, "Is there a shorter way to show possession?" The word students' can show ownership of laughter. To form the possessive of a plural noun that end in -s or -es, I add an apostrophe after the -s.*

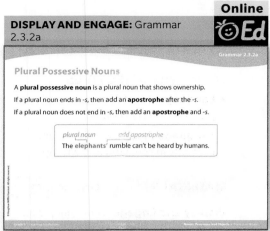

DISPLAY AND ENGAGE: Grammar 2.3.2a — Online Ed

Grammar 2.3.2a

Plural Possessive Nouns

A **plural possessive noun** is a plural noun that shows ownership.
If a plural noun ends in -s, then add an **apostrophe** after the -s.
If a plural noun does not end in -s, then add an **apostrophe** and -s.

plural noun	add apostrophe

The elephants' rumble can't be heard by humans.

Engage and Apply

- Complete items 1–5 on <u>Display and Engage: Grammar 2.3.2b</u> with students.

- Have students ask themselves if there is a shorter way to show possession.

- Have students complete <u>Printable: Grammar 2.3.2</u> for practice with plural possessive nouns.

- Have students edit a writing draft for the correct usage of plural possessive nouns.

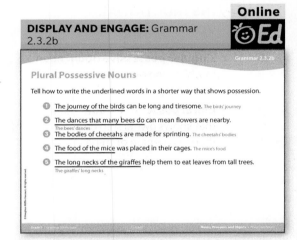

DISPLAY AND ENGAGE: Grammar 2.3.2b — Online Ed

Grammar 2.3.2b

Plural Possessive Nouns

Tell how to write the underlined words in a shorter way that shows possession.

1. The <u>journey of the birds</u> can be long and tiresome. The birds' journey
2. The <u>dances that many bees do</u> can mean flowers are nearby. The bees' dances
3. The <u>bodies of cheetahs</u> are made for sprinting. The cheetahs' bodies
4. The <u>food of the mice</u> was placed in their cages. The mice's food
5. The <u>long necks of the giraffes</u> help them to eat leaves from tall trees. The giraffes' long necks

 ENGLISH LEARNER SUPPORT: Scaffolded Practice

SUBSTANTIAL

Have students insert a plural possessive noun in sentence frames, such as:

The _____ chairs were placed in rows. **girls'**
The _____ toys are in the box. **cats'**

MODERATE

Review with students the difference between singular and plural possessive nouns. Remind students that apostrophes are typically included in possessive nouns. Work with students to identify the bold words in these sentences as plural possessive nouns or plural nouns.

- *The* **boys** *jumped in the water with joy.* **plural**
- *The* **girls'** *shoelaces became untied.* **plural possessive**
- *Both* **boys** *had a lot of fun that day.* **plural**

LIGHT

Have students work with partners to write sentences about something that happened today, using plural possessive nouns.

NOUNS, PRONOUNS, AND OBJECTS • POSSESSIVE NOUNS

LEARNING OBJECTIVES

- **Language** Identify singular and plural possessive nouns.
- **Language** Use possessive nouns correctly in speaking and writing.

MATERIALS	Online

Display and Engage *Grammar 2.3.3a, 2.3.3b*

Printable *Grammar 2.3.3*

 INSTRUCTIONAL VOCABULARY

- **singular possessive noun** noun in which one person or thing owns something
- **plural possessive noun** noun that shows ownership by more than one person or thing

Connect and Teach

- Show **Display and Engage: Grammar 2.3.3a**. Review with students singular and plural possessive nouns.

- Write the following on the board: *The campers' long trip had just begun. The car's fuel tank was filled with gas.*

  THINK ALOUD *I ask, "How can I tell if a possessive noun is singular or plural?" For most plural possessive nouns, like campers', the apostrophe is at the end of the word. Singular possessive nouns, like car's, have an 's.*

Engage and Apply

- Complete items 1–5 on **Display and Engage: Grammar 2.3.3b** with students.

- Have students ask themselves how they can tell if a possessive noun is singular or plural.

- Have students complete **Printable: Grammar 2.3.3** for practice with possessive nouns.

- Have students edit a writing draft for the correct usage of possessive nouns.

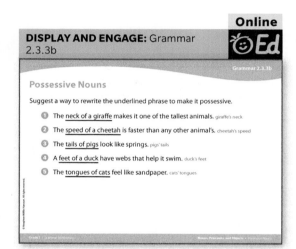

DISPLAY AND ENGAGE: Grammar 2.3.3a — Online Ed

Grammar 2.3.3a

Possessive Nouns

A possessive noun shows ownership.

A singular possessive noun has an apostrophe and an -s to show possession.

A plural possessive noun has an apostrophe after the s, or if the plural noun does not have an s, an apostrophe and then -s.

singular noun   add apostrophe (') and -s
The elephant's ears were huge!

plural noun   add apostrophe
The elephants' trunks were long.

DISPLAY AND ENGAGE: Grammar 2.3.3b — Online Ed

Grammar 2.3.3b

Possessive Nouns

Suggest a way to rewrite the underlined phrase to make it possessive.

1 The neck of a giraffe makes it one of the tallest animals. giraffe's neck
2 The speed of a cheetah is faster than any other animal's. cheetah's speed
3 The tails of pigs look like springs. pigs' tails
4 A feet of a duck have webs that help it swim. duck's feet
5 The tongues of cats feel like sandpaper. cats' tongues

EL **ENGLISH LEARNER SUPPORT: Scaffolded Practice**

SUBSTANTIAL

Have students insert a possessive noun in sentence frames, then tell whether the noun is singular or plural. For example:
The _____ shirt has stripes. girl's, singular
The _____ leashes are hanging by the door. dogs', plural

MODERATE

Review with students the difference between singular and plural possessive nouns. Remind students that apostrophes are typically included in possessive nouns. Work with students to identify the bold words in these sentences as singular or plural possessive nouns.

- *The **boys'** sneakers are lined up on the floor. plural possessive*

- *The **girl's** hair is brown. singular possessive*

- *Both **boys'** socks have red stripes. plural possessive*

LIGHT

Have students work with partners to write sentences about the classroom, using a mix of singular and plural possessive nouns.

NOUNS, PRONOUNS, AND OBJECTS • POSSESSIVE NOUNS

LEARNING OBJECTIVES

- **Language** Identify and write singular and plural possessive nouns.
- **Language** Use possessive nouns correctly in speaking and writing.

MATERIALS

Online Ed

Display and Engage *Grammar 2.3.4a, 2.3.4b*

Printable *Grammar 2.3.4*

INSTRUCTIONAL VOCABULARY

- **singular possessive noun** noun in which one person or thing owns something
- **plural possessive noun** noun that shows ownership by more than one person or thing

Review Possessive Nouns

- Show **Display and Engage: Grammar 2.3.4a**. Remind students that adding an apostrophe + s forms the **singular possessive** of many nouns. Adding an apostrophe to the end of a plural noun forms the **plural possessive** of many nouns. Review examples of each.

- Work with students to complete the exercises on **Display and Engage: Grammar 2.3.4b**.

- Have students complete **Printable: Grammar 2.3.4** for more practice with possessive nouns.

- Have students edit a writing draft for the correct usage of possessive nouns.

ENGLISH LEARNER SUPPORT: Scaffolded Practice

SUBSTANTIAL
Review with students the difference between singular and plural possessive nouns. Have students identify where the apostrophe should go in the bold word to make it the singular possessive.

- *The **owls** feathers are brown.* owl's
- *The **dogs** fur is black.* dog's
- *The **turtles** shell is brown.* turtle's

MODERATE
Remind students that apostrophes are typically included in possessive nouns. Work with students to write a possessive noun to fit in the blank.

- *The _____ hoot sounded through the woods.* owl's
- *The _____ leash was pink.* dog's
- *The _____ fur was different colors.* rabbit's

LIGHT
Have students work with partners to write sentences about animals, using possessive nouns.

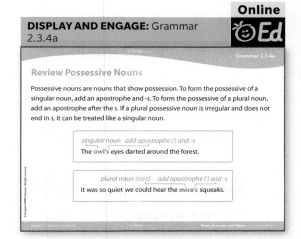

DISPLAY AND ENGAGE: Grammar 2.3.4a

Online Ed

Review Possessive Nouns

Possessive nouns are nouns that show possession. To form the possessive of a singular noun, add an apostrophe and -s. To form the possessive of a plural noun, add an apostrophe after the s. If a plural possessive noun is irregular and does not end in s, it can be treated like a singular noun.

singular noun add apostrophe (') and -s
The owl's eyes darted around the forest.

plural noun (no s) add apostrophe (') and -s
It was so quiet we could hear the mice's squeaks.

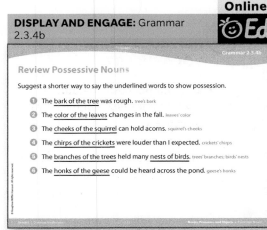

DISPLAY AND ENGAGE: Grammar 2.3.4b

Online Ed

Review Possessive Nouns

Suggest a shorter way to say the underlined words to show possession.

1. The bark of the tree was rough. tree's bark
2. The color of the leaves changes in the fall. leaves' color
3. The cheeks of the squirrel can hold acorns. squirrel's cheeks
4. The chirps of the crickets were louder than I expected. crickets' chirps
5. The branches of the trees held many nests of birds. trees' branches; birds' nests
6. The honks of the geese could be heard across the pond. geese's honks

NOUNS, PRONOUNS, AND OBJECTS • POSSESSIVE NOUNS

LEARNING OBJECTIVES

- **Language** Identify and write singular and plural possessive nouns.
- **Language** Use possessive nouns correctly in speaking and writing.

MATERIALS	Online

Display and Engage *Grammar 2.3.5*

Printable *Grammar 2.3.5*

 **INSTRUCTIONAL VOCABULARY**

- **singular possessive noun** noun in which one person or thing owns something
- **plural possessive noun** noun that shows ownership by more than one person or thing

Connect and Teach

- Show **Display and Engage: Grammar 2.3.5**. Remind students that they can make their writing more concise by using possessive nouns to show that a person or thing owns something.

Engage and Apply

- Write the following phrases on the board. Have partners rewrite the phrase to make it more concise.

  » *the book owned by Sheila* Sheila's book

  » *the fur of the cat* the cat's fur

  » *the flames of the candle* the candles' flames

- Then have students write a sentence for each possessive. Invite students to share their sentences with the class.

- Have students complete **Printable: Grammar 2.3.5** for practice forming possessive nouns.

- Have students return to a piece of their writing. In pairs, have them look for sentences that they can combine or revise using a possessive noun. Explain that combining sentences helps make writing less choppy. Have volunteers share their improvements.

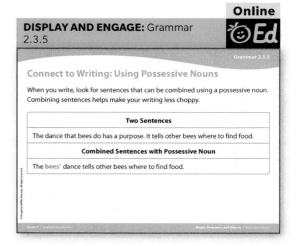

EL ENGLISH LEARNER SUPPORT: Support Revision

SUBSTANTIAL

Write: *The mane of the horse was brown. The shoes on the feet of the horse needed to be put back on the hooves of the horse.*

- Say: *Some of the phrases in these sentences can be made shorter by using possessives.* Then write: *The horse's mane was brown. The horse's shoes needed to be put back on the horse's hooves.* Ask: *How are these sentences different? The second is shorter and less choppy because it uses possessive nouns.*

MODERATE

Write: *The red barn owned by the farmer was where he kept the saddles of the horses.*

- Say: *I want to revise the sentence to be shorter and use possessive nouns.*

Work with students to rewrite the sentence to use fewer words to show possession. *The farmer's red barn was where he kept the horses' saddles.*

LIGHT

Have students write two complete sentences about a horse that use singular and/or plural possessive nouns.

LEARNING OBJECTIVES

- **Language** Identify subject pronouns.
- **Language** Use subject pronouns correctly in speaking and writing.

MATERIALS	Online

Display and Engage *Grammar 2.4.1a, 2.4.1b*

Printable *Grammar 2.4.1*

INSTRUCTIONAL VOCABULARY

- **pronoun** takes the place of a noun
- **subject pronoun** takes the place of a noun used as the subject of a sentence

Connect and Teach

- Show **Display and Engage: Grammar 2.4.1a**. Explain that a **pronoun** is a word that takes the place of a noun. A **subject pronoun** takes the place of a noun used as the subject of a sentence. Write these singular subject pronouns on the board: *I, you, she, he, it*. Then write these plural subject pronouns: *we, you, they*.

- Model replacing nouns with subject pronouns in this sentence: *Jessica emptied the box.*

  THINK ALOUD *To identify the subject of a sentence and the subject pronoun that might replace it, I ask, "Who or what is the subject of the sentence? What word can you replace the subject with?" The word* Jessica *is the subject. I can replace it with the subject pronoun* She.

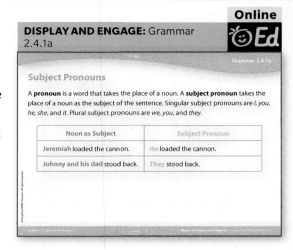

DISPLAY AND ENGAGE: Grammar 2.4.1a

Online Ed

Engage and Apply

- Complete items 1–6 on **Display and Engage: Grammar 2.4.1b** with students.

- Have students write one sentence with a singular subject pronoun and another with a plural subject pronoun.

- Have students complete **Printable: Grammar 2.4.1** for practice with subject pronouns.

- Have students edit a writing draft for the correct usage of subject pronouns.

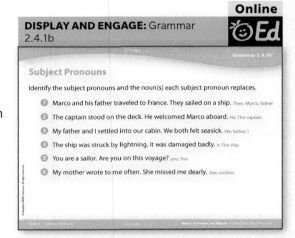

DISPLAY AND ENGAGE: Grammar 2.4.1b

Online Ed

ENGLISH LANGUAGE SUPPORT: Facilitate Language Connections

Point out the cognate in the vocabulary list. Students can see the word *noun* in *pronoun*. A pronoun should be used to avoid writing the same noun over and over.

Scaffolded Practice

SUBSTANTIAL

Use these sentence frames to demonstrate how to use subject pronouns in the place of proper names.

Mr. Lee sees Mrs. Lee on the bus.

_____ *sees Mrs. Lee on the bus.* He

MODERATE

Use the sentence frames to demonstrate how to use subject pronouns in the same sentence. For example:

Mr. Lee see Mrs. Lee on the bus.

_____ *sees Mrs. Lee on the bus.* He

Mr. and Mrs. Lee see the boys on the bus.

_____ *see the boys on the bus.* They

LIGHT

Guide students in writing two sentences one, with a subject pronouns.

LEARNING OBJECTIVES

- **Language** Identify object pronouns.
- **Language** Use object pronouns correctly in speaking and writing.

MATERIALS   Online ⊙Ed

Display and Engage *Grammar 2.4.2a, 2.4.2b*

Printable *Grammar 2.4.2*

INSTRUCTIONAL VOCABULARY

- **object pronoun** takes the place of a noun used after a verb or a preposition

Connect and Teach

- Show **Display and Engage: Grammar 2.4.2a**. Explain that an **object pronoun** takes the place of a noun used after an action verb or after words such as *to, for, with, in,* or *out.* Review the object pronouns *me, him, her, them,* and *us.* Remind students that some sentences have plural objects that are replaced by plural object pronouns.

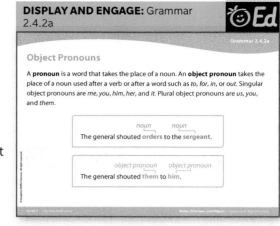

- Model the correct use of object pronouns in the sample sentence: *The chef shouted to the waiter.*

  THINK ALOUD *To identify the correct use of object pronouns, I ask, "Whom or what is receiving the action of the sentence?" The chef shouted (action) to the waiter. (whom) Using the list of plural object pronouns, I can replace the waiter with the singular object pronoun him.*

Engage and Apply

- Complete items 1–8 on **Display and Engage: Grammar 2.4.2b** with students.

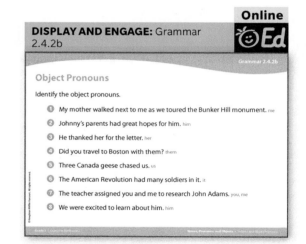

- Write the following sentence on the board. Have students replace nouns with the object pronouns. *The girl put the dishes in the sink. She, them*

- Have students complete **Printable: Grammar 2.4.2** for practice with object pronouns.

- Have students edit a writing draft for the correct usage of object pronouns.

🗨 ENGLISH LANGUAGE SUPPORT: Scaffolded Practice

SUBSTANTIAL

Use these sentence frames to demonstrate how to use object pronouns in the place of proper names.

I saw Mrs. Jones in the hall.
I saw _____ in the hall. her
Lila teaches Marisa and me after school.
Lila teaches _____ after school. us

MODERATE

Use the sentence frames to demonstrate how to use object pronouns to avoid repetition.

I saw Mrs. Jones in the hall. I gave _____ the homework assignment. her
Lila teaches Marisa and me after school. She helps _____ with math. us

LIGHT

Guide students in writing two sentences, one with proper names and one with an object pronoun that helps avoid repetition.

LEARNING OBJECTIVES

- **Language** Identify pronoun-antecedent agreement.
- **Language** Use pronoun-antecedent agreement correctly in speaking and writing.

MATERIALS
Online

Display and Engage *Grammar 2.4.3a, 2.4.3b*

Printable *Grammar 2.4.3*

 **INSTRUCTIONAL VOCABULARY**

- **antecedent** the noun or nouns that the pronoun replaces and refers back to

Connect and Teach

- Show **Display and Engage: Grammar 2.4.3a**. Use the example to explain that the **antecedent** of a pronoun is the noun or nouns that the pronoun replaces.

- Write the following sentence on the board: *The social studies teacher was good, even though she gave really difficult tests.*

- Explain that *she* is the pronoun because it refers to the noun *teacher*. *Teacher* is the antecedent because it is the noun to which the pronoun is referring. Explain the importance of making sure pronouns agree in number and gender with the antecedent.

DISPLAY AND ENGAGE: Grammar 2.4.3a
Online

Grammar 2.4.3a

Pronoun-Antecedent Agreement

The **antecedent** of a pronoun is the noun or nouns that the pronoun replaces. A pronoun must agree with its antecedent in number and gender.

> *singular, female subject*
> **Abigail Adams** wrote letters to her husband.

> *singular, female subject pronoun*
> **She** wrote almost every week.

Engage and Apply

- Complete items 1–5 on **Display and Engage: Grammar 2.4.3b** with students.

- Write the following sentence on the board. Have students substitute a pronoun for the repeated noun and then identify its antecedent. *The toy was broken into bits because the toy fell off the table.* **it; the toy**

- Have students complete **Printable: Grammar 2.4.3** for practice with pronouns and antecedents.

- Have students edit a writing draft for the correct pronoun-antecedent agreement.

DISPLAY AND ENGAGE: Grammar 2.4.3b
Online

Grammar 2.4.3b

Pronoun-Antecedent Agreement

Identify the subject and object pronouns and their antecedents.

1. General George Washington and his men crossed the Delaware River. The journey was difficult for them. them-Washington and his men
2. Our class took a history test on Friday. We studied for three days. We-Our class
3. Our principal has a painting of George Washington in his office. It holds great meaning for him. him-principal; it-painting
4. The soldiers trudged through the wintery weather. It was hard on them. It-weather; them-soldiers
5. Abigail Adams wrote many letters to her husband. He enjoyed receiving them from her. he-husband; them-letters; her-Abigail Adams

EL **ENGLISH LANGUAGE SUPPORT: Scaffolded Practice**

SUBSTANTIAL

Work with students to identify the pronoun and its antecedent.

- *The coach wrote an invitation and sent it to his team.* **pronoun: it; antecedent: an invitation**
- *The coach was having a party. He wanted to celebrate the victory.* **pronoun: he; antecedent: The coach**

MODERATE

Work with students to tell whether the pronoun in each sentence below is a subject pronoun or an object pronoun. Have them name its antecedent.

- *The coach wrote an invitation and sent it to his team.* **object pronoun; antecedent: an invitation**
- *The coach was having a party. He wanted to celebrate the victory.* **subject pronoun; antecedent: The coach**

LIGHT

Give students a short paragraph. Have them identify the pronouns in the text as well as their antecedents.

LEARNING OBJECTIVES

- **Language** Review subject and object pronouns.
- **Language** Use subject and object pronouns correctly in speaking and writing.

MATERIALS Online

Display and Engage *Grammar 2.4.4a, 2.4.4b, 2.4.4c*

Printable *Grammar 2.4.4*

 INSTRUCTIONAL VOCABULARY

- **pronoun** takes the place of a noun
- **subject pronoun** takes the place of a noun used as the subject of a sentence
- **object pronoun** takes the place of a noun used after a verb or a preposition
- **antecedent** the noun or nouns that the pronoun replaces and refers back to

Review Subject and Object Pronouns

- Show **Display and Engage: Grammar 2.4.4a** and then **Grammar 2.4.4b**. Remind students that a **subject pronoun** takes the place of a noun used as the subject of a sentence. An **object pronoun** takes the place of a noun used after an action verb or after a preposition. Pronouns must agree with their **antecedents** in gender and number.

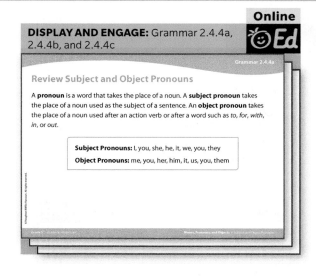

DISPLAY AND ENGAGE: Grammar 2.4.4a, 2.4.4b, and 2.4.4c

Grammar 2.4.4a

Review Subject and Object Pronouns

A **pronoun** is a word that takes the place of a noun. A **subject pronoun** takes the place of a noun used as the subject of a sentence. An **object pronoun** takes the place of a noun used after an action verb or after a word such as *to, for, with, in,* or *out.*

Subject Pronouns: I, you, she, he, it, we, you, they
Object Pronouns: me, you, her, him, it, us, you, them

- Work with students to complete the exercises on **Display and Engage: Grammar 2.4.4c**.

- Have students complete **Printable: Grammar 2.4.4** for more practice with subject and object pronouns.

- Have students edit a writing draft for the correct usage of subject and object pronouns.

EL ENGLISH LANGUAGE SUPPORT: Scaffolded Practice

SUBSTANTIAL

Have students replace the noun in the subject of each sentence with a subject pronoun.

- *The players applauded Henry.* **They applauded Henry.**
- *Jill gave Ava the letter.* **She gave Ava the letter.**

MODERATE

Have students replace the noun in the subject and the proper noun in the predicate with subject or object pronouns.

- *The players applauded Henry.* **They applauded him.**
- *Jill gave Juan the letter.* **She gave him the letter.**

LIGHT

Have students work with partners to write a few sentences about something they learned in school today. Have students use subject and object pronouns to avoid repetition. Remind them that pronouns must agree with their antecedents.

NOUNS, PRONOUNS, AND OBJECTS • SUBJECT AND OBJECT PRONOUNS

LEARNING OBJECTIVES

- **Language** Use subject and object pronouns correctly.
- **Language** Use subject and object pronouns correctly in speaking and writing.

MATERIALS　　Online

Display and Engage *Grammar 2.4.5*

Printable *Grammar 2.4.5*

 INSTRUCTIONAL VOCABULARY

- **pronoun** takes the place of a noun
- **subject pronoun** takes the place of a noun used as the subject of a sentence
- **object pronoun** takes the place of a noun used after a verb or a preposition
- **antecedent** the noun or nouns that the pronoun replaces and refers back to

Connect and Teach

- Show **Display and Engage: Grammar 2.4.5**. Tell students that using pronouns correctly can make writing clearer and more interesting to read.

- Point out that an important part of writing and revising is checking whether there is pronoun-antecedent agreement.

Engage and Apply

- Display the following sentences. Guide students in using pronouns to replace nouns. Then have students identify the subject and object pronouns.

  » *When John was young, John went to an amusement park.* **When John was young, he went to an amusement park.** *(he, subject pronoun)*

  » *Zoe got a new bike. Zoe loved riding her bike with her cousins. Zoe rode to the park with her cousins.* **Zoe got a new bike. She loved riding her bike with her cousins. She rode to the park with them.** *(She, subject pronoun; them, object pronoun)*

- Have students complete **Printable: Grammar 2.4.5** for practice using subject and object pronouns.

- Have students return to a piece of their writing. In pairs, have them look for repeated words they can replace with pronouns. Encourage them to rewrite their sentences using subject and object pronouns. Remind students to use correct pronoun-antecedent agreement. Have volunteers share their improvements.

 ENGLISH LANGUAGE SUPPORT: Support Revision

SUBSTANTIAL

Explain that to make writing interesting, it is important to avoid repeating words. Instead of using the same noun over and over, for example, students can replace one or more of them with a pronoun.

- Write: *I, you, he, she, it, we, they*. Explain that these are subject pronouns. They can be the subject of a sentence.

- Write: *me, you, him, her, it, us, them*. Explain that these are object pronouns. They can be the object of a verb or a preposition.

MODERATE

Write: *Div talked to the artists. Div asked if Div could help the artists. The artists said Div could help the artists.*

- Explain that these sentences can be made more fluent and interesting if the nouns are not repeated. Instruct students to copy the sentences, replacing repeated nouns with pronouns.

LIGHT

Have students write a paragraph about something they've read recently using subject and object pronouns. Have the students underline the pronouns in their paragraph.

LEARNING OBJECTIVES

- **Language** Identify indefinite pronouns.
- **Language** Use pronouns correctly in speaking and writing.

MATERIALS	Online

Display and Engage: *Grammar 2.5.1a, 2.5.1b*

Printable *Grammar 2.5.1*

INSTRUCTIONAL VOCABULARY

- **indefinite pronoun** refers to a person or thing that's not identified

Connect and Teach

- Show **Display and Engage: Grammar 2.5.1a**. Remind students that a pronoun is a word that takes the place of a noun. An **indefinite pronoun** refers to a person or thing that is not identified. Tell students that words, such as *someone, something, anyone, everything, both, all, either, each, nothing, anything,* and *neither* are indefinite pronouns.

- Model identifying indefinite pronouns in this example sentence: *Someone went to the cafeteria.*

  THINK ALOUD *To identify the indefinite pronoun, I ask, "What pronoun refers to a person or thing that is not identified?" The word Someone does not identify who went to the cafeteria.*

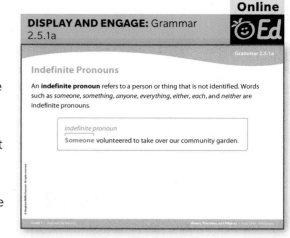

DISPLAY AND ENGAGE: Grammar 2.5.1a

Online

Indefinite Pronouns

An **indefinite pronoun** refers to a person or thing that is not identified. Words such as *someone, something, anyone, everything, either, each,* and *neither* are indefinite pronouns.

> *indefinite pronoun*
> Someone volunteered to take over our community garden.

Engage and Apply

- Complete items 1–8 on **Display and Engage: Grammar 2.5.1b** with students.

- Write the words *anyone, either, few, both,* and *all* on the board. Ask students to provide sentences using each indefinite pronoun.

- Have students complete **Printable: Grammar 2.5.1** for practice with indefinite pronouns.

- Have students edit a writing draft for the correct usage of indefinite pronouns.

DISPLAY AND ENGAGE: Grammar 2.5.1b

Online

Indefinite Pronouns

Identify the indefinite pronouns.

1. We have to get someone to replace our community gardener. someone
2. Everyone was happy with the work that he did. Everyone
3. I don't know if anyone answered our ad in the newspaper. anyone
4. The gardener either got another job or no longer wants to volunteer. either
5. We would do anything to make him stay. anything
6. Everybody knows it can be difficult to volunteer a lot of time. Everybody
7. I hope everything goes well with him in the future. everything
8. Each of the other gardeners had a lot of fun at the job. Each

ENGLISH LEARNER SUPPORT: Scaffolded Practice

SUBSTANTIAL

Use the following sentences to demonstrate that an indefinite pronoun replaces a person or thing that is not identified.

Someone came to the class.
Does anyone want to help?

MODERATE

Use the sentence frames below to guide students to use indefinite pronouns.

_____ came to the class. *Some; Few; All*
Does _____ want to help? *somebody; everybody; someone*

LIGHT

Have students complete a sentence starter using one or more of the following indefinite pronouns: *anyone, everything, both.* For example, *Our principal said that _____.*

NOUNS, PRONOUNS, AND OBJECTS • MORE KINDS OF PRONOUNS

LEARNING OBJECTIVES

- **Language** Identify possessive pronouns.
- **Language** Use possessive pronouns correctly in writing and speaking.

MATERIALS   Online

Display and Engage: *Grammar 2.5.2a, 2.5.2b*

Printable *Grammar 2.5.2*

 **INSTRUCTIONAL VOCABULARY**

- **possessive pronoun** shows ownership

Connect and Teach

- Show **Display and Engage: Grammar 2.5.2a**. Explain that a **possessive pronoun** replaces a possessive noun and shows ownership. Tell students that words such as *my, your, his, her, its, our, their, mine, yours,* and *theirs* are possessive pronouns.

- Model identifying possessive pronouns in this sample sentence: *Our town has a theater with a new café.*

  THINK ALOUD *To identify the possessive pronoun, I ask, "What is the pronoun in the sentence that shows ownership?" I see that the word Our appears before the word town. Our shows ownership by telling whose town it is. I think Our is the possessive pronoun.*

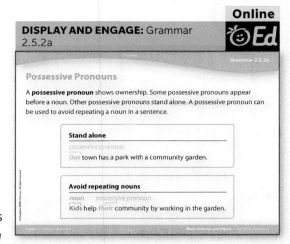

DISPLAY AND ENGAGE: Grammar 2.5.2a   Online 🍊Ed

Grammar 2.5.2a

Possessive Pronouns

A **possessive pronoun** shows ownership. Some possessive pronouns appear before a noun. Other possessive pronouns stand alone. A possessive pronoun can be used to avoid repeating a noun in a sentence.

Stand alone
possessive pronoun
Our town has a park with a community garden.

Avoid repeating nouns
noun   possessive pronoun
Kids help their community by working in the garden.

Engage and Apply

- Complete items 1–6 on **Display and Engage: Grammar 2.5.2b** with students.

- Write the following sentences on the board. Have students orally complete the sentences with a possessive pronoun.
  - » *Peter and Carla read _____ report about recycling.* **their**
  - » *We will plant bulbs in _____ schoolyard.* **our**
  - » *Lena wrote a letter to _____ state representative.* **her**

- Have students complete **Printable: Grammar 2.5.2** for practice with possessive pronouns.

- Have students edit a writing draft for the correct usage of possessive pronouns.

DISPLAY AND ENGAGE: Grammar 2.5.2b   Online 🍊Ed

Grammar 2.5.2b

Possessive Pronouns

Identify the possessive pronouns.

1 Where are your tomatoes? your
2 Those cucumbers are mine. mine
3 Any citizen can contribute to our garden. our
4 The shovel is hers. hers

Suggest a possessive pronoun to replace the repeated noun.

5 Josh offers Josh's vegetables to everyone. his
6 The volunteers need people to help the volunteers. them

EL **ENGLISH LEARNER SUPPORT: Facilitate Language Connections**

Explain that possessive pronouns are used differently in some languages. For example, in Spanish, the possessive pronoun *su* is used to replace both masculine and feminine nouns. In Russian, the possessive of a noun depends on the gender of the noun it describes, rather than the noun the pronoun replaces. Provide additional practice forming statements using possessive pronouns, for example: *His book is on the desk. Her soccer game was canceled.*

Scaffolded Practice

SUBSTANTIAL / MODERATE
Use the sentence frames below to guide students to use possessive pronouns.
Shirley carried _____ book to class. **her**
Luis picked up _____ pen. **his**

LIGHT
Have students revise sentences to use possessive pronouns to avoid repetition. For example, *Tamara carried Tamara's violin* can be revised to *Tamara carried her violin.*

LEARNING OBJECTIVES

- **Language** Identify interrogative pronouns.
- **Language** Use interrogative pronouns correctly in speaking and writing.

MATERIALS
Online

Display and Engage: *Grammar 2.5.3a, 2.5.3b*

Printable *Grammar 2.5.3*

INSTRUCTIONAL VOCABULARY

- **interrogative pronoun** begins a question

Connect and Teach

- Show **Display and Engage: Grammar 2.5.3a**. Tell students that **interrogative pronouns** are words used to begin questions. Point out that the words *who, what,* and *which* are interrogative pronouns.

- Model identifying interrogative pronouns in this example sentence: *What are your favorite sports at the school?*

  THINK ALOUD *To identify an interrogative pronoun, I look to see if a pronoun begins a sentence. Then I ask, "What pronoun begins the question in this sentence?" What is the interrogative pronoun.*

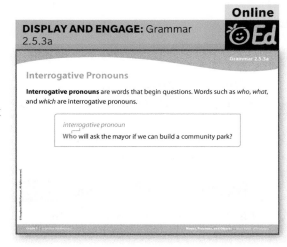

DISPLAY AND ENGAGE: Grammar 2.5.3a

Online Ed

Grammar 2.5.3a

Interrogative Pronouns

Interrogative pronouns are words that begin questions. Words such as *who, what,* and *which* are interrogative pronouns.

interrogative pronoun
Who will ask the mayor if we can build a community park?

Engage and Apply

- Complete items 1–6 on **Display and Engage: Grammar 2.5.3b** with students.

- Have student pairs work together. Tell one partner to point to an object in the classroom and say one of the three interrogative pronouns: *who, what,* or *which.* Have the other partner make up a question about the object, using the interrogative pronoun.

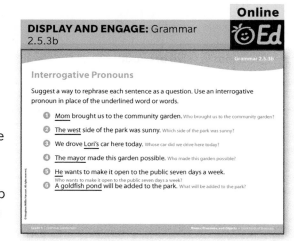

DISPLAY AND ENGAGE: Grammar 2.5.3b

Online Ed

Grammar 2.5.3b

Interrogative Pronouns

Suggest a way to rephrase each sentence as a question. Use an interrogative pronoun in place of the underlined word or words.

1. <u>Mom</u> brought us to the community garden. Who brought us to the community garden?
2. <u>The west side</u> of the park was sunny. Which side of the park was sunny?
3. We drove <u>Lori's</u> car here today. Whose car did we drive here today?
4. <u>The mayor</u> made this garden possible. Who made this garden possible?
5. <u>He</u> wants to make it open to the public seven days a week. Who wants to make it open to the public seven days a week?
6. <u>A goldfish pond</u> will be added to the park. What will be added to the park?

- Have students complete **Printable: Grammar 2.5.3** for practice with interrogative pronouns.

- Have students edit a writing draft for the correct usage of interrogative pronouns.

EL **ENGLISH LANGUAGE SUPPORT: Scaffolded Practice**

SUBSTANTIAL

Use the following sentences to demonstrate that an interrogative pronoun takes the place of a person or thing in a question. Ask students to identify the interrogative pronoun in each question.

Who has my book?

Which book did you read?

MODERATE

Use the sentence frames below to guide students to use interrogative pronouns.

_____ has my book? *Who*

_____ was that sound? *What*

LIGHT

Have students write two sentences that ask a question and use interrogative pronouns. For example: *What is your name?*

LEARNING OBJECTIVES

- **Language** Identify indefinite, possessive, and interrogative pronouns.
- **Language** Use pronouns correctly in speaking and writing.

MATERIALS   Online

Display and Engage: *Grammar 2.5.4a, 2.5.4b, 2.5.4c*

Printable *Grammar 2.5.4*

INSTRUCTIONAL VOCABULARY

- **indefinite pronoun** refers to a person or thing that's not identified
- **possessive pronoun** shows ownership
- **interrogative pronoun** begins a question

Review Pronouns

- Show <u>Display and Engage: Grammar 2.5.4a</u> and then <u>Grammar 2.5.4b</u>. Review with students that a *pronoun* is a word that replaces a noun. An **indefinite pronoun** refers to a person or thing that is not identified. A **possessive pronoun** shows ownership or possession. An **interrogative pronoun** begins a question.

- Work with students to complete the exercises on <u>Display and Engage: Grammar 2.5.4c</u>.

- Have students complete <u>Printable: Grammar 2.5.4</u> for more practice with pronouns.

- Have students edit a writing draft for the correct usage of pronouns.

DISPLAY AND ENGAGE: Grammar 2.5.4a, 2.5.4b, and 2.5.4c

Online
Ed

Grammar 2.5.4a

Review Pronouns

A **pronoun** is a word that takes the place of a noun. There are several kinds of pronouns. Words such as *someone* and *something* refer to a person or thing that is not identified. These pronouns are called **indefinite pronouns**.

> *indefinite pronoun*
> Anyone can become a gardener here.

Pronouns that replace possessive nouns are called **possessive pronouns**.

> *possessive pronoun*
> Mr. McGowan never had his own yard.

ENGLISH LEARNER SUPPORT: Scaffolded Practice

SUBSTANTIAL

Ask students to identify each group of words as indefinite, possessive, or interrogative pronouns.

- *my, mine, hers, his* possessive pronouns
- *someone, anyone, somewhere* indefinite pronouns
- *who, what, which* interrogative pronouns

MODERATE

Write the following sentences on the board: *Everyone at school read about Darnell's idea. What is his idea? Darnell wants to do something with the old basketball court.*

Help students identify the indefinite pronouns in the sentences. (*Everyone; something*) Then have them identify the interrogative pronoun and the possessive pronoun. (*What; his*)

LIGHT

Have students complete a sentence starter using one or more of the following pronouns: *hers, anyone, what, everything, ours, both*. For example, *Our music teacher said that* _____.

CONNECT TO WRITING: USING INDEFINITE, POSSESSIVE, AND INTERROGATIVE PRONOUNS

LEARNING OBJECTIVES

- **Language** Identify indefinite, possessive, and interrogative pronouns.
- **Language** Use pronouns correctly in speaking and writing.

MATERIALS   Online

Display and Engage: *Grammar 2.5.5*

Printable *Grammar 2.5.5*

 **INSTRUCTIONAL VOCABULARY**

- **indefinite pronoun** refers to a person or thing that's not identified
- **possessive pronoun** shows ownership
- **interrogative pronoun** begins a question

Connect and Teach

- Show **Display and Engage: Grammar 2.5.5**. Tell students that an important part of revising is using pronouns correctly.

- Point out that using the correct pronouns in writing will make the ideas clear to readers. Using pronouns also eliminates some repetition.

Engage and Apply

- Display the following sentences. Have students identify the underlined pronouns as indefinite, possessive, or interrogative.

  » *Who is his teacher?* interrogative; possessive

  » *Neither wanted to go to the meeting.* indefinite

  » *What does everyone want for lunch?* interrogative; indefinite

  » *All are welcome to our meeting.* indefinite; possessive

- Have students complete **Printable: Grammar 2.5.5** for practice using indefinite, possessive, and interrogative pronouns.

- Have students return to a piece of their writing. In pairs, have them look for repeated words they can replace with pronouns. Encourage them to rewrite their sentences using indefinite, possessive, and interrogative pronouns. Have volunteers share their improvements.

DISPLAY AND ENGAGE: Grammar 2.5.5

Online Ed

Grammar 2.5.5

Connect to Writing: Using Indefinite, Possessive, and Interrogative Pronouns

Possessive pronouns can help you avoid repeating proper nouns in your writing. When you use possessive pronouns, be sure that your readers will be able to understand to whom each possessive pronoun refers.

Excessive Use of Proper Noun	Improved with Possessive Pronouns
Carla will present Carla's proposal at the council meeting tonight. Carla's mother and aunt will attend the meeting, along with Carla's cousin.	Carla will present her proposal at the council meeting tonight. Her mother and aunt will attend the meeting, and Carla's cousin will be there, too.

EL **ENGLISH LEARNER SUPPORT: Support Revision**

SUBSTANTIAL/MODERATE

Write the following sentences on the board: *Darnell and Linda gave speeches. Darnell's and Linda's opinions were different.*

- Say: *Let's use a possessive pronoun to make the second sentence sound more natural.*

- Refer to the list of possessive pronouns: *my, your, her, its, our,* and *their.* Ask: *Which possessive pronoun can we use to replace Darnell's and Linda's?* their

LIGHT

Have students write two sentences about something they've read this week. Ask them to use both possessive nouns and pronouns in the sentences.

LEARNING OBJECTIVES

- **Language** Identify direct objects.
- **Language** Use direct objects correctly in speaking and writing.

MATERIALS	Online

Display and Engage *Grammar 2.6.1a, 2.6.1b*

Printable *Grammar 2.6.1*

 **INSTRUCTIONAL VOCABULARY**

- **direct object** the word that receives the action of the verb

Connect and Teach

- Show **Display and Engage: Grammar 2.6.1a**. Explain that a **direct object** is a word in the predicate that receives the action of the verb.

- Model identifying the direct object in the example: *Jake bought his sister a new book.*

  THINK ALOUD *To identify the direct object, I ask, "What word tells who or what receives the action of the verb?"* Sister *is the direct object because it receives the action of the verb* bought.

> **Online**
> **DISPLAY AND ENGAGE:** Grammar 2.6.1a
>
> Direct Objects
>
> A **direct object** is a word in the predicate that receives the action of the verb.
>
> verb   direct object
> The boy helped his mother with the chores.

Engage and Apply

- Complete items 1–8 on **Display and Engage: Grammar 2.6.1b** with students.

- Have students identify the direct object of each sentence below:

  » *Monica liked her cat.* **her cat**

  » *The cat purred near Monica's sister.* **Monica's sister**

- Have students complete **Printable: Grammar 2.6.1** for practice with direct objects.

- Have students edit a writing draft for correct usage of direct objects.

> **Online**
> **DISPLAY AND ENGAGE:** Grammar 2.6.1b
>
> Direct Objects
>
> Identify the action verb of each sentence. Then identify the direct object of each sentence.
>
> 1. The boy chopped enough wood for a week. chopped; wood
> 2. The farmer plowed the field for the corn. plowed; field
> 3. Maddie and Sean picked berries for jam. picked; berries
> 4. Dylan read a story to his brother. read; story
> 5. The girl walked the dog along the river. walked; dog
> 6. That night his head hit the pillow, and he was asleep. hit; pillow
> 7. The next day Aiko painted the barn. painted; barn
> 8. No wonder the boy welcomed his father back gratefully. welcomed; father

---

EL **ENGLISH LEARNER SUPPORT: Facilitate Language Connections**

In some languages, such as Spanish, direct objects can come before the verb, after the verb, and can even be attached to the end of the verb. Point out that in English, the direct object nearly always follows the verb.

Scaffolded Practice

SUBSTANTIAL

Use the frames to demonstrate how to generate direct objects in sentences.

Sanjay chopped _____. **vegetables**

Lori bought a _____. **book**

Guide students to generate sentences with direct objects. The answers provided are sample responses.

MODERATE

Use the sentence frames from the Beginning section to demonstrate direct objects. Guide students to generate their own sentences for direct objects. Then have them exchange sentences with another student and identify the direct objects in each other's sentences.

LIGHT

Have pairs of students look through classroom books to find examples of direct objects. Ask them to identify the direct object and the action verb in the sentence.

LEARNING OBJECTIVES

- **Language** Identify compound direct objects in sentences.
- **Language** Use direct and indirect objects correctly in speaking and writing.

MATERIALS   Online

Display and Engage *Grammar 2.6.2a, 2.6.2b*

Printable *Grammar 2.6.2*

 **INSTRUCTIONAL VOCABULARY**

- **compound direct object** words that receive the action of the same verb

Connect and Teach

- Show **Display and Engage: Grammar 2.6.2a**. Tell students that when more than one word in a sentence receives the action of the verb, that sentence contains a **compound direct object**.

- Model identifying the compound direct object in the example sentence: *My sister bakes pies and cakes.*

  THINK ALOUD *To identify the direct objects, I ask, "What words tell who or what receives the action of the verb?" Pies and cakes are the direct objects because they receive the action of the verb bakes.*

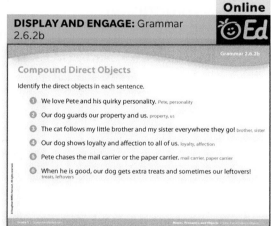

DISPLAY AND ENGAGE: Grammar 2.6.2a

Compound Direct Objects

A **direct object** receives the action of a verb. Some sentences contain more than one direct object, or a **compound direct object**.

compound direct object
My dog Pete requires care and attention.

Engage and Apply

- Complete items 1–6 on **Display and Engage: Grammar 2.6.2b** with students.

- Write the following sentences on the board. Have students orally identify the compound direct object in each sentence.

  » *Roxy bought a jacket and scarf.* **jacket and scarf**

  » *Ricardo lost his gloves and hat.* **gloves and hat**

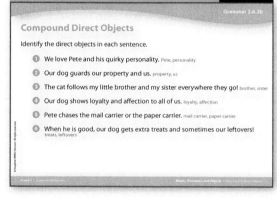

DISPLAY AND ENGAGE: Grammar 2.6.2b

Compound Direct Objects

Identify the direct objects in each sentence.

1. We love Pete and his quirky personality. Pete, personality
2. Our dog guards our property and us. property, us
3. The cat follows my little brother and my sister everywhere they go! brother, sister
4. Our dog shows loyalty and affection to all of us. loyalty, affection
5. Pete chases the mail carrier or the paper carrier. mail carrier, paper carrier
6. When he is good, our dog gets extra treats and sometimes our leftovers! treats, leftovers

- Have students complete **Printable: Grammar 2.6.2** for practice with compound direct objects.

- Have students edit a writing draft for correct usage of compound direct objects.

EL **ENGLISH LEARNER SUPPORT: Scaffolded Practice**

SUBSTANTIAL/MODERATE

Use the frames to demonstrate direct and compound direct objects. Use the sample answers to demonstrate direct objects, then have students come up with their own direct objects to fill in the blanks.

The farmer chased _____ and _____ through the woods. **dogs and birds**
Workers painted _____ and _____. **the barn and house**

Guide students to tell who or what receives the action of the verb in each sentence.

LIGHT

Provide students with the sentence frames below, and have them combine them into one sentence with a compound direct object.

The farmer gathered the _____.
The farmer then gathered the _____.

INDIRECT OBJECTS

LEARNING OBJECTIVES

- **Language** Identify indirect objects.
- **Language** Use indirect objects correctly in speaking and writing.

MATERIALS   Online

Display and Engage *Grammar 2.6.3a, 2.6.3b*

Printable *Grammar 2.6.3*

INSTRUCTIONAL VOCABULARY

- **indirect object** tells to or for whom or what the action is done

Connect and Teach

- Show **Display and Engage: Grammar 2.6.3a**. Explain that an **indirect object** usually tells to or for whom/what the action of the verb is done.

- Model identifying the indirect object in the sample sentence: *The shop owner gave Max a dollar.*

  THINK ALOUD *To identify the indirect object, I ask, "To whom or what or for whom or what is the action of the verb done?" Gave is the verb. The shop owner gave to Max a dollar. Max is the indirect object.*

Engage and Apply

- Complete items 1–8 on **Display and Engage: Grammar 2.6.3b** with students.

- Have volunteers generate sentences with indirect objects, and write them on the board. Then have other volunteers identify the indirect objects and explain the reasons for their choices.

- Have students complete **Printable: Grammar 2.6.3** for practice with indirect objects.

- Have students edit a writing draft for correct usage of direct and indirect objects.

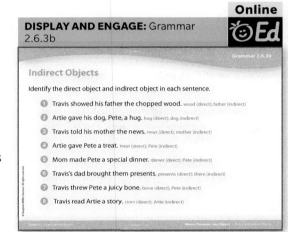

DISPLAY AND ENGAGE: Grammar 2.6.3a — Online Ed

Indirect Objects

Some sentences have both a direct and an indirect object. The direct object receives the action of the verb. The **indirect object** tells to or for whom or what the action of the verb is done. The indirect object comes before the direct object in a sentence.

indirect object   direct object
The dog gave Angelo a lick.
Angelo names the person to whom the lick was given.

DISPLAY AND ENGAGE: Grammar 2.6.3b — Online Ed

Indirect Objects

Identify the direct object and indirect object in each sentence.
1. Travis showed his father the chopped wood. wood (direct); father (indirect)
2. Artie gave his dog, Pete, a hug. hug (direct); dog (indirect)
3. Travis told his mother the news. news (direct); mother (indirect)
4. Artie gave Pete a treat. treat (direct); Pete (indirect)
5. Mom made Pete a special dinner. dinner (direct); Pete (indirect)
6. Travis's dad brought them presents. presents (direct); them (indirect)
7. Travis threw Pete a juicy bone. bone (direct); Pete (indirect)
8. Travis read Artie a story. story (direct); Artie (indirect)

EL ENGLISH LEARNER SUPPORT: Scaffolded Practice

SUBSTANTIAL

Have students identify the indirect object in several sentences. For example:
The farmer gave the chickens feed. chickens
The farmer handed his helper the corn. helper
Guide students to generate sentences with indirect objects, emphasizing that they tell to whom or what the action of the verb was done.

MODERATE

Use the same sentences to demonstrate indirect objects. Guide students to generate sentences with indirect objects. Then have them exchange sentences with another student and identify the indirect objects in each other's sentences.

LIGHT

Provide students with the sentence frames below, and have them finish the sentences with a direct and indirect object.
The farmer gave _____ .
Sarah gave _____ .

LEARNING OBJECTIVES

- **Language** Identify direct and indirect objects.
- **Language** Use direct and indirect objects correctly in speaking and writing.

MATERIALS   Online 

Display and Engage *Grammar 2.6.4a, 2.6.4b, 2.6.4c*

Printable *Grammar 2.6.4*

 INSTRUCTIONAL VOCABULARY

- **direct object** the word that receives the action of the verb
- **compound direct object** words that receive the action of the same verb
- **indirect object** tells to or for whom or what the action is done

Review Direct and Indirect Objects

- Show **Display and Engage: Grammar 2.6.4a** and **Grammar 2.6.4b**. Remind students that a **direct object** is the word in the predicate that receives the action of a verb. A **compound direct object** is made up of two or more words that receive the action of the same verb. An **indirect object** usually tells to whom or what the action of the verb is done.

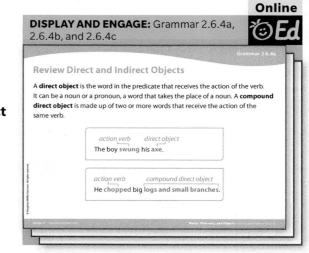

- Work with students to complete the exercises on **Display and Engage: Grammar 2.6.4c**.

- Have students complete **Printable: Grammar 2.6.4** for more practice with direct and indirect objects.

- Have students edit a writing draft for correct usage of direct and indirect objects.

ENGLISH LEARNER SUPPORT: Scaffolded Practice

SUBSTANTIAL

Remind students that the direct object is the person or thing that receives an action. Provide this example: *The dog chewed the bone.* Ask students to identify the direct object in the sentence. *bone*

MODERATE

Display the following sentences. Work with students to identify each direct object and indirect object, noting any compound direct objects.

- *Travis heard a scream.* **scream** (*direct object*)
- *The dog protected the boy and the girl.* **boy and girl** (*compound direct object*)
- *Mom gave her sons some food.* **sons** (*indirect object*); **food** (*direct object*)

LIGHT

Provide students with the sentence frames below, and have them complete the sentences with a direct and indirect object.

Miranda gave _____ .
Tom showed _____ .

NOUNS, PRONOUNS, AND OBJECTS • DIRECT AND INDIRECT OBJECTS

LEARNING OBJECTIVES

- **Language** Identify direct and indirect objects.
- **Language** Use direct and indirect objects correctly in writing and speaking.

MATERIALS — Online Ed

Display and Engage *Grammar 2.6.5*

Printable *Grammar 2.6.5*

 **INSTRUCTIONAL VOCABULARY**

- **direct object** the word that receives the action of the verb
- **compound direct object** words that receive the action of the same verb
- **indirect object** tells to or for whom or what the action is done

Connect and Teach

- Show **Display and Engage: Grammar 2.6.5**. Tell students that combining sentences to create a compound direct object can improve the flow of their writing. Using indirect objects can make writing more precise.

- Explain that an important part of revising is to eliminate choppy writing by combining sentences where it makes sense.

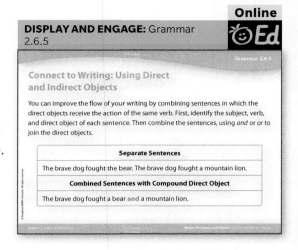

DISPLAY AND ENGAGE: Grammar 2.6.5

Online Ed

Grammar 2.6.5

Connect to Writing: Using Direct and Indirect Objects

You can improve the flow of your writing by combining sentences in which the direct objects receive the action of the same verb. First, identify the subject, verb, and direct object of each sentence. Then combine the sentences, using *and* or *or* to join the direct objects.

Separate Sentences
The brave dog fought the bear. The brave dog fought a mountain lion.

Combined Sentences with Compound Direct Object
The brave dog fought a bear **and** a mountain lion.

Engage and Apply

- Display the following sentences. Guide students to combine them by creating compound direct objects.

  » *We helped my mother plant lettuce. We also helped my mother plant peas. **We helped my mother plant lettuce and peas.***

  » *They built a fence around the school. They built a separate student exit. **They built a fence around the school and a separate student exit.***

- Using the samples above as models, ask volunteers to write pairs of sentences on the board that each contain direct objects. Then have all students combine the pairs to write sentences with compound direct objects. Call for volunteers to share their revised sentences. Then have students add indirect objects to one or more of the sentences.

- Have students complete **Printable: Grammar 2.6.5** for practice with direct objects.

- Have students return to a piece of their writing. In pairs, have them look for repeated words and phrases they can combine into one sentence. Encourage them to rewrite their sentences using compound direct objects. Have volunteers share their improvements.

(EL) ENGLISH LEARNER SUPPORT: Support Revision

SUBSTANTIAL

Write: *Jack grabbed the bat.*

- Help students identify the verb and direct object. Ask: *What is the verb, or action word, in this sentence?* Take responses, and then confirm that the verb is *grabbed*.
- Ask: *What noun is affected by the verb?* Solicit responses, and then confirm that the noun is *bat*.
- Have students identify the verb and direct object in other sentences.

MODERATE

Ask students to choose one story or article they have read recently to summarize in a paragraph. Have them include and underline three or four direct or indirect objects in the paragraph.

LIGHT

Write the following sentence on the board: *Travis shouldered an ax.*

Underline *shouldered* and circle *ax*. Ask students to draw an arrow pointing from the action to the noun that receives the action. Then have students write their own sentence with a direct and indirect object. Then have them trade papers with a partner to identify the direct and indirect objects in the sentence.

VERBS • VERBS

LEARNING OBJECTIVES

- **Language** Identify linking and action verbs.
- **Language** Use verbs correctly in writing and speaking.

MATERIALS	Online

Display and Engage *Grammar 3.1.1a, 3.1.1b*

Printable *Grammar 3.1.1*

 INSTRUCTIONAL VOCABULARY

- **linking verb** connects a subject of a sentence to information about it
- **action verb** tells what the subject does, did, or will do

Connect and Teach

- Show **Display and Engage: Grammar 3.1.1a**. Explain that a verb states the existence or action of a subject. **Linking verbs**, such as the verbs *be, become,* or *seem*, do not describe an action. Instead, they link the subject to more information about the subject, as in the sentence "I am cold." Linking verbs serve an important but limited purpose. Whenever possible, good writers try to use **action verbs**, which convey the subject's activities.

- Model identifying action verbs in this sentence: *The dog ran into the woods.*
  THINK ALOUD *To identify the action verb, I ask* What has the subject of the sentence done? Ran *is what the subject,* the dog, *did, so it is the action verb.*

Online
DISPLAY AND ENGAGE: Grammar 3.1.1a

Grammar 3.1.1a

Linking and Action Verbs

An **action verb** shows what the subject does, did, or will do.
A **linking verb** connects the subject of the sentence to the predicate or object.

action verb
The tree kangaroo climbed out on the branch.

linking verb
The tree kangaroo looked unusual.

Engage and Apply

- Complete items 1–8 on **Display and Engage: Grammar 3.1.1b** with students.

- Write the verbs *run, walk, write, yell, perform,* and *sleep* on the board. Ask volunteers to think of other action verbs that could be synonyms for these words. Have them use the synonyms in sentences.

Online
DISPLAY AND ENGAGE: Grammar 3.1.1b

Grammar 3.1.1b

Linking and Action Verbs

Identify the action verb or linking verb in each sentence.

1. The tree kangaroo jumped from the branch. jumped (action)
2. I traveled to the forests of Papua New Guinea. traveled (action)
3. The scientists tracked the animal. tracked (action)
4. The workers felt very tired. felt (linking)
5. The tree kangaroo appeared short and squat. appeared (linking)
6. The men built a fence around the tree. built (action)
7. After a few minutes, the animal awakened. awakened (action)
8. The tree kangaroo is a wild animal. is (linking)

- Have students complete **Printable: Grammar 3.1.1** for practice with action and linking verbs.

- Have students edit a writing draft using action and linking verbs correctly.

EL ENGLISH LEARNER SUPPORT: Facilitate Language Connections

In Cantonese, Hmong, Vietnamese, Tagalog, and Haitian Creole, verbs do not change to show tense. Instead, adverbs or expressions of time indicate when an action has taken place.

Scaffolded Practice

SUBSTANTIAL

Tell students that you are going to perform an action. Then, walk across the room. Point out that *walked* is a verb that describes that action. It is an action verb. Have students name other verbs they know, allowing them use their home language. Ask students to repeat the words in English as well.

MODERATE

Demonstrate other actions, and help students identify the verbs for those actions.

LIGHT

Write be, become, and seem. Remind students these are called linking verbs and that they link the subject with information about the subject. Model each linking verb. Marta is happy. The trees become leafless in winter. The room seems quieter now. Have students use linking verbs in their own sentences.

MAIN AND HELPING VERBS

LEARNING OBJECTIVES

- **Language** Identify main and helping verbs.
- **Language** Use verbs correctly in writing and speaking.

MATERIALS

Online

Display and Engage *Grammar 3.1.2a, 3.1.2b*

Printable *Grammar 3.1.2*

 INSTRUCTIONAL VOCABULARY

- **main verb** conveys the most important action, state, or condition in a sentence
- **helping verb** adds detail to the main verb

Connect and Teach

- Show **Display and Engage: Grammar 3.1.2a**. Explain that a **main verb** is the most important verb in a sentence. It tells what the subject is thinking or doing. **Helping verbs** come before main verbs and add details.

- Model identifying the main verb and helping verb in the following sentence: *He may receive a package tomorrow.*

  THINK ALOUD *To identify the helping verb and main verb, I ask Which verb describes the action and which verb helps it? May is the helping verb and receive is the main verb because it describes the action of the subject.*

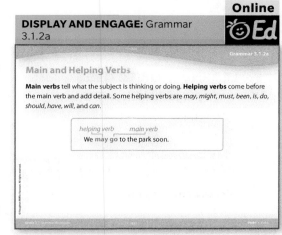

DISPLAY AND ENGAGE: Grammar 3.1.2a

Online Ed

Engage and Apply

- Complete items 1–8 on **Display and Engage: Grammar 3.1.2b** with students.

- Have students choose three helping verbs and write a sentence with each.

- Have students complete **Printable: Grammar 3.1.2** for practice with main and helping verbs.

- Have students edit a writing draft using main and helping verbs correctly.

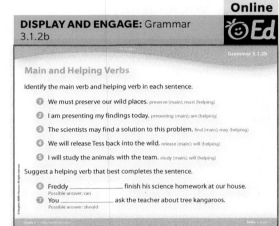

DISPLAY AND ENGAGE: Grammar 3.1.2b

Online Ed

 ENGLISH LEARNER SUPPORT: Scaffolded Practice

SUBSTANTIAL

Write sentences on the board and have students identify the main and helping verbs in each.

- *I may go to the park today.* main: *go*; helping: *may*
- *I can walk three miles.* main: *walk*; helping: *can*

MODERATE

Have volunteers demonstrate an activity, such as walking or jumping, and then work with them to write a sentence that uses a main and helping verb about that activity.

LIGHT

Have volunteers demonstrate an activity such as walking or jumping. Then have students write a complete sentence that uses a main and helping verb.

LEARNING OBJECTIVES

- **Language** Identify verb tenses.
- **Language** Use verbs correctly in writing and speaking.

MATERIALS	Online

Display and Engage *Grammar 3.1.3a, 3.1.3b*

Printable *Grammar 3.1.3*

 INSTRUCTIONAL VOCABULARY

- **verb tense** a verb form that conveys time, sequence, state, or condition

Connect and Teach

- Show **Display and Engage: Grammar 3.1.3a**. Explain that verbs appear in different tenses. Examples include the **present tense**—something happening right now—and the **past tense**, which is something that happened in the past. Explain that **verb tenses** can help convey time, sequence, condition, and states.

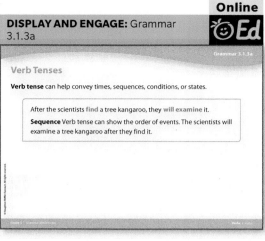

Online Ed

DISPLAY AND ENGAGE: Grammar 3.1.3a

Grammar 3.1.3a

Verb Tenses

Verb tense can help convey times, sequences, conditions, or states.

> After the scientists find a tree kangaroo, they will examine it.
>
> **Sequence** Verb tense can show the order of events. The scientists will examine a tree kangaroo after they find it.

- Model identifying whether the verb tense conveys time, sequence, state, or condition in this sentence: *The boys searched the woods near the baseball field for the missing ball.*

  THINK ALOUD *To identify how tenses can be used to convey time, sequence, state, or condition, I ask* Do the verb tenses help convey time, sequence, condition, or state? *In the example, the tense indicates time because* searched *is a past tense verb.*

Engage and Apply

- Complete items 1–6 on **Display and Engage: Grammar 3.1.3b** with students.

- Ask students to write sentences that use verb tenses to convey time, sequence, condition, and states. Then have students trade sentences with partners who will identify the way verb tenses are used.

Online Ed

DISPLAY AND ENGAGE: Grammar 3.1.3b

Grammar 3.1.3b

Verb Tenses

For each of the following sentences, identify whether the verb tenses are helping to convey time, sequence, condition, or state.

1. The scientists captured a tree kangaroo. time
2. The tree kangaroos moved higher when the men started climbing. sequence
3. The lab was to have sent results after the samples were collected and submitted. condition
4. The crew will be finished in a little while. state
5. The students will study about Papua New Guinea for homework. time
6. The class will have explored tree kangaroos in an earlier lesson. sequence
7. The scientist will have been in the rain forest three weeks by then. state

- Have students complete **Printable: Grammar 3.1.3** for practice with verb tenses.

- Have students edit a writing draft using the correct verb tenses.

EL **ENGLISH LEARNER SUPPORT: Scaffolded Practice**

SUBSTANTIAL

Write sentences on the board and have students identify the verb.

- *Roger found an old coin in the park.*
- *He will check a book about coins out of the library.*

MODERATE

Review the terms *time, sequence, condition,* and *state*. Work with students to find a sentence in a book and identify whether the verb tense used in the sentence conveys time, sequence, condition, or state.

LIGHT

Have students choose *time, sequence, condition,* or *state* and then have them write a sentence that uses verb tense to convey that idea.

VERBS • VERBS

LEARNING OBJECTIVES

- **Language** Review linking and action verbs, main and helping verbs, and verb tenses.
- **Language** Use verbs correctly in writing and speaking.

MATERIALS	Online

Display and Engage *Grammar 3.1.4a, 3.1.4b*

Printable *Grammar 3.1.4*

 INSTRUCTIONAL VOCABULARY

- **main verb** conveys the most important action, state, or condition in a sentence
- **helping verb** adds detail to the main verb
- **verb tense** a verb form that conveys time, sequence, state, or condition

Review Verbs

- Show **Display and Engage: Grammar 3.1.4a**. Remind students that **action verbs** show mental or physical activity. **Linking verbs** connect the subject to adjectives, nouns, or pronouns that follow the verb. Verbs may include **helping verbs** that clarify the meaning of the main verb and help to show tense. Review with students how **verb tense** can be used to convey time, sequence, state, or condition. Then have students complete the activity on **Display and Engage: Grammar 3.1.4b**.

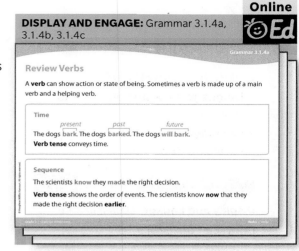

DISPLAY AND ENGAGE: Grammar 3.1.4a, 3.1.4b, 3.1.4c

Online Ed

- Have students write sentences using helping and linking verbs and tenses that show time, sequence, states, and conditions. Use these sentences as models.

  » *The photographer was happy.* was, linking; past, state

  » *We will go to the park.* will, helping; will go, action; future, time

- Have students complete **Printable: Grammar 3.1.4** for more practice with verbs.

- Have students create a four-column chart in their notebooks, with the headings *Linking Verbs, Action Verbs, Main Verbs,* and *Helping Verbs*. Have partners page through reading selections of classroom library books and add examples to each column.

- Have students edit a writing draft using the correct forms of actions verbs, main verbs, helping verbs, and linking verbs.

EL **ENGLISH LEARNER SUPPORT: Scaffolded Practice**

SUBSTANTIAL

Remind students that most verbs are action or linking. Provide examples of each such as: *ran, helped, saw* (action); *are, were, became* (linking).

MODERATE

Present the English terms for the types of verbs that students have learned: action verbs, linking verbs, main verbs, and auxiliary (helping) verbs. Note that the words *action* and *auxiliary* are cognates of the Spanish terms *accion* and *auxiliar*. Display the following sentences. Work with the group to identify each verb type.

- *Many sea turtles swim long distances.* (action verb: *swim*)

- *Turtles are a kind of reptile.* (linking verb: *are*)

- *The vet has treated the turtle.* (auxiliary verb: *has*; main verb: *treated*)

LIGHT

Have volunteers perform an action, such as walking or picking something up. Then have students write a complete sentence that describes the action. Have them identify the main verb and any helping or linking verbs.

VERBS · VERBS

LEARNING OBJECTIVES

- **Language** Choose strong verbs to convey ideas.
- **Language** Use verbs correctly in writing and speaking.

MATERIALS	Online

Display and Engage *Grammar 3.1.5*
Printable *Grammar 3.1.5*

 **INSTRUCTIONAL VOCABULARY**

- **action verb** tells what the subject does, did, or will do

Connect and Teach

- Show **Display and Engage: Grammar 3.1.5**. Explain that properly formed sentences help the reader understand the text and stay focused on the topic. Every properly formed sentence must contain a subject and a predicate.

- Point out that an important part of writing and editing is making sure that verbs are used correctly.

DISPLAY AND ENGAGE: Grammar 3.1.5   Online

Connect to Writing: Using Linking and Action Verbs

You can make your writing strong by using verbs that convey details and information vividly and accurately. Use linking and action verbs to share details about time, sequence, and condition.

Sentence with Vague Verb	Sentence with Exact Verb
The squirrel went up into a tree at some point.	The squirrel had scrambled up into a tree yesterday.
I watched the tree branches the other day.	I will peer into the tree branches tomorrow if I can.

Engage and Apply

- Display the following sentences. Guide students in identifying the verbs and their types.

  » *David seemed pleased by the news about the new animal tracking devices.*

  » *Louise had worked in the forest for years.*

  » *I have read a magazine article about trees.*

- Have students complete **Printable Grammar 3.1.5** for practice with action and linking verbs.

- Have partners write a short narrative that includes verb tenses showing times, sequences, states, and conditions. Tell partners to exchange papers with another pair and check that verb tenses were used correctly.

EL **ENGLISH LEARNER SUPPORT: Support Revision**

SUBSTANTIAL

Write sentences on the board and underline the verbs:
Lia has wrote her paper in the library.
Miguel have walks to the school.
We is read the assigned chapter.

Work together to identify the verb tense errors in each sentence. Review linking verbs and present and past tense as you discuss each sentence and revise it.

MODERATE

Have students revisit a piece of their past writing and identify several sentences that use linking verbs and verbs in the present and past tense. Have student pairs review the sentences for correct verb use, and revise where needed.

LIGHT

Have students review a piece of past writing and identify sentences that need revision due to incorrect verb tense. Have them revise and ask volunteers to share revision examples with the group.

LEARNING OBJECTIVES

- **Language** Identify present and past tense verbs.
- **Language** Use verb tenses correctly in writing and speaking.

MATERIALS
Online

Display and Engage Grammar 3.2.1a, 3.2.1b

Printable Grammar 3.2.1

 INSTRUCTIONAL VOCABULARY

- **present tense** tells what is happening now or over and over
- **past tense** tells what happened in the past

Connect and Teach

- Show **Display and Engage: Grammar 3.2.1a**. Explain that verb tense tells when an action takes place. Explain that **present tense** tells what the subject in a sentence is doing right now. A verb that tells what has already happened is in the **past tense**.

- Model identifying the tense of the verb in the example sentence: *We walk to the store.*

    THINK ALOUD *To identify the verb tense as present or past, I ask* When is the action occurring? Is it happening now, or is it over? *Because the verb is in the present tense, I know the action is taking place now. If I were to add* -ed *to walk, it would be in the past tense.*

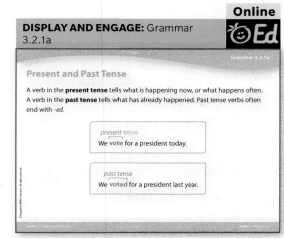

DISPLAY AND ENGAGE: Grammar 3.2.1a · Online · Ed

Present and Past Tense

A verb in the **present tense** tells what is happening now, or what happens often. A verb in the **past tense** tells what has already happened. Past tense verbs often end with -ed.

present tense
We vote for a president today.

past tense
We voted for a president last year.

Engage and Apply

- Complete items 1–8 on **Display and Engage: Grammar 3.2.1b** with students.

- Write the following verbs on the board. Have students identify each as present tense or past tense and then change it to the other tense.
    kick present; kicked
    laughed past; laugh
    chewed past; chew

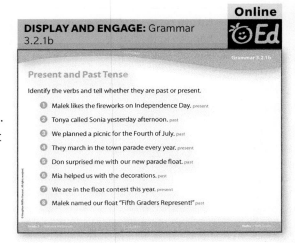

DISPLAY AND ENGAGE: Grammar 3.2.1b · Online · Ed

Present and Past Tense

Identify the verbs and tell whether they are past or present.

1. Malek likes the fireworks on Independence Day. *present*
2. Tonya called Sonia yesterday afternoon. *past*
3. We planned a picnic for the Fourth of July. *past*
4. They march in the town parade every year. *present*
5. Don surprised me with our new parade float. *past*
6. Mia helped us with the decorations. *past*
7. We are in the float contest this year. *present*
8. Malek named our float "Fifth Graders Represent!" *past*

- Have students complete **Printable: Grammar 3.2.1** for practice with present and past tense.

- Have students edit a writing draft using the present and past tenses.

 ENGLISH LEARNER SUPPORT: Faciliate Language Connections

In English, the past tense is usually formed using *-ed* at the end of a verb, and the future tense is formed by adding *will* before the verb. In many languages, including Spanish, each subject uses a different ending in the past and future tenses.

Scaffolded Practice

SUBSTANTIAL
Use the following sentence frames to demonstrate how to use simple past and present verb tenses.
The king _____ the country. (present tense) *rules*
The king _____ the country. (past tense) *ruled*

MODERATE
Have students complete these sentence frames orally using the correct verb tense.
The king now _____ the country. rules
The colonists _____ tea into Boston harbor. dumped

LIGHT
Ask students to use present and past verbs to make sentences about yesterday and today.

LEARNING OBJECTIVES

• **Language** Identify future tense.
• **Language** Use verb tenses correctly in writing and speaking.

MATERIALS	Online

Display and Engage *Grammar 3.2.2a, 3.2.2b*

Printable *Grammar 3.2.2*

 INSTRUCTIONAL VOCABULARY

• **future tense** tells what will happen in the future

Connect and Teach

• Show **Display and Engage: Grammar 3.2.2a**. Explain that a verb in the **future tense** tells what will happen. Point out that future-tense verbs use the helping verb *will* before the action word.

• Model identifying the future tense in the example sentence: *We will visit the museum next month.*

   THINK ALOUD *To identify the future tense, I ask* Is the action something that is going to happen? *In this example, we haven't gone to the museum yet, so it's in the future tense.*

Engage and Apply

• Complete items 1–5 on **Display and Engage: Grammar 3.2.2b** with students.

• Write the following sentences on the board and have students change the verbs to future tense. Point out that some other words also may need to change.
   I read that history book last year. I will read that history book next year.
   Carlos studies every day. Carlos will study every day.

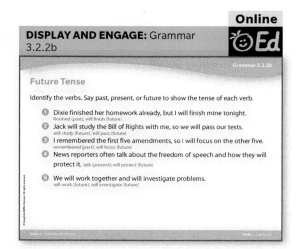

• Have students complete **Printable: Grammar 3.2.2** for practice with future tense.

• Have students edit a writing draft using the future tense.

EL **ENGLISH LEARNER SUPPORT: Scaffolded Practice**

SUBSTANTIAL
   Use the following sentence frame to demonstrate how to use simple future tense.
   The king _____ the country. (future tense) *will rule*

MODERATE
   Have students complete these sentence frame orally using the correct verb tense:
   The king _____ soldiers next week. will send

LIGHT
   Ask students to make sentences using the future tense.

VERBS • VERB TENSES

LEARNING OBJECTIVES

- **Language** Identify and understand consistent use of tenses.
- **Language** Use verb tenses correctly in writing and speaking.

MATERIALS   Online

Display and Engage *Grammar 3.2.3a, 3.2.3b*

Printable *Grammar 3.2.3*

 INSTRUCTIONAL VOCABULARY

- **present tense** tells what is happening now or over and over
- **past tense** tells what happened in the past
- **future tense** tells what will happen in the future

Connect and Teach

- Show **Display and Engage: Grammar 3.2.3a**. Explain to students that **verb tenses** show when actions happen.

- Tell students that it is important to use verb tenses consistently when communicating the order of actions or events. Inappropriate shifts in verb tense or aspect should be corrected to avoid confusion.

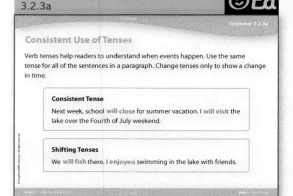

- Model identifying consistent tense: *Next week, I will write my history report. Then school will close for summer vacation.*

  THINK ALOUD *To identify whether the tense is consistent, I ask Does the paragraph make sense? Is the order of events clear? Both actions will take place in the future. The sentences make sense.*

Engage and Apply

- Complete the item on **Display and Engage: Grammar 3.2.3b** with students.

- Ask students to fix the verb-tense error in the second part of the following sentence. *Roberto will read the book, then he wrote his report.* Roberto will read the book, then he will write his report.

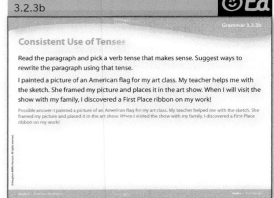

- Have students complete **Printable: Grammar 3.2.3** for practice with future tense.

- Have students edit a writing draft using consistent verb tenses.

EL **ENGLISH LEARNER SUPPORT: Scaffolded Practice**

SUBSTANTIAL

Review present and past tense verb forms. Write the sentences on the board and have students identify the tense and tell whether it is consistent.

I went to the park yesterday. The weather was lovely. past tense; the tense is consistent

MODERATE

Write the sentences on the board and have students identify the error in tense of the second sentence.

I went to the park yesterday. The weather will be lovely. was

Discuss why it is important to have consistent verb tense when communicating. *to avoid confusion; to be clear*

LIGHT

Have students write a few sentences about something they did the day before. Remind them to keep the tense of their verbs consistent. Have partners review sentences and discuss how to correct any errors.

LEARNING OBJECTIVES

- **Language** Review present, past, and future verb tenses.
- **Language** Use verb tenses correctly in writing and speaking.

MATERIALS	Online

Display and Engage *Grammar 3.2.4a, 3.2.4b*

Printable *Grammar 3.2.4*

 INSTRUCTIONAL VOCABULARY

- **present tense** tells what is happening now or over and over
- **past tense** tells what happened in the past
- **future tense** tells what will happen in the future

Review Verbs

- Show **Display and Engage: Grammar 3.2.4a**. Remind students that a verb that tells what is happening right now is in the **present tense**. A verb that tells what has already happened is in the **past tense**. A verb that tells what is going to happen is in the **future tense**. Remind students to keep their verb tenses consistent. Inappropriate shifts in verb tense can confuse readers. Then have students complete the activity on **Display and Engage: Grammar 3.2.4b**.

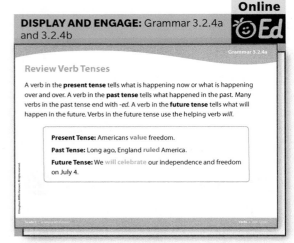

DISPLAY AND ENGAGE: Grammar 3.2.4a and 3.2.4b

Online

Review Verb Tenses

A verb in the **present tense** tells what is happening now or what is happening over and over. A verb in the **past tense** tells what happened in the past. Many verbs in the past tense end with -ed. A verb in the **future tense** tells what will happen in the future. Verbs in the future tense use the helping verb will.

> **Present Tense:** Americans value freedom.
> **Past Tense:** Long ago, England ruled America.
> **Future Tense:** We will celebrate our independence and freedom on July 4.

- Write the following paragraph on the board. Have students identify and correct the inappropriate shifts in verb tense.

  Brenda dropped her tools at home and will walk to Alex's house. She knocked on the door when she arrived, but there is no answer. "I wonder where he is?" Brenda thought. She decided to wait for a few minutes on the porch. will walk/walked; is/was

- Have students complete **Printable: Grammar 3.2.4** for more practice with verb tenses.

- Have students edit a writing draft using correct and consistent verb tenses.

EL **ENGLISH LEARNER SUPPORT: Scaffolded Practice**

SUBSTANTIAL

Remind students that "tense" in this context means the time that is being described. Provide these examples of present, past, and future tense:

The fans arrive at the stadium.

The game started at noon.

The fans will cheer for their team.

Have students identify the tense of at least one of the sentences.

MODERATE

Review the idea that verb tenses indicate the moment that an action is performed. Present these sentences. Have students identify the tense of each verb.

- *We will watch a film tomorrow about the car industry.* (future)

- *We watched a film about Henry Ford last week.* (past)

- *We watch films in school every week.* (present)

LIGHT

Have students write one sentence each using past, present, and future tense. Ask volunteers to share examples of each tense.

LEARNING OBJECTIVES

- **Language** Choose verb tenses to convey ideas.
- **Language** Use verb tenses correctly in writing and speaking.

MATERIALS Online

Display and Engage *Grammar 3.2.5*

Printable *Grammar 3.2.5*

INSTRUCTIONAL VOCABULARY

- **present tense** tells what is happening now or over and over
- **past tense** tells what happened in the past
- **future tense** tells what will happen in the future

Connect and Teach

- Show <u>**Display and Engage: Grammar 3.2.5**</u>. Explain to students that maintaining consistent and correct **verb tense** is an important part of sentence fluency.

- Remind students that ensuring consistent and correct verb tenses is an important part of revising.

DISPLAY AND ENGAGE: Grammar 3.2.5

Online
Ed

Grammar 3.2.5

Connect to Writing: Using the Correct Verb Tense

Your readers will be confused if you shift the verb tense within a sequence of events you are writing about. Tell readers whether events are happening, have already happened, or will happen in the future by choosing the correct tense and using it consistently.

Shifting Tenses	Consistent Tense
When my family visited Washington, DC, last summer, we see the Lincoln Memorial. We toured the Capitol and will visit the Washington Monument. We have a great time!	When my family visited Washington, DC, last summer, we saw the Lincoln Memorial. We toured the Capitol and visited the Washington Monument. We had a great time!

Engage and Apply

- Display the following sentences and guide students to make the verbs consistent. *King George's messengers tell him about the tea party. The king ordered the soldiers to retaliate.* First sentence: replace *tell* with *told*; second sentence: change *ordered* to *orders*

- Have students independently correct the tense in the following sentences. *John Adams will lead the colonists before the war. He is elected president later.* John Adams led; He was

- Have students complete <u>**Printable: Grammar 3.2.5**</u> for practice with verb tenses.

- Tell students that as they revise their writing, they should look for inconsistent use of verb tense. Have students revise a piece of writing to make sure they are using the same verb tense throughout. Tell partners to exchange papers with another pair and check that verb tenses were used correctly.

EL ENGLISH LEARNER SUPPORT: Support Revision

SUBSTANTIAL

Explain that verbs show time through tenses. Write: *Past Tense, Present Tense,* and *Future Tense.*

- Write: *A government repeals a law.* Say: *This use of the verb* repeal *shows that something happens now, in the present.*
- Write: *In 1770, the government repealed the law.* Say: *This use of the verb* repeal *shows that something happened before, in the past.*
- Write: *Next year, the government will repeal the law.* Say: *This use of the verb* repeal *shows that something will happen in the future.*

MODERATE

Write: *last year, today,* and *tomorrow.* Have students fill in the blank in each sentence with the correct time word to match the verb tense.

- *The musician played music _____. last year*
- *The musician will play music _____. tomorrow*
- *The musician plays music _____. today*

LIGHT

Have students write sentences about their favorite kind of music, using past, present, and future tenses of different verbs. Have volunteers share sentences.

LEARNING OBJECTIVES

- **Language** Identify and use regular verbs.
- **Language** Use regular and irregular verbs correctly in speaking and writing.

MATERIALS   Online

Display and Engage *Grammar 3.3.1a, 3.3.1b*

Printable *Grammar 3.3.1*

 INSTRUCTIONAL VOCABULARY

- **regular verb** add -*ed* or -*d* to its present tense to show action that happened in the past; may use helping verbs *has, have, had*

Connect and Teach

- Show **Display and Engage: Grammar 3.3.1a**. Explain that a verb is a **regular verb** if adding -*ed* or -*d* to its present-tense form to create the past tense form. A regular verb also ends with -*ed* when used with the helping verbs *has, had,* or *have.*

- Model identifying regular verbs in the example sentences: *The campers hiked around the lake. They had looked for the entrance to the road.*

  THINK ALOUD *To identify the regular verb, I ask* Does adding -*ed* or -*d* form the past tense? Does the verb have a helping verb? *The past-tense verb* hiked *is formed by adding* -d *to* hike, *so it's a regular verb. The past-tense verb* looked *is formed by adding* -ed, *and it has a helping verb.*

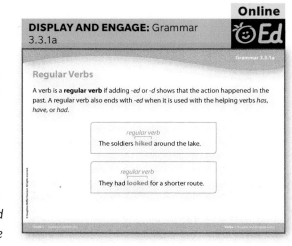

DISPLAY AND ENGAGE: Grammar
3.3.1a

Online
Ed

Regular Verbs

A verb is a **regular verb** if adding -*ed* or -*d* shows that the action happened in the past. A regular verb also ends with -*ed* when it is used with the helping verbs *has, have,* or *had.*

regular verb
The soldiers **hiked** around the lake.

regular verb
They had **looked** for a shorter route.

Engage and Apply

- Complete items 1–8 on **Display and Engage: Grammar 3.3.1b** with students.

- List the following verbs on the board. Work with students to identify the present or past tense form of each one.
  named name
  prepared prepare
  followed follow
  camp camped
  ignore ignored
  shimmer shimmered

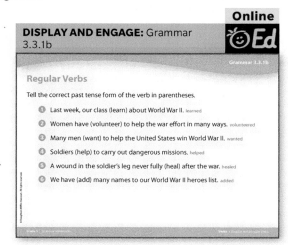

DISPLAY AND ENGAGE: Grammar
3.3.1b

Online
Ed

Regular Verbs

Tell the correct past tense form of the verb in parentheses.

1. Last week, our class (learn) about World War II. learned
2. Women have (volunteer) to help the war effort in many ways. volunteered
3. Many men (want) to help the United States win World War II. wanted
4. Soldiers (help) to carry out dangerous missions. helped
5. A wound in the soldier's leg never fully (heal) after the war. healed
6. We have (add) many names to our World War II heroes list. added

- Have students complete **Printable: Grammar 3.3.1** for practice with regular verbs.

- Have students edit a writing draft using the correct forms of regular verbs.

EL **ENGLISH LEARNER SUPPORT: Scaffolded Practice**

SUBSTANTIAL

Work with students to orally complete these sentence frames to demonstrate how to use the regular verb *walk* in present and past tense. Remind students about the endings -*ed* and -*d* and the helping verbs that create the past tense.
Today, I _____ to school. walk
In the past, I only _____ on my street. walked

MODERATE

Work with students to write a sentence frame for each of these pairs of verbs.
volunteer/volunteered
walk/walked

LIGHT

Have students create their own sentence frames for several regular verbs. Then ask students to complete the sentence frames of another student. Have volunteers share their sentences.

VERBS • REGULAR AND IRREGULAR VERBS

LEARNING OBJECTIVES

- **Language** Identify and use irregular verbs.
- **Language** Use regular and irregular verbs correctly in speaking and writing.

MATERIALS	Online

Display and Engage *Grammar 3.3.2a, 3.3.2b*

Printable *Grammar 3.3.2*

 INSTRUCTIONAL VOCABULARY

- **irregular verb** form the past tense by changing a vowel; some forms need to be memorized

Connect and Teach

- Show <u>Display and Engage: Grammar 3.3.2a</u>. Point out that the past tense of an **irregular verb** is not formed by adding *-ed* or *-d* to its present tense. Explain that students will need to memorize the past tense forms of irregular verbs.

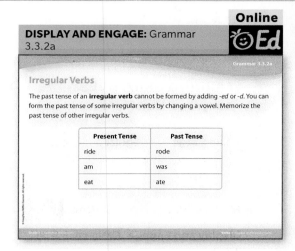

DISPLAY AND ENGAGE: Grammar 3.3.2a

Online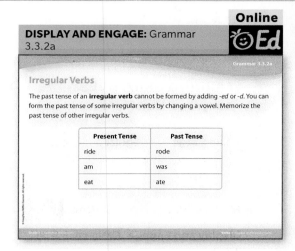

Irregular Verbs

The past tense of an **irregular verb** cannot be formed by adding *-ed* or *-d*. You can form the past tense of some irregular verbs by changing a vowel. Memorize the past tense of other irregular verbs.

Present Tense	Past Tense
ride	rode
am	was
eat	ate

- Model how to identify verbs as regular or irregular using the following sentences: *We picked apples from the tree. I ate an apple as we walked home.*

  THINK ALOUD *To identify verbs as regular or irregular, I ask* Does forming the past tense by adding *-ed* or *–d* make a word that makes sense or that I recognize? *The past-tense verb* walked *is formed by adding -ed to* walk, *so it's a regular verb. The verb* ate *is the past-tense form of* eat, *so it is an irregular verb.*

Engage and Apply

- Complete items 1–8 on <u>Display and Engage: Grammar 3.3.2b</u> with students.

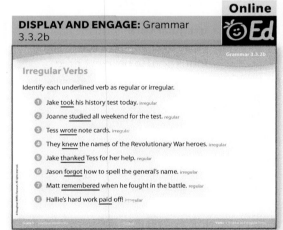

DISPLAY AND ENGAGE: Grammar 3.3.2b

Online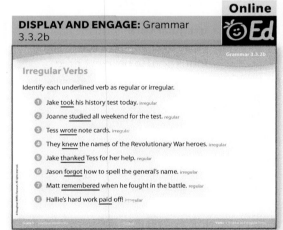

Irregular Verbs

Identify each underlined verb as regular or irregular.

1. Jake <u>took</u> his history test today. *irregular*
2. Joanne <u>studied</u> all weekend for the test. *regular*
3. Tess <u>wrote</u> note cards. *irregular*
4. They <u>knew</u> the names of the Revolutionary War heroes. *irregular*
5. Jake <u>thanked</u> Tess for her help. *regular*
6. Jason <u>forgot</u> how to spell the general's name. *irregular*
7. Matt <u>remembered</u> when he fought in the battle. *regular*
8. Hallie's hard work <u>paid</u> off! *irregular*

- Write the following words on the board. Have students provide the past-tense forms of the verbs.
  become became
  forget forgot
  drive drove

- Have students complete <u>Printable: Grammar 3.3.2</u> for practice with irregular verbs.

- Have students edit a writing draft using the correct forms of irregular verbs.

 ENGLISH LEARNER SUPPORT: Scaffolded Practice

SUBSTANTIAL

Work with students to orally complete these sentence frames to demonstrate the correct usage of irregular verbs. Tell students that *fight* is in the present tense and *fought* is in the past tense.
Today, citizens _____ for their freedom. fight
In the past, citizens _____ for their freedom. fought
Review a list of irregular verbs with students and invite them to keep a list of their own.

MODERATE

Work with students to write a sentence frame for each of these pairs of verbs.
ran/run
fight/fought
Have students help you start a class chart of irregular verbs and their present- and past-tense forms.

LIGHT

Have students create their own sentences for several irregular verbs. Invite students to share their sentences.

VERBS • REGULAR AND IRREGULAR VERBS

LEARNING OBJECTIVES

- **Language** Identify and use the past tense form of irregular verbs.
- **Language** Use regular and irregular verbs correctly in speaking and writing.

MATERIALS   Online

Display and Engage *Grammar 3.3.3a, 3.3.3b*

Printable *Grammar 3.3.3*

INSTRUCTIONAL VOCABULARY

- **irregular verb** form the past tense by changing a vowel; some forms need to be memorized

Connect and Teach

- Show **Display and Engage: Grammar 3.3.3a**. Review with students how to find the past-tense forms of regular and irregular verbs. Use examples such as *begin/began*, *think/thought*, and *is/was* to show how the past tense of irregular verbs is formed.

- Point out that students can use a dictionary to find the past tense of irregular verbs.

Engage and Apply

- Complete items 1–7 on **Display and Engage: Grammar 3.3.3b** with students.

- Call out several present-tense forms of irregular verbs. Work with students to use a dictionary to find the past-tense forms of these words.

- Have students write a sentence for each verb, using its past tense form.

- Have students complete **Printable: Grammar 3.3.3** for practice with irregular verbs.

- Have students edit a writing draft using the correct past tense form of irregular verbs.

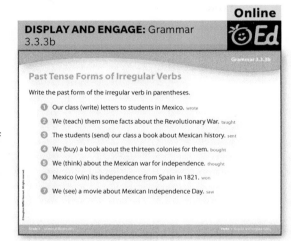

DISPLAY AND ENGAGE: Grammar 3.3.3a   **Online** *Ed*

Grammar 3.3.3a

Past Tense Forms of Irregular Verbs

An **irregular verb** does not add *-ed* to its present form to show action that happened in the past. The past tense of an irregular verb is formed in different ways. You can use a dictionary to find the past tense of an irregular verb.

Present Tense	Past Tense
begin	began
catch	caught
throw	threw

DISPLAY AND ENGAGE: Grammar 3.3.3b   **Online** *Ed*

Grammar 3.3.3b

Past Tense Forms of Irregular Verbs

Write the past form of the irregular verb in parentheses.

1. Our class (write) letters to students in Mexico. wrote
2. We (teach) them some facts about the Revolutionary War. taught
3. The students (send) our class a book about Mexican history. sent
4. We (buy) a book about the thirteen colonies for them. bought
5. We (think) about the Mexican war for independence. thought
6. Mexico (win) its independence from Spain in 1821. won
7. We (see) a movie about Mexican Independence Day. saw

EL ENGLISH LEARNER SUPPORT: Scaffolded Practice

SUBSTANTIAL

Work with students to find the past tense form of the irregular verb. Encourage students to use a dictionary if they need it.

catch caught
break broke

MODERATE

Have students find the past tense form of the irregular verb. Encourage students to use a dictionary if they need it.

bring brought
find found

Then have students use each past-tense form in a sentence.

LIGHT

Have students write two sentences using the past tense of an irregular verbs. Have volunteers share sentences.

LEARNING OBJECTIVES

- **Language** Review regular and irregular verbs.
- **Language** Use regular and irregular verbs correctly in speaking and writing.

MATERIALS   Online

Display and Engage *Grammar 3.3.4a, 3.3.4b*

Printable *Grammar 3.3.4*

INSTRUCTIONAL VOCABULARY

- **regular verb** add *-ed* or *-d* to its present tense to show action that happened in the past; may use helping verbs *has, have, had*
- **irregular verb** form the past tense by changing a vowel; some forms need to be memorized

Review Verbs

- Show **Display and Engage: Grammar 3.3.4a**.

- Remind students that a verb is a regular verb if adding *-ed* or *-d* shows that the action happened in the past.

- Review that the past tense of an irregular verb cannot be formed by adding *-ed* or *-d*. Some irregular verbs can be changed to past tense by changing a vowel. Others need to be memorized.

- Display the following verb groups: *ride, rode, have ridden; eat, ate, have eaten; say, said, have said; do, did, have done.* Assign pairs of students one verb group and ask them to write a sentence for each of its forms.

- Write these sentences on the board and guide students to choose the correct verb to complete each.

  » *Joseph has (went, gone, go) to the store.* gone

  » *She (gave, given, give) him the list.* gave

- Work with students to complete the exercises on **Display and Engage: Grammar 3.3.4b**.

- Have students complete **Printable: Grammar 3.3.4** for practice with regular and irregular verbs.

- Have students edit a writing draft using the correct forms of regular and irregular past tense verbs.

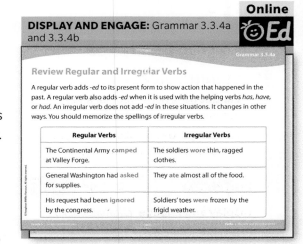

DISPLAY AND ENGAGE: Grammar 3.3.4a and 3.3.4b   Online

Grammar 3.3.4a

Review Regular and Irregular Verbs

A regular verb adds *-ed* to its present form to show action that happened in the past. A regular verb also adds *-ed* when it is used with the helping verbs *has, have,* or *had.* An irregular verb does not add *-ed* in these situations. It changes in other ways. You should memorize the spellings of irregular verbs.

Regular Verbs	Irregular Verbs
The Continental Army camped at Valley Forge.	The soldiers wore thin, ragged clothes.
General Washington had asked for supplies.	They ate almost all of the food.
His request had been ignored by the congress.	Soldiers' toes were frozen by the frigid weather.

ENGLISH LEARNER SUPPORT: Scaffolded Practice

SUBSTANTIAL

Remind students that irregular verbs do not follow regular rules. The only way to know how to change their tenses is to memorize the different forms of those verbs. Provide examples from the lessons for students to review. Model how to find past-tense forms using a dictionary.

MODERATE

Review with students that irregular verbs do not follow the usual rules of grammar. Display the following sentences. Work with students to identify each irregular verb and its present-tense form.

- *The soldier fought in the battle.* fought

- *He gave other soldiers help, too.* gave

- *He has become an American hero.* has become

LIGHT

Have students look through classroom books to find examples of irregular past-tense verbs. Have them make a list and trade it with a partner to check and review.

VERBS • REGULAR AND IRREGULAR VERBS

LEARNING OBJECTIVES

- **Language** Choose regular and irregular verbs to convey ideas.
- **Language** Use regular and irregular verbs in speaking and writing.

MATERIALS	Online

Display and Engage *Grammar 3.3.5*
Printable *Grammar 3.3.5*

 INSTRUCTIONAL VOCABULARY

- **regular verb** add *-ed* or *-d* to its present tense to show action that happened in the past; may use helping verbs *has, have, had*
- **irregular verb** form the past tense by changing a vowel; some forms need to be memorized

Connect and Teach

- Show **Display and Engage: Grammar 3.3.5**. Tell students that paying attention to word choice can make their writing clearer and more interesting to read. Discuss the two examples below.
  Example 1: Jason asked for more help.
  Example 2: Jason yelled for more help.

- The second example is better because it uses a more specific form of a past-tense verb.

- Point out that an important part of revising is choosing words to communicate action precisely. Remind students to pay attention to the correct past-tense forms of verbs as well.

Engage and Apply

- Display the following sentences. Have students work with partners to rewrite the sentences, improving word choice.

  » *The nurse* <u>helped</u> *the patients by giving them water.* aided; assisted

  » *The patients* <u>liked</u> *the nurse.* appreciated; admired

  » *The nurse* <u>kept</u> *the patients from feeling sick.* prevented

- Point out regular and irregular verbs and discuss the past-tense forms.

- Have students complete **Printable: Grammar 3.3.5** for practice using exact verbs.

- Tell students that as they revise their writing, they should look for opportunities to incorporate exact verbs in their sentences. Have students revise a piece of writing to use more exact verbs. Tell partners to exchange papers with another pair and check that verb tenses were used correctly.

EL **ENGLISH LEARNER SUPPORT: Scaffolded Practice**

SUBSTANTIAL

Review regular and irregular verbs. *Write: The British retreat. Molly runs to the cannon.* Tell students these sentences show present action. *Write: The British _____. Molly _____ to the cannon.* Help students name the past-tense forms of the verbs. (*retreated, ran*) Review more examples of regular and irregular verbs.

MODERATE

Write the following sentences. Then have partners rewrite them in the past tense.

- *In the winter, the soldiers camp in the snow.*
- *The army goes out on patrol.*
- *Some of the soldiers freeze to death.*

LIGHT

Have students write original sentences using these past-tense verbs about a book they are reading this week. Have volunteers share sentences and give examples of past-tense regular and irregular verbs.

VERBS *BE* AND *HAVE*

LEARNING OBJECTIVES

- **Language** Identify the verbs *be* and *have*.

- **Language** Use the verbs *be* and *have* correctly in writing and speaking.

MATERIALS	Online

Display and Engage *Grammar 3.4.1a, 3.4.1b*

Printable *Grammar 3.4.1*

 INSTRUCTIONAL VOCABULARY

- **irregular verb** a verb that does not follow the regular rules of verb forms

Connect and Teach

- Show <u>Display and Engage: Grammar 3.4.1a</u>. Explain that the verbs *be* and *have* are **irregular verbs** that change when the subject changes. The subject and verb must agree in number and tense.

- Model identifying the verb *be* in the example sentence: *We are studying the deserts.*

  THINK ALOUD *To identify the correct form of* be, *I ask What tense is the verb? How many are in the subject? The verb* are *is in the present tense. We say that the subject is plural.*

- Model identifying the verb *have* in the example sentence: *She had read an interesting book about the Mojave Desert.*

  THINK ALOUD *To identify the correct form of the verb* have, *I ask What tense is the verb? How many are in the subject? The verb* had *is in the past tense. The word* she *is singular.*

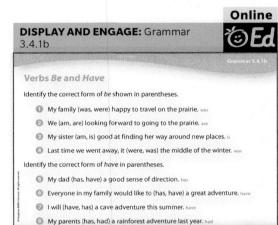

DISPLAY AND ENGAGE: Grammar 3.4.1a

Online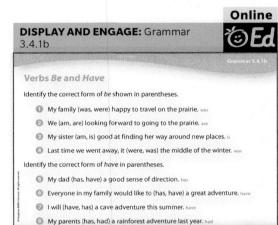

Verbs *Be* and *Have*

The verbs *be* and *have* are irregular verbs. They change forms when the subject changes.

The subject and verb in a sentence must agree in number and tense.

verb be
The mountains are my favorite place to travel.

verb have
I don't have a good sense of direction.

Engage and Apply

- Complete items 1–10 on <u>Display and Engage: Grammar 3.4.1b</u> with students.

- Work with students to identify the correct forms of *be* and *have* in these sentences.
  She (are, is) learning about mountain lions.
  We (had, has) a great time on the river.

- Have students complete <u>Printable: Grammar 3.4.1</u> for practice with *be* and *have*.

- Have students edit a writing draft using the correct forms of the verbs *be* and *have*.

DISPLAY AND ENGAGE: Grammar 3.4.1b

Online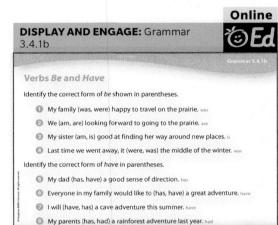

Verbs *Be* and *Have*

Identify the correct form of *be* shown in parentheses.

1. My family (was, were) happy to travel on the prairie. was
2. We (am, are) looking forward to going to the prairie. are
3. My sister (am, is) good at finding her way around new places. is
4. Last time we went away, it (were, was) the middle of the winter. was

Identify the correct form of *have* in parentheses.

5. My dad (has, have) a good sense of direction. has
6. Everyone in my family would like to (has, have) a great adventure. have
7. I will (have, has) a cave adventure this summer. have
8. My parents (has, had) a rainforest adventure last year. had

 ENGLISH LEARNER SUPPORT: Facilitate Language Connections

The verb *be* can be left out of a sentence in Cantonese, Hmong, Vietnamese, and Haitian Creole. If students say *I happy* instead of *I am happy*, provide extra practice with sentences containing forms of *be*. For example: *I was hungry. We were hungry.*

Scaffolded Practice

SUBSTANTIAL/MODERATE

Use the following sentences to demonstrate how to use the correct form of *be* and *have*.
The girl (is, am) good at hiking. is
She (has, have) taken several hikes. has
Sarah _____ taken several hikes. has

LIGHT

Have students describe people or things using the correct form of *be* and *have*. Provide them with sentence frames such as:
I _____. The mountains _____.

VERBS · THE VERBS *BE* AND *HAVE*

LEARNING OBJECTIVES

- **Language** Identify verb phrases with *be* and *have*.
- **Language** Use the verbs *be* and *have* correctly in writing and speaking.

MATERIALS   Online

Display and Engage *Grammar 3.4.2a, 3.4.2b*

Printable *Grammar 3.4.2*

 INSTRUCTIONAL VOCABULARY

- **verb phrase** the part of a sentence that shows action; the whole phrase acts as a verb

Connect and Teach

- Show **Display and Engage: Grammar 3.4.2a**. Point out that many phrases use the verbs *be* and *have*. Explain that a verb phrase is a part of the sentence that shows the action. The whole verb phrase acts as a verb.

- Model identifying the verb phrase in the example sentence: *Shaina is learning about desert habitats.*

  THINK ALOUD *To identify the verb phrase, I ask* What part of this sentence has the verb? *I see that* is learning *shows the action of the sentence. The verb phase is* learning *is a form of* be.

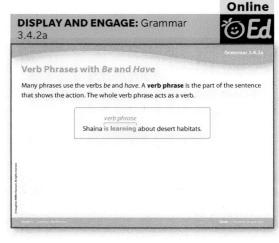

Online

DISPLAY AND ENGAGE: Grammar
3.4.2a

Grammar 3.4.2a

Verb Phrases with *Be* and *Have*

Many phrases use the verbs *be* and *have*. A **verb phrase** is the part of the sentence that shows the action. The whole verb phrase acts as a verb.

> *verb phrase*
> Shaina is learning about desert habitats.

Engage and Apply

- Complete items 1–10 on **Display and Engage: Grammar 3.4.2b** with students.

- Display the following sentences to students and read them aloud. Then, have students identify the verb phrase to a partner.

  The clouds are moving across the sky. **are moving**

  My sister and I have seen eagles fly by. **have seen**

  You have learned how to watch quietly. **have learned**

- Have students complete **Printable: Grammar 3.4.2** for practice with *be* and *have*.

- Have students edit a writing draft using verb phrases with *be* and *have*.

Online

DISPLAY AND ENGAGE: Grammar
3.4.2b

Grammar 3.4.2b

Verb Phrases with *Be* and *Have*

Identify the verb phrase in each sentence.

1. I am taking my compass out of my backpack. am taking
2. We are passing this same rock over and over again. are passing
3. You have to show me the way to our car. have to show
4. It had to be a rainy day today. had to be
5. The wet plant leaves were dripping on my head. were dripping
6. After we get home, I am going to throw away my map. am going
7. The map had not helped me at all. had not helped
8. We have to get a better map for our next trip. have to get

---

ENGLISH LEARNER SUPPORT: Scaffolded Practice

SUBSTANTIAL

Use the following sentences to demonstrate how to use the correct form of *be* and *have*.

The girl (is, am) eating a snack. is

She (has, have) made snacks for everyone. has

MODERATE

Write the sentence frame and guide students to use the correct form of *have*.

Sarah _____ baked a loaf of bread. has

LIGHT

Have students describe people or things using the correct form of *be* and *have* in verb phrases. Provide them with sentence frames such as:

I _____. The shop _____.

VERBS • THE VERBS *BE* AND *HAVE*

LEARNING OBJECTIVES

- **Language** Identify and use consistent verb tenses.
- **Language** Use the verbs *be* and *have* correctly in writing and speaking.

MATERIALS	Online

Display and Engage *Grammar 3.4.3a, 3.4.3b*

Printable *Grammar 3.4.3*

INSTRUCTIONAL VOCABULARY

- **verb phrase** the part of a sentence that shows action; the whole phrase acts as a verb

Connect and Teach

- Show **Display and Engage: Grammar 3.4.3a**. Explain that when using the verbs *be* and *have*, students should remember to use verb tenses consistently. In order for sentences to be correct, the verb must be in the same tense as the verb phrase.

- Model making the verb and the verb phrase the same tense:
  She is going to like where I am taking her.

- Explain that *is going* is in the present tense; therefore, *am taking* also must be in the present tense.

Engage and Apply

- Complete items 1–10 on **Display and Engage: Grammar 3.4.3b** with students.

- Display the following subjects. Have students identify the present and past forms of *be* and *have* for each subject.
  The sailor is, was, has, had
  My parents are, were, have, had
  You are, were, have, had
  I am, was, have, had

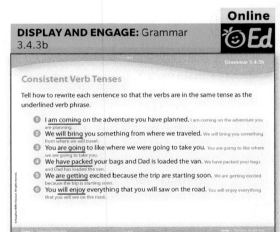

DISPLAY AND ENGAGE: Grammar 3.4.3a

Online Ed

Grammar 3.4.3a

Consistent Verb Tenses

When using the verbs *be* and *have*, remember to use verb tenses consistently. In order for your sentences to be correct, the verbs must be in the same tense.

Not correct
I had asked Laura to come with us, but she had to go to swim class that day.

Correct
I had asked Laura to come with us, but she had gone to swim class that day.

DISPLAY AND ENGAGE: Grammar 3.4.3b

Online Ed

Grammar 3.4.3b

Consistent Verb Tenses

Tell how to rewrite each sentence so that the verbs are in the same tense as the underlined verb phrase.

1. I am coming on the adventure you have planned. *I am coming on the adventure you are planning.*
2. We will bring you something from where we traveled. *We will bring you something from where we will travel.*
3. You are going to like where we were going to take you. *You are going to like where we are going to take you.*
4. We have packed your bags and Dad is loaded the van. *We have packed your bags and Dad has loaded the van.*
5. We are getting excited because the trip are starting soon. *We are getting excited because the trip is starting soon.*
6. You will enjoy everything that you will saw on the road. *You will enjoy everything that you will see on the road.*

- Have students complete **Printable: Grammar 3.4.3** for practice with *be* and *have*.

- Have students edit a writing draft using the correct forms of the verbs *be* and *have*.

 ENGLISH LEARNER SUPPORT: Scaffolded Practice

SUBSTANTIAL
Use the following sentence to demonstrate how to use verb tenses consistently.
The girls were playing a game and _____ studying for the test this morning. **were**

MODERATE
Write the sentence frame and guide students to use the correct form of *have*.
He _____ created a new game idea. **has**

LIGHT
Have students describe people or things using the correct form of *be* and *have* in the correct tense. Provide them with sentence frames such as:
I _____. At the park _____.

LEARNING OBJECTIVES

- **Language** Review the verbs *be* and *have*.
- **Language** Use the verbs *be* and *have* correctly in speaking and writing.

MATERIALS   Online

Display and Engage *Grammar 3.4.4a, 3.4.4b*

Printable *Grammar 3.4.4*

 INSTRUCTIONAL VOCABULARY

- **main verb** the verb in a verb clause that carries the main meaning or action
- **helping verb** a verb that helps make clear the tense, mood, or person of the main verb
- **irregular verb** a verb that does not follow the regular rules of verb forms
- **subject-verb agreement** a rule stating that subjects and verbs must be both singular or both plural

Review the Verbs *Be* and *Have*

- Show **Display and Engage: Grammar 3.4.4a**.

- Review with students that the verbs *be* and *have* are irregular verbs. Explain that the subject and verb must agree in number and tense. In addition, verbs and verb phrases also must be in the same tense in order for sentences to be correct.

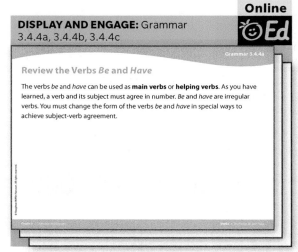

DISPLAY AND ENGAGE: Grammar
3.4.4a, 3.4.4b, 3.4.4c

Online
Ed

Grammar 3.4.4a

Review the Verbs *Be* and *Have*

The verbs *be* and *have* can be used as **main verbs** or **helping verbs**. As you have learned, a verb and its subject must agree in number. *Be* and *have* are irregular verbs. You must change the form of the verbs *be* and *have* in special ways to achieve subject-verb agreement.

- Work with students to complete the exercises on **Display and Engage: Grammar 3.4.4b**.

- Have students write three sentences using a form of *be* or *have* as a main or helping verb. Then have partners check each other's sentences.

- Have students complete **Printable: Grammar 3.4.4** for more practice with the verbs *be* and *have*.

- Have students edit a writing draft using the correct forms of the verbs *be* and *have*.

 ENGLISH LEARNER SUPPORT: Scaffolded Practice

SUBSTANTIAL

To remind students that the verbs *be* and *have* are irregular, provide examples of *be* and *have* functioning in different ways. For example: *We are late.* (*are* as a linking verb) *I have two dollars.* (*have* as an action verb) *The phone is ringing.* (*is* as a helping verb) *No one has asked me.* (*has* as a helping verb) Give other example sentences and have students identify the linking or helping verb in each sentence.

MODERATE

Remind students that they have encountered these kinds of verbs: action verbs, linking verbs, main verbs, and helping verbs. Present the verb *be*, which can function as both a linking and a helping verb. Display the following sentences. Help students tell whether each underlined form of *be* is used as a linking verb (linking the predicate to the subject) or a helping verb (accompanying a main verb).

- *Francis is an older boy.* *is, linking*
- *The children are alone in the wilderness.* *are, linking*
- *They are escaping from the Comancheros.* *are, helping*
- *The wind was blowing wildly.* *was, helping*

LIGHT

Have students write a sentence each using *be* and *have*, paying special attention to how they are using the verb (helping, linking, or main) and whether they have used the same tense.

VERBS • THE VERBS *BE* AND *HAVE*

LEARNING OBJECTIVES

- **Language** Choose the verbs *be* and *have* to convey ideas.
- **Language** Use the verbs *be* and *have* correctly in writing and speaking.

MATERIALS   Online **Ed**

Display and Engage *Grammar 3.4.5*

Printable *Grammar 3.4.5*

 INSTRUCTIONAL VOCABULARY

- **irregular verb** a verb that does not follow the regular rules of verb forms

Connect and Teach

- Show **Display and Engage: Grammar 3.4.5**. Explain that students must remember to use the correct forms of *be* and *have*.

- Remind students to keep the verb tense consistent so that their paragraphs make sense.

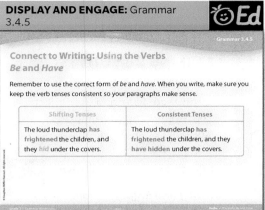

DISPLAY AND ENGAGE: Grammar 3.4.5   Online **Ed**

Grammar 3.4.5

Connect to Writing: Using the Verbs *Be* and *Have*

Remember to use the correct form of *be* and *have*. When you write, make sure you keep the verb tenses consistent so your paragraphs make sense.

Shifting Tenses	Consistent Tenses
The loud thunderclap has frightened the children, and they hid under the covers.	The loud thunderclap has frightened the children, and they have hidden under the covers.

Engage and Apply

- Display the following sentences. Have students give the correct form of *be* and *have*.

  » *The bear (has, have) already been seen.* has

  » *I (were, was) hiding in the trees.* was

- Display the sentences. Have students make the verb tenses correct.

  » *The hike (is, are) cancelled for today.* is

  » *I (has, have) taken a walk in the meadow.* have

- Have students write two sentences using the correct form of *be* and two sentences using the correct form of *have*. Then have partners read their sentences to each other.

- Have students complete **Printable: Grammar 3. 4.5** for practice with *be* and *have*.

- Tell students that as they revise their writing, they should look for correct use of *be* and *have*. Have students revise a piece of writing to use *be* and *have* correctly. Tell partners to exchange papers and check that verb tenses were used correctly.

EL **ENGLISH LEARNER SUPPORT: Scaffolded Practice**

SUBSTANTIAL

Remind students that *be* and *have* are often used as helping verbs. Say: *Remember that there are several forms of* be *and* have. *Forms of* be *include* is, am, was, *and* were. *Forms of* have *include* has, have, *and* had. Share example sentences and help students identify the forms of *be* and *have*.

MODERATE

Have students look through a story they have read for sentences with helping verbs in them. Have partners copy these sentences, circle the helping verbs, and underline the main verbs.

LIGHT

Write: *The children were running from the outlaws.* Circle the helping verb *were*. Underline the main verb *running*.

- Explain that *have* also can be used after *could, should, would,* or *must*. Write: *The outlaws could have seen the children's tracks in the dirt.* Circle the helping verb *have*.

- Have partners write sentences with the helping verbs *be* and *have*. Then have partners read their sentences to each other.

LEARNING OBJECTIVES

- **Language** Identify perfect tenses.
- **Language** Form and use perfect tenses correctly in writing and speaking.

MATERIALS Online **Ed**

Display and Engage *Grammar 3.5.1a, 3.5.1b*

Printable *Grammar 3.5.1*

 INSTRUCTIONAL
VOCABULARY

- **perfect tense** a group of tenses with *has*, *have*, or *had* as a helping verb
- **present perfect tense** includes *has* or *have* as a helping verb

Connect and Teach

- Show **Display and Engage: Grammar 3.5.1a**. Explain that the **present prefect tense** uses *has* or *have* as a helping verb with the past participle form of the main verb. The helping verb and main verb together form the present perfect tense.

- Model identifying the present perfect tense in the example sentence: *She has seen many bears.*

  THINK ALOUD *To identify the present perfect tense, I ask* Is the helping verb in the present tense? Is the main verb in the past participle form? *The verb has in this sentence is in the present tense. The main verb,* seen, *is in the participle form. This sentence is in the present perfect tense.*

Engage and Apply

- Complete items 1–8 on **Display and Engage: Grammar 3.5.1b** with students.

- List the following main verbs on the board. Have students use *have* or *has* to change the main verbs to present perfect tense.
  eat has eaten
  hike have hiked
  run has run
  climb have climbed
  jump has jumped
  sit have sat

- Have students complete **Printable: Grammar 3.5.1** for practice with perfect tenses.

- Have students edit a writing draft using present perfect tense correctly.

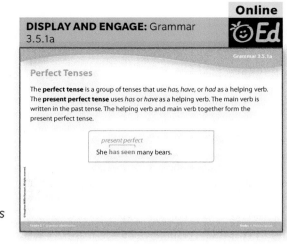

DISPLAY AND ENGAGE: Grammar 3.5.1a

Online **Ed**

Perfect Tenses

The **perfect tense** is a group of tenses that use *has, have,* or *had* as a helping verb. The **present perfect tense** uses *has* or *have* as a helping verb. The main verb is written in the past tense. The helping verb and main verb together form the present perfect tense.

present perfect
She has seen many bears.

DISPLAY AND ENGAGE: Grammar 3.5.1b

Online **Ed**

Perfect Tenses

Suggest how to rewrite each sentence to show the present perfect tense correctly.

1. She has try to get more blueberries. She has tried to get more blueberries.
2. We has wanted a blueberry pie for weeks. We have wanted a blueberry pie for weeks.
3. The boys have eat every pie I bake. The boys have eaten every pie I baked.
4. I think I have see that bear walking in the woods. I think I have seen that bear walking in the woods.
5. It have been a tradition for us to pick berries at the farm. It has been a tradition for us to pick berries at the farm.
6. We have love walking in the woods for a long time. We have loved walking in the woods for a long time.

 ENGLISH LEARNER SUPPORT: Scaffolded Practice

SUBSTANTIAL
Use the following sentence frames to demonstrate how to use perfect tenses.
Her sister (had, have) played a game. had
The bear cubs (has, have) run away. have

MODERATE
Write the following sentence frames and guide students to use perfect tenses.
Her sister (had, have) hoped to see the bear. had
The flowers (has, have) looked beautiful this spring. have
I will (had, have) walked through the woods. have

LIGHT
Have students use the perfect tense to describe a scene from a story they've read. Provide them with sentence frames, such as the following:
The girl _____.
The boy _____.

LEARNING OBJECTIVES

- **Language** Identify past perfect tenses.
- **Language** Form and use perfect tenses correctly in writing and speaking.

MATERIALS	Online

Display and Engage *Grammar 3.5.2a, 3.5.2b*

Printable *Grammar 3.5.2*

 INSTRUCTIONAL VOCABULARY

- **past perfect tense** includes *had* as a helping verb

Connect and Teach

- Show **Display and Engage: Grammar 3.5.2a**. Tell students that the **past perfect tense** uses *had* as a helping verb with a main verb in the past participle form. Together, the helping verb and main verb form the past perfect tense.

- Model identifying the past perfect tense in the example sentence: *Leo had looked for chipmunks on the hike.*

  THINK ALOUD *To identify the past perfect tense, I ask* Is the helping verb had? Is the main verb in the past participle form? *I see the helping verb* had, *and the main verb,* looked, *is in the past participle form. This shows me that the sentence is in the past perfect tense.*

Engage and Apply

- Complete items 1–8 on **Display and Engage: Grammar 3.5.2b** with students.

- Have students complete the following sentence frames using the past perfect tense.
  The rain _____ (start) to fall. **had started**
  The mountain paths _____ (fill) with mud puddles. **had filled**

- Have students complete **Printable: Grammar 3.5.2** for practice with past perfect tense.

- Have students edit a writing draft using past perfect tense correctly.

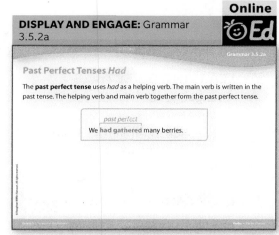

🗨 **ENGLISH LEARNER SUPPORT: Scaffolded Practice**

SUBSTANTIAL
Use the following sentence frames to demonstrate how to use past perfect tense.
She _____ played a game. **had**
He _____ seen a bear in the woods. **had**

MODERATE
Write the following sentence frames and guide students to use perfect tenses.
She _____ a bear in the woods. **had seen**
He _____ to be a bear. **had pretended**
She _____ the bear was scary. **had thought**

LIGHT
Have students write a few sentences using past perfect tense about something that had happened one time.

VERBS • PERFECT TENSES

LEARNING OBJECTIVES

- **Language** Identify past perfect tenses.
- **Language** Form and use perfect tenses correctly in writing and speaking.

MATERIALS   Online

Display and Engage *Grammar 3.5.3a, 3.5.3b*

Printable *Grammar 3.5.3*

INSTRUCTIONAL VOCABULARY

- **future perfect tense** includes *will have* as a helping verb

Connect and Teach

- Show **Display and Engage: Grammar 3.5.3a**. Explain that the **future perfect tense** uses *will have* as a helping verb with a past-participle form of the main verb. Tell students that the helping verb and main verb form the future present tense.

- Model identifying the future perfect tense in the example sentence: *We will have gathered many berries.*

  THINK ALOUD *To identify the future perfect tense, I ask Is the helping verb* will have? *Is the main verb in the past participle form? I see* will have, *which is in the future tense. The main verb,* gathered, *is in the past participle form. I know that the sentence is in the future perfect tense.*

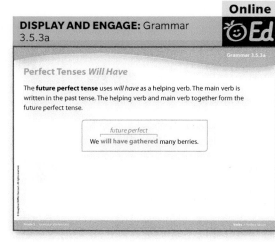

Engage and Apply

- Complete items 1–10 on **Display and Engage: Grammar 3.5.3b** with students.

- Display the following sentences. Have students change the verb phrase to the future perfect tense.
  My dad has taught me to put up a tent.
  will have taught
  We have roasted hot dogs over the fire.
  will have roasted

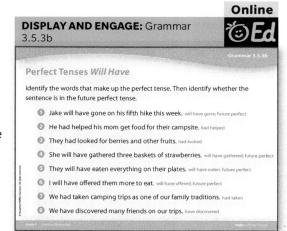

- Have students complete **Printable: Grammar 3.5.3** for practice with future perfect tense.

- Have students edit a writing draft using the correct forms of the future perfect tense.

EL ENGLISH LEARNER SUPPORT: Scaffolded Practice

SUBSTANTIAL

Use the following sentence frames to demonstrate how to use the future perfect tense.
She _____ gone to the park. will have
He _____ ridden his bike for ten miles. will have

MODERATE

Write the following sentence frames and guide students to use the future perfect tense.
She _____ the play with the bear. will have seen
I _____ three plays this year. will have seen
She _____ in two new plays. will have starred

LIGHT

Have students use the future perfect tense to write a few sentences. Have students trade papers and identify the helping verb and main verb.

VERBS • PERFECT TENSES

LEARNING OBJECTIVES

- **Language** Review perfect tenses.
- **Language** Form and use perfect tenses correctly in writing and speaking.

MATERIALS	Online

Display and Engage *Grammar 3.5.4a, 3.5.4b*

Printable *Grammar 3.5.4*

INSTRUCTIONAL VOCABULARY

- **perfect tense** a group of tenses with *has, have,* or *had* as a helping verb
- **present perfect tense** includes *has* or *have* as a helping verb
- **past perfect tense** includes *had* as a helping verb
- **future perfect tense** includes *will have* as a helping verb

Review Perfect Tenses

- Show **Display and Engage: Grammar 3.5.4a**.

- Review with students that the verbs *be* and *have* are irregular verbs. Point out that the subject and the verb must agree in number and tense. Explain that a special ending must be added to irregular verbs used with *has, have,* or *had*.

- Work with students to complete the exercises on **Display and Engage: Grammar 3.5.4b**.

- Have students write three sentences using the perfect tenses for the verbs *make, break,* and *take*.

- Have students complete **Printable: Grammar 3.5.4**.

- Have students edit a writing draft using the correct form of the present perfect, past perfect, and future perfect tenses.

DISPLAY AND ENGAGE: Grammar
3.5.4a, 3.5.4b

Online
@Ed

Grammar 3.5.4a

Review Perfect Tenses

You have already learned the simple verb tenses: *past, present,* and *future*. English has another group of tenses called the **perfect tenses**. All perfect-tense verbs include *has, have,* or *had* as a helping verb. A verb in the **present perfect tense** includes *has* or *have* as a helping verb. A verb in the **past perfect tense** includes *had* as a helping verb. A verb in the **future perfect tense** includes *will have* as a helping verb.

> **Present Perfect:** Two bears have eaten some berries.
> **Past Perfect:** Two bears had eaten some berries.
> **Future Perfect:** Two bears will have eaten some berries.

ENGLISH LEARNER SUPPORT: Scaffolded Practice

SUBSTANTIAL

To remind students that the perfect tenses include present perfect, past perfect, and future perfect, provide examples of each:

- present perfect tense: *Jeanne has entered the class reading challenge.*
- past perfect tense: *She had entered it last year, too.*
- future perfect tense: *She will have read twelve books by December.*
  Guide students to identify the helping verb and main verb in each sentence.

MODERATE

Present the verb *have*. Explain to students that *have* can be used as a helping verb, or it can be used as a main verb to show possession. Display the following sentences. Help students tell whether each form of *have* is used as a helping verb or as a main verb showing possession.

- *The mother bear has protected her cubs.* helping
- *The building has a new elevator.* main

LIGHT

Have students use the perfect tense to write a few sentences about something they've read this week.

VERBS • PERFECT TENSES

LEARNING OBJECTIVES

- **Language** Choose perfect tenses to convey ideas.
- **Language** Form and use perfect tenses correctly in writing and speaking.

MATERIALS Online

Display and Engage *Grammar 3.5.5*
Printable *Grammar 3.5.5*

 INSTRUCTIONAL VOCABULARY

- **perfect tense** a group of tenses with *has, have,* or *had* as a helping verb

Connect and Teach

- Show **Display and Engage: Grammar 3.5.5**. Tell students that they need to use the correct forms of regular and irregular verbs when they write sentences containing perfect tenses.

Engage and Apply

- Review with them that subject and verb must agree when using the perfect tenses.

- Display the following sentences. Have students write the correct form of the regular or irregular verb.

  » *The fire has (go) out.* **gone**

  » *My family has (hike) back down the mountain.* **hiked**

- Display these sentences. Have students write the sentence using the correct form of the verb.

  » *I will have (sleep) in a tent for three nights.* **slept**

  » *We have (love) every moment of our camping trip.* **loved**

  » *My parents have (pack) the car.* **packed**

- Have students complete **Printable: Grammar 3.5.5** for practice with perfect tenses.

- Tell students that as they revise their writing, they should make sure they are using verb tenses correctly. Have them review a piece of writing and change any verbs that are in the incorrect tense. Tell partners to exchange papers and check that verb tenses were used correctly.

Online **Ed**

DISPLAY AND ENGAGE: Grammar 3.5.5

Connect to Writing: Using Perfect Tenses

You know that regular verbs add *-ed* when used with *has, have,* or *had.* You must add a special ending to irregular verbs used with *has, have,* or *had.* Use the correct forms of regular and irregular verbs when you write sentences in the perfect tenses.

Incorrect	Correct
Tamara has ate some berries.	Tamara has eaten some berries.
Her mom had gave them to her.	Her mom had given them to her.
By the morning, Tamara will have leaved for school.	By the morning, Tamara will have left for school.

EL **ENGLISH LEARNER SUPPORT: Scaffolded Practice**

ALL LEVELS Explain that the different perfect tenses describe different types of actions in the past. Write and read aloud: *Our families have lived on this land for over 75 years.* Underline *have lived.* Explain that this is the present perfect tense. Say: *Verbs in the present perfect tense describe events that began in the past and continue in the present.*

- Write and read aloud: *The Jackson family had lived near the lake for many years before they moved to the city.* Underline *had lived.* Say: *This action is past perfect.* Explain that verbs in the past perfect tense describe events that began in the past and also ended in the past.

- Write and read aloud: *The students will have completed their readings on Native Americans by next week.* Underline *will have completed.* Say: *This action is future perfect.* Explain that verbs in the future perfect tense describe events that began in the past but will be finished in the future.

Have students write sentences about the past using perfect tenses. Encourage them to use signal words such as *first* and *then* to show the passage of time.

LESSON 3.6.1   EASILY CONFUSED VERBS

LEARNING OBJECTIVES

- Identify and correctly use easily confused verbs.
- Use easily confused verbs correctly in writing and speaking.

MATERIALS   Online Ed

Display and Engage *Grammar 3.6.1a, 3.6.1b*

Printable *Grammar 3.6.1*

Connect and Teach

- Show **Display and Engage: Grammar 3.6.1a**. Explain that some verbs have meanings that are related but not the same. Tell students that it is important to know the exact meaning of these verbs so that they will not use them incorrectly.

- Model correct verb usage in an example sentence: *Joseph learned how to use a lasso.*

    THINK ALOUD *To identify the correct usage of the verb in the sentence, I ask* What definition fits the sentence? How does the sentence sound if you say it aloud? *The definition of the verb learn is "to receive instruction from someone." The verb is used correctly because Joseph could receive instruction about how to use a lasso. The sentence also sounds correct when read aloud.*

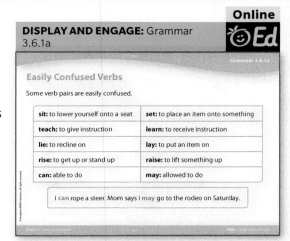

DISPLAY AND ENGAGE: Grammar 3.6.1a   Online Ed

Easily Confused Verbs

Some verb pairs are easily confused.

sit: to lower yourself onto a seat	set: to place an item onto something
teach: to give instruction	learn: to receive instruction
lie: to recline on	lay: to put an item on
rise: to get up or stand up	raise: to lift something up
can: able to do	may: allowed to do

I can rope a steer. Mom says I may go to the rodeo on Saturday.

Engage and Apply

- Complete items 1–8 on **Display and Engage: Grammar 3.6.1b** with students.

- Have students choose two pairs of verbs from the exercises and write sentences for each word. Have them use the Thinking Questions to check that they are using the verbs correctly.

- Have students complete **Printable: Grammar 3.6.1** for practice with easily confused verbs.

- Have students edit a writing draft using easily confused words correctly.

DISPLAY AND ENGAGE: Grammar 3.6.1b   Online Ed

Easily Confused Verbs

Identify the correct verb in each sentence.

1. Roping cattle is hard work, and not everyone (can, may) do it. can
2. The cowboys (rose, raised) at dawn and ate their breakfast. rose
3. The cattle did not generally (lie, lay) down at the end of the day. lie
4. (Rising, Raising) his hand, the rancher greeted the cowboys. Raising
5. The rancher (sit, set) his plate down and went to check on the horses. set
6. If young men and women did not (teach/learn) how to fend for themselves, they could not have survived the Wild West. learn

EL ENGLISH LEARNER SUPPORT: Facilitate Linguistic Connections

Many languages, such as English, have their own spelling/usage traps. Have students provide examples of confusing verbs, terms, and phrases in their own languages. Help students develop situational skits that will allow them to practice using the easily confused verbs. Explain that in some cases, they simply have to memorize the correct verbs and practice using them in context, as native English speakers do.

Scaffolded Practice

SUBSTANTIAL

Work with students to orally complete these sentence frames using easily confused verbs.
The cowboy was not going to _____ on the saddle. **sit**
Instead, he _____ a bucket of oats in front of the horse. **set**

MODERATE

Work with students to complete these sentence frames using easily confused verbs. As students complete the sentence frames, ask them to read the sentences aloud.
The old vaquero _____ roping skills to the young cowboys. **teaches**
The young cowboys are eager to _____ how to handle a horse. **learn**

LIGHT

Guide students as they choose three word pairs from the Display and Engage and write sentences containing each easily confused verb.

LEARNING OBJECTIVES

- Identify and correctly use easily confused verbs.
- Use easily confused verbs correctly in writing and speaking.

MATERIALS   Online

Display and Engage *Grammar 3.6.2a, 3.6.2b*

Printable *Grammar 3.6.2*

Connect and Teach

- Show **Display and Engage: Grammar 3.6.2a**. Explain to students that they will be learning about some other words that are often confused. Point out that these words are not verbs, and they have similar meanings.

- Model correct usage of *good* in this example sentence: *Sophie did good rounding up the herd.*

  THINK ALOUD *To identify correct usage, I ask* What definition fits the sentence? What part of speech is needed? *The word* good *describes how Sophie performed rounding up the herd. But* good *is an adjective, not an adverb. So, the sentence should read,* Sophie did well *rounding up the herd.*

> **Online**
> **DISPLAY AND ENGAGE:** Grammar
> 3.6.2a
>
> Grammar 3.6.2a
>
> **Identify Easily Confused Verbs**
>
> Some words are easily confused. Study the meanings of these words to avoid misusing them.
>
> **Good** is an adjective used to describe nouns or pronouns.
> **Well** is an adverb used to describe verbs.
> **There** is an adverb that means "that location or place."
> **Their** is a possessive pronoun that shows who or what owns something.
> **They're** is the contraction of "they are."
> **Whose** is a possessive pronoun that shows who or what owns something.
> **Who's** is the contraction of "who is."

Engage and Apply

- Complete items 1–8 on **Display and Engage: Grammar 3.6.2b** with students.

- Have students choose a pair of commonly confused verbs from either Display and Engage. Tell them to write sentence frames, leaving out the target word. Have partners exchange sentences and complete the frames.

- Have students complete **Printable: Grammar 3.6.2** for practice with commonly confused verbs.

- Have students edit a writing draft using the correct easily confused words.

> **Online**
> **DISPLAY AND ENGAGE:** Grammar
> 3.6.2b
>
> Grammar 3.6.2b
>
> **Identify Easily Confused Verbs**
>
> Identify the word in parentheses that correctly completes the sentence.
>
> ① (Whose/Who's) horse is this? Whose
> ② The cowboys have received (there/their/they're) supper. their
> ③ The vaqueros did a (good/well) job teaching the young cowboys. good
> ④ (There/Their/They're) going to ride this afternoon. They're
> ⑤ (Whose/Who's) turn is it to build the fire? Whose
> ⑥ The cowboys set up camp over (their/there/they're). there
> ⑦ He aimed (good/well) and hit his target. well
> ⑧ (Whose/Who's) making dinner tonight? Who's

 ENGLISH LEARNER SUPPORT: Scaffolded Practice

SUBSTANTIAL

Work with students to orally complete these sentence frames using easily confused words.
What do you see over _____. there
_____ going to see a movie tomorrow. They're

MODERATE

Work with students to complete these sentence frames using easily confused words. As students complete the sentence frames, ask them to read the sentences aloud.
I did _____ on the test. well
The book was _____. good

LIGHT

Guide students as they choose from *good/well*, *they're/their/there*, or *whose/who's* and write sentences containing each easily confused word.

VERBS • EASILY CONFUSED VERBS

LEARNING OBJECTIVES

- Identify and correctly use easily confused verbs.
- Use easily confused verbs correctly in writing and speaking.

MATERIALS	Online

Display and Engage *Grammar 3.6.3a, 3.6.3b*

Printable *Grammar 3.6.3*

Connect and Teach

- Show <u>Display and Engage: Grammar 3.6.3a</u>. Use the examples to explain how to use parts of speech to determine whether a word is used correctly. Discuss how students can create and use memory tricks to help them choose correct words.

- Display the following sentences.
  Marina gave a good reason for being late.
  Joseph went over there.

  THINK ALOUD *To determine how a word should be used I ask* What is the part of speech of the word? *The word* good *is an adjective that describes the noun* reason. *Knowing the parts of speech can help me choose the right words to use. The word* there *is an adverb that refers to a location or place.*

Engage and Apply

- Complete items 1–8 on <u>Display and Engage: Grammar 3.6.3b</u> with students.

- Write the following words on the board:
  can / may
  lie / lay
  whose / who's
  good / well
  there / their

- Have students provide sentences orally that use these words correctly. Challenge students to identify the verbs.

- Have students complete <u>Printable: Grammar 3.6.3</u> for practice with commonly confused verbs.

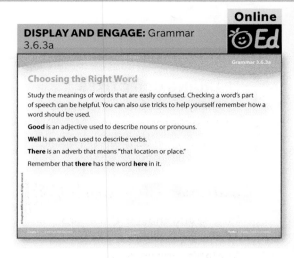

DISPLAY AND ENGAGE: Grammar 3.6.3a

Online Ed

Grammar 3.6.3a

Choosing the Right Word

Study the meanings of words that are easily confused. Checking a word's part of speech can be helpful. You can also use tricks to help yourself remember how a word should be used.

Good is an adjective used to describe nouns or pronouns.

Well is an adverb used to describe verbs.

There is an adverb that means "that location or place."

Remember that **there** has the word **here** in it.

DISPLAY AND ENGAGE: Grammar 3.6.3b

Online Ed

Grammar 3.6.3b

Choosing the Right Word

Identify the word in parentheses that correctly completes the sentence.

1. The cowboys (rise/raise) at dawn every morning. rise
2. (Whose/Who's) going to keep watch tonight? Who's
3. The vaqueros shared (there/their/they're) food with each other. their
4. The cowboys rode (good/well) across the prairies. well
5. She wanted to (teach/learn) us how to round up the mustangs. teach
6. Cowboys wore chaps to protect (there/their/they're) legs from rope burns. their
7. He took a drink and then (sit/set) the cup on the ground. set
8. The young calves sometimes (lie/lay) down next to their mothers. lie

---

(EL) ENGLISH LEARNER SUPPORT: Scaffolded Practice

SUBSTANTIAL

Work with students to orally complete these sentence frames using easily confused words.
I feel tired so I will _____ down. lie
You can _____ the book on the counter. lay

MODERATE

Work with students to complete these sentence frames using easily confused words. As students complete the sentence frames, ask them to read the sentences aloud.
I _____ count to ten in Spanish. can
You _____ take a break from your homework. may

LIGHT

Guide students as they choose a word pair from the list on the board and write sentences containing each easily confused word.

LEARNING OBJECTIVES

- Identify easily confused verbs and choose the correct word.
- Use easily confused verbs in writing and speaking.

MATERIALS   Online

Display and Engage *Grammar 3.6.4a, 3.6.4b*

Printable *Grammar 3.6.4*

Review Easily Confused Verbs

- Show **Display and Engage: Grammar 3.6.4a**. Review with students that some words have meanings that are related but different. Explain that knowing the meanings and parts of speech of these words can help students use them correctly.

- Work with students to complete the exercises on **Display and Engage: Grammar 3.6.4b**.

- Have students complete **Printable: Grammar 3.6.4** for more practice with easily confused words.

- Have students edit a writing draft using the correct easily confused words.

DISPLAY AND ENGAGE: Grammar
3.6.4a, 3.6.4b, 3.6.4c

Online
Ed

Grammar 3.6.4a

Review Easily Confused Words

Some pairs of verbs have such closely related meanings that they are easily confused. Most of these verbs are **irregular verbs**. A few are **helping verbs**. By studying the meanings of both verbs, you can avoid using the wrong one in your speaking and writing.

 ENGLISH LEARNER SUPPORT: Scaffolded Practice

SUBSTANTIAL

To remind students that some verbs can be easily confused, provide examples of some of the most commonly confused: *lie/lay; sit/set; can/may.*

MODERATE

Explain to students that every language has words and word forms that are confusing. Encourage students to use verbs and verb phrases that they understand and that are appropriate to their writing tasks.

LIGHT

Guide students to write sentences using *may/can* or another easily confused word pair.

LESSON 3.6.5

VERBS • EASILY CONFUSED VERBS

LEARNING OBJECTIVES

- Identify and correctly use easily confused verbs.
- Use easily confused verbs correctly in writing and speaking.

MATERIALS   Online

Display and Engage *Grammar 3.6.5*

Printable *Grammar 3.6.5*

Connect and Teach

- Show **Display and Engage: Grammar 3.6.5**. Remind students that following the rules for conventions makes their writing clear and easy for readers to understand.

- Point out that an important part of revising is using easily confused verbs and other words correctly.

Engage and Apply

- Review the definitions and usage of the easily confused verbs. Reinforce how some easily confused verbs are irregular verbs and a few are helping verbs.

- Display these sentences. Have students rewrite them using the correct verb.
  You can relax if you have put the saddles away. **You may relax if you have put the saddles away.**
  You may play the harmonica very well. **You can play the harmonica very well.**
  He didn't know anything about how to rise cattle. **He didn't know anything about how to raise cattle.**

- Have students complete **Printable: Grammar 3.6.5** for practice with easily confused verbs.

- Tell students that as they revise their work, they should correct verbs and words that are easily confused. Have students revise a piece of writing with a special eye for making sure their writing is clear and accurate. Tell partners to exchange papers and check that easily confused words were used correctly.

Online Ed

DISPLAY AND ENGAGE: Grammar 3.6.5

Grammar 3.6.5

Connect to Writing: Using Verbs Correctly

You know that some pairs of verbs have meanings that are related but different. These verbs are easily confused with each other. When you proofread your writing, it is important to pay special attention to these verbs.

Incorrect Verbs	Correct Verbs
I sit my book on my desk and open it. Then I lie my pencil neatly next to the book. I'm ready for Ms. Lopez to learn us about the Wild West.	I set my book on my desk and open it. Then I lay my pencil neatly next to the book. I'm ready for Ms. Lopez to teach us about the Wild West.

EL ENGLISH LEARNER SUPPORT: Grammar Practice

CONNECT AND TEACH Write verb pairs on the board: *can/may, sit/set, teach/learn, lie/lay,* and *rise/raise.* Use each pair in an example sentence, such as: *I will teach you the song, and you will learn it.*

ENGAGE AND APPLY Have partners read the following sentences aloud. Have them choose the correct verb in parentheses.

- *The sun (rises/raises) every morning. rises*
- *I (can/may) ride a horse better than a cowboy. can*
- *Could you please (learn/teach) me about the Old West? teach*
- *I love to (lie/lay) on the ground and look at the stars. lie*

CONNECT TO WRITING Have students write sentences about cowboys that contain easily confused verbs. Have them read the sentences aloud to a partner.

LEARNING OBJECTIVES

- Identify adjectives and descriptive adjectives.
- Use adjectives and articles correctly in writing and speaking.

MATERIALS	Online

Display and Engage *Grammar 4.1.1a, 4.1.1b*

Printable *Grammar 4.1.1*

 INSTRUCTIONAL VOCABULARY

- **adjective** gives information about a noun
- **descriptive adjective** tells what kind or origin

Connect and Teach

- Show **Display and Engage: Grammar 4.1.1a**. Explain that an **adjective** gives information about a noun, such as how many and what kind. One special kind of **descriptive adjective** tells the origin of the person, place, or thing it describes.

- Model identifying the adjectives used in the example sentences: *I read twelve comics. I read spine-tingling episodes. I read the Japanese comic last.*

   THINK ALOUD *To identify adjectives, I ask* Which word gives information about a noun? *(twelve; spine-tingling; Japanese)* Does it describe the noun or tell the origin of the noun? Twelve *tells how many;* spine-tingling *tells what kind;* Japanese *is a descriptive adjective that tells the origin of the comic.*

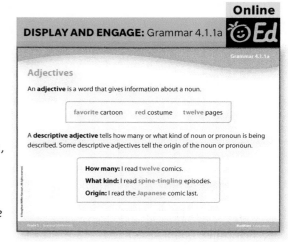

DISPLAY AND ENGAGE: Grammar 4.1.1a

Adjectives

An **adjective** is a word that gives information about a noun.

| favorite cartoon | red costume | twelve pages |

A **descriptive adjective** tells how many or what kind of noun or pronoun is being described. Some descriptive adjectives tell the origin of the noun or pronoun.

How many: I read twelve comics.
What kind: I read spine-tingling episodes.
Origin: I read the Japanese comic last.

Engage and Apply

- Complete items 1–8 on **Display and Engage: Grammar 4.1.1b** with students.

- Write the following nouns on the board.

pencil	book
picture	chalk
paper	rules

- Work with students to brainstorm adjectives that might describe each noun. *Sample answers: wooden pencil; French book; pretty picture; white chalk; yellow paper; school rules*

- Have students complete **Printable: Grammar 4.1.1** for practice with adjectives.

DISPLAY AND ENGAGE: Grammar 4.1.1b

Adjectives

Identify the descriptive adjectives that give information about the underlined nouns.

1. Newspapers print many <u>cartoons</u>. many
2. The people who draw cartoons are talented <u>artists</u>. talented
3. The original <u>drawings</u> for cartoons are often valuable. original, valuable

Identify the descriptive adjective that tells the origin of each underlined noun.

4. Many read a comic that takes place in an Asian <u>city</u>. Asian
5. A Spanish <u>woman</u> helps a lost girl get home. Spanish
6. The Italian <u>character</u> was a hero, too. Italian

 ENGLISH LEARNER SUPPORT: Scaffolded Practice

Explain Terms About Language Point out the cognate in the list above. Then explain that an adjective adds more information about a noun.

SUBSTANTIAL
Explain to students that an adjective describes a noun. Work with students to complete the following sentence frames using adjectives:
The comic book had _____ pages. sixteen
Greg carried _____ boxes. big

MODERATE
Work with students to complete the sentence frames using adjectives that tell what kind. *tiny; cardboard*

LIGHT
Ask students to use adjectives to orally describe objects in the room, telling how many and what kind. Example:
There are ten *books on the shelf.*
There are ten red *books on the shelf.*

LEARNING OBJECTIVES

- Identify adjectives and descriptive adjectives.
- Use adjectives and articles in writing and speaking.

MATERIALS   Online 🖥Ed

Display and Engage *Grammar 4.1.2a, 4.1.2b*

Printable *Grammar 4.1.2*

📖 INSTRUCTIONAL VOCABULARY

- **adjective** gives information about a noun
- **linking verb** connects the subject in a sentence to an adjective describing it; some are forms of the verb "to be," such as *is, are, am,* and *was*

Connect and Teach

- Show <u>**Display and Engage: Grammar 4.1.2a**</u>. Explain that a linking verb may connect the subject in a sentence to an adjective describing it. Some linking verbs are forms of the verb "to be," such as *is, are, am,* and *was*.

- Model identifying the linking verbs used in the example sentences: *The food in the cafeteria smells good. Greg is happy to write comic books.*

  THINK ALOUD *To identify a subject, linking verb, and adjective describing the subject, I ask* What is the subject? What is the adjective? What word connects the subject to the adjective? *The subjects are* food *and* Greg. *The adjectives are* good *and* happy. Smells *and* is *connect the subjects and adjectives.*

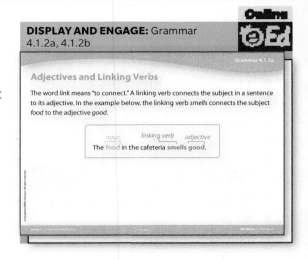

DISPLAY AND ENGAGE: Grammar
4.1.2a, 4.1.2b

Engage and Apply

- Complete items 1–6 on <u>**Display and Engage: Grammar 4.1.2b**</u> with students.

- Write the following sentence frames on the board. Have students identify the linking verb and add an adjective.
  The painting seems _____. seems; vibrant
  The screen looks _____. looks; high
  Some painters feel _____. feel; happy

DISPLAY AND ENGAGE: Grammar
4.1.2c

- Have students complete <u>**Printable: Grammar 4.1.2**</u> for practice with adjectives and linking verbs.

💬 ENGLISH LEARNER SUPPORT: Scaffolded Practice

SUBSTANTIAL

Work with students to complete the following sentence frames using adjectives:
The big book looks _____. heavy
The artists feel _____ about their project. excited

MODERATE

Work with students to complete the sentence frames above by identifying the linking verb and choosing an adjective. *looks; feel*

LIGHT

Ask students to use adjectives to orally describe objects in the room, using a linking verb and an adjective. Example:
The chalkboard looks dark green.
The clock is round.

MODIFIERS • ADJECTIVES

LEARNING OBJECTIVES

- Identify adjectives and articles.
- Use adjectives and articles correctly in writing and speaking.

MATERIALS	Online
Display and Engage *Grammar 4.1.3a, 4.1.3b*	
Printable *Grammar 4.1.3*	

 INSTRUCTIONAL
VOCABULARY

- **adjective** gives information about a noun
- **article** type of adjective that refers to a specific noun or a general noun

Connect and Teach

- Show **Display and Engage: Grammar 4.1.3a**. Explain that the words *a*, *an*, and *the* are articles. Point out that **articles** are kinds of adjectives that refer to and give information about a noun.

- Model identifying articles used in the example sentences: *Please pass me an apple. I would like the red one.*
  THINK ALOUD *I ask* Is the noun general or specific? *In the first sentence, it is general. In the second, it is specific.*

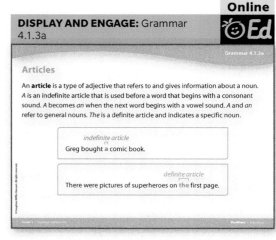

DISPLAY AND ENGAGE: Grammar
4.1.3a

Online
Ed

Grammar 4.1.3a

Articles

An **article** is a type of adjective that refers to and gives information about a noun. *A* is an indefinite article that is used before a word that begins with a consonant sound. *A* becomes *an* when the next word begins with a vowel sound. *A* and *an* refer to general nouns. *The* is a definite article and indicates a specific noun.

indefinite article
Greg bought a comic book.

definite article
There were pictures of superheroes on the first page.

Engage and Apply

- Complete items 1–6 on **Display and Engage: Grammar 4.1.3b** with students.

- Display several short phrases containing an adjective and a noun. Have students respond orally using the articles *a*, *an*, or *the*, as appropriate, to describe the noun. *standing in _____ cafeteria line* the
  took _____ big bite of his sandwich a
  _____ ink-jet printer an
  developed _____ master plan a

DISPLAY AND ENGAGE: Grammar
4.1.3b

Online
Ed

Grammar 4.1.3b

Articles

Fill in the blank with the correct article, *a* or *an*.

1. The storeowner said that it was _____ amusing story. an
2. I wanted to buy _____ comic book for my cousin. a
3. I hear this comic is part of _____ popular series. a

Complete the sentence with the correct article, *a* or *the*.

4. Making _____ comic book is simple! a
5. _____ collection was the most popular in the store. The
6. It was fun exploring _____ new comic shop in our neighborhood. the

- Have students complete **Printable: Grammar 4.1.3** for practice with adjectives and articles.

ENGLISH LEARNER SUPPORT: Scaffolded Practice

SUBSTANTIAL
Work with students to complete the following sentence frames using an article:
Did you find _____ book to read? a
I have _____ band's new record. the

MODERATE
Work with students to complete the sentence frames using articles:
I checked out _____ book from _____ library. a; the
_____ artist painted _____ mural. The; a

LIGHT
Ask students to write two sentences about something that happened today. Have them think about whether they should use *the* or *a*. Have them circle the articles in their sentences.

MODIFIERS • ADJECTIVES

LEARNING OBJECTIVES

- Identify adjectives and descriptive adjectives.
- Use adjectives and articles correctly in writing and speaking.

MATERIALS	Online

Display and Engage *Grammar 4.1.4a, 4.1.4b*

Printable *Grammar 4.1.4*

INSTRUCTIONAL VOCABULARY

- **adjective** gives information about a noun
- **linking verb** connects the subject in a sentence to an adjective describing it; some are forms of the verb "to be," such as *is, are, am,* and *was*
- **article** type of adjective that refers to a specific noun or a general noun

Review Adjectives and Articles

- Show **Display and Engage: Grammar 4.1.4a**.

- Review that an **adjective** is a word that describes a noun. A **linking verb** connects the subject in a sentence to an adjective that tells about it. Point out that an **article** is a type of adjective that refers to a specific noun or a general noun. Review with students the different kinds of adjectives.

 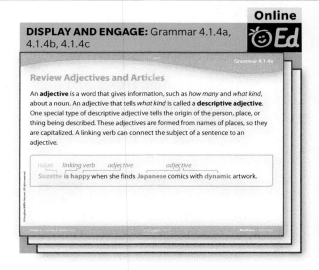
- Work with students to complete the exercises on **Display and Engage: Grammar 4.1.4b**.

- Have students complete **Printable: Grammar 4.1.4**.

- Have students edit a writing draft using adjectives and articles correctly.

ENGLISH LEARNER SUPPORT: Scaffolded Practice

SUBSTANTIAL
Remind students that an adjective gives information about a noun. Provide examples of adjectives in this sentence: *I used my sharpest pencil to draw a final, perfect copy.* adjectives: *sharpest, final, perfect*

MODERATE
Display the following sentences. Help students locate each adjective and the noun that each one tells about.
The tiny book told about a bold superhero. adjectives: *tiny, bold;* nouns: *book, superhero*
Some Japanese comics are popular here. adjectives: *Some, Japanese, popular;* noun: *comics*

LIGHT
Ask students to find a paragraph in a book and identify all the adjectives and articles they can find.

MODIFIERS • ADJECTIVES

LEARNING OBJECTIVES

- Identify adjectives and descriptive adjectives.
- Use adjectives and articles correctly in writing and speaking.

MATERIALS	Online

Display and Engage *Grammar 4.1.5*

Printable *Grammar 4.1.5*

 **INSTRUCTIONAL VOCABULARY**

- **adjective** gives information about a noun
- **article** type of adjective that refers to a specific noun or a general noun

Connect and Teach

- Show **Display and Engage: Grammar 4.1.5**. Tell students that using precise descriptive adjectives helps create clear images for the reader.

- Point out that an important part of revising is using descriptive adjectives correctly.

Engage and Apply

- Display the following sentences. Have partners work together to provide adjectives to describe the nouns. Tell students to choose the correct article, when necessary.

  Greg illustrated a/an _____ comic book.

  It was about a/an _____ man and his _____ friends.

  The _____ man and his _____ friends saved some _____ people from a/an _____ monster.

- Have students complete **Printable: Grammar 4.1.5** for practice with adjectives and articles.

- Tell students that as they revise their work, they should use interesting descriptive adjectives to create clear images. Have students revise a piece of writing to add more descriptive adjectives. Tell partners to exchange papers and give suggestions for where new description could be added.

EL ENGLISH LEARNER SUPPORT: Grammar Practice

Connect and Teach Explain that writers can combine sentences by using *and* to join adjectives when those adjectives follow a form of *be*.

- Write: *The comic books were short and sturdy.*

- Have a student underline the adjectives in the sentence.

Engage and Apply Help students create sentences with combined adjectives. Have them share their sentences. Then have them suggest new adjectives for each other's sentences.

Connect to Writing Have students write two sentences about comics that contain adjectives.

- Students should circle the adjectives and point to each noun they modify.

- Then have students define adjectives in their own words.

MODIFIERS • ADVERBS

LEARNING OBJECTIVES

- Identify adverbs and the verbs they describe.
- Use adverbs in writing and speaking.
- Identify and adjust incorrect verb tenses.

MATERIALS	Online ⓔ **Ed**

Display and Engage *Grammar 4.2.1a, 4.2.1b*

Printable *Grammar 4.2.1*

 INSTRUCTIONAL VOCABULARY

- **adverb** describes a verb
- **frequency** tells how often
- **intensity** tells how much

Connect and Teach

- Show **Display and Engage: Grammar 4.2.1a**. Explain that an **adverb** is a word that tells something about a verb. Some adverbs tell *how, when,* or *where.* Many adverbs end in *-ly.*

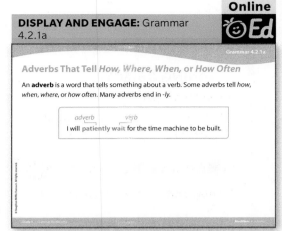

- Model identifying what verb the adverb describes in the example sentence: *I will wait patiently for the time machine to be built.*

  THINK ALOUD *To identify the adverb in the sentence, I'll ask* What is the verb? What word tells how, when, or where about the verb? *The verb is* will wait. *Patiently tells how the subject will wait. So* patiently *must be the adverb.*

Engage and Apply

- Complete items 1–10 on **Display and Engage: Grammar 4.2.1b** with students.

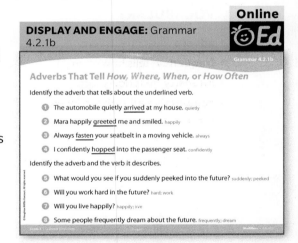

- List the following verbs on the board. Work with students to identify adverbs that might describe each one.

  walk briskly
  wandered slowly
  thought quickly
  stood silently
  jumped suddenly

- Have students complete **Printable: Grammar 4.2.1** for practice with adverbs.

- Have students edit a writing draft using the correct forms of adverbs.

EL **ENGLISH LEARNER SUPPORT: Scaffolded Practice**

Explain Terms About Language Point out the cognate in the list above. Then explain that:

- An adverb adds more information about a verb.

SUBSTANTIAL
Work with students to identify the adverbs in the following short sentences:
Stella speaks slowly. slowly
Jim plays today. today
Use gestures, pantomime, and simplified language to demonstrate how the adverb adds meaning to the sentence.

MODERATE
Provide the sentence frame below, and have students complete it with an adverb. Then have them demonstrate the adverb.
I speak _____. slowly, quickly, loudly

LIGHT
Tell students that most adverbs are formed by adding *-ly* to adjectives. Write the following adjectives on the board. Work with students to form adverbs and to use them in sentences.
quick   *silent*
slow   *loud*
correct

MODIFIERS • ADVERBS

LEARNING OBJECTIVES

- Identify conjunctive adverbs.
- Use adverbs correctly in writing and speaking.

MATERIALS	Online

Display and Engage *Grammar 4.2.2a,*
4.2.2b

Printable *Grammar 4.2.2*

 INSTRUCTIONAL VOCABULARY

- **adverb** describes a verb
- **frequency** tells how often
- **intensity** tells how much
- **conjunctive adverbs** connects ideas

Connect and Teach

- Show **Display and Engage: Grammar 4.2.2a**. Explain that adverbs can tell more about an action in a sentence, but that some adverbs work differently by connecting ideas in a sentence. Explain that **conjunctive adverbs** make writing clearer and that punctuation such as semicolons and commas are often needed.

- Model identifying conjunctive adverbs: *My brother is allergic to dogs; otherwise, we would have a dog as a pet.*

  THINK ALOUD *When I read the sentence, I see that there are two ideas here:* allergic to dogs *and* would have a dog as a pet. *The word* otherwise *connects the two ideas. If the brother was not allergic to dogs, the family would have a dog as a pet. I notice the semicolon before the adverb. This is a clue that it is a conjunctive adverb.*

- Explain that some conjunctive adverbs can introduce an idea, such as *We didn't go out to eat. Instead, we made homemade pizzas.* Point out the comma and that the word *Instead* still connects two ideas: not going out to eat and making pizzas at home.

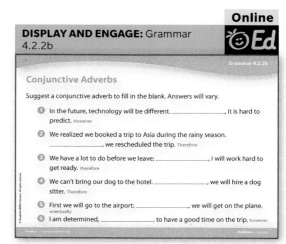

Engage and Apply

- Complete items 1–6 on **Display and Engage: Grammar 4.2.2b** with students.

- Write several conjunctive adverbs on the board, such as *likewise, similarly, also, finally, next, besides,* and *meanwhile*. Work with students to use the adverb in a sentence, noting the punctuation needed. Have volunteers share which two ideas are connected.

- Have students complete **Printable: Grammar 4.2.2** for practice with adverbs of frequency and intensity.

- Have students edit a writing draft using the correct forms of adverbs.

 ENGLISH LEARNER SUPPORT: Scaffolded Practice

ALL LEVELS Review the concept of connecting two ideas with conjunctive adverbs by pointing out clauses. Write the sentence on the board: *The sky is black and thunder roared; however the rain never fell.* Explain that each clause is one idea: it looked like it would rain, but it never did. Then point out how the conjunctive adverb works to connect or join them. Review the meanings of conjunctive adverbs to reinforce the connection.

MODIFIERS • ADVERBS

LEARNING OBJECTIVES

- Identify adverbs and the verbs they describe.
- Use adverbs correctly in writing and speaking.
- Identify and adjust incorrect verb tenses.

MATERIALS   Online ⊙ Ed

Display and Engage *Grammar 4.2.3a, 4.2.3b*

Printable *Grammar 4.2.3*

 INSTRUCTIONAL VOCABULARY

- **adverb** describes a verb
- **frequency** tells how often
- **intensity** tells how much
- **conjunctive adverbs** connects ideas

Connect and Teach

- Show **Display and Engage: Grammar 4.2.3a**. Explain that an adverb needs to make sense when it describes a verb.

- Model recognizing when an adverb makes sense in these example sentences: *He happily buys science fiction books. He perfectly buys science fiction books.*

  THINK ALOUD *To identify which adverb makes sense, I ask* Does the adverb describe the action in the sentence? *I see that the adverb* happily, *in the first sentence, describes the action. The adverb* perfectly *does not describe the action.*

- Remind students that conjunctive adverbs are useful tools in making their writing more clear. These adverbs connect ideas in sentences.

Engage and Apply

- Complete items 1–8 on **Display and Engage: Grammar 4.2.3b** with students.

- Display the following sentence pairs that use adverbs correctly and incorrectly. Have students determine when the adverb makes sense describing the verb.
  Nicole quickly made seventeen changes to her invention before lunch. correct
  Nicole softly made seventeen changes to her invention before lunch. incorrect

- Have pairs look in the week's reading for examples of conjunctive adverbs. Have students discuss how ideas are connected and how the adverb makes the writing clearer.

- Have students complete **Printable: Grammar 4.2.3** for practice with adverbs.

- Have students edit a writing draft using the correct forms of adverbs.

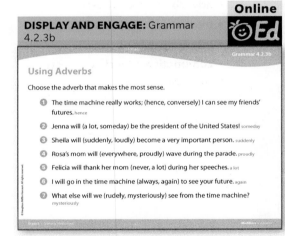

 ENGLISH LEARNER SUPPORT: Scaffolded Practice

SUBSTANTIAL
Work with students to identify the adverbs in the following sentences:
I worked hard on the homework assignment. **hard**
I waited patiently for my grade. **patiently**

MODERATE
Provide the sentence frame below, and have students complete it with an adverb.
I sing _____. **loudly, badly, well**

LIGHT
Have students write two sentences describing something they did recently, using an adverb in each sentence. Have them act or pantomime if they struggle to come up with an adverb.

LEARNING OBJECTIVES

- Identify adverbs and the verbs they describe.
- Use adverbs correctly in writing and speaking.

MATERIALS	Online

Display and Engage *Grammar 4.2.4a, 4.2.4b*

Printable *Grammar 4.2.4*

 INSTRUCTIONAL VOCABULARY

- **adverb** describes a verb
- **frequency** tells how often
- **intensity** tells how much
- **conjunctive adverb** connects two ideas

Review Adverbs

- Show **Display and Engage: Grammar 4.2.4a**.

- Review with students that an adverb is a word that describes a verb. Adverbs tell how, when, or where an action happens. Many adverbs end with -*ly*. Adverbs of frequency tell how often. Adverbs of intensity tell how much.

- Review that conjunctive adverbs work by connecting ideas in sentences. Review that conjunctive adverbs can connect clauses in one sentence. A semicolon is used. Then review that a conjunctive adverb can connect two sentences. A comma is used. Display and discuss these examples:
The fog rolled in thick and white; consequently, drivers had a hard time seeing the road. I forgot to read the chapter last night. Nonetheless, I was able to answer a few questions in class.

- Work with students to complete the exercises on **Display and Engage: Grammar 4.2.4b**.

- Have students complete **Printable: Grammar 4.2.4**.

- Have students edit a writing draft using the correct forms of adverbs.

DISPLAY AND ENGAGE: Grammar 4.2.4a, 4.2.4b, 4.2.4c

 Online

Review Adverbs

A word that describes a verb is an **adverb**. Adverbs tell *how, when, where,* or *how often* an action happens. Many adverbs end with -*ly*. Be sure that the adverb that describes a verb makes sense.

How	The time machine buzzed loudly.
When	Soon the door opened.
Where	I took a deep breath and stepped inside.
How often	I sometimes feel cramped in small spaces.

EL ENGLISH LEARNER SUPPORT: Scaffolded Practice

SUBSTANTIAL

Provide students with examples of verbs that tell *how, where,* or *when*: how-*smoothly*; where-*here*; when-*now*.

MODERATE

Review the idea that an adverb is a word that can modify a verb, an adjective, or another adverb. An adverb can tell how, where, or when. Because the use of adverbs is such a broad topic, concentrate on adverbs that modify verbs. Explain that many English adverbs that tell how end in -*ly*. However, many other adverbs have no special ending. Point out the adverb in each sentence below. Help students identify what it tells about the verb.

- *Peter answered slowly. how*
- *Was he playing outside? where*
- *He will put on his costume soon. when*

LIGHT

Have students write two sentences describing something they saw recently using adverbs. Remind students to use words that tell *how, when,* or *where*.

MODIFIERS • ADVERBS

LEARNING OBJECTIVES

- Identify adverbs and the verbs they describe.
- Use adverbs correctly in writing and speaking.

MATERIALS   Online Ed

Display and Engage *Grammar 4.2.5*

Printable *Grammar 4.2.5*

 INSTRUCTIONAL VOCABULARY

- **adverb** describes a verb
- **frequency** tells how often
- **intensity** tells how much
- **conjunctive adverb** connects two ideas

Connect and Teach

- Show **Display and Engage: Grammar 4.2.5**. Tell students that using precise adverbs to make descriptions more vivid helps readers visualize images clearly.

- Point out that an important part of revising is using precise adverbs.

Engage and Apply

- Display the following sentences. Guide students to provide adverbs to describe the verbs.

  Paulo was _____ convinced to work on designing a robot. **easily**

  Jocelyn departed _____ after the science fair. **immediately**

  Grace _____ traveled to conventions in a modified bus. **frequently**

- Have students complete **Printable: Grammar 4.2.5** for practice with adjectives and articles.

- Tell students that as they revise their work, they should look for opportunities to use adverbs to make their writing more interesting. Have students revise a piece of writing to add more adverbs. Remind students to consider using conjunctive adverbs to connect ideas. Tell partners to exchange papers and give suggestions.

 ENGLISH LEARNER SUPPORT: Grammar Practice

Connect and Teach Write: *Jonas sighed. It was a loud sigh.* Explain that writers can combine short sentences, such as these, by using adverbs.

- Write: *Jonas sighed loudly.* Have a student underline the suffix *-ly*.

Engage and Apply Guide students in combining sentences with adverbs by providing these sentence pairs:

- *The bell rang. It was a loud ring.* The bell rang loudly.
- *The man coughed. It was a quiet cough.* The man coughed quietly.

Connect to Writing Have students write three short sentences on the topic of time travel. Then have them combine the sentences into one, using adverbs.

DISPLAY AND ENGAGE: Grammar 4.2.5

Online Ed

Grammar 4.2.5

Connect to Writing: Using Adverbs

To make your descriptions more vivid, try using precise adverbs. By doing so, you can make your writing more lively and create details that help readers visualize images clearly.

Less Precise Adverb	More Precise Adverb
The detective walked slowly down the street.	The detective walked stealthily down the street.

MODIFIERS • MAKING COMPARISONS

LEARNING OBJECTIVES

- Identify comparative/superlative forms.
- Use comparative/superlative forms correctly in writing and speaking.

MATERIALS	Online

Display and Engage *Grammar 4.3.1a, 4.3.1b*

Printable *Grammar 4.3.1*

INSTRUCTIONAL VOCABULARY

- **comparative adjective** an adjective used in a comparison of two people, places, or things
- **superlative adjective** an adjective used in a comparison of more than two persons, places, or things

Connect and Teach

- Show **Display and Engage: Grammar 4.3.1a**. Explain that **comparative adjectives** compare two people, places, or things by adding *-er* to the adjective or using *more* before the adjective. **Superlative adjectives** compare more than two people, places, or things by adding *-est* to the adjective or using *most* before the adjective.

- Model identifying the comparative adjective in the example sentence: *Traveling in a covered wagon is more difficult than traveling in a car.*

  THINK ALOUD *To identify the comparative adjective, ask* How many things are being compared in the sentence? *There are two things being compared in this sentence: traveling in a covered wagon and traveling in a car. The adjective used in this comparison is* more difficult.

Engage and Apply

- Complete items 1–10 on **Display and Engage: Grammar 4.3.1b** with students.

- List the following adjectives on the board. Have students write sentences using comparative and superlative forms of the adjectives.

pretty	new
tall	old
deep	cold

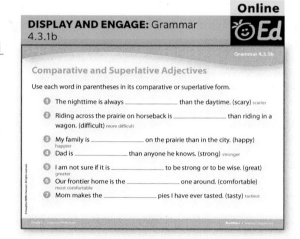

- Have students complete **Printable: Grammar 4.3.1** for practice with comparative and superlative adverbs.

- Have students edit a writing draft using the correct forms of superlatives.

(EL) ENGLISH LEARNER SUPPORT: Facilitate Linguistic Connections

Many languages express comparisons using words that mean *more* and *than*, rather than endings, such as *-er*. For example, Spanish uses *más que*. Provide additional practice making comparisons, for example, *smaller, smallest, more important, most important*.

Scaffolded Practice

SUBSTANTIAL
Use the following sentence to demonstrate how to use a comparative/superlative adjective.
Traveling takes (long, longer) when the weather is bad. longer

MODERATE
Use the following sentences to demonstrate how to use comparative/superlative adjectives.
I think history is the _____ subject. (good) best
Traveling takes _____ when it rains. (long) longer

LIGHT
Have students describe people, places, or things using comparative/superlative adjectives. Provide them with sentence frames, such as *I love _____ the most.*

MODIFIERS • MAKING COMPARISONS

LEARNING OBJECTIVES
- Identify comparative/superlative forms.
- Use comparative/superlative forms correctly in writing and speaking.

MATERIALS	Online

Display and Engage *Grammar 4.3.2a, 4.3.2b*

Printable *Grammar 4.3.2*

 INSTRUCTIONAL VOCABULARY

- **comparative adverb** formed by putting *more* in front of an adverb and used to compare two people, places, or things
- **superlative adverb** formed by putting *most* in front of an adverb and used to compare more than two persons, places, or things

Connect and Teach

- Show **Display and Engage: Grammar 4.3.2a**. Tell students that the words *good* and *bad* have special comparative and superlative forms.

- Model using the superlative forms of *good* in the example sentence: *The wagon was the best at keeping them dry.*

  THINK ALOUD *To identify when to use the superlative forms of* good, *I ask* How many things are being compared in the sentence? *More than two things are being compared in this sentence since the wagon is being compared with everything else that might keep them dry.* Best *is the superlative form of* good.

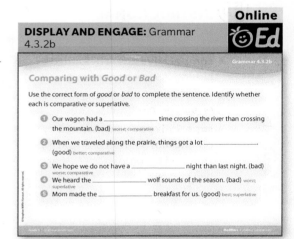
DISPLAY AND ENGAGE: Grammar 4.3.2a — Online Ed

Engage and Apply

- Complete items 1–10 on **Display and Engage: Grammar 4.3.2b** with students.

- Display the following sentences and read them aloud. Then, have students complete the sentences using the comparative or superlative form of the adjective.
  The trip was (bad) than their other trips. worse
  The wagon rolled (good) after it was fixed. better

- Have students complete **Printable: Grammar 4.3.2** for practice with good and bad.

- Have students edit a writing draft using the correct forms of comparative adjectives.

 ENGLISH LEARNER SUPPORT: Scaffolded Practice

SUBSTANTIAL
Use the following sentences to demonstrate how to use comparative and superlative forms of *good* and *bad*.
The train ride went (good) than other trips I have taken. better
My vacation was (good). the best

MODERATE
Use the following sentences to demonstrate how to use comparative and superlative forms of *good* and *bad*.
I think math is the _____ subject. (bad) worst
My _____ subject is English. (good) best

LIGHT
Have students write a sentence about something they've read using the comparative and superlative forms of *good* and *bad*.

MODIFIERS • MAKING COMPARISONS

LEARNING OBJECTIVES

- Identify comparative/superlative forms.
- Use comparative/superlative forms correctly in writing and speaking.

MATERIALS   Online ⊙Ed

Display and Engage *Grammar 4.3.3a, 4.3.3b*

Printable *Grammar 4.3.3*

 INSTRUCTIONAL VOCABULARY

- **comparative adverb** formed by putting *more* in front of an adverb and used to compare two people, places, or things
- **superlative adverb** formed by putting *most* in front of an adverb and used to compare more than two persons, places, or things

Connect and Teach

- Show **Display and Engage: Grammar 4.3.3a**. Point out that when making the comparative form of an adverb ending in -*ly,* you add *more* in front of the adverb. Explain that you add the word *most* in front of an adverb ending in -*ly* to make the superlative form.

- Model making the adverb into the comparative form:

  The horses moved _____ quickly than the wagons. **more**

  To use the adverb *quickly* in the comparative form, add the word *more.* Explain that *more quickly* is the comparative adverb.

Engage and Apply

- Complete items 1–10 on **Display and Engage: Grammar 4.3.3b** with students.

- Display the following sentences. Have students change the adverb to be comparative or superlative.

  Pioneers slept _____ soundly once they arrived. **more**

  Children need to walk the _____carefully near the river. **most**

 DISPLAY AND ENGAGE: Grammar
4.3.3a

Online
⊙Ed

Grammar 4.3.3a

Comparing with Adverbs

Adverbs have comparative forms. Add the word *more* in front of an adverb to make the comparative form. Add the word *most* in front of an adverb to make the superlative form.

> *comparative*
> We felt **more happily** about this morning's sunrise than the others.

> *superlative*
> We felt **most happily** about the sunset.

DISPLAY AND ENGAGE: Grammar
4.3.3b

Online
⊙Ed

Grammar 4.3.3b

Comparing with Adverbs

Use the correct form of the adverb in parentheses to complete the sentence. Identify whether each is comparative or superlative.

1. We felt _____ about leaving our home than leaving the city. (sadly) *more sadly; comparative*
2. We laughed _____ when my brother told jokes. (happily) *most happily; superlative*
3. Jenny cheers _____ about our big trip than I do. (excitedly) *more excitedly; comparative*
4. We will have to travel _____ than on other trips. (carefully) *more carefully; comparative*
5. I worry _____ than my little sister. (seriously) *more seriously; comparative*
6. Dad talks _____ to us. (comfortingly) *most comfortingly; superlative*
7. Mom says we will travel _____ than other families on the frontier. (bravely) *more bravely; comparative*

- Have students complete **Printable: Grammar 4.3.3** for practice with good and bad.

- Have students edit a writing draft using the correct forms of comparative adverbs.

EL **ENGLISH LEARNER SUPPORT: Scaffolded Practice**

SUBSTANTIAL

Use the following sentences to demonstrate how to use *more/mostly.*

I am _____ finished with the homework. **mostly**

I ran _____ quickly than I had before. **more**

MODERATE

Use the following sentences to demonstrate how to use adverbs and *more/mostly.*

I am _____ with the homework. **mostly finished**

I ran _____ than I had before. **more quickly**

LIGHT

Have students write two sentences using *more* or *mostly.*

MODIFIERS • MAKING COMPARISONS

LEARNING OBJECTIVES

- Identify comparative/superlative forms.
- Use comparative/superlative forms in writing and speaking.

MATERIALS   Online

Display and Engage *Grammar 4.3.4a, 4.3.4b*

Printable *Grammar 4.3.4*

 INSTRUCTIONAL VOCABULARY

- **comparative adverb** formed by putting *more* in front of an adverb and used to compare two people, places, or things
- **superlative adverb** formed by putting *most* in front of an adverb and used to compare more than two persons, places, or things

Review Making Comparisons

- Show **Display and Engage: Grammar 4.3.4a**.

- Review with students that comparative adjectives compare two people, places, or things by adding *-er* to the adjective or using *more* before it. Superlative adjectives compare more than two people, places or things by adding *-est* to the adjective or using *most* before it.

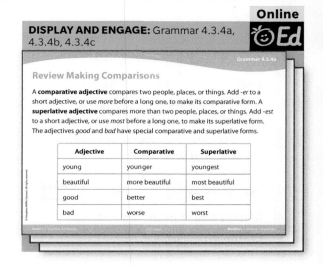

DISPLAY AND ENGAGE: Grammar 4.3.4a, 4.3.4b, 4.3.4c

Online

Review Making Comparisons

A **comparative adjective** compares two people, places, or things. Add -er to a short adjective, or use *more* before a long one, to make its comparative form. A **superlative adjective** compares more than two people, places, or things. Add -est to a short adjective, or use *most* before a long one, to make its superlative form. The adjectives *good* and *bad* have special comparative and superlative forms.

Adjective	Comparative	Superlative
young	younger	youngest
beautiful	more beautiful	most beautiful
good	better	best
bad	worse	worst

- Work with students to complete the exercises on **Display and Engage: Grammar 4.3.4b**.

- Have students complete **Printable: Grammar 4.3.4**.

- Have students edit a writing draft using the correct forms of superlatives.

ENGLISH LEARNER SUPPORT: Scaffolded Practice

SUBSTANTIAL

To remind students that comparative adjectives and adverbs compare two, while superlative adjectives and adverbs compare more than two, provide examples of each:
- comparative adjective: *Jill is* shorter *than Amy.*
- superlative adjective: *She is the* shortest *girl in the line.*
- comparative adverb: *Aaron walked* more slowly *than Chris.*
- superlative adverb: *He walked the* most slowly *of all.*

MODERATE

Review the idea that both adjectives and adverbs can show comparison. Display the following sentences. Help students locate adjectives and adverbs that show comparison.
- *Frank is the younger brother.* younger—adjective modifying brother
- *He grew faster than anyone in his family.* faster—adverb modifying grew
- *The twins are the youngest children of all.* youngest—adjective modifying children
- *The twins walked the most slowly of all the children.* most slowly—adverb modifying walked

LIGHT

Have students write a few sentences comparing two activities they did this week. Encourage them to use comparative and superlative adjectives.

MODIFIERS • MAKING COMPARISONS

LEARNING OBJECTIVES

- Identify comparative/superlative forms.
- Use comparative/superlative forms in writing and speaking.

MATERIALS Online

Display and Engage *Grammar 4.3.5*

Printable *Grammar 4.3.5*

 INSTRUCTIONAL VOCABULARY

- **comparative adverb** formed by putting *more* in front of an adverb and used to compare two people, places, or things
- **superlative adverb** formed by putting *most* in front of an adverb and used to compare more than two persons, places, or things

Connect and Teach

- Show **Display and Engage: Grammar 4.3.5**. Explain that students need to remember to add *-er* or use *more* before the adjective for comparative adjectives. Tell them that for superlative adjectives, they need to add *-est* or use *most* before the adjective.

Online Ed

DISPLAY AND ENGAGE: Grammar 4.3.5

Connect to Writing: Using Comparisons Correctly

You can sometimes make comparisons, sentences, or ideas in your writing clearer by using comparative and superlative forms of adjectives and adverbs.

Less Clear	More Clear
I am eight year old. I have a sister and a brother.	I am eight years old. I have an older brother and an older sister. My sister is oldest of us all.

Engage and Apply

- Have students give a correct adjective form.

  The _____ tree branch blew down and broke. (long) longest
  Mom makes the _____ campfire at night. (good) best
  I don't like the wind but the dust is _____. (bad) worse
  I am _____ about picking berries than about wading in the creek. (excited) more excited

- Have students write sentences using comparative and superlative forms of the adjectives *tall* and *good*. Have partners read their sentences to one another.

- Have students complete **Printable: Grammar 4.3.5** for practice with making comparisons.

- Tell students that as they revise their work, they should make their ideas clearer by using comparative and superlative forms. Have students revise a piece of writing to add more comparative and superlative adjectives. Tell partners to exchange papers and give suggestions.

EL **ENGLISH LEARNER SUPPORT: Grammar Practice**

Connect and Teach Explain that students will use *-er* and *-est* to compare people and things.
Say: *We will use the word tall to compare two students in the class.*
Write this sentence frame using the names of students in the class: *Rachel is _____ than Frank.*
Ask: *What do we add at the end of the adjective tall to compare two people?* -er *What is the complete word?* taller *What is the complete sentence?* Rachel is taller than Frank.

- Repeat the process, having students compare Rachel to all the rest of the children. *Rachel is the tallest of all.*

Engage and Apply Guide students in creating additional comparisons of animals using *small*.

Connect to Writing Draw three stick figures of increasing heights. Have students express comparisons in sentences using the words *tall, taller,* and *tallest.*

LEARNING OBJECTIVES

- Recognize and explain the role of prepositional phrases in sentences.
- Use prepositional phrases correctly in writing and speaking.
- Use academic and domain-specific words appropriately in writing and speaking.

MATERIALS   Online Ed

Display and Engage *Grammar 4.4.1a, 4.4.1b*

Printable *Grammar 4.4.1*

 INSTRUCTIONAL VOCABULARY

- **preposition** shows relationships of location, time, or direction
- **prepositional phrase** begins with a preposition and ends with a noun or pronoun; adds detail

Connect and Teach

- Show **Display and Engage: Grammar 4.4.1a**. Explain that **prepositions** are words that show relationships between other words in a sentence. Point out that, like adverbs, prepositions convey relationships of location, time, or direction. They also can help add details in the way adjectives do. Tell students that some common prepositions are *above, after, at, during, for, through, in, on, of, to,* and *with*.

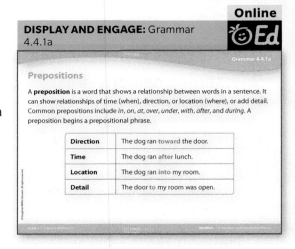

DISPLAY AND ENGAGE: Grammar 4.4.1a   Online ⊙Ed

Grammar 4.4.1a

Prepositions

A **preposition** is a word that shows a relationship between words in a sentence. It can show relationships of time (when), direction, or location (where), or add detail. Common prepositions include *in, on, at, over, under, with, after,* and *during*. A preposition begins a prepositional phrase.

Direction	The dog ran toward the door.
Time	The dog ran after lunch.
Location	The dog ran into my room.
Detail	The door to my room was open.

- Model identifying the preposition in the following sentence: *The dog ran after lunch.*
  THINK ALOUD *To identify the preposition, I ask* What words tell about time, direction, or location, or add detail? *I see the words* after lunch. *They tell me when, or what time, the dog ran. I know that* after *is a common preposition. I'll try using my knowledge of common prepositions with the other sentences.*

Engage and Apply

- Complete items 1–10 on **Display and Engage: Grammar 4.4.1b** with students.

- List prepositions on the board. Have students provide a phrase using each one. Ask them to tell under which heading their phrases should be categorized: *direction, location, time,* or *detail*.

DISPLAY AND ENGAGE: Grammar 4.4.1b   Online ⊙Ed

Grammar 4.4.1b

Prepositions

Identify the preposition in each sentence and tell whether the preposition shows *time, direction, location,* or *detail*.

1. The dog ran to the basement. to; direction
2. She upset the backpack of homework. of; detail
3. I chased after her. after; direction
4. The dog was naughty during the birthday party. during; time
5. She knows she is the hit of the party. of; detail
6. We won't scold her at the moment. at; time
7. We will take her to obedience school tomorrow! to; direction
8. Next time I will keep the homework in my bedroom. in; location

- Have students complete **Printable: Grammar 4.4.1** for practice with prepositions.

- Have students edit a writing draft using prepositions correctly.

EL **ENGLISH LEARNER SUPPORT: Facilitate Linguistic Connections**

Common Spanish prepositions include *con* (with), *en* (in, on), *entre* (between), *sin* (without), and *sobre* (on, over). Provide additional practice with prepositions and prepositional phrases, for example, *on the wall, off the floor*.

Scaffolded Practice

SUBSTANTIAL
Use the following sentence frames to demonstrate the use of prepositions.
She stopped _____ the store. at
He played basketball _____ an hour. for

MODERATE
Work with students to use the sentence frames to identify the prepositional phrases and explain their use.

LIGHT
Have students describe the relationship of objects in the classroom by creating sentences using prepositional phrases. *Example: The teacher's desk is located in the corner.*

LEARNING OBJECTIVES

- Recognize and explain the role of prepositional phrases in sentences.
- Use prepositional phrases in writing and speaking.
- Use academic and domain-specific words appropriately in writing and speaking.

MATERIALS   Online

Display and Engage *Grammar 4.4.2a, 4.4.2b*

Printable *Grammar 4.4.2*

 INSTRUCTIONAL VOCABULARY

- **preposition** shows relationships of location, time, or direction
- **prepositional phrase** begins with a preposition and ends with a noun or pronoun; adds detail

Connect and Teach

- Show <u>Display and Engage: Grammar 4.4.2a</u>. Explain that a **prepositional phrase** begins with a preposition and ends with a noun or pronoun. Point out that the noun or pronoun is the object of the preposition. Tell students that prepositional phrases add meaning and details to many types of creative and informational writing.

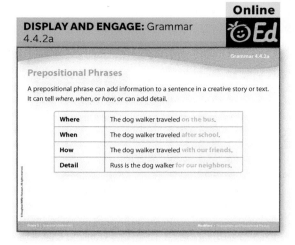

- Model identifying the prepositional phrase in this example sentence: *Russ is the dog walker for our neighbors.*

  THINK ALOUD *I ask* What is the prepositional phrase in the sentence? What information does it add? *I can identify the preposition,* for. *I see that the phrase ends with the noun* neighbors. *The prepositional phrase is* for our neighbors. *This prepositional phrase adds detail by telling whose dogs Russ walks.*

Engage and Apply

- Complete items 1–10 on <u>Display and Engage: Grammar 4.4.2b</u> with students.

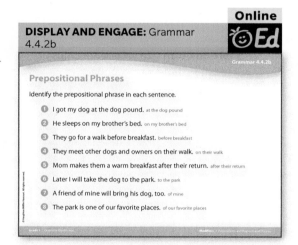

- Have students find sentences with prepositional phrases in a story they have read. Ask partners to discuss the preposition's function in each sentence.

- Have students complete <u>Printable: Grammar 4.4.2</u> for practice with prepositions.

- Have students edit a writing draft using the correct forms of prepositional phrases.

 ENGLISH LEARNER SUPPORT: Scaffolded Practice

SUBSTANTIAL

Display these sentences and have students identify the prepositional phrase.
She gave her homework to the teacher. to the teacher
He went to the movies after school. after school

MODERATE

Use the following sentence frames to demonstrate the use of prepositional phrases.
She went _____. to school, to the store
We found a kitten _____. on the street, in the park

LIGHT

Have students write two sentences to describe a place they've visited recently. Have them include a prepositional phrase in each sentence.

LESSON
4.4.3

COMBINING SENTENCES

LEARNING OBJECTIVES

- Recognize and explain the role of prepositional phrases in sentences.
- Use prepositional phrases correctly in writing and speaking.

MATERIALS	Online

Display and Engage *Grammar 4.4.3a, 4.4.3b*

Printable *Grammar 4.4.3*

INSTRUCTIONAL VOCABULARY

- **preposition** shows relationships of location, time, or direction
- **prepositional phrase** begins with a preposition and ends with a noun or pronoun; adds detail

Connect and Teach

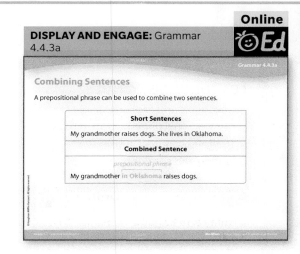

Online Ed

DISPLAY AND ENGAGE: Grammar 4.4.3a

- Show **Display and Engage: Grammar 4.4.3a**. Tell students that two short sentences about the same subject can be combined into one sentence by moving important information from one sentence to the other in the form of a prepositional phrase.

- Model how to combine sentences by moving the prepositional phrase: *My grandmother raises dogs. She lives in Oklahoma.*

  THINK ALOUD *To help me combine two or more short sentences, I ask* What is the prepositional phrase in the sentences? How can it be used to combine the sentences? *The prepositional phrase is* in Oklahoma. *This can be moved to the first sentence to create one sentence that says the same thing.* My grandmother in Oklahoma raises dogs.

Engage and Apply

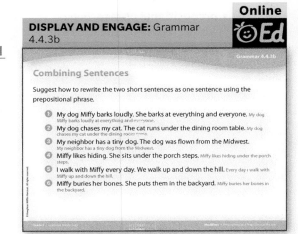

Online Ed

DISPLAY AND ENGAGE: Grammar 4.4.3b

- Complete items 1–10 on **Display and Engage: Grammar 4.4.3b** with students.

- Display these sentences:
  My dog spends time outside. He sits on the porch. My cat watches birds. There are birds in the yard.

- Have students combine each set of sentences into one.
  My dog spends time outside on the porch. My cat watches birds in the yard.

- Have students complete **Printable: Grammar 4.4.3** for practice with prepositions.

- Have students edit a writing draft that combines sentences correctly.

ENGLISH LEARNER SUPPORT: Scaffolded Practice

SUBSTANTIAL

Work with students to combine these sentences.
I went outside. I walked to the park. I went outside to walk to the park.

MODERATE

Have students suggest ways to combine the sentences.
I read a book. It was about birds. I read a book about birds.

LIGHT

Have students go back to the sentences they've written this week. Have them look for ways they can use prepositional phrases to combine sentences.

LEARNING OBJECTIVES

- Recognize and explain the role of prepositional phrases in sentences.
- Use prepositional phrases correctly in writing and speaking.

MATERIALS   Online

Display and Engage *Grammar 4.4.4a, 4.4.4b*

Printable *Grammar 4.4.4*

 INSTRUCTIONAL VOCABULARY

- **preposition** shows relationships of location, time, or direction
- **prepositional phrase** begins with a preposition and ends with a noun or pronoun; adds detail

Connect and Teach

- Show **Display and Engage: Grammar 4.4.4a**.

- Remind students that prepositional phrases add information to sentences in a piece of writing. This information tells *when, where, how,* or gives other details. Review that prepositional phrases begin with a preposition and end with a noun or pronoun. These phrases can be used to combine two short sentences into one longer sentence.

DISPLAY AND ENGAGE: Grammar 4.4.4a and 4.4.4b

Grammar 4.4.4a

Review Prepositions and Prepositional Phrases

Prepositions are words that show relationships between other words in a sentence. Some common prepositions are *above, after, at, during, for, through, in, of, to,* and *with.* Prepositions convey location, time, or direction. **Prepositional phrases** begin with a preposition and end with a noun or pronoun. They add meaning and details to sentences.

Direction	A dog walker was moving toward the park.
Time	She had been walking three dogs for an hour.
Location	She stopped at the smallest dog's home.
Detail	A woman with red hair happily patted her dog.

- Work with students to complete the exercises on **Display and Engage: Grammar 4.4.4b**.

- Have students complete **Printable: Grammar 4.4.4**.

- Have students edit a writing draft that uses prepositions and prepositional phrases correctly.

EL ENGLISH LEARNER SUPPORT: Scaffolded Practice

SUBSTANTIAL
Remind students that a prepositional phrase is a group of words that begins with a preposition and ends with a noun or a pronoun. Provide examples of prepositional phrases that tell *when, where,* or *how.* When: *in the evening;* Where: *beside the riverbank;* How: *by herself.*

MODERATE
Review the idea that a preposition is a word that links other words in a sentence. A prepositional phrase is a group of words that begins with a preposition and ends with a noun or a pronoun. A prepositional phrase can provide more information, telling *when, where,* or *how.* Display the following sentences. Guide students to identify the prepositional phrase. Have them tell whether the preposition tells *when, where,* or *how.*
- *The soldiers found the dog in Germany.* **in Germany, tells where**
- *B.J. was a hero during the war.* **during the war, tells when**
- *The boy delivered newspapers by bicycle.* **by bicycle, tells how**

LIGHT
Have students describe an event they participated in recently. Have them write a few sentences that tell *when, where,* or *how* using prepositions and prepositional phrases.

LEARNING OBJECTIVES

- Recognize and explain the role of prepositional phrases in sentences.
- Use prepositional phrases correctly in writing and speaking.

MATERIALS   Online

Display and Engage *Grammar 4.4.5*

Printable *Grammar 4.4.5*

 INSTRUCTIONAL VOCABULARY

- **preposition** shows relationships of location, time, or direction
- **prepositional phrase** begins with a preposition and ends with a noun or pronoun; adds detail

Connect and Teach

- Show **Display and Engage: Grammar: 4.4.5**. Remind students that combining two short sentences by moving a prepositional phrase can improve the flow of their sentences. Discuss these two examples.

Short Sentences

I feed my dog. He eats one meal in the evening.

Longer Sentence

I feed my dog one meal in the evening.

DISPLAY AND ENGAGE: Grammar 4.4.5

Online Ed

Grammar 4.4.5

Connect to Writing: Using Prepositions and Prepositional Phrases

In your writing, you can combine two short sentences by using a prepositional phrase. If two sentences tell about one subject, you can combine them by moving a prepositional phrase from one sentence to the other.

Short Sentences	
	prepositional phrase
Our dog Growler chased a squirrel. Growler ran	into Mrs. Castillo's garden.

Combined Sentence	
	prepositional phrase
Our dog Growler chased a squirrel	into Mrs. Castillo's garden.

- Point out that an important part of revising all types of writing is combining sentences using a prepositional phrase.

Engage and Apply

- Have partners write two short sentences. One should include a prepositional phrase. Have them exchange papers and rewrite each other's sentences as one longer sentence.

- Have students complete **Printable: Grammar 4.4.5** for practice with combining sentences.

- Tell students that as they revise their work, they should look for ways to combine sentences to make their writing smoother. Have students revise a piece of writing to combine sentences where appropriate. Tell partners to exchange papers and give suggestions.

EL **ENGLISH LEARNER SUPPORT: Grammar Practice**

Connect and Teach   Remind students that a prepositional phrase provides more information in a sentence. It always begins with a preposition and ends with either a noun or a pronoun.

Engage and Apply   Have students find the prepositional phrases in the following sentences.

- *The dog jumped over the fence.* **over the fence**
- *Peg walked around her neighborhood.* **around her neighborhood**
- *Peg wrote ideas in her notebook.* **in her notebook**

Connect to Writing   Provide these prepositions: *above, behind, in front of, around, under, with, next to.* Have students write sentences about the classroom, using prepositional phrases.

LEARNING OBJECTIVES

- **Language** Use coordinating conjunctions.
- **Language** Combine sentences using conjunctions correctly in reading and writing.

MATERIALS   Online

Display and Engage *Grammar 5.1.1a, 5.1.1b*

Printable *Grammar 5.1.1*

 INSTRUCTIONAL VOCABULARY

- **conjunctions** words that connect other words or groups of words in a sentence
- **coordinating conjunction** a conjunction that joins two words, groups of words, or sentences

Connect and Teach

- Show **Display and Engage: Grammar 5.1.1a**. Explain that **conjunctions** are words that connect other words or groups of words in a sentence.

- Tell students that when *and, but*, and *or* connect sentence parts that are alike, they are called **coordinating conjunctions**. They can be used to connect similar words, phrases, or clauses within a sentence. They also can connect two sentences to make a compound sentence.

- Model identifying conjunctions in the example sentence: *Some desert animals are endangered and need our protection.*

  THINK ALOUD *To identify coordinating conjunctions, I ask:* What word's function is to connect other words or groups of words in the sentence? *The conjunction* and *joins two predicates:* are endangered *and* need our protection.

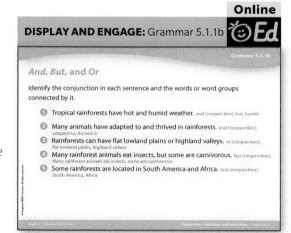

Online
Ed

DISPLAY AND ENGAGE: Grammar 5.1.1a

And, But, and Or

Conjunctions are words that connect other words or groups of words in a sentence. The coordinating conjunctions *and, but,* and *or* join sentence parts that are alike.

conjunction
Some rainforest animals are endangered and need our protection.

Engage and Apply

- Complete items 1–5 on **Display and Engage: Grammar 5.1.1b** with students.

- Write these sets of words and phrases on the board: *took a trip to the park/ listened to the ranger; the fifth grade/the sixth grade; informative/interesting.* Have students join them with coordinating conjunctions and use them in sentences.

DISPLAY AND ENGAGE: Grammar 5.1.1b

Online
Ed

And, But, and Or

Identify the conjunction in each sentence and the words or word groups connected by it.

1. Tropical rainforests have hot and humid weather. *and (conjunction); hot, humid*
2. Many animals have adapted to and thrived in rainforests. *and (conjunction); adapted to, thrived in*
3. Rainforests can have flat lowland plains or highland valleys. *or (conjunction); flat lowland plains, highland valleys*
4. Many rainforest animals eat insects, but some are carnivorous. *but (conjunction); Many rainforest animals eat insects, some are carnivorous*
5. Some rainforests are located in South America and Africa. *and (conjunction); South America, Africa*

- Have students complete **Printable: Grammar 5.1.1** for practice with coordinating conjunctions.

 ENGLISH LEARNER SUPPORT: Facilitate Language Connections

Tell students that a conjunction is a word that joins other words together. Explain that conjunctions serve the same function in many languages, which is to "connect."

Scaffolded Practice

SUBSTANTIAL

Write this sentence on the board: *We enjoyed our trip to the park, but* _____. Have students complete the sentence in a way that creates a compound sentence.

MODERATE

Write sentence frames with *and* and *but*, leaving out the words that follow the coordinating conjunction. Guide students to finish each sentence.

LIGHT

Have students write original compound sentences without the comma and coordinating conjunction. Have them exchange papers with a partner to complete.

LEARNING OBJECTIVES

- **Language** Use coordinating conjunctions.
- **Language** Combine sentences using conjunctions correctly in speaking and writing.

MATERIALS   Online

Display and Engage *Grammar 5.1.2a, 5.1.2b*

Printable *Grammar 5.1.2*

 INSTRUCTIONAL VOCABULARY

- **coordinating conjunction** a conjunction that joins two words, groups of words, or sentences

Connect and Teach

- Show **Display and Engage: Grammar 5.1.2a**. Explain that **coordinating conjunctions** are used to create compound sentences. Tell students that two sentences with the same subject or related to the same idea can be joined with a comma and the coordinating conjunction *and*. Two sentences with contrasting ideas can be combined with a comma and the conjunction *but* or *or*.

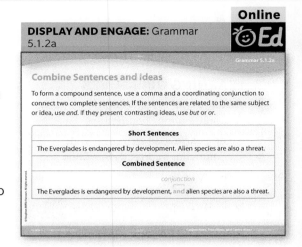

Online
Ed

DISPLAY AND ENGAGE: Grammar 5.1.2a

Grammar 5.1.2a

Combine Sentences and Ideas

To form a compound sentence, use a comma and a coordinating conjunction to connect two complete sentences. If the sentences are related to the same subject or idea, use *and*. If they present contrasting ideas, use *but* or *or*.

| **Short Sentences** |
| The Everglades is endangered by development. Alien species are also a threat. |

| **Combined Sentence** |
| *conjunction* |
| The Everglades is endangered by development, and alien species are also a threat. |

- Model how to form a compound sentence using a conjunction to combine two ideas: *The Everglades is endangered by development. Alien species are also a threat.*

  THINK ALOUD *To form a compound sentence, I ask:* How are the two sentences related? What conjunction can I use to connect them? *Both sentences relate to threats to the Everglades, so the conjunction* and *can be used to connect them.*

Engage and Apply

- Complete items 1–6 on **Display and Engage: Grammar 5.1.2b** with students.

- Have volunteers write compound sentences on the board. Ask other students to explain the function of the conjunctions.

- Have students complete **Printable: Grammar 5.1.2** for practice with coordinating conjunctions.

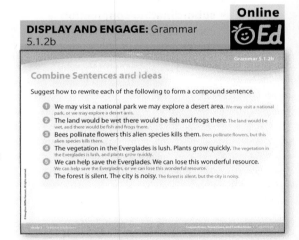

Online
Ed

DISPLAY AND ENGAGE: Grammar 5.1.2b

Grammar 5.1.2b

Combine Sentences and ideas

Suggest how to rewrite each of the following to form a compound sentence.

1. We may visit a national park we may explore a desert area. We may visit a national park, or we may explore a desert area.
2. The land would be wet there would be fish and frogs there. The land would be wet, and there would be fish and frogs there.
3. Bees pollinate flowers this alien species kills them. Bees pollinate flowers, but this alien species kills them.
4. The vegetation in the Everglades is lush. Plants grow quickly. The vegetation in the Everglades is lush, and plants grow quickly.
5. We can help save the Everglades. We can lose this wonderful resource. We can help save the Everglades, or we can lose this wonderful resource.
6. The forest is silent. The city is noisy. The forest is silent, but the city is noisy.

 ENGLISH LEARNER SUPPORT: Scaffolded Practice

SUBSTANTIAL

Write these sentence on the board:

We went to the park. We enjoyed our trip.

Have students suggest ways to use conjunctions to combine the sentences.

MODERATE

Write a few sentences on the board and have students rewrite them to combine sentences and ideas.

LIGHT

Have students review a piece of their writing to look for places they can combine sentences and ideas. Have them revise to use conjuctions to combine ideas.

LEARNING OBJECTIVES

- **Language** Identify coordinating and subordinating conjunctions.
- **Language** Use sentences with conjunctions correctly in writing and speaking.

MATERIALS	Online

Display and Engage *Grammar 5.1.3a, 5.1.3b*

Printable *Grammar 5.1.3*

 INSTRUCTIONAL VOCABULARY

- **subordinating conjunction** a conjunction that combines two clauses into a complex sentence

Connect and Teach

- Show <u>Display and Engage: Grammar 5.1.3a</u>. Explain that a **subordinating conjunction** makes one part of a sentence dependent on the other part. List common subordinating conjunctions: *while, because, although, if, since.* Tell students that connecting two sentences with a subordinating conjunction forms a complex sentence.

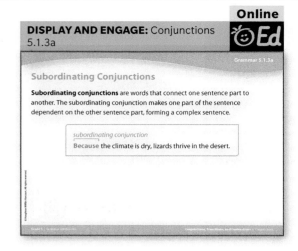

DISPLAY AND ENGAGE: Conjunctions
5.1.3a

- Model identifying the dependent part of the sentence and the subordinating conjunction in this complex sentence: *Because the climate is dry, lizards thrive in the desert.*

  THINK ALOUD *To identify a subordinating conjunction, I ask:* Which part of the sentence is dependent on the other part? Lizards thrive in the desert *could form a complete sentence. It is not dependent.* Because the climate is dry *is dependent on the other part of the sentence.* Because *is the subordinating conjunction.*

Engage and Apply

- Complete items 1–4 on <u>Display and Engage: Grammar 5.1.3b</u> with students.

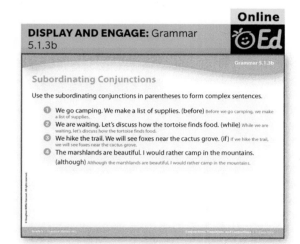

DISPLAY AND ENGAGE: Grammar
5.1.3b

- Have students write complex sentences using subordinating conjunctions. Have partners identify the conjunctions and dependent sentence parts.

- Have students complete <u>Printable: Grammar 5.1.3</u> for practice with subordinating conjunctions.

 ENGLISH LEARNER SUPPORT: Scaffolded Practice

SUBSTANTIAL

Write this sentence on the board and have students identify the subordinating conjunction. Students may point to or say *because* as they are able.

I love the park because there are many things to do there.

MODERATE

Write a few short sentences on the board and have students suggest ways to combine the sentences using subordinating conjunctions.

I love the park.

There are many things to do there.

There is a nice playground.

We play there.

The weather is nice.

LIGHT

Have students review a piece of their writing to look for places they can combine sentences and ideas. Have them revise to add dependent clauses with subordinating conjunctions.

LEARNING OBJECTIVES

- **Language** Review coordinating and subordinating conjunctions.
- **Language** Use sentences with conjunctions correctly in writing and speaking.

MATERIALS

Online Ed

Display and Engage *Grammar 5.1.4a, 5.1.4b, 5.1.4c*

Printable *Grammar 5.1.4*

 INSTRUCTIONAL VOCABULARY

- **conjunctions** words that connect other words or groups of words in a sentence

Review Conjunctions

- Show **Display and Engage: Grammar 5.1.4a**. Then show **Display and Engage: Grammar 5.1.4b**. Remind students that **conjunctions** are words that connect other words or groups of words in a sentence. Review coordinating and subordinating conjunctions and how they can be used to form compound and complex sentences.

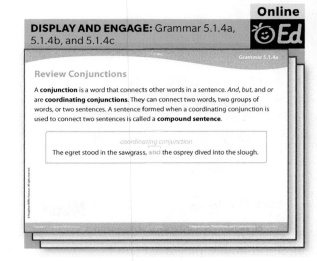

Online
 Ed

DISPLAY AND ENGAGE: Grammar 5.1.4a, 5.1.4b, and 5.1.4c

Grammar 5.1.4a

Review Conjunctions

A **conjunction** is a word that connects other words in a sentence. *And, but,* and *or* are **coordinating conjunctions.** They can connect two words, two groups of words, or two sentences. A sentence formed when a coordinating conjunction is used to connect two sentences is called a **compound sentence.**

coordinating conjunction
The egret stood in the sawgrass, and the osprey dived into the slough.

- Work with students to complete the exercises on **Display and Engage: Grammar 5.1.4c**.

- Have students complete **Printable: Grammar 5.1.4**.

🗨 ENGLISH LEARNER SUPPORT: Scaffolded Practice

SUBSTANTIAL

Remind students that conjunctions can be either coordinating or subordinating. Provide examples, such as *since* (subordinating), *and* (coordinating), *although* (subordinating), and *but* (coordinating). Use examples of sentences with both types of conjunctions and have students identify each type by pointing to or saying the conjunction. You may use classroom books for students to find examples.

MODERATE

Present these examples of coordinating conjunctions (*and, but, or*) and subordinating conjunctions (*because, if, although, when, as, since*). Have students identify the conjunction in each sentence below.

- *Because the wetlands were endangered, people worked to restore them.* **Because; subordinating**

- *An osprey is a kind of hawk, and it eats fish.* **and; coordinating**

LIGHT

Have students write one sentence that uses a coordinating conjunction and one that uses a subordinating conjunction.

CONJUNCTIONS, TRANSITIONS, AND CONTRACTIONS • CONJUNCTIONS

LEARNING OBJECTIVES

- **Language** Use coordinating and subordinating conjunctions.
- **Language** Use sentences with conjunctions correctly in speaking and writing.

MATERIALS   Online 😊 *Ed*

Display and Engage *Grammar 5.1.5*

Printable *Grammar 5.1.5*

 INSTRUCTIONAL VOCABULARY

- **conjunctions** words that connect other words or groups of words in a sentence

Connect and Teach

- Show **Display and Engage: Grammar 5.1.5**. Remind students that using coordinating and subordinating conjunctions to connect short sentences can help make their writing flow more smoothly.

- Tell students that when they revise, they need to look for run-ons in their writing and correct them. Remind them that both types of conjunctions can be used to eliminate run-on sentences by forming compound or complex sentences.

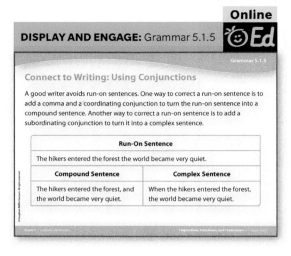

DISPLAY AND ENGAGE: Grammar 5.1.5

Connect to Writing: Using Conjunctions

A good writer avoids run-on sentences. One way to correct a run-on sentence is to add a comma and a coordinating conjunction to turn the run-on sentence into a compound sentence. Another way to correct a run-on sentence is to add a subordinating conjunction to turn it into a complex sentence.

Run-On Sentence	
The hikers entered the forest the world became very quiet.	
Compound Sentence	**Complex Sentence**
The hikers entered the forest, and the world became very quiet.	When the hikers entered the forest, the world became very quiet.

Engage and Apply

- Display this run-on sentence on the board: *The water flows from the Everglades to the ocean it does not flow naturally.*

- Have students use coordinating and subordinating conjunctions to correct the run-on sentence. Have them share their new compound and complex sentences. *(compound) The water flows from the Everglades to the ocean, but it does not flow naturally.*
(complex) Although the water flows from the ocean to the Everglades, it does not flow naturally.

- Have students write to a partner to explain the function of the coordinating and subordinating conjunctions in their sentences.

- Have students complete **Grammar 5.1.5** for practice with conjunctions.

- Tell students that as they revise their work, they should look for ways to combine ideas with conjunctions. Have students look for opportunities to use conjunctions to form compound or complex sentences as they revise their paragraphs. Tell partners to exchange papers and check that conjunctions were used correctly.

EL **ENGLISH LEARNER SUPPORT:** Scaffolded Practice

ALL LEVELS Write: *The hiker sees water. The hiker sees trees.* Ask: *How can I combine these two sentences?* Write: *The hiker sees water and trees.* Underline *and* and say: *And is a connecting word. We use it to add extra information. Connecting words are called* conjunctions.
Write the following sentence frames. Have students add the conjunction that completes each sentence. *We should conserve paper _____ plastic.* **and** *Should we throw away plastic bags, _____ should we recycle them?* **or** *Sometimes we remember to conserve, _____ at other times we forget.* **but**
Have students write sentences about their two favorite foods. Have them use all three of the conjunctions they learned.

CONJUNCTIONS, TRANSITIONS, AND CONTRACTIONS • TRANSITIONS

LEARNING OBJECTIVES

- **Language** Use transitions to link ideas.
- **Language** Use transitions correctly in writing and speaking.

MATERIALS	Online

Display and Engage Grammar 5.2.1a, 5.2.1b

Printable Grammar 5.2.1

INSTRUCTIONAL VOCABULARY

- **transition** word or phrase that links sentences and ideas

Connect and Teach

- Show **Display and Engage: Grammar 5.2.1a**. Explain that a **transition** is a connecting word or phrase that shows how details or ideas are related. Tell students that transitions can be single words, such as *however* and *although*, or phrases, such as *for example* and *in addition*.

- Model how to identify the transition in the example sentence: *We sang the national anthem, after practicing it.*

  THINK ALOUD *To find the transition in the sentence, I ask:* Which word or group of words links ideas? *The two ideas are* We sang the national anthem *and* practicing it. *The word that connects both ideas is* after.

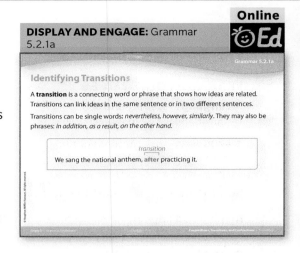

DISPLAY AND ENGAGE: Grammar 5.2.1a **Online Ed**

Identifying Transitions

A **transition** is a connecting word or phrase that shows how ideas are related. Transitions can link ideas in the same sentence or in two different sentences.

Transitions can be single words: *nevertheless, however, similarly*. They may also be phrases: *in addition, as a result, on the other hand*.

transition
We sang the national anthem, after practicing it.

Engage and Apply

- Complete items 1–6 on **Display and Engage: Grammar 5.2.1b** with students.

- Write these sentences on the board, and have students identify each transition.

  Jack has a great voice; however, he is too shy to sing the anthem. **however**

  Lily, though, is a person who loves to lead the class. **though**

- Have students complete **Printable: Grammar 5.2.1** for practice with transitions.

DISPLAY AND ENGAGE: Grammar 5.2.1b **Online Ed**

Identifying Transitions

Choose the transition that logically completes the blank in each sentence.

first	next	in contrast	then	like	as a result

1. We saluted the flag, and _____ we sang the national anthem. then
2. Singing the national anthem, _____ saluting the flag, is a sign of patriotism. like
3. _____, the teacher sings the anthem. First
4. _____ the class joins in. Next
5. My voice is weak _____ to Henrietta's, which is loud. in contrast
6. _____ of our practices, we are pretty good. As a result

 ENGLISH LEARNER SUPPORT: Facilitate Language Connections

Remind students that transition words are important in all kinds of writing. Point out that other languages also use transition words. Ask students to name words in their first language that are used for transitions, such as *first, later, meanwhile, in addition,* and *however*. Explain that words in English serve the same purpose.

Scaffolded Practice

SUBSTANTIAL

Write these sentences on the board and work with students to choose appropriate transitions to link them.

Sybil alerted the men. _____ she rode home. **Then**

He wanted to help his country, _____ he enlisted. **so**

MODERATE

Give students a choice of transitions for each of the sentence sets. Have them choose the correct word or phrase and rewrite each sentence.

LIGHT

Write several transitions on the board. Have partners take turns using them in sentences.

LEARNING OBJECTIVES

- **Language** Identify and use transitions to link ideas.
- **Language** Use transitions correctly in writing and speaking.

MATERIALS	Online

Display and Engage *Grammar 5.2.2a, 5.2.2b*

Printable *Grammar 5.2.2*

 INSTRUCTIONAL VOCABULARY

- **transition** word or phrase that links sentences and ideas

Connect and Teach

- Show **Display and Engage: Grammar 5.2.2a**. Explain that **transitions** signal certain types of relationships between ideas, such as time order, cause and effect, or comparison and contrast. Tell students that it is important to choose the transition that clarifies the relationship between the details in a sentence or paragraph.

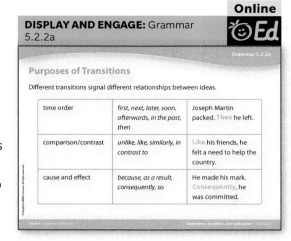

- Model how to identify the relationship between ideas in this example sentence: *Like his friends, he felt a need to help his country.*

  THINK ALOUD *To understand the relationship between the ideas in the sentence, I ask:* What is the transition? How does it relate the ideas? *The transition in this sentence is* Like. *This transition signals comparison.*

Engage and Apply

- Complete items 1–5 on **Display and Engage: Grammar 5.2.2b** with students.

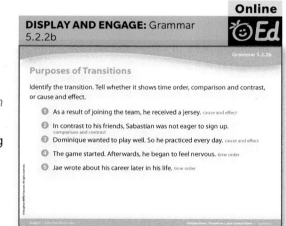

- Write these transitions on the board: *in addition, as a result, first, then, similarly.* Have pairs of students take turns using each transition in a sentence.

- Have students complete **Printable: Grammar 5.2.2** for practice with transitions.

 ENGLISH LEARNER SUPPORT: Scaffolded Practice

SUBSTANTIAL

Write these sentences on the board and guide students to identify the transitions and their purpose.

Like Sybil, Dan was good at riding horses. **Like; compare**

As a result, they often competed. **As a result; cause and effect**

MODERATE

Have students use a transition to complete the sentence frames.

_____ *Sybil, Dan was good at riding horses.* **Like**

_____, *they often competed.* **As a result**

LIGHT

Write several transitions that show comparison on the board, such as *like, similarly, in addition.* Have partners take turns using them in sentences.

LEARNING OBJECTIVES

- **Language** Identify and use transitions to link ideas.
- **Language** Use transitions correctly in writing and speaking.

MATERIALS   Online

Display and Engage *Grammar 5.2.3a, 5.2.3b*

Printable *Grammar 5.2.3*

 INSTRUCTIONAL VOCABULARY

- **transition** word or phrase that links sentences and ideas

Connect and Teach

- Show **Display and Engage: Grammar 5.2.3a**. Explain that writers use **transitions** to organize and communicate their ideas clearly. Point out that narrative writing frequently contains time-order transitions. Opinion writing often relies upon cause-and-effect transitions, as well as words and phrases that help to build an argument. Informative writing may use comparison-and-contrast transitions or others.

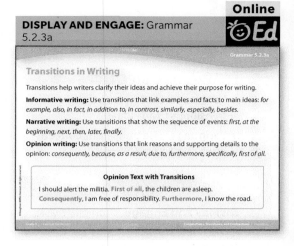

- Model how to choose accurate transitions for the example given on the projectable.

  THINK ALOUD *To identify which transitions should be used, I ask:* What is the purpose of my writing? Which transitions will show the organization of my ideas? *The purpose of the sentences is to persuade. Transitions, such as* first of all, consequently, *and* furthermore, *help to build the argument.*

Engage and Apply

- Complete items 1–4 on **Display and Engage: Grammar 5.2.3b** with students.

- As a class, choose one of the prompts and write a short paragraph using the transitions.

- Have students complete **Printable: Grammar 5.2.3** for practice with transitions.

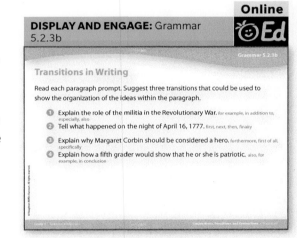

 ENGLISH LEARNER SUPPORT: Scaffolded Practice

SUBSTANTIAL

Have students select another prompt from Display and Engage: Grammar 5.2.3b and guide them to choose appropriate transitions.

MODERATE

Have students use transitions to complete the sentence frames.

_____, I had a math test in school._____, I read a new story in English class.

LIGHT

Have students write three sentences about something they did today. Encourage them to use transitions to show organization in their writing.

LEARNING OBJECTIVES

- **Language** Review how to use transitions to link ideas.
- **Language** Use transitions correctly in writing and speaking.

MATERIALS	Online

Display and Engage *Grammar 5.2.4a, 5.2.4b, 5.2.4c*

Printable *Grammar 5.2.4*

 INSTRUCTIONAL VOCABULARY

- **transition** word or phrase that links sentences and ideas

Review Transitions

- Show **Display and Engage: Grammar 5.2.4a** and then **Grammar 5.2.4b**. Review the functions of **transitions** and their importance in different types of writing.

- Work with students to complete the exercises on **Display and Engage: Grammar 5.2.4c**.

- Have students complete **Printable: Grammar 5.2.4**.

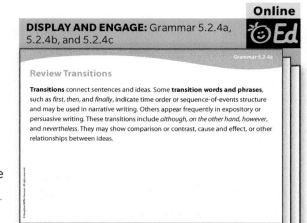

DISPLAY AND ENGAGE: Grammar 5.2.4a, 5.2.4b, and 5.2.4c

Online

Grammar 5.2.4a

Review Transitions

Transitions connect sentences and ideas. Some **transition words and phrases**, such as *first, then,* and *finally,* indicate time order or sequence-of-events structure and may be used in narrative writing. Others appear frequently in expository or persuasive writing. These transitions include *although, on the other hand, however,* and *nevertheless.* They may show comparison or contrast, cause and effect, or other relationships between ideas.

 ENGLISH LEARNER SUPPORT: Scaffolded Practice

SUBSTANTIAL

Remind students that transitions can be helpful to keep events in time order. Provide these examples of such transitions: *before, after, the next day, finally*. Help students think of what they did in class during the week. Work together to write sentences about the week using these transitions. Read the sentences aloud.

MODERATE

Remind students that transition words are useful because they link ideas in a sentence. Present the following sentences. Help students identify the transitions.

*We read the book although it was difficult. **although***
*In addition, we watched the film. **In addition***
*We compared the two later. **later***

LIGHT

Have students write a short paragraph about something that happened this week. Encourage them to use transitions to show organization in their writing.

LEARNING OBJECTIVES

- **Language** Choose transitions to link ideas in writing.
- **Language** Use transitions correctly in writing and speaking.

MATERIALS	Online

Display and Engage *Grammar 5.2.5*
Printable *Grammar 5.2.5*

INSTRUCTIONAL VOCABULARY

- **transition** word or phrase that links sentences and ideas

Connect and Teach

- Show **Display and Engage: Grammar 5.2.5**. Explain that good writers always include **transitions** to help their readers understand how ideas are related and to eliminate choppiness from their writing.

- Point out that when students revise, they should look for places where they can insert transitions to clarify the relationships between ideas. They also should make sure that the transitions they have included indicate logical relationships.

- Tell students that when transitions appear at the beginning of sentences, they are often followed by commas.

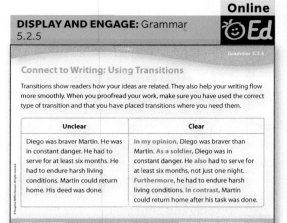

Engage and Apply

- Display the following pairs of sentences. Have students work with a partner to rewrite the sentences with a transition that logically links the ideas.
  The horse stumbled. She fell off. She fell off when the horse stumbled.
  He walked ten miles. He rested in camp. He walked ten miles. Then he rested in camp.

- Have students complete **Printable Grammar 5.2.5** for practice with transitions.

- Tell students to be sure to include transitions when they edit their work.

 ENGLISH LEARNER SUPPORT: Scaffolded Practice

SUBSTANTIAL/MODERATE

Remind students that transitions are words or phrases that help to connect ideas or sentences. They can show relationships, such as time, cause and effect, or comparison and contrast.
Write: *First, he watched for the signal. Later, he mounted his horse.* Ask students to identify the transition words. Explain that the words *First* and *Later* are transitions that show the sequence of the events, or the time relationship.

LIGHT

Write these sentences on the board. Have students identify the transition in each sentence.
Because of the signal, he knew they were coming by sea. **Because**
Finally, he could start his journey. **Finally**
He was tired; nevertheless, he was happy. **nevertheless**
Have students write a paragraph summarizing a story they read this week. Have them circle the transitions that they use in their paragraphs.

LEARNING OBJECTIVES

- **Language** Identify and use contractions.
- **Language** Use contractions correctly in writing and speaking.

MATERIALS   Online

Display and Engage *Grammar 5.3.1a, 5.3.1b*

Printable *Grammar 5.3.1*

 INSTRUCTIONAL VOCABULARY

- **contraction** joins two small words
- **apostrophe** punctuation mark
- **negative** a word that means "no"

Connect and Teach

- Show **Display and Engage: Grammar 5.3.1a**. Explain that **contractions** with *not* are made by joining a verb, such as *are, can,* and *do,* with the word *not*. The **apostrophe** takes the place of the letter *o* in the word *not*. Some **negative** contractions have irregular forms.

- Model identifying contractions with *not* in the example sentence: *It'll be a great story if there isn't a sad ending.*

  THINK ALOUD *To identify a contraction with* not, *I look for words with the letter* n, *an apostrophe, and the letter* t. *I ask:* Which contraction is made with the word not? *The contraction* isn't *uses the word not.*

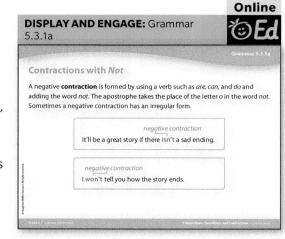

Engage and Apply

- Complete items 1–6 on **Display and Engage: Grammar 5.3.1b** with students.

- List the following words on the board. Have students combine the words with *not* and call out the contraction. Make sure they include the placement of the apostrophe. *is, should, do, could, are, have (isn't, shouldn't, don't, couldn't, aren't, haven't)*

- Have students complete **Printable: Grammar 5.3.1** for practice with contractions with *not*.

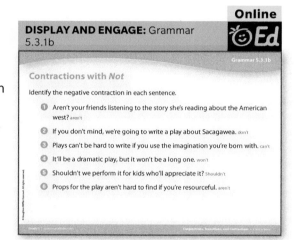

 ENGLISH LEARNER SUPPORT: Scaffolded Practice

SUBSTANTIAL

Tell students that negative contractions are made by joining a verb with the word *not*. Explain that the *o* in the word *not* can be replaced by an apostrophe ('). Show them the examples below.
do not/don't
are not/aren't
have not/haven't

MODERATE

Have students use contractions to fill in the missing words below. Then have students read each sentence aloud to see if it makes sense.
Why _____ you going to school today? aren't
I _____ have any more food to share. don't/didn't
I _____ spent any more money. haven't

LIGHT

Write verbs on the board with *not*. Have students combine the words and spell out the contractions, including the apostrophe. Have partners read their contractions aloud to see if they are correct.

LEARNING OBJECTIVES

- **Language** Identify contractions and use apostrophes with pronouns.
- **Language** Use contractions and apostrophes correctly in writing and speaking.

MATERIALS	Online 

Display and Engage *Grammar 5.3.2a, 5.3.2b*

Printable *Grammar 5.3.2*

 INSTRUCTIONAL VOCABULARY

- **contraction** joins two small words

Connect and Teach

- Show **Display and Engage: Grammar 5.3.2a**. Point out to students that some **contractions** are made by combining a pronoun with a verb. An apostrophe is used to replace the missing letters.

- Model identifying contractions with pronouns in the example sentence: *They're trying to find a faster route.*

  THINK ALOUD *To identify a contraction that combines a pronoun with a verb, I look for words with a pronoun and an apostrophe. I ask:* Which word is made up of a pronoun and a verb? *The word* They're *is the correct answer.*

Engage and Apply

- Complete items 1–8 on **Display and Engage: Grammar 5.3.2b** with students.

- List the following word pairs on the board. Work with students to combine the pronouns and verbs into contractions. Make sure they include the correct placement of the apostrophe. *he will, you will, we are, they are, you are, she would, they would, you would*

- Have students complete **Printable: Grammar 5.3.2** for practice with contractions with pronouns.

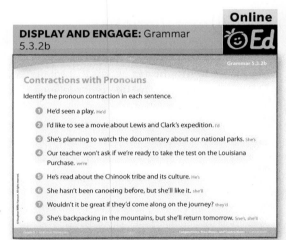

DISPLAY AND ENGAGE: Grammar 5.3.2a — Online Ed

Contractions with Pronouns

A **pronoun contraction** is made up of a pronoun and a verb. An **apostrophe** is used in place of the dropped letter or letters.

> pronoun contraction
> They're trying to find a faster route.

DISPLAY AND ENGAGE: Grammar 5.3.2b — Online Ed

Contractions with Pronouns

Identify the pronoun contraction in each sentence.

1. He'd seen a play. He'd
2. I'd like to see a movie about Lewis and Clark's expedition. I'd
3. She's planning to watch the documentary about our national parks. She's
4. Our teacher won't ask if we're ready to take the test on the Louisiana Purchase. we're
5. He's read about the Chinook tribe and its culture. He's
6. She hasn't been canoeing before, but she'll like it. she'll
7. Wouldn't it be great if they'd come along on the journey? they'd
8. She's backpacking in the mountains, but she'll return tomorrow. She's, she'll

EL ENGLISH LEARNER SUPPORT: Scaffolded Practice

SUBSTANTIAL

Tell students that contractions can combine a pronoun and a verb. Show them the examples below.

he is/he's
he would/he'd
they were/they're

Guide them to form a sentence with the pronoun and verb, and then restate the sentence with the contraction in place of the pronoun and verb.

MODERATE

Have students use contractions to fill in the missing words below. Then have students read each sentence aloud to see if it makes sense.

_____ going to school today. I'm, He's, She's, We're, You're, They're
_____ like to bring snacks. I'd, He'd, She'd, We'd, You'd, They'd
_____ going to enjoy the day. I'm, He's, She's, We're, You're, They're

LIGHT

Have students write two sentence with contractions that use a pronoun and a verb. Have partners read their contractions aloud to see if they are correct.

LESSON 5.3.3

PRONOUN CONTRACTIONS AND HOMOPHONES

LEARNING OBJECTIVES

- **Language** Identify and use pronoun contractions and homophones.
- **Language** Use contractions and apostrophes correctly in writing and speaking.

MATERIALS

Online

Display and Engage *Grammar 5.3.3a, 5.3.3b*

Printable *Grammar 5.3.3*

 INSTRUCTIONAL VOCABULARY

- **homophones** words that sound alike, but have different spellings and meanings

Connect and Teach

- Show <u>Display and Engage: Grammar 5.3.3a</u>. Point out that contractions can combine two words using an apostrophe to replace missing letters.

- Tell students that some contractions sound like other words, such as *it's/its, they're/there/their, who's/whose*. Remind students that they have to be careful to spell correctly to avoid **homophone** errors.

- Tell students that a contraction can say the same thing using one word instead of two. Model shortening a sentence: *We are not wearing our hiking boots today. We're not/We aren't wearing our hiking boots today.*

  THINK ALOUD *To shorten a sentence, I ask:* Which words can be combined to make a contraction? *The words* We *and* are *can be shortened to* We're. *The words* are *and* not *can be shortened to* aren't.

Engage and Apply

- Complete items 1–5 on <u>Display and Engage: Grammar 5.3.3b</u> with students.

- Tell students that homophones sound alike, but have different spellings and meanings. Write *you're* and *your* on the board. Explain that *you're* means "you are," but *your* means "something that belongs to you." Continue with other word pairs, such as: *its/it's; we'll/wheel*.

- Have students complete <u>Printable: Grammar 5.3.3</u> for practice with contractions and homophones.

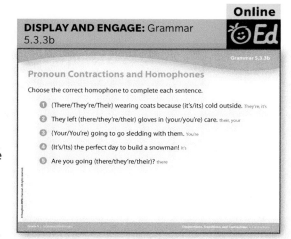

DISPLAY AND ENGAGE: Grammar 5.3.3a — Online Ed

Pronoun Contractions and Homophones

When writing contractions, use an apostrophe to replace letters. Do not use double negatives, or two negative words together. Do not use the contraction *ain't*.

Some contractions are homophones, or words that sound the same but are spelled differently. These include *you're/your, it's/its, they're/there/their*. *You're, it's,* and *they're* are contractions (*you are, it is, they are*). Be careful to spell correctly when you form contractions.

DISPLAY AND ENGAGE: Grammar 5.3.3b — Online Ed

Pronoun Contractions and Homophones

Choose the correct homophone to complete each sentence.

1. (There/They're/Their) wearing coats because (it's/its) cold outside. They're, it's
2. They left (there/they're/their) gloves in (your/you're) care. their, your
3. (Your/You're) going to go sledding with them. You're
4. (It's/Its) the perfect day to build a snowman! It's
5. Are you going (there/they're/their)? there

ENGLISH LEARNER SUPPORT: Scaffolded Practice

SUBSTANTIAL

Write the word pairs on the board and review the meaning of each word until students understand how they differ.

it's/its
they're/there
you're/your

MODERATE

Have students use contractions to fill in the missing words below. Then have students read each sentence aloud to see if it makes sense.

_____ going to take a turn next. *You're*
There's going to be a party. _____ next Tuesday. *It's*
_____ going to be at the party. *They're*

LIGHT

Have students write two sentence with contractions they reviewed today. Have partners read their contractions aloud to check for homophone errors.

CONJUNCTIONS, TRANSITIONS, CONTRACTIONS • CONTRACTIONS

LEARNING OBJECTIVES

- **Language** Review contractions.
- **Language** Use contractions correctly in writing and speaking.

MATERIALS	Online

Display and Engage *Grammar 5.3.4a, 5.3.4b, 5.3.4c*

Printable *Grammar 5.3.4*

 **INSTRUCTIONAL VOCABULARY**

- **contraction** joins two small words

Review Contractions

- Show **Display and Engage: Grammar 5.3.4a** and then **Grammar 5.3.4b**.

- Remind students that a negative **contraction** is made by joining a verb with the word *not*, using an apostrophe instead of *o*. Contractions can be made by combining a pronoun and a verb. Some contractions are homophones.

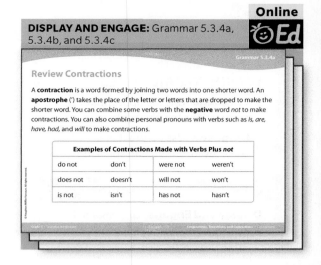

- Work with students to complete the exercises on **Display and Engage: Grammar 5.3.4c**.

- Have students complete **Printable: Grammar 5.3.4**.

EL **ENGLISH LEARNER SUPPORT: Scaffolded Practice**

SUBSTANTIAL

Review with students that contractions can be made by combining words and using apostrophes to replace missing letters. Provide examples of contractions, such *as: aren't* (are and not); *couldn't* (could and not); *they're* (they and are); *we'll* (we and will). As they are able, have students identify the words that were combined to make each contraction.

MODERATE

Explain to students that contractions appear most often in speech and in informal writing. Have students work together using contractions to make a sign to post on the door when the class is not in the room. For example, *We're not in the room. We're at the library. We'll be back soon.* Encourage students to use contractions when writing dialogue, when quoting a speaker, and when writing informal assignments, such as personal narratives.

LIGHT

Have students write a short paragraph using contractions. Have partners read their contractions aloud to check for homophone errors.

CONJUNCTIONS, TRANSITIONS, CONTRACTIONS • CONTRACTIONS

LEARNING OBJECTIVES

- **Language** Choose appropriate contractions to convey ideas.
- **Language** Use contractions correctly in writing and speaking.

MATERIALS	Online

Display and Engage *Grammar 5.3.5*
Printable *Grammar 5.3.5*

 INSTRUCTIONAL VOCABULARY

- **contraction** joins two small words

Connect and Teach

- Show **Display and Engage: Grammar 5.3.5**. Tell students that forming **contractions** correctly and avoiding double negatives is important to keeping their writing clear and easy to read.

- Point out that an important part of revising is to make sure that apostrophes are placed correctly.

Engage and Apply

- Review the rules for joining two words to make a contraction, combining a verb with the word *not* to make a negative, and making contractions with personal pronouns and verbs.

- Display the following paragraph. Have students find words that can be combined into a contraction.
  Lewis and Clark did not have a map of the Louisiana Territory. They could not have known what they would find. Still, their expedition and the journals they kept tell us a lot about the land we are living in. **didn't, couldn't, they'd, we're**

- Have students complete **Printable: Grammar 5.3.5** for practice with contractions.

- Tell students that as they revise, they should check to make sure that their contractions are used correctly.

 ENGLISH LEARNER SUPPORT: Scaffolded Support

SUBSTANTIAL
Remind students that apostrophes can be used in place of letters when forming contractions. Give them sample sentences with pronouns and verbs that they can turn into contractions by using an apostrophe.

MODERATE
Have partners read the following sentences aloud. Have them write the words that the contractions replace.
Explorers don't know what they will find. **do not**
Lewis wasn't worried when he first met the Shoshone. **was not**
You're sure that Lewis and Clark traveled 8,000 miles? **You are**
I'd like to learn more about how Sacagawea helped Lewis and Clark. **I would**
They haven't read Lewis's and Clark's journals. **have not**

LIGHT
Have students identify several contractions in a story they read this week. Then, with a partner, have students write sentences with contractions describing the selection's photographs and illustrations.

LEARNING OBJECTIVES

- **Language** Use and explain the function of quotations.
- **Language** Use proper capitalization and punctuation for direct quotations correctly in speaking and writing.

MATERIALS	Online

Display and Engage *Grammar 6.1.1a, 6.1.1b*

Printable *Grammar 6.1.1*

 INSTRUCTIONAL VOCABULARY

- **direct quotation** the exact words a character or person says
- **quotation marks** punctuation marks at the beginning and end of a direct quotation

Connect and Teach

- Show <u>Display and Engage: Grammar 6.1.1a</u>. Explain that a **direct quotation** is the exact words of a speaker or writer. Tell students that **quotation marks** are placed at the beginning and end of a direct quotation. End punctuation marks for the quotations—periods, exclamation points, and question marks—are placed inside the quotation marks. The first word in a quotation that is a complete sentence is capitalized.

  THINK ALOUD *To identify and punctuate the direct quotation, I ask: Does the sentence give a speaker's exact words? How can I separate the exact words from the rest of the sentence? A comma and quotation mark are used to separate the speaker's exact words from the rest of the sentence.*

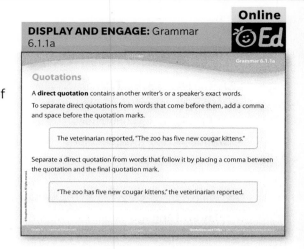

DISPLAY AND ENGAGE: Grammar 6.1.1a

Online

Quotations

A **direct quotation** contains another writer's or a speaker's exact words.

To separate direct quotations from words that come before them, add a comma and space before the quotation marks.

> The veterinarian reported, "The zoo has five new cougar kittens."

Separate a direct quotation from words that follow it by placing a comma between the quotation and the final quotation mark.

> "The zoo has five new cougar kittens," the veterinarian reported.

Engage and Apply

- Complete items 1–6 on <u>Display and Engage: Grammar 6.1.1b</u> with students.

- Hold a conversation with a volunteer. Have other students write down what is said and punctuate the quotations correctly.

- Have students complete <u>Printable: Grammar 6.1.1</u> for practice with quotation marks.

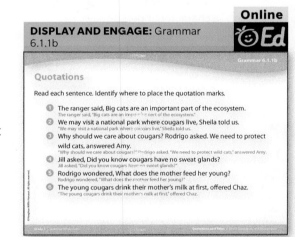

DISPLAY AND ENGAGE: Grammar 6.1.1b

Online

Quotations

Read each sentence. Identify where to place the quotation marks.

1. The ranger said, Big cats are an important part of the ecosystem.
   The ranger said, "Big cats are an important part of the ecosystem."
2. We may visit a national park where cougars live, Sheila told us.
   "We may visit a national park where cougars live," Sheila told us.
3. Why should we care about cougars? Rodrigo asked. We need to protect wild cats, answered Amy.
   "Why should we care about cougars?" Rodrigo asked. "We need to protect wild cats," answered Amy.
4. Jill asked, Did you know cougars have no sweat glands?
   Jill asked, "Did you know cougars have no sweat glands?"
5. Rodrigo wondered, What does the mother feed her young?
   Rodrigo wondered, "What does the mother feed her young?"
6. The young cougars drink their mother's milk at first, offered Chaz.
   "The young cougars drink their mother's milk at first," offered Chaz.

- Have students edit a writing draft using the correct form of quotations.

 ENGLISH LEARNER SUPPORT: Facilitate Language Connections

It is common when printing dialogue in Spanish to dispense with quotation marks and use a long dash (—), sometimes known as an em dash (*raya* in Spanish), to indicate the beginning and end of the quotation or a change in speaker.

Scaffolded Practice

SUBSTANTIAL

Say: *I like this class.* Then write the sentence on the board, explaining that it is a direct quotation because you said it. Place quotation marks in the proper spots. Then say and write another direct quotation on the board and have students explain where they would put the quotation marks.

MODERATE

Flip through a story with dialogue that students have already read and guide them to read the direct quotations, explaining that the characters said those exact words.

LIGHT

Have students copy a short section of dialogue from a story, leaving out the quotation marks and other punctuation. Then have partners exchange sentences and add the correct punctuation marks.

QUOTATIONS AND TITLES • DIRECT QUOTATIONS AND INTERJECTIONS

LEARNING OBJECTIVES

- **Language** Recognize and explain the function of text quotations.
- **Language** Use text quotations correctly in speaking and writing.

MATERIALS   Online

Display and Engage *Grammar 6.1.2a, 6.1.2b*

Printable *Grammar 6.1.2*

 INSTRUCTIONAL VOCABULARY

- **direct quotation** the exact word a character or person says

Connect and Teach

- Show **Display and Engage: Grammar 6.1.2a**. Remind students that **direct quotations** include someone else's words. Explain that they can use direct quotations when using text evidence in their writing to support a key point. Words, phrases, or sentences copied directly from another source always appear in quotation marks.

- Use this example to model how students can weave parts of a direct quotation into their own writing: *The article stated that they are "seldom seen."*

  THINK ALOUD *To decide how to include a direct quotation from a source, I ask: What part of the text do I want to quote? How can I include it smoothly in my writing? The words* seldom seen *are taken directly from the text to describe the cougars. This phrase cannot stand alone and must be built into the writer's own sentence.*

DISPLAY AND ENGAGE: Grammar 6.1.2a   Online ⊙Ed

Grammar 6.1.2a

Text Quotations

One way to present information from another source is to quote the author's words directly. When you use phrases or sentences from another text, copy the words and internal punctuation marks exactly as they appear in the original source. Then enclose them in quotation marks.

Quoted Phrase
The author describes the big cats as being "seldom seen."

Quoted Sentence
The article stated, "They are seldom seen."
The article stated that "they are seldom seen."

Engage and Apply

- Complete items 1–3 on **Display and Engage: Grammar 6.1.2b** with students.

- Have students work in pairs to take direct quotations from a classroom book and present them in their own sentences. Have volunteers write their sentences on the board.

- Have students complete **Printable: Grammar 6.1.2** for practice with quotation marks.

- Have students edit a writing draft using text quotations correctly.

DISPLAY AND ENGAGE: Grammar 6.1.2b   Online ⊙Ed

Grammar 6.1.2b

Text Quotations

The direct quotations are underlined. Suggest how to rewrite the sentences using correct punctuation.

1. The article stated that most cougars are <u>voracious carnivores</u>. The article stated that most cougars are "voracious carnivores."
2. Cougars live throughout North America. <u>They have been able to adapt to a variety of habitats.</u> "They have been able to adapt to a variety of habitats."
3. They make sounds <u>ranging from contented purrs to ferocious hisses and growls</u>. They make sounds "ranging from contented purrs to ferocious hisses and growls."

 ENGLISH LEARNER SUPPORT: Scaffolded Practice

SUBSTANTIAL

Work with students to find a quotation in a textbook. Then have them complete the sentence frame.

According to _____, " _____ "

MODERATE

Have students find a quotation in a book and complete the sentence frame on their own.

LIGHT

Have students find a quotation in a book and record it. Then have them exchange with partners to make sure they used quotation marks correctly.

LEARNING OBJECTIVES

- **Language** Use and explain the function of interjections.
- **Language** Use interjections and dialogue correctly in speaking and writing.

MATERIALS
Online

Display and Engage *Grammar 6.1.3a, 6.1.3b*

Printable *Grammar 6.1.3*

 **INSTRUCTIONAL VOCABULARY**

- **interjection** single word or group of words used to express a feeling or emotion

Connect and Teach

- Show <u>Display and Engage: Grammar 6.1.3a</u>. Tell students that **interjections** are words or phrases that show emotion. When these words occur in dialogue, they usually appear at the beginning of a sentence and are followed either by an exclamation point or a comma.

- Explain that sometimes writers split dialogue into two parts. Both parts begin and end with quotation marks. Unless the second part begins with a proper noun, the first word is not capitalized.

- Mention that in between the two parts of a split quotation, the writer usually tells who is speaking, what the speaker is doing, or how he or she is speaking.

- Show an example of an interjection that forms the first part of the split quotation.

DISPLAY AND ENGAGE: Grammar 6.1.3a

Online Ed

Grammar 6.1.3a

Interjections and Dialogue

Interjections such as *Hey, Ouch,* and *Wow* show emotion. They are followed by exclamation points or commas.

Split quotations are direct quotations divided into two parts. Begin and end both parts with quotation marks. Capitalize and punctuate the first part like a regular quotation. Place a comma, a space, and quotation marks before the first word of the second part.

interjection   split quotation

"Wow," Bill exclaimed, "that documentary about the cougars was awesome!"

Engage and Apply

- Complete the activity on <u>Display and Engage: Grammar 6.1.3b</u> with students.

- Have students return to the projectable and identify the function of each interjection.

- Have students complete <u>Printable: Grammar 6.1.3</u> for practice with quotation marks.

- Have students edit a writing draft using text quotations correctly.

DISPLAY AND ENGAGE: Grammar 6.1.3b

Online Ed

Grammar 6.1.3b

Interjections and Dialogue

Discuss how to rewrite the following dialogue. Add quotation marks and punctuate and capitalize each sentence correctly.

Hey, Bill, said Andy thoughtfully we should do our report on cougars in our state.

Perfect! We could show slides, Bill replied and we could create handouts.

Guess what! I have a new software program, Andy said that will help us make signs.

Cool! I think we're all set said Bill, and I can't wait to start

"Hey, Bill," said Andy thoughtfully, "we should do our report on cougars in our state."
"Perfect! We could show slides," Bill replied, "and we could create handouts."
"Guess what! I have a new software program," Andy said, "that will help us make signs."
"Cool! I think we're all set," said Bill, "and I can't wait to start!"

 ENGLISH LEARNER SUPPORT: Scaffolded Practice

SUBSTANTIAL

Have students look at a passage of dialogue in a short story or novel to identify examples of split quotations.

MODERATE

Have students ask partners how their day is, then record their responses using quotation marks. Encourage students to use interjections.

LIGHT

Have students write a few lines of dialogue, and then exchange them with partners to check that quotation marks are used correctly.

QUOTATIONS AND TITLES • DIRECT QUOTATIONS AND INTERJECTIONS

LEARNING OBJECTIVES

- **Language** Review the function of direct quotations and interjections.
- **Language** Use direct quotations and interjections correctly in speaking and writing.

MATERIALS   Online

Display and Engage *Grammar 6.1.4a, 6.1.4b, 6.1.4c*

Printable *Grammar 6.1.4*

INSTRUCTIONAL VOCABULARY

- **direct quotation** the exact word a character or person says
- **interjection** single word or group of words used to express a feeling or emotion

Review Direct Quotations and Interjections

- Show **Display and Engage: Grammar 6.1.4a** and then **Grammar 6.1.4b**. Review how to punctuate **direct quotations** with students. Remind them that if a quoted sentence is split into two parts, a comma and quotation marks end the first part. A comma, space, and then quotation marks follow the interrupting phrase. Then read the information on **interjections** aloud. Discuss the various functions of interjections in sentences.

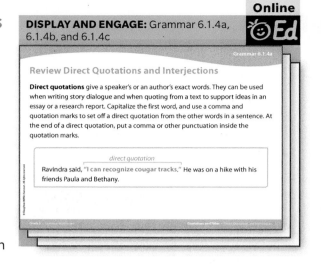

- Work with students to complete the exercises on **Display and Engage: Grammar 6.1.4c**.

- Have students complete **Printable: Grammar 6.1.4**.

- Have students edit a writing draft using text quotations correctly.

EL ENGLISH LEARNER SUPPORT: Scaffolded Practice

SUBSTANTIAL

Remind students that when writing quotations, the punctuation—commas, periods, exclamation points, and question marks—should be placed inside the quotation marks.

MODERATE

Display the following examples without the internal punctuation. Help students identify the words of dialogue and add the missing punctuation.

"Cougars are a species of wild cat," said my teacher.

She added, "A cougar can weigh more than a person."

LIGHT

Have students find a few quotations they like and write them in sentences. Have them exchange their papers with partners to check that they used quotation marks correctly.

QUOTATIONS AND TITLES • DIRECT QUOTATIONS AND INTERJECTIONS

LEARNING OBJECTIVES

- **Language** Use and explain the function of quotations and interjections.
- **Language** Use proper capitalization and punctuation for direct quotations.

MATERIALS   Online

Display and Engage *Grammar 6.1.5*

Printable *Grammar 6.1.5*

INSTRUCTIONAL VOCABULARY

- **direct quotation** the exact word a character or person says
- **interjection** single word or group of words used to express a feeling or emotion

Connect and Teach

- Show <u>**Display and Engage: Grammar 6.1.5**</u>. Explain that good writers make sure they have punctuated their **direct quotations** correctly. An important part of revising is inserting commas, quotation marks, and other punctuation marks where they are needed.

- Remind students that including direct quotations from texts or other sources will lend support to their key points. These quotations must be copied exactly and punctuated accurately.

- Point out that **interjections** also must be punctuated correctly. Those that convey strong emotion are followed by an exclamation point. Others can be set off by a comma.

Engage and Apply

- Ask student pairs to write dialogue that includes the correct spacing, quotation marks, and punctuation, as well as interjections. Have volunteers write their dialogue on the board and explain the function of the interjections that they used.

- Have students complete <u>**Printable: Grammar 6.1.5**</u> for practice with quotation marks.

- Tell students that as they revise their work, they should look for places to add quotations to support their main ideas.

 ENGLISH LEARNER SUPPORT: Scaffolded Practice

ALL LEVELS Review that a direct quotation shows someone's exact words. An interjection is a word or phrase that shows emotion. Interjections are often found in quotations. Write: *"Wow!" Margo said. "Cats are awesome predators."*

Ask: *What were Margo's exact words? How do you know?*

Circle the quotation marks in the quotation. Say: *These are quotation marks. We put one set to show where a quotation starts. We put the other set to show where the quotation ends.*

Choose an activity in which all the students have participated together. Encourage students to use an interjection and a comment about the activity. Work together to write students' responses, using quotation marks and punctuation. For example, *"Wow!" Jean said. "That test was difficult!"*

LEARNING OBJECTIVES

- **Language** Know the rules for capitalization of and use of italics in titles.
- **Language** Use capitalization and italics in titles correctly in writing.

MATERIALS	Online

Display and Engage *Grammar 6.2.1a, 6.2.1b*

Printable *Grammar 6.2.1*

 **INSTRUCTIONAL VOCABULARY**

- **title** the name of a book or other creative work
- **italic** a type style in which words slant to the right
- **underline** to place a line under a word

Connect and Teach

- Show **Display and Engage: Grammar 6.2.1a**. Explain that writing **titles** requires following some special rules. The titles of books, movies, plays, and newspapers belong in **italics**. When writing by hand, **underline** these titles, which is the proofreading mark that indicates italics.

- Explain that italics are sometimes used in writing to emphasize certain words. Not all words students see in italics will be titles.

  THINK ALOUD *To show the mechanics of writing a title, I ask:* When writing by hand, how would you show that *The Girl Who Rode Like the Wind* is a book title? The Girl Who Rode Like the Wind

Engage and Apply

- Complete items 1–6 on **Display and Engage: Grammar 6.2.1b** with students.

- Provide for students examples of type that is printed in italics. Use the student book or other materials. Have students practice identifying type that is printed in italics. Then have them write two sentences containing book titles.

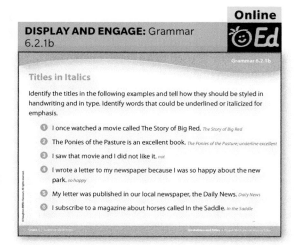

- Have students complete **Printable: Grammar 6.2.1** to practice formatting titles.

- Have students edit a writing draft using titles in italics correctly.

EL **ENGLISH LEARNER SUPPORT: Facilitate Language Connections**

Capitalization is handled differently in several languages, including Spanish. The initial word and important words are not necessarily capitalized in a title. Remind students that the initial word and all important words are capitalized in a title in English.

Scaffolded Practice

SUBSTANTIAL

Introduce the terms, *title* and *italic,* from this lesson. Display the following sentence typed on paper:

The title of the book is *The Black Stallion*.

Then handwrite the same sentence to introduce the term *underline*:

The title of the book is The Black Stallion.

MODERATE

Have students complete the following sentence to introduce a key term from this lesson.

The _____ of a book should be in italics. *title*

LIGHT

Have students demonstrate their understanding of the key terms involved in writing titles. Provide them with a sentence frame, such as:

A movie title would appear in _____ or with _____. *italics; underlining*

LEARNING OBJECTIVES

- **Language** Use underlining, quotation marks, or italics to indicate titles.
- **Language** Use quotation marks for titles correctly in writing.

MATERIALS	Online

Display and Engage *Grammar 6.2.2a, 6.2.2b*

Printable *Grammar 6.2.2*

 INSTRUCTIONAL VOCABULARY

- **title** the name of a book or other creative work

Connect and Teach

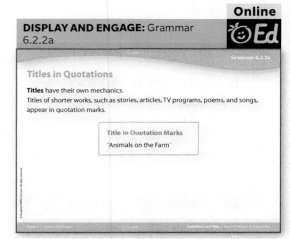

DISPLAY AND ENGAGE: Grammar 6.2.2a · Online Ed

- Show **Display and Engage: Grammar 6.2.2a**. Tell students that not all **titles** are written with underlining or in italic. Titles of shorter works, such as stories, poems, articles, TV programs, or songs, appear in quotation marks.

- Model how to write titles of shorter works by presenting this example of a TV program title: *Animals on the Farm*

  THINK ALOUD *To write a title properly, I ask:* How would you show that *Animals on the Farm* is the name of a television program? *"Animals on the Farm"*

Engage and Apply

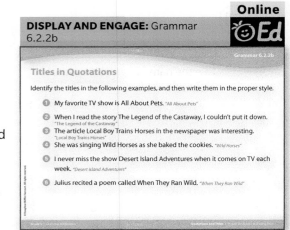

DISPLAY AND ENGAGE: Grammar 6.2.2b · Online Ed

- Complete items 1–6 on **Display and Engage: Grammar 6.2.2b** with students.

- Ask partners to quiz each other about types of titles, asking which are treated with quotation marks and which are treated with underlining or italics. Have students use a computer to type sentences that contain poem, article, and book titles.

- Have students complete **Printable: Grammar 6.2.2** for practice with formatting titles.

- Have students edit a writing draft using titles correctly.

ENGLISH LEARNER SUPPORT: Scaffolded Practice

SUBSTANTIAL

Have students choose a short story and write the title. Ask what kind of formatting it needs. *(quotation marks)*

MODERATE

Have students choose a short story, novel, TV show, or movie and write the title. Work with them to format the title correctly.

LIGHT

Have students write a sentence describing the most interesting thing they read or saw that week, including the title. Have partners exchange papers to check whether the title is formatted correctly.

LEARNING OBJECTIVES

- **Language** Know when to use underlining, quotation marks, or italics to indicate titles.
- **Language** Use capitalization of titles correctly in writing.

MATERIALS Online

Display and Engage *Grammar 6.2.3a, 6.2.3b*

Printable *Grammar 6.2.3*

 INSTRUCTIONAL VOCABULARY

- **title** the name of a book or other creative work

Connect and Teach

- Show **Display and Engage: Grammar 6.2.3a**. Tell students that **titles** have capitalization rules. The first and last words in titles begin with a capital letter. Most other words also begin with a capital letter. However, the following words do not have a capital letter, unless they begin or end a title: articles such as *a, an, the*; coordinating conjunctions such as *and, or, but*; and prepositions such as *at, on, into*.

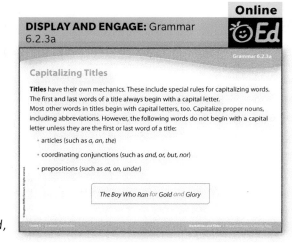

DISPLAY AND ENGAGE: Grammar 6.2.3a Online Ed

Capitalizing Titles

Titles have their own mechanics. These include special rules for capitalizing words. The first and last words of a title always begin with a capital letter. Most other words in titles begin with capital letters, too. Capitalize proper nouns, including abbreviations. However, the following words do not begin with a capital letter unless they are the first or last word of a title:

- articles (such as *a, an, the*)
- coordinating conjunctions (such as *and, or, but, nor*)
- prepositions (such as *at, on, under*)

The Boy Who Ran for Gold and Glory

- Capitalize prepositions longer than four letters, such as *about, after,* and *between*.

- Model how to capitalize titles by presenting this example: *the boy who ran for gold and glory*.

  THINK ALOUD *To write a title properly, I ask:* How would you use capital letters in the title, *the boy who ran for gold and glory? The Boy Who Ran for Gold and Glory*

Engage and Apply

- Complete items 1–6 on **Display and Engage: Grammar 6.2.3b** with students.

- Write *horse, but, the, at, stallion, and ride* on the board. Help students determine whether they would be capitalized if they were not the first or last word in a title.

- Have students complete **Printable: Grammar 6.2.3** for practice with formatting titles.

- Have students edit a writing draft using titles correctly.

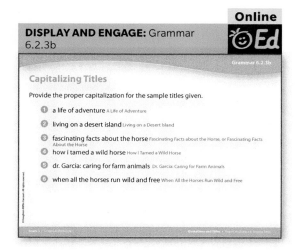

DISPLAY AND ENGAGE: Grammar 6.2.3b Online Ed

Capitalizing Titles

Provide the proper capitalization for the sample titles given.

1. a life of adventure A Life of Adventure
2. living on a desert island Living on a Desert Island
3. fascinating facts about the horse Fascinating Facts about the Horse, or Fascinating Facts About the Horse
4. how i tamed a wild horse How I Tamed a Wild Horse
5. dr. Garcia: caring for farm animals Dr. Garcia: Caring for Farm Animals
6. when all the horses run wild and free When All the Horses Run Wild and Free

ENGLISH LEARNER SUPPORT: Scaffolded Practice

SUBSTANTIAL

Write a title without any capitalization and have students identify which words should be capitalized. As they tell which words, discuss whether the word is the first or last in the title or a preposition longer than four letters, such as *about, after,* and *between*. If so, the word should be capitalized. Then ask if the word is an article such as *a, an, the*; coordinating conjunction such as *and, or, but*; preposition such as *at, on, into*. If so, then the word should not be capitalized.
My Side of the Mountain
Because of Winn-Dixie

MODERATE

Have students suggest titles of books they have read and work with them to decide which words should be capitalized.

LIGHT

Have students name their favorite book and write the title. Remind them to use capital letters. Have partners exchange papers to tell whether the titles are capitalized correctly.

LESSON 6.2.4

LEARNING OBJECTIVES

- **Language** Review rules for using underlining, quotation marks, or italics to indicate titles.
- **Language** Use rules for proper mechanics of titles correctly in writing.

MATERIALS

Online

Display and Engage *Grammar 6.2.4a, 6.2.4b*

Printable *Grammar 6.2.4*

 **INSTRUCTIONAL VOCABULARY**

- **title** the name of a book or other creative work

Review Proper Mechanics and Writing Titles

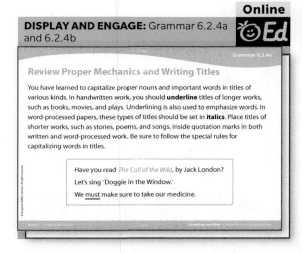

DISPLAY AND ENGAGE: Grammar 6.2.4a and 6.2.4b

Online Ed

Review Proper Mechanics and Writing Titles

You have learned to capitalize proper nouns and important words in titles of various kinds. In handwritten work, you should **underline** titles of longer works, such as books, movies, and plays. Underlining is also used to emphasize words. In word-processed papers, these types of titles should be set in *italics*. Place titles of shorter works, such as stories, poems, and songs, inside quotation marks in both written and word-processed work. Be sure to follow the special rules for capitalizing words in titles.

Have you read *The Call of the Wild*, by Jack London?
Let's sing "Doggie in the Window."
We must make sure to take our medicine.

- Show **Display and Engage: Grammar 6.2.4a**. Review with students that **titles** have special rules writers must follow. Titles of longer works are underlined when written by hand, or are set in italics when printed. Shorter works are placed in quotation marks. Titles use capital letters at the beginning of words. Most words are capitalized.

- Work with students to complete the exercises on **Display and Engage: Grammar 6.2.4b**.

- Have students complete **Printable: Grammar 6.2.4**.

- Have students edit a writing draft using titles correctly.

 ENGLISH LEARNER SUPPORT: Scaffolded Practice

SUBSTANTIAL/MODERATE

To remind students that titles of longer works are written with italics or are underlined if handwritten, and titles of shorter works are written with quotation marks, provide examples of each: *The Black Stallion* (novel); "Genius" (poem). Use books of poetry or a magazine to show the difference between longer and shorter works. Write the title of the magazine in italics or underlined. Write the titles of the poems or articles with quotation marks. Help students distinguish between other longer and shorter works and how they should be written by displaying these writing forms.

novel longer work, written with italics

short story shorter work, written with quotation marks

play longer work, written with italics

song shorter work, written with quotation marks

poem shorter work, written with quotation marks

LIGHT

Have students write a few sentences describing a novel and a short story, including the title. Have partners exchange papers to determine whether the titles are formatted correctly.

QUOTATIONS AND TITLES • PROPER MECHANICS AND WRITING TITLES

LEARNING OBJECTIVES

- **Language** Choose and write titles with italics, underlining, or quotations.
- **Language** Use proper mechanics when writing titles.

MATERIALS   Online

Display and Engage *Grammar 6.2.5*

Printable *Grammar 6.2.5*

INSTRUCTIONAL VOCABULARY

- **title** the name of a book or other creative work

Connect and Teach

- Show **Display and Engage: Grammar 6.2.5**. Explain to students that they should use the proper mechanics when referring to **titles** in their writing. These mechanics include using italics or underlining to identify books, movies, and longer works, and using quotations to identify shorter works. Titles have special rules for capitalization.

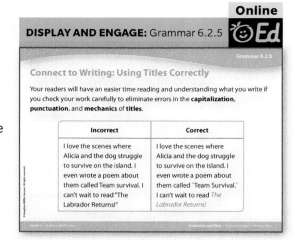

DISPLAY AND ENGAGE: Grammar 6.2.5   Online   **Ed**

Connect to Writing: Using Titles Correctly

Your readers will have an easier time reading and understanding what you write if you check your work carefully to eliminate errors in the **capitalization, punctuation,** and **mechanics** of **titles.**

Incorrect	Correct
I love the scenes where Alicia and the dog struggle to survive on the island. I even wrote a poem about them called Team survival. I can't wait to read "The Labrador Returns!"	I love the scenes where Alicia and the dog struggle to survive on the island. I even wrote a poem about them called "Team Survival." I can't wait to read *The Labrador Returns!*

Engage and Apply

- Have students identify whether the title described should be in italics, underlining, or quotes.

  » *A book about a young boy's adventures* italics or underlining

  » *A short story in a book* quotation marks

  » *A magazine about travel* italics or underlining

  » *A song about a black horse* quotation marks

- Have students write titles without proper capitalization or styling, identifying each title's type. Have partners correct these titles.

- Have students complete **Printable: Grammar 6.2.5** for practice with writing titles.

- Tell students that as they revise, they should make their ideas clearer by checking their work carefully for proper mechanics, including the mechanics for writing titles.

EL ENGLISH LEARNER SUPPORT: Scaffolded Practice

ALL LEVELS Write the following titles on the board and ask students to work in mixed-proficiency groups to identify how they would type each one on a computer.

the raven (poem) "The Raven"

the star-spangled banner (song) "The Star-Spangled Banner"

old yeller (novel) Old Yeller

romeo and juliet (play) Romeo and Juliet

Then have students write the title of a favorite book, movie, song, and story using proper capitalization and mechanics.

PUNCTUATION IN COMPOUND AND COMPLEX SENTENCES

LEARNING OBJECTIVES

- Use commas and semicolons to separate and set off sentence elements.
- Use commas and semicolons correctly in writing.

MATERIALS	Online

Display and Engage *Grammar 7.1.1a, 7.1.1b*

Printable *Grammar 7.1.1*

 INSTRUCTIONAL VOCABULARY

- **semicolon** mark of punctuation used to link or separate parts of a sentence
- **comma** mark of punctuation used to separate elements in a sentence

Connect and Teach

- Show <u>Display and Engage: Grammar 7.1.1a</u>. Explain that, in a compound sentence, a **comma** is placed after the first independent clause and before the coordinating conjunction. In a complex sentence, the comma is placed between the independent and dependent clauses.

- Model how to decide where to place the comma in the example sentence: *Many sailors suffered from injuries and the captain worried about safety.*

  THINK ALOUD *To identify how to punctuate the sentence, I ask:* Is this a compound or complex sentence? Where is the independent clause? *This sentence has two independent clauses, so it is a compound sentence. I should place the comma after* injuries *and before* and.

- Explain that a **semicolon** joins two independent clauses that are related: *Some people take notes on tablets; others write in a paper notebook.* The two ideas are connected, so a comma wouldn't be enough to separate the ideas.

- Point out that semicolons are also used to separate clauses that use commas: *Some people only write on a computer; but others, for many reasons, prefer to write with a pen or pencil.*

Engage and Apply

- Complete items 1–8 on <u>Display and Engage: Grammar 7.1.1b</u> with students.

- Review dependent and independent clauses with students. Have them identify whether the clauses in each sentence are dependent or independent and how that determines where the comma or semicolon should be placed.

- Have students complete <u>Printable: Grammar 7.1.1</u> for practice with commas.

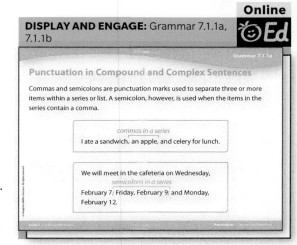

 ENGLISH LEARNER SUPPORT: Scaffolded Practice

SUBSTANTIAL

Write several sentences on the board that lack necessary commas. Read each aloud, pausing slightly where a comma should be placed. Have students take turns coming to the board to insert each comma.

MODERATE

On the board, write several sentences that contain commas. Guide students to identify each comma's function in the sentence.

LIGHT

Have students write two sentences about something they read this week that include commas or semicolons. Ask them to write their sentences on the board.

INTRODUCTORY ELEMENTS

LEARNING OBJECTIVES

- Use commas to separate and set off sentence elements.
- Use commas correctly in writing.

MATERIALS   Online ⓞ*Ed*

Display and Engage *Grammar 7.1.2a, 7.1.2b*

Printable *Grammar 7.1.2*

INSTRUCTIONAL VOCABULARY

- **comma** mark of punctuation used to separate elements in a sentence

Connect and Teach

- Show **Display and Engage: Grammar 7.1.2a**. Explain that commas set off introductory elements from the rest of the sentence. Tell students that these introductory elements might be words, for example, *yes* or *no*; phrases; or even clauses.

- Model how to identify and correctly punctuate introductory elements with this example: *On the first page, there was a list of important dates.*

  THINK ALOUD *To decide whether a comma is necessary, I ask:* Is there a word or group of words that introduces the sentence but is not part of the main sentence? *The phrase* On the first page *introduces the sentence. It should be set off by a comma.*

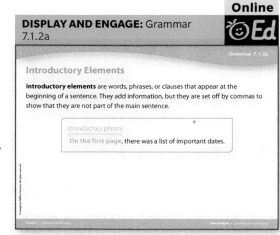

DISPLAY AND ENGAGE: Grammar 7.1.2a

Online ⓞ*Ed*

Grammar 7.1.2a

Introductory Elements

Introductory elements are words, phrases, or clauses that appear at the beginning of a sentence. They add information, but they are set off by commas to show that they are not part of the main sentence.

introductory phrase
On the first page, there was a list of important dates.

Engage and Apply

- Complete items 1–8 on **Display and Engage: Grammar 7.1.2b** with students.

- List common introductory words and phrases on the board. Have students take turns using each one in an original sentence. Write their sentences on the board and work together to punctuate them correctly.

- Have students complete **Printable: Grammar 7.1.2** for practice with commas.

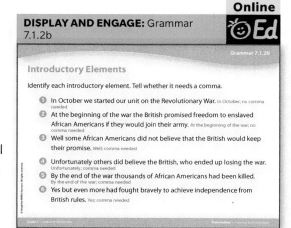

DISPLAY AND ENGAGE: Grammar 7.1.2b

Online ⓞ*Ed*

Grammar 7.1.2b

Introductory Elements

Identify each introductory element. Tell whether it needs a comma.

1. In October we started our unit on the Revolutionary War. In October; no comma needed
2. At the beginning of the war the British promised freedom to enslaved African Americans if they would join their army. At the beginning of the war; no comma needed
3. Well some African Americans did not believe that the British would keep their promise. Well; comma needed
4. Unfortunately others did believe the British, who ended up losing the war. Unfortunately; comma needed
5. By the end of the war thousands of African Americans had been killed. By the end of the war; comma needed
6. Yes but even more had fought bravely to achieve independence from British rules. Yes; comma needed

💬 ENGLISH LEARNER SUPPORT: Scaffolded Practice

SUBSTANTIAL

Write several sentences with introductory phrases (such as *On Tuesday* or *When I finish my homework*) on the board that lack necessary commas. Read each aloud, pausing slightly where a comma should be placed. Have students take turns coming to the board to insert each comma.

MODERATE

On the board, write several sentences with introductory elements followed by commas. Guide students to identify each comma's function in the sentence.

LIGHT

Have students write two sentences about something they read this week that include an introductory element followed by a comma. Ask them to write their sentences on the board.

LEARNING OBJECTIVES

- Use commas to separate and set off sentence elements.
- Use commas correctly in speaking and writing.

MATERIALS   Online 🍊Ed

Display and Engage *Grammar 7.1.3a, 7.1.3b*

Printable *Grammar 7.1.3*

INSTRUCTIONAL VOCABULARY

- **comma** mark of punctuation used to separate elements in a sentence

Connect and Teach

- Show **Display and Engage: Grammar 7.1.3a**. Explain that **commas** are used to set off names or nouns that indicate direct address, as well as short questions inserted at the end of sentences.

- Model how to identify and correctly punctuate direct address and tag questions with this example: *Leo, I enjoyed that history unit, didn't you?*

  THINK ALOUD *To identify where commas are necessary, I ask:* Is there a name in the sentence that shows that someone is being addressed? Is there a short question joined on to the end of a sentence? *In the example sentence, Leo is being spoken to. Therefore, his name should be set off by a comma. A short question is at the end of the sentence. That needs a comma, too.*

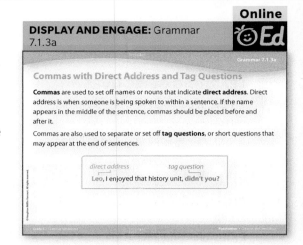

DISPLAY AND ENGAGE: Grammar 7.1.3a   Online 🍊Ed

Grammar 7.1.3a

Commas with Direct Address and Tag Questions

Commas are used to set off names or nouns that indicate **direct address**. Direct address is when someone is being spoken to within a sentence. If the name appears in the middle of the sentence, commas should be placed before and after it.

Commas are also used to separate or set off **tag questions**, or short questions that may appear at the end of sentences.

>   direct address   tag question
> Leo, I enjoyed that history unit, didn't you?

Engage and Apply

- Complete items 1–8 on **Display and Engage: Grammar 7.1.3b** with students.

- Say the following sentences to the class: *Please read page 10 aloud, Joe. Make sure you speak loudly, won't you?*

- Call on volunteers to write their sentences on the board.

- Have students complete **Printable: Grammar 7.1.3** for practice with commas.

- Have students edit a writing draft using the correct forms of direct address and tag questions.

DISPLAY AND ENGAGE: Grammar 7.1.3b   Online 🍊Ed

Grammar 7.1.3b

Commas with Direct Address and Tag Questions

Identify each direct address or tag question. Tell where the comma should go.

1. George Washington Carver was an amazing man wasn't he?
   George Washington Carver was an amazing man, wasn't he?
2. Sandra did you read the same book I did?
   Sandra, did you read the same book I did?
3. You have time to ask questions class before you take the test.
   You have time to ask questions, class, before you take the test.
4. I wondered if there were other African American inventors like George Washington Carver that we could read about Ms. Temple. I wondered if there were other African American inventors like George Washington Carver that we could read about, Ms. Temple.
5. I will give you a reading list at the end of class Jack.
   I will give you a reading list at the end of class, Jack.
6. That would be great wouldn't it?
   That would be great, wouldn't it?

🇪🇱 ENGLISH LEARNER SUPPORT: Facilitate Linguistic Connections

A tag question is a short question tagged on at the end of a sentence and set off by a comma. Cantonese, Khmer, Korean, and Vietnamese do not have exact equivalents of tag questions. Give students additional practice in recognizing and punctuating sentences with tag questions, providing examples, such as these: *You wanted another piece of cake, didn't you? It would be great to have a day off, wouldn't it?*

Scaffolded Practice

SUBSTANTIAL

Write several sentences with direct address and/or tag questions on the board that lack necessary commas. Read each aloud, pausing slightly where a comma should be placed. Have students take turns coming to the board to insert each comma.

MODERATE

On the board, write several sentences with direct address followed by commas or tag questions preceded by commas. Guide students to identify each comma's function in the sentence.

LIGHT

Have students write two sentences giving instructions to do something that include a direct address and a tag question. Ask them to write their sentences on the board.

LEARNING OBJECTIVES

- Review commas and semicolons.
- Use commas and semicolons correctly in speaking and writing.

MATERIALS	Online

Display and Engage *Grammar 7.1.4a, 7.1.4b*

Printable *Grammar 7.1.4*

 INSTRUCTIONAL VOCABULARY

- **semicolon** mark of punctuation used to link or separate parts of a sentence
- **comma** mark of punctuation used to separate elements in a sentence

Review Commas and Semicolons

- Show **Display and Engage: Grammar 7.1.4a**.
- Review the placement of commas in sentences with students. Have students read the example sentences and discuss the function of the comma in each sentence.
- Display example of sentences using semicolons and discuss why semicolons are needed.

    » *Dogs are very popular pets; cats come in a close second in popularity.* A semicolon links two independent clauses that are closely related.

    » *Ray watches basketball and soccer; Ray's brother, who studied karate for years, thinks basketball and soccer are too fast-paced.* A semicolon separates the clauses with commas, keeping the writing clear.

- Work with students to complete the exercises on **Display and Engage: Grammar 7.1.4b**.
- Have students complete **Printable: Grammar 7.1.4**.
- Have students edit a writing draft using commas and semicolons correctly.

DISPLAY AND ENGAGE: Grammar 7.1.4a and 7.1.4b

Online

Review Commas and Semicolons

Both **commas** (,) and **semicolons** (;) are punctuation marks used within sentences. They help readers understand the meaning of a sentence by clearly separating different parts.

Separate items in a series or list: We need eggs, milk, and bread.

Set off introductory words and phrases: By 1871, the war was almost over.

Indicate a name used in direct address: Maria, can you imagine being on a ship in the middle of a battle?

Set off a tag question at the end of a sentence: That was an important battle, wasn't it?

Separate items in a series or list with commas: We need eggs, milk, and bread; we also need soap, shampoo, and lotion.

EL **ENGLISH LEARNER SUPPORT: Scaffolded Practice**

SUBSTANTIAL
Have students find a passage in a book and look at any commas in the passage. Discuss the placement of the commas and their function in each sentence.

MODERATE
Have students find a passage in a book and look for commas. Guide students to identify each comma's function in the sentence.

LIGHT
Have students write a paragraph about something they did at school this week. Have partners exchange papers to check that commas are used correctly.

PUNCTUATION • COMMAS AND SEMICOLONS

LEARNING OBJECTIVES

- Use commas to separate and set off sentence elements.
- Use commas correctly in writing.

MATERIALS   Online

Display and Engage *Grammar 7.1.5*

Printable *Grammar 7.1.5*

 INSTRUCTIONAL VOCABULARY

- **semicolon** mark of punctuation used to link or separate parts of a sentence
- **comma** mark of punctuation used to separate elements in a sentence

Connect and Teach

- Show **Display and Engage: Grammar 7.1.5**. Explain that a good writer uses commas and semicolons to make his or her meaning clear to readers.

- Point out that an important part of revising is to check your writing carefully to be sure that commas and semicolons are placed correctly.

Engage and Apply

- Display the following sentences. Work with students to punctuate the first sentence correctly. Then have them work with a partner to correct the last two sentences.

  » *Well Captain Smith we have furled the sails dropped the anchor and prepared the lifeboats.* Well, Captain Smith, we have furled the sails, dropped the anchor, and prepared the lifeboats.

  » *Life on board ship during the Revolutionary War would have been difficult wouldn't it?* Life on board ship during the Revolutionary War would have been difficult, wouldn't it?

  » *Yes give me a modern-day cruise ship going to Venice Italy Miami Florida or Bar Harbor Maine instead!* Yes, give me a modern-day cruise ship going to Venice, Italy; Miami, Florida; or Bar Harbor, Maine instead!

- Have students complete **Printable: Grammar 7.1.5** for practice with commas.

- Tell students that as they revise their work, they should look for places to use commas to separate elements in their sentences.

 ENGLISH LEARNER SUPPORT: Scaffolded Practice

SUBSTANTIAL

Review that commas and semicolons indicate a pause in a sentence. Explain that they separate ideas that are connected. Share simple ideas in a list and model how to use commas and semicolons to connect them.

MODERATE

Review that writers use commas and semicolons to make their writing clear.

- Write: James carried gunpowder, water, and other supplies. Point out that the commas separate items in a series. Say: *If the items in the series already contain commas, then use semicolons.*
- Tell students that commas also separate introductory elements from the rest of the sentence, as in: *Yes, he certainly improved.* Add that commas set off short tag questions, as in: *They were right, weren't they?*

LIGHT

Write these sentences on the board. Have partners punctuate them correctly.

- *I want to take notes make a timeline and study the text before the test.*
- *Pass me the pen Bella.*
- *He was very young to be in the war wasn't he?*

LEARNING OBJECTIVES

- Use commas with introductory words and phrases, names, and in a series.
- Use introductory words correctly in speaking and writing.

MATERIALS   Online 🍊 *Ed*

Display and Engage *Grammar 7.2.1a, 7.2.1b*

Printable *Grammar 7.2.1*

INSTRUCTIONAL VOCABULARY

- **comma** a punctuation mark used to show a pause or separation of ideas within a sentence
- **introductory word/phrase** a word or phrase preceding the comma in a sentence

Connect and Teach

- Show **Display and Engage: Grammar 7.2.1a**. Explain that a **comma** follows an **introductory word or phrase**.

- Model: *After cleaning and labeling, fossils can be used to answer many questions.*

  THINK ALOUD *To decide if a comma is needed in a sentence, I ask:* Is there a word or phrase that begins the sentence? Is there a place in the sentence where I would naturally pause? *I pause after the phrase* After cleaning and labeling, *so a comma is needed.*

Engage and Apply

- Complete items 1–8 on **Display and Engage: Grammar 7.2.1b** with students.

- Work with students to identify where the comma should go. Point out that the comma is placed after an introductory phrase.

- Have students complete **Printable: Grammar 7.2.1** for practice with commas.

- Have students edit a writing draft using the correct introductory punctuation.

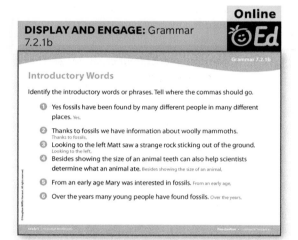

ENGLISH LEARNER SUPPORT: Scaffolded Practice

SUBSTANTIAL

Display and read the sentence. Have students point to the place where the comma belongs. *Yes I do want a sandwich.* Then have students write the sentence, placing it where it belongs.

MODERATE

Ask students a question. Guide them to write an answer using an introductory phrase.

LIGHT

Have students write an answer to a question using an introductory word or phrase.

LEARNING OBJECTIVES

- Use commas with names.
- Use commas with names correctly in writing.

MATERIALS   Online

Display and Engage *Grammar 7.2.2a, 7.2.2b*

Printable *Grammar 7.2.2*

Connect and Teach

- Show <u>Display and Engage: Grammar 7.2.2a</u>. Explain how commas are used to set apart a name.

- Model this sentence: *That's amazing, Mrs. Parker, that even kids have found fossils.*

    THINK ALOUD *To tell if a comma is needed with names, I ask: Is the person who is being spoken to addressed by name in the sentence? Where in the sentence do I naturally pause? Mrs. Parker is addressed, so a comma is needed before and after her name.*

- Point out that some abbreviations and acronyms are proper nouns, so they are capitalized and treated like names in an introductory phrase. Give examples: *I've had the symptoms, Dr. Scott, for two weeks. The White House's residents, POTUS and FLOTUS, are moving in.*

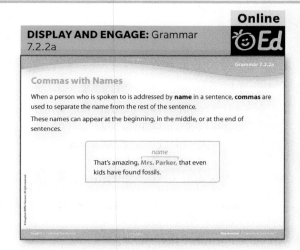

DISPLAY AND ENGAGE: Grammar 7.2.2a   Online **Ed**

Commas with Names

When a person who is spoken to is addressed by **name** in a sentence, **commas** are used to separate the name from the rest of the sentence.

These names can appear at the beginning, in the middle, or at the end of sentences.

name
That's amazing, Mrs. Parker, that even kids have found fossils.

Engage and Apply

- Complete items 1–8 on <u>Display and Engage: Grammar 7.2.2b</u> with students.

- Remind students that commas should go after a person's name. Have students choose where to place the commas in each sentence.

- Have students complete <u>Printable: Grammar 7.2.2</u> for practice with commas.

- Have students edit a writing draft using commas with names correctly.

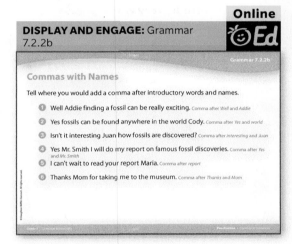

DISPLAY AND ENGAGE: Grammar 7.2.2b   Online **Ed**

Commas with Names

Tell where you would add a comma after introductory words and names.

1. Well Addie finding a fossil can be really exciting. *Comma after Well and Addie*
2. Yes fossils can be found anywhere in the world Cody. *Comma after Yes and world*
3. Isn't it interesting Juan how fossils are discovered? *Comma after interesting and Juan*
4. Yes Mr. Smith I will do my report on famous fossil discoveries. *Comma after Yes and Mr. Smith*
5. I can't wait to read your report Maria. *Comma after report*
6. Thanks Mom for taking me to the museum. *Comma after Thanks and Mom*

 ENGLISH LEARNER SUPPORT: Scaffolded Practice

SUBSTANTIAL
Display and read the sentence. Have students point to the place where the comma belongs. *Will we stop for lunch Mrs. Lopez.* Then have students write the sentence, placing the comma where it belongs.

MODERATE
Guide students to write a sentence about something they would like to do, addressing a partner or classmate.

LIGHT
Have students write a sentence telling someone in the class something they would like to do.

LEARNING OBJECTIVES

- Use commas with introductory words and phrases, names, and in a series.
- Use commas correctly in writing.

MATERIALS	Online

Display and Engage *Grammar 7.2.3a, 7.2.3b*

Printable *Grammar 7.2.3*

 **INSTRUCTIONAL VOCABULARY**

- **comma** a punctuation mark used to show a pause or separation of ideas within a sentence
- **introductory word/phrase** a word or phrase preceding the comma in a sentence

Connect and Teach

- Show **Display and Engage: Grammar 7.2.3a**. Review where to add **commas** after **introductory words and phrases** and when people are addressed directly in a sentence.

- Tell students that commas should also be used to separate **nouns in a series**.
  THINK ALOUD *When deciding if I should use a comma, I ask:* Are there three or more nouns in a list? *If there are, I need to separate them with commas.*

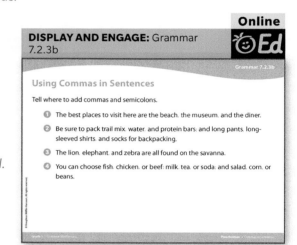

Engage and Apply

- Complete items 1–8 on **Display and Engage: Grammar 7.2.3b** with students.

- Write the following sentence on the board: *Within two days Heather he will know what he wants to do with the fossil.*

- Work with students to identify where commas belong in the sentence.

- Have students complete **Printable: Grammar 7.2.3** for practice with commas.

- Have students edit a writing draft using commas with names correctly.

EL ENGLISH LEARNER SUPPORT: Scaffolded Practice

SUBSTANTIAL

Display and read the sentence. Have students point to the place where the commas belong. *I would like turkey cheese and tomatoes on my sandwich.* Then have students write the sentence, placing the commas where they belong.

MODERATE

Guide students to write a sentence listing ingredients for something they like to make.

LIGHT

Have students write a sentence telling someone how to make something. Remind them to use commas if more than two nouns are used in a series.

PUNCTUATION • COMMAS IN SENTENCES

LEARNING OBJECTIVES

- Review commas with introductory words and phrases, names, and in a series.
- Use commas correctly in writing.

MATERIALS	Online

Display and Engage *Grammar 7.2.4a, 7.2.4b*

Printable *Grammar 7.2.4*

 **INSTRUCTIONAL VOCABULARY**

- **comma** a punctuation mark used to show a pause or separation of ideas within a sentence
- **introductory word/phrase** a word or phrase preceding the comma in a sentence

Review Commas in Sentences

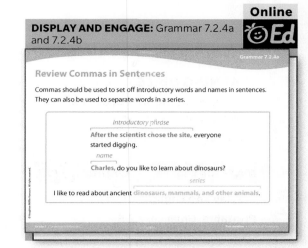

DISPLAY AND ENGAGE: Grammar 7.2.4a and 7.2.4b

- Show **Display and Engage: Grammar 7.2.4a**. Review the placement of commas in sentences with students. Have students read the example sentences and discuss the function of the comma in each sentence.

- Display sentences without commas and ask students to help you place them. Once the commas are placed, discuss the purpose of each comma.

  » *The director of the sports team, Coach Chen, visited with young players today.* name

  » *When we go to the movies, we always get popcorn.* introductory words
  My favorite physician, Dr. Abby, is retiring this year. name

- Review that abbreviations and acronyms can be proper nouns. Remind students to capitalize them and use commas as in other sentences with names.

- Work with students to complete the exercises on **Display and Engage: Grammar 7.2.4b**.

- Have students complete **Printable: Grammar 7.2.4**.

EL **ENGLISH LEARNER SUPPORT: Scaffolded Practice**

SUBSTANTIAL
Have students review a piece of their own writing and identify places where commas should go.

MODERATE
Have students review a piece of their own writing and identify places where commas should go. Guide students to rewrite the sentences, placing commas in the correct places.

LIGHT
Have students review the sentences they wrote this week. Have them exchange with partners and tell whether they each used commas correctly.

LEARNING OBJECTIVES

- Use commas with introductory words and phrases, names, and in a series.
- Use commas correctly in writing.

MATERIALS	Online

Display and Engage *Grammar 7.2.5*

Printable *Grammar 7.2.5*

 INSTRUCTIONAL VOCABULARY

- **comma** a punctuation mark used to show a pause or separation of ideas within a sentence
- **introductory word/phrase** a word or phrase preceding the comma in a sentence

Connect and Teach

- Show **Display and Engage: Grammar 7.2.5**. Remind students that sentences can be combined using introductory phrases. Sometimes the wording needs to change. Discuss the examples below.

- *Mary uses a small brush. The brush cleans her fossils.*
  Using a small brush, Mary cleans her fossils.

DISPLAY AND ENGAGE: Grammar 7.2.5

Connect to Writing: Using Commas in Sentences

When you edit, look for sentences that may be missing commas. Remember to include commas to set off introductory words, names, and words in a series.

> Yes, friends, the Tyrannosaurus Rex was a fearsome beast. He had huge teeth, a powerful tail, and strong legs.

- Point out that the second example is clearer and smoother.

Engage and Apply

- Have students write a short paragraph about a fossil they would like to find. Remind them to use commas.

- Have students complete **Printable: Grammar 7.2.5** for practice with commas.

- Tell students that as they revise their work, they should look for places to use commas to separate elements in their sentences

EL **ENGLISH LEARNER SUPPORT: Scaffolded Practice**

SUBSTANTIAL/MODERATE

Review that writers use commas to make their writing clear.

- Write: *James carried gunpowder, water, and other supplies.* Point out that the commas separate items in a series.
- Tell students that commas also separate introductory words and phrases from the rest of the sentence, as in: *Yes, that is better.* Add that commas set off names, as in: *Would you like some, Mary?*

LIGHT

Write these sentences on the board. Have partners punctuate them correctly.

- *I need lettuce tomatoes and carrots for a salad.*
- *Can I have the salt Lisa.*
- *Before we get started I want to say a few words.*

LEARNING OBJECTIVES

- Use commas with appositives in sentences.
- Use appositives correctly in speaking and writing.

MATERIALS
Online Ed

Display and Engage *Grammar 7.3.1a, 7.3.1b*

Printable *Grammar 7.3.1*

 INSTRUCTIONAL VOCABULARY

- **appositive** a noun, noun phrase, or series of nouns placed next to another word or phrase to identify or rename it, set off by commas

Connect and Teach

- Show **Display and Engage: Grammar 7.3.1a**. Explain that commas are used to set off an **appositive**.

- Model using the sentence, *The buck, an adult male deer, had beautiful antlers.*

  THINK ALOUD *To decide when to use commas in a sentence, I ask: Is there a phrase that follows a noun? Does the phrase identify or explain the noun? An adult male deer identifies the subject. I set it off in commas in the sentence.*

Engage and Apply

- Complete items 1–8 on Display and **Engage: Grammar 7.3.1b** with students.

- Work with students to set off appositives with commas.

- Have students complete **Printable: Grammar 7.3.1** for practice with commas.

- Have students edit a writing draft using appositives correctly.

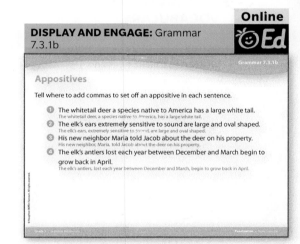

DISPLAY AND ENGAGE: Grammar 7.3.1a — Online Ed

DISPLAY AND ENGAGE: Grammar 7.3.1b — Online Ed

 ENGLISH LEARNER SUPPORT: Scaffolded Practice

SUBSTANTIAL
Have students copy this sentence, adding commas in a series: *I like red blue and pink.* Read the sentence together. Then explain that appositives tell more about the noun in a sentence. Display this sentence: *The insect, a green grasshopper, jumped across the sidewalk.* Guide students to understand that *a green grasshopper* identifies *The insect* and that commas separate the noun and appositive.

MODERATE
Have partners write a sentence about three foods. Invite partners to add commas for the series of nouns. Then display a sentence with an appositive and work together to add commas in the correct places. For example: *My brother, the youngest sibling in my family, is always late to dinner.*

LIGHT
Have partners write sentences using words in a series and sentences with appositives. Invite volunteers to share their sentences.

PUNCTUATION • MORE COMMAS

LEARNING OBJECTIVES
- Use commas in sentences.
- Use commas correctly in writing.

MATERIALS Online

Display and Engage *Grammar 7.3.2a, 7.3.2b*

Printable *Grammar 7.3.2*

 INSTRUCTIONAL VOCABULARY

- **series** a list of three or more items written in the same form

Connect and Teach

- Show **Display and Engage: Grammar 7.3.2a**. Explain other uses for commas. Have students read the chart. Explain that commas are used in a **series** of items.

- Model inserting the commas in the sample sentence on the projectable after *plants, moss, and leaves.*

  THINK ALOUD *To decide where to add commas in the sentence, I ask:* Are there three or more items in a series? *There are four items in a series. A comma should be placed after each item except the last one.*

- Review that commas are also used in dates, places, and interjections. Display these examples and discuss the comma placement.
  I was born on Wednesday, December 17.
  I live in Phoenix, Arizona.
  Wow, it is really hot in Arizona!

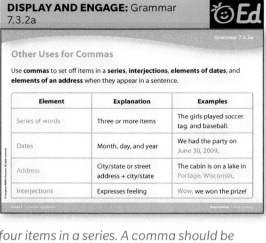

DISPLAY AND ENGAGE: Grammar 7.3.2a

Online Ed

Other Uses for Commas

Use **commas** to set off items in a **series, interjections, elements of dates,** and **elements of an address** when they appear in a sentence.

Element	Explanation	Examples
Series of words	Three or more items	The girls played soccer, tag, and baseball.
Dates	Month, day, and year	We had the party on June 30, 2009.
Address	City/state or street address + city/state	The cabin is on a lake in Portage, Wisconsin.
Interjections	Expresses feeling	Wow, we won the prize!

Engage and Apply

- Complete items 1–8 on **Display and Engage: Grammar 7.3.2b** with students.

- Work with students to add commas to the correct place in each sentence.

- Have students complete **Printable: Grammar 7.3.2** for practice with commas.

- Have students edit a writing draft using the correct form of commas in a series.

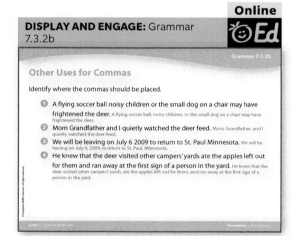

DISPLAY AND ENGAGE: Grammar 7.3.2b

Online Ed

Other Uses for Commas

Identify where the commas should be placed.

1. A flying soccer ball noisy children or the small dog on a chair may have frightened the deer. A flying soccer ball, noisy children, or the small dog on a chair may have frightened the deer.
2. Mom Grandfather and I quietly watched the deer feed. Mom, Grandfather, and I quietly watched the deer feed.
3. We will be leaving on July 6 2009 to return to St. Paul Minnesota. We will be leaving on July 6, 2009, to return to St. Paul, Minnesota.
4. He knew that the deer visited other campers' yards ate the apples left out for them and ran away at the first sign of a person in the yard. He knew that the deer visited other campers' yards, ate the apples left out for them, and ran away at the first sign of a person in the yard.

 ENGLISH LEARNER SUPPORT: Scaffolded Practice

SUBSTANTIAL
Have students copy this sentence, adding commas: *The event will take place on September 9 2019 in Chicago Illinois.* Read the sentence together.

MODERATE
Have partners write a sentence about a place they will visit. Remind them to use commas to separate words in a series, dates, and addresses.

LIGHT
Have partners write sentences using dates and addresses.

LEARNING OBJECTIVES
- Use commas in sentences.
- Use commas in sentences correctly in writing.

MATERIALS   Online

Display and Engage *Grammar 7.3.3a, 7.3.3b*

Printable *Grammar 7.3.3*

INSTRUCTIONAL VOCABULARY

- **appositive** a noun, noun phrase, or series of nouns placed next to another word or phrase to identify or rename it, set off by commas
- **series** a list of three or more items written in the same form

Connect and Teach

- Show **Display and Engage: Grammar 7.3.3a**. Review with students how to use **commas** correctly in sentences with **appositives**, items in **series**, dates, interjections, and with city and state information.

- Explain that commas should be used to separate two adjectives modifying the same noun and before a direct quotation.

  THINK ALOUD *When I think about whether a sentence needs a comma, I ask: Does the sentence include a series of items? Does it have a date, or name of a city or state? These are the places that commas should be used.*

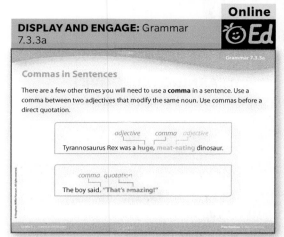
Engage and Apply

- Complete items 1–8 on **Display and Engage: Grammar 7.3.3b** with students.

- Write this sentence on the board: *Wow Maria Todd and Nicholas first met Ernest Blake the scientist on July 1 2008.*

- Work with students to identify where commas are needed. *Is there a phrase that follows a noun? Does it identify or explain the noun?* Commas should set off the phrase *the scientist*; use commas after *Wow, Maria, Todd, Blake,* and *July 1.*

- Have students complete **Printable: Grammar 7.3.3** for practice with commas.

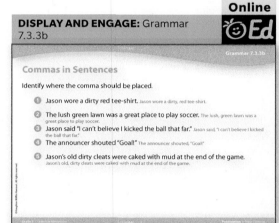
ENGLISH LEARNER SUPPORT: Scaffolded Practice

SUBSTANTIAL
Have students copy this sentence, adding commas: *The shiny new bicycle will be delivered on January 10 2019.* Read the sentence together.

MODERATE
Display sentences that require commas for series, dates, places, appositives, and interjections. Have small groups work together to place commas. Discuss the commas as a group.

LIGHT
Have students write three sentences that use commas in different ways. Have partners trade sentences and discuss the reason the commas are needed.

PUNCTUATION • MORE COMMAS

LEARNING OBJECTIVES
- Review how to use commas in sentences.
- Use commas correctly in writing.

MATERIALS   Online

Display and Engage *Grammar 7.3.4a, 7.3.4b*

Printable *Grammar 7.3.4*

Review Commas

- Show **Display and Engage: Grammar 7.3.4a**.

- Review the placement of commas in sentences with students. Have students read the example sentences and discuss the function of the comma in each sentence.

- Make a list of some of the ways commas are used in sentences:
  Appositives
  Series of Nouns
  Interjections
  Dates
  Places
  Work together to write sentences for each category, inviting volunteers to explain the placement of the commas. Remind students that commas indicate a pause in a sentence and also separate information so a sentence is easier to understand.

- Work with students to complete the exercises on **Display and Engage: Grammar 7.3.4b**.

- Have students complete **Printable: Grammar 7.3.4**.

- Have students edit a writing draft using commas correctly with appositives, series, dates, and places.

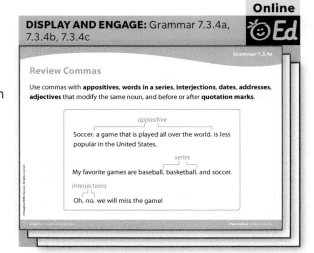

DISPLAY AND ENGAGE: Grammar 7.3.4a, 7.3.4b, 7.3.4c

Online Ed

Grammar 7.3.4a

Review Commas

Use commas with **appositives**, **words in a series**, **interjections**, **dates**, **addresses**, **adjectives** that modify the same noun, and before or after **quotation marks**.

appositive
Soccer, a game that is played all over the world, is less popular in the United States.

series
My favorite games are baseball, basketball, and soccer.

interjections
Oh, no, we will miss the game!

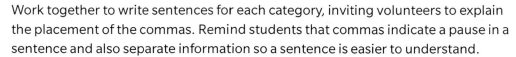

ENGLISH LEARNER SUPPORT: Scaffolded Practice

SUBSTANTIAL
Have students copy this sentence, adding commas: *The new bicycle a red model 9TX is available from the shop.* Read the sentence together.

MODERATE
Have partners write a sentence about something they did this week. Remind them to use commas to separate elements in the sentence.

LIGHT
Have students write two sentences about something they would like to buy. Have partners exchange papers to check that each used commas correctly.

PUNCTUATION • MORE COMMAS

LEARNING OBJECTIVES
• Use commas in a series when writing.
• Use commas correctly when writing.

MATERIALS   Online Ed

Display and Engage *Grammar 7.3.5*
Printable *Grammar 7.3.5*

 INSTRUCTIONAL VOCABULARY

• **series** a list of three or more items written in the same form

Connect and Teach

• Show **Display and Engage: Grammar 7.3.5**. Remind students that sentences that share a subject can be combined to make a **series**. Discuss the examples below.
  The wild deer watched the humans fearfully. They raised their tails in alarm. Then they fled.
  The wild deer watched the humans fearfully, raised their tails in alarm, and then fled.

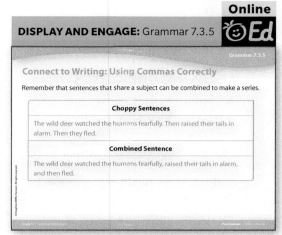

DISPLAY AND ENGAGE: Grammar 7.3.5

Connect to Writing: Using Commas Correctly

Remember that sentences that share a subject can be combined to make a series.

Choppy Sentences
The wild deer watched the humans fearfully. Then raised their tails in alarm. Then they fled.

Combined Sentence
The wild deer watched the humans fearfully, raised their tails in alarm, and then fled.

• Point out that the second example is clearer and smoother. Discuss how the commas separate the information and allow the reader to pause.

Engage and Apply

• Have partners work together to write a sentence combining three short, choppy sentences in a series.

• Have students complete **Printable: Grammar 7.3.5** for practice with commas.

• Tell students that as they revise their work, they should look for places to add commas to separate elements in their sentences.

EL **ENGLISH LEARNER SUPPORT: Scaffolded Practice**

SUBSTANTIAL
Review that writers use commas to make their writing clear.
• Write: *James, the coach, carried water for the players.* Point out that the commas separate the appositive in the sentence.
• Tell students that commas are also used in dates and addresses. *The first professional basketball game was held on November 1, 1946, in Toronto, Ontario, Canada.*

MODERATE
Write these sentences on the board. Have partners punctuate them correctly.
• *She was born on October 1 1954.*
• *I'd like to visit Los Angeles California.*
• *The New York Knicks my favorite team have a game next week.*

LIGHT
Have partners write two sentences each that are missing commas. Have them exchange papers and correctly punctuate each other's sentences.

PUNCTUATION · OTHER PUNCTUATION

LEARNING OBJECTIVES
- Identify and use colons.
- Use colons correctly in writing.

MATERIALS	Online

Display and Engage *Grammar 7.4.1a, 7.4.1b*

Printable *Grammar 7.4.1*

 INSTRUCTIONAL VOCABULARY

- **colon** a punctuation mark (:) that introduces a list, separates hours and minutes, or follows the greeting in a business letter

Connect and Teach

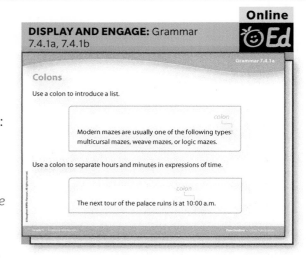

DISPLAY AND ENGAGE: Grammar 7.4.1a, 7.4.1b — Online

- Show **Display and Engage: Grammar 7.4.1a**. Explain a **colon** and its uses.

- Model using a colon in this sentence: *Modern mazes are usually one of the following types: multicursal mazes, weave mazes, or logic mazes.*

  THINK ALOUD *To decide when to use colons, I ask: Does the sentence include a list, hours and minutes, or the greeting in a business letter? If it includes a list, is the list formally introduced? This will help me realize when to use a colon.*

Engage and Apply

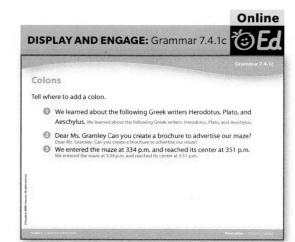

DISPLAY AND ENGAGE: Grammar 7.4.1c — Online

- Complete items 1–8 on **Display and Engage: Grammar 7.4.1b** with students.

- Work with students to place colons in the correct place in each sentence.

- Have students complete **Printable: Grammar 7.4.1** for practice with colons.

- Have students edit a writing draft using colons correctly.

EL **ENGLISH LEARNER SUPPORT: Scaffolded Practice**

SUBSTANTIAL
Say *colon* while modeling correct colon placement by adding the mark to a sample sentence. Use gestures or visuals to clarify sentence meaning. Then say this sentence aloud and have students write it, placing the colon correctly: *She had a meeting at 2:00 p.m.*

MODERATE
Repeat the above. Then have partners write additional sentences using colons.

LIGHT
Have students write sentences using colons and parentheses.

**LESSON
7.4.2**

PARENTHESES

LEARNING OBJECTIVES

• Identify and use parentheses.

• Use parentheses correctly in writing.

MATERIALS	Online ⊙*Ed*

Display and Engage *Grammar 7.4.2a, 7.4.2b*

Printable *Grammar 7.4.2*

INSTRUCTIONAL VOCABULARY

• **parentheses** punctuation marks that come before and after a word or phrase that is inserted into a sentence but is not essential to the meaning of the sentence

• **hyphen** punctuation mark used to connect words or parts of words

• **dash** punctuation mark used to show new or additional ideas in a sentence

Connect and Teach

• Show **Display and Engage: Grammar 7.4.2a**. Explain that **parentheses** set off information.

• Model using this sentence: *The encyclopedia (Volume 11) has information about mazes.*

  THINK ALOUD *To decide if I need to use parentheses in a sentence, I ask: Is the information that interrupts the sentence of major importance to the meaning of the sentence?*

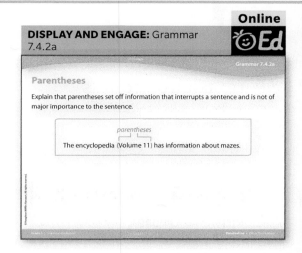

DISPLAY AND ENGAGE: Grammar 7.4.2a

Online ⊙*Ed*

Grammar 7.4.2a

Parentheses

Explain that parentheses set off information that interrupts a sentence and is not of major importance to the sentence.

parentheses

The encyclopedia (Volume 11) has information about mazes.

• Explain that **hyphens** connect words and word parts, such as *My ten-year-old sister is a math whiz!* Explain that a **dash** looks like a long hyphen, but it separates ideas.
  We could not figure out when—or where—to go to dinner.
  Liz might come to the party—you never know!

Engage and Apply

• Complete items 1–8 on **Display and Engage: Grammar 7.4.2b** with students.

• Work with students to place parentheses in the correct place in each sentence.

• Display some examples of sentences that need dashes and have students tell you where to place them.

• Have students complete **Printable: Grammar 7.4.2** for practice with parentheses.

• Have students edit a writing draft using parentheses correctly.

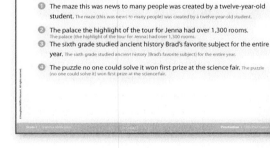

DISPLAY AND ENGAGE: Grammar 7.4.2b

Online ⊙*Ed*

Grammar 7.4.2b

Parentheses

Tell where to add parentheses.

1. The maze this was news to many people was created by a twelve-year-old student. The maze (this was news to many people) was created by a twelve-year-old student.
2. The palace the highlight of the tour for Jenna had over 1,300 rooms. The palace (the highlight of the tour for Jenna) had over 1,300 rooms.
3. The sixth grade studied ancient history Brad's favorite subject for the entire year. The sixth grade studied ancient history (Brad's favorite subject) for the entire year.
4. The puzzle no one could solve it won first prize at the science fair. The puzzle (no one could solve it) won first prize at the science fair.

ⓔ ENGLISH LEARNER SUPPORT: Scaffolded Practice

SUBSTANTIAL

Say *parentheses* while modeling correct parentheses placement by adding the marks to a sample sentence. Use gestures or visuals to clarify sentence meaning.

Then say this sentence aloud and have students write it, placing the parentheses correctly: *The dog (a German shepherd) rarely barked.*

MODERATE

Repeat the above. Then have partners write additional sentences using parentheses.

LIGHT

Have students write sentences using parentheses.

PUNCTUATION • OTHER PUNCTUATION

LEARNING OBJECTIVES

- Identify colons and parentheses in sentences.
- Use colons and parentheses correctly in writing.

MATERIALS	Online

Display and Engage *Grammar 7.4.3a, 7.4.3b*

Printable *Grammar 7.4.3*

 INSTRUCTIONAL VOCABULARY

- **colon** a punctuation mark (:) that introduces a list, separates hours and minutes, or follows the greeting in a business letter
- **hyphen** punctuation mark used to connect words or parts of words
- **dash** punctuation mark used to show new or additional ideas in a sentence
- **parentheses** punctuation marks that come before and after a word or phrase that is inserted into a sentence but is not essential to the meaning of the sentence

Connect and Teach

- Show **Display and Engage: Grammar 7.4.3a**. Review **colons** and **parentheses**. Then explain that hyphens are sometimes used to connect compound adjectives.

  THINK ALOUD *To decide what kind of punctuation to use in a sentence, I ask: Does the sentence include a list, hours, minutes, or a greeting? If so, I use a colon.* Does the sentence include information that should be set off from the rest of the sentence? *If so, I use parentheses.*

- Explain that hyphens are used to connect words, such as compound adjectives and numbers. Display examples: *well-groomed dog; forty-nine.*

- Share that hyphens are also used to separate words at the end of a line. Explain that words are separated by syllables. Display examples in books and magazines of words that are separated by a hyphen as a line continues. Point out the syllables and how the word was divided by the hyphen.

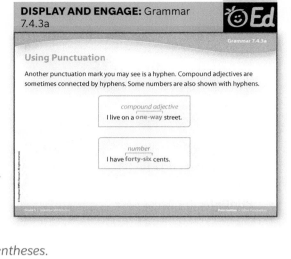

Online Ed

DISPLAY AND ENGAGE: Grammar 7.4.3a

Grammar 7.4.3a

Using Punctuation

Another punctuation mark you may see is a hyphen. Compound adjectives are sometimes connected by hyphens. Some numbers are also shown with hyphens.

compound adjective
I live on a **one-way** street.

number
I have **forty-six** cents.

Engage and Apply

- Complete items 1–8 on **Display and Engage: Grammar 7.4.3b** with students.

- Display this sentence: *Ancient Egyptians (my favorite history topic) built the following: pyramids, temples, and statues.*

- Work with students to explain why the punctuation is needed. *A colon is needed to set off a list formally introduced by the following. My favorite history topic is not essential to the meaning of the sentence; it is extra information.*

- Have pairs search for examples of hyphens in magazines and the week's reading. Have students discuss the reason for the hyphen.

- Have students complete **Printable: Grammar 7.4.3** for practice with colons.

- Have students edit a writing draft using punctuation correctly.

Online Ed

DISPLAY AND ENGAGE: Grammar 7.4.3b

Grammar 7.4.3b

Using Punctuation

Identify where punctuation may be missing and suggest which punctuation to add.

1. Forty two books were overdue this week. Forty-two books were overdue this week.
2. The well known author is signing books at the library. The well-known author is signing books at the library.
3. The librarian saw that twenty five people signed up to volunteer. The librarian saw that twenty-five people signed up to volunteer.
4. I checked out a book about man eating alligators. I checked out a book about man-eating alligators.

 ENGLISH LEARNER SUPPORT: Scaffolded Practice

SUBSTANTIAL
Say *hyphen* while modeling correct hyphen placement by adding the mark to a sample sentence. Use gestures or visuals to clarify sentence meaning. Then say this sentence aloud and have students write it, placing the hyphen correctly: *The play was a one-woman show.*

MODERATE
Repeat the above. Then have partners write additional sentences using a compound adjective.

LIGHT
Have students write sentences using hyphenated compound adjectives.

PUNCTUATION • OTHER PUNCTUATION

LEARNING OBJECTIVES

- Identify and use colons and parentheses in sentences.
- Use punctuation correctly in writing.

MATERIALS   Online

Display and Engage *Grammar 7.4.4a, 7.4.4b*

Printable *Grammar 7.4.4*

 INSTRUCTIONAL VOCABULARY

- **colon** a punctuation mark (:) that introduces a list, separates hours and minutes, or follows the greeting in a business letter
- **hyphen** punctuation mark used to connect words or parts of words
- **dash** punctuation mark used to show new or additional ideas in a sentence
- **parentheses** punctuation marks that come before and after a word or phrase that is inserted into a sentence but is not essential to the meaning of the sentence

Review Punctuation

- Show **Display and Engage: Grammar 7.4.4a**. Review the placement of **colons**, **parentheses**, and **hyphens/dashes** in sentences. Have students read the example sentences and discuss the function of the punctuation mark in each sentence.

- Have pairs search classroom books for example of colons, parentheses, hyphens, and dashes. Ask pairs to copy the examples and discuss how each punctuation mark makes the sentences clearer.

- Work with students to complete the exercises on **Display and Engage: Grammar 7.4.4b**.

- Have students complete **Printable: Grammar 7.4.4**.

- Have students edit a writing draft using punctuation correctly.

DISPLAY AND ENGAGE: Grammar 7.4.4a, 7.4.4b, 7.4.4c

Online

Grammar 7.4.4a

Review Punctuation

Colons can introduce a list, separate hours and minutes in expressions of time, and be included after a greeting in a business letter.

colon

Soccer practice starts at 4:00 p.m. sharp.

colon

Bring all necessary equipment: cleats, knee pads, and practice uniform.

(EL) **ENGLISH LEARNER SUPPORT: Scaffolded Practice**

SUBSTANTIAL

Read a sentence aloud, and then write it on the board as students suggest punctuation for it.
The possible topics for the research paper (on a history topic) are: ancient Rome, the American Revolution, or the history of China.

MODERATE

Repeat the above. Then have partners write additional sentences using colons and parentheses.

LIGHT

Have students write two sentences using parentheses and/or colons.

PUNCTUATION • OTHER PUNCTUATION

LEARNING OBJECTIVES

- Use puncuation marks in writing.
- Use the correct punctuation when writing.

MATERIALS	Online

Display and Engage *Grammar 7.4.5*

Printable *Grammar 7.4.5*

INSTRUCTIONAL VOCABULARY

- **colon** a punctuation mark (:) that introduces a list, separates hours and minutes, or follows the greeting in a business letter
- **hyphen** punctuation mark used to connect words or parts of words
- **dash** punctuation mark used to show new or additional ideas in a sentence
- **parentheses** punctuation marks that come before and after a word or phrase that is inserted into a sentence but is not essential to the meaning of the sentence

Connect and Teach

- Show **Display and Engage: Grammar 7.4.5**. Remind students to proofread their writing. Discuss these examples.

  Alicia enjoys the following puzzles mazes, brain teasers only the hard ones, and logic problems.

  Alicia enjoys the following puzzles: mazes, brain teasers (only the hard ones), and logic problems.

- The second example is correct because it sets off the list with a **colon** and encloses information that interrupts in **parentheses**.

- Review the functions of colons, parentheses, **hyphens**, and **dashes** in sentences and remind students that using these punctuation marks can make their writing clearer.

Engage and Apply

- Have partners work together to review their writing to find missing punctuation.

- Have students complete **Printable: Grammar 7.4.5** for practice with punctuation.

- Tell students that as they revise their work, they should look for places to add punctuation to their sentences.

EL ENGLISH LEARNER SUPPORT: Scaffolded Practice

SUBSTANTIAL

Review that writers use colons and parentheses to make their writing clear.

- Write: *The coach (who wore a yellow jersey) made sure all players had the following: plenty of water, good shoes, and enough pads.* Point out that the parentheses and the colon set off parts of the sentence.

MODERATE

Write these sentences on the board. Have partners punctuate them correctly.

- *My mother a doctor works long hours.*
- *To finish the project I need the following glue paint and paper.*

LIGHT

Have partners write two sentences each that are missing punctuation. Have them exchange papers and correctly punctuate each other's sentences.

SPELLING • FREQUENTLY MISSPELLED WORDS

LEARNING OBJECTIVES

- Use and identify homophones.
- Spell frequently misspelled words correctly in writing.

MATERIALS	Online

Display and Engage *Grammar 8.1.1a, 8.1.1b*

Printable *Grammar 8.1.1*

INSTRUCTIONAL VOCABULARY

- **homophone** words that sound the same but are spelled differently and have different meanings

Connect and Teach

- Show <u>**Display and Engage: Grammar 8.1.1a**</u>. Explain that **homophones** are words that sound the same but are spelled differently and have different meanings. Have students read the example sentences. Work with them to define the called-out words.

  THINK ALOUD *To think about commonly misspelled words when writing, I ask:* Is this the correct spelling for this meaning, or am I using a homophone?

Engage and Apply

- Complete items 1–8 on <u>**Display and Engage: Grammar 8.1.1b**</u> with students.

- Work with students to identify the correct spelling based on the context of the sentence.

- Have students complete <u>**Printable: Grammar 8.1.1**</u> for practice with homophones.

- Have students edit a writing draft to correct any commonly misspelled words.

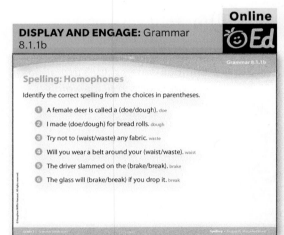

Online Ed

DISPLAY AND ENGAGE: Grammar
8.1.1a

Spelling: Homophones

Homophones are words that sound alike but are spelled differently and have different meanings. Make sure you use the correct spelling for the correct meaning.

The king sat on his throne.
The ball was thrown by the pitcher.

I bought new clothes for school.
Please close the door when you leave.

Online Ed

DISPLAY AND ENGAGE: Grammar
8.1.1b

Spelling: Homophones

Identify the correct spelling from the choices in parentheses.

1. A female deer is called a (doe/dough). doe
2. I made (doe/dough) for bread rolls. dough
3. Try not to (waist/waste) any fabric. waste
4. Will you wear a belt around your (waist/waste)? waist
5. The driver slammed on the (brake/break). brake
6. The glass will (brake/break) if you drop it. break

 ENGLISH LEARNER SUPPORT: Scaffolded Practice

SUBSTANTIAL

Students may be able to identify similar sounding words in their native language to compare to homophones in English. Give students a pair of homophones and work with them to look up the words in a dictionary.

sweet/suite
wear/where

MODERATE

Repeat the above. Then have partners choose a word pair and write a sentence using each word.

LIGHT

Have students write two sentences that include homophones.

SPELLING • FREQUENTLY MISSPELLED WORDS

LEARNING OBJECTIVES

- Identify and use words with endings.
- Spell frequently misspelled words correctly in writing.

MATERIALS	Online

Display and Engage *Grammar 8.1.2a, 8.1.2b*

Printable *Grammar 8.1.2*

 INSTRUCTIONAL VOCABULARY

- **endings** letters added to the end of a word to change the word's meaning

Connect and Teach

- Show **Display and Engage: Grammar 8.1.2a**. Explain that **endings** *-er, -or,* or *-ar* often indicate a person or thing that does something. For example, a builder builds. Point out that sometimes these endings show objects that do something, such as a skyscraper.

- Encourage students to look up words in a dictionary if they are unsure of the spelling.

  THINK ALOUD *Before I look up a word in the dictionary for the correct spelling, I ask: Am I spelling the ending of the word correctly?*

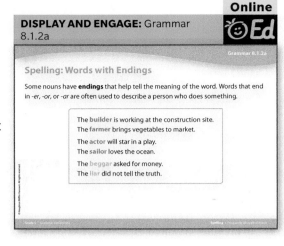

Engage and Apply

- Complete items 1–8 on **Display and Engage: Grammar 8.1.2b** with students.

- Work with students to identify a word that would fit in the blank in this sentence. *We visited the bakery and watched the _____ make breads.* **baker**

- Have students complete **Printable: Grammar 8.1.2** for practice with spelling.

- Have students edit a writing draft to spell the endings of words correctly.

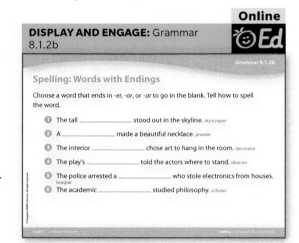

 ENGLISH LEARNER SUPPORT: Scaffolded Practice

SUBSTANTIAL
Have students suggest a few careers. Then have them look up the spellings of each career in a dictionary.

MODERATE
Repeat the above. Then have partners work together to write a sentence using one of the careers they looked up.

LIGHT
Have students write a sentence about a career. Encourage them to pick a career that ends in *-er* or *-or.*

LESSON 8.1.3

LEARNING OBJECTIVES

- Use frequently misspelled words correctly in writing.

MATERIALS — Online ⊙ Ed

Display and Engage *Grammar 8.1.3a, 8.1.3b*

Printable *Grammar 8.1.3*

INSTRUCTIONAL VOCABULARY

- **suffix** ending with a meaning that is added to a word; suffixes change the meaning of the word they are added to

Connect and Teach

- Show **Display and Engage: Grammar 8.1.3a**. Explain that **suffixes** are endings that change the meaning of the word. Review the suffixes -*tion*, -*able*, and -*ive*.

- Encourage students to look up words in a dictionary if they are unsure of the spelling.

  THINK ALOUD *To help me find the correct spelling of a suffix in the dictionary, I ask: Am I spelling the beginning part of the word correctly?*

Engage and Apply

- Complete items 1–8 on **Display and Engage: Grammar 8.1.3b** with students.

- Work with students to identify a word that would fit in the blank in this sentence. *The reference book gave me valuable _____ for my report.* information

- Have students complete **Printable: Grammar 8.1.3** for practice with spelling.

- Have students edit a writing draft using the correct spellings of suffixes.

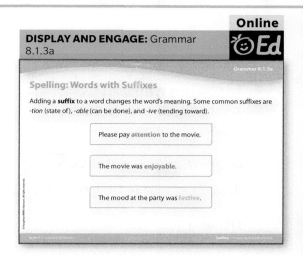

DISPLAY AND ENGAGE: Grammar 8.1.3a — Online ⊙ Ed

Spelling: Words with Suffixes

Adding a **suffix** to a word changes the word's meaning. Some common suffixes are -*tion* (state of), -*able* (can be done), and -*ive* (tending toward).

Please pay **attention** to the movie.

The movie was **enjoyable**.

The mood at the party was **festive**.

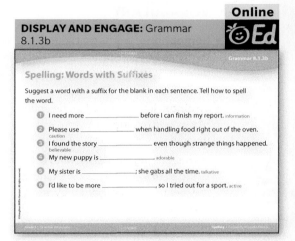

DISPLAY AND ENGAGE: Grammar 8.1.3b — Online ⊙ Ed

Spelling: Words with Suffixes

Suggest a word with a suffix for the blank in each sentence. Tell how to spell the word.

1. I need more _____ before I can finish my report. information
2. Please use _____ when handling food right out of the oven. caution
3. I found the story _____ even though strange things happened. believable
4. My new puppy is _____. adorable
5. My sister is _____; she gabs all the time. talkative
6. I'd like to be more _____, so I tried out for a sport. active

ENGLISH LEARNER SUPPORT: Scaffolded Practice

SUBSTANTIAL
Work with students to identify words that have the suffixes -*tion*, -*able*, and -*ive*. For example: *information, agreeable, creative.* Discuss their definitions.

MODERATE
Repeat the above. Then have partners work together to write a sentence using one of the words.

LIGHT
Have students write a few sentences using a word with a suffix.

LEARNING OBJECTIVES

• Use frequently misspelled words correctly in writing.

MATERIALS	Online

Display and Engage *Grammar 8.1.4a, 8.1.4b*

Printable *Grammar 8.1.4*

 INSTRUCTIONAL VOCABULARY

• **homophone** words that sound the same but are spelled differently and have different meanings

• **endings** letters added to the end of a word to change the word's meaning

• **suffix** ending with a meaning that is added to a word; suffixes change the meaning of the word they are added to

Review Spelling

• Show <u>Display and Engage: Grammar 8.1.4a</u>. Review **homophones**, **endings**, and **suffixes**. Remind students that if they are ever unsure about the correct spelling of a word, they can look it up in a glossary or dictionary.

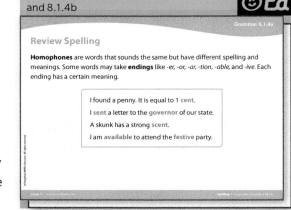

Online

DISPLAY AND ENGAGE: Grammar 8.1.4a and 8.1.4b

Grammar 8.1.4a

Review Spelling

Homophones are words that sounds the same but have different spelling and meanings. Some words may take **endings** like -er, -or, -ar, -tion, -able, and -ive. Each ending has a certain meaning.

I found a penny. It is equal to 1 cent.
I sent a letter to the governor of our state.
A skunk has a strong scent.
I am available to attend the festive party.

• Display a list of homophones and say each word aloud with students. Have students identify the differences in the spelling of each homophone set. Then discuss the difference in meaning. Use a homophone pair incorrectly in sentences, such as *doe/dough*. Discuss how using the wrong homophone makes the sentences unclear.

• Display a list of common suffixes, such as: *-able, -ful, -less.* Add the suffixes to words, modeling how the meaning of each word changes. For example: *presentable, careful, thoughtless.* Repeat with the endings *-er, -or,* and *-ar. (teacher, creator, actor)*

• Work with students to complete the exercises on <u>Display and Engage: Grammar 8.1.4b</u>.

• Have students complete <u>Printable: Grammar 8.1.4</u>.

• Have students edit writing using the correct spellings of commonly misspelled words.

 ENGLISH LEARNER SUPPORT: Scaffolded Practice

SUBSTANTIAL
Work with students to make a list of words they have heard but are unsure of how to spell. Work with them to look up the spelling of each word in a glossary or dictionary.

MODERATE
Repeat the above. Then have partners work together to write a sentence using one of the words.

LIGHT
Repeat the Beginning activity. Then have students write a few sentence using two words they looked up.

SPELLING • FREQUENTLY MISSPELLED WORDS

LEARNING OBJECTIVES

- Spell words correctly in writing.
- Use frequently misspelled words correctly in writing.

MATERIALS	Online

Display and Engage *Grammar 8.1.5*
Printable *Grammar 8.1.5*

Connect and Teach

- Show **Display and Engage: Grammar 8.1.5**. Explain that all words should be spelled correctly in final drafts.

- Point out that an important part of revising is to check your writing carefully to be sure that words are spelled correctly.

- Remind students to review the spelling of words with endings, and to check the meaning of the word with the ending added.

- Review that homophones are words that sound the same but are spelled differently. Remind students to check that the correct spelling is used to avoid confusion.

DISPLAY AND ENGAGE: Grammar 8.1.5 • Online Ed

Connect to Writing: Using Correct Spelling

When you edit, read every word carefully to make sure it is spelled correctly. The spell-checker on your computer may find spelling errors, but it will not show you homophone errors.

> The boards on the floor made a creak.
> The creek outside burbled.

> We are not allowed to use phones at dinner.
> Please read that line aloud.

Engage and Apply

- Have students look back at one of their previous drafts and reread to make sure all words are spelled correctly. Remind them that if they are unsure of how something should be spelled, they can look it up in a dictionary.

- Have students complete **Printable: Grammar 8.1.5** for practice with frequently misspelled words.

- Tell students that as they revise their work, they should look for misspelled words and correct them.

EL ENGLISH LEARNER SUPPORT: Scaffolded Practice

SUBSTANTIAL
Review that writers spell words correctly and fix words they see that are spelled incorrectly.
- Write: *The princess sat on a thrown.*
Say: *Which word is spelled incorrectly? What is the correct spelling? thrown/throne*
Give students additional examples.

MODERATE
Have students revisit a previous piece of writing and identify any misspelled words. Then have students rewrite a sentence or two from the piece to correct the misspellings.

LIGHT
Have partners write two sentences using words they used this week. Then have partners read each other's sentences to check for spelling mistakes.

Resources

Online

FIND MORE ONLINE!

Into Reading Scope and Sequence

Rubrics

Standards Correlations

Instructional Vocabulary Glossary

Language Transfer

Index

Professional Learning

Look up these professional resources to learn more about the research foundations for *Into Reading: Writing Workshop*.

Calkins, Lucy. *The Art of Teaching Writing*. Portsmouth, NH: Heinemann, 1994.

Calkins, Lucy, Amanda Hartman, and Zoe Ryder White. *One to One: The Art of Conferring with Young Writers*. Portsmouth, NH: Heinemann, 2005.

Calkins, Lucy. *A Guide to the Writing Workshop: Primary Grades*. Portsmouth, NH: Heinemann, 2017.

Carroll, Joyce Armstrong. *The Best of Dr. JAC*. Spring, TX: Absey & Company, Inc., 1998.

Carroll, Joyce Armstrong. *Dr. JAC's Guide to Writing with Depth*. Spring, TX: Absey & Company, Inc., 2002.

Carroll, Joyce Armstrong. "Finding the Genesis for a Thesis." *School Library Monthly* 29, no. 6 (March 2013):17–19.

Carroll, Joyce Armstrong. "Teaching the Thesis." *School Library Monthly* 29, no. 2 (November 2012):18–20.

Carroll, Joyce Armstrong, and Jill Aufill. *Authentic Strategies for High-Stakes Tests: A Practical Guide for English Language/Arts*. Spring, TX: Absey & Company, Inc., 2007.

Carroll, Joyce Armstrong, Kelley Barger, Karla James, and Kristy Hill. *Guided by Meaning in Primary Literacy: Libraries, Reading, Writing, and Learning*. Santa Barbara, CA: Libraries Unlimited, 2016.

Carroll, Joyce Armstrong, and Edward E. Wilson. *Acts of Teaching: How to Teach Writing: A Text, A Reader, A Narrative*. 2nd Ed. Portsmouth, NH: Heinemann, 2008.

Carroll, Joyce Armstrong, and Edward E. Wilson. *Brushing Up on Grammar: An Acts of Teaching Approach*. Santa Barbara, CA: Libraries Unlimited, 2010.

Cruz, M. Colleen. *The Unstoppable Writing Teacher: Real Strategies for the Real Classroom*. Portsmouth, NH: Heinemann, 2015.

Dawson, Peg, and Richard Guare. *Smart but Scattered: The Revolutionary "Executive Skills" Approach to Helping Kids Reach Their Potential*. New York, NY: Guilford Press, 2009.

Durlak, Joseph A., Celene E. Domitrovich, Roger P. Weissberg, and Thomas P. Gullotta, eds. *Handbook of Social and Emotional Learning: Research and Practice*. New York, NY: Guilford Press, 2016.

Durlak, Joseph A., Roger P. Weissberg, Allison B. Dymnicki, Rebecca D. Taylor, and Kriston B. Schellinger. "The Impact of Enhancing Students' Social and Emotional Learning: A Meta-Analysis of School-Based Universal Interventions." *Child Development* 82, no. 1 (January/February 2011): 405–432.

Dweck, Carol S. *Mindset: The New Psychology of Success*. New York, NY: Ballantine Books, 2007.

Fisher, Douglas, and Nancy Frey. *Better Learning Through Structured Teaching: A Framework for the Gradual Release of Responsibility*. 1st ed. Association for Supervision & Curriculum Development, 2008.

Gartland, Lauren B., and Laura B. Smolkin. "The Histories and Mysteries of Grammar Instruction: Supporting Elementary Teachers in the Time of the Common Core." *The Reading Teacher* 69, no. 4 (January/February 2016): 391–399.

Gerde, Hope. K., Gary. E. Bingham, and Barbara A. Wasik. "Writing in Early Childhood Classrooms: Guidance for Best Practices." *Early Childhood Education Journal* 40, no. 6 (2012): 351–59.

Graham, Steve. "Want to Improve Children's Writing? Don't Neglect Their Handwriting." *American Educator* (Winter 2009–2010): 20–27, 40.

Graham, Steve, Alisha Bollinger, Carol Booth Olson, Catherine D'Aoust, Charles MacArthur, Deborah McCutchen, and Natalie Olinghouse. *Teaching Elementary School Students to Be Effective Writers*. Washington, DC: Institute of Education Sciences, 2012.

Graham, Steve, and Karen R. Harris. "A Path to Better Writing: Evidence-Based Practices in the Classroom." *The Reading Teacher* 69, no. 4 (January/February 2016): 359–365.

Graham, Steve, and Karen Harris. *Writing Better: Effective Strategies for Teaching Students with Learning Disabilities*. 1st ed. Baltimore, MD: Brookes Publishing, 2005.

Graham, Steve, Karen Harris, and Michael Hebert. *Informing Writing: The Benefits of Formative Assessment*. Washington, DC: Carnegie Corporation of New York, Alliance for Excellent Education, 2011.

Graham, Steve, and Dolores Perin. *Writing Next: Effective Strategies to Improve Writing of Adolescents in Middle and High Schools—A Report to Carnegie Corporation of New York.* Washington, DC: Alliance for Excellent Education, 2011.

Harris, Karen, Steve Graham, Linda Mason, and Barbara Friedlander. *Powerful Writing Strategies for All Students.* 1st ed. Baltimore, MD: Brookes Publishing, 2007.

Horn, Martha, and Mary Ellen Giacobbe. *Talking, Drawing, Writing: Lessons for Our Youngest Writers.* Portland, ME: Stenhouse Publishers, 2006.

Kirby, Amanda, and Lynne Peters. *100 Ideas for Supporting Pupils with Dyspraxia and DCD.* London: Bloomsbury Academic, 2007.

Lonigan, Christopher. J., and Timothy Shanahan. "Executive Summary." *Developing Early Literacy: Report of the National Early Literacy Panel.* Washington, DC: National Institute for Literacy, 2009.

McGrath, Constance. *The Inclusion-Classroom Problem Solver: Structures and Supports to Serve All Learners.* Portsmouth, NH: Heinemann, 2007.

Mo, Ya, Rachel A. Kopke, Lisa K. Hawkins, Gary A. Troia, and Natalie G. Olinghouse. "The Neglected 'R' in a Time of Common Core." *The Reading Teacher* 67, no. 6 (March 2014): 445–453.

Richards, Regina G. *When Writing's a Problem: Understanding Dysgraphia & Helpful Hints for Reluctant Writers.* Riverside, CA: RET Center Press, 2015.

Richards, Todd L., Virginia W. Berninger, Pat Stock, Leah Altemeier, Pamela Trivedi, and Kenneth R. Maravilla. "Differences Between Good and Poor Child Writers on fMRI Contrasts for Writing Newly Taught and Highly Practiced Letter Forms." *Reading and Writing* 24, no. 5 (May 2011): 493–516.

Rogers, Katie, and Julia Simms A. *Teaching Argumentation: Activities and Games for the Classroom.* Bloomington, IN: Marzano Research, 2015.

Serravallo, Jennifer. *The Writing Strategies Book: Your Everything Guide to Developing Skilled Writers.* Portsmouth, NH: Heinemann, 2017.

Sloan, Megan. *Into Writing: The Primary Teacher's Guide to Writing Workshop.* Portsmouth, NH: Heinemann, 2009.

Teaching Elementary School Students to Be Effective Writers Practice Guide Summary. Washington, DC: Institute of Education Sciences, September 23, 2014.

Troia, Gary A., ed. *Instruction and Assessment for Struggling Writers: Evidence-Based Practices.* Challenges in Language and Literacy. New York, NY: Guilford Press, 2010.

Troia, Gary A. "Research in Writing Instruction: What We Know and What We Need to Know." In *Shaping Literacy Achievement: Research We Have, Research We Need*, edited by Michael Pressley, Allison K. Billman, Kristen H. Perry, Kelly E. Reffitt, and Julia Moorhead Reynolds, 129–156. New York City: Guilford Press, 2007.

Troia, Gary A., and Steve Graham. "Effective Writing Instruction Across the Grades: What Every Educational Consultant Should Know." *Journal of Educational and Psychological Consultation* 14 (2003): 75–89.

Troia, Gary A., and Steve Graham, eds. *Students Who Are Exceptional and Writing Disabilities: Prevention, Practice, Intervention, and Assessment. Exceptionality: a Special Education Journal.* London: Routledge, 2017.

Troia, Gary A., Rebecca K. Shankland, and Anne Heintz, eds. *Putting Writing Research into Practice: Applications for Teacher Professional Development.* New York, NY: Guilford Press, 2010.

Van Sluys, Katie. *Becoming Writers in the Elementary Classroom: Visions and Decisions.* Principles in Practice. Urbana, IL: National Council of Teachers of English, 2011.

Washington, Julie. "Language Development in Young Children." Early Learning Webinars. Houghton Mifflin Harcourt, October 20, 2016. http://www.hmhco. com/classroom/ evaluate-and-sample/webinars/professional-webinars/ early-learning?elqTrackId=36 6ad0c9423e486691852cd55a 08e45b&elqaid=3697 &elqat=2.

Winn, Maisha T., and Latrise Johnson. *Writing Instruction in the Culturally Relevant Classroom. Principles in Practice.* Urbana, IL: National Council of Teachers of English, 2011.

Credits

Handwriting

Individual students have various levels of handwriting skills, but they all have the desire to communicate effectively. To write correctly, they must be familiar with concepts of

- size (tall, short)
- open and closed letters
- capital and lowercase letters
- manuscript vs. cursive letters
- letter and word spacing
- punctuation

Explain Stroke and Letter Formation

Tell students that most manuscript letters are formed with a continuous stroke, so students will not often pick up their pencils when writing a single letter. Explain that when they begin to use cursive handwriting, students will have to lift their pencils from the paper less frequently and will be able to write more fluently. Provide students with a copy of the manuscript and cursive handwriting models on pages R7–R9 for future reference.

Teach Writing Position

Establishing the correct posture, pen or pencil grip, and paper position for writing will help prevent handwriting problems.

Posture Tell students to sit with both feet on the floor and with hips to the back of the chair. They can lean forward slightly but should not slouch. Ask them to make sure their writing surface is smooth and flat. It should be at a height that allows their upper arms to be perpendicular to the surface and their elbows to be under their shoulders.

Writing Instrument Have students use an adult-sized number-two lead pencil for their writing assignments. Explain that as they become proficient in the use of cursive handwriting, they can use pens to write final drafts.

Paper Position and Pencil Grip Explain to students that as they write in cursive, the position of the paper plays an important role. The paper should be slanted along the line of the student's writing arm, and the student should use his or her nonwriting hand to hold the paper in place. Tell them to hold their pencils or pens about one inch from the tip.

Then ask students to assume their writing position. Check each student's position, providing adjustments as necessary.

Develop Handwriting

The best instruction builds on what students already know and can do. Given the wide range in students' handwriting abilities, a variety of approaches may be needed. Use the following activities as you choose to provide regular handwriting practice to students of all proficiency levels.

ANCHOR CHART: Cursive Handwriting

Online
Ed

Anchor Chart

Write in Cursive

Project or display **Anchor Chart: Cursive Handwriting**. Point out the characteristics of cursive writing and the differences from the manuscript alphabet, as needed. Then duplicate for each student the model of the cursive alphabet on page R7. Have students trace each lowercase and uppercase letter. Then have students write each letter in both lowercase and uppercase on a separate sheet of lined paper.

Handwriting (continued)

Slant Letters Correctly Tell students that most cursive letters slant very slightly to the right. Have them practice writing the lowercase alphabet. Tell them to check that they have slanted their letters correctly by drawing a faint vertical line through the middle of each letter. If they have correctly slanted each letter, the lines will all be parallel to each other.

Letter Spacing Explain to students that when writing in cursive, they should leave an equal amount of space between each letter in a word. Tell students that if they leave too little or too much space between letters, their writing will be difficult to read. Write the following words on the board and have students write them on a sheet of lined paper: *batch, reject, vanish, sloppy, rhythm*.

Word Spacing Tell students that it is important to leave the correct amount of space between each word in a sentence. Tell students to leave a space about the width of a pencil between words. Demonstrate how to do this. Then have students practice letter and word spacing by writing phrases that describe the weather, such as *hot and dry*.

Join Uppercase and Lowercase Letters Tell students that when writing most proper nouns in cursive, they must join an uppercase and a lowercase letter. Have students practice joining uppercase and lowercase letters by writing the following state names: Alabama, California, Florida, New York. Then explain that some uppercase letters, such as D, P, T, V, and W, do not join with a lowercase letter. Have students practice writing the following proper nouns, making sure not to join the first and second letter: Dallas, Phoenix, Texas, Virginia, Washington.

Answer Questions Have students practice writing sentences by answering "how" questions about things they see and do on a daily basis. For example, you might ask, *How do you get to school?* Tell students to write their answers in complete sentences and use their best cursive writing.

Write Sentences Have students write five original sentences about their daily routines. Remind them to slant their letters correctly and to leave the correct amount of space between the letters in each word and between each word in a sentence. Have them trade papers with a classmate and give feedback on the legibility of their partner's cursive writing.

Write a Paragraph Have students write an original paragraph about a favorite book, sport, or other activity. Remind them to use the correct posture for writing, paying special attention to leaving appropriate spacing between letters in a word and between words in a sentence.

Assess Handwriting

To assess students' handwriting skills, review samples of their written work. Note whether they use correct letter formation and appropriate size and spacing. Note whether students follow the conventions of print, such as correct capitalization and punctuation. When writing messages, notes, and letters, or when publishing their writing, students should write legibly in cursive, leaving appropriate spacing between letters and words to make the work readable for their audience.

HANDWRITING Cursive Alphabet

A B C D E F G H
I J K L M N O P
Q R S T U V W
X Y Z

a b c d e f g h
i j k l m n o p
q r s t u v w
x y z

HANDWRITING Manuscript Alphabet

A B C D E F G H
I J K L M N O P
Q R S T U V W
X Y Z

a b c d e f g h
i j k l m n o p
q r s t u v w
x y z

CONTINUOUS STROKE Manuscript Alphabet

A B C D E F G H
I J K L M N O P
Q R S T U V W
X Y Z

a b c d e f g h
i j k l m n o p
q r s t u v w
x y z